Women
and the
American
Labor Movement

D1120428

Women and the American Labor Movement

From the First Trade Unions to the Present

Philip S. Foner

THE FREE PRESS
A Division of Macmillan Publishing Co., Inc.
NEW YORK

Collier Macmillan Publishers
LONDON

The Free Press
A Division of Macmillan Publishing Co., Inc.
866 Third Avenue, New York, N.Y. 10022

Collier Macmillan Canada, Inc.

Printed in the United States of America

printing number
1 2 3 4 5 6 7 8 9 10

Library of Congress Cataloging in Publication Data

Foner, Philip Sheldon
   Women and the American labor movement.

   Bibliography: p.
   Includes index.
   1. Women in trade-unions—United States—History.
2. Women—Employment—United States—History. I. Title.
HD6079.2.U5F652   1982   331.4   82-70913
ISBN 0-02-910470-X (pbk.)   AACR2

To Roslyn, Elizabeth, and Laura

Contents

Preface and Acknowledgments

As LONG AGO AS 1922 Arthur M. Schlesinger, Sr., in *New Viewpoints in American History* pointed out our need for an intensive study of American women. Research in women's history is in full swing today. Scholars have been investigating the history of the American women's movement in its various phases. In published and unpublished studies, monographs and interpretative essays, overall accounts of the American women's movement from a political, social, and cultural standpoint have been appearing in increasing number.

Workingwomen, however, do not loom large in the new scholarship dealing with the American women's movement just as they do not occupy an important place in most histories of the American labor movement. While women are not new to the American work force, their role in this capacity has been largely neglected. In the more than fifty years since Alice Henry published *Women and the Labor Movement* (1923) and Theresa Wolfson issued *The Woman Worker and the Trade Unions*, only one new study has appeared, the 1977 work by Barbara Mayer Wertheimer, *We Were There: The Story of Working Women in America*, which runs from colonial times to 1912.

For the most part historians of women and the American labor movement have relied on standard printed sources. But today there exist many repositories throughout the United States that house materials relevant to workingwomen. Prominent among them are the Arthur and Elizabeth Schlesinger Library of the History of Women in America, formerly the Women's Archives, at Radcliffe College, Cambridge, Massachusetts, the Sophia Smith Collection at Smith College, Northampton, Massachusetts, the Manuscripts Division of the Library of Congress and the National Archives in Washington, D.C., the Tamiment Institute Library at New York University, and others. The use of these repositories have resulted in several doctoral dissertations on workingwomen leaders and on organizations which throw new and valuable light on the history of women and the labor movement. This volume is vastly indebted to the important collections in these and other repositories.

Anyone today who writes labor history knows that it means more than the history of organized labor and that the history of working-class experience must go beyond emphasis on workers on the job and in their collective organizations and actions. But we most certainly do not know all we need to know about workingwomen and the American labor movement, and we cannot content ourselves with glorifying inchoate dissatisfaction while at the same time underemphasizing organized resistance. This resistance, moreover, is a fitting answer to the tendency to view women's past as one of undifferentiated subjection and passive victimization, in short, a chronicle of failure.

Women have been active in their own behalf since the earliest days of the factory system, often against what must have seemed insurmountable odds. Far from being passive, many women were militant and aggressive in their attempts to improve their working conditions. In a number of important industries, it was the militancy and perseverance of women workers that laid the foundations of trade unionism. This in the face of the double obstacle of employer-public hostility and the indifference of most male-dominated unions.

In analyzing the history of American workingwomen, I have tried to take into account both their status as women and their status as workers, and tried to understand the ways women's experiences as workers were different from those of men. Throughout, too, I have sought to point up the unique experience and problems of black women in the work force.

Nevertheless, it is impossible to separate the story of workingwomen from that of working men and from major events in social, economic, and political history that had profound effects on changes in women's work, as well as from changes going on in American society generally. Therefore, after reexamining the appropriateness of traditional periodization in the history of workingwomen, I have decided to follow the conventional marking of time-periods. In doing so, I have sought to identify a "woman's issue" within a larger historical content.

The present volume is an abbreviated version of my two-volume *Women and the American Labor Movement* (The Free Press, 1980 and 1981), volume I covering the period from colonial times to the eve of World War I, and volume II the era from World War I to the present. Readers who wish to study a more complete history of women and the American labor movement will find the two-volume work totaling close to 1,500 pages suitable and readily available.

A work of this nature would have been impossible to produce without the kind cooperation of many libraries, historical societies, institutions and individuals. I owe a deep gratitude to the staffs of the libraries of Radcliffe College, New York University, University of Illinois, Tamiment Institute of New York University, Northeastern University, University of Maryland, University of Chicago, University of Texas, Austin, University of California, Berkeley, University of California, Los Angeles, University of California, Santa Cruz, University of Pennsylvania, Georgetown University, Northwestern University, Columbia University, Lincoln University, Wayne State University, Detroit, University of Florida, Gainesville, University of Delaware, University of Wisconsin, Madison, University of Wisconsin, Milwaukee, Catholic University of America, Boston Public Library, New York Public Library, Library of Congress, Newberry Library, Chicago, Library Company of Philadelphia, Lynn Public Library, Detroit Public Library, Augusta Public Library, Cohoes Public Library, San Antonio Public Library, New Orleans Public Library, New York State Labor Library, State House Library, Boston, American Institute for Marxist Studies, New York, Tennessee State Library and Archives, American Federation of Labor Library, Library of Trade Union Women's Studies, Cornell University, Amalgamated Clothing Workers of America Library, United States Department of Labor Library, Rhode Island Historical Society, New Hampshire Historical Society, Maryland Historical Society, Pennsylvania Historical Society, Illinois Historical Society, and State Historical Society of Wisconsin.

I owe sincere thanks to Ken Lawrence of the Deep South People's History Project and to Ron Benson, Millersville State College, for kindly furnishing me with copies of several important documents. Ron Benson; Lislotte Gage of the University of Hannover, Germany; Carl Gersuny of the University of Rhode Island; Robert E. Snyder of Syracuse University; Josephine Pacheco of George Mason University; and Dennis Clark Dickerson, Myrna Fichtenbaum, Sherna Gluck, Robert Korstadt, Peter Lowber, Sally Miller, Albert Prago, and Dale Rosen kindly furnished me copies of their own work in the field. I wish to thank Tillie A. Pevzner, Institute for Retired Professionals, The New School for Social Research, for assistance in checking newspaper sources.

Portions of the manuscript have been read, and valuable suggestions offered, by Sally M. Miller, Ted Werntz, and Janet Ridgway of Working Women. My brother Moe Foner furnished me with important material relating to the history of Local 1199. My brother Henry Foner read the entire manuscript, and helped in other ways. I owe him a special debt of gratitude.

1

The First Trade Unions

IN 1824 WOMEN PARTICIPATED IN the first factory strike along with men. A year later there occurred the first strike in which women alone participated. This was the strike for higher wages of "the Tailoresses of New York." While we do not know much about the events leading up to the strike,[1] we do know a great deal about the conditions that caused it.

Women in Jacksonian America had few rights and little power. Their role in society was sharply limited. While propertyless white men were becoming part of the electorate, women were denied the vote; their property rights were restricted, and they were excluded from most trades and professions.[2] In particular, they were systematically eliminated from medical practice. Although most of the colonies' original healers were women (a tradition that existed in England and Europe until the execution of some 4 million "witches" from 1749 to 1755 effectively thinned the ranks of female health practitioners), by the end of the Revolutionary War a male medical elite had begun to band together against women through a complex campaign for licensing and other legislation, harassment, restrictive medical school admission policies, propaganda about the alleged biological frailty and emotional instability of women, and the repeated assertion that women's proper sphere was home and hearth. By the 1820s all but three states had set up licensing requirements for midwives that made medical school a prerequisite, and no women were admitted to regular medical schools. Except for a brief resurgence of women healers ("irregular" doctors) during the Popular Health movement in the second half of the nineteenth century, women were all but excluded from the field until the early 1900s.[3]

In short, in Jacksonian America, women were largely confined to the domestic realm, where their duty was to be submissive and patient and to cultivate and spread virtue. While men could be both competitive and aggressive as they dealt with the harsh reality of the worlds of business and politics, women, from their place in the home, were supposed to provide the soothing, taming, and gentle energy that would help ensure harmony and social order—a counterpoint to the "ruggled individualism" that accompanied the rise of industrial capitalism and westward expansion.[4]

The "cult of true womanhood"—the belief that women are mysteriously but definitively different from men and can realize their womanliness only in the uniquely female role of bearing and nurturing children—was spread through a host of popular novels, sermons, etiquette books, manuals, and new ladies' magazines.[5] Women were counseled to be submissive and good-natured, to avoid politics, and to concentrate their energies on domestic tasks. These tasks were said to have their own political importance.[6] Thus, while not participating directly in political life, a woman was described as performing her civic duties through her role as "the Republican mother" who raised and educated the nation's children and was therefore responsible for preserving the civic virtues.[7] Said The Lady at Home, a popular book of the day: "Even if we cannot reform the world in a moment, we can begin by reforming ourselves and our households. It is woman's mission. Let her not look away from her own little family circle for the means of producing moral and social reforms, but begin at home."[8]

Thus, while industrialization brought lower-class women into the factories as unskilled labor, middle-class women were excluded from the newly formed professions by both prejudice and cultural restraints. Paradoxically, however, they had more leisure time than women in any previous generation. The tasks that had been assigned to them in colonial society—the manufacture of food and clothing, the education of children, home nursing, and medical care—were now institutionalized outside the home. Many of them, therefore, turned their energies to reform activities and literary pursuits.[9]

What of the thousands of poor women who could not stay at home and cultivate virtue—unmarried or orphaned young women, widows who had to support themselves and their children, and wives whose husbands could not work because of illness? They simply had to work.

During the colonial period, nearly all clothing not intended for home use was either made to order or sold by the person who made it. What turned women sewers into wage workers was the development of ready-made clothing and the wholesale trade. The demand for cheap, ready-made clothing came largely from the army and navy and from Southern slaveholders. Producing cheap clothing for Southern slaves proved to be a profitable enterprise for Northern capitalists. The growing industry, centered in New York, Philadelphia, and Boston, was further aided by the tariffs imposed on imported clothing in 1816 and 1828. By 1835 "every country village within 100 miles of New York became as busy as a beehive with tailors and tailoresses."[10]

Most of the work was done either at home or in small shops, called "slop shops," under miserable conditions. The name derived from the waterfront shops in the eastern seaboard cities that catered to the clothing needs of sailors waiting for their ships to leave. In these shops women produced on demand shirts and pants made of sturdy fabric. Since payment was at a piece rate, there was terrible pressure on the workers to increase their output by toiling longer hours. Meanwhile, agents for the shops traveled about the countryside distributing cut parts of the garment to women who assembled them at home. They played off the out-of-town sewers against the women in the city shops to keep rates low. Little skill was required for most of the work, and the women were deliberately kept unskilled by the employers. It was difficult to gain access to the better-paying, more highly skilled sections of the trade, such as dressmaking and millinery. Apprentices were compelled to keep sewing and were not taught the art of design.[11]

In 1828 Matthew Carey, an Irish immigrant who had amassed a fortune in Philadelphia's publishing business and had devoted himself to philanthropy, began a crusade on behalf of working women, especially tailoresses and seamstresses. In pamphlets, essays, and letters to the press, he revealed the wages and conditions of women sewers. But even Carey did not fully grasp the stark reality of the situation. In an 1831 pamphlet he estimated the average wages of sewing women at $1.25 a week, whereupon a committee of these women notified him that earnings were usually $1.12½ a week and often fell below that figure. In his revised publication, Carey revealed that a skilled sewer, constantly employed, working early and late, could make no more than nine shirts a week. Since two-thirds of her pay went for rent, this would leave her only 40 cents—or 6 cents a day—for food, clothing, fuel, and other necessities. A woman who had children or a sick husband to look after and thus could not put in full time might have 4 cents a day to meet her needs.[12]

Women in Boston made even less than those in Philadelphia. In 1830 the average weekly wage for a fully employed woman was the same in both cities, but rent in Boston was higher, with rooms generally costing $1 a week. In New York City, the situation was even worse. A physician in that city who saw many of these women as patients wrote: "To say that the wages paid by clothing store keepers to seamstresses are inadequate to their support is but a cold and imperfect statement of the truth." He found women making duck trousers for a store "at FOUR CENTS A PAIR; and cotton shorts at SEVEN CENTS A PIECE." When he asked the women if they could live on such pay, the answer was in one word: "Impossible!"[13]

A tailoress described her plight and that of her sisters in a letter to the press:

> Only think of a poor woman, confined to her seat fifteen hours out of twenty-four to make a pair of... pantaloons, for which she receives only twenty-five cents. And indeed, many of them are not able to make a pair in much less than two days. ...
>
> Only think of twelve and a half cents for making a shirt, that takes a woman a whole day, if she attends to any other work in her family. There a poor soul must sit all day in this dark weather, and burn candles half her time, and injure her health, to lay in coal for the approaching winter. How shall she clothe her poor children, or even feed them at this rate? Yet there are many poor women of my acquaintance, that are placed in the disheartening situation I have mentioned; and many of them are widows, with a number of children. And the tailors scold us when we bring home the work, and some of them say the work is done ill, and then take out half the price, or give us nothing if they think fit, and at the same time they sell their clothing much dearer than they did some time ago, and God help us, we have to submit to the injustice.[14]

Matthew Carey appealed several times to rich ladies and gentlemen to provide relief by hiring these women at higher wages. He protested: "I have known a lady to expend a hundred dollars on a party; pay thirty or forty dollars for a bonnet, and fifty for a shawl; and yet make a hard bargain with a seamstress or washerwoman, who had to work at her needle or at the washing tub for thirteen or fourteen hours a day to make a bare livelihood for herself and a numerous family of small children."[15] "A Working Woman" was even blunter. She used the term "beating-down ladies" to describe "these fine people" ("who never had a care in their minds [but] to make their parties equal to those of their associates, and their dress more recherché"), because they were constantly "beating down" prices and helping to aggravate the poverty of the seamstresses.[16]

The low wages paid to seamstresses (as well as to domestics and washerwomen) forced them to face "the alternatives of begging—applying to the overseers of the poor—stealing—or starving." We might add another," wrote philanthropist Carey, "but we forbear."[17] That other option was prostitution. In 1835, a year after it was founded, the New York Female Moral Reform Society reached the conclusion that many of the city's poor workingwomen, even though they were basically moral, were being forced to turn to prostitution because of ruthless economic exploitation.[18] The New York *Daily Sentinel*, the first daily labor paper in the United States, reached the same conclusion:

> What wretched, wretched state of things is this which confronts our working women! How the miserable sufferers endure it, or in what way they procure

bread and water for their support, God only knows. That many of them, after struggling for years against honest pride, at last become inmates of the work-house, we have daily evidence. That some, maddened to despair by the utter hopelessness of living reputably in comfort, should stoop to the last, most degrading of resorts for support, and fit themselves to become inmates of the Magdalen Asylum [for prostitutes], can we wonder?[19]

While the New York tailoresses began as early as 1825 to try to find a way to combat the anguish, desperation, and powerlessness that characterized their lives, it was not until six years later that their efforts took the form of sustained activity. On February 11, 1831, the New York *Daily Sentinel* carried two items relating to women who worked with the needle. One, simply called "Facts," read: "A Tailor in Chatham street, who advertises for 'twenty or thirty' seamstresses, offers the applicants, for making shirts, *seven cents* each. Oak wood is *five dollars* a load." The other, headed "Meeting of Tailoresses," reported that "from two to three hundred females" had met in Mott Street "to form an association for the purpose of taking measures for bettering their conditions." The report also revealed that the tailoresses had agreed to form an association and had chosen one committee to draft a constitution and another to come up with a plan of action. There had also evidently been some discussion of a strike, since a correspondent who was present reported that many women who had families to support and who depended entirely on their labor to do so had indicated that they would not be able to hold out long enough "to make the stand effectual, unless they were provided for," as a result of which it was decided to raise a fund to support people in such circumstances.[20]

The United Tailoresses' Society of New York, as the new organization was called, met weekly. At one of its early meetings, the society aroused considerable attention because Mrs. Lavinia Wright, its secretary, had raised the issue of women's rights. The *Boston Evening Transcript* paid no attention to the conditions that prompted the tailoresses to form their union, but it was quick to condemn Wright's "clamorous and unfeminine" declaration of the rights of women, which, according to the newspaper, it was "obvious Providence never destined her to exercise." The *Transcript* advised the tailoresses to confine themselves to "their scissors and pincushions, their tape and foot stoves."[21]

Despite such objections, the United Tailoresses' Society continued to meet, and discussions of the rights of women continued to take place at the meetings. "Let us turn a deaf ear to the slanders of our enemies, for enemies we have, no doubt," boldly declared Sarah Monroe, a leader of the society, at one of its meetings. "If we are true to ourselves and each other, they cannot harm us." While she did not minimize the difficulties they faced, she urged her sisters not to be discouraged: "If we do not come forth in our own defense, what will become of us? . . . Let us trust no longer to the generosity of our employers; seeing that they are men in whose heads or hearts the thought of doing justice to a fellow being never seems to enter." Only by organizing themselves and standing up boldly for their rights, she went on, would they be able to secure for themselves "an adequate and permanent reward" for their labors. And she concluded:

> It needs no small share of courage for us, who have been used to impositions and oppression from our youth up to the present day, to come before the public in defense of our rights; but, my friends, if it is unfashionable for the men to bear oppression in silence, why should it not also become unfashionable with the women. Or do they deem us more able to endure hardship than they themselves?[22]

In June, 1831, the United Tailoresses' Society of New York prepared its own list of wages and declared that its members would not work for less than the amounts listed. When the employers rejected the new scale, the United Tailoresses, sixteen hundred strong, went out on strike. They continued to hold out through June and July, combating "difficulties from which men might have shrunk."[23] Their struggle was ridiculed in the commercial press, which echoed the employers' argument that since women, unlike men, were "exempt" from the need to support families, their demand for wages similar to those of men was ridiculous. The society's secretary responded:

> Now this is either a sad mistake, or a wilful oversight; for how many females are there who have families to support, and how many single men have none, and who, having no other use for the fruits of their employers' generosity, they, childlike, waste it, while the industrious mother, having the care of a helpless offspring, finds (with all the economy she is necessitated to practice) the scanty reward of her labors scarcely sufficient to support nature![24]

The labor press, led by the New York *Working Man's Advocate* and the New York *Daily Sentinel* (both edited by George Henry Evans), carried editorials and correspondence offering the striking tailoresses both support and advice about how they might win. One suggestion was to call "a meeting of the male population" to propose a boycott by the men trade unionists of all tailors who had not accepted the United Tailoresses' wage scale. Another urged a campaign against the use of prison labor and the labor of people in almshouses, which undercut the wages of seamstresses and tailoresses. Still another was that the members of the society collect funds by subscription among themselves to set up a cooperative store, which would provide employment at "liberal wages," with sick pay and retirement benefits for the subscribers. One correspondent urged the society to present a petition to the ministers of all churches asking them to "plead their cause with the people" and take up collections for the strikers. "Then," he concluded, "it will be seen who are and who are not friends of the widows and orphans, and of suffering, unprotected females."[25]

Unfortunately, the advice produced little in the way of funds, and the male trade unions showed little interest in the suggestion of a boycott of employers who refused to accept the proposed wage scale. Nor did an appeal to clergymen produce any results. "Where now are you disinterested philanthropists," asked the *Daily Sentinel* angrily, "your Magdalen people, who make such a wonderful display of reclaiming two or three dozen females from vice, while *two or three thousand*, at this present moment, are unable to obtain the necessaries of life by honest industry?"[26] But, as before, the appeal fell on deaf ears. The result was that when the society's members resolved to "adhere steadfastly to their own bill of prices" and sent a committee of three to inform the employers of this determination, the employers refused to make any concessions whatsoever. On July 25, 1831, the tailoresses voted to return to work and to "draw up an Address to the public stating their reasons for adopting this course."[27]

In this address, the society described the hardships and inadequate wages that had compelled its members to strike and announced that, despite the defeat, they would continue to meet and would even launch a cooperative clothing establishment. But that project never became a reality, and the last heard of the organization was the following announcement in the New York *Daily Sentinel* of September 5, 1831: "The monthly meeting of the United Tailoresses' Society to be held this Monday evening at 7 o'clock at Congress Hall, corner of the Bowery and Hester Street. Phebe Scott, President; Louisa M. Mitchell, Secretary."

Baltimore's trade unions were more inclined to help the tailoresses and seamstresses of that city than were their counterparts in New York. When the sewing women organized the Female Union Society of Tailoresses and Seamstresses of Baltimore on September 20, 1833, drew up a bill of wages, and voted to strike on October 1 if their demands were not met, they received assurances of support from the city's unions. The Baltimore journeymen tailors called a special meeting to aid the women in their strike.[28] Unfortunately, because of a scarcity of reports in the contemporary press, we do not know the outcome of the strike or even what happened to the Female Union Society. But the men and women workers of Baltimore retained a unified front. In September, 1835, the United Men and Women's Trading Society, a joint organization of men and women workers, came into existence in that city.[29]

In 1832, after four years of incessant campaigning on behalf of higher wages for women workers in Philadelphia, Matthew Carey was forced to concede that his appeals had gone largely unheeded and abandoned the cause as "impracticable." So indeed it seemed until 1835, when the workingwomen themselves began to organize. In June, 1835, eighteen women met and planned a large meeting for all workingwomen of the city. They invited Carey to preside, and he eagerly accepted, acknowledging in doing so that he had naively believed that all that was needed to improve conditions for workingwomen was to "excite public sympathy" for their sufferings. He had, he admitted, been "miserably mistaken," but he hoped that now, through their own struggles, the workingwomen would gain the success they deserved.[30]

The meeting was attended by an overflow crowd of about five hundred workingwomen from all the sewing trades and several others as well. Several clergymen and philanthropists were also present, but no trade union of men workers was represented. After speeches describing "the injustices and oppression of the poor, honest, and industrious working women of Philadelphia," the women formed the Female Improvement Society for the City and County of Philadelphia—the first citywide federation of workingwomen that embraced women from several trades. Committees were chosen from each trade to draw up wage scales. At the next general meeting, other committees were charged with submitting the new wage demands to the employers and publicizing the names of those who acceded. A special committee was appointed to protest the low pay received by women for sewing army clothes and to call upon the Secretary of War to remedy the situation.[31]

The secretary replied that he could do nothing more than submit the petition to the commissary general of purchase, writing that, while the government did not wish to oppress the "indigent but meritorious females employed in its service," the issue was one of "much delicacy," since it was "so intimately connected with the manufacturing interests and the general prices of this kind of labour in the city of Philadelphia."

The standard for "this kind of labour" was determined by the Provident Society, one of Philadelphia's charities, which paid seamstresses 12½ cents a shirt. Both private employers and the U.S. War Department consequently paid the same wage for the work. So when the seamstresses pleaded in their petition that such a price reduced them "to the degradation of pauperism," the Secretary of War could defend the practice by arguing that he was doing only what charitable institutions were doing, and it was not proper for him to disturb the existing structure. Fortunately, a number of employers were not so sensitive, and the women did win a series of wage increases.[32]

Women shoebinders were among the groups of women workers who united to fight for improved conditions in these early years. Although the factory system and modern machinery were still to affect the making of shoes, the trade was undergoing important changes. In 1800 the household served as the basic unit of shoe production. The master shoemaker (and head of the household) purchased the leather and supervised production in a small shop called a "ten-footer" behind his family's cottage. Working under him were a group of (usually younger) journeymen who brought their own kits of tools with them and received from the master not only wages but room and board, firewood, and clothing. Within the master's house, his wife and daughters, working as binders, hand-stitched the upper part of the shoe. His sons, serving as apprentices and entrusted with a variety of odd jobs, completed the work team.

By the 1830s household shoe production had given way to the central shop. The master, who had fashioned his finished goods on customer order or else sold them to a small shopkeeper, had fallen victim to his supplier and distributor. Merchants with access to credit and an eye to expanding markets created a new production system. While household manufacture remained important, the merchant-owned central shop was becoming dominant in the field. Skilled cutters prepared leather for the merchant. Rural and village women and girls hand-stitched uppers for him. Journeymen bottomers, who owned little more than their tools but still retained essential skills, tacked the upper to the sole. They worked for the merchant but labored at home or in "ten-footers." The merchant's delivery wagons would bring the leather to the women to be sewn, and the merchant marketed the finished product.[33]

Massachusetts was a center for shoemaking, with Lynn at its hub. As early as 1829 there were 1,500 women binding and trimming shoes in Lynn, and, as the demand for lower-priced shoes grew, women from all the surrounding villages became shoebinders.[34] Women shoebinders were paid on a piecework basis, often in scrip redeemable at certain dry goods stores. At first the wages in Lynn were comparatively high, but by 1833 they had begun to fall, and the women decided to do something to maintain their standards. The *Lynn Record* of January 1, 1834, heralded the New Year with a story under the startling head: "The Women Are Coming."

> Alas for the Shoe Manufacturers! We tender our sympathy and condolence but in vain. It is all over with you! You may as well strike your flag, and give up the ship, first and last. The powers that be are against you. *Men* may commence an enterprize and become disheartened—they put the hand to the plough, and look back. Not so, the women—they know no defeat. We would as soon invade the armies of Philip of Macedon, as theirs, and with more hope of success. *We intend to be on the popular side*—on the side of *power*, right or wrong, and therefore cannot help you. Our advice is: agree with your adversary quickly. The women want money and must have it—you must give it to them, *that* you must: and you may as well make no bones of doing it at once, as to have your bones broken, and do it afterward.

In a more serious vein, the *Lynn Record* went on to report that about a thousand women had gathered in convention at the Friends' Meeting House in Lynn, and at this gathering, "probably the largest ever held in

New England," they had formed the Female Society of Lynn and Vicinity for the Protection of Female Industry. In a manifesto to the public, they insisted that it was only just that "equal rights should be extended to all—to the weaker sex, as well as to the stronger," that the "disadvantages which nature and custom have entailed upon females, as to the common transactions and business of life; are sufficiently great of necessity, without the addition of others, which are unnecessary and unjust." Hence they had been "driven by necessity to seek relief, impressed with the belief that women as well as men have certain inalienable rights, among which is the right at all times of 'peaceably assembling to consult upon the common good.'" Despite the concession to the prevailing opinion as to the relative strength of the two sexes, the *Lynn Record* correctly noted that the demand for equal rights for women was very advanced for the time and that probably no other meeting place would have tolerated such a stand. But at the Friend's Meeting House "the *liberty of speech* is not all on one side, the women, as well as men are here permitted to *speak out*."

The constitution of the Female Society provided for quarterly meetings, established a relief fund and quarterly dues cf 12½ cents, and provided for a wage scale to be voted on quarterly. Every member had to agree to work only at the agreed-upon wages, and members could be censured or expelled for violating this pledge.[35]

Once organized, the women shoebinders of Lynn went out on strike for a new wage scale. Two days after the strike began, the women of Saugus, "encouraged by the example of the ladies of Lynn," formed their own organization. The 125 members adopted the wage demands of their Lynn sisters, presented them to their employers, and won their acceptance.[36] But the Lynn manufacturers responded to the demand of the Lynn women with the cry that to raise wages would ruin the town. The women replied: "We can only say that we regard the welfare of the town as highly as anyone can do; and that we consider it to consist, not in the aggrandizement of a few individuals, but in the general prosperity and the welfare of the industrious and laboring classes."[37]

The Lynn strike continued for over two months. In March the Female Society announced that most of its demands had been agreed to, and the shoebinders returned to work under a new wage scale. Apart from the militancy and solidarity of the women strikers, their victory was aided by the fact that they were fully supported by the men's Cordwainers' Union, whose members raised funds for the strike and agreed not to work for any shoe manufacturer who did not meet the women's demands. Perhaps as a token of its gratitude, the Female Society chose two men to serve as its delegates to the Boston Trades' Union, the city central labor organization. But the society was not represented for long; by June, 1833, it was reported to be facing difficulty in maintaining its existence, with most of its members again working "under price" or not paying dues.[38]

The women shoebinders and corders of Philadelphia were able to maintain their organization after they organized and struck. In March, 1836, five hundred corders and binders formed the Female Boot and Shoe Binders Society, and even though they were not organically united, they struck together with the men's cordwainers' union for a rate advance. Denouncing the "detestable machinations of the employers to crush a suffering class of females," the journeymen announced: "Although they may forget they have mothers, we have resolved to take them [the women] under our protection, to flourish or sink with them." Even if they won their own demands, the men declared, they would not return to work until the women had won theirs. They formed a committee to solicit donations for the corders and binders and urged all unionists to "join their sisters in the holy cause of bettering their conditions."[39]

The *National Laborer,* Philadelphia's leading labor paper, urged full support of the women strikers and, in appealing to "trade unionists to come manfully forward to their succor," observed admiringly, "They well deserve generous aid, for they have stood out boldly for their rights, with an unanimity the other sex might truly be proud of."[40] Contributors to the strike fund included the shoemakers of Wilmington, Delaware, and the hand loom weavers of Philadelphia. Matthew Carey raised money and spoke in behalf of the strikers. The outcome of the strike is unknown, but it must have ended in some victory, since in June, 1836, the Female Boot and Shoe Binders Society published its constitution and invited all binders and corders to join this "large and growing society."[41]

There are other examples, in this period, of rampant exploitation of women wage earners—those making straw hats, cigars, and artificial flowers, as well as umbrella sewers and bookbinders—and of the attempts of these women to organize against it. Unfortunately, because of lack of records, we know little about these early efforts. Few lasting organizations of women workers emerged in this period. The women's associations were even shorter-lived than the male trade unions of the period, generally coming into existence during a time of struggle and fading after a strike was won or lost. It was an experience that was to be repeated many times throughout American labor history.

Despite the frequent defeat of hopes and the temporary nature of these first associations, the efforts of women workers to organize themselves into protective organizations during this time are significant. They are closely connected with the general rise in American labor activity, and the tactics used by women workers were similar to those employed by unions in other trades. Like their brothers, fathers, husbands, and sons, they met, drew up wage scales, and pledged not to work for any employer who would not agree to pay the wages being demanded. A committee would usually present the wage scale to the employers, and other committees would publicize the women workers' case to the public. By the time women workers organized, these had already become tried and tested methods of the trade unions. As the sewing women of Baltimore put it at their first meeting in September, 1833: "We know of no method so likely to procure us relief as that which has of late been successfully practiced by the mechanics of this city."[42]

Still, the painful truth is that the major reason women workers were so late in organizing compared with men is that the early trade unions, with few exceptions, were hostile to women workers, viewing them as a competitive threat instead of as potential allies, and refused to organize them. Thus, in the main, women were compelled to organize themselves.

The first trade unions were set up by skilled craftsmen who converted their mutual aid societies, organized to assist members in time of illness, to ones that could conduct struggles for higher wages and shorter hours. Their members were workers in a single craft, often working in a small shop and performing most of the work required to produce a product. But the 1790s marked both the beginnings of a national market and the rise of the merchant capitalists who furnished credit and materials to local producers and put pressure on them to increase their production. The small shops with skilled craftsmen producing for a local market soon gave way to larger shops with more and more workers and with one employer, manufacturing for markets in the South and West. As competition for these markets increased, employers reduced wages and increased working hours. They also divided workers into teams in order to speed up the work through specialization and division of labor. And they began to replace adult men with young boys and girls and adult women to do the work at one-fourth or one-half the men's wages.

The early trade unions fought vigorously against the growing division of labor and tried to prevent the hiring of more and more apprentices and unskilled workers who "will work for what they can get." As they saw it, the more women workers hired, the more the wages of the skilled male workers would suffer. They saw the women as part of a reserve of cheap labor being used against them, and they often blamed the women instead of their employers for their plight.

Thus the first trade unions, established in the 1790s, were for men only.* So, too, were the Democratic-Republican societies, in which the early trade unions were active. While the societies, in advancing the

---

*The Philadelphia Benevolent Society stated in its 1802 constitution that "women as well as men may become subscribers to the *Benevolent Society* and every member shall have an equal voice in questions relative to the management thereof." (*Rules and Regulations of the Philadelphia Benevolent Society* [Philadelphia, 1802], p. 23.) But when the male craftsmen who belonged to the society organized their specific unions, they all excluded women.

cause of Jeffersonianism, regularly toasted "the fair daughters" of America, none of these fair daughters was invited to join.[43]

From refusing to include women, the early trade unions moved to exclude them from the trades. In 1819 the Journeymen Tailors of New York went out on strike to keep master tailors from hiring women. In the printing trade, unions took similar action: the Typographical Society of Philadelphia forced one printer to renounce a plan to hire women compositors, and the printers of Boston joined together to drive "the girls from the business of setting type."[44]

The introduction of machinery intensified the trend toward division of labor. Skilled craftsmen were increasingly confronted with machines that could do their work in less time and robbed them of the advantage they had enjoyed over unskilled workers. Since women and children were the first to be hired to tend the machines in the new factories, many male workers associated "female labor" with the developing factory system and the cheapening of the value of skilled labor. This was made clear in the 1819 walkout of New York journeymen tailors against the use of seamstresses in their profession. They insisted that since women possessed inherently inadequate abilities, their labor insulted the trade. Here is how one such tailor explained it in a letter to the New York *Evening Post:*

> A journeyman tailor not above the level of mediocrity cannot make a super-fine plaincoat to pass the ordeal of criticism—much less many other garments that might be named; yet this very man can make waistcoats and pantaloons and that, too, with more judgment and solidity than a woman can; *hence* we infer that women are incomplete, and if incomplete, they ought to disclaim all right and title to the avocation of tailor.[45]

In their pursuit of self-esteem, the mechanics upheld their dignity by refusing to work side by side with women. Although revolutionary changes in transportation and technology had greatly altered the usual patterns of labor, many skilled craftsmen saw the entrance of women into the job market as the major source of their problems. They tended to the view that women belonged in the home, where they would be supported by male workers, and not in the world of trades and industry, where they added "unfair competition." A strike declaration of 1809 argued that American society had an overriding obligation to provide its workingmen with sufficient compensation for their labor so that their wives and daughters would not have to work.[46]

The *Mechanics' Free Press* of Philadelphia devoted considerable space to the argument that women should remain at home, and it became an ardent supporter of the "cult of true womanhood." One of the articles, entitled "Female Society," pointed to the proper role women should play:

The advantages of female society are numerous, and extend themselves over almost every custom and every action of social life. It is to social intercourse with women, that men are indebted for every effort they make to please and be agreeable.... In our sex, there is a kind of constitutional or masculine pride which hinders us from yielding, in points of knowledge or of humor, to each other. Though this may be designed by nature for several useful purposes, yet it is often the source, also, of a variety of evils, the most dangerous to the peace of society; but we lay it entirely aside in our connections with woman.... Hence we may rest assured, that it is the conversation of virtuous and sensible women only, that can properly fit us for society; and that by abating the ferocity of our more irascible passions, can lead us on in that gentleness of deportment distinguished by the name of humanity. The tenderness we have for them softens the ruggedness of our nature.[47]

It is a measure of the contradictory attitude toward women held by many male workers of the period that in 1829 the Mechanics' Union of Trade Associations of Philadelphia, the first city central labor body in the United States and the sponsor of the *Mechanics' Free Press,* invited Frances Wright to deliver the Fourth of July address to the workers of its city. Wright, a young Scottish woman, was one of the first to speak about women's rights and thus was an outstanding example of what the "cult of true womanhood" was against. For days thereafter, the workingmen of Philadelphia (and later those in other cities who read the address) echoed her concluding statement that, valuable as the Declaration of Independence was, it would not serve the interests of the American people unless it was rewritten to add certain guarantees to its basic principles; namely, that each child had a natural right to a free education, each man and woman to the fruits of their labor, and each aged person to retirement in comfort: "Until this oversight be rectified, the revolution we this day commemorate will be incomplete and insufficient, the 'declaration' contained in this instrument will be voided."[48]

But since Frances Wright, although an ardent champion of labor, was not herself a workingwoman, she did not pose a threat to the skilled craftsmen who had invited her to address them and who published and distributed her Fourth of July speech. In any case, the fact is that for several years after they were founded, the early labor papers ignored the workingwoman. In 1830, three years after the *Mechanics' Free Press* was launched, "A Working Woman" complained to the Boston *Working Man's Advocate:*

> You come out to support and advocate the rights of Working Men, their wrongs are trumpeted from paper to paper, from city to city, from the "Literary Emporium" to the "Ancient Domain." Thus far you are right. "This ought ye to have done, and not leave the other undone." Know ye not that a large portion of the females of our country come under the denomination of Working Women—that they are oppressed and injured as deeply as are the Men?

George Henry Evans was so struck by this complaint that he reprinted the letter in his New York *Daily Sentinel* and vowed to devote space in his papers to correcting the omission.[49] The *Daily Sentinel*, the *Working Man's Advocate*, and the *Man*—all edited and published by Evans in New York—devoted considerable space to the conditions and activities of workingwomen, supported them editorially, and opened their columns to correspondence from workingwomen and their sympathizers. Among the causes Evans promoted was the establishment in New York City of a "Women's Library," to be composed "of the writings in favor of women, and books best calculated to improve the minds and disposition of females."[50]

Evans even went so far as to challenge the prevailing view of the male trade unions that women should not be allowed to enter new trades. He supported Matthew Carey's idea of increasing the number of occupations open to women in strong words:

> And these [occupations] are much better paid than any which we self-styled lords of the creation have hitherto left to the gentler sex. We are quite willing to flatter women, to profess love and devotion for them, to call them angels and fifty other foolish names; but we are not willing, it seems, to let them share with us those profitable employments which are perfectly adapted to their sex's strength. It is very true that such changes in female labor might tend to lower men's wages, and still more to overstock occupations already more than supplied with hands. But such an argument ought not to weigh as a feather in the balance. If we are to suffer, let us suffer equally and together.[51]

Other labor papers did not go that far, but they did begin to pay more attention to workingwomen. The *National Laborer* of Philadelphia argued that *special* attention must be paid to these workers: "There is no portion of the community whose condition demands our immediate attention more than the female operatives of this country."[52]

The more enlightened approach of the labor press of the 1830s helps to explain the greater support of women workers by male trade unionists during that decade. It also helps to explain the fact that one of the labor parties of the period—the Association of the Working People of New Castle, Delaware (a community with a labor paper alert to the problems of workingwomen)[53]—even demanded the enfranchisement of women.[54]

As we have seen, when factory workers organized and "turned out," their actions were publicized and supported by workers in other trades. In much the same spirit, the cigarmakers of Philadelphia resolved during their ten-hour strike in 1835 that the wages paid to "females engaged in segar making is far below a fair compensation for their labor." They invited the females "in a body to strike with us."[55] And, as we have seen, the Philadelphia men's Cordwainers' Union struck together with the female corders and binders and resolved to take the women "under our protection to flourish or sink with them."

It can be argued that however supportive these male trade unionists were, they appeared to have shared the sexist attitudes of the time that the women were weaker, gentler, and more dependent, and needed male protection. It can also be argued that in these (and other) cases of male supportive help, women were firmly established in the occupations, so that the men had everything to gain and nothing to lose by helping them win better conditions. But however imperfect the motives may have been, these instances of cooperation disprove the view that *all* male trade unionists of the period were hostile to women workers.[56]

This is not to say that even the more enlightened male trade unionists took a consistent position on the issue of workingwomen. While many expressed concern that if women continued to operate under existing oppressive working conditions, the effect on their own health and that of future generations would be harmful to the nation, they still felt that if women were to enter trades where conditions were better, performing work then done by men, "wages would gradually sink to almost nothing."[57] To their minds, the solution was for workingwomen to return to the home. Thus, the president of the Philadelphia Trades' Assembly appealed to working women in 1835 to unite and "form a female traders' union" to battle for higher wages and shorter hours, until they succeeded in working only half as long as they did at the time. At that point there would be more work for men to do, and since they would be paid better for this work,

> ultimately you will be what you ought to be, free from the performance of that kind of labor which was designed for man alone to perform. Then will you who are wives be able to devote your time to your families and your homes; then you will be able to attend to the cultivation of your mind, and impart virtuous instruction to your children; then you will be able to appreciate the value and realize the blessings of the connubial state. And you who are unmarried can then enjoy those innocent amusements and recreations, so essential to health, and qualify yourselves for the more sober duties of wives, mothers, and matrons.[58]

These often contradictory attitudes toward women workers of the period came to a head at the third convention of the National Trades' Union in 1836. There the Committee on Female Labor presented the first trade union report in American history dealing with women workers. It recommended that men admit women workers into their unions or encourage the women to form separate unions, with "one auxiliary to the other," so that "in case of difficulties they [the women] would be governed by their [the men's] laws and receive their support." It also called upon the convention, "from feelings of humanity," to "recommend to the different Unions the propriety of assisting with their advice and influence, the female operatives throughout the United States, in ameliorating their present unhappy situation, under the female system of labor." But the committee saw these actions only as temporary necessities to "curb the excess before we destroy the evil." Its main point was that the existing system of employing women was a blot on the "escutcheon on the character of American freemen, [which] if not checked by some superior cause . . . will entail ignorance, misery and degradation on our children, to the end of time." The solution for women and the nation was inherent in the nature of women: "The physical organization, the natural responsibilities, and the moral sensibility of women, prove conclusively that her labors should be only of a domestic nature." Unfortunately, the report went on, women were "very blind as to their real interest," and imagined that efforts to destroy the vicious system under which they were forced to leave the home were "destructive to their interest." It was therefore necessary to educate such women, and indeed all workingwomen, to understand that under existing conditions the woman

> in a measure stands in the way of the male when attempting to raise his prices or equalize his labor; and that there her efforts to sustain herself and family are actually the same as tying a stone around the neck of her natural protector, Man, and destroying him with the weight she has brought to his assistance. This is the true and natural consequence of female labor, when carried beyond the necessities of the family.

Thus, the report, which opened with the most advanced position of any trade union movement of that era, closed with the exposition of a backward attitude that women continue to confront today. The Committee on Female Labor urged male trade unionists to "act the part of men" and seek the gradual destruction of the "unnatural policy of placing females in a different element from that designed by nature."[59]

In 1834 Seth Luther, perhaps the most enlightened labor leader of the period on the issue of women workers, pointed out: "It is quite certain that unless we have the female sex on our side, we cannot hope to accomplish any object we have in view."[60] Few workingmen of the period were ready to take the necessary steps to achieve such an alliance of working people. But whatever the attitudes of male workers, women would continue to enter the work force in increasing numbers and would continue their attempts to organize themselves into protective organizations.

2

Factory Women, Their Unions,
and Their Struggles

THE ECONOMIC CRISIS OF 1837 dealt a devastating blow to American trade unionism. Production practically came to a standstill, and thousands upon thousands of workers were thrown out of jobs. With one-third of the working class unemployed and most of the others working only part-time, the trade unions of the 1830s found it impossible to keep their heads above water. One after another, local societies, city centrals, and the national trade unions passed out of existence, taking with them the first labor newspapers.[1]

Throughout the Northeast, mills closed down as the words of a bitter song rang through the region:

> "The mill has shut down! Good God, shut down!"
> It has run at loss this many a day.
> Far worse than flood or fire in the town
> Will be the famine, now the mill has shut down.
> But to shut mills down is the only way,
> When they run at a loss, the mill owners say.
> God help the hands to whom it meant bread!
> With the mill shut down they'd better be dead![2]

When the mills reopened in the early 1840s, there emerged both a new type of factory operative and a new form of struggle against oppressive conditions. Before the crisis, most factory women came from the nearby farms, and their earnings in the factories were not their sole means of support. They could leave whenever they desired. Under these circumstances, their demonstrations were bound to be more in the nature of temporary, short-lived outbursts than sustained trade union activity. But in the 1840s a more or less permanent working class gradually began to emerge in the factories. A good many New England farmers had lost their farms during the depression of 1837–1840. "As the New England farms disappeared," writes Norman F. Ware, "the freedom of the mill operatives contracted. They could no longer escape.... A permanent factory population became a reality."[3] Or, as a contemporary labor journal emphasized in the summer of 1845, the workers in the mills were composed "of a large share of poverty's daughters whose fathers do not possess one foot of land, but work day by day for the bread that feeds their families. Many are foreigners free to work ... according to the mandates of heartless power, or go to the poor house, beg or do worse."[4]

Once the female factory operatives became the primary wage earners in the family, they became fully committed to improving their conditions systematically rather than through brief "turnouts." The factory operatives of Lowell, Manchester, Dover, Nashua, Fall River, and Waltham, already famous for their cultural and literary activities, were now to earn a new reputation. They were the ones who, in the mid-1840s, formed the first trade unions of industrial women in the United States—the Female Labor Reform Associations—and furnished the first women trade unionists of note in this country: Sarah G. Bagley, Huldah J. Stone, and Mehitabel Eastman.[5] By their ability, militancy, and hard work, these women leaders won the respect of the men who led the New England labor movement. They served as delegates to labor conventions and, along with men, became officers of regional labor organizations. They moved about the towns and villages of New England, soliciting subscriptions for the labor press, and they played a leading role in the great struggle initiated by the male operatives of Fall River for a ten-hour day. They gave impetus, as well, to a number of other important reforms, including the emancipation of slaves, the abolishment of capital punishment, and temperance. Moreover, these militant mill workers were among the real pioneers in the movement for women's rights. They were pressing for full citizenship for women, through voice and pen, at precisely the same time that Elizabeth Cady Stanton, the Grimké sisters, Susan B. Anthony, and other middle-class women were active, and they used many of the same arguments.

During the 1840s newspapers, magazines, and foreign travel books continued to paint glowing pictures of life in the Lowell mills, stressing the point that, unlike the workers in the manufacturing plants of Europe, those in the Lowell mills were living in a veritable paradise, cared for more as "pupils at a great seminary than as hands by whose industry profit is to be made out of capital."[6] Even Harriet H. Robinson, the famous Lowell mill operative, in her reminiscences, described what she called the "bright side" of the existence led by the women factory workers in Lowell. However, she conceded at the end: "Undoubtedly there might have been another side to this picture, but I have described the side I knew best."[7] What she may have meant was that factory work had a "bright side" compared with conditions in the rural communities from which the young women had moved, and in other occupations where conditions were even worse—a point that a number of scholars have recently stressed in arguing that the favorable contemporary accounts of life and work in the factories should be taken seriously.[8] But in the contemporary literature on the "Lowell System," there never was "another side." The entire emphasis was placed on the "Beauty of Factory Life." It was summed up in a poem entitled "Song of the Factory Girls" (published at the mill owners' expense):

> Oh, sing me the song of the Factory Girl!
> So merry and glad and free!
> The bloom in her cheeks, of health how it speaks,
> Oh! a happy creature is she!
> She tends the loom, she watches the spindle,
> And cheerfully toileth away,
> Amid the din of wheels, how her bright eyes kindle,
> And her bosom is ever gay.
>
> . . . . .
>
> Oh, sing me the song of the Factory Girl!
> Whose fabric doth clothe the world,
> From the king and his peers to the jolly tars
> With our flag o'er all seas unfurled.
> From the California's seas, to the tainted breeze
> Which sweeps the smokened rooms,
> Where "God Save the Queen" to cry are seen
> The slaves of the British looms.[9]

Ironically, by 1845 workers in the oft-maligned English system labored four to six fewer hours a week and had two more holidays a year than the Americans, and most British operatives were required to tend fewer looms.[10] Ironically, too, for several years the female operatives themselves helped to propagate the myth of New England's factory paradise. The young women in the Lowell mills formed "improvement circles"—little clubs in which they produced sketches, essays, and short tales modeled on those in the popular periodicals of the day. The circles were fostered and encouraged by both the clergymen of Lowell and the mill owners, who looked with favor upon their employees' devoting themselves to culture rather than to complaining about their conditions in the mills and acting to remedy them.

Out of one of these little clubs emerged the *Lowell Offering*. Under the supervision of Reverend Charles Thomas, pastor of the Second Universalist Church, four small quartos of sixteen pages each, containing the literary efforts of factory operatives, made their appearance at irregular intervals between October, 1840, and March, 1841. The major emphasis in these issues was to dispel the notion that factory work was degrading and that the mill operatives were exploited.

Soon the *Lowell Offering* was attracting national and international attention. Another improvement circle in Lowell, guided by the Reverend Thomas Thayer, pastor of the First Universalist Church, began a rival publication in April, 1841, called the *Operatives' Magazine*. Unlike the *Offering*, it did not advertise itself as exclusively female but "solicited communications from the operatives of both sexes." Printed by William Schouler, an agent of the mill owners, the *Operatives' Magazine*, like the *Offering*, had no intention of criticizing factory conditions or urging the factory operatives to unite to change them. In August, 1842, Schouler became the proprietor of the *Lowell Offering* and united the *Operatives' Magazine* with that more famous publication.

Still another magazine that espoused the escapist outlook of factory operatives was the *Olive Leaf, and Factory Girls' Repository*, published in Cabotville, Massachusetts.[11] But the *Lowell Offering*, with Harriet Farley and Harriot F. Curtis, both former mill operatives, as coeditors, advanced the view most clearly. It carried the words "A Repository of Original Articles Written by Females Employed in the Mills" and for several years was accepted as the voice of the mill workers. William Scoresby, a visitor from England, called it "the ninth wonder of the world, considering the source from which it comes." Charles Dickens, in his *American Notes*, referred to it as the "first clear notes of real life in America."* An American returning from England reported: "The *Lowell Offering* is probably exciting more attention in England, than any other American publication. It is talked of in the political as well as literary world." And in France, Adolphe Thiers solemnly proclaimed to the Chamber of Deputies that the magazine proved that in a democracy, labor could possess a mind and soul as well as a body.[12]

At the height of its fame, the tone of the *Lowell Offering* was set by Harriet Farley. One of ten children of a Congregational minister in New Hampshire, she had had to seek work at the age of fourteen to help support the family. After working at straw plaiting, binding shoes, tailoring, and other trades, she had entered the Lowell mills and joined an improvement circle. She first won attention in December, 1840, when the *Lowell Offering*, then edited by Abel C. Thomas, printed her reply, signed "A Factory Girl," to an attack by transcendentalist Orestes A. Brownson (in his magazine *Boston Quarterly Review*) on textile mill owners and their exploitation of factory labor. Brownson observed: "We

---

*Dickens added: "Of the merits of the *Lowell Offering* as a literary production, I will only observe, putting entirely out of sight the fact of the articles having been written by these girls after the arduous labors of the day, that it will compare advantageously with a great many English Annuals."

know no sadder sight on earth than one of our factory villages presents, when the bell at break of day, or at the hour of breakfast or dinner, calls out its hundreds of thousands of operatives." Factory work, he wrote, was enough "to damn to infamy the most worthy and virtuous girl." Farley defended the mill owners, attacking Brownson as a "slanderer," and called work in the textile mills "one of the most lucrative female employments." Her defense of the corporations came to the attention of Amos Lawrence, Lowell textile magnate, and in the fall of 1842 he assisted her financially so that she could leave the mill and devote herself to the editorship of the *Offering*. A year later Harriot F. Curtis joined her as coeditor.[13]

It was not long before the factory owners sent a written tribute to the editors, praising the "worthy enterprise" in which they were engaged.[14] For the editors of the *Lowell Offering* were not in the least concerned with wages, hours, and working conditions. As stockholders multiplied and greater profits were demanded, the wages of the Lowell operative were reduced more and more and a speedup of work and a longer day became the rule. "Since 1841," declared the *Lowell Advertiser* of October 28, 1845, "the operatives' wages have been cut down twice directly, besides being cut down indirectly by requiring them to do at least 25 percent extra work." The operatives, tending as many as three looms, worked indoors for long hours daily, pausing only for two hastily gulped meals. They were off only on Sundays and on four holidays during the year. Even Saturday evenings were denied them—the boardinghouses refused to allow lamps to be lighted so that the girls would retire early in preparation for church on Sunday. Moreover, Lowell set the pattern for all mills using the Waltham system, and agreements existed among employers to follow the wage rates and production speed of the machines adopted at Lowell.[15]

But none of this found its way into the pages of the *Lowell Offering*. "We could do nothing to regulate the price of wages of the world," wrote Harriet Farley. "We would not if we could, at least we would not make that a prominent subject in our pages, for we believe there are things of even greater importance." As for hours and working conditions, these were matters over which workers had "no control." Improvements would come as a result of the kindheartedness of the factory owners, who would "in their own good time introduce the ten-hour system, and will not this be a noble deed?"[16]

What were the "things of even greater importance"? All that really mattered, said Farley, was to "elevate, instruct and purify the mind and soul of the workers; to give them an outlet for the spiritual and emotional needs of the soul; to provide them with sweetness and light." Let the factory girls, therefore, continue to meet in improvement circles where they could read and study. Armed with learning and culture, they could protect themselves from the crushing power of the machine, which dehumanized the worker and robbed her of dignity and self-assurance. At the same time, they would prove to the world that there was "Mind Among the Spindles" and that a factory girl was the equal in learning and culture of the lady who stayed at home in leisure and comfort and did not soil her hands with work. As long as the mind and the soul were free, what did it matter what happened to the body? The philosophy of the factory girls should be that of the Apostles: "Having food and raiment, let us be therewith content."[17]

Writing of Harriet Farley's editorship of the *Lowell Offering*, Norman F. Ware points out that she "began by defending the operatives against attacks that were levelled at the corporations, and finished by defending the corporations at the expense of the operatives."* Nor did contemporary labor reformers fail to recognize this. They criticized the *Offering*'s editor for being deferential to employers and indifferent to the real needs of the factory operatives. When, they asked, would the *Offering* begin to reflect the real problems of these workers?[18]

However, the factory operatives themselves remained silent, no doubt influenced by the prevailing view that it was not fitting for mere female employees to question a magazine supported by the men who owned the mills. It was Sarah G. Bagley who broke this silence. She initiated a public debate that made it widely known that the world-famous magazine did not meet with the approval of all the female operatives it was supposed to represent.

Bagley, the first woman labor leader in American history, was probably born in Meredith, New Hampshire, and received a common-school education before moving to Lowell in 1836. She was employed in the Hamilton Manufacturing Company for six and a half years, and then in the Middlesex Factory, for about two years. For four of her eight years as a weaver, Bagley conducted a free evening school after working hours for the factory women, who were so eager to acquire an education that they were called the "culture-crazy girls."[19]

Bagley joined the Lowell Improvement Circle and wrote articles on the "Pleasures of Factory Life" for the *Lowell Offering*. As wages declined, working conditions deteriorated, and especially as the speed of machine operations increased rapidly, she became increasingly discontented with conditions in the mills and began to contribute articles to the *Offering* that were critical of the corporations. Later, denied access to this timid magazine, she voiced her anger at an Independence Day rally in 1845

---

*An anthology of the *Lowell Offering* which does not offset Norman J. Ware's evaluation is in Benita Eisler, ed., *The Lowell Offering: Writings by New England Mill Women (1840–1845)*, Philadelphia and New York, 1978. Several issues of what is called *New Lowell Offering*, produced at the University of Lowell by women students, faculty, and staff, have appeared since the Spring of 1977.

at Woburn, Massachusetts, attended by two thousand workingmen. When one of the speakers praised the *Offering*, Bagley took the platform and, according to the reporter for the *Lowell Advertiser*, "made some statements . . . which will do much to correct the impression abroad that it is the organ of the 'Factory Operatives'—stating that she had written articles in relation to the condition of the operatives, and their insertion had been invariably *refused!*"[20]

Bagley's attack on the *Offering* was widely reported, and Harriet Farley promptly responded through Schouler, the editor of the *Lowell Courier*, denying that she had ever rejected any article by Bagley. If any had been refused, Farley declared, it must have been while Mr. Thomas was in charge of the *Offering*. This started a debate between Bagley and Farley in the columns of the *Lowell Express* in which the mill operative challenged the editor to cite one article she had published that was critical of corporation policies and conduct. When Farley refused, Bagley called her a "mouthpiece of the corporations" (August 7, 1845). On this note the debate ended, but undoubtedly Bagley's attacks won support among the factory operatives. Late in 1845, despite assistance from the corporations and their agents, the *Offering* died for lack of support. Bagley greeted the news with the statement: "Peace to its slumbers, and if it should ever witness a morn of resurrection, may it be prepared to take a high stand among the redeemed as the bold defender of the rights of the people."[21]

Even before the *Lowell Offering* surrendered to the attacks of factory operatives, the women had acted to set up their own magazines and periodicals. In 1842 a fortnightly periodical, the *Factory Girl*, saw the light of day in New Market, New Hampshire. It was edited by men, but they were assisted "by several operatives of undoubted ability," and most of its contents were by young factory women. In 1842 the *Wampanoag, and Operatives' Journal* came into existence in Fall River, Massachusetts, edited by Frances Harriet Whipple.* In 1844 the *Factory Girl's Garland*, published by a man but edited by female factory operatives, appeared in Exeter, New Hampshire. Exeter was also the site for the *Factory Girls' Album and Operatives' Advocate*, which began publication in 1846. Although published by a man, it too was edited entirely by "an association of females who are operatives in the factories, and consequently qualified to judge the wants of those whose cause they will advocate."[22]

On November 7, 1845, the *Voice of Industry*, originally published by

---

*Frances Harriet Whipple, a native of Rhode Island, became active in the movement led by Thomas Dorr for a more democratic suffrage in that state, and was also a leading figure in the Rhode Island antislavery movement, writing poetry for the cause. Whipple's interest in labor is indicated by the fact that in addition to editing the *Wampanoag, and Operatives' Journal* during its year of existence (1842–1843), she was also the author of a pro-labor novel, *The Mechanic* (1841).

William F. Young in Fitchburg, Massachusetts, but now issued in Lowell, carried the notice:

> We cordially invite the Factory Girls of Lowell, and the operatives and working people generally, whether they agree with us or not, to make the *Voice* a medium of communication; for it is your paper, through which you should be heard and command attention. The press has been too long monopolized by the capitalist non-producers, party demagogues and speculators, to the exclusion of the people, whose rights are as dear and valid.

So many factory operatives made the *Voice* their "medium of communication" that it soon came to be known as "the factory girl's *Voice*." In May, 1846, the paper was taken over entirely by the young women in the factories.[23]

These new periodicals carried their share of genteel poetry, stories, and advice on general conduct, but they also spoke out vigorously in defense of the factory operatives and their efforts to improve their conditions. Moreover, through their columns, the young women began to demolish the myth of the "Beauty of Factory Life" in letters, articles, and poetry describing the actual conditions in the mills. Liberal papers like the *Manchester Democrat* also opened their columns to letters and articles from factory operatives describing the conditions they faced in the mills. "What Are We Coming To?" asked Octavia in the *Factory Girl* of March 1, 1843:

> I can hardly clear my way, having saved from four weeks steady work, but three hundred and ninety-one cents. And yet the time I give to the corporation, amounts to about fourteen or fifteen hours. We are obliged to rise at six, and it is about eight before we get our tea, making fourteen hours. What a glorious privilege we enjoy in this boasted republican land, don't we? Here am I, a healthy New England Girl, quite well-behaved bestowing just half of all my hours, including Sundays, upon a company, for less than two cents an hour, and out of the other half of my time, I am obliged to wash, mend, read, reflect, go to church!!! &c. I repeat it, what are we coming to?

Other letters told of girls who, "scarcely paid sufficient to board themselves," were forced to abandon their virtue to obtain favors. They told of managers who, finding the girls "languorous" in the morning, conceived the "brilliant" plan of forcing them to work on empty stomachs. They told of wage reductions of 40 percent in mills earning enormous profits; of workers forced to accept their wages in scrip, which meant a loss of about 50 percent in the value of these wages. Many letters complained of the unbearable speedups and pointed out that whereas ten years earlier the girls had tended two looms, making from 216 to 324 picks a minute,* they were now forced to tend four looms, making 480

---

*The process of pushing the pick the desired distance from the last one inserted previously.

picks a minute, "the increased work being done by labor and the profit
going to capital." The letters protested vehemently against the blacklist
system employed by all corporations to terrorize the factory workers and
the "curse" of the premium system, under which bonuses were given to
overseers and second hands (assistant overseers) who were able to get
more work out of the operatives. A special target were the widely circulated reports telling of factory women who had accumulated sufficient
savings to move west and purchase farms. "An Operative" replied:

> In the first place our average amount of wages is two dollars per week; then
> allowing for every day's labor, without sickness, and without rest, we have, at
> the close of the year, one hundred and four dollars. Out of this sum, for the
> "preservation of health," we must be supplied with comfortable clothing,
> suitable for toil with constant wear and tear; not to put on to merely loll upon
> sofas. No small amount is paid out for the mere article of shoes; for this
> running six times a day back and forth from the mill to our boarding houses,
> over stone sidewalks, takes off our *soles*. Then come rubbers, umbrellas,
> shawls, bonnets, &c., for everyday use; and this is not all;—we are required
> by our corporation rules to attend church regularly, and if we comply, a pew
> rent is added to our expenditures, of about five or six dollars. And what
> church is there in the city that would receive us upon their velvet cushions in
> our mill attire? Not one, I believe, could be found. Then comes the expense
> of a better suit, a Sunday garb, to appear decent in the eyes of the commu-
> nity. And to follow it out and really not to be niggardly or mean, we must
> contribute to the various *professedly* charitable objects of the day.

"How long," she asked, "do you think it would take us to become independent at this rate, go out west and buy us farms?"[24]

In addition to demolishing the romance of factory life, the operatives
used these publications to point out that it was impossible to take a
neutral position "while manufacturers and operatives were diametrically
opposed in their pecuniary interests." This note of class-consciousness
was sounded in many forms, including poetry and what was called "New
Definitions":

> Overseer—A servile tool in the hands of an Agent; who will resort to the
> lowest, meanest and most groveling measures, to please his Master, and to fill
> the coffers of a soulless Corporation.
> Operative—A person who is employed in a Factory, and who generally
> earns three times as much as he or she receives.
> Contemptible—For an overseer to ask a girl what her religious sentiments
> are, when she applies to him for employment.
> Oppressive—To make two men to do the work of three, without making
> any addition to their wages.[25]

The importance of the factory magazines cannot be overemphasized.
Workers smuggled them into the mills, and they were read eagerly and
passed along. These magazines stimulated the type of resistance described in the *Factory Girls' Album* of September 19, 1846:

> Dialogue of a Lowell girl with the overseer of a factory:—"Well, Mr. Buck, I

am informed that you wish to cut down my wages?" "Yes, such is my determination." "Do you suppose that I would go into that room to work again, at lower price than I received before?" "Why, it's no more than fair and reasonable, considering the hard times." "Well, all I have to say is, that before I'll do it, I'll see you in Tophet, pumping thunder at three cents a clap!" It is needless to say that she was not invited to resume her duties.

Behind such resistance were the first unions of female factory workers—the Female Labor Reform Associations.

The first and most important Female Labor Reform Association was organized in January, 1845, in Lowell, Massachusetts, by twelve workers in the cotton mills. Within six months, its membership had grown to five hundred and was rising steadily. "Our numbers have been daily increasing," said its president and one of its founders, Sarah G. Bagley, in May, 1845, "our meetings generally well attended, and the real zeal of the friends of equal rights and justice has kindled anew."[26]

The constitution of the association, adopted at the January, 1846, meeting, reflected the operatives' desire to improve factory conditions and their quality of life. It pledged to work for the ten-hour day and for improvements in sanitary and lighting conditions in the textile factories. It called upon all the operatives "to throw off the shackles" that prevented them "from rising to that scale of being for which God designed us," and required every member to pledge herself "to labor *actively* for reform in the present system of labor."

The association at first relied on moral suasion to gain its goals, but it declared in its 9th Article: "The members of this Association disapprove of all hostile measures, strikes and turn outs until all pacific measures prove abortive, and then that it is the imperious duty of everyone to assert and maintain that independence which our brave ancestors bequeathed us, and sealed with their blood."[27] Representatives of the Lowell association attended mass meetings of factory women in the mill towns of Manchester, Dover, and Nashua, New Hampshire. In each of these places, Female Labor Reform Associations were organized. The Lowell union also contacted factory women in western Pennsylvania, and they soon formed the Female Labor Reform Association of Allegheny and Pittsburgh.

An appeal from the Lowell association, addressed to all workingwomen in America, urged them to organize for the struggle for a better life. It was necessary, it said, to have "a complete union among the worthy toilers and spinners of our nation": "By organizing associations and keeping up a correspondence throughout the country, and arousing the public mind to a just sense of the claims of humanity we hope to roll on the great tide of reformation until from every fertile vale and towering hill the response shall be echoed and reechoed: Freedom—Freedom for all!"[28]

The Lowell Female Labor Reform Association did not achieve a nationwide organization of working women, but it was the first and probably the only mid-nineteenth-century association to organize women workers outside a local area. Its influence even extended to workingwomen in the trades.

The factory magazines and the *Voice of Industry* devoted most of their attention to the conditions of the factory operatives and to efforts to improve them, but they were not indifferent to the problems of other workingwomen. On August 28, 1845, the *Voice of Industry* announced: "We are publishing a series of articles from the *New York Tribune* upon the state of 'female labor' in that city, which develop a most deplorable degree of servitude, privation and misery among this helpless and dependent class of people." The articles revealed that while these workingwomen were living "half fed, half clothed, and half sheltered [in] cooped up, ill-ventilated cellars and garrets, [their] ill-rewarded and slavish toil [had] raised to lordly wealth, a herd of merchants and speculators who add nothing to the real wealth of the country."* The *Voice* urged these "terribly exploited women" to emulate their sisters in the factories by organizing to improve their conditions. It was delighted to report a series of strikes of seamstresses, and commented: "We hope the rebellion will sweep the whole country. . . . Shame upon man when weak and friendless women were compelled to appear before the public and give tongue to their wrongs." The *Voice* was especially pleased to report the formation of the Female Industrial Association of New York as another of the Female Labor Associations of the period.

The New York Association was organized at an 1845 meeting attended by seven hundred women who were determined to win better wages "by appealing to the public at large and showing the amount of their suffering." Noting that a speech by Elizabeth Gray (subsequently elected president) signified the emergence of an articulate spokeswoman for "suffering female workers of New York," the *Voice* approvingly quoted her statement that the Association was open to all, "for only by a firm cooperation could they accomplish what they are laboring for."[29]

The Female Industrial Association of New York did include representatives of almost all the women's trades: tailoresses, plain and coarse sewers, shirtmakers, bookfolders and stitchers, capmakers, straw workers, dressmakers, crimpers, and fringe- and lacemakers. The preamble to the association's constitution stated:

*The *Tribune* articles, entitled "Labor in New York: Its Circumstances, Conditions and Rewards," were probably the most detailed picture of white working women in any ante-bellum city. Beginning with an examination of the status of the ten thousand seamstresses in the city, the articles went on to deal with straw braiders, artificial-flower makers, shoebinders, bookfolders, bookbinders, map colorers, curled-hair manufacturers, dressmakers, huckster women, milliners, umbrella and parasol makers, and domestic servants (*New York Tribune*, Aug. 18, 20, 22, 25, 26, 28, 29; Sept. 3, 5, 9, 11, 13, 15, 16, 17; Oct. 4; Nov. 8, 11, 18, 1845).

Whereas, the young women attached to the different trades in the city of New York having toiled a long time for a remuneration totally inadequate for the maintenance of life, and feeling the truth of the gospel assertion that "the laborer is worthy of his hire," have determined to take upon themselves the task of asserting their rights against unjust and mercenary employers.[30]

The *Voice* carried only one other report on the Female Industrial Association of New York. On September 4, 1846, it noted that President Elizabeth Gray had conceded at an association meeting that the organization had met with little response from the public to its pleas for justice, and that the employers had refused to meet with association representatives or to make any changes in the conditions of the working women.

But the campaign of the Female Industrial Association of New York to convince the public of the need for reform was insignificant in scope compared with that conducted by the various Female Labor Reform Associations of the factory girls, and especially by the Lowell association. To further this work, the Lowell association appointed a committee to expose and counteract the false impressions created by the newspapers and corporation apologists. "The Press," Sarah G. Bagley declared, "takes every effort to slander our efforts and ridicule our operations." When the labor weekly *Voice of Industry* was in financial difficulty, early in 1846, the Lowell Female Labor Reform Association purchased the press and type and continued the publication with Bagley as chief editor. Forced to work fourteen or more hours a day in the mills, Bagley and other association members could not continue to issue the paper by themselves and had to turn it over to a man. But the association's officers still continued on the publishing committee and conducted speaking tours among mill workers and mechanics throughout New England to solicit subscriptions for the *Voice of Industry*.[31]

The Lowell Female Labor Reform Association also made its point of view known through the "Female Department" of the *Voice of Industry*, the first newspaper column edited and produced by workingwomen. The "Female Department," directed by Bagley, featured articles and poetry on a wide range of subjects of interest to women and regularly carried notices of meetings of the association. Under its masthead of the "Female Department" appeared the words, "As is Woman, so is The Race." Some of the articles, letters, and poetry in the column were written by men, including James Russell Lowell and John Greenleaf Whittier, but most of it was by women, for, as Bagley pointed out in the "Introductory," it had been deemed advisable to have a medium "devoted to the females of our country and through which they shall be heard." She also emphasized: "Our department devoted to woman's thoughts will also defend woman's rights, and while it contends for physical improvement, it will not forget that she is a social, moral, and religious being. It will not be neutral, because it is female, but it will claim to be heard on all subjects that affect her intellectual, social or religious condition."[32]

The Lowell association also established an "Industrial Reform Lyceum" to discuss controversial subjects ignored by the regular town lyceum. It organized fairs, May parties, and social gatherings at which copies of the *Valentine Offering*, a collection of articles and poems written by factory women, were sold. One of its most important activities was the publication and distribution of a series of "Factory Tracts," which were "to give a true exposition of the Factory system and its effects upon the health and happiness of the operatives." Written by the mill women, the tracts did more perhaps than any other publication to expose the myth of the factory paradise of New England. In "Some of the Beauties of Our Factory System—Otherwise Lowell Slavery," a mill operative who signed herself "Amelia" described in detail the long, tedious hours, the speedups, the low wages, the tyrannical boardinghouse system, and the blacklisting in the factories, and then asked: "Now, reader, what think you? Is not this the height of the beautiful and are not we operatives an ungrateful set of creatures that we do not properly appreciate, and be highly thankful for such unparalleled generosity on the part of our employers?"[33]

But "Amelia" was not content merely to expose the evils of "Lowell slavery." She called upon her sisters "for action—*united and immediate action.*" Her plea was not in vain. Not only did more operatives join the association, but when the Massachusetts Corporation in Lowell ordered weavers to tend four instead of three looms, and at the same time reduced wages one cent for each piece of work, the association called a meeting of the factory women to protest this order. The workers drew up a pledge resolving that they would not tend a fourth loom unless they received a wage increase in ratio to the increased work and that any worker who signed the pledge and then violated it should have her name published in the *Voice of Industry* as a traitor to the working class. Every weaver who worked for the corporation signed the pledge, and not a single girl violated the agreement. The company was forced to rescind its order.[34]

"Amelia" was also the author of "The Summons," one of the most widely published of the many songs and poems by members of the female labor reform associations. It went in part:

> Ye children of New England!
>   The summons is to you!
> Come from the workshop and the field,
>   With steadfast hearts and true.

. . . . .

'Tis mockery in the sight of God,
 To say that land is blest
Where millions bow beneath the rod
 Of tyranny oppressed.

For bread, where famished children cry,
 And none their want supplies—
Where toiling thousands live and die
 In ignorance and vice.

Then in the name of God come forth,
 To battle with the foe;
Nor stay ye till our hands have laid
 Each proud oppressor low.[35]

The chief "oppressor" was the mill owner, but there were many others in American society who had to be fought. Some operatives charged the abolitionists with taking a stand against slavery in the South while ignoring what they considered worse slavery in the factories of the North.*[36] But most factory women disagreed, and, indeed, they became known as the "Pretty Friends of the Slave."[37] "Should We Keep Quiet About Slavery?" asked "A Factory Girl," and she answered in a resounding negative. Another expressed the same idea in a poem:

Hast thou ever asked thyself
 What is it to be a slave?
Bought and sold for sordid pelf,
 From the cradle to the grave!

After describing the daily humiliations and sufferings inflicted upon slaves, especially women, she concluded:

Such is slavery! Couldst thou bear
 Its vile bondage? Oh! my brother,
How, then, canst thou, wilt thou dare
 To inflict it on another![38]

The Lowell Female Labor Reform Association participated officially in antislavery meetings and circulated antislavery petitions among the factory women.[39] The female associations also aided the drive to bring

*Such an attitude was expressed in the concluding verse of a poem, "The Factory Girl" published in the *Voice of Industry*, Dec. 11, 1845, describing the death of a factory woman from starvation:

That night a chariot passed her,
 While on the ground she lay;
The daughters of her master
 An evening visit pay—
Their tender hearts were sighing,
 As negroes' woes were told;
While the white slave was dying,
 Who gained their father's gold!

relief to the starving peasants of Ireland during the tragic potato famine
and became active in the movement to abolish capital punishment. The
temperance organizations in the mill cities were made up largely of the
factory women.[40] The female operatives became associated, too, with the
Utopian Socialist movement organized by the followers of Charles
Fourier in America; Sarah G. Bagley was elected vice-president and
Mary Emerson, another official of the Lowell Female Labor Reform
Association, secretary of the Lowell Union of Association.*

When the Lowell Female Labor Reform Association announced the
launching of its "Female Department" in the *Voice of Industry,* it pointed
out bluntly: "Our department devoted to woman's thoughts will also
defend woman's rights." This it did throughout its existence, as did the
other publications that carried the writings of the factory operatives. In
its entire publication history, the *Offering* carried only one article devoted to the issue of women's rights, and even Harriet H. Robinson, a
champion of the *Offering,* conceded that the approach in that article was
a timid one.[41] While the single article in the *Offering* touched delicately
on the need for greater status for women in society, the author warned
her sisters not to move too far from their "proper sphere," lest they risk
losing "the grace of their own sex" without acquiring any of the superior
qualities of the opposite sex. But the militant factory girls insisted that
women had the right to aspire to every place in society occupied by men
and condemned the entire establishment of laws and customs that prevented them from doing so.[42] The *Lowell Offering* and the other genteel
publications of the factory women viewed marriage as a means of escape
from the laboring class—especially marriage to the rich son of a mill
owner[43]—but the militant factory women cautioned against marrying
men of money who were spoiled by their upbringing and had no true
understanding of the needs of workingwomen. Marriage to a working-
class man was considered preferable, but in any case, the factory women
were advised not to marry the first eligible man who came along but
rather to make certain that the prospective husband would be as atten-
tive to and respectful of their rights once married as he was during
courtship. In "Rights of Married Women," an "Indignant Factory Girl"
condemned the entire structure that caused a woman "to lose her indi-
viduality" in marriage, and insisted that if men and women could not
function as true equals in the marital state, it would be better that each

*The basic concept of Charles Marie François Fourier (1772–1837), French Utopian So-
cialist, was the Phalanx, around which a new social order would grow. His movement was
known in the United States as Associationism, and his followers included Albert Brisbane
and Horace Greeley. Among significant colonies incorporating Fourierite principles were
Brook Farm and Hopedale. For the influence of Fourierism on the American labor
movement in the 1840s, see Philip S. Foner, *History of the Labor Movement in the United
States* (New York, 1955)1: 174–78.

"live a life of heroic isolation in calm self-reliance." For the woman, it was "better than submission," she wrote, concluding:

> No relation is true that *makes* one soul subservient to another, none is true which does not rather tend to the elevation and equalization of both parties. The same lie which reveals itself in slavery, is at the bottom of our marriage institution,—the governing of one nature by its loss to the will of another, and they must both pass under the renovating hand, now that they have been bared to the marching eye of this Age.[44]

Practically every argument put forth by the middle-class women's rights pioneers was advanced in the publications of the militant factory women. In addition, they contributed a working-class point of view. Thus, they insisted on equal pay for men and women performing the same work. One wrote: "If a certain amount of labor is performed, it can make no difference by any manner of rational reasoning, by whom the labor is done. It is folly to argue that labor performed by females is not in every respect done as well as by men, and there is no earthly reason why they should not receive as much." There was only one principle that should prevail in a democracy:

> The labor of one person ought to command the same price as the labor of another person, provided it be done as well and in the same time, whether the laborer be a man or woman. A thousand of type, properly set in a stick and deposited on a galley, a thousand stitches in a waistcoat, by a girl, are worth as much to a master tailor or printer, as if the work be done by a man,—and ought to be paid as well.

There was even a pioneer proposal for what is now called affirmative action: "Those who have employment fit for women, to bestow, ought to give them preference; for there are fewer occupations of which they are capable, and they need help and encouragement more than men."[45]

A prominent Lowell physician, who signed himself "Spectator," published a series of articles sneeringly criticizing the factory women for forming labor reform associations and agitating for women's rights instead of properly educating themselves to function as women had always operated—as "the power behind the throne," manipulating men to get from them what they wanted and compelling them to do as they wished. A member of the Female Labor Reform Association, signing herself "Operative," took on "Spectator" and challenged the entire concept of the "power behind the throne," arguing:

> Man forms our customs, our laws, our opinions for us. He forms our customs, by raising a cry against us, if he thinks we overstep our prescribed limits. Woman is never thought to be out of her *sphere*, at home; in the nursery, in the kitchen, over a hot stove cooking from morning till evening—over a wash-tub, or toiling in a cotton factory 14 hours per day. But let her for once step out, plead the cause of right and humanity, plead the wrongs of her

slave sister of the South or of the operative of the North, and even attempt to teach the science of Physiology, and a cry is raised against her, "out of her sphere."

Not so with man, she went on; he could fill any position, and everything he did was accepted as "within the range of man's sphere." Pointing specifically to the disfranchisement of women, she noted: "Man forms our laws, and by them we must abide, although we have no voice in making them," and she added: "Man forms our opinions, for he has the keys of knowledge in his own possession. Our colleges of education are founded expressly for him—and all offices, scientific, as well as political, military and ecclesiastical, man fills." She asked why all the offices in public institutions were filled by men; why men got paid more for the same work that women did; why women were deprived of the opportunity to guide the nation as well as men. "Will 'Spectator' tell?" she inquired, and went on to observe: "I think I have proved that the 'power behind the throne' is powerless."

With respect to "Spectator's" suggestion that the factory girls educate themselves properly, she commented briefly:

> I would sincerely thank "Spectator" for marking out for us a course of study, and would be happy to pursue it, if I had books and *time* to peruse them—but my excuse must be that I am still an
> OPERATIVE.[46]

Much has been written about the middle-class women of the 1840s who defied convention by traveling about for various causes of the period and who, in the process, advanced the movement for women's rights. But not enough has been said about the pioneer women labor leaders who performed the same function at the same time. In their letters to the *Voice of Industry* relating their travels to various towns and villages to collect subscriptions for the labor paper, Sarah Bagley, Huldah Stone, and Mehitabel Eastman described the hostile reaction of middle-class men who charged them with being "unfeminine."[47] But they refused to be intimidated; on the contrary, they used the criticism to advance the cause of women's rights. Reporting an attack upon her by a middle-class man who was infuriated when "*a female*" dared to approach him with the request that he subscribe to the *Voice of Industry*, Huldah Stone wrote to the various female labor reform associations:

> There, my sisters, now will you not hang your heads in disgrace, and abandon the cause of equal rights at once and forever? "Why," said he, "no man that has any *influence*, or that is of any use to the cause will take it. Females are out of *their place* while soliciting names to a working man's paper." . . . From my very soul I *pity* such a man—one who holds the female sex in such low estimation as to make such an assertion. . . . I suppose he is one of those who would wish to have "*the woman*" a domestic animal, that is, know-

ing just enough to cook his victuals, mend his feetings, rock the cradle and keep the house in order; and if she wished for any further information, why she must ask her Lord and Master! An *equal* she must not be. She must not engage in any great and noble enterprise to benefit her own and the other sex, *even* if she could accomplish twice as much as a man, for she would be "out of place." She must not dare go forth . . . to labor in order to sustain a paper devoted entirely to the interests of the thousands of females who are toiling beyond anything which their physical natures can endure, in close, unhealthy atmospheres, and to hard working laborers who receive just enough to keep soul and body in the same latitude, for fear of getting out of place![48]

The women labor leaders who advanced the cause of women's rights in various towns and villages were ignored by the educated women of leisure on whom the early feminist movement depended. Hence the mill women sent no delegates to the 1848 Woman's Rights Convention at Seneca Falls, New York, and those who met there did not speak on the most immediate economic issues of concern to these exploited working-women. Yet when they read the Declaration of Sentiments adopted by the Seneca Falls convention in the *New Era of Industry* (successor to the *Voice of Industry*), particularly the list of impositions upon woman by man, beginning with the fact that he had never permitted her "to exercise her inalienable right to the elective franchise," as well as the assertion that women "do insist upon an admission into all the rights and privileges which belong to them as citizens in the United States," the mill women must indeed have felt that the convention spoke for them, too. Through the journal known as the *Factory Girls' Voice* they declared: "We rejoice in that convention as a significant indication of the tendencies of this age."[49]

Like the middle-class women of the period, working-class women found it difficult to obtain respect from middle-class men. But they did gain it from working-class men, as Bagley, Stone, and Eastman noted in their letters. Mill superintendents ordered Stone out of the factories, but the men working in the mills received her cordially and subscribed to the paper. An agent forced Eastman to leave when she tried to sell subscriptions to the men at work, but, she reported, he "could not extend his authority any further and I went on with my business and was well treated throughout the premises."[50] To be sure, workingmen had the same interest in advancing the labor reform cause, especially the ten-hour day, as did the women, and they were fully aware that the organizations the pioneer women labor leaders represented gave the cause great impetus. Nevertheless, their response to the working-class women stood in sharp contrast to the reaction of middle-class men to middle-class women activists of the time.

The issue that, more than any other, united workingwomen and workingmen of the 1840s was the struggle for the ten-hour day. Many mechanics had gained the ten-hour day during the 1830s, but the New England workers had not shared the gains of the shorter workday movement of the preceding decade, and many of those outside of New England who had won the ten-hour day had lost it during the years of the economic crisis.[51] The vast majority of workers—male mechanics and female operatives alike—still worked twelve to fourteen hours a day. A fourteen-hour day was in many cases a twelve-and-a-half-hour working day when two mealtimes were deducted. Nevertheless, there were operatives who worked a full fourteen or fifteen hours a day, and those women who did not live in boardinghouses and had to shop for food and cook meals had to spend additional hours in their second, unpaid job.[52]

Advocates of the ten-hour movement of the 1840s developed a philosophy of their own to justify their demand and win public support, vividly expressed in the magazines and periodicals issued by or in behalf of the factory operatives. In letters and articles, the factory women emphasized the fact that because of the physical and mental effects of the existing hours of labor, the average worker could not expect to live long or hope to devote energies to anything but endless toil.[53]

Some ten-hour advocates even regarded the lessening of the hours of labor as "the primary social step" toward the achievement of a new social order. As the workers became more enlightened, they reasoned, they would grasp more clearly the necessity of putting an end to the existing economic system and would join eagerly in the crusade for a cooperative society. Still, if we were to select a single statement that summed up the position of the advocates of the ten-hour day, the following by Huldah Stone (who, incidentally, expressed the view in 1845 that *eight* hours should be the normal working day), would do as well as any:

> Is it really necessary that men and women should toil and labor twelve, sixteen, and even eighteen hours, to obtain the mere sustenance of their physical natures? Have they no other wants which call as loudly for satisfaction as those? Call ye this *life*—to labor, eat, drink and die, without knowing anything, comparatively speaking, of our mysterious natures—of the object of our creation and preservation and final destination? No! 'tis not *life*. It is merely existing in common with the inanimate and senseless part of creation.[54]

"I verily believe," replied one mill owner, "there are a large number of operatives in our cotton mills who have too much spare time now." To reduce the working hours, he went on, "would increase crime, suffering, wickedness and pauperism." When workers refused to accept this argument and continued to insist on a ten-hour day, the capitalists struck back viciously with discharges and blacklists. Corporation agents threatened to blacklist all women who joined the Lowell Female Labor Reform Association and with it the crusade for the ten-hour day. Sarah Bagley wrote: "Deprive us, after working thirteen hours, of saying our lot is a hard one! We will make the name of him who dares the act stink with every wind."[55]

Ten-hour advocates differed with respect to the methods to be employed to secure the shorter workday. Some called for a huge campaign to convince legislators that incessant toil was inconsistent with the health, happiness, and liberty of the laborer and the welfare of the community and that laws should be passed restraining employers from hiring workers for more than ten hours a day. Others believed that groups of workers should concentrate on achieving agreement with their employers and establishing the ten-hour day in their own shops or factories. Still others favored the adoption of methods used successfully by workers in England in their struggle for shorter hours. This plan of action, popularized by John C. Cluer, an English weaver and labor organizer who had come to this country early in the 1840s, included three points: first, a convention of workers and manufacturers to discuss and agree on a program for the reduction of working hours; if the convention failed, a petition campaign to the legislatures; and finally, if that method also failed to bring results, a general strike, or, as it was popularly called, a "Second Independence Day." The general strike would take place on July 4, with all New England workers declaring their "independence of the oppressive manufacturing power."[56]

In the main, however, the movement for the ten-hour day depended on legislative action. In 1840 the ten-hour system had been established for federal government employees by executive order of President Van Buren. To do the same thing for employees of private concerns involved the state legislatures that had chartered them. The problem was to organize enough mass pressure to overcome the control exercised over the legislatures by the corporations.

How much pressure would be needed was graphically illustrated in 1842 and 1843, when the Massachusetts legislature ignored petitions for a ten-hour day forwarded by mill workers. In the fall of 1844, however, a new labor organization—the New England Workingmen's Association—came into being, which gave vigorous support to the crusade for a shorter workday.[57] Sarah Bagley represented the Lowell Female Labor Reform Association at the 1845 convention of the new association. Nor was she just a silent delegate; she delivered a forceful appeal for joint activity of men and women workers for the ten-hour day. Conceding that there were those who disapproved of such conduct by a woman, she declared: "For the last half a century, it has been deemed a violation of woman's sphere to appear before the public as a speaker, but when our rights are trampled upon and we appeal in vain to legislators, what shall we do but appeal to the people?" Were "the daughters of New England" to be told again by the powers that were that "they have no political rights and are not subject to legislative action"? "It is for the workingmen of this country to answer these questions— what shall we expect at your hands in the future?" In short, it was for the delegates to answer the question of whether or not their sisters and daughters should also enjoy the blessings of shorter hours, even though they could not vote.

The members of the Female Labor Reform Association claimed "no exalted place" in the labor movement, said Bagley, but wished, "like the heroines of the Revolution . . . to furnish the soldiers with a blanket or replenish their knapsacks from our pantries." In behalf of the union of factory women, she presented the Workingmen's Association with a silk banner on which was inscribed the motto: "Union for Power—Power to bless humanity."[58]

Despite her modest claims, the male delegates to the convention knew enough about the militant and inspired leadership of Sarah Bagley to elect her vice-president of the association—the highest position occupied by a woman in the labor movement anywhere in the world at that time—and to assign her the leading role in the campaign for the ten-hour day.* In the months that followed, the drive for the ten-hour day—sparked by the Lowell Female Labor Reform Association and the *Voice of Industry* and headed by Bagley—blanketed the mill towns with petitions. Thousands of signatures, most of them of workingwomen, were obtained.[59]

Upon receiving the petitions, the Massachusetts House of Representatives' Committee on Manufacturing decided to hold hearings. Its chairman, William Schouler—proprietor of the *Lowell Courier,* an important backer of the *Lowell Offering,* and a leading spokesman for the corporation—informed the petitioners, most of them women, that they would have to appear to testify in defense of the ten-hour day, "or we shall be under the necessity of laying it aside." Evidently he was confident that "maidenly modesty" would prevent the militant factory women from appearing in public before a legislative committee in the statehouse in Boston—but he quickly discovered that he had underestimated their militancy. When the committee hearings opened, Bagley and other operatives were on hand, and their testimony provided a dramatic picture of the working life of a female factory operative. One operative's testimony was described in part as follows:

---

*Two other leaders of the Female Labor Reform Associations were elected officials of the New England Workingmen's Association: Huldah J. Stone as recording secretary and Mehitabel Eastman as secretary.

She complained of the hours for labor being too many, and the time for meals too limited. In the summer season, the work is commenced at 5 o'clock a.m., and continued till 7 o'clock p.m., with half an hour for breakfast and three-quarters of an hour for dinner. During eight months of the year, but half an hour is allowed for dinner. The air in the room she considered not to be wholesome. . . . About 130 females, 11 men, and 12 children work in the room with her. . . . Thinks that there is no day when there are less than six of the females out of the mill from sickness. Has known as many as thirty.

Despite the overwhelming evidence presented by witnesses of the pressing need for a ten-hour day, the report of the investigating committee, written by Schouler, was opposed to any legislation. It insisted that "a law limiting the hours of labor, if enacted at all, should be of a *general nature;* it should apply to individuals or copartnerships as well as to corporations." It conceded that there were abuses in the factory system but expressed confidence that these could be eliminated without legislation, for "here labor is on an equality with capital, and indeed controls it, and so it ever will be while free education and free institutions exist." The report concluded by asking that "the petitions be referred to the next General Court."[60]

When the report was made public, Harriet Farley timidly rebuked the committee. Calling the petition to the legislature both "proper and dignified," she went on to ask: "Might not an arrangement have been made which would have shown some respect to the petitioners, and a regard for the ease and comfort of the operatives?"[61] The *Lowell Advertiser* criticized Farley for her restraint and charged the committee with inconsistency in conceding the existence of abuses while at the same time insisting that it was not up to the legislature to deal with them. As for the statement that labor was "on an equality with capital," it asked:

Why do not laborers reform the abuses of which they complain, instead of applying for protection to a Legislature that tells them that they are abused, but that the Legislature can't help them? Why does capital take the Lion's share and compel the laborers to put up with the Jackal's? . . . Capital is the Lion! and the terms he imposes *must* be submitted to.[62]

The *Voice of Industry* and the Lowell Female Labor Reform Association charged that the petitions had been rejected because the committee had been bought by the corporations. When William Schouler later ran for reelection to the legislature, the Lowell association denounced him as "a corporation machine or tool" and urged the male workers to defeat him. When the returns were in, the association published a resolution expressing its "grateful acknowledgement to the voters of Lowell" for "consigning William Schouler to the obscurity he so justly deserves."[63]

While the campaign for a ten-hour law was going forward in Massachusetts, the factory women in western Pennsylvania, members of the

Female Labor Reform Association of Allegheny City and Pittsburgh, were so incensed by legislative stalling that they decided to take matters into their own hands. On September 15, 1845, five thousand workers went on strike for the ten-hour day. They held out for almost a full month, at which point some of the women, desperate, decided to go back to work. But they did not remain at work long. Strikers went from factory to factory, broke open the gates, seized the workers at the machines, and dragged them outside. At the largest of the mills—Blackstock's factory—they were joined by the "men's auxiliary." An on-the-spot reporter for the *Pittsburgh Journal* describes what happened at Blackstock's:

> They [the factory girls] were now in full force. A whole legion of men and boys accompanied them as auxiliaries, to be used in case they were required. Thus prepared, flushed with conquest... they marched to *the scene of the great struggle*—the Battle of Blackstock's.
>
> On their arrival, they saluted the enemy with three shouts of defiance and a universal flourish of sticks and bonnets. After a minute or two spent in reconnoitre, they moved forward in a solid column of attack, on the... pine gate of the yard.
>
> In a moment the gate was forced open. But the defenders were determined on a heroic defence, and the assailants were thrown back and the gate again closed. A second time the assault was made with a similar result.
>
> Both parties now took time for breath, and opened negotiations. The factory girls demanded the instant expulsion of the girls at work. The people inside obstinately refused the terms, and both parties again prepared to decide the matter by the uncertain chances of the field.
>
> "They say they won't—let's try again!" and encouraging each other with loud cries, the legions marched to the imminent breach. For a moment, the combat was a doubtful one. The garrison made a stubborn resistance—but what could you expect from pine boards?... The gate gave way—"hurrah! hurrah!," and in a moment the yard was filled, the fortress was taken by storm, and the garrison were prisoners of war.

The following day the same paper carried this report:

> We are informed that the manufacturers have expressed a great deal of dissatisfaction with reference to the conduct of the Police, on Monday, during the disturbances. It seems to us that this is unjust. It was utterly impossible for any ordinary police force to have maintained order. There were hundreds of male friends of the operatives standing round—ready to interfere whenever it should become necessary... "let 'em hit one of them gals if they dare, and we'll fetch them out of their boots!" said a grim double-fisted fellow on our right, while they were breaking open Blackstock's.[64]

Although the male workers supported the women strikers, they did not, as in the 1830s, regard the women as too fragile to be able to conduct a militant struggle by themselves. The "factory Amazons," as the

Pittsburgh Journal described them, broke down the fences and walls barring them from those who continued to work and won their strike by themselves. The men stood around waiting to help if needed.

The sight of hundreds of women daring to break open the factory gates and toss out the strikebreakers by sheer force so antagonized conservative middle-class groups that the factory women found it impossible to gain public support. The employers were adamant, contending that they could not decrease working hours as long as New England mills continued to operate on a thirteen- or fourteen-hour basis. They promised, however, that the moment the ten-hour day was instituted in the New England mills, they would introduce it in Pennsylvania.

The Pittsburgh workers then turned to their sisters and brothers in New England and urged them to intensify their fight for the ten-hour day, assuring them that in western Pennsylvania arrangements had been made "for continuing the warfare." Upon receiving this plea, the Lowell Female Labor Reform Association invited John C. Cluer to discuss his plan for a ten-hour day at their meeting. Cluer outlined his three-stage idea and was "enthusiastically received."[65]

In conjunction with the New England Workingmen's Association, the Lowell Female Labor Reform Association once again circulated petitions, once again gathered thousands of signatures, and once again presented them to the legislature. Once again, too, the petitions were rejected. Now completely infuriated, the Lowell association set July 4, 1846, as the day for a general strike for the ten-hour day. But the movement received little support. The fact that five thousand workers in western Pennsylvania had been unable to gain a victory despite their militant struggle discouraged many workers in New England, and the idea faded away.[66]

The petition crusade for a ten-hour law continued in Massachusetts, but the Senate committee appointed to consider the petitions once again advanced the principle that a ten-hour law applicable only to corporations would be unjust. Although it admitted that the legislature had the power to define the number of hours that should constitute a day's labor, the committee insisted that "it could not deprive the citizen of [the right to make his own] contract." Furthermore, it went on, any restriction would "injure business, and the result will be, the laborer is sure to suffer."[67]

Only in New Hampshire was the petition crusade for a ten-hour law successful. There, the campaign gained thousands of petition signatures under the leadership of Mehitabel Eastman, the factory operative who was president of the Manchester Female Labor Reform Association, a coeditor of the *Voice of Industry*, and secretary of the New England Workingmen's Association. The signatures were backed up by mass meetings sponsored jointly by the Female Labor Reform Associations of Manchester, Dover, and Nashua, and the male operatives and mechanics.[68]

In urging the enactment of a ten-hour law, the legislative committee in New Hampshire argued that a shortening of the workday would be advantageous to the employers, for they "would realize a greater profit, even in less time, from laborers more vigorous and better able to work, from having had suitable time to rest."[69] Evidently the New Hampshire employers were not entirely convinced by the logic of this argument, for, at their insistence, clauses were inserted into the statutes permitting employers to draw up special contracts with workers for more than ten hours. Even before the laws were passed, employers submitted these contracts to their workers and informed them that they had the alternative of signing and continuing to work or refusing to sign and going jobless. They also threatened to blacklist the workers who refused to sign.

In spite of the terror of the blacklist, the workers fought valiantly to preserve the ten-hour laws by agreeing among themselves not to sign the special contracts. A mass meeting held on August 24, 1847, in Manchester's City Hall was described as "filled to overflowing with the factory girls prominent among those in the large audience." Female and male operatives alike pledged never to sign the special contracts, and the Manchester Democrat editorialized: "The meeting illustrates that both male and female operatives are capable of uniting effectively for a common cause."[70]

But the workers in New Hampshire were unable to maintain their pledge. The power of the corporations was too great. Workers who refused to sign were discharged, and when they went elsewhere to seek employment, they found all doors closed to them.[71]

In 1847 a ten-hour day became law in England without any provisions for special contracts permitting a longer workday. It was not until 1874 that a comparable law was passed in Massachusetts! Little wonder, then, that the Lowell Female Labor Reform Association, pointing to the difference in the situations of the factory worker in monarchical England, with its ten-hour day, and democratic America, with its fourteen-hour day, declared bitterly that "the fourteen hour system of Labor, adopted in the American Factories ... makes the system of Factory Life and labor but little better than physical assassination."[72]

During these developments, the manufacturing of shoes was still more or less what it had been in the 1830s: household manufacture was still important, and the putting-out (or domestic) system was still dominant. Rural and village women and girls still hand-stitched uppers for the merchant while the journeymen bottomers retained their skills as they tacked the uppers to the soles. They still worked for the merchant who controlled the trade and set wages and conditions. How oppressive these conditions were, even in the preindustrial period of shoemaking in the 1840s, is revealed by the fact that in 1850, Lynn health officials reported that the life expectancy of Massachusetts shoemakers was far lower than that of Massachusetts farmers—forty-three as contrasted with sixty-five years.

But worse was still to come. Starting in the 1850s, the factory with its mechanization brought about changes in the shoe industry, just as it had already done in textiles. Large-scale factory production in the shoe industry began in 1852 with the utilization of the sewing machine, invented six years earlier, for stitching on the upper portion of boots and shoes. The sewing machine drew women into the factories, and the hand workers were largely replaced by female machine operators: binders, stitchers, basters, and gummers. Workshops still turned out shoes along with the factories, and skilled journeymen were still important. (The McKay stitcher, with its power pegging machinery, was not introduced until 1862.) But the handwriting was on the wall for the skilled shoemaker.[73]

In 1860 the workshops and factories of Lynn produced 4½ million pairs of women's and children's shoes. Still, the wages of the shoe workers had been sharply reduced. While the cost of living rose, wage cut followed wage cut. After a reduction in the fall of 1859, men were earning $3 a week. Wages for women were even lower, many women earning as little as $1 a week for as much as sixteen hours of work a day.[74]

The horror of what the factory system portended for Lynn was brought home starkly on January 10, 1860, when news reached the city that because of faulty construction, the Pemberton Mill of Lawrence, built in 1853, had collapsed, killing five hundred women and men operatives. In sermons the following Sunday, Lynn's ministers refused to attribute the mill disaster to an "Act of God" but instead put the blame on the mill owners' greed in failing to provide adequate safety precautions for the workers and to supervise the hasty construction properly. Were the shoe workers in Lynn's factories to face the same fate? The words of the song "The Fall of the Pemberton Mill" sent a shudder through Lynn.

> Not a moment's warning, I presume
> Of their impending, awful doom;
> The Pemberton Mills came tumbling down
> With souls five hundred to the ground.
>
> Through Lawrence streets, by old and young,
> The awful cry of fire was rung.[75]

On February 1, 1860, the *Lynn News* reported a meeting of shoe-makers "to take measures to secure an advance upon the present low rates of wages." The paper expressed its sympathy: "We certainly think that something ought to be done to secure to the workmen full compensation for their labor. They are the true wealth of this city, and one dollar taken from their just earnings is so much taken from the value of our real estate, from the revenue of our city government, and from the appropriation for educational purposes."

When the manufacturers turned down the workers' request for higher wages and refused to meet with their communities, the workers chose Washington's Birthday, 1860, for the beginning of the strike, in the hope that "his history of patience and endurance, may inspire every one that has pledged his honor to persevere in the cause so vital to themselves and their families." The *Lynn News* reported that the shoe workers had enthusiastically supported the decision to strike, and again expressed support: "When we place ourselves in their position, we can sympathize with all their trials, and feel the justice of all their demands."[76]

Two weeks later, the women binders and stitchers of Lynn joined the strike. At a mass meeting held before their decision to strike, a list of prices for various kinds of work presented by a committee of women workers was discussed and a canvassing committee was appointed to enlist all female workers. Another meeting held the following evening was so well attended that many could not get into the hall. Alonzo G. Draper, one of the leading figures in the strike, assured the women that the outcome of the struggle depended on their decision, "for if the ladies refused to bind and stitch, the bosses must either accede to the strikers' demands or go out of town." He urged the women to join the strike, "unless they could secure a permanent advantage by compelling the manufacturers to sign their list of prices." Draper's plea was endorsed by a Mrs. Greenleaf, described by one reporter as a "Jewish shoebinder, member of the canvassing committee." The reporter wrote: "She considered their cause as a sacred one and precisely similar to that of the Jewish patriarchs who left Egypt because they were obliged to work for nothing and furnish their own materials."

After some discussion, the binders voted to strike on March 7, 1860, if the new price scale was not accepted, and to mark the decision with a great procession. They also voted to invite the Lynn City Guard and Light Infantry to escort the procession. Before adjourning, the meeting appointed committees to visit Swampscott, Salem, Marblehead, Danvers, Ipswich, and other towns to "invite the binders of those places to join the strike and sign the pledge of adherence to the list of prices."[77]

Despite his sneering tone at the militant spirit displayed at the meeting, the reporter for the *New York Times* could not help expressing admiration for the women shoe workers:

> Every one of the fifteen hundred women at the meeting pledged herself to turn out, and to urge her friends to do the same. Draper was not mistaken in calling this the decisive step. Woe to the scab, be it male or female, who appears in the streets of Lynn henceforth. No unkindly greeting will be uttered, no act of violence perpetrated, but what is worse, withdrawal of all sympathy, either in word or deed, by the determined female strikers.

Later, after meeting with the "Female Committee," the *Times* reporter wrote that they had reached the decision to have the "girls call upon the scabs and endeavor to inoculate them with their own love of freedom, and tell them that the treatment they might expect from their old friends would be worse than the small-pox."[78] A special "Scab Committee" was appointed to visit homes in the different wards to make certain that no one was strikebreaking "by binding or gumming, or finishing on the sly."[79]

Elsewhere in the shoe towns, the women workers joined enthusiastically in the struggle. Many a reporter who observed the spirit of the women strikers was convinced that the strike could only end in victory. Thus, a correspondent for the *New York Herald* wrote from Marblehead, Massachusetts: "The women are talking about taking part in the strike—and what the Marblehead women undertake they are bound to succeed in accomplishing." He wrote of the women strikers in Lynn: "They assail the bosses in a style which reminds one of the amiable females who participated in the first French Revolution."[80]

Yet mingled with the reports commending the spirit of the women strikers were repeated comments that their conduct violated the cultural code that women should not venture beyond the kitchen hearth and church pew. Editorial writers thundered that the shoemakers' strike was living proof of the demoralizing influence of the women's rights movement. Were not these female strikers asserting that they were struggling for equal pay for equal work? Surely, socialism would be the next step![81] Ironically, unlike the factory women of Lowell and Manchester, the female shoebinders of Lynn showed little interest in the political and legal aspects of the women's rights movement. Their activity appears to have been confined to the economic sphere. The male strikers responded by organizing a "vigilance committee" to make certain that only those reporters who wrote of the "female strikers with respect" would be permitted to attend their meetings. The women strikers endorsed this action and voted not to admit reporters to their open meetings who "misrepresented or burlesqued" them.[82]

Reporters had predicted that the women strikers' procession on

March 7 would "be the feature of the strike," and so it was. For a week before the scheduled date, after it had become clear that the employers had rejected the women workers' new price list, Lynn, Marblehead, South Reading, Saugus, and Swampscott came alive with the painting of banners and the enrollment of female strikers. On Tuesday morning, March 6, a delegation of Lynn women shoe workers presented a banner to the strikers' Executive Committee on behalf of all the women who had voted to join the strike. One one side, the banner bore a likeness of Washington and the words: "With the spirit of '76 we hope to gain the day. Perseverance is our motto. We all unite in the grand strike to aid our friends and brothers." On the reverse side was a painting of two hearts united with the words: "The strikers. Let our hearts beat as one, in the spirit of '76. Stand firm, and victory is sure."

In presenting the banner, Ellen Darlin, one of the strike leaders, denounced the "avarice of the manufacturers who, in their haste to be rich, have abridged the wages of the workers, until they are now not only in danger of losing the fruits of their past labors, but of being reduced to a condition little superior to that of bond slaves." She concluded: "And not only are the wages of the workmen abridged, but those of the workwomen are also reduced far below a just compensation. These things have forced us into action, against our inclinations, and we rejoice to see that the workmen have taken a stand against such oppression."

Accepting the banner on behalf of the men strikers of Lynn, David N. Johnson declared: "May we ever regard it as an emblem of woman's interest and devotion in every worthy cause—for I express no unmeaning compliment when I say that without woman's sympathy and cooperation, no noble work was ever consummated. May your hopes and ours be realized."[83]

A leading speaker at the mass meeting held on the eve of the procession was Reverend Thomas Driver, the city's black preacher. He told the women that he "always liked the looks of the Lynn girls, but now he was proud of them." He knew their condition and was convinced that they were "worse off than the slaves in the South." He reported that he had recently visited nine slave states, had witnessed the evils of slavery, and had become a "confirmed Abolitionist." But, he added: "I find there are white as well as black slaves; there are slaves in this state and in this city worse, far worse, in their condition than the black slaves at the South. The only difference is that they can't sell you. Thank God for that!" These remarks created a "great sensation," and Reverend Driver was wildly applauded,[84] as was the canvassing committee, which reported to the meeting that 1,711 signatures had been obtained in support of the bill of wages and that all would strike.[85]

"The great feature of Wednesday, March 7, was the women's procession," began an account in the *Lynn Weekly Reporter*. The parade was scheduled to start at ten o'clock in the morning, and by the first break of light, a deputation of men and women strikers, firemen, and military from Marblehead, South Reading, Swampscott, and Saugus arrived in Lynn. At eight o'clock a driving snowstorm set in, and by ten the streets seemed impassable. But, nothing daunted, the procession began on time, and, escorted by a detachment of musket-bearing militia and the Lynn Cornet Band, eight hundred women strikers started at Lynn Common and marched for several hours in the falling snow past the central shops on Lynn's major thoroughfares. At the head of their procession, they carried a banner with the inscription: "AMERICAN LADIES WILL NOT BE SLAVES. GIVE US A FAIR COMPENSATION AND WE LABOUR CHEERFULLY."

Other banners, representing the different wards, carried the slogans: "Our Union is Complete: Our Success Certain!" "Weak in Physical Strength but Strong in Moral Courage, We Dare Battle for the Right, Shoulder to Shoulder with our Fathers, Husbands, and Brothers!" "We Scorn to Labor For Half Prices!" "May Revolution Never Cease While Tyranny Exists!" "We Strike For Our Rights!" A banner carried by Ward 7 bore a poetic slogan:

> We could not live and pay our fare,
> When binding shoes at one cent a pair.

The women strikers were followed by male strikers, who marched in the order of their wards, and then by delegations from the other shoe towns. A female drummer accompanied the Marblehead delegation of men and women strikers "and excited great enthusiasm." At the common, the procession broke up and the women moved to the Lyceum Hall, where a collation had been prepared by sympathetic citizens.

Despite the stormy weather, the whole vicinity of the common had been densely packed with people and carriages, and at least ten thousand people witnessed the parade. "The demonstration appears to have given the highest satisfaction, and is very properly regarded as a great success," the Lynn *News* concluded.[86]

Ten days later, the women again paraded in Lynn, this time in the sunshine. Delegations from Salem, Marblehead, Newburyport, and other towns joined them, while the fire companies of Lynn, Marblehead, and several other shoe towns marched along. Ten thousand strikers paraded that day in a procession almost two miles long, and many thousands more, including schoolchildren who had been dismissed for the day, lined the way.

There were five processions in all, and each time the spirit of the strikers remained firm. The employers tried to break the strike by threatening the German and Irish workers that the state legislature would deprive them of the vote. The German workers of Natick met and unanimously resolved: "That neither the fear of losing our political influence nor the threats of our would-be masters will deter us from adhering to the rules of the Natick strikers until the battle is fought and victory won." The German shoebinders adopted a resolution supporting the stand taken by their husbands and fathers and also resolved "to uphold the cause of the battle of justice against oppression."[87] Although most of the strikers were descendents of eighteenth-century rural and village Yankees, the immigrant shoe workers identified with them and the spirit of earlier American struggles for freedom.

In response to an appeal by the Lynn employers, State Attorney General Phillips came to the shoe town and convinced the mayor to call out the militia and the Boston police to quell minor disturbances. The workers massed at the railroad station and greeted the Boston police with jeers, hisses, and shouts. Eight thousand people were there, and the women strikers carried banners reading, "Go Back Home," "You Are Not Wanted Here," and "No Outside Police." The town officials who had called in the militia and police were later voted out of office.[88]

Community support for the strikers was widespread. Hungry men and women were fed at collations, and, over the objections of the employers, the Overseers of the Poor dispensed wood and coal to the strikers—"to those even who refuse to go to work when they could earn from $1.50 to $2.00 per day," wrote an indignant employer who was having no success in recruiting scabs.[89]

Nowhere was support for the strikers more in evidence than among the clergy. When a group of manufacturers informed Reverend Charles C. Shackford, pastor of the Second Congregational (Unitarian) Church, that they expected him to deliver a sermon criticizing the women strikers for defying St. Paul's injunction that women should be passive and silent, he told the group that he believed them to be in the wrong and urged them to accept the strikers' demands.* Father John Strain also refused to condemn the women strikers, and advised "every Catholic shoemaker not to lift a hammer while the Yankees were standing out for higher wages; and if any of the Yankees did not remain firm, to influence them, if possible, to be true to the objects of the strike." And Reverend Driver spoke out again and again for the strikers, telling his congregation; "You, my colored brethren, know how to sympathize with labor unrequited. The poor journeyman is the bird picked. He is now the cider juice in the press under the screw."[90]

*St. Paul's exact words were: "Let your women keep silence in the churches: for it is not permitted unto them to speak; but they are commanded to be under obedience, as also saith the law. And if they will learn anything, let them ask their husbands at home: for it is a shame for women to speak in the church" (1 Cor. 14:34–35).

The Lynn strike attracted nationwide attention, and meetings of support were held in New York and Philadelphia by sympathetic workingmen and workingwomen. Abraham Lincoln and Stephen Douglas, then competing for the presidency, commented on it. Douglas blamed the strike on the "irrepressible conflict" doctrine of William H. Seward, with its "inflammatory attack" on the rights of property in slaves. Lincoln, on the other hand, declared in his New Haven speech of March 6, 1860: "I am glad to see that a system of labor prevails in New England under which laborers can strike when they want to, where they are not obliged to labor whether you pay them or not. I like the system which lets a man quit, when he wants to, and wish it might prevail everywhere. One of the reasons why I am opposed to slavery is just here."[91]

But the strike was taking its toll of the strikers. On April 10, after thirty manufacturers had signed a written agreement advancing wages over 10 percent, more than a thousand workers—men and women— went back to work. The employers involved refused to recognize the unions that were organized during the strike, while other manufacturers refused either to recognize the unions or to sign written agreements. Some of the strikers held out for another week or two, but they finally returned to work without written agreements. After all the workers had gone back, they held a mass meeting at which they announced that their principal objective—a fair remuneration for their labor—had been achieved and that, having formed a permanent association for the protection of their interests during the strike, they would continue the struggle until the owners recognized their organization. And although they did not invite the binders or other women shoe workers into their association, they expressed gratitude to them for their faithfulness to the labor cause and announced their determination to work jointly with them and any organizations they might form.[92]

During the Civil War (1861–1865), women played an increasingly important role in the production of goods.[93] Because of the shortage of male workers and the wartime industrial expansion, over 100,000 new jobs were available for women in factories, sewing rooms, and arsenals. For the first time women were employed as government clerks, being hired in 1852 by General Elias Spinner, treasurer of the United States, for the Treasury Department. In 1864 Congress appropriated the salaries for these women. But the appropriation set a maximum of $600 a year for female clerks, while male clerks earned from $1,200 to $1,800 a year.[94]

Private employers drew the appropriate conclusions and began to hire women in print- and cigar shops, telegraph offices, department stores, and light manufacturing—at no more than 50 percent of the wages men received for the same work. Indeed, it was predicted that, if the trend continued, men's wages would be brought down to the level of women's by the end of the war.[95]

This prospect compelled the labor movement to take greater interest in women workers and to pay more attention to the improvement of their conditions. Hence, when working women's unions were formed in a number of cities during the war, they received the cooperation of many workingmen's unions in these cities.[96]

Most of the working women's unions vanished before the war's end. But the Working Women's Protective Unions, organized by philanthropists in New York City, Chicago, Detroit, and St. Louis to provide legal protection for workingwomen (especially seamstresses), remained in existence until the 1880s.[97]

3

The National Labor Union

IN THE WINTER of 1864–1865, as victory for the Union forces seemed imminent, the demand arose that workingwomen should make way for the returning soldiers by quitting the jobs they had filled during the war years, replacing men who had left for the front, and should prepare, instead, to marry. It was claimed that the men returning from the front would provide a stabler labor force than women who were working only temporarily and would sooner or later leave to marry and raise families. A group of workingwomen in Ohio, faced with the threat of loss of their jobs, met the argument head on. "Whom are we to marry when so many have died in the cruel war?" they asked in a letter to the *Boston Daily Evening Voice.* "And what about those of us who gave our husbands to die for the country?"

> To hear some very proper persons discourse upon woman's sphere and influence, one would imagine that all women are blessed with comfortable homes, having nothing to do but cultivate amiability and gladden the hearts of those to whom they are bound by the ties of relationship.
>
> Many are shocked that we should insist on trying to keep our occupations, and charge us with masculinity. Perhaps it would be more feminine to fold our hands and starve in graceful indolence; or pass through life an object of charity.[1]

Unfortunately, logic had little effect. When the war ended, in April, 1865, the veterans of the Union Army became the army of the unemployed. Immediately, female clerks in Washington began to be discharged, and private employers, faced with a sudden cessation of war contracts, followed the pattern set by the government. With so many unemployed men looking for work at any wages, the advantage of cheaper female labor disappeared, at least for the time being.[2]

The *Boston Daily Evening Voice* pleaded in vain that since "so few avenues are open to women," they should be retained wherever they could work as efficiently as men: "We believe the welfare of the country depends as much, to say the least, upon the elevation of woman as upon the elevation of workingmen." Nor was it only the nation's welfare that was at stake, but its morality as well. For what alternative was there for so many women, suddenly thrown into the ranks of the unemployed, except "total moral ruin"?[3] But the only response to this plea was the accumulation of daily reports of "increasing numbers of unemployed females."[4]

Except for the *Boston Daily Evening Voice,* not a single labor journal spoke out against the indiscriminate discharge of workingwomen to make room for returning war veterans. Indeed, it seemed that most men and most trade unions still regarded women workers as nothing more than irritants who threatened to drive down wages by taking jobs at substandard rates when they should have remained at home, and who were now aggravating the difficulties created by postwar unemployment. Apart from a local here and there, virtually every trade union still refused to admit them to membership.

Nevertheless, the immediate postwar years did bring some startling changes. Workingwomen did not just wait for men to approve of their presence or assist them but organized themselves. Even ballet dancers in New York City met in November, 1865, "to discuss the feasibility of a strike," and resolved to demand a raise in their pay from $5 to $9 a week. When they were turned down, they struck until they won their demand.[5] One group of workingwomen in particular won the admiration and respect of male unionists by their militancy and effective organization. They were the laundresses of Troy, New York, who contributed the next important woman labor leader after Sarah G. Bagley to American labor history—Kate Mullaney.

Laundry work had long been one of the lowest-paying occupations for women. In 1829 a Philadelphia laundress was reported to be receiving $10 for washing eight dozen articles of clothing a week, less the cost of soap, starch, fuel to heat the water, and replacement of buttons. In the 1850s, steam laundries made their appearance in the hotels of New York, and as machinery began to take over the work of individual washerwomen, laundresses' rates fell still lower.[6]

Troy, New York, where the detachable collar was invented and introduced in the 1820s, rapidly became the center for the manufacture of collars and cuffs for men's shirts and of shirts and ladies' blouses that carried detachable collars. But washing, starching, and ironing the collars and cuffs were as important as making them, and several hundred Troy women were engaged in the processes involved: washing with soap; bleaching with chloride of soda; adding dilute of sulfuric acid to further bleach the collars; and again washing in suds; boiling; rubbing and rinsing; bluing and rolling; starching (with thin starch to be followed by a thick starch); drying; and finally ironing.[7] An 1865 description of Troy told of the laundresses whose daily work required them "to stand over the washtub and over the ironing table with furnaces on either side, the thermometer averaging 100 degrees, for wages averaging $2.00 and $3.00 a week." This they did for twelve to fourteen hours a day![8]

One of these Troy women was Kate Mullaney, and some time during the summer of 1865, she brought together about two hundred of the laundresses to form the Troy Collar Laundry Union. The immediate issue that sparked the meeting was the introduction of starching machines, which were scalding hot to handle and which cut prices for starching almost in half.[9]

Not far from where the laundresses met secretly were the offices of the local unions of the Iron Molders' International Union and the Sons of Vulcan (skilled iron puddlers). Both organizations had become defunct early in the war but had been revitalized, had grown steadily, and had won agreements that satisfied their members' demand for higher wages. "Why not follow this example?" the fiery Kate Mullaney asked her sisters. The laundresses responded. By the beginning of 1866, the union had succeeded in increasing their wages to $8 to $14 a week, although their workday remained twelve to fourteen hours long. By this time the laundresses had gained a reputation among male unionists as "the only *bona fide* female union in the country." Respect for the Troy laundresses mounted when the labor press in April, 1866, carried the story that the female union had contributed $1,000 to the striking molders of their city. The Troy Trades' Assembly showed its respect by inviting the union to affiliate, and even added a whole section of books relating to women to its Labor Free Library and Reading Room.[10]

Laundresses made labor history in 1866 in still another way. The Jackson (Miss.) *Daily Clarion* of June 24, 1866, carried on its front page the text of a startling "Petition of the Colored Washerwomen" to the mayor, informing him that "the subject of raising the wages" had been considered at a meeting on June 18 and the following resolution unanimously adopted:

> That on and after the foregoing date, we join in charging a uniform rate for our labor, that rate being an advance over the original price by the month or day the statement of said price to be made public by printing the same, and anyone belonging to the class of washerwomen, violating this, shall be liable to a fine *regulated by the class.* . . .
> The prices charged are:
> > $1.50 per day for washing
> > $15.00 per month for family washing
> > $10.00 per month for single individuals

The petition is historic; it represents the first known collective action of free black workingwomen in American history, as well as the first labor organization of black workers in Mississippi. The editor of the *Daily Clarion,* hardly able to believe his eyes, responded to the black washerwomen that he regarded "the agitation as ill-timed, unfortunate and calculated to injure instead of better their condition." He assured the white community that it need not believe black women of Jackson capable of such audacity:

> We believe it originated with one or two Northern adventurers who have come here to fill their pockets at the expense of the ignorant negro, under the pretense of philanthropy and benevolence. Whether one of the said adventurers presided at the conclave of the washerwomen, we are not advised, but he acted as their amanuensis, and it is said the petition comes up in his writing.[11]

The editor was soon to see evidence that the tradition of organizing to reduce their grievances, begun by the black washerwomen of his city, would be picked up by black workingwomen throughout the country.

In 1866 there was another first in the history of workingwomen: for the first time a national labor federation pledged support to all workingwomen.

It will be recalled that in 1836, the National Trades' Union, the first national labor federation, had denounced the employment of women outside the home. In 1864 an attempt was made to establish a national labor federation—the International Assembly of North America—but it failed. At the founding convention in Louisville, however, the trade unionists expressed support for workingwomen, but only for women sewers, and even then it was on the ground of labor's moral responsibility to "the poor, the helpless and the oppressed of the weaker sex."[12] While this was a definite advance from the attitude of 1836, it was still a very short step. Two years later a new effort at forming a national labor federation was more successful, and the position on women workers was far more advanced. To be sure, of the seventy-seven delegates representing thirteen states and the District of Columbia who met in Baltimore on August 20, 1866, to create the National Labor Union, none was a woman or represented an organization with a large female membership. But the women workers did have their champions among the men present in Baltimore—such as Richard F. Trevellick of Detroit and Andrew C. Cameron of Chicago. William H. Sylvis, cofounder of the National Labor Union and the foremost labor leader of the era, was their leading advocate.

Sylvis, though lacking formal education, had risen to the position of president of the Iron Molders' International Union in 1863 and had transformed the union into the largest and most effective trade union of the period. During his frequent organizing tours throughout the country (on the meagerest financial resources), Sylvis obtained a firsthand picture of the sufferings of workingwomen as well as a healthy respect for their contributions to the labor movement, wherever they were permitted to make them. He attended the great picnic of the Troy Trades' Assembly to raise money for their library and reading room, and in a letter to *Fincher's Trades' Review* he emphasized that it was the workingwomen who had made its success possible. He hoped thereby to convince the "old fogies" in other cities to begin making common cause with workingwomen.[13]

Like most other male trade unionists of the period, Sylvis believed that while it was the duty of organized labor to protect female workers, women did not basically belong in the labor force and should return to "the domestic circle." If women had to leave their exalted position as wives and mothers, he believed, it should be for the trades that were traditionally women's occupations, where they would not compete with men. This was his chief motivation in behalf of the sewing women.

But Sylvis learned from the class struggle, in which he believed devoutly, and his opinions changed. Although he never completely gave up the belief that the presence of women in the labor market was a violation of the natural social order of things, he saw only too clearly that the number of workingwomen had increased greatly during the Civil War and that even though many had been discharged at the war's end, they were in industrial life to stay. If the wage standards of the mechanics were to be defended, all women workers, and not just the sewing women, had to be organized into unions and their wage standards equalized with those of the men.

Sylvis went even beyond this approach to the understanding that none of labor's broader objectives could be achieved without the cooperation of workingwomen. He had come to the conclusion that trade unions by themselves could not solve the problems of the workers under capitalism. The inability of the Iron Molders' Union to preserve its gains in the face of postwar depression and unemployment led Sylvis to search for new ways to solve the problems of workers. He began to emphasize the need to broaden the constituency of the labor movement to include both blacks and women, to establish international labor solidarity, to encourage independent political action by labor, and to form producers' cooperatives in order to replace the existing wage system with a more equitable social order. To achieve these goals, the cooperation of the workingwoman was essential, especially if she gained the right to vote: "How can we hope to reach the social elevation for which we all aim without making women the companion of our advancement?"[14]

Under Sylvis' influence, the National Labor Union adopted a progressive approach toward women workers. The 1866 convention pledged "individual and undivided support to the sewing women, factory operatives, and daughters of toil," and made it clear that in so doing, it was not acting solely out of sympathy with the workingwomen but also in the self-interest of the male workers. An *Address of the National Labor Congress to the Workingmen of the United States* tackled the issue of "Female Labor." It conceded that "prejudices" existed against the employment of women, but insisted that the position of the laboring classes on the issue had been "grossly misrepresented." It was natural that male workers had objected to the introduction of female labor "when used as a means to depreciate the value of their own." The employers' action, under the pretext of "disinterested 'philanthropy,'" was intended not so much to elevate woman as to achieve "the degradation of man," by bringing "the labor of one . . . into competition with another." Declaring boldly that the time had come for a clear statement of labor's stand on the issue, the *Address* went on:

> We claim that if they are capable to fill the positions now occupied by the stronger sex—and in many instances they are eminently qualified to do so—they are entitled to be treated as their equals, and receive the same compensation for such services. That they do not is *prima facie* evidence that their employment is entirely a question of self-interest, from which all other considerations are excluded. Why should the seamstress or female factory operative receive one-third or one-half the amount demanded by and paid to men for the performance of the same work? Yet that such is the case, is a fact too well established to require corroboration.
>
> We trust, therefore, that the workingmen of America will protest against this iniquitous system, and lend their powerful influence to effect a reform, and in no manner can they do so more thoroughly than by aiding in the formation of those labor associations in which experience has demonstrated their own safety lies.[15]

Implementation of the address was left to the various trade unions. Only one union responded—the Cigar Makers' International Union. The CMIU was organized in 1864 with a constitution that prohibited both women and blacks from membership. Meanwhile, as we have noted, the large-scale introduction of molds for the forming of cigars (formerly the most important aspect of skill involved in cigarmaking) brought large numbers of women into the trade. At first the male cigarmakers reacted to this threat in fairly typical fashion: in 1866 they debated whether or not they should allow women to work in union shops, with the majority arguing that they should be eliminated from the industry and sent back home where they belonged.[16] But in 1867, in response to the twin pressure of competition from female labor and the action taken by the National Labor Union, the cigarmakers amended their constitution. A third factor may well have been the fear of independent organizing by women. During the war the Lady Segar Makers in Providence had unionized, and in September, 1864, they voted to boycott a nonunion employer.[17] The possibility that similar unions of women might be established outside the control of the Cigar Makers' International Union may have helped convince recalcitrant members that they ought to change their union's constitution. Whatever may have motivated the action, the fact is that the CMIU was the first national union to admit women to membership, and it went the whole way by permitting blacks to join as well. It is not clear whether the women and blacks were to be organized into separate locals or integrated with the existing membership. Nonetheless, the action taken by the Cigar Makers International Union in 1867 was a pioneer step in the organization of both women and blacks.[18]

The National Labor Union's 1866 pledge to workingwomen may have made little impact on the male unionists of the country, aside from the cigarmakers, but it did pave the way for an alliance between the labor and women's rights movements. Although this alliance was of brief duration, it had important repercussions on both participants.

The women in the alliance were feminists led by Elizabeth Cady Stanton and Susan B. Anthony. In the immediate postwar atmosphere, Stanton and Anthony, along with other woman suffragists, expected that they would be rewarded for their wartime patriotism and for having suspended their suffrage demands for the duration by being included in the expansion of the franchise, along with ex-slaves. They envisaged the emergence of the movements for black suffrage and women suffrage as a united front coalescing in a single demand for universal adult suffrage. A movement did arise to achieve this goal. In May, 1866, the American Equal Rights Association was organized with the aim of securing the suffrage for black men and all women. Frederick Douglass was chosen as one of the three vice-presidents, and both Stanton and Anthony were active in its leadership. The association launched a campaign to petition Congress, then in the process of molding the Fourteenth Amendment, to include suffrage of women and black men.

But it soon became clear—at least to male abolitionists, black and white, to most black women, and to some white feminists—that it would be impossible for both women and black men to gain the ballot at this stage. Radical Republicans were engaged in a difficult struggle with President Johnson and his allies, prominent among whom were the former slaveowners, for a meaningful freedom for the ex-slaves. They became convinced that to advocate woman suffrage would not only further complicate their already difficult task but would also guarantee defeat of their effort to enfranchise the freedmen. They were able to convince a number of feminists, Lucy Stone among them, that suffrage for the black men should take priority, and that the struggle for woman suffrage should be delayed until the former was obtained, after which a campaign for the right of all women to vote could get under way.[19]

But Stanton and Anthony and the women they influenced refused to go along. Instead, they broke with their former allies in the abolitionist camp and launched an independent movement, hoping to gain new support for their efforts to achieve the immediate enfranchisement of women. Whether or not they acted in the best interests of their own cause by breaking with the abolitionists is a matter of some disagreement among historians,[20] but there is no disputing the fact that the split in the feminist movement led Stanton and Anthony to look elsewhere for allies. This search for support had two direct consequences. One was the beginning of feminist attention to the cause of the woman worker in an effort to create a mass base of working-class feminism. The other was their search for coalition with the labor movement, through the National Labor Union, by means of which the feminists could more readily come into contact with workingwomen and, at the same time, create a new political party to support the woman suffrage cause. The fact that this could only be done through the defeat of the Republican Party, and with it the Radical Republican program of Reconstruction, was a matter of no concern to the Stanton-Anthony group. Even further, they were prepared to ally themselves with the bitterest racist enemies of black suffrage, if necessary. to accomplish their aims. Included among these was an eccentric railroad promoter and financier, George Francis Train, a well-known white racist, who now became a champion of woman suffrage. To Train, this latest cause was a convenient weapon to be used against the specter of black domination, which, in his terms, would reduce American society to the level set by "ignorant negroes."[21]

None of this troubled Stanton and Anthony. On the contrary, when Train offered them financial backing for a newspaper to be called *The Revolution*, through which they could build a new constituency for woman suffrage, they eagerly accepted. As early as November, 1866, Anthony had said that the "working women of the country are with us. Say to them that with the ballot in their hands, they can secure equal pay for their work, and the demand for the ballot will be as strong as that of the black man today."[22] With the split developing in the suffrage movement, the workingwomen became even more important to Anthony, and she looked to the new publication as a means of transforming her rhetoric into action.

The first issue of the *Revolution* came off the press on January 8, 1868, and ten thousand copies of the sixteen-page weekly were sent throughout the country under the frank of James Brooks, the proslavery, Copperhead Democratic Congressman from New York. The magazine announced that it was devoted to principle, not policy: to suffrage, irrespective of color or sex; to equal pay for equal work; the eight-hour day; the abolition of party despotism; currency reform; unrestricted immigration; and the regeneration of American society. Its slogan was "Down with politicians, up with people." On the day the *Revolution* made its publishing debut, Train left for England, where he was arrested and imprisoned for pro-Irish activities. Thereafter, the paper depended almost entirely on the resources of Anthony and Stanton, particularly the former. Having read themselves out of the abolitionist-feminist coalition, they were unable to obtain any assistance from that quarter. But by advocating an eight-hour day and equal pay for equal work, and by calling attention to women's substandard wages and supporting unions and strikes, they were able to gain the support of the labor press and of a number of the leaders of the National Labor Union—especially Sylvis, Cameron, and Trevellick.[23]

The NLU leaders were impressed by the argument, emphasized in every issue of the *Revolution,* that without the ballot workingwomen would never be able to resolve the two major disadvantages from which they suffered: inequality of wages with men and inability to enter the trades and professions. Not only would the vote serve to dignify both woman and her labor, but it would enable her to back up her economic struggles with political action—to battle with both hands and not with one tied behind her back. The editors of the *Revolution* argued that both men and women workers suffered from the oppression of capital and that both were defrauded of their "just dues." But in the struggle to redress their grievances, workingwomen were victims of a disability not shared by their fellow sufferers: lack of access to the ballot box.[24] To Sylvis, Cameron, and Trevellick, who were already envisioning an independent labor party, the *Revolution*'s editors pointed out that "all their efforts of self-extraction and elevation" would be for naught if they did not include workingwomen in their plans.[25]

The NLU leaders were also impressed by the attention paid to their organization by the *Revolution.* At the time the paper was launched, the NLU was foundering, partly because of an economic recession during 1867 and 1868. With the elevation of Sylvis to the NLU presidency and the return of prosperity in mid-1868, the federation began to flourish. An indefatigable organizer, Sylvis spread the NLU's message throughout the country, and the *Revolution* reported his progress with delight, noting that he had "visited nearly all the cities, towns, and villages in the United States, attended hundreds of meetings, public and private, and made the acquaintance of many hundred thousand workingmen." Sylvis was portrayed as the prototype of the new labor leader—a man who combined remarkable organizing talent with a broad vision of the labor movement as the vanguard for all the oppressed. The *Revolution* analyzed and then endorsed every one of the NLU planks: the eight-hour day, land reform, opposition to monopolies, producer and consumer cooperatives, currency reform, and support of trade unionism. "The principles of the National Labor Union are our principles," the editors proclaimed. "We see on the surface of this great movement the portent of bright days and hear a voice that shall be heard by all the

people's servants in Washington, and by the selfish, hard-hearted op-
pressors everywhere." It hailed the commencement of "the contest between labor and capital," and confidently predicted that the NLU would
lead the entire working class, women included, in the impending struggle.[26]

The unsuccessful attempts of the *Revolution*'s editors to win support
for woman suffrage from the Republican Party leadership served to
further cement their ties with the NLU leaders, who were themselves
turning against the Republican Party, which they identified as the political party of the class responsible for the oppression of the urban industrial workers. In Sylvis' words, the new "money" power made no
distinctions—sexual, racial, or any other—in exploiting its victims: "The
working people of our nation, white and black, male and female, are
now sinking to a condition of serfdom." To defeat this money power and
end its control over the national government required the defeat of its
political tool and agent, the Republican Party.[27] As Ellen Carol Dubois
points out: "Stanton and Anthony criticized the Republican Party on
different grounds but they shared with labor a rejection of its claim to be
'the party of progress.' "[28] Hence their readiness to support and campaign for the Democratic Party, the party of the former slaveowners, if it
would incorporate their demands into its platform.[29]

But both the *Revolution* editors and the NLU leaders were unsuccessful in their efforts to get the 1868 Democratic convention to adopt their
respective positions—for woman suffrage, in the case of Stanton and
Anthony, and, in the case of the NLU spokesmen, for the eight-hour
day, a greenback currency system, the granting of public lands to actual
settlers rather than to corporations, and the speedy and noninflationary
payment of the national debt. While the platforms of both petitioners
met the same fate, for the women suffragists it had not been a wasted
effort. During the Democratic convention, they met with leaders of the
National Labor Union and arranged for Sylvis and other spokesmen to
contribute articles to the *Revolution* on the need for a labor-centered third
party.[30] For its part, the *Workingman's Advocate*, official organ of the NLU,
carried a series of articles in September, 1868, by "Mrs. M. Wynkoop,"
urging "the wives of workingmen" to concern themselves with extra-
domestic activities. The articles included tributes to the "woman's rights
women" and their "noble mission." They urged workingmen's wives to
apply the same devotion to the cause of labor reform as the "woman's
rights women" had given to the suffrage:

> You, wives of the working men, have a great work before you. If you will be
> persuaded to do it earnestly and well, our millionaires on the one hand, with
> their vast hoarded treasures, that have been wrung out of the flesh and
> nerves of the masses; and our wearied men and women on the other, with
> worn out bodies and broken spirits, who are ready to lay down their burden

of life, almost as soon as they have taken it up, will be only in the history of the past.*[31]

The *Revolution* began publishing its call a month before the 1868 NLU convention met, inviting unions and all organizations that worked for the "amelioration of the condition of those who labor for a living" to attend.[32] Susan B. Anthony was determined to have women represented, and she succeeded. When the congress convened, the only women who requested delegate status were those whom Anthony had brought with her: Mary Kellogg Putnam, Mary McDonald, Elizabeth Cady Stanton, and Anthony herself. Anthony came with credentials from the Working Women's Association #1, an organization she had formed in the offices of the *Revolution* just a week before the congress "for the purpose of doing everything possible to elevate women and raise the value of their labor." Its membership consisted of the women typesetters and clerks employed by the *Revolution*, together with Stanton, Anthony, and Mary McDonald. However, Stanton came to the NLU representing not the Working Women's Association but the Woman Suffrage Association of America, another organization that was put together for the convention. Mary Kellogg Putnam, daughter of Edward Kellogg, the monetary reformer, came as a representative of Working-women's Association #2, which Anthony also set up. Mary McDonald represented the Women's Protective Labor Union Association of Mt. Vernon, New York, likewise organized just before the congress.† Thus outfitted with hastily prepared credentials, the "Sentimental Reformers" (as David Montgomery calls them) descended upon the NLU Congress in New York City on September 21, 1868.[33]

The Committee on Credentials seated Anthony, Putnam, and McDonald without protest, despite the fact that none of them was really a workingwoman. However, when Stanton presented credentials from the Woman Suffrage Association, the committee decided to refer the matter to the entire assembly on the ground that it was not a labor organization. During the discussion, those who opposed the seating of Stanton, mainly delegates from the building trades, argued on this ground. They also made it clear, however, that their real target was the

---

*With the advice of Eugene V. Debs to "get the railroaders' wives interested in the Brotherhood," Ida Husted Harper wrote a monthly column from 1883 to 1894 ("The Woman's Department") in the *Locomotive Firemen's Magazine,* official organ of the Brotherhood of Locomotive Firemen, which Debs edited. Ray Ginger, *The Bending Cross: A Biography of Eugene V. Debs* (New Brunswick, N.J., 1949), p. 31; Nancy Barker Jones, "A Forgotten Feminist: The Early Writings of Ida Husted Harper, 1878-1894," *Indiana Magazine of History,* 73(1977): 79-101.

†"Despite its title," Ellen Carol Dubois notes, "the Mt. Vernon Association was made up of property-owning women who demanded the right to vote on the basis of their role as taxpayers." ("A New Life: The Development of an American Woman Suffrage Movement, 1860-1869" [Ph.D. dissertation, Northwestern University, 1975], p. 203.)

issue of woman suffrage. Sylvis argued for seating Stanton, hastening to add that doing so would not constitute an endorsement of women's suffrage. He paid tribute to her as "one of the boldest writers of her age . . . [who] has done more than anybody I know to elevate her class and my class, too, and God knows they need elevation." Anthony spoke in Stanton's defense, directing her argument to those who opposed woman suffrage: "She considered that the improvement of the condition of woman was only to be accomplished through the means of giving them the ballot. Hence the Woman Suffrage Association of America, more than any other, had for its object the amelioration and elevation of the women who work for a living."

Many trade unionists were persuaded by her speech, and when the question was put, Stanton was seated by a vote of forty-five to eighteen. The next day, however, eighteen delegates representing the building trades threatened to leave the convention if her delegate status was allowed to stand. To prevent a split in the NLU, the congress engineered a compromise. It refused to rescind Stanton's credentials, but passed a resolution asserting that in admitting her as a delegate, the NLU "does not regard itself endorsing her particular ideas, or committing itself to the position of Female Suffrage." Still another defeat was suffered by the suffragists when the delegates rejected a recommendation of the Committee on Female Labor, headed by Anthony, that their resolution should include the phrase "secure the ballot."[34]

Yet the remainder of the report by the Committee on Female Labor was truly historic. It urged the extension of eight-hour demands to women workers, equal pay for equal work, and trade unions for working women. It also encouraged women "to learn trades, engage in business, join our labor unions, or form protective unions of their own, and use every other honorable means to persuade or force employers to do justice to women by paying them equal wages for equal work."[35]

When the report (without any reference to the ballot) was adopted by the congress, the National Labor Union became the first labor federation in world history to vote for equal pay for equal work. Indeed, to Karl Marx, this stand made the NLU one of the most significant organizations in the world labor movement. Thus, he wrote to a friend in America:

> Great progress was evident in the last Congress of the National Labor Union in that among other things it treated working women with complete equality—while in this respect the English, and the still more gallant French, are burdened with a spirit of narrow-mindedness. Anybody knows, if he knows anything about history, that great social changes are impossible without the feminine ferment. Social progress can be measured exactly by the social progress of the fair sex.[36]

In many ways, as Marx pointed out, the women had been treated "with complete equality." They had been granted delegate status at a national labor assembly, and only in the case of one had there even been a dispute over the credentials; the women had participated in every phase of the congress. Nor had they limited themselves to feminist issues—they had spoken at length on resolutions relating to strikes, currency reform, and political action. Anthony and Putnam had been appointed to the resolutions committee, and the subject of workingwomen had been frequently discussed. In his keynote address, President Whaley had spoken at length about the problems of workingwomen and about the necessity of raising their wages so that the general wage level could be uplifted. He called for equal pay for equal work and for trade union encouragement and assistance to women's labor organizations. Vice-President Jessup, himself from New York, reported favorably on Anthony's recent efforts to organize workingwomen in New York City and said that the workingwomen's associations she had formed had a "good prospect of success." The convention had mandated a committee to report on female labor, appointed Anthony its chairperson, and included Jessup among its members, as an indication of the importance it placed on the issue. Finally, the convention commended Kate Mullaney, president of the Collar Laundry Union of Troy, for her "indefatigable efforts" on behalf of female laborers, and appointed her special assistant secretary to correspond with workingwomen and coordinate national efforts to form workingwomen's associations.*[37]

The convention also moved toward the creation of an independent, labor-based political party and adopted a platform for the party that included a pledge of "undivided support for sewing women and daughters of toil in this land." Anthony had strongly supported the formation of an independent labor party because, she argued, Democrats and Republicans alike were in the hands of finance capital. She predicted "that they will never propose or bring about any measure for workingmen of real permanent benefit."[38] Despite the convention's coolness on the issue of women's suffrage, Stanton and Anthony were convinced that with Sylvis and most of the NLU's other leaders actively supporting independent political action by labor, they would soon endorse suffrage for women in order to strengthen the ranks of the new labor party.[39]

Most of the women who attended the convention were deeply impressed. In their minds, the very seating of women delegates marked "a new era in Workingmen's conventions," while the appointment of Mullaney to organize workingwomen proved that "the recognition of woman

*Kate Mullaney was also elected second vice-president of the NLU, but the action had to be annulled because the first vice-president came from the same state. It is not clear if she attended the convention, since she is not listed among those given delegate status.

[was] to be future policy of the National Labor Congress." Evaluating the convention for the *Revolution,* Stanton wrote that the men of labor "have inaugurated the grandest movement of the century." And now it was clear that workingwomen were to be part of that movement![40]

It was not so clear whether black workingwomen would be included. At no point in the discussions on workingwomen was there a single reference to black women. However, the delegates had elected Sylvis president, and in his letters to the *Working Man's Advocate* while on an organizing tour for the NLU, Sylvis told of black workers, mostly men but some women, too, organizing unions in Baltimore, Mobile, Charleston, Savannah, and Philadelphia and engaging in militant strikes. He warned those unions that declared strikes in protest against the employment of black workers that their "fanatical bigotry" jeopardized the future of the labor movement, for it was "impossible to degrade one group of workers without degrading all." Besides, he pointed out, labor must realize that the black man now had the suffrage in the South, would soon gain it in the North, and would even hold the balance of political power in the nation: "If we can succeed in convincing these people to make common cause with us . . . we will have a power . . . that will shake Wall Street out of its boots." It did not require much imagination, he declared, to picture the consequences for the American working class if women were enfranchised in addition to black men, and if they joined in the crusade against Wall Street. Such a development, Sylvis insisted, was now overdue. "Why," he asked, "should women not enjoy every social and political privilege enjoyed by men? The time, I hope, is not far when universal suffrage and universal liberty will be the rule over the world."[41]

In December, 1868, Sylvis and the Executive Committee of the NLU met in Washington, D.C., and, in a precedent-shattering action, extended a formal invitation to all persons interested in the labor movement, regardless of color or sex, to attend the annual convention in Philadelphia the following August.[42] The national labor federation, which had already seated four women as delegates in 1868, was to mark a new era by seating nine blacks in 1869. None of the black delegates was a woman, and the nine black male trade unionists voted unanimously with the majority of the delegates to prevent the seating of a white woman delegate—Susan B. Anthony.

The issue came to a head when Anthony's credentials as a delegate from the Working Women's Association were challenged by John Walsh of Local #6 of the National Typographical Union, on the familiar ground that the association was not a *"bona fide* labor organization," plus the new charge that Anthony had "striven to procure places for girls from which men had been discharged"—in other words, had acted as a recruiter of strikebreakers. He supported his charges with details of

Anthony's activities during a printers' strike, and with a letter from Augusta Lewis detailing her unfortunate experiences in the Working Women's Association. (Both events are discussed in the next chapter.) The dispute came to the floor, where Anthony, permitted the right to respond to the charges against her because she had been a delegate to the 1868 congress, admitted the charge relating to the printers' strike and justified her action by the statement that this was the only way women could get experience in the trade: "The result was that some forty or fifty girls served with Gray and Green* and others, during a few months while the strike was in progress."[43]

Anthony's chief champion was Austin Puett, an Indiana attorney, and he did her cause more harm than good by dismissing with contempt the trade unionists' anger over strikebreaking. He proclaimed his faith in the universal equality of rights and his hope that everyone would "enter upon the grand platform of competition, and I do not care whether he is a 'rat' or a mouse." This was too much for Delegate Walsh to stand, and he declared angrily that Puett had not only demonstrated a total ignorance of trade union principles but "convinced me that he is not a workingman or he would know what a 'rat' is." Walsh also favored "Equal rights for all," he said, but not for "a rat or a renegade." He then went on to voice a typically sexist sentiment that had nothing to do with the issues at hand. "The lady goes in for taking women away from the wash tub," he cried, "and in the name of heaven, who is going there if they don't? I believe in a woman's doing her work, men marrying them, and supporting them."[44]

In her final defense before the convention, Anthony raised the feminist argument. She insisted that the real reason her seating was opposed was that women did not have the right to vote. If women had the franchise, they would be respected, admitted to the trades, and treated with equality. "All women in this country are under the power of men," she concluded. "We ask for a change, we ask for a change."[45]

It took three days for the delegates to reach a decision—a clear indication that there was no simple issue involved in the conflict over Anthony's credentials. Actually, the first vote was fifty-five to fifty-two in favor of her admission. Anthony concluded that these "55 men felt they were voting for Woman Suffrage."[46] This was an exaggeration; the fifty-five men were voting to keep the alliance between the National Labor Union and the woman reformers from breaking apart.

In the end it took a threat by the printers to withdraw to bring about Anthony's exclusion. A day after the first vote, the Typographical Union said bluntly that it would pull out of the congress if Anthony's credentials were accepted. Andrew Cameron tried to work out an acceptable

---

*Gray and Green was the job printing firm that printed the *Revolution*.

compromise but failed, and the second and final vote was sixty-three to twenty-eight to reject Anthony's credentials and eject her from the convention.[47]

A number of the delegates told the press that Sylvis, who had died less than a month before the convention, might have been able to find an amicable solution. The *American Workman,* a Boston labor paper, agreed. Sylvis, it maintained, would have had the issue fought out in the New York Typographical Union and not at the NLU convention. It was also convinced that "it was a narrow spirit which sought to entrap her in the meshes of technical quibbling, or hold her amenable in open convention to the rigid rulings of local trade-unions."

Sylvis may have been free of such a "narrow spirit," it went on, but unfortunately many male unionists were not. Some still believed women to be inferior to men and mentally and temperamentally unfit to vote. Others believed that suffrage was only incidental, and that in advocating equal pay for equal work, the NLU had "acknowledged all the correlative rights of women, including property and suffrage." Still others maintained that it would take too long to secure female suffrage and insisted that "our business is with those who are already voters." The *American Workman* concluded, "He must be a short-sighted person who cannot see that labor reform needs the support of the women of the country, irrespective of their views upon the matter of the ballot."[48]

The editor of the Boston labor paper was also troubled by the fact that "the colored delegates, whose cause she [Anthony] has so long advanced, were as a unit against her admission—a fact which I cannot understand."[49] The editor obviously did not know that Anthony had cut her ties with blacks several years before the NLU convention and had increasingly antagonized them by her willingness to ally herself with any group, no matter how racist, so long as it would give lip service to woman suffrage. These relations degenerated still further when she increasingly criticized the granting of the ballot to the "brutish and ignorant Negro man" and argued that woman suffrage would serve as a bulwark against "Negro rule" in the South.[50]

It should be noted that not all women were excluded from the 1869 NLU convention. Martha Wilbridge, from the Excelsior League of Massachusetts, was admitted and placed at the head of one of the important committees. Even a devoted friend of Anthony's praised the convention for having declared itself in favor of the principle that women deserve to be dealt with "as worthy of recognition on terms of the fullest equality."[51]

Several female delegates, including a white—Mary A. S. Carey—were admitted to the founding convention of the Colored National Labor Union, which opened in Washington, D.C., on December 6, 1869. However, the delegation from Newport to the Rhode Island State Labor Convention, which chose delegates for Washington, included a woman only after a letter of complaint was received from "A Colored Woman of Newport." She said she "was much disappointed in that all your delibera-tions, speeches and resolutions, which were excellent so far as the men are concerned, the poor woman's interests were not mentioned, or re-ferred to." She then asked a pertinent question:

> . . . are we to be left out? we who have suffered all the evils of which you justly complain? Are our daughters to be denied the privilege of honestly earning a livelihood, by being excluded from the milliner, dressmaker, tailor, or dry goods store, in fact every calling that an intelligent, respectable, industrious female may strive to obtain, and this merely because her skin is dusky? These privileges are all denied colored females of Newport. However well they may be fitted for other positions, they are compelled to accept the meanest drudgeries or starve. . . .
>
> Therefore the colored women of Newport would ask your meeting and Convention that is to assemble next Monday to remember us in your deliber-ations so that when you mount the chariot of equality, in industrial and mechanical pursuits, we may at least be permitted to cling to the wheels.

Chastened by this deserved rebuke, Newport's black workers set up a committee, which nominated "a lady to represent the city of Newport in the coming State Convention."[52]

On the second day of the Colored National Labor Union's conven-tion, a tax of $2 was proposed to be levied on each delegate to cover expenses. When Mrs. Colby, delegate from the District of Columbia, asked "if the ladies were to be included in the persons taxed," she was told that "there was no distinction to be made on account of race, sex, or color." However, since it was felt that female delegates might not be able to afford so steep a tax, the tax for all delegates was reduced to $1, and the principle of equality was retained. Shortly thereafter, Isaac Myers, who was to be elected first president of the union, introduced a resolu-tion urging, among other points, that the new labor organization dedi-cate itself to carrying out "the learning of trades and professions by our children without regard to sex." After this proposal was adopted, Mrs. Carey, the white female delegate from Detroit, addressed the convention at considerable length on the issue of "the rights of women and the justice of their recognition by the sterner sex." At the conclusion of her remarks, the chairperson of the Committee on Female Suffrage offered a resolution that the new organization, "profiting by the mistakes hereto-fore made by our white fellow citizens in omitting women as co-workers in such societies," should cordially include black women in the invitation to further and organize cooperative societies. The committee report made it clear that in that body's opinion, "no subject bearing upon the industrial relations of the colored people to the community requires more earnest consideration." The report suggested that the solution to the plight of the women workers lay in "organized effort, whether in associations with men or in societies of their own." It recommended that women "learn trades" and engage in whatever honorable callings would have a tendency to "enlarge their sphere and influence of labor." The report expressed confidence that once women had demonstrated their willingness to form associations, they "could not fail to impress upon the sterner sex the importance of removing all barriers to the full recognition and success of woman as an important industrial and moral agent in the field of human activities and responsibilities."

The convention unanimously adopted the resolution and report submitted by the Committee on Woman's Labor. The Colored National Union thereby took, in several respects, a stronger stand in defense of equal rights of women in industry and trade unions than its white counterpart. Yet the *Revolution* failed to inform its readers that the black labor delegates had taken this advanced position in favor of equality for women workers.[53]

When the *American Workman* said that the *Revolution* had remained "constantly in support" of the NLU since the 1868 congress, it was exaggerating the case. In truth, the Stanton-Anthony journal's enthusiasm for the NLU had begun to wane even before the 1869 congress. In contrast to its active campaign to recruit women for the 1868 NLU meeting, the *Revolution* carried only one notice, without comment, about the 1869 convention.[54] Four women associated with the *Revolution* had attended the 1868 congress; only Anthony went to the 1869 convention, and even she had to be persuaded by NLU representatives that despite the death of suffragism's strongest ally in the organization— William H. Sylvis—it was still worth her while to attend.[55]

The point is that Stanton and Anthony were interested in the labor movement mainly as a force to advance the cause of woman suffrage, and even their work among workingwomen was centered on building a new base for the suffrage movement. The experience at the 1869 NLU congress convinced the *Revolution*'s editors that an alliance with the labor movement to advance the woman suffrage cause was nothing but an illusion. Stanton, never as enthusiastic about the possibilities of that alliance as Anthony, wrote that the National Labor Congress' action "has proved what the *Revolution* has said over and over again, that the worst enemies of woman's suffrage will ever be the laboring masses of men."[56]

But not many workingwomen shared this attitude. Their faith in the National Labor Union as a vehicle through which they might redress their grievances was still strong enough in 1870 for the Massachusetts Working Women's League and the Working Women's Labor Union for the State of New York—the only two statewide organizations of female workers established in the post–Civil War period—to place themselves "under the protection of the National Labor Union." The founding convention of the New York Working Women's Labor Union, held in

March, 1870, adopted a series of resolutions denouncing the fact that women and children had to work longer than ten hours a day, deploring strikes "except as a last resort toward the maintenance of our rights," endorsing the cooperative movement "as the true way in which the wealth of the country can be more equally distributed," urging the creation of a paper "devoted to our interests as *bona fide* working women," and calling for the establishment of a Labor Exchange in New York City to help women procure employment. Finally, the convention appealed directly to the workingmen of the nation through the National Labor Union "to come forward and aid us in this work of reform ... as we believe our interests are identical and our objects are one."[57]

Two men active in the NLU—Alexander Troup and William J. Jessup—were present at the convention and conveyed the appeal to the NLU congress, which thereupon urged male unionists to respond to the appeal and "welcome [women] entering into just competition with men in the industrial race of life."[58]

Four women delegates were present at the 1870 and 1871 conventions of the National Labor Union. In 1870 Mrs. E. O. G. Willard of the Sewing Girls' Union of Chicago was elected second vice-president. A year later, Mrs. Willard, representing the Working Women's Union of the same city, was reelected.[59]

The National Labor Union never took a stand in favor of woman suffrage before it passed into history in 1873, but it did reaffirm its position in favor of economic rights for workingwomen, including their right to receive equal pay with men for equal work. The 1871 congress put it in these words: "*Resolved,* That this organization cheerfully recognizes the right of women everywhere to learn and engage in any profession, trade or occupation which they may desire, and that for any certain amount of work they should receive the same pay as men."[60]

4

The Knights of Labor

IN 1869 nine Philadelphia garment cutters, whose union had been shattered and its members blacklisted, formed a secret society, which they named the Noble Order of the Knights of Labor. Its founder, Uriah H. Stephens, became master workman, the title of the presiding officer. Stephens placed great emphasis on solidarity. Labor, he argued, had to be powerful and unified in order to cope with the strength of organized capital. Since all workers had common interests, they should logically belong to a common society and be united by bonds of "universal brotherhood." "I do not claim any power of prophecy," he is reported to have said, "but I can see ahead of me an organization that will cover the globe. It will include men and women of every craft, creed, and color; it will cover any race worth saving."[1]

But Stephens, though far in advance of many of the members of the early Knights, was so obsessed with the value of secrecy and with the sexist view that women could not keep secrets that, while he favored the inclusion of all male workers and mentioned women, he did not advocate opening membership to women. They were excluded from the Knights for more than a decade. Meanwhile, the Molly Maguire episode had the effect of discrediting secret organizations,* and the Catholic

---

*The Molly Maguires was a secret society of Irish workers, named for a legendary Irish revolutionary, which operated in the mining regions of Pennsylvania, and was accused of plotting the assassination of mine superintendents and others whose policies they resented. Today many labor historians argue that there was no society in America calling itself the Molly Maguires; that the name was tagged to the Ancient Order of Hibernians by the coal operators and their allies in order to crush any organization in the mining industry, and that the Pinkerton agency hired to ferret out the so-called criminals actually committed many of the crimes. Ten miners, all Irish, were hanged as ring-leaders in the "conspiracy" after a biased trial.

On January 16, 1879, the government of Pennsylvania granted a pardon to Jack Kehoe, the miners' leader and one of the ten men executed.

clergy would not countenance secret oaths. Faced with this opposition, Knights leaders moved to eliminate some secret parts of their ritual in 1878. These efforts were consummated at the General Assembly meeting held in Detroit in September, 1881, where delegates voted to abolish oaths and other secret aspects by the beginning of the following year. Terence V. Powderly, who had replaced Stephens as master workman, predicted that making the Knights' names and objectives public would result in an increase in the order's membership.[2]

If nothing else, the new policy removed one obstacle to the admission of women. More important was the fact that the census of 1880 revealed that the population of the country had increased by 30 percent in the preceding decade, but the number of males over sixteen years of age employed in manufacturing had increased by less than 25 percent while that of females over fifteen had increased by 64 percent. The 2,647,000 women gainfully employed in 1880 constituted 15.2 percent of the nation's work force, and employers were still continuing to replace men with women at lower wages. By 1890 there were 4,005,500 gainfully employed women, making up 17.2 percent of the total labor force. This figure included almost 300,000 girls under fifteen years of age.

About a quarter of the 4 million women workers in 1890 were housekeepers, stewards, hostesses, or family servants. Women factory workers were distributed as follows:[3]

Clothing manufacture	389,231	Tobacco	10,868
Laundries and cleaning	109,280	Printing	9,322
Cotton textiles	92,394	Silk and rayon	9,211
Other textiles	42,420	Carpets and rugs	7,674
Shoes	21,007	Hats	6,357
Containers and boxes	14,126		

At its first national convention in 1878, the Knights delegates discussed the impact on men's wages of unskilled females working as machine operators. In an effort to protect the men, they included in the Knights' constitution the provision that one of the order's goals would be to secure "for both sexes equal pay for equal work," as the National Labor Union had done ten years earlier. But the Knights' constitution still made no provision for the admission of women.

At the 1879 convention Philip Van Patten, a socialist, introduced a resolution to permit women to become members and to organize local assemblies under the same conditions as men. After some quibbling over details, the resolution received the necessary two-thirds approval, but it was tabled until the next assembly. At the 1880 General Assembly, Powderly was authorized to convene a committee to prepare regulations and a ritual for the induction of women. He never convened the committee, explaining later that "a separate ritual will bespeak inequality, lead to confusion and is unnecessary." It actually *was* unnecessary, for early in 1881, when male shoe workers of Local Assembly 64 in Philadelphia refused to accept a wage cut, management turned to the unorganized female shoe workers and cut wages 30 to 60 percent. Under the leadership of Mary Stirling, the women struck. Local Knights organizer Harry Skeffington promptly inducted the strikers into the order. Garfield Assembly 1684, the first local composed exclusively of women, was chartered in September, 1881. Its members elected Stirling to the District Assembly, which sent her to the General Assembly that year.[4]

Once the doors were opened, the number of women's assemblies grew sharply. One other women's local was formed in 1881; 3 in 1882; 9 in 1883; 13 in 1884; 46 in 1885; and 121 in 1886. The organizational structure of the Knights of Labor provided for two types of local assemblies under the jurisdiction of the broader District Assembly, and women participated in both. When a small community did not contain sufficient workers in a given trade to form a separate local, it formed a mixed local, including all eligible Knights. Many of these mixed locals contained only women members. The Garfield Assembly was the first of these, but the idea caught on, so that by 1887, the majority of the female locals were of this type. In the large cities, organizers encouraged workers in specific trades to form separate trade assemblies. In New York, Chicago, Fall River, and other large centers, such trade assemblies included both men and women. Still, it was not automatic that assemblies should include both sexes. "L.A. 5426 which has hitherto been composed entirely of men requests permission to admit women," Charles Lichtman, a member of the General Executive Board, wrote to Powderly. "I have told them it needed dispensation from you and that to save them time I would request one from you. The address of the R[ecording] S[ecretary] is Will C. Bailey, Riverside, California. Will you please attend to this?" Powderly granted the dispensation, but in some cases, even this did not solve the problem. John A. Forsythe, the recording secretary of Assembly No. 2317 in Seymour, Indiana, complained to Powderly:

Our Assembly is a "mixed" one of about 140 members, all men workers. Recently, new by-laws were adopted fixing the price of initiation for ladies, and eight good and true women, ladies in the best sense of the term and wives of honest workers, have been proposed and balloted in due form and each one has been rejected.

The Assembly has good reason to believe that, in each instance, these black balls were cast by the same individuals. . . . The majority is powerless to repair the very great injury that has been done.

The questions we, as true Knights, desire you to answer at your earliest convenience are:

1. What, if anything, can we do according to law in the matter?

2. Are men who, professing to be Knights, will skulk behind the ballot box, and in the way and with the weapon of a coward, assault good and true

women in the virtue dearest to the heart of every true wife, mother or daughter, her reputation and social standing, worthy to be recognized as Knights?

3. Must the very large majority of our Assembly, who recognize the true principles of Knighthood—the equality of woman—submit to the action of the very small minority in thus ruling her out of our circle?

The rejection of these women has aroused the most intense indignation and, for the good of the Order, we ask you, as our acknowledged and honored head, to point us, if possible, to some way out of the difficulty.

Powderly praised the Assembly's majority for upholding the "true principles of Knighthood," and granted dispensation to overrule the blackballs. The "eight good and true women" were initiated as members of Assembly No. 2317.[5]

Figures on the number of women members in the order vary. The highest estimate was made by M. B. E. Kelley in 1898. "One hundred and fifty, even two hundred thousand would probably be quite within bounds," Kelley wrote, but quickly added that this "must be pure guesswork." The most acceptable estimate is that in 1886, when the Knights' membership was at its highest point, there were about 50,000 women members, constituting 8 or 9 percent of the total membership.

Who were these female Knights? A breakdown of the occupations of the women assemblies in 1886 reveals that nineteen of the ninety-one assemblies listed were composed of shoe workers; seventeen of mill operatives; twelve of housekeepers; five each of sewers, tailoresses, and laundresses; four each of knitters, collar and shirt ironers, and dress- and cloakmakers; two each of hatters, weavers, and paper-box makers; and one each of bookbinders, carpetmakers, cigarmakers, farmers, feather curlers, gold cutters, lead pencil workers, and rubber workers. There was one assembly of Bohemian women in Chicago, and fifteen of black women whose occupations were housekeepers, farmers, chambermaids, and laundresses.* Clearly the Knights did not limit the order's membership to wage earners; a few women's assemblies had both middle-class and working-class women as members. An example is the Myrtle Assembly in Baltimore, a women's union to which middle-class women also belonged; however, workingwomen held all the offices.[6]

The first union of female government employees in Washington, D.C., joined the Knights of Labor in 1883, the same year that the Civil

---

*Assemblies of black domestics existed in Washington, D.C., Norfolk, Virginia, Wilmington, North Carolina, and Philadelphia. However, the Atlanta black washerwomen who formed an association in a black church in 1880 and a year later struck for a dollar per dozen pounds of wash, were not affiliated with the Knights of Labor. Three thousand washerwomen struck, but threats from landlords to raise the rent of all strikers and arrests by police broke the strike (David M. Katzman, *Seven Days A Week: Women and Domestic Service in Industrializing America*, New York, 1978, p. 196).

Service Act made a limited number of government posts in Washington subject to competitive examinations. For the first time, women were encouraged to compete directly with men for jobs in the federal government. The Pendleton Act, as the Civil Service Act was then known, represented a first step in the fight for equality for women in government employment, although the 1870 measure permitting department heads to pay women less than men for identical work was still in effect. When the first test under the Civil Service Act was administered in 1883, the highest score was achieved by Mary Frances Hoyt, a Vassar College alumna, who was appointed to a $900 clerkship on September 5. But she actually received only $600, while men already in the post were paid the higher amount. Secretary of the Interior Henry M. Teller found a simple solution to the problem—he refused to employ any women in the Department of the Interior.

In September, 1882, women clerks in a number of government departments formed the Women's National Labor League, with Charlotte Smith as president and Elizabeth S. Bryant as secretary. The League affiliated with the Knights of Labor in February, 1883, giving the Knights of Labor an assembly of female government employees in the nation's capital.[7]

Since shoe and textile workers were an important part of the female membership in the Knights, it is not surprising that the largest part of that membership was in Massachusetts. In the year and a half preceding 1887, no fewer than 13,200 Bay State women were admitted to the Knights, 80 percent of them in the shoe and textile industries. The largest center was Lynn, where the women shoemakers, former Daughters of St. Crispin, were affiliated as assemblies of the Daughters of Labor and the Ladies' Stitching Association. Women Knights were part of the ten thousand members of the labor movement in Lynn at a time when the total number of workingpeople in the city was not much more than fifteen thousand.[8]

Women garment workers made up another important element in the Knights, and in several cities they formed viable union organizations under the banner of the order. By 1886 women garment workers in Chicago had organized two local trade assemblies—Local No. 7170 for women cloakmakers and Local No. 7707 for tailoresses. Additional garment workers participated in trade assemblies supported by both men and women. Other local assemblies for female garment workers operated in New York City, Rochester, Toledo, Newark, Baltimore, and St. Louis.

The reason these women joined the Knights is illustrated by the case of Rebecca, a New York city workingwoman, who wrote a series of letters to the editor of *John Swinton's Paper* concerning her plight and that of her fellow employees. She worked at a sewing machine in a underclothing factory from eight until six for a salary of $5 a week. Rebecca ended her first letter with a plaintive question on behalf of herself and her sister in the factory: "*How* do we live on $5 a week with good girlish appetites for nice things, good girlish fondness for nice clothes and ornaments, and good girlish liking for dances, excursions, and holidays—how do we get along?"

Her next letter informed the editor that a reduction in business had caused a corresponding reduction in the work force at her place of employment from a peak of one hundred to thirty. Those who remained had to work ever more quickly. Still, she complained, the employer treated them like dogs and used terms like "liar," "hussy," and "lazy good-for-nothing" in shouting at them. Although he insisted that they start work punctually, he delayed ringing the bell in the evening in order to steal a few minutes from them. Rebecca concluded the letter with the news that she and her sister had been "laid off."

In her next letter Rebecca reported that she and her sister had obtained work as apronmakers. The girls now earned $3.60 a week each, working from six in the morning until ten at night. After a month's absence, Rebecca returned to her former job. Conditions had grown worse in the interim. Not only did the workroom now lack adequate heating, but the employer prohibited the girls from warming themselves in the hall room during the lunch period. They also received violent scoldings if they so much as looked up from their work.

Rebecca concluded her series of letters by stressing the need for organizing the workingwomen into trade unions in order to eliminate the injustice, capricious and insulting behavior, and repeated humiliations she had described and to introduce fair wages and decent conditions. The impulse for organization, she pointed out, must come from outside, since the girls lacked the time needed for effective organization and were resigned to a daily life of drudgery.

In the next issue of *John Swinton's Paper* a letter from a reader advised Rebecca to join the Knights of Labor and listed the address where she and her fellow workingwomen could become members of the order. Within two weeks, the girls in Rebecca's factory had all joined the Knights.[9]

While the Knights did not wage a consistent campaign to eliminate racism in the order's ranks, it did bring large numbers of black workers into the predominantly white labor movement for the first time. The constitution promulgated for all local assemblies in 1884 declared that the order made no distinction with respect to "nationality, sex, creed, or color." It has been estimated that of a total membership in 1886 exceeding 700,000, no fewer than 60,000 were black.

The Knights of Labor included both all-black assemblies and those of mixed black and white membership. Although segregated locals were predominant, especially in the South, even some locals below the Mason-Dixon line were mixed. The Knights began organizing in the South in 1878, assigning fifteen organizers to the area, and Negroes as well as whites were asked to join. The blacks either formed or joined locals of longshoremen, miners, iron- and steelworkers, and farm workers.[10]

A number of women's locals were organized in Atlanta, Richmond, Durham, Memphis, Raleigh, and Jacksonville, usually composed of domestic workers and seamstresses. Nearly all these locals were segregated, but there were a few integrated locals of female Knights in the South. Ida B. Wells, a black journalist and teacher, soon to become internationally famous as a crusader against lynching, wrote in the Memphis *Watchman* in 1887:

> I was fortunate enough to attend a meeting of the Knights of Labor.... I noticed that everyone who came was welcomed and every woman from black to white was seated with the courtesy usually extended to white ladies alone in this town. It was the first assembly of the sort in this town where color was not the criterion to recognition as ladies and gentlemen. Seeing this I could listen to their enunciation of the principle of truth and accept them with a better grace.[11]

By 1887 the order's black recruits came primarily from rural areas in the South, where black men and women formed assemblies together in an effort to escape the evils of tenant farming and sharecropping, low wages, low per capita income, high illiteracy, poor public services, lynching, the convict-labor system, and chain gangs. The Knights, whose program stressed land reform, increased education, and workers' cooperatives, held out the only hope to landless blacks in an agrarian society, barred from textile, tobacco, furniture, and other industries and oppressed and dominated by landlord-merchant power. Lack of capital generally prevented the successful operation of black Southern cooperatives, but black members of the Knights were able to establish a number of them. Usually the first floor of the union hall was the site of a cooperative store. The Knights, moreover, provided blacks with the mutual-benefit and social functions—picnics, banquets, socials, and the like—associated with the churches and fraternal societies in which black women had traditionally played an important role. Since the Knights appeared more willing than any other organization of the era to extend to blacks a measure of both acceptance and dignity, the blacks eagerly joined.[12]

Young black men in Chicago set up a tailoring establishment after their employer locked them out for attending a labor parade. By soliciting subscriptions, they raised the $400 needed to begin production. Nine months later they had produced $36,000 worth of garments. In Baltimore and New York, women operated cooperative shirt factories, while women in Waterford, New York, ran a collar-and-cuff factory. Black women in Richmond operated a cooperative laundry under the auspices of the Knights of Labor.

In spite of the hostility of its leadership to the strike as a weapon, the Knights of Labor attained its greatest membership as a result of the order's role during strikes.* The first major strike conducted by the Knights was that of the telegraphers against Western Union in 1883. It was also the first K. of L. strike in which men and women struck together. The telegraphers were defeated after a three-months walkout; many were refused reemployment and were blacklisted. "The Ostracized Female Operators," read the headline of a story in a New York paper early in September, 1883, reporting that a fund was being raised in behalf of the telegraphers who had gone out on strike against Western Union and who had been refused reemployment. "Aid is especially asked for the ostracized female operators, who have been persistently rejected when applying for their old positions. These ladies, however, have no desire to live in idleness, and ask those who sympathize with them to give them notice of any situations that can be obtained."[13]

Taking his cue from Western Union, a Philadelphia shoe manufacturer discharged the grievance committee and every officer of the Garfield Assembly in his shop. The male Knights in Philadelphia advised the members of the assembly not to resist, but the female Knights rejected their advice. They decided that unless they fought the issue through and established a precedent of opposing discrimination against union members, the organization of women workers would suffer. They therefore called the shop on strike, and after a bitter struggle, succeeded in reinstating every one of their members.[14]

In most cases, women shoe workers received more support from male Knights than those in Philadelphia. On April 25, 1885, shoe manufacturers Brennan & White in Williamsburgh (Brooklyn) discharged all women employees belonging to the Knights' shoemakers' union. When the male workers walked out in protest, scabs were hired, given loaded revolvers, and told to "shoot to kill" if necessary to protect themselves against strikers' violence. At the same time, Brennan & White had the women blacklisted in other Williamsburgh shoe factories and sought female convicts from the Kings County Prison as replacements.

When some convicts refused to work, the women strikers issued a

---

*The great growth of the Knights of Labor followed its victory over Jay Gould in the strike on the Southwestern railroad system, involving 10,000 miles of railroad and 4,500 workers. When Gould yielded on March 16, 1885, the spectacular triumph over one of the greatest capitalists of the day brought thousands of new workers into the ranks of the K. of L. Between July, 1885, and October, 1886, membership in the Knights of Labor jumped from 110,000 to over 700,000.

statement praising them and assuring the manufacturers that with the "power" of the union, they would triumph: "We will live to witness the day of our victory." And they did. A boycott declared by the New York Protective Association (controlled by District Assembly No. 49 of the Knights of Labor) and Brooklyn's Central Labor Union came to the aid of the strikers. Shoe laster John Flynn described how it worked in the local neighborhoods. Committees of men and women strikers "go right into our neighborhood, where we live and tell our mothers and sisters not to buy the company's shoes." Before long, Brennan & White reinstated all the strikers and signed an agreement with the union representing the women in their shop.[15]

A boycott also helped women hatters at Berg's hat factory in Orange, New Jersey, who were fired when they decided to form a local of the Knights in the spring of 1885. The boycott instituted by the Knights and other trade unionists caused Berg to back down.[16]

In 1881 a union of cloakmakers joined a newly organized group of dressmakers and proceeded to ally themselves with New York City's Knights. Although this particular organization was short-lived and excluded women in the trades, many of the same men launched a second effort in 1882, once again forming a local trade assembly of the Knights of Labor. When the order permitted women to join, they invited women to join them. Although none of these workers—men or women—had ever participated in a strike, they gathered in July, 1883, in Standard Hall to listen to speeches favoring a walkout, delivered in both German and English. The rallying cry for these Polish Jews, Germans, and Bohemians became "When men and women cannot earn enough to live they must strike." Women workers met separately upstairs and expressed their determination to stand together with the men.

More than 750 workers, about half of them women, agreed to go out on strike for a $2.50 daily wage rate and a ten-hour day. They also insisted that piece rates be reconstructed so that operators who were paid according to that system could earn $15 a week.

After women in the remaining shops still working joined the walkout, the manufacturers acceded to the workers' demands. By August, 1883, the successful strikers had returned to work. While the New York clothing workers' strike was not the first Knights of Labor strike to unite men and women—the telegraphers had already done this in their strike against Western Union—it was the first such strike to end in victory.[17]

Not all the women in the clothing trade were as militant as those in New York City. Lizzie Swank, organizer of an assembly of women garment workers in Chicago, was working in an unorganized factory whose owner first cut prices paid for piecework, then introduced a new rule that work would not be credited to an employee's book until it was returned from the buttonhole maker and presser. As a result, some workers had to go without any income for from two to four weeks, meanwhile falling behind in their rent and facing eviction from their boardinghouses. Swank suggested that they complain to the manufacturer. When each girl voiced her fear of approaching him individually, Swank suggested that they pass around a petition listing their complaints. She wrote the petition; 150 signatures were collected, and only four workers refused to sign. The signers agreed that if even one woman was fired, all the others would walk out. When the women presented the petition, the supervisor called them "silly hussies," and the manufacturer called them ingrates who did not appreciate the generous benefits he provided his workers. Then he singled out four, including Swank and her sister, the group's spokeswomen, and fired them. Not one of the other 146 girls who had signed the petition defended their discharged sisters or walked off the job, as they had agreed to do.[18]

However, on May 3, 1886, during the great eight-hour strikes in Chicago, Lizzie Swank led several hundred sewing women in a strike for the eight-hour day, and they closed down shop after shop along Sedgwick and Division streets. The *Chicago Tribune* of May 4, 1886 called them "Shouting Amazons," and reported: "Between 300 and 400 girls and women were affected with a malignant form of the eight-hour malady yesterday morning." One women told the *Tribune* reporter: "We'll never give in. Never, never, until we get our demands. We want eight hours with ten hours pay." The paper noted that when the march was over, the women signed up to join the Knights of Labor.

In 1882 men, women, and children employed by the Harmony Company Cotton mills in Cohoes, New York, struck against a wage cut—the fourth reduction in seven years. The majority of the strikers were Irish and French-Canadian women, and after six months, the company brought in Protestant Swedish families to replace the Catholic strikers. The strikers responded directly and vigorously, gathering at the mill entrances to "greet" the scabs with stones. The strike was crushed by a combination of police protection for the scabs and starvation. However, the strikers joined the Knights of Labor, and within a year the mill was compelled to rescind the fourth wage cut. The working-class community of Cohoes elected to the State Assembly one of the men who had worked with the women strikers in 1882 and was head of the K. of L. in the city.[19]

The 1884 strikes of women members of the Knights in the textile mills of Fall River and Worcester, in the hat factories of South Norwalk, Connecticut, and of tobacco workers in the Durham, North Carolina, plant of W. Duke Sons and Company were outstanding for the militancy and perseverance of the strikers. One of the most memorable strikes of the decade of militant strikes was conducted in 1885 by women Knights in the carpet-weaving industry. There were some men involved in the strike of three thousand carpet weavers employed by Alexander Smith's Sons in Yonkers, New York, but 90 percent of the strikers were young women. The strike began on February 20, 1885, when Smith refused to reinstate a 10 percent wage reduction (imposed the previous December), to pay wages already due, and to rehire at least twenty women who had been fired for membership in the Knights. The company's stringent factory discipline was another cause of the strike. In late March the strikers' executive committee issued a statement listing the principal demands, together with a long discussion of company fines for actions that the women considered harmless. The committee's complaints were quite specific:

> If a girl is caught looking out of a window her loom is stopped, and she is sent to the boss to explain, and very often she is docked for it. If a girl is discharged from one department she cannot get employment in any other without first begging of her former boss permission to go to work, and they are not allowed to talk to one another during working hours, *or at noon time,* under penalty of being discharged.... They are not allowed to eat dinner together; even two sisters working in two different departments are not allowed to eat their meals together in the factory.[20]

On the eve of the strike, only seven hundred of the women were members of the union, but immediately after the struggle began, all 2,500 women joined the Knights. Unable to hire enough replacements, the company closed down for a few weeks in April and May. When the mills reopened, few strikers accepted Smith's offer to rehire all but those who had begun the walkout three months earlier. The company did find between three and four hundred girls who would work, but the strikers fought to prevent them from entering the plants. The police attacked the pickets and seized three of the women strikers—Ellen Tracy, Lizzie Wilson, and Mary Carey—and charged them with "walking upon Nepperhan Avenue" near the struck mills. The women were haled into court in a police wagon and held for trial.

The arrest of the women strikers aroused tremendous indignation in Yonkers. At a mass protest meeting at Getty Square, resolutions were adopted denouncing "the action of the police as being despotic," and pledging "moral support" to the strikers. Fearing that no jury would convict the women, the court ruled that the strikers could be tried without a jury, but an appeal to the higher courts reversed this decision, and the trial was held before a jury.

As a mark of admiration for the brave conduct of the three young women Knights, and as a token of respect "for the whole striking sisterhood of Yonkers," the entire labor movement of New York City joined in a testimonial meeting sponsored by the powerful Central Labor Union and the Excelsior Labor Club. Delegates from every New York union were among the two thousand people of both sexes who packed the hall for the meeting. Seated on the platform were the honored guests—the three young women members of the K. of L. from Yonkers. Next to them was seated John Swinton, who had been designated to present them with medals in honor of their militancy and courage. The medals carried these words below the insignia of an American eagle:

IN HONOR
of the
ARREST OF A PICKET
in the
YONKERS STRIKE
May 18, 1885

As the Yonkers officials had feared, the jury quickly acquitted the young women.[21]

Meanwhile, the strikers used the boycott against the stores selling Smith's carpets. *John Swinton's Paper* reported (with tongue in cheek) that the women strikers sometimes used "a father or mother, sister, brother or lover to help them. They never say that a man or store is *boycotted*— that is 'un-American' and they don't believe in it—but some tradesmen could tell a wonderful tale and the quiet 'ostracism' (that's an odd word) will result in displacing 'capital' in Yonkers."[22]

Although the strike ended late in August, 1885, without the union's being recognized, the wage cut was rescinded, the fining system was completely revised, and several other grievances of the workers were remedied. The strikers' militancy brought increased respect for women workers both among employers and in the labor movement.[23]

Wives of members of the order and women Knights were also of great assistance to male Knights engaged in strikes and boycotts. They helped on the picket lines, gave scabs the "ditch-degree" and "water cure" (throwing strikebreakers into ditches and dousing them with dishpans of water), and in Cleveland's Rolling Mill strike, they threw "stones, pieces of slag, stone and cinder" at both the strikebreakers and the police who protected them.

"Women as Boycotters" was the title of an article dealing with the effectiveness of the boycott as used by the Knights. The writer noted that since women did all or most of the buying for the family, it was they who determined the success or failure of a boycott. He cited the case of grocers who refused to sell the bread of an antiunion baker, and pointed out that "it was the women Knights who visited his customers and successfully forced compliance with the boycott." The experience of the Knights in both the shoe and garment industries suggests to David Montgomery

that effective unionization of women operatives was likely to have a remarkably radicalizing impact on the organization. In Philadelphia, Toronto, Cincinnati, Beverly, and Lynn both the resistance of the manufacturers to unionism and the level of mutuality exhibited by the workers leapt upward noticeably when the women shoe workers organized along with the men.

Small wonder, then, that Powderly observed that women "are the best men in the Order."[24]

While women occupied positions of leadership in the Knights of Labor, it was in no way commensurate with their number in and contributions to the order. Powderly received frequent requests from women assemblies that they be allowed to induct men as assembly officers because of the women's lack of experience in leadership roles. "These requests were so numerous," James J. Kenneally notes, "that they were treated as routine, and a special form was designated for granting the required dispensation." But Powderly drew the line on the number of men who could function as such officials: "I will not grant dispensation to more than one male member to act as officer of a women's Assembly. Alfred Murray may act as M[aster] W[orkman] but that is all. The others can give as good advice to women officers out of office as in it and it will help the new Assembly much better than if they sat around and let the men do the work of running the Assembly."[25]

A number of assemblies responded sympathetically to women who aspired to leadership positions. Some women members held several posts. Mrs. Elizabeth C. Williams-Patterson was variously organizer for Local Assembly No. 2999 of San Francisco, state lecturer and organizer for the Knights of Labor of Illinois, editor of the *Labor Signal*, the K. of L. paper in Indianapolis, and state lecturer and organizer for the state of Indiana. She was praised as "an expounder and teacher of the principles of the Order," and, said a union circular, "Her enthusiasm and faith in the work are unsurpassed, and never fail to cause both women and men, yes, and children to consecrate themselves to the holy cause. Victor Hugo says 'the 19th century is the century for woman's work,' and no one can rouse women to the necessities of the hour like Sister Patterson."[26]

The highest post occupied by women in the Knights of Labor was that of master workman of a District Assembly. The first to do so was Mrs. Elizabeth Rodgers, who was chosen master workman of a Chicago women's assembly in 1881 and master workman of District No. 24 in the same city in 1886. She presided over the entire Knights' organization in the Chicago area outside of the stockyards, and her district encompassed fifty thousand men and women. In reporting the selection of "A Woman Master Workman," the *New York Times* observed that although Rodgers was only thirty-nine and the mother of eleven children, eight of whom were living, she had "yet managed to make a reputation as a labor reformer." She had served as supreme judge of District No. 24 and as a delegate to the Trades Assembly.

Leonora M. Barry, who headed a District Assembly of nearly a thousand women Knights in upstate New York, was also elected a master workman in 1886. Elizabeth Morgan was elected master workman of Local Assembly No. 1789 of Chicago in 1887, and Mrs. Mary Elizabeth Lease—the famous female orator who urged Kansas farmers to "raise less corn and more hell" was elected master workman of "one of the largest Local Assemblies in the State of Kansas"[27] in 1891.

Rodgers and Barry were among the sixteen women delegates (out of a total of 660) at the General Assembly of 1886, held in Richmond, Virginia. The other fourteen included one salesclerk, six shoe workers, five textile operatives, one dressmaker, and one ironer. Rodgers was listed as a housewife and Barry as a machine hand. Rodgers brought her youngest child, a two-week-old girl, to the convention. (The delegates presented a gold watch to the child and nominated Rodgers to the post of general treasurer, an honor she declined.) In an interview with Frances Willard, the temperance leader and herself a member of the order, Rodgers paid tribute to her husband, George, a leader of the Knights in Chicago, for making her role in the order possible. "My husband always believed that women should do anything they liked that was good and which they could do well," she said proudly. "But for him I would never have got on so well as a Master Workman. I was the first woman in Chicago to join the Knights. They offered us the chance, and I said to myself, 'There must be a first one, and so I'll go forward.'"[28]

The Richmond convention made history for working women. It was at this convention that the Knights of Labor became the first labor organization in America to establish a Department of Woman's Work. It appointed a woman as general investigator to head this department.

So many female assemblies had sprung up in towns and cities throughout the United States that by 1885 the General Assembly meeting in Hamilton, Ontario, authorized the creation of a Committee on Woman's Work. The committee, composed of Mary Hanaflin (a salesclerk) and Lizzie Shute and Mary Sterling (both shoe workers), undaunted by lack of experience, sent out a questionnaire to all local assemblies with women members asking how many members they had, what trades they represented, how many hours constituted a day's work, the average wage paid them, whether the laws concerning child labor were enforced, and if the local had representation in the district. The results were distressing. Ten hours, the committee found, constituted the average workday, and women workers earned an average of $5 per week, although the shoe trade paid more. Laws prohibiting child labor were rarely enforced, and when boys and girls were employed, the girls were "obliged to work more steadily and for less pay than the boys."

When Mary Hanaflin supplemented the report with an address to the assembled Knights in Richmond, she insisted that the first task confronting workingwomen was not to secure the franchise but rather to achieve decent working conditions, and that unionization was the key to this achievement. She proposed wide-ranging investigations to determine the most serious problem areas for workingwomen, to be followed by a strong campaign to publicize the appalling working conditions and additional measures to bring women into the organization.* It was in response to this report that the delegates established the Department of Woman's Work and created the office of general investigator. The object of the department was "to investigate the abuses to which the female sex is subjected by unscrupulous employers, and to agitate the principles which our Order teaches of equal pay for equal work, and of the abolition of child labor."[29]

The Knights appointed Leonora M. Barry, an enthusiastic Knight and outstanding orator, as general investigator. Born in Cork, Ireland, Barry had come to the United States as a young girl. Her family had settled in St. Lawrence County in upstate New York, where she married and had three children. Widowed at an early age, she went to work as a machine hand in an Amsterdam, New York, hosiery mill in order to support herself and her children. She had received *65 cents* for her first week's work. She joined the Knights in 1884 and by September, 1886, had risen to become master workman. The following month, she represented her district at the General Assembly in Richmond.[30]

Operating full-time and with her salary and expenses paid by the order, Barry set out immediately on her mission "to free from the remorseless grasp of tyranny and greed the thousands of underpaid women and girls in our large cities, who, suffering the pangs of hunger, cold and privation, ofttimes yield and fall into the yawning chasm of immorality." For the next three years she conducted an extensive correspondence and traveled throughout the country organizing, investigating, and lecturing. In 1888 she reported to the convention delegates that in one eleven-month period "there have come to the Woman's Department ... 537 applications for my presence, 213 of which have been filled by actual service, and all others answered from the office. Communications requesting advice and information, 789, all of which have been answered by the faithful and efficient secretary, Mary A. O'Reilly."[31]

Barry delivered more than five hundred lectures and organized half a dozen new women's locals, in addition to increasing membership in the

---

*Actually, some work of this kind was already being carried on in Chicago. As statistician of the women's assembly in that city, Lizzie Swank assumed the task of gathering facts on wages, sanitary conditions in workrooms, and hours of labor. Other members visited workshops and talked to both employers and workers in an effort to uncover abuses and then bring them to public attention. Although they were hampered in their efforts by employer opposition and by workers' fear to cooperate, Swank and her colleagues did bring to light the conditions in the Chicago garment industry. The majority of women earned between $1 and $10 a week for a ten to twelve-hour day.

old ones and organizing scores of male workers as well. An account of one of her lectures in the *New London* (Conn.) *Telegraph* went:

> There was quite a large attendance in Lawrence Opera House last night to hear Mrs. L. M. Barry, general instructor of the Knights of Labor. . . . She is a pleasing and forcible speaker with a perfect knowledge of the demands of labor and how they best can be secured. She clearly illustrated the aims of the Knights of Labor and the advantages of forming assemblies, both male and female, and touched upon all phases of the various social and other elements that have a bearing upon the labor question, with some good advice regarding the guidance of political affections.[32]

A number of male Knights, however, resented Barry's work and refused to cooperate with her. She also aroused the opposition of several Catholic priests, one of whom, Father Peter C. McEnroe of Mahoney City, Pennsylvania, denounced her as "Lady Tramp" and called the order "a vulgar, immoral society" for encouraging women to act as organizers. Barry met the attack head on in a stinging letter to Father McEnroe in which she denounced his "slanderous attack" upon her "character and motives as representative of a grand and noble Order pledged to the support of humanity," and defended her right as "an Irishwoman, a Catholic and an honest woman" to serve the cause of her fellow workers.[33]

Despite his usual sensitivity to criticism by Catholic priests, Powderly defended Barry and encouraged her to extend her activity. He did advise her, however, not to spend any time lecturing to and organizing for men:

> The men in this Order have, in my estimation, acted selfishly in encroaching upon your time as they did. Devote every moment to the service of women for their affairs have been kept too long in the background and no one ever had the opportunity you have at hand to make the indignation heaped on defenceless woman a burning question in the near future. To do so you must waste no more time on men, except it be to secure their intercession in behalf of struggling women.[34]

Barry frequently combined her educational trips for the Knights with speaking engagements for women's suffrage and temperance groups. "When I found an opportunity of laying before other organizations of women, the cause of their less fortunate sisters and moulding a favorable sentiment, I felt I was doing that which is an actual necessity, as woman is often unconsciously woman's oppressor," she declared. Barry's speech before the National Woman's Suffrage Association "roused the convention more than that of any other person." Representing the Knights, she attempted to explain the order's goals to the middle-class delegates: "We are trying to teach the outside world that the working woman has feelings, has sensitiveness, has her heart's longings and de-

sires for the better things of life." Any industrial system or society that
prevented some women from participating in it must be abolished because it was false. It was upon the working class that the suffragists
should rely for their most consistent and effective allies. The Knights of
Labor, she said, "are educating our men to know what the ballot means,
not only for the working man, but for the working man's wife and
sister."* Still, it was not enough to battle for the suffrage and other legal
advances:

> Do not, I ask you, in the name of justice, in the name of humanity, do not
> forget to give your attention and some of your assistance to the root of all
> evil, the industrial and social system that is so oppressive, which has wrought
> the chain of circumstances in which so many have become entangled, and
> which has brought the once fondly-loved mother to the position of the twelve
> or fourteen-hour toiler of today. If you would protect the wives and mothers
> of the future from this terrible condition we find these in today, give them
> your assistance.[35]

Barry delivered three reports to annual gatherings of the Knights'
General Assembly—in 1887, 1888, and 1889. All three are of great importance in the history of workingwomen, but perhaps their outstanding
feature is the space devoted to the conditions of workingwomen in various cities throughout the United States.† She paid particular attention to
conditions in the garment industry, describing the women garment
workers as "huddled together in close, stifling back-rooms, where the
machine operatives furnish their own machines, and in most cases,

---

*Although the 1886 K. of L. General Assembly adopted the position of the Committee on
Woman's Work that "there is more important work for women to do before they are
prepared to vote in the affairs of the Nation," the order did endorse the demand for
woman suffrage, and leading Knights often spoke from the same platform as Susan B.
Anthony and Elizabeth Cady Stanton. Anthony was inducted into the order. (*Proceedings
of the K. of L. General Assembly,* 1886, p. 288; Terence V. Powderly, *The Path I Trod* [New
York, 1940], p. 389; Elizabeth S. Bryant to Powderly, 1 February 1883, Terence V.
Powderly Papers, Catholic University of America.) However the Knights refused to endorse the 1890 suffrage campaign in South Dakota, and the organization's stand helped
to defeat the proposal.

†In none of her reports to the General Assemblies did Barry deal with black women.
However, in a letter to Powderly from Montgomery, Alabama, on March 29, 1889, she
complained: "These southern people beat the D- - - - for internal wrangling and quarrels.
They are all ignorant, the best of them, narrow-minded and bigoted and stand in their
own light. It is a constant struggle for supremacy with them. Bro. Powderly, if it be in any
way possible for you to appoint a colored man for lecture it is a dire necessity that you
should do so as in some places the white K. of L. would not allow the Colored K. of L. to
come into the hall where I was giving a public lecture. Of course, you know how I fumed
inwardly at this violation of Knighthood laws, but what could I do? You can't force public
sentiment; it must be molded or won by degrees." (Terence V. Powderly Papers, Catholic
University of America.) Barry seems to have been unaware that the Knights' leadership
made no attempt to educate Southern white workers on the need to combat segregation
and the importance of racial equality.

thread . . . for 5 cents a pair [of pants]. They are then turned over to the finisher who puts on the buttons, makes button-holes and puts on buckles for 5 cents a pair; 6 pairs is an average day's work."

Barry condemned the "contract sweating middlemen" (contractors who obtained cut goods from manufacturers and recruited workers to complete the garments at a rate lower than the one he received when he returned the finished garments), and blamed them for bringing ruin and misery to the workers. The contractor who employed five operatives made 30 cents per unit, or $1.50 a day, while each worker received only 30 cents per day. "Men's vests are contracted out at 10 cents each, the machine operative receiving 2½ cents and the finisher 2½ cents each, making 5 cents a vest for completion." Since twenty vests constituted a day's work, a contractor who employed five operatives reaped $1 a day for doing nothing, while his "victim has 50 cents for eleven and twelve hours of her life's energies."[36]

Barry described female employees in a Philadelphia corset factory who had to pay a 10-cent fine for eating, laughing, singing, or talking while on the job. When an employee in a Newark corset factory reported even one minute late, she was locked out and fined two hours' pay "for wasted time." A clothing manufacturer in Terre Haute, Indiana, demanded that his female operatives pay 25 cents a week for the steam required to operate their machinery and for the needles they used. He also insisted that employees, whose weekly pay ranged between $2 and $6, pay for necessary repairs to their machines. Even the experienced Barry was shocked to discover practices such as those prevailing in an Auburn, New York, establishment in which

> upon accepting a position, an employee was compelled to purchase a sewing machine from the proprietress who is an agent for the Sm- - Co. This must be paid for in weekly payments of 50 cents, if the operative makes $3.00. If at any time before the machine was paid for (through a reduction of the already meager wages) she was dismissed—as a consequence of the enforcement of some petty tyrannical rule, sickness, anger, or any other cause—she forfeited the machine and any money paid on it, and the machine was resold to the next applicant. She must also purchase the thread for doing the work, as the proprietress is the agent for the thread company. It takes 4 spools of thread at 50 cents a spool to do $5 worth of work and when $2 is paid for thread and 50 cents for the machine, the unfortunate vicitm has $2.50 wherewith to board, do the laundry, and care for herself generally, and it is only the experts who can make even this.

But even this blatant exploitation paled compared with what she found in a linen mill in Paterson, New Jersey. There, "the women stood on a stone floor with water from a revolving cylinder flying constantly against the breast. They had in the coldest weather to go home with underclothing dripping because they were allowed neither space nor a few moments of time in which to change their clothing."[37]

Barry compiled the first nationwide statistics on women's work and found that they earned from $2.50 to $3 for a work week of eighty-four hours.[38] The information she gathered was turned over to the newly established state bureaus of labor.* But unlike the labor bureaus, Barry did not content herself with merely accumulating statistics and describing working conditions.† She also emphasized the need to change those conditions through unionism. She soon discovered, however, that there were many obstacles to be overcome in organizing workingwomen. The three major ones were the opposition of employers, the opposition of male Knights, and the opposition of workingwomen. She had expected the first, but the last two came as a shock to her. On November 15, 1887, she wrote to Powderly:

> I have been racking my brain for months past to try and devise some means or method whereby I might create an interest in our Order among working women. I have found the one stumbling block to be what good will it do us? And as these minds seem to have been trained in such narrow grooves that it was impossible for them to see or understand the benefits accruing from organization without some present benefit, I have formulated a plan which, with your sanction, I propose to suggest and endeavor to make a success in every possible locality.

Barry's plan called for every local assembly having women members to appoint a committee of three, which would meet and found a "Workingwomen's Beneficial and Protective Association to be governed and conducted by the Order of the K. of L." The convention would set the fee for membership and monthly dues, and the sum to be paid per week in case of sickness or accident. The association would have a Protective Committee to which any member might come "with any grievance or wrong done them by an employer, such as defrauding of wages, unjust

---

*In 1869 Massachusetts created the first department to collect and correlate labor statistics, under the leadership of Carroll D. Wright (later the first U.S. Commissioner of Labor). By ten years later, six states had labor bureaus, which proceeded to gather a wealth of information about labor conditions, including those of workingwomen.

†Investigators for state labor bureaus refused to recommend any action to remedy the abuses they exposed. Some felt that their duty simply required them to present the material in raw form, together with the complaints of workingwomen, without any official recommendation whatever. Even Carroll D. Wright, while he sympathized with the women, maintained that "no suggestion might be made by which these girls' wages might be improved," since their pay depended on the natural laws of economics which neither legislative fiat nor trade unionism could repeal. Probably the only solution to the problems of workingwomen, Wright suggested, was through humanitarian appeals to employers, the opening of religious and social facilities for workingwomen, and the establishment of respectable boardinghouses for them.

fines, etc., said committee to investigate the matter and be empowered to procure the necessary legal advice and counsel to prevent it."
"What do you think of it?" Barry asked Powderly. Apparently she never found out, since after her letter was received, it was stamped "No Answer Required." In any case, Barry reached the conclusion that the existing locals were not doing enough to convince women that the Knights merited their support,[39] and she did not hesitate to make this point in her reports to the general assemblies. Insisting that women workers would remain degraded as long as "the selfishness of brothers in toil continues," Barry warned that

> within the jurisdiction of our District Assemblies starvation and sin are knocking at, aye, and have gained entrance at the doors of thousands of victims of underpaid labor. And the men who have pledged themselves to the "assistance of humanity" and the "abolition of poverty" are so engrossed in the pursuit of their own ambitious desires, that upon their ears the wail of woe falls unheeded, and the work of misery still goes on.

The longer she traveled, the more convinced she became that the K. of L. platform of "equal pay for equal work" was a mockery, and she challenged delegates to either erase the plank from the platform or turn their attention toward upholding it. She pleaded: "O brothers of the Knights of Labor, I implore you by your love for mothers, wives and daughters . . . to uproot the corrupt system that is making slaves—not alone in poverty, but slaves to sin and shame—of those who by right of divine parentage we must call sisters."[40]

Barry did not absolve workingwomen themselves from responsibility for their continued exploitation. She discovered that many women workers dreaded having others learn that they worked in factories. "If there is one cause more than another that fastens the chains on Baltimore working-women," she reported, "it is their foolish pride, they deeming it a disgrace to have it known that they are engaged in honest toil." This unfortunate attitude enabled employers to pay inadequate wages and provide intolerable working conditions. Again, not only did employers refuse her permission to investigate their premises, but frequently cautious friends of workingwomen would warn them against discussing their conditions with her lest their employer retaliate. In addition to what she called "the habit of submission and acceptance without question of any terms offered them," many workingwomen were reluctant to participate in union activities because they expected to be married soon. "All this," Barry concluded, "is the result or effect of the environment and conditions surrounding women in the past and present, and can be removed only by constant agitation and education."[41]

Not all Barry's experiences were discouraging. In some cities she found enthusiastic, well-organized groups of women and others eager to join them. The women members of the Detroit assembly were "intelligent, earnest, and active; they are a power for good." The women's assembly in Minneapolis evidenced "the clear brain and honest heart of its members, although a great deal of work remained for the women of that mid-western city."[42]

Experiences like these caused Barry to maintain for two years her enthusiasm and optimism about the potential for the Woman's Department. She concluded her report to the 1888 General Assembly on this encouraging note: "Ten thousand organized women today look to the Woman's Department for counsel, advice and assistance. It is their hope, their guiding star."[43]

But by the time she attended the 1889 General Assembly, her optimism had faded. The Order's influence had declined sharply and there was little she could do to stem the tide. Her annual report for 1889 reflected both her disappointment and her sense of defeat.

First, Barry startled the delegates by confessing that she had always believed woman's place was in the home. "If it were possible," she said, "I wish that it were not necessary to women to learn any trade but that of domestic duties, as I believe it was intended that man should be the breadwinner." But since this was impossible under existing conditions, she believed "women should have every opportunity to become proficient in whatever vocation they choose to find themselves fitted for."* What really stunned the delegates, however, was Barry's request that they disband the Woman's Department. After a careful analysis of the obstacles she had had to confront in three years of investigating and organizing, Barry concluded that she had not achieved the results she had hoped for. She suggested that the organization terminate her position as investigator and eliminate her department: "There can be no separation or distinction of wage workers on account of sex and a separate department for the interests of women is a direct contradiction of this." She agreed to continue serving the order, but refused to "stand at the head of something that, owing to the failure of the women to organize more thoroughly, does not exist except in name."[44]

*Barry clung to this position through the remainder of her life. Interviewed by Marguerite Martyn for the St. Louis Post-Dispatch long after she had left the Knights of Labor, she was asked: "How do you reconcile your belief in woman suffrage with your disapproval of the modern tendency to desert the home?" "I do not admit that suffrage makes women desert their homes," she replied. "History of states where women vote proves they do not aspire to office. The few who do would express the ambition for public notice in some other direction if not in this." She went on to argue that what government needed "is the subtle touch which we cannot describe except to call it womanliness. . . . The home is the cradle in which the nation is rocked, reared and fostered." (Undated clipping in Leonora M. Barry Lake Folder, Sophia Smith Collection, Smith College Library.)

Barry's recommendation is especially puzzling in view of a letter to Powderly on October 4, 1888, in which she had written:

As to wishing the Woman's Department abolished, I never have nor ever will. First, because it is an absolute necessity as an encouragement to our working women, many of whom look to the department as their guiding star. Second, because I am prepared to show that it has done as much good for the Order as any other, and more than some other departments.

Still another reason was that it would deprive her secretary, Mary A. O'Reilly, of a livelihood on which she and her children depended. From other correspondence, it appears that a number of the top leaders of the Knights, especially John W. Hayes of the General Executive Board, were pressing for abolition of the Woman's Department and for Barry's removal. When Powderly failed to stand up for her, Barry told him frankly that she had become "disheartened and bitter." Evidently she was also discouraged by Powderly's insistence that she not speak to men, for she wrote: "I ask you to release me from the stricture of talking to women only as I can best reach them through men."[45] Just what she meant is not clear, but she was correct in noting the opposition to the Woman's Department and to the two women who ran it. As early as November 5, 1887, the *Labor Enquirer,* the K. of L. paper published in Chicago, sneered that "creating two fat jobs for the sisters will do little towards lifting the burdens from the workingwomen's shoulders. So far the effect of the Woman's Department has only been to increase the list of office-holders."

Despite all this, Barry's recommendation was not accepted; the Woman's Department continued, and Barry herself continued as "General Instructor and Director of Woman's Work," lecturing and investigating. Then, in November, 1889, Powderly informed her that "owing to the straitened circumstances in which the Order is placed," she had to stop traveling and would have to concentrate on activity in Philadelphia, "and work among the women of that city until such time as you have effected an organization among them." He added ominously: "What we most require at present is an organization; without it the bills of the Order cannot be paid, and until we have it no lecturing can be done at the expense of the Order."[46]

Barry followed his advice and continued organizing in the Philadelphia area until November, 1890, when she married Oliver R. Lake, a St. Louis printer and fellow Knight. In a letter to the 1890 General Assembly, signed L. M. Barry Lake, she urged the delegates to select her successor. She also wished the new investigator success in "women's struggle for justice, equity and complete emancipation from political and industrial bondage."[47]

An effort was made to continue the Woman's Department, and the office Barry vacated was offered to Alzina P. Stevens, the only woman delegate to the 1890 convention*—a far cry from the sixteen women delegates who had attended the 1886 Assembly. When she declined the post, the Woman's Department of the Knights of Labor was abolished.

On the surface, nothing much seemed to have been accomplished by Barry's four years of investigating, speaking, and organizing. But she had brought to public attention a full picture of the abysmal conditions of workingwomen and had collected a body of statistics and descriptions that were to prove useful in future struggles. While Barry herself never again worked actively for the labor movement,† Mary A. O'Reilly, the secretary of the Woman's Department, continued to work in the order for three more years. When Pennsylvania passed its first factory inspection law, she became deputy factory inspector, one of the first women to hold such a post, and continued in the position for six years.[48]

After 1886, when the Knights of Labor reached the pinnacle of its success, with its membership rolls reaching nearly 700,000, the order began a rapid decline. The tremendous employer counteroffensive that followed the Haymarket Affair‡ wiped out the order's substantial membership gains and left many locals in severe distress. Lockouts, blacklists, arrests, and imprisonment were used to drive workers out of the Knights.[49] But many workers were also driven out by the order's leadership, and among them were many of the most militant women Knights.

In the spring of 1886, the District Assembly in the area of Troy, New York, had eighty-eight local assemblies. The Joan of Arc Assembly, made up of "collar girls," had a membership of more than four thousand. Some were veterans of the Troy Collar Workers' Union of the 1860s, but the majority were newly recruited.[50]

Early in May, committees of the Joan of Arc Assembly met with representatives of the Collar Manufacturers' Association and asked for a

---

*Stevens was master workman of a women's assembly in Chicago and owner and editor of her own newspaper. She was later appointed assistant factory inspector for Illinois.

†Leonora M. Barry Lake continued to lecture after her retirement from the Knights of Labor, speaking at conventions of suffragists and for the Chautauqua circuit on a number os subjects. Asked if she had "some pet reform," she replied: "If any, it is on behalf of working women." (Interview in *St. Louis Post-Dispatch,* undated clipping in Leonora M. Barry Lake Folder, Sophia Smith Collection, Smith College Library.)

‡The Haymarket Affair resulted from the explosion of a dynamite bomb in the midst of a squadron of police attempting to disperse a peaceful labor meeting in Chicago, on May 4, 1886. Seven police were killed and some sixty were wounded. During a wave of hysteria, eight men, all anarchists and alleged anarchists, were arrested and placed on trial. Though no evidence proved their connection with the actual bomb-throwing, they were tried for their opinions only and condemned to death. Four were hanged on November 11, 1887, one committed suicide in prison (or was murdered by the prison guards), one was sentenced to 15 years imprisonment, and two had their sentence commuted to life imprisonment.

wage increase for the "collar girls," who had suffered a series of wage reductions, and for a new price list that would equalize wages throughout the city. The manufacturers rejected both demands and offered only the existing price schedule. At this point, 250 Joan of Arc laundresses employed by George P. Ide & Company went on strike to restore a wage cut put into effect the previous year. Immediately, thirty-one of the largest companies in Troy notified the Knights of Labor that they were going to institute their own price schedules regardless of the order. They also warned the "laundry employees of George P. Ide & Company who have struck for increased wages" to return to work on Monday morning, May 17: "And in case the said employees do not return to work on said date, however much we regret the necessity of so doing, we each and all agree to close the manufacturing department of our factories on Tuesday, May 18, at 6 p.m., and remain closed until all differences are adjusted."[51]

The lockout threatened over fifteen thousand people who either were employed in the Troy collar factories or worked in their homes on collars and shirts, as well as those who made boxes for the factories. "The grave importance of the situation is easily to be seen," the Troy *Northern Budget* commented. "A shut-down will throw out of employment thousands of the best class of working people in the city and vicinity." It added: "The striking girls express their determination to stay out until their demands are granted," and noted that the Knights of Labor of the entire district had promised full support, and had let the paper know that "the Knights of Labor are people who wear shirts and collars" and were well experienced in the art of boycotting. Since the plan was to start a cooperative factory if the laundry workers were locked out, there would be collars and shirts for the boycotters to purchase.[52]

On May 19, 1886, all the collar factories closed down. That same day the locked-out "collar girls" paraded through the streets of Troy carrying signs that charged the manufacturers with attempting "to beat back their workers to the condition of slaves."[53] A group of "collar girls" wrote a letter to the Troy *Northern Budget* in which they accused "outside agitators" of being responsible for the lockout. "We ask the striking laundry girls of Geo. P. Ide & Co. to be considerate and return to work," the "loyal" workers went on, "for judging by our own experience, their employers will deal justly with them." Once they had returned, the manufacturers would call off the lockout, and all could be working again under employers who would be, in the future as in the past, "kind and considerate, ready and willing to listen to any grievances that the girls wished to bring to them."[54]

The great majority of the "collar girls" indignantly repudiated the statement that they had been provoked by "outside agitators." They reminded the few who had defended the employers that "more men have been made wealthy in Troy by the shirt and collar business than by any other, and that in some instances they have become independently rich within five years, just from the income of this business." But the workers who were responsible for their wealth "still live in poverty" and were even "forced to accept wage reductions." When their sisters struck against this tyranny, the very men they had made rich threatened "to deprive all of their workers of their ability to earn their daily bread." Already they were sending agents to Albany to replace the locked-out girls. But they should understand that "the locked-out employees will never permit new help to work," that "Troy never has given protection to its manufacturers when there was trouble with the working women, and it will not do it now if the collar factories attempt to open with new girls."[55]

This warning had its effect. No attempt was made to introduce strikebreakers into the factories. The manufacturers relied instead on starving out the workers. But on June 12, a month after the lockout began, the Joan of Arc Assembly met in front of the Troy City Hall and adopted the following resolutions:

> Resolved, That we can never accept the schedule of prices offered us by the Combined Manufacturers' Association, for the reason that that schedule is the result of a persistent and long continued system of cutting down prices, until they have reached a point far below the real value of our services, and are actually insufficient for our necessary support, and
>
> That whenever our employers are ready to give us a fair price for our labor, we are ready to go back to work; also
>
> Resolved, That we return our sincere and hearty thanks to our brothers and sisters of the locals belonging to our district assembly who have so promptly and generously sent us money, which our committees are now using to supply the needs of hundreds of those who are deprived of work in consequence of this unjust and cruel lockout, and we duly appreciate the promise that this supply shall be continued until this lockout is at an end.[56]

Unfortunately, the promise had to be repudiated at the bidding of the Knights' top leadership. On June 21, John W. Hayes, leading member of the K. of L. General Executive Board, came to Troy and proposed an agreement under which the "collar girls" would return to work at existing wages while a committee continued to negotiate a new agreement. The manufacturers rejected even this proposal, insisting that they would never reopen their laundries until the strikers returned unconditionally. Without consulting the Joan of Arc Assembly or any of the striking women, Hayes replied: "Since you refuse to accept our proposition, we will accept yours, and thereby prove to the public that we have more interest in the welfare of the city than the combined capital of the Collar and Shirt Manufacturers' Association." To the laundry workers, Hayes issued the following notice: "You are hereby ordered to re-

turn to work tomorrow, Wednesday, June 24, at your respective places."
And he sent notices to the entire District Assembly ordering locals to give
no further assistance to the locked-out workers.[57]

On June 25, 1886, the "collar girls" returned to the laundry factories,
but within two months the Joan of Arc Assembly had ceased to exist.
Most of its members had left the Knights of Labor in disgust, and their
action was widely publicized among other assemblies of women members
of the order.[58]

Black women Knights, too, were driven out of the order by a combination of employers' terror and the policies of the Knights' leadership.
In October–November, 1887, black male and female sugar workers in
Louisiana, members of the Knights of Labor, struck for wages of $1.25 a
day without board or $1 a day with board, and for wages to be paid every
two weeks in money. They were arrested, evicted from their cabins, and
shot down in cold blood by state militiamen and vigilantes hired by the
sugar planters. With no assistance from the national leadership of the
Knights of Labor, most of the strikers were forced to return to work on
the old terms.[59] Some of them left the order, but other blacks remained
steadfast members. However, the K. of L. leadership eventually drove
them out, too. Frightened by the fact that the order in the South was fast
becoming an all-black organization, they retreated from the stand mod-
erately in favor of racial equality they had taken early in the Knights'
history. By 1894 the retreat was in full swing.

The Knights announced that the only solution for the black problem
was to raise federal funds to deport blacks to the Congo Basin, Liberia,
"or some other parts of Africa," and Grand Master Workman James R.
Sovereign, Powderly's successor, was instructed by the General Executive Board to mobilize support for an appropriation of funds to deport
blacks.[60] Blacks were outraged. "Negroes have been residents of this
country for two hundred and forty years and are as much American
citizens as anybody," the Chicago Colored Women's Club announced. "If
this country is too small for the Knights of Labor and the Negro, then let
the Knights leave."[61] The Knights—or what remained of the order—
stayed, but blacks left the organization in utter disgust. The once-great
Knights of Labor, the only organization in American life that had challenged the patterns of discrimination and segregation up to that time,
had joined all other institutions in relegating black Americans to an
inferior status.[62]

By 1895 the membership of the Knights of Labor had plummeted to
twenty thousand. Although it continued to exist thereafter, it ceased to
be a viable labor organization after 1895.[63]

The Knights of Labor was the largest labor organization in nineteenth-century America. At its height, the order had twelve thousand

locals distributed in every metropolis, in virtually every industrial center, large or small, and in hundreds of small towns and rural villages, mine patches, and country crossroads. Of all places in America with populations over one thousand in the decade from 1880 to 1890, half had at least one local assembly of the Knights of Labor, while many major urban centers had over a hundred. Locals varied in size from just over ten members to over a thousand. Assemblies were formed in a thousand distinct occupations, ranging from urban and rural day labor to factory and artisan labor. Membership composition was diverse, with hundreds of assemblies consisting entirely of women or blacks or members of individual ethnic groups.

After an early reluctance to accept women as members, the Knights opened the doors of the house of labor to more women than had any organization up to that time, and to more than many who succeeded the order. For black women, especially, it represented a milestone in labor history. Thousands of women found a sisterhood in the Knights, and through it they fought some of the most militant battles of the 1880s. Out of the Knights emerged a cadre of courageous and tireless female leaders—Leonora M. Barry, Lizzie Swank, Elizabeth Rodgers, Mary Hanaflin, Mary A. O'Reilly, Lizzie H. Shute, Mary Sterling, Bridget O'Keefe, and others—who worked valiantly to improve the lot of workingwomen.

It is difficult to estimate the effect of the Knights of Labor on the conditions of women workers. The New Jersey commissioner of labor declared in 1886: "Since the girls have joined the Knights of Labor here they make the same wages as the men."[64] But Leonora M. Barry's findings indicate that no other commissioner of labor could make the same statement.

The Knights did win the reputation as the first labor organization to place women on an equal footing with men. "In all our assemblies, local, district, state, trade, and general," Mary Hanaflin told a woman's convention, "woman has an equal voice, when a member, with her brother trade unionist." But here, too, there was another side to the story. In many assemblies, male Knights did not favor the organization of women and did not accord them "an equal voice." Eventually, the Knights denied black women any semblance of equality. Grand Master Workman Powderly seems to have been a consistent champion of the necessity and justice of organizing women workers and devoted a portion of the *Journal of United Labor,* the Knights' official organ, to news of women's activities and articles on workingwomen. But he was in advance of many Knights on this issue, and he constantly had to remind his fellow members of the order of their verbal commitment to equality of men and women.[65]

Not a few women Knights were passive and shied away from complaining about conditions of their employment and fighting to improve them. At the same time, many were militant and defied both convention and male supremacists in the order. While Lizzie Swank in Chicago often encountered passivity and a reluctance to stand up for their rights among women workers, another observer at a Chicago women's assembly reported that "timid young girls—girls who have been overworked from their cradles—stand up bravely and in steady tones, swayed by conviction and the wrongs heaped upon their comrades, talk nobly and beautifully of the hope of redress to be found in organization."[66]

The *Los Angeles Union* exaggerated when it said: "The Knights of Labor is the only organization we know which encourages the membership of ladies, demands for women exact equality, and insists on equal pay for equal work."[67] But while the Knights as a whole did not challenge the traditional ideas about woman's sphere, many assemblies did advocate "the true principle of Knighthood—the equality of women."*

For a brief period the Knights of Labor broke down sexual, ethnic, racial, trade, and skill barriers in an attempt to mobilize men and women, black and white, skilled and unskilled, in a union of all the toilers. While this brief period did not fundamentally change the status or conditions of workingwomen, it did bring forth a number of female labor leaders who were to carry their knowledge and experience with them into the next period in the history of organized labor and the woman worker.[68]

*The Ladies' Social Assembly of Olneyville, a mill town in Rhode Island, composed of female members of the Knights of Labor who had gained the reputation of being among "the hardest workers" for the Order, established "a most remarkable institution, a 'socialistic' day nursery in one of Olneyville's largest churches, for the women mill workers to leave their children in safe charge." (Paul Buhle, "The Knights of Labor in Rhode Island," *Radical History Review*, vol. XVII, Spring, 1978, p. 58.)

5

The American Federation
of Labor

THE DRAMATIC UPSURGE in labor organization in the mid-1880s was linked to the meteoric rise of the Knights of Labor, but it continued even after that organization's rapid descent into oblivion. In fact, even while the K. of L. was disintegrating, the new American Federation of Labor was experiencing a slow but steady growth. First organized as the Federation of Organized Trades' and Labor Unions of the United States and Canada, it was renamed and reorganized in 1886. By 1892 the thirteen original member unions had increased to forty.[1]

No women were present at the founding convention of the federation in 1881, but the debate over the new organization's name indicated the intent to include workingwomen. Originally it was proposed that the organization be called "The Federation of Organized Trades' Unions of the United States of America and Canada," and that it be composed of trade unions only. But one delegate, speaking for the majority, pointed out that the convention's purpose was to found an organization that would take into its folds "the whole labor element of this country," not just skilled workers, and not solely men. For that reason, he proposed the name "Federation of Organized Trades' and Labor Unions," with the skilled workers entering through the trade unions and the unskilled and semiskilled, of whom women formed a great percentage, coming in through the so-called labor unions. The proposal was adopted.[2]

At its 1882 convention the federation extended an invitation to all women's organization to join and assured them that they would be represented at future sessions "upon an equal footing with trade organizations of men."[3] The following year Mrs. Charlotte Smith, president of the Women's National Industrial League, was admitted as a delegate and addressed the convention.* She appealed to the delegates to advise, cooperate, and assist in the formation of women's unions, and pledged that women would stand by male unionists, making a concerted effort against their common foes. The convention responded by drafting "An Address to Working Girls and Women," urging them to organize and unite with the federation in establishing the principle that "equal amounts of work should bring the same prices whether performed by man or woman." A convention delegate supported the appeal with the assertion that treacherous employers who exploited female workers, especially seamstresses and factory operatives, could only be thwarted if the workingwomen of the land would "array themselves under the banner of united labor."[4] At the 1885 convention, the delegates repeated the appeal to the workingwomen of this country to protect themselves by organizing into unions of their respective trades or callings and authorized the legislative committee to assist women in organizing wherever the opportunity offered itself.[5]

But beyond recognizing the problems faced by women workers, adopting lofty pronouncements calling for them to join unions, and reasserting the principle of "equal pay for equal work," the AFL made little concrete progress for workingwomen during the 1880s. Moreover, Samuel Gompers, the first president of the AFL, and, with the exception of one year (1895), the head of the federation until his death in 1924, was frank enough to acknowledge that enforcement of "equal pay for equal work regardless of sex" would probably help men more than women, since many women workers had been hired precisely because they could be paid lower wages than men.[6] Only two national affiliates of the AFL—the Cigar Makers' Union and the Typographical Union—accepted women as members, and others actually passed resolutions prohibiting them from joining. Only one woman delegate appeared at any AFL convention prior to 1891, and women were conspicuously absent at meetings of affiliated local unions. Gompers was able to do little to help them because of the federation's policy of trade union autonomy and noninterference.[7]

In the main, women workers, being relatively unskilled, did not fit into the craft unions of the AFL, and to the degree that they were

---

*Mrs. Smith, it will be recalled, had helped found the union of female government employees affiliated with the Knights of Labor, but it was quite common for unionists to hold dual affiliation with both the Knights and the federation during the latter organization's early years. Mrs. Smith appeared before the U.S. Senate Committee on Education and Labor in 1883, where she attacked the Western Union Company for its low wage scales for women and urged the women of the nation to donate funds for the striking Western Union women. (U.S. Senate Committee on Education and Labor, *Report Upon the Relations Between Capital and Labor* [Washington, D.C., 1884] 1: 442.)

organized in the early federation, the tendency was to set up separate
unions for women workers. Indeed, it was not uncommon for AFL
organizers to form two unions in a shop or factory—one for women and
one for men—and to arrange for negotiations with employers to be
conducted by a joint committee representing both unions. The women
workers frequently complained that they got the worst end in such an
arrangement, since "the men think that the girls should not get as good
work as the men and should not make half as much money as a man."[8]
Very few women were willing to join such unions, and the plan was
quickly abandoned.

Practically the entire history of the American Federation of Labor
and women workers in the 1880s was written by one organization: the
Ladies' Federal Labor Union No. 2703 in Chicago. Its founder and
guiding spirit was Elizabeth Chambers Morgan, wife of Chicago's leading socialist, Thomas J. Morgan. Born in Birmingham, England, in
1850, she came from a family of ten children and parents who were
factory operatives. Her formal education ended at the age of eleven,
when she went to work in a factory. After marrying Morgan in 1868, she
emigrated with her husband to Chicago. In September, 1874, she became a charter member of the Sovereigns of Industry, a society concerned mainly with establishing consumers' cooperatives for the distribution of the necessities of life among wage earners and "designed for
the laboring classes, especially working men and women."[9] Women were
active in the Sovereigns, and she became a secretary of the Chicago
Assembly. The Sovereigns disappeared before the end of the decade,
and Elizabeth Morgan continued her labor activity in the Knights of
Labor. She was one of the first women admitted into the Knights and
became, as we have noted, master workman of the Chicago Assembly. She
was also one of the earliest Knights to leave the order, resigning in
disgust in 1887 over the leadership's increasing conservatism. In June,
1888, she led a small group of Chicago women in organizing the Ladies'
Federal Labor Union No. 2703. It was a mixed union, composed of
typists, seamstresses, dressmakers, clerks, music teachers, candymakers,
gum makers, and other female workers. The year it was organized, it
received both a charter from the American Federation of Labor and
state recognition as a legal corporation.[10]

Elizabeth Morgan quickly earned a high place among those women
who have made distinguished contributions to the American labor
movement. She was secretary of the Ladies' Federal Labor Union and its
delegate to the Chicago Trade and Labor Assembly, a citywide association of trade unions. She did excellent work in recruiting members into
the Ladies' Federal Labor Union and, through it, in organizing other
workingwomen into unions.[11] Although her limited education required
that she seek assistance in polishing her literary style, she wrote the

recruiting leaflet "The Aims and Objects of Ladies' Federal Labor Union No. 2703," which began:

> Without organization for self protection, with the many disadvantages of sex, and the helplessness of childhood, the female and child workers are the victims of every avaricious, unscrupulous and immoral employer. The Ladies' Federal Union has been organized to prevent to some extent, the moral, physical and mental degradation of women and children employed as wage workers in this city.

This it hoped to accomplish by "the organization of all women"; by investigating the complaints brought by women and children "against unjust and inhuman employers, and by every honorable means, attempt[ing] to remove the wrongs complained of"; by securing the enforcement of local and state laws that would tend to improve the conditions of employment of women and children, and agitating for the enactment of further legislation; by obtaining "the aid and co-operation of the great labor organizations of this city and country, and the active assistance of the many women's organizations"; by discussing the labor question for "intellectual improvement"; by assisting members in case of sickness or accident; and by "social enjoyment." All workingwomen were eligible for membership; the initiation fee was 25 cents, and dues were 5 cents a week. Sickness benefits were $3 a week. Morgan supplemented the leaflet with speeches outlining the advantages of unionism for workingwomen. One argument she raised was far in advance of her time: she pointed out that unions would make women "self-reliant" so they "need not marry worthless husbands for a home and the bare necessities of life."[12]

By February, 1892, the Ladies' Federal Labor Union had brought into being twenty-four women's organizations, including unions of bookbinders, shirtmakers and cloakmakers, watchmakers, and shoe workers. When ten women of one craft had been recruited into the federal union, they set up a union of their own, received a charter from the AFL, and began to organize other women in their trade. Nearly all these unions were organized by Mrs. Morgan, who, although so small in stature that she had "to climb on a chair to light a gas jet," was a woman with "a face every line of which betoken[ed] energy, shrewdness and determination."[13]

After 1891 Mrs. Morgan acquired "a national reputation."[14] In her monthly reports to the Chicago Trade and Labor Assembly, she called for the mandatory schooling of children under fourteen, the arrest of truants, the prohibition of child labor, the appointment of women to the school board, and the designation of factory inspectors. All her proposals were adopted by the assembly and forwarded to the state legislature.[15] In the late summer of 1888, the *Chicago Times* ran a series of articles entitled "City Slave Girls," depicting the misery of women employed in factories and workshops.[16] Stirred by this exposé, Mrs. Morgan persuaded the Ladies' Federal Labor Union to establish a committee to determine the authenticity of the articles and to seek the cooperation of the Trade and Labor Assembly and various women's groups in combating these evils.[17]

After the investigation confirmed the accuracy of the *Chicago Times* articles, the committee formed the Illinois Women's Alliance to protect workingwomen and children. The alliance was composed of the Ladies' Federal Labor Union and a number of women's groups with suffrage, medical, literary, religious, and temperance interests. The coalition aimed "to prevent the moral, mental, and physical degradation of women and children as wage-workers" by enforcing the existing factory ordinances and compulsory education laws and by seeking the enactment of such new laws as might be necessary. Morgan was a member of the alliance's executive committee and also chairman of the Trade Assembly delegation to the alliance.[18]

The Women's Alliance compiled an impressive record of achievement. It thoroughly exposed the weakness of Illinois's Compulsory Education Act of 1883, under which children between the ages of eight and fourteen were supposed to be in school for not less than twelve weeks each year. Since the law had no effective enforcement provisions, it was virtually useless, and the alliance found thousands of school-age children roaming the streets and working in factories and stores. It obtained the passage of an improved law in 1889, which required children to begin school at age seven, extended the minimum time spent in school to sixteen weeks a year, and, most important, provided for enforcement through truant officers appointed by the school board, with fines for violations. Thousands of Chicago's children were taken from the streets and factories and placed in the schools. But the alliance soon discovered that there was an insufficient number of public schools in the city to educate them. "Children cannot be driven into schools which have no existence," it pointed out. The alliance therefore led the mass campaign that resulted in the construction of new schools.[19]

The organization also secured passage of a city ordinance empowering the commissioner of health to appoint five women factory inspectors; it sponsored a clothing drive for school-age children from poverty-stricken families; and, after a long struggle, it obtained the appointment of an alliance member to the Board of Education. With Elizabeth Morgan as chairperson, the alliance's Committee on Child Labor worked for a comprehensive child labor law and succeeded in gaining both a local ordinance and a general child labor law in the state legislature prohibiting the employment of children under fourteen years of age. Unfortunately, a combination of a lack of enforcement provisions and exemption clauses rendered the laws practically worthless.[20] But the five women factory inspectors appointed as a result of pressure by the Women's Alliance won international fame for their accomplishments. The "No. 5" issue of the *Eight Hour Day*, a four-page flier published in Zurich on April 10, 1890, carried a report from "North America" proudly noting that "five women inspectors in Chicago have fulfilled their tasks during the past year," and went on: "They have succeeded in compelling the larger shopowners to provide seats for women clerks, as prescribed by law. Moreover the women inspectors have told the clerks that if they are fired for using the seats they should file a complaint with the city's Health Department." Evidently the women workers had feared a blacklist if they complained. But Chief Inspector Ruth Young had sent notices to all the shops warning against reprisals, and the *Eight Hour Day* reported that "the women have seats." "The work of the Women's Alliance," the flier concluded, had in this case paid off.

The victories scored by the Women's Alliance sponsored by the AFL Ladies' Federal Labor Union No. 2703, under the leadership of its dynamic secretary, Elizabeth Morgan, were evidence of what a coalition of trade union and middle-class women could accomplish. Similar coalitions were beginning to emerge in a number of other cities, generally composed of Working Girls' Clubs, Working Women's Improvement Associations, Working Women's Societies, Social Settlements, and Consumers' Leagues.

In 1884 a small group of young workingwomen in New York City banded together to form the Working Girls' Club, to gain cultural enrichment through talks on literary, religious, and moral questions. Grace M. Dodge, a young heiress, became a prime mover in the undertaking and helped set up Working Girls' Clubs in other cities. By 1885 there were branches in Brooklyn, Philadelphia, and Boston, all dedicated to providing young workingwomen with opportunities "for moral intercourse and the development of higher and nobler aims." Girls fourteen and older were eligible to join the clubs. Those over sixteen paid a 25-cent initiation fee and monthly dues of 25 cents, while girls in the fourteen-to-sixteen age group participated in Junior Clubs and paid lower dues. Once enrolled, a member could use the club's comfortably furnished rooms and its circulating library, piano, and writing supplies. She could also attend frequent lectures, "entertainments," and sewing and embroidery classes, and had the privilege of joining dressmaking, cooking, millinery, and school extension classes upon the payment of nominal fees. Through the efforts of Dodge and other wealthy benefactors, the New York members enjoyed the use of two summer houses on Long Island, for which they paid only $3 for weekly board.

The Working Girls' Clubs could not have survived without the financial support of middle-class philanthropists, and participation in the clubs' varied cultural, educational, and recreational activities did bring working girls and middle-class women together. But many young women who worked long hours in shops and factories could not find the spare time to participate in these social activities. Nor did the clubs do anything to improve the economic status or conditions of the girls so that they could find the time to participate. In the main, the rich women who formed these clubs and financed the boardinghouses for young women workers "were concerned primarily with imbuing their members with good work habits and genteel notions of femininity." The very names given to the clubs—"Endeavor Club," "Enterprise," and "Steadfast," for example—reflect their outlook. Moreover, a collection of essays by the members published by the Working Girls' Clubs, entitled *Thoughts of Busy Girls, Who Have Little Time for Study, Yet Find Much Time for Thinking*, offers still another insight into the movement's orientation. In the spirit of the *Lowell Offering*, the collection contained essays on such topics as "What Constitutes an Ideal Womanhood and How to Attain It," and "Purity and Modesty: Two Words of Value." The themes repeated throughout the essays were those of self-sacrifice, gentleness, and tenderness.[21]

The subject of trade unionism was neither discussed in the essays nor broached at the lectures and forums. The *American Hebrew*, a publication that was hostile to organized labor, hailed the formation in October, 1888, of the "Emma Lazarus Working Girls' Club" in the vestry room of the Shearith Israel synagogue on West Nineteenth Street in New York City. The club, named in honor of the Jewish poet whose poem is inscribed on the Statue of Liberty, aimed at seeking "the elevation of the Jewish working girls by their own efforts." But such "elevation" through unions was not to be discussed.[22]

The Chicago Working Women's Improvement Association, on the other hand, did make a serious effort to acquaint workingwomen with the benefits of trade union membership. Founded in 1887 by professional and wage-earning women, the association received advice and support from the social workers of Hull House, one of the pioneer settlement houses in the United States.[23]

The settlement house movement, which spread rapidly throughout the United States, was inspired by the establishment of Toynbee Hall in London in 1884. The idea was for men and women who had recently graduated from universities to set up a "settlement" in a slum, share the problems of the poor, and work with them to reform neighborhood conditions. By 1891 there were six such settlements in the United States, but by 1900 the number had grown to over a hundred, by 1905 to over two hundred, and to over four hundred by 1910.

Two of the oldest settlements were in Chicago: Hull House, established in 1889 by Jane Addams and Ellen Gates Starr, and Chicago Commons, founded in 1894 by Reverend Graham Taylor. Alice Hamilton, a pioneer in industrial medicine, remembered that "at Hull House we got into the labor movement as a matter of course without realizing how or when."[24] Labor unions met regularly at Hull House (as they did at Denison House and South End in Boston, and at University and Henry Street settlements in New York). The constitution of University Settlement pledged "to bring men and women of education into closer relations with the laboring classes for their mutual benefit," and the same principle was adopted by many, though by no means all, of the settlement houses. In addition to working for labor and social welfare legislation, many settlement house workers took an active part in strikes and helped organize unions, especially among working girls and women. While there was inevitably some patronizing of working-class women by the upper-and middle-class settlement workers, the relationship, in the main, was of benefit to the female workers.[25]

Jane Addams welcomed the formation of the Chicago Working Women's Improvement Association and encouraged the group to hold its meetings at Hull House. There they were joined by Florence Kelley, socialist daughter of Republican Congressman William D. Kelley of Pennsylvania. Miss Kelley had been educated at Cornell University and the University of Zurich. While in Europe, she had made contact with Friedrich Engels and continued to correspond with the cofounder of scientific socialism after her return to the United States. Kelley had joined the Knights of Labor, and after its decline, she became part of the Hull House settlement workers. That group helped Elizabeth Morgan in organizing unions among the workingwomen of Chicago.[26]

At about the same time, a group of well-to-do sympathizers in New York City, particularly Josephine Shaw Lowell and Louisa Perkins, was meeting with young workingwomen to discuss the problems of woman workers and the techniques needed to end the abuses they suffered. The principal working-class woman at the meetings was an Irish garment worker, Leonora O'Reilly. In 1881, at the age of eleven, Leonora was forced to leave school and go to work in a New York collar factory, earning $1 per dozen finished collars. In three years, when the rate had declined to 50 cents a dozen, O'Reilly joined the Knights of Labor and participated in her first strike.[27]

That same year she assembled a group of fellow collarmakers on New York's Lower East Side to discuss their grievances and explore possible remedies. In time she met Lillian Wald, Stanton Coit, and Felix Adler, who were soon to organize the settlement movement in New York. They helped O'Reilly put the group on a more solid foundation and participated in discussions on how to build unionism among the exploited workingwomen in New York City. The group was soon joined by shopwomen and factory operatives, among whom were Alice L. Woodbridge and Ida Van Etten. Woodbridge had been a stenographer and saleswoman but had been obliged to give up several lucrative positions because of improper advances by her employers. Van Etten, a former garment worker and a member of the Socialist Labor Party, had tried unsuccessfully to organize women into independent unions after she had "discovered" the sweatshop system during a visit to a tenement workshop on New York's Lower East Side:

> In every room were crowded together from six to ten men and women, four to five machines, with a cooking stove at white heat for the use of the pressers. Women with white pinched faces, unkempt hair, dressed in ragged, dirty, "unwomanly" rags, were working from sixteen to eighteen hours a day for a pittance from 50 to 75 cents. No word of mine can picture to you the horror of it—the dirt, the squalor, the food these people eat, the clothes they wear, the air they breathe, and more pitiful than all, their weary faces, out of which all hope and joy had long since been banished. All made up a scene that would linger in the mind, like Dore's pictures of Dante's inferno.[28]

Ida Van Etten joined the club of workingwomen and, together with O'Reilly, Woodbridge, and Mrs. Lowell, helped organize the Working Women's Society. Its objectives, according to a *New York Times* story were: "to found trades' organizations in trades where they at present do not exist, and to encourage and assist labor organizations to the end of increasing wages and shortening hours." In due time the society discovered that it could not remedy the deplorable working conditions of saleswomen and cashiers in department stores through unionism; the women were too young (most of them being between fourteen and twenty years of age), and with the decline of the Knights of Labor and the dominance of craft unionism in the American Federation of Labor, they lacked the skill to be accepted by any of the existing craft unions. As an alternative, it was decided to organize the shoppers in an effort to improve the conditions of these women workers. Out of this determination emerged the first Consumers' Leagues.[29]

Unlike the Working Girls' Clubs, the Working Women's Society believed that through unionization, workingwomen could increase their wages, shorten working hours, and end cruel and tyrannical treatment on the part of employers and their managers.[30] The problem was to transmit this understanding to the existing trade union apparatus and to convince it to organize workingwomen.

Early in 1891 Ida Van Etten undertook, on behalf of the Working Women's Society, to attempt to move the AFL in the direction of doing more for workingwomen. She prepared a circular urging the AFL to appoint a special organizer to bring the message of unionism to workingwomen and to appropriate the necessary funds for the campaign. She also asked President Gompers for permission to appear before the AFL Executive Council to press the need for the organizing campaign and to assure the trade unionists that the Working Women's Society would do its share in organizing and rallying public support for strikes by workingwomen.[31]

The pressure of the New York Working Women's Society helped produce results. Gompers invited two women to address the 1891 convention. Eva McDonald Valesh, an organizer for the Minnesota Farmers' Alliance and editor of a fortnightly paper published for the Trades Assemblies in the twin cities of Minneapolis and St. Paul, vividly described the evils encountered by the workingwomen of the nation and pointed up the crying need for organization among them. She told the delegates: "If men seriously expect higher wages or shorter hours, they must, for their own self-preservation, organize the women, making them valuable allies instead of a source of danger." She was followed by Ida Van Etten, representing the New York Working Women's Society, who stressed the need for the immediate appointment of women organizers to bring exploited workingwomen into the federation. She concluded:

> It can readily be seen that women workers either must become organized and receive not only equal pay for equal work, but also equal opportunities for working, or they will, by degrees, naturally form an inferior class in every trade in which they enter; a class more poorly paid, and who will, in consequence, work longer hours; who will receive less consideration from their employers, and who will be without means of redress, even in those grievances which are most degrading to their womanhood. In this condition they will be a constant menace to wages; they will be used, in case of strikes and lockouts, to supply the places of union men; and, in short, we shall witness the horrible spectacle of workers whose interests are identical being used against each other for the purpose of lowering the general condition of the class.
>
> The bitterness with which employers oppose the organization of women furnishes the best evidence of their present value in supplying them with ignorant, unthinking and consequently cheap laborers.

The speeches were greeted by loud applause, and the convention appointed Valesh and Van Etten to a three-member committee on women's work (with Valesh as chairperson and Van Etten as secretary), to consider the AFL's engaging a woman to "lecture to working women of the land" and encourage female membership in the federation. The committee recommended that the Executive Council appoint such a woman, to be called the national organizer for women, at a salary of $1,200 a year plus expenses, and make her a member of the council. The convention failed to take decisive action on the recommendation, but at least the door had been opened.[32]

Meanwhile, other forces were helping to bring more women into the AFL. Organizers for the federation began circulating copies of Ida Van Etten's pamphlet *The Condition of Women Workers Under the Present Indus-*

trial System, and issues of the Working Women's Society's periodical, *Far and Near,* "with a view of organizing the girls who toil in the shops and mills."[33] New federal labor unions of women workers came into being and were chartered by the AFL in Toledo, Ohio, Terre Haute, Indiana, and Emporia, Kansas. The Anchor Federal Labor Union No. 5568 of Emporia circulated the following resolutions adopted on the occasion of the death of Carrie Bowen, one of its founders:

> *Whereas,* From being compelled to work in an unhealthy place, thereby impairing her constitution so that when disease attacked her she could not successfully resist it, we have lost through death our beloved sister, Carrie Bowen, therefore be it
>
> *Resolved* by Anchor Federal Labor Union that though we shall miss her from our midst, we will not mourn, for we trust that God in his Love for his children has prepared better surroundings for her in the land beyond than the toiling masses enjoy in this,
>
> *Resolved,* that we call upon all working girls to follow her example in joining with organized labor, thereby assisting in doing away with a system of wage slavery that compels the common people, whom Christ loved so well, to work under surroundings detrimental to health and the cause of taking thousands off before their time.
>
> > A thousand factories taking lives
> > A thousand different ways
> > So that the Rich and Robbing class
> > May pass sweet pleasant days.[35]

The AFL also chartered directly unions of women workers in a specific industry. The most important of these was the union of collar and shirt workers in Troy, New York.

From 1886, when they had dissolved the Joan of Arc Assembly in disgust over having been sold out by the Knights of Labor leadership, until the beginning of 1891, the "collar girls" of Troy had been without a union. During these same years, reductions imposed by the United Shirt and Collar Company had brought wages down to an average of 50 cents a day. "Many of us," wrote Mary S. Evaline, spokeswoman for the "collar girls" at United, "have others dependent on our work, and this wholesale attack on our wages can only result in privation and want to those who are near and dear to us."[36]

On January 6, 1891, the collar, cuff, and shirt workers employed at the Lansingburgh factory of United struck. Within a few days the strike spread to other factories in Troy, and with five hundred girls on strike, a good section of the shirt and collar industry was tied up. The State Branch of the AFL, responding to an appeal from the strikers, sent several representatives into the area. The strikers then formed a union under the AFL and elected Mary Evaline, the twenty-three-year-old strike leader, president and Dora Sullivan vice-president.

The United Shirt and Collar Company was a powerful concern with sales of close to $1 million annually. When it refused to discuss a settlement with the strikers, the State Branch of the AFL issued a boycott against its products. The company promptly capitulated. A committee composed of the strike leaders and the state AFL drew up a new scale of wages for United. This scale served as a basis for other companies involved in the strike, and it was to serve similarly for all shirt and collar establishments in Albany and Glens Falls. The State Branch of the AFL resolved "to ask all members of labor organizations to withhold their patronage from such firms who fail to pay their employees such reasonable rates of wages as they may demand in accordance with the scale of prices accepted by the United Shirt and Collar Co."[37]

On February 1, 1891, the *Troy Northern Budget* announced the end of the strike, describing it as having "perhaps attracted more attention and sympathy for the strikers . . . than any fight which has occurred between capital and labor in this vicinity for many years. . . . The girls go to work under an increased schedule of prices and they have won a victory." On the same day, H. J. Ogden, AFL general organizer in Utica and first vice-president of the New York State Branch, wrote jubilantly to Gompers: "You have no doubt learned the result of the collar girls strike at Troy. It was a great victory for the girls and the Federation. . . . We expect to have seven thousand of them organized in the very near future under the banner of the Federation."[38]

To achieve this goal, the state branch engaged Mary Evaline as a special organizer with the power to establish local unions of collar and cuff workers. A few months later the national AFL commissioned Dora Sullivan as a "general organizer" for the workingwomen of Troy and vicinity. By November, 1891, there were six unions in the collar, cuff, and shirt industry of Troy, all affiliated with the AFL. Several unions in the industry, composed of female operatives, were also organized in the principal shirt manufacturing centers at Albany, Cohoes, Glens Falls, and Greenwich, New York.[39]

The year 1891 also witnessed affiliation with the AFL of a national union with a substantial membership of women—the United Garment Workers of America, the first national union in the men's clothing industry. The women's garment industry, on the other hand, had neither a national union in the 1890s nor a substantial number of women members in those local unions that did exist.* Most of the women's clothing industry in the 1890s was characterized by what came to be known as

*The term "garment industry" at this time covered several dozen needle trades, including not only men's and women's ready-made clothing, but also the millinery, men's hat and cap, neckwear, and corset industries. The term "garment worker" included both highly skilled craftsmen, such as cutters; semiskilled sewing machine operators; and unskilled manual workers, such as button seamstresses and thread trimmers.

"seasonal unionism"—that is, local unions that were formed during sudden, unpremeditated strikes when the season began and manufacturers introduced new styles. Eventually the opposing parties reached a temporary agreement. But enthusiasm for the union lasted only during this brief bargaining interval. After the agreement was reached, members lost interest until the following year.

Still, as the individual unions came and went and the strikes were won and lost, a body of experience was being accumulated. On October 9, 1888, the United Hebrew Trades was founded by the Jewish socialists in the garment trade to centralize and stabilize the trade union movement in order to deal effectively with the "sweating system" and other evils. Each of the "seasonal unions" usually included a women's branch; in the strikes that led to the season agreement, women were among the most militant strikers, and they were naturally included in the unions that emerged after the strikes were settled. The Jewish workingwomen also joined the unions established by the United Hebrew Trades. But the men who dominated these unions made only token efforts to organize women workers. Organizers in the women's clothing industry complained that Jewish women made poor union material because of their preoccupation with marriage. They cited examples of women who were good strikers but quit the union after the strike ended with a contract that included the women—conveniently ignoring the many men in the unions who did precisely the same thing. For their part, the young women garment workers, working at the tasks that required the least skill and experience, found that their path to the more skilled jobs was blocked by the men who dominated the unions. Small wonder, then, that they regarded the unions as having little value for them.[40]

In early April, 1891, forty-seven cutters and tailors from the five largest men's clothing manufacturing centers met in New York City and founded the United Garment Workers of America. The UGW immediately affiliated with the AFL. Although the convention delegates had united to form a new national union, they had chosen a leadership that hardly reflected the views of a great many of the clothing workers who were to be members of the union. This conflict was destined to cause controversy and discord that was to plague the UGW throughout its history. The union members back home were mainly immigrant workers, Jewish socialists, who demanded sweeping social and economic changes in society. But the delegates had chosen as their leaders conservative, American-born workers who supported a "pure and simple" trade unionism and rejected socialist demands for broad social changes.

Although the UGW was as thoroughly dominated by men as were the local unions in the women's clothing industry, it was more willing to open its doors to women workers. At its founding convention, the UGW determined to fight the contracting evil and the growing production of clothing in tenement sweatshops under intolerable, nonunion conditions by issuing a label for clothing to designate that it had been made by workers who received adequate wages and worked a limited number of hours per day in acceptable surroundings. In order to receive the label, a manufacturing establishment had first to recognize the UGW as a legitimate bargaining agent, and all employees in the shop had to be union members. Consequently, UGW organizers felt a greater pressure to recruit women workers than did organizers for the unions in the women's garment industry. Encouraged by the UGW to join, women entered the union in sizable numbers. On June 26, 1892, Charles F. Reichers, UGW national secretary, informed Gompers "that three-fifths of the United Garment Workers of America consist of women, two Locals No. 8 & 16 are entirely composed of young girls, and No. 18 of Newburgh, N.Y. which is mixed has about 400 women in good standing."[41]

Actually, while UGW organizers encouraged women to organize, men usually assumed the leadership positions in the newly formed locals. Often when union leaders demanded that manufacturers pay higher wages and shorten the hours of work, they requested such improvements only for the cutters and operators, skilled jobs held by men, and ignored the women buttonhole makers and finishers, who worked longer hours for lower wages.[42]

The organization of women in the United Garment Workers resulted more from the activity of women than from that of men organizers, and nearly all these women were working for the AFL rather than the UGW. Dora Sullivan's work as "general organizer" for the AFL was confined to the collar-and-shirt industry. Meanwhile, Gompers was receiving requests from women workers for a woman to be a general organizer for various other industries. The correspondents complained that male organizers often omitted women from the agreements drawn up with employers, and that even when they were interested in organizing women, they were often ineffective because they "used strong language" and were "guilty of drunkenness." Male organizers themselves conceded that they had trouble in reaching women workers after working hours:

> If a girl is living at home, it is not quite so awkward, but if she is in lodgings, I can't possibly ask to see her in her own room. If I talk to her at all, it will be out in the street, which is not pleasant, especially if it is snowing or freezing or blowing a gale. It is not under these conditions that a girl is likely to see the use of an organization or be attracted by its happier or more social side.[43]

Then in April, 1892, evidently acting on the recommendation of the three-member committee appointed by the 1891 AFL convention, Gompers appointed Mary E. Kenney as a general organizer for the federation, with no limitation on the trades in which she would do her organizing work. Born in 1864 to Irish immigrant parents, Kenney had dropped out of school after the fourth grade, when her father was killed in an accident on the job, and went to work in a bindery to help support her ailing mother. In 1887, for an average of sixty-five hours of labor a week, she received $2. Still she was fired when she demanded a raise, and she had to begin again in a new shop where conditions were even worse. As she recalled:

> Every woman in the bindery worked from Friday morning at 7 through the night till Saturday afternoon at 4. In spite of the strain, we all tried to work with good spirit, but many girls' heads began dropping on the table by midnight from sheer exhaustion. I held out till about 3:30 in the morning. Then I sat on the floor, leaned up against the wall and gave up for about 15 minutes.

Kenney rebelled against such treatment and almost singlehandedly began organizing her fellow workers. She had participated in a Chicago Working Girls' Club but found the members' preoccupation with social outings meaningless and went instead to the Ladies' Federal Labor Union No. 1703. With the assistance of Elizabeth Morgan, she organized the Chicago Bindery Workers' Union, one of the offshoots of the Ladies' Federal Union.

Inevitably she met Jane Addams, and, after an initial period of distrust, became convinced that the social settlement people at Hull House were also interested in the cause of the working class. She later recalled that it "was one of the greatest moments of my life when I discovered that there were really people outside of workers who cared." Through Jane Addams, Kenney met Henry Demarest Lloyd, a Midwest reformer, who in 1891 was working on *Wealth Against Commonwealth*, a classic exposé of monopoly, and Clarence Darrow, the pro-labor lawyer. With Lloyd's support and the encouragement of Hull House, Kenney began organizing the shirtwaist workers and assisting them in their strikes for improved working conditions and higher wages. She even burst into Marshall Field's office to protest the fact that workers at his factory received only $4.85 a week for a ten-hour day and in addition were required to pay for the ice in their water and to clean the factory's floors. When Field refused to correct these injustices, she threatened to publicize these wretched working conditions through the press. A few days later, the practice of requiring workers to pay for ice and sweep the factory floors was abolished.[44]

Gompers met Kenney in 1891 during a visit to Chicago and was impressed with her, and when he decided to appoint a woman general organizer for the AFL without restricting her scope, he asked whether Kenney would come to New York to help organize women workers in the East. Kenney headed for New York on May 26, 1892. All during that hot summer, she shuttled back and forth between New York City and Troy, where she tried to organize some of the unorganized "collar girls" and straighten out a serious dispute that had arisen between Dora Sullivan and her followers and the AFL Executive Council.

The conflict arose over the introduction of the McKay Starching Machine in the laundries of Miller, Hall & Hartwell in Troy. Sullivan and the union members working for the firm insisted that if the machine was to be used the company should guarantee against reducing either wages or the number of women employed. When it refused, the women went on strike and Sullivan asked the AFL Executive Council to boycott the firm's products. The Executive Council complied, but later charged Sullivan and her supporters with having ordered the strike and the boycott over the objection of most of the members of the union, a charge she heatedly denied and on which she was supported in an affidavit by a group of union members. Ordered by Gompers to attend a hearing on the issue in New York City, Sullivan refused on the ground that the union could not afford the cost. Kenney was unable to resolve the dispute. Eventually the strike was lost, and Gompers suspended the charter of the Collar, Cuff and Shirt Starchers' Union No. 5577.[45]

Kenney also shuttled between Massachusetts and New York, signing up and educating garment workers, bindery workers, women printers, shoemakers, carpet weavers, and textile operatives. On September 28, 1892, she wrote a report on her activities to Gompers:

I began work as organizer May 31st in New York City. June 2nd I called a meeting of undergarment workers. The meeting was a failure. June 21st I held a meeting of bindery girls, the following meeting we organized a union. Up to the time I left New York they were not in a position to take out a charter in the A. F. of L. I addressed three social clubs of working women in New York, July 29th. The Garment Workers held a meeting and formed a Union. August 2nd left New York for Troy. Held a large meeting in Troy in which a number of non-union girls joined after the meeting. August 16th held a mass-meeting of shirt makers and bindery girls in Albany. A large number of nonunion shirt makers joining the Union and promising at their next business meeting to take out a charter in the A. F. of L.

Thursday the 18th the bindery girls of Albany formed a Union. I left Troy August 26th for New York. The following week I worked in the office of the A. F. of L. addressing envelopes for Homestead.* August 27th I left New York for Boston. While here the first week I failed to call any meeting or address any owing to Labor Day. Sept. 7th I addressed a social club of working women. Sept. 16th the Custom Tailoresses Union. Sept. 23rd a

---

*The reference is to the historic Homestead strike of 1892 by the Amalgamated Association of Iron, Steel, and Tin Workers, called to oppose wage cuts instituted by the Carnegie Steel Company at its Homestead, Pennsylvania, plant.

mass-meeting of working women of various trades, tonight, Sept. 28th, the bindery girls hold a meeting to form a Union which I am sure of a Union. Thursday, Sept. 29th, I speak in Middleboro to shoe workers, Friday, Sept. 30th at Haverhill to shoe workers, Saturday, Oct. 1st, women carpet workers weavers. I have an engagement for Oct. 6th to address a mass-meeting of all the Club members together. Oct. 7th the Printers Union arranged a meeting for me to address the women of their trade....

I have met and talked with several girls of different trades and callings and believe that the time is near when their trades will be organized, even if women are slow in so doing. The extreme hot weather has put the work back very much.[46]

Working with Leonora O'Reilly, Kenney helped organize Local No. 16 of the United Garment Workers. Kenney and O'Reilly found the new union members, most of them Jewish women, to be bright, effective speakers, interested in union activities.[47] These young women were now part of the national union as a result of the activities of two militant female organizers, not because of the UGW men, who had repeatedly refused their assistance.

In Boston, with the aid of John F. O'Sullivan, a leading union organizer (whom she later married), Kenney helped seventy-five Irish-American women who worked at the Plymouth Rock clothing factory form Women's Tailors' Union No. 37 of the UGW.[48] She also formed a federation of trade union women modeled after Chicago's Federal Ladies' Union No. 2703. From Boston Kenney wrote to Gompers on September 15: "I don't believe organization of women can be accomplished as readily as men. To me it seems slow, and if I had my choice of organizing either, I would take the men every time—it would make a better showing. I believe though much can be done for the women and I also do the best I can."[49]

While her "best" was good enough for Gompers, the other members of the AFL Executive Council were disappointed. When Gompers recommended on September 30 that Kenney's commission as general organizer be renewed, he was voted down. Chris Evans, United Mine Workers leader and AFL secretary, informed Gompers bluntly that the federation "is not in a condition financially to keep a woman organizer in the field without better hope of success than at present indicated." Kenney's efforts, he said, were "worthy of commendation, yet the fact remains that they have proved futile." John B. Lennon, of the Journeymen Tailors' Union, the AFL treasurer, suggested that Kenney be paid her salary until October 29 and "return fare to Chicago so as to give her time to secure employment."[50]

Kenney took her dismissal philosophically, but she warned Gompers that if the AFL was serious about organizing women, it had better appoint more rather than fewer female organizers: "I believe that the key to the situation in organization of women is that they need their leaders with them all the time." The advice was lost on Gompers. In his report to the 1892 AFL convention, he commended Kenney for her five months' organizing work, describing her activities as "missionary in nature," but failed to request either her reappointment or the appointment of another woman organizer.[51]

Back in Chicago, Kenney started a cooperative garment factory, helped financially by Lloyd, Darrow, and Jane Addams. She lived at Hull House, doing volunteer work for the Women's Cloak Makers' Union, distributing literature on the eight-hour day and beginning to pick up the work she had abandoned the previous May in the continuing campaign against the sweatshops.[52]

The sweatshop campaign had started in the summer of 1891. On August 20 Elizabeth Morgan wrote to Gompers: "The union cloak makers are having lots of trouble with the sweaters and the Trade Assembly put this work in the hands of committee Mr. M. H. Madden and myself. So we made a raid into 15 shops so far, and such things we see is a disgrace to the city and workmen. . . . The committee is not yet finished their visits to these sweaters shops."[53] Thus began what was to develop into one of the most important and influential reports in American labor history, which eventually called the attention of the entire nation to the evils of the sweating system.

Although the sweatshop had existed before the large Eastern European immigration at the end of the nineteenth century, it became more fully established in the garment industry as a result of the influx of the immigrants. "There are not many things an unskilled foreigner, knowing no English, can do," wrote Ray Stannard Baker at the turn of the century, "but almost any man or woman can sew." The sweaters, contractors paid by the large manufacturing companies to finish products begun in their factories, hired the cheapest nonunion labor possible (usually immigrant women and children) to do piecework, such as hand sewing, in their tenement dens. Since he was paid according to the number of finished products he returned to the manufacturer, the sweater literally "sweated" the work out of his employees by working them twelve to fifteen hours a day. Once they found that they were able to have work done at less cost outside the factories, the manufacturers stopped hiring piece workers entirely and cut the wages of their regular employees.

The immigrants had come to America in search of a better way of life. Instead, they found the sweatshop. "Nowhere in the world at any time, probably," Baker concluded, "were men and women worked as they were in the sweatshop—the lowest paid, most degrading employment. The sweatshop employer ground all the work he could from every man, woman and child under him."*⁵⁴

By 1891 the sweating system, whose very existence was denied by the manufacturers, had become so entrenched in Chicago that it was both undermining the conditions of women workers and preventing their unionization. Early in August the wages of Chicago's female cloakmakers, members of the Ladies' Federal Labor Union, were cut by 40 percent. Morgan took the case of the cloakmakers' drastic cut to the Chicago Trades and Labor Assembly and argued that an intensive campaign against sweating was absolutely imperative. She called for an immediate investigation to expose the true conditions and disprove the manufacturers' repeated denials. The assembly responded by appointing a "Committee on Abuses" to investigate the sweatshop problem, made up of Elizabeth Morgan and M. H. Madden, also a member of the assembly. An officer of the city's Health Department, the city attorney, an official of the Cloak Makers' Union, and members of the local press (to whom advance notices had been sent) accompanied the committee on its fact-finding tour. As a result, Chicago newspapers began to run front-page stories denouncing the sweating system whose existence they had been dismissing for years.⁵⁵

Elizabeth Morgan used the committee's visits to the tenement shops to fill a serious gap in the prior campaigns against the sweating system— the absence of reliable statistics. She began with the report of the Labor Assembly committee's visits to the sweatshops, *The New Slavery: Investigation into the Sweating System . . . as Applied to the Manufacture of Wearing Apparel,* and continued in speeches and testimony before a congressional committee. In the report, Morgan published previously unknown and unobtainable information on twenty-six sweating establishments, detailing the name and address of each sweater, his employer, the type of work, the sanitary conditions, the working space, the number of men, women, and children employed, and their hours and wages. She included the names of such highly respectable Chicago stores as Siegel & Cooper and Marshall Field's.

About a third of the report was devoted to vivid descriptions of the overcrowded dens of filth, vermin, and disease where women (nearly half the labor force) and children under fourteen years of age ("some . . . as young as 5 years") toiled from ten to fourteen hours a day. The conditions at specifically identified sweatshops were set forth in detail partly because Morgan was convinced that humanitarian arguments in favor of closing the sweatshops would have little appeal "to a

---

*For a picture of sweatshops (native style and immigrant style), which reinforces the point that the post-1880 immigrants did not bring the sweatshop to the United States but found it here, see Leon Stein, *Out of the Sweatshop: The Struggle for Industrial Democracy* (New York, 1977).

selfish public." But when "dainty ladies" of the middle and upper classes learned that they were being exposed to diphtheria, scarlet fever, and other contagious diseases spread by workers with "fevered hands, infected with the spatter of the consumptive," they would be more willing to join the campaign to close down these "pestilence-breeding sweat holes."

Morgan closed her pamphlet with a plea for enforcement of the city child labor and inspection ordinances, warning that if the laws were not enforced, Chicago citizens would be guilty of "murdering" a whole class of laborers who were "working in but ONE-TENTH of the space required by law . . . and one-fifteenth the space provided for criminals in our jails."[56]

On September 6, 1891, the Chicago Trades and Labor Assembly received Morgan's findings with "cries of indignation." A Chicago paper, *Rights of Labor,* printed it first in two issues.[57] Ten thousand copies later published by the assembly were snapped up, leaving "a number of people . . . begging for more."[58] Mrs. Morgan then used the Committee on Child Labor of the Illinois Women's Alliance to continue the investigation of sweatshops. During February and March, 1892, the committee exposed a number of new sweatshops.

In March, 1892, learning that Congress was preparing to investigate the sweating system, Morgan sent a copy of her Trade Assembly report to the special committee appointed to conduct the inquiry. The congressmen, impressed, decided to start their inquiry in Chicago and invited Morgan to be the first witness. Unfortunately, she was the only person to testify against the sweaters, while fifteen other witnesses, all "manufacturers and wholesale dealers in clothing," testified in their behalf. "I cannot understand this," Morgan wrote to Gompers. "Here the Tailors and Cloak Makers were present at the Trade Assembly Sunday and I ask them to be on hand Monday, when Labor has a good chance to use their force . . . and then . . . I alone a woman, have to do all their work. It is a disgrace to Labor Men of Chicago."[59] (Evidently, Elizabeth Morgan did not yet realize that the men who headed these unions were mainly concerned with the more skilled workers, who were male and, despite their public avowals to the contrary, were not too concerned about the plight of the women who made up a vast majority of the sweatshop workers.) In any case, the Chicago press concluded that Morgan was a "valuable witness," that her testimony "was listened to with a great deal of interest," that her use of statistics and specific examples and "intelligent and thoroughgoing statements" convinced the committee that Congress should "bring about a remedy for the evils complained of."[60]

"'Abolish the sweating system' was the keynote of the mass-meeting which filled Central Music hall yesterday," began the lead article on the front page of the *Chicago News-Record* of February 20, 1893. It was to take a number of such meetings, together with tireless activity on the part of Elizabeth Morgan, Mary S. Kenney, and Florence Kelley, the strong support of trade unions and Hull House residents, and the cooperation of Illinois's great liberal governor John Peter Altgeld, before victory was won. But in June, 1893, the Illinois legislature passed the Factory and Workshop Inspection Act, or, as it became known, the Sweatshop Act. That pioneer law set sanitary standards for certain types of sweatshop manufacturing and regulated the labor of children and the working hours of women. Section 5 of the Act, for which Elizabeth Morgan fought hard and long, limited the employment of women in any factory or workshop to eight hours a day, six days a week.*[61]

All the while that she was investigating and exposing sweatshops and lobbying for antisweatshop legislation and for an eight-hour law for women, Elizabeth Morgan was also serving as secretary of the Federal Ladies' (now Women's) Union No. 2703, organizing unions of working-women in the Chicago area—watchmakers in Elgin, women shoe workers in Chicago, and various types of factory operatives—addressing strike meetings of these workers, and mobilizing relief for strikers.[62] The 1894 AFL convention gave Elizabeth Morgan a standing ovation in recognition of her strenuous efforts on behalf of workingwomen and children. She was the only female delegate at the convention and accepted the nomination for first vice-president, marking the first time a woman had run for high federation office. Although the incumbent, Peter J. McGuire, was one of the founders of the AFL and had been reelected to that post each year since 1890, Morgan received 226 votes against his 1,865 in a totally male-dominated convention. The convention paid her further tribute by endorsing her three basic proposals: state compulsory education laws to be instituted everywhere, and, if already on the statute books, to be fully enforced; an eight-hour law for women and children employed in manufacturing establishments to be enacted by all states; and abolition of the sweating system and tenement house manufacturing by state action.[63]

Morgan was pleased with the convention's action, but she would have been more pleased had there been more female delegates at the convention and had there been a woman general organizer functioning at the

*The Illinois Manufacturers Association challenged the constitutionality of the eight-hour law for women in the courts. Elizabeth Morgan organized and chaired a public debate on "the justice, necessity, and legality" of the law, but on March 15, 1895, the Illinois Supreme Court found Section 5 of the Sweatshop Act unconstitutional. The unanimous opinion was the first court decision in the United States against the eight-hour law, and Earl Beckner notes that it "effectually closed the question of legislative restriction of the hours of employment of women for a number of years." (Mrs. T. J. Morgan to Gompers, 20 April 1894, *AFL Corr.*; Earl R. Beckner, *History of Labor Legislation in Illinois* [Chicago, 1929], p. 190.)

time the gathering met. She had been unhappy over the failure to extend Mary Kenney's organizing commission and had pleaded with Gompers for more female organizers.[64] But the AFL had remained without a woman general organizer until December, 1893, when Gompers commissioned Miss E. E. Pitt, a member of the Typographical Union in Boston. Pitt had done considerable work in her spare time organizing the women garment workers, and, at the request of the Boston AFL office, which urged that she be empowered to "extend her field of operations . . . among the women of other trades," Gompers commissioned her to begin "organizing women regardless of their trades or callings."[65]

In January, 1894, Gompers recommended to the AFL Executive Council that four additional women organizers be appointed, but he was quickly voted down. The Council gave four reasons for its negative stand. First, a financial one: "That on account of the present depression in trade that action on the appointment of four female organizers be deferred until a more propitious time." Then it was argued that it would not be possible to find qualified women to fill the four jobs. Again, the argument was raised that the money could be spent more effectively by hiring men as organizers. And finally, specific requests for organizing help were being received from unions composed entirely of men, these requests had to be filled and promised more than the vague suggestion that additional women organizers might be successful in organizing more women. On top of this, the council insisted that Pitt's work as organizer of women be cut short because of lack of funds, and she was allowed to carry on for only a few additional months. By the time the AFL convention met in 1894, the federation was once again without a woman general organizer.[66]

Even though the federation maintained a corps of "several hundred organizers" in the field, Gompers and his lieutenants took few additional concrete steps after 1892 to promote the organization of women.[67] The bulk of the AFL was made up of national trade unions that were basically craft in structure and were interested solely in the organization of skilled workers. They persistently ignored the resolutions adopted at federation conventions calling for the organization of women workers. In its issue of July 5, 1893, the *Coast Seamen's Journal,* official organ of the Sailors' Union of the Pacific, explained this indifference when it editorialized:

> Mentally and physically, women are incapable as a sex of achieving great things, but they are capable of being instrumental in making it impossible for men to be what nature intended them to be—the providers and protectors of women and children. The labor movement, which is the only movement that can possibly accomplish anything in the way of social reform, has the special responsibility of giving every man a chance to earn sufficient money to provide for a wife and family. Once that has been accomplished, the issue of women in industry and in the unions will soon cease to exist.

6

The Women's
Trade Union League

In *Century of Struggle: The Woman's Rights Movement in the United States*, Eleanor Flexner notes: "The Years between 1903 and the entry of the United States into the first World War in 1917 saw the growth of the first unions composed largely of women. These unions remain a stable part of the American labor movement down to the present time."[1] Although the Women's National Union Label League and women's auxiliaries of men's unions were active in 1903, it was a new organization—the National Women's Trade Union League, founded by middle-class reformers and working-class women in that year—that became the first national body dedicated to organizing women workers.

During the 1880s and 1890s an increasing number of middle-class women turned their attention toward those of their sex who worked in factories, shops, and tenements. Since the Civil War, when the Workingwomen's Protective Union was established by New York *Sun* editor Moses Beach and financed by philanthropists to aid New York seamstresses, there had been rich and professional people who sought to help women workers. Although they were all too often visionary, impractical, condescending, and paternalistic, these reform advocates did represent a break from most pre-war middle-class reformers, especially among women, who ignored the hardships of female workers and considered their life style unladylike. To be sure, even many of the postwar reformers believed that women's normal occupation was in the home, that their employment, especially of wives, violated natural law, and, further, that the children of such women would be unfit citizens and workers. Even some of the reformers who were most outspoken in advancing the rights and dignity of labor remained convinced that women should not work outside the home.

Nevertheless, most of the reformers ultimately came to the realization that the women were working to support themselves or their families, and not, as many employers maintained, for "pin money." This, in turn, led to a recognition of the need to help them change the miserable conditions under which they worked.[2]

During the 1890s, there was an increase in the number of middle-class women, frequently college-educated, who came to this conclusion, who demonstrated a real concern for workingwomen, and who directed their energies to assisting them. The various reformers arrived at varying answers in seeking effective means for helping workingwomen. Some believed that if the female laborer became better educated and worked hard, she could win her employer's appreciation and, with it, higher wages. Others felt that employers could be persuaded to improve working conditions through appeals to their wives. Still others lobbied for remedial legislation, while some set up programs and organizations that encouraged self-sufficiency and independence. Another group established residence in working-class neighborhoods and assisted trade union organizers in their work. Some even temporarily abandoned their professional lives in order to experience the life of workingwomen. They then exposed the terrible conditions they discovered, in the hope of convincing others that these conditions could and should be changed. Another group believed that consumers could be persuaded to boycott firms that refused to provide minimum standards of decency for their workers. Then there was the controversy between those who believed that the answer lay in women's trade unions and those who felt that such trade unions were impractical because the work was too temporary and the labor supply too great and women could or could not organize effectively. The answer, this group felt, lay in legislation limiting working hours and establishing minimum wages.

Some of the activities of the 1890s were transitory and represented nothing more than titillation for bored women with nothing else to do. Some reformers abandoned their efforts during the mid-decade depression, just when the need was greatest. But most continued their activities, and not a few came to view social work as a chance to do something really useful.

Regardless of their motivations or the length of their activity, most of the middle-class reformers agreed on two main points: first, that individual women could not be blamed for their poverty or immorality—the fault lay with society, not with individuals; and secondly, that these evils could be eradicated by harmonious accommodation between working-women and their employers, without conflict or any fundamental change in society, such as the overthrow of capitalism and the establishment of socialism. For all their avowed interest in improving workingwomen's lives, the middle-class women who participated in these various efforts never actively cooperated with wage-earning women when they chose to use economic weapons like the strike to win advances.[3]

To be sure, Socialist men and women who were associated with upper- and middle-class social reformers in these activities neither shared their naive beliefs nor rejected labor's economic weapon. But they did not insist on the acceptance of their views as a condition of the collaboration. In fact, some Socialists were convinced that even with their rejection of class conflict and sweeping social goals, the social reformers were able to accomplish more for workingwomen than the Socialists themselves. Writing to Frederick Engels from Hull House on May 27, 1893, Florence Kelley emphasized the importance of the work being done by the settlement houses "among the wage earners." While conceding that Socialists, too, were "active," she noted that they were "practically unorganized and very few at best." She herself continued to advance Socialist ideas through articles, pamphlets, reports, and papers, but she found that she could accomplish more for workingwomen through her work in Hull House than in the Socialist movement.[4]

Kelley went on to organize branches of the Consumers' League in Chicago, along with her other important work. In 1898 she represented the Chicago office at the national convention of the Consumers' League, and in 1899 she was chosen its first executive officer. She became the driving force behind the National Consumers' League and by 1903 had helped to set up fifty-three units and three college societies in eighteen states. By that time forty-seven factories in eleven states were utilizing the Consumers' League's label, attesting to the fact that these employers' labor standards met league stipulations.[5] In some cities, the league was also able to reach agreements with the larger department stores that they would stay open late for only two weeks before Christmas. Elsewhere they lobbied for state laws prohibiting the work of girls under sixteen years of age after nine o'clock at night.

Yet the relationship between the Consumers' League and the trade unions was anything but friendly. The unions feared that the league's award of its label to nonunion firms made organization even more difficult. At the 1903 AFL convention, Gompers criticized the league as an organization of well-intentioned young ladies who issued the label when they found working conditions sanitary but who ignored wages and hours.[6] Florence Kelley herself eventually came to recognize the limitations of the Consumers' League's "white lists" (which served as a method for screening and recommending products and stores for shoppers) and sought out new means for aiding workingwomen.[7]

Meanwhile, two groups that had participated in the settlement house movement were becoming more and more convinced that the trade union was the most promising vehicle for improving the economic status of workingwomen. These groups comprised middle-class advocates of social justice who had seen at first hand the need for labor organization and workingwomen who were themselves active in unions.[8]

As Gertrude Barnum, an upper-class activist in the Women's Trade Union League, explained:

> I myself have graduated from the Settlement into the trade union. As I became more familiar with the conditions around me, I began to feel that while the Settlement was undoubtedly doing a great deal to make the lives of working people less grim and hard, the work was not fundamental. It introduced into their lives books and flowers and music, and it gave them a place to meet and see their friends or leave their babies when they went out to work, but it did not raise their wages or shorten their hours. It began to dawn on me, therefore, that it would be more practical to turn our energies toward raising wages and shortening hours.[9]

Nevertheless, only a minority of the settlement house workers concerned themselves with helping women form trade unions. Those who did had become discouraged by the slow approach of social reform organizations and by the elitism of traditional charity work. A major problem lay in winning the cooperation of male unionists in recruiting workingwomen into existing unions. The average male trade unionist regarded the middle-class social worker as more concerned with gathering statistics than with improving the workers' lot. It was not to be easy to convince such men that the social reformers were sincerely interested in improving the economic status of workingwomen through trade unionism, especially since the hostility to the middle-class women often served as an excuse for the male unionists to do nothing themselves to organize women.

During the 1890s settlement houses became regular features in large cities. A number of settlement houses were hostile to trade unions and refused to support the labor movement, but this was not true of the large social settlements. Labor unions met regularly at Chicago's Hull House, at Denison House and South End House in Boston, and at University and Henry Street Settlements in New York. Many union locals of women were founded at Hull House, Denison House, and the Henry Street Settlement, and while settlement house workers generally tended to favor the peaceful resolution of labor disputes, all three settlement houses supported the strikes of the women workers they had helped to organize and, in general, endorsed strikes that they felt were justified.

Eventually the settlement workers won the support and cooperation of young, militant workingwomen in the effort to organize unions of women workers. In fact, most of the women's unions that existed at the beginning of the twentieth century had been organized by these militant women workers, often with the help of a social settlement.[10]

In 1901, after lengthy hearings, the Industrial Commission issued a report linking prostitution to low wages and demanding equal pay for equal work. The commission pointed out that evidence presented before it indicated that unions had helped to improve the welfare of working-women, and it placed the burden of implementing its recommendation on the existing trade unions.[11] But the American Federation of Labor, the major body uniting these unions, had already amply demonstrated that it was not prepared to fulfill this function. Except for adopting routine convention resolutions sympathetic to women, the AFL practically ignored the needs of 5 million female workers.

Both groups in the settlement houses—the social reformers and the workingwomen—realized that most existing trade unions, because of their emphasis on organizing only skilled workers, failed to reach the women who needed their assistance most. Even the garment industry unions, which included more women than most other unions, accepted the disparity in wages between men and women and did little to encourage women to assume leadership positions. Nearly all unions—Socialist and non-Socialist alike—were handicapped by the belief that women's sojourn in the world of work was temporary; that their real goal was marriage; and that they were too passive and too inarticulate to contribute a high degree of commitment to unionism. With these premises, these union leaders reasoned that it would be a waste of the union's time and money to attempt to organize them.

The settlement house groups knew that while there were elements of truth in this analysis, it was not the whole truth. The most recent decades had demonstrated that many female workers were receptive to unionization, and the militancy of the women in strikes proved that they could teach male unionists a thing or two about struggle. Certainly, the militancy of the women garment workers disproved many of the myths surrounding workingwomen.

In 1902 the militancy of the women in the garment shops found its way into the streets of the working-class neighborhoods. In mid-May, Jewish women, most of them housewives on New York's East Side, but also including a sprinkling of women in the garment trades, formed the "Ladies Anti-Beef Trust Association" to protest the rapidly rising price of kosher meat and the betrayal of a boycott of wholesale distributors by the Jewish retail butchers. (After the wholesalers had yielded and reduced prices, the retail butchers refused to pass the lowered prices on to the consumers.) The outraged women boycotted the retail butchers, battered those butcher shops that remained open, threw meat into the streets, poured kerosene on it, and prevented nonboycotters from buying meat. "Eat no meat while the Trust is taking meat from the bones of your children and women," read a Yiddish circular decorated with a skull and crossbones.[12]

Dozens of women were beaten by the police, arrested, fined, or jailed. Rebecca Ablowitz, one of the women boycotters, engaged in the following exchange with the magistrate:

> Why do you riot?
> Your Honor, we know our wounds. We see how thin our children are and that our husbands haven't strength to work. . . .
> But you aren't allowed to riot in the street.
> We don't riot. But if all we did was to weep at home, nobody would notice it; so we have to do something to help ourselves.[13]

Like the women who struck the garment shops, the women who boycotted Jewish butchers were denounced by the commercial press. The New York *World* described them as "a pack of wolves," and the *New York Times* devoted its lead editorial on May 24, 1902, to them:

> The class of people . . . who are engaged in this matter have many elements of a dangerous class. They are very ignorant. . . . They do not understand the duties or the rights of Americans. They have no inbred or acquired respect for law and order as the basis of the life of the society into which they have come. . . . Resistance to authority does not seem to them necessarily wrong, only risky, and if it ceases to be risky, the restraint it can have on their passions is very small; practically it disappears. . . . The instant they take the law into their own hands, the instant they begin the destruction of property, and assail peaceable citizens and the police, they should be handled in a way that they can understand and cannot forget. . . . Let the blow fall instantly and effectually. . . .
> These rioters were plainly desperate. They meant to defy the police and were ready for severe treatment. They did not get treatment nearly severe enough, and they are therefore far more dangerous than they were before.

But to the workers at New York's Henry Street Settlement and University Settlement, these women were upholding the best in the American tradition of protest against greed, and had demonstrated by their militancy that lower-class women were neither passive nor inarticulate. One of these settlement workers was William English Walling, the son of a prominent doctor, grandson of a Kentucky millionaire. At Hull House Walling had become increasingly interested in trade unionism, eventually, he was to become a prominent member of the Socialist Party. For the time being, he decided that he could make his best contribution to social reform through the settlement.

In 1902 Walling became a resident at University Settlement. His interest in the plight of poor women was heightened by his personal observation of the activities of the "Ladies Anti-Beef Trust Association," whose angry demonstrations took place just outside the settlement. More than ever convinced that workingwomen could organize effectively and fight for decent conditions, and having read accounts of the British Women's Trade Union League, which had been organized in 1874 and had had considerable success in organizing women workers—or so it was reported in the United States—he decided to study its work at first hand. In 1903, with the support of Lillian Wald and Florence Kelley of the Henry Street Settlement, Walling went to England to learn more about the League.[14]

As Allen F. Davis notes, the organization of the Women's Trade Union League is "an interesting example of the cross-fertilization of reform ideas between the United States and Great Britain."[15] The impetus for the formation of the British Women's Trade Union League came from two temporarily successful American women's trade unions: the New York Parasol and Umbrella Makers' Union and the Women's Typographical Union. Emma Ann Paterson, an Englishwoman who was active in the suffrage movement and became honorary secretary of her local Workingmen's Club and Institute, had been impressed, while traveling in the United States in 1873, by these two unions of women in New York. She returned to England "fired with the idea of urging her countrywomen to form trade unions,"* and, together with other interested women, formed the British Women's Protective and Provident League in 1874. She remained its honorary secretary until 1886, when she was succeeded by Clementine Black.[16]

"The Women's Trade Union Provident League is a society of people who give time or work or money to try and establish trade unions among women," Clementine Black wrote in the *Women's Union Journal* of 1888. "That is, and always has been, its first and main object."[17] But up to this point, the league had not accomplished very much in pursuit of its objective. To be sure, it had helped to form societies of women workers, such as female typists, in the late 1870s, but most of them had been short-lived and were at no time part of the established trade union movement of the day.[18] Meanwhile, the number of women workers in British industry had multiplied, as did the exploitation to which they were subjected. According to the 1881 Census, almost one-third of the total labor force in England between the ages of twenty and sixty-five were women. They formed the majority in the textile trades, and, including girls under twenty years of age, there were more than 1,750,000 females employed in various industries, with another 2 million in domestic and other services. Their earnings were roughly 50 percent of the male rate.[19]

On July 5, 1888, despite their fear of dismissal and the lack of funds, sixty-two East End women matchmakers struck. Within two weeks, with

---

*Although a pioneer in the field of organizing female workers, Paterson was adamantly opposed to special legislation for their protection. Indeed, when a Home Office Enquiry in 1873 "recommended a reduction of women's hours from 60 to 54 and a bill to this effect came before Parliament, the opposition of the 'feminists' led by Paterson killed it" (Harold Goldman, *Emma Paterson* [London, 1974], p. 73).

the assistance of the Women's Trade Union Provident League, which collected £400 for the strike fund and sent down a corps of organizers to help form a union and hold it together, and aided further by the arbitration of the London Trades Council, these female strikers won major concessions. Fines and deductions were abolished, wages were raised, and, most important of all, these unskilled female workers formed the Matchmakers' Union. It remained "the largest union composed entirely of women and girls in England" for many years, with a membership of 800, of whom 650 regularly kept up their weekly contributions. In their history of British trade unionism, the Webbs wrote that the celebrated "match-girls' strike" of 1888 "turned a new leaf in Trade Union annals. Hitherto success had been in almost exact proportion to the workers' strength."[20]

This was followed by the great 1889 strike of gas workers in London. During this strike, Eleanor Marx-Aveling (daughter of Karl Marx) formed the first women's branch of the National Union of Gas Workers and General Labourers. The Executive Council of the Gasworkers formally admitted the Silvertown Women's Branch and its secretary, Mrs. Marx-Aveling, into the union. In May 1890, when the first Annual Conference of the National Union of Gasworkers and General Labourers took place, the union already had some forty thousand members in eighty-nine branches, including two composed entirely of women. Eleanor Marx-Aveling was elected a member of the fifteen-member Executive Board by acclamation. On a motion from the floor, moved by both a male delegate and a woman representative, a resolution was adopted that the union should include in its demands, wherever possible, that women should receive the same wages for doing the same work as men.[21]

As these developments were occurring, Clementine Black wrote to the editor of the London *Times* on behalf of the Women's Protective and Provident League, pointing out that

> under whatever system workpeople are employed, the want of a proper trade organization among them inevitably tends to the existence of conditions of employment in every respect unjust and repressive. It is, the League submits, largely to a development of its work in the formation of women's unions that the public must look for a removal of these industrial conditions, which are not only a disgrace to our civilization, but are fraught with elements in the highest degree dangerous to the peace and well-being of society.[22]

The success of the strikes of women workers and their incorporation into the existing unions had its impact on the league's name. In 1874, "fearing that storms of opposition would be aroused if the words 'Trades Union' were introduced,"[23] the league's founders had adopted what they hoped would be an inoffensive title—the Women's Protective and Provident League. Since then, however, trade unionism had become one of the facts of public life, especially with the emergence of the "new unionism," which organized the unskilled. The strikes of 1888 and 1889—first of the match workers, then of the dockers and the gas workers—hastened this development. In September, 1888, the league's name was changed to the Women's Trade Union Provident League. And in December, 1890, the league changed its name again to the Women's Trade Union League, which it remained until its fusion into the larger trade union movement in 1919.[24]

Three decades after Emma Paterson had founded the British league, William English Walling visited England to study its operations. Early in 1903 he met members of the British Women's Trade Union League and other trade union leaders and learned how the organization encouraged women to join existing men's unions. He was especially impressed by the fact that the British league united both upper-class and working-class women in a common effort to organize women into their own unions and integrate them into established men's locals. Walling became convinced that a similar organization could improve conditions for American workingwomen, and he carried the idea back to the United States.[25]

Filled with enthusiasm, Walling went to Boston in November, 1903, to attend the annual AFL convention. Walling explained his plan to form an American Women's Trade Union League to the recently widowed Mary Kenney O'Sullivan, and she enthusiastically agreed to help him. The two—one a wealthy reformer and the other a working-class labor leader (both settlement house residents)—worked out the tentative plan for the new organization designed specifically to help workingwomen enter unions. They arranged for a meeting in Faneuil Hall and invited AFL Executive Council members and convention delegates whose trades included large numbers of women.[26]

The meeting, held on November 14, included several AFL delegates and a number of Boston settlement workers. The group selected Walling, O'Sullivan, and Nellie B. Barker, of the Women's Label League, to draft a constitution. In addition, O'Sullivan and Walling agreed to visit Boston settlement houses to explain their program and gather support. Walling had insisted that the new league must have the support of the American Federation of Labor, and he and O'Sullivan conferred with Gompers during the AFL convention. "When they submitted to me a proposal, I gave it my hearty approval and participated in the necessary conferences," Gompers wrote later in his autobiography. Actually, the statement was an exaggeration on both counts. He gave the proposal only passive support and appointed Max Morris of the AFL Executive Council to attend the conference.

On November 17, 1903, four leading Boston settlement house workers—Vida Scudder, Helena S. Dudley, Robert Woods, and Philip

Davis—together with a number of union officials, including Max Morris, met with Walling and O'Sullivan. After some discussion, the participants decided that before the proposed organization could undertake a recruiting drive in a particular industry, it must first contact the national union possessing jurisdiction over these women. They also adopted a resolution requiring that the proposed Women's Trade Union League should, wherever possible, affiliate with the central labor body in a given locality. Finally, they decided to request that the AFL employ a full-time woman organizer.[27]

Two days later a third meeting was convened. This time Harry White, president of the United Garment Workers, Michael Donnelly, president of the Amalgamated Meat Cutters & Butcher Workmen, and John F. O'Brien, president of the Clerks International Protective Union, met with other members of the trade unions and the settlement workers—among them, Mary Morton Kehew of the Women's Educational and Industrial Union, Emily Balch and Helena S. Dudley of Denison House, and Philip Davis of Civic Service House. With the exception of Nellie Parker, an AFL delegate from a Boston women's union, all of the labor delegates were men. By contrast, nearly all the participants from the Boston settlement houses and reform groups were women.[28]

Before this meeting adjourned, the new organization had a name— the Women's National Trade Union League (changed in 1907 to the National Women's Trade Union League)—a set of officers, and a constitution. To lend prestige to the new organization, the unionists and reformers suggested that several nationally known figures be asked to serve as officers. Mary Morton Kehew, a wealthy Bostonian long known in social reform circles and the former president of the General Federation of Women's Clubs, was selected as the league's first president and Mary Kenney O'Sullivan as secretary. Jane Addams agreed to serve as the league's vice-president. Mary McDowell, a University of Chicago settlement resident, was asked to fill a position on the Executive Board, in recognition of her work in organizing women in the meat-packing industry. Also elected to the Executive Board were Lillian Wald, who, during the 1890s, had worked to organize small women's unions of New York City garment finishers and buttonhole makers; Leonora O'Reilly, New York settlement worker and United Garment Worker organizer; Mary Freitas, a textile worker from Lowell, Massachusetts; and Ellen Lindstrom, a long-time Chicago unionist and former walking delegate for the Special Order Clothing Workers and the United Garment Workers.* There were two settlement workers and three trade unionists, one of whom was also a settlement worker, on the Executive Board.[29]

The constitution of the new organization stated that its object "shall

---

*A walking delegate was a trade unionist who was sent to labor areas or groups to encourage organization of workers.

be to assist in the organization of women workers into trade unions."
(Shortly thereafter. there was added, "and thereby to help secure conditions necessary for healthful and efficient work and to obtain a just
return for such work.") Anyone was eligible to be a member upon declaring "himself or herself willing to assist those trade unions already existing, which have women members, and to aid in the formation of new
unions of women wage workers." Nonunion members (called "allies"
because of the antilabor connotation of the term "nonunionist") were
eligible not only to join the league but to hold any office. However, the
constitution stipulated that membership on the Executive Board was to
be divided as follows: "The majority . . . shall be women who are, or have
been, trade unionists in good standing, the minority of those well known
to be earnest sympathizers and workers for the cause of trade
unionism."[30]

The ally was described as one who "must have patience, lofty faith
and unalterable humility. It is the girls who must ever be the movement,
but the ally can help immensely. She has often time, money, and the
touch with the outside world." This was Walling's definition and reflected his concern that the new organization would be dominated by
upper-class allies. This concern was already evident in the provision that
workingwomen were to hold the majority of Executive Board positions.
It was also reflected in Walling's warning to Leonora O'Reilly that the
upper-class allies must rid themselves of any trace of the "Lady with
something to give her sisters." They were, he advised, to step aside and
make way for working-class members in the leadership of the organization. He urged that they learn about trade unionism, labor organizing,
and working conditions from the women who had firsthand experience
in such matters. Finally, unlike the charity organizers and even many
settlement house workers of the period, the allies were advised to let
their working-class colleagues define their own goals and avoid the
temptation to impose upon them a middle-class culture or life style, or to
use the league as an instrument for social control.[31]

Walling was also concerned about relations with the AFL. The founders of the new organization considered asking for a formal endorsement from the federation but decided to delay until "the League should
have accomplished some definite work."[32] However, the desire for ties
with the AFL was reflected in the provision that an annual conference
would be held jointly with the federation's convention.

The newly formed group was encouraged by the fact that Gompers
had permitted O'Sullivan to announce the league's formation from the
podium of the AFL convention, although they noted that the federation
president was somewhat less enthusiastic in his introduction of O'Sullivan than he was in introducing Martha Moore Avery for an attack on
socialism. While he remained silent after O'Sullivan's remarks, he pre-

sented Avery with a small bouquet, which he ostentatiously fastened to her dress.

The scarcity of women delegates at the convention was another cause for the league's lack of enthusiasm for immediate affiliation. There were only five women among the 496 AFL members present, and while they succeeded in getting the convention to adopt resolutions calling for special efforts to organize women, for the appointment of at least one female organizer, and for endorsement of woman suffrage, as the women knew all too well, as far as female workers were concerned, in the AFL there was a great difference between resolutions and action. A final damper on the enthusiasm of the league's founders came when Gompers did not view the organization's formation as sufficiently newsworthy to merit mention in the *American Federationist* of December, 1903, even though the issue was full of convention news.

Still, it was with a good deal of optimism that the league's charter members returned to their own cities to set up local branches. After all, the organization had been born in a moment of ebullience, at the very height of gains in union members during the period from 1897 to 1904.* Branches were rapidly formed in New York, Boston, and Chicago. In each case, the birth took place in a settlement house—in New York at University Settlement, in Chicago at Hull House, and in Boston at Denison House. In each case, too, the settlement workers sought to enlist the support of labor leaders. It took considerable work on the part of Leonora O'Reilly to overcome the hostility of the Central Labor Union toward the New York League and win even token cooperation. In Boston and Chicago the union leaders were more receptive. John Fitzpatrick, president of the Chicago Federation of Labor, not only endorsed the League, but praised it for not being afraid to blaze new trails.[33]

When the Women's Trade Union League held its first annual meeting in October, 1904, league members were even more optimistic than they had been in March. They enthusiastically agreed to work for the eight-hour day and for a limitation on the work week to fifty-eight hours; to achieve legislation preventing the hiring of workers with false promises; and to help displaced workers find new jobs. Several promising possibilities emerged from a wide-ranging discussion of techniques that might be used to further the league's goals. Members reaffirmed their determination to cooperate with existing trade unions in organizing women and to attempt to organize workers in trades that were not

*Between 1897 and 1901 the total membership of American trade unions more than doubled, rising from 447,000 to 1,124,000. But this was only the beginning. From 1900 to 1904, union membership more than doubled, rising from 868,500 to 2,072,270, with the AFL tripling its membership from 548,300 to 1,676,200 (Philip S. Foner, *History of the Labor Movement*, New York, 1964 3:27).

yet unionized. They agreed, too, to appear before women's clubs whenever the opportunity arose, to explain the aims of their new organization. Finally, they planned the establishment of a bureau of information
that would offer members ready access to statistics and data on investigations of factory conditions.[34]

In 1905 the center of power in the league shifted from New York to
Chicago, when Ellen M. Henrotin, a wealthy Chicago woman, was
chosen national president, a post she held until 1907. That year Margaret Dreier Robins replaced Henrotin as president of the national
league, and served in that capacity from 1907 to 1922.

From its inception, the WTUL's primary objective was to encourage
women to form unions or to join existing locals and then to affiliate to
the appropriate AFL national union. But AFL principles and practices
repeatedly frustrated the organization's efforts to achieve that objective.
In one respect, women suffered more from these principles and practices than even black men. Although the AFL agreed, as a "solution" to
racial discrimination by its affiliates, to charter black workers excluded
from all-white unions—thereby giving its blessing to Jim Crow trade
unionism—it refused to accord even this possibility to women. The result, the leagues were often compelled to report sadly, was that the
women they had helped to organize were forced to abandon the union,
"and as a group, [were] lost to organized labor."[35]

In 1907–1908 the New York League reported: "While the Women's
Trade Union League has been working for the organization of women
into trade unions, it has recognized that the direct work of organization
will be done by the women themselves and that its own work is largely
educational."[36] A year later, in 1909, a revolution began in the garment
trades that was to prove the validity of this estimate. However, the role of
the Women's Trade Union League in this series of the most famous
women's struggles in American labor history was destined to be far more
than just "educational."

7

The Waistmakers' Revolt

ON NOVEMBER 24, 1909, eighteen thousand waistmakers in Manhattan and Brooklyn walked out of nearly five hundred shops. By the end of the day, more than twenty thousand workers were on strike.

The women working in New York City's dress and waistmaking shops astonished the nation by staging this dramatic strike. This great uprising served as a catalyst for workers in other branches of the industry. And it spearheaded the drive that turned the shells of unions into mass organizations, thereby laying the foundation for stable and lasting organizations in the women's and men's clothing industries and for the widespread unionization of women workers.

The manufacture of shirtwaists was a comparatively new branch of the garment trade. It had developed rapidly after 1900, especially in New York and Philadelphia, and by 1909 there were about six hundred waist and dress shops in New York City, employing from 35,000 to 40,000 workers. About 80 percent of them were young women between the ages of sixteen and twenty-five, most of them unmarried, two-thirds of them Jewish, with a couple of thousand Italians and a few hundred blacks. Men accounted only for about 20 percent of the workers, but they occupied the high-paying jobs that demanded special skill and experience.[1]

While dress- and waistmakers experienced the typical economic inequities that were prevalent throughout the industry, working conditions in this segment of the industry were better than those in other branches. Since most of the shops had been set up comparatively recently, they were more sanitary than those in the rest of the industry. Most work rooms contained windows that provided adequate lighting. Wages, too, were generally higher than those in other branches of the trade. However, they varied both from shop to shop and within shops, depending on skill and on the prevailing system of work. Despite the fact that by the end of 1909 the industry was prosperous, wage rates had fallen steadily since the 1908 depression. Thus, early in 1908 a woman machine operator on waists could earn as much as $12 or $13 a week at piece rates, whereas late in 1909 she was lucky to make $9 or $10. In addition, some workers received their wages directly from inside subcontractors who negotiated individually with the manufacturer.* This system inevitably created inequities in the pay scale. Some women received only $3 or $4 per week, while others, who worked directly for the manufacturer, received as much as $15 or $20 per week. As in other branches, wages fluctuated because of the seasonal nature of the industry. The workers' annual income was cut considerably by enforced idleness for three months of the year. One contemporary study declared that the average weekly wage for the industry was $9, but seasonal layoffs brought the average down to only $5—and this was for fifty-six to fifty-nine hours' work each week, with only the usual rate for overtime.[2]

The inside subcontractors exploited the very young women through an oppressive system of apprenticeship. Workers were subjected to strict discipline: subcontractors and examiners levied fines for lateness and for sewing errors. "In the shops we don't have names," declared one waistmaker, "we have numbers." Manufacturers charged for needles and thread—often as much as $1.50 a week—as well as for electric power, for the chairs the workers sat on, and for the lockers in the shops, all at a substantial profit. They fined their employees for being a few minutes late or for accidentally spoiling a piece of cloth. A ticket system prevailed, under which a worker, after completing a task or piece, would receive a tag, which was turned in at the end of a period as the basis for calculating her wages. Workers complained that the manufacturers deliberately made the tags very small, in the hope that some of the workers would lose them. This is exactly what often happened, and as a result the worker received pay for only part of her output.

Because the industry operated on a piecework basis, the employer or his agent could easily show favoritism to "cooperative" workers by giving them larger bundles of work. To top it all off, the entire system was characterized by tyrannical bosses, nagging, pettiness, espionage, favoritism, rudeness, and discourtesy.[3]

Local No. 25 of the ILGWU had jurisdiction over the waistmakers. Founded in 1906 by seven young women and six men, the local had

---

*Subcontracting was a variation of the traditional contracting system in the garment trades. Like the contractor, the subcontractor contracted with a manufacturer to complete a specified amount of work for an agreed-upon price. Like the contractor, too, he supervised a team of workers in completing the bundles of garments. Unlike the contractor, however, the subcontractor did not own a shop but worked in the manufacturers' large inside establishments. Subcontractors, not manufacturers, were responsible for paying their workers, and when manufacturers lowered rates, the subcontractors passed the decrease on to their teams of workers.

failed to attract many members. Just four weeks before the strike, union officers noted that the membership had barely reached eight hundred workers, described as irregular and unenthusiastic. Few of them had any knowledge of union organization. To be sure, Women's Trade Union Leaguers, especially East Side organizer Rose Schneiderman, had helped small groups of dressmakers learn the principles and practices of unionism and had convinced a group to affiliate with Local No. 25 in 1908. However, men controlled the union, holding all the officers and eight of the fifteen positions on the Executive Board.[4]

Nevertheless, unrest had been building steadily and visibly for at least a year before the uprising. Throughout late 1908 and 1909 walk-outs became increasingly frequent in the large waist factories in the Washington Square area. Confrontations between manufacturers and workers over wage and piece-rate cuts, subcontracting, and the practice of charging workers for electricity, needles, and other materials became increasingly sharp.

In late July, 1909, the two hundred employees of the Rosen Brothers ladies' waist shop walked out on strike in protest against inadequate pay scales. During the strike, thugs assaulted pickets, and the police, obviously acting at the employers' request, arrested women who shouted "scab" at strikebreakers. However, the strikers' perseverance brought results, for on August 26, Rosen Brothers capitulated. The victorious strikers gained full union recognition and a 20 percent wage increase.[5]

Early in September, one hundred and fifty young women walked out of the Leiserson factory, accusing their employer of paying starvation wages. The strike spread to the Triangle Waist Company (which was to become nationally infamous in 1911 because of the tragic fire on its premises). After Triangle's owners learned that a few of their employees had joined the union, they promptly locked out the entire shop of five hundred workers and advertised for replacements. The infuriated employees literally besieged Local No. 25's headquarters and signed up en masse with the union.[6]

Although some magistrates conceded that New York State law sanctioned the right to picket, they countenanced arrests and beatings of the strikers, many of them teenagers. Every day, scores of pickets were fined or sentenced to the workhouse. On the other hand, the magistrates discharged entire contingents of thugs arrested for assaulting young strikers, in spite of their criminal records.[7]

Despite the militancy of the strikers, it was clear that shop-by-shop strikes would not work and that only by tying up the entire trade during the busy season could the workers gain their demands. On October 21, 1909, a general meeting of union members declared for a general strike in the trade, demanding an immediate 10 percent increase in wages and recognition of the union by the employers.[8]

Meanwhile the striking women of Local No. 25 received new moral and material support. The United Hebrew Trades, the central organization of Jewish unionists in the city, began a fund-raising appeal among trade unionists and succeeded in obtaining pledges from the working shirtwaist employees to give 10 cents each on behalf of the strikers. The Women's Trade Union League of New York City, which had been helping the strikers from the outset of the walkouts, now established a corps of forty-eight volunteers, generally women from the upper middle classes, who accompanied pickets in order to prevent their unwarranted arrests. They were attacked by the police on the picket line along with the strikers, and some were even arrested. But when the police learned that they were dealing with socially prominent women, they changed their tactics. Mary Dreier, the league's president, was arrested by accident and quickly released when her identity was discovered in court. The arresting officer apologized humbly, asking, "Why didn't you tell me you was a rich lady? I'd never have arrested you in the world." Such obvious bias in favor of the rich was widely publicized by the WTUL and was contrasted with police outrages committed against the strikers, thereby arousing public sympathy for the girls. The police, in turn, grew resentful of the league's support of the strike and kept asking why educated women insisted on involving themselves with lower-class working-women strikers.[9]

During the weeks of the shop strikes, about two thousand workers joined the union, and hundreds crowded the cramped union office daily with talk of a general strike. Now the union, too, began to consider calling a general strike. Because the New York WTUL had been active in assisting the workers in the Triangle, Leiserson, and Rosen strikes, and because any large undertaking would require the league's financial assistance, the union shared its deliberations with that organization. The two organizations met on November 22 to discuss the question of an industry-wide walkout, as well as to protest actions of the struck companies and the police. Among the speakers scheduled to address the rank-and-file workers were Samuel Gompers, Mary Dreier, Meyer London, and Ernest Bohm, secretary of the New York City Central Federated Union.[10]

On the night of the meeting Cooper Union auditorium was packed with an overflow crowd of shirtwaist workers. For over two hours, as the tension in the auditorium mounted, the workers listened to one speaker after another urging caution and moderate action. Gompers reminded the audience that he always looked upon strikes as the method of last resort. He cautioned the workers against acting too hastily, adding, however: "If you cannot get the manufacturers to give you what you want, then strike. And when you strike, let the manufacturers know that you are on strike." Wild applause followed this remark, but there was still no action for a general strike.

Finally, after hearing one moderate voice after another, a young workingwoman leaped to her feet and asked for the floor. The workers in the audience recognized her as one of the most militant rank-and-filers—Clara Lemlich from Leiserson's, where the workers had already been on strike for eleven weeks. They knew, too, that she had just returned from the hospital after having been brutally beaten on the picket line. Barely five feet tall and not more than twenty years old, she spoke in impassioned Yiddish—the native tongue of the majority of the shirtwaist workers—and proceeded to berate the cautious speakers who had held the platform during the evening. She concluded: "I have listened to all the speakers, and I have no further patience for talk. I am one who feels and suffers from the things pictured. I move we go on a general strike!"

Instantly, the crowd was on its feet—adult women, men, and teenagers—cheering, stamping, crying approval. Chairman Feigenbaum called for a vote. Three thousand voices shouted their unanimous approval, waving hats, handkerchiefs, and other objects.

"Do you mean faith?" cried the chairman. "Will you take the old Hebrew oath?"

Three thousand right arms shot up, and three thousand voices repeated the oath: "If I turn traitor to the cause I now pledge, may this hand wither from the arm I now raise."

Meanwhile, messengers carried the news of the meeting to the other halls where the waistmakers had gathered. There the strike vote was ratified just as enthusiastically,[11] and thus began the famous labor struggle that has become known as the "Uprising of Twenty Thousand,"* "women's most significant struggle for unionism in the nation's history."[12]

Both Local No. 25 and the WTUL were stunned by the waistmakers' response to the general strike call. At most, they had expected four or five thousand Jewish workers to strike.[13] Instead, on the first day, eighteen to twenty thousand shirtwaist workers came out in response to the strike call. Women by the thousands stormed the small union office on

*Estimates of the number of strikers range from the New York State Department of Labor Bureau of Mediation and Arbitration figure of fifteen thousand to Local No. 25's estimate of forty thousand. The estimate of thirty thousand is based on Helen Marot's calculation based on WTUL records. (Helen Marot, "A Woman's Strike: An Appreciation of the Shirtwaist Makers of New York," *Proceedings of the Academy of Political Science, City of New York* 1 [1910]: 122. The report on the strike in the *Annual Report of the Women's Trade Union League of New York, 1909–1910,* is entitled "The League and the Strike of the Thirty Thousand" [New York, 1910], p. 11.)

Clinton Street to enroll in Local No. 25. Soon, nearly thirty thousand operators, cutters, pressers, and finishers were on strike. Although four-fifths of the female strikers were Jewish, several thousand Italian and nonimmigrant women participated as well.*

Many small waist manufacturers, unable to stand even a short interruption during the busy season, were soon parading to union headquarters to sign agreements with the union. These agreements included a provision for a union shop; a fifty-two-hour week; limitation of overtime work; equal division of work among union members; and a price list of changing styles to be fixed by conference between employer, employee, and union representatives. In addition, the employers promised to employ only contractors who used union labor; to furnish machines, needles, thread, and other supplies; and to allow a weekly check of their payroll by union officials. Any party violating the agreement would have to pay a $300 penalty. By the time the strike was hardly four days old, almost half of the original twenty thousand strikers had won improved conditions, including union contracts, and had returned to work.[14]

Because many employers made quick settlements, Local No. 25 and the WTUL were optimistic that the strike would be short and spectacularly successful. But the employers who settled at once were those who could not afford a protracted work stoppage. The larger firms that dominated the industry were determined to fight it out to the bitter end. They formed the Association of Waist and Dress Manufacturers of New York and, on November 27, declared open war against the union, recruiting strikebreakers and vowing to hold out against a settlement. A member of the association warned that a trade agreement with the union was not "worth the paper it was written upon" and urged employers who had signed such agreements to repudiate them. It warned that only manufacturers who opposed unionism would be eligible for membership in the employers' organization. "We insist upon the open shop," the president declared, "and from that stand we will not budge."[15]

Thus, very early, the strike settled down to a protracted campaign of siege warfare against the larger firms. It required a good deal of spirit and devotion to unionism to maintain this siege. The winter of 1909–1910 was exceptionally cold and snowy in New York City. Many a frostbitten young picket was taken directly to the hospital or clinic. In addition, the ILGWU, then only nine years old, was not yet firmly established and had a scanty treasury, so that regular strike benefits were few and far between and the strikers were hard put to meet their rent and

*Helen Marot calculated that the overwhelming majority of the strikers were Russian-Jewish women. She broke down the ethnic backgrounds of the strikers as follows: 20,000 to 21,000 Russian-Jewish women, 6,000 Jewish men (cutters and pressers), 2,000 Italian women, and approximately 1,000 native-born American women (ibid.).

grocery bills. Most of the original $60,000 strike fund and the funds collected during the strike had to be used to pay the fines of women convicted by biased magistrates.[16]

The members of the association tried to break the strike by exploiting Jewish and Italian antagonisms and sought to drive a wedge between the girls by keeping black workers on the job, importing professional strikebreakers, and arranging with out-of-town plants, particularly in Philadelphia, to supply them with goods. But they depended primarily on brute force, arrests, and convictions. By December 22, 1909, over seven hundred pickets had been arrested; nineteen were sentenced to the workhouse on Blackwell's Island on charges of disorderly conduct and vagrancy, and the rest were fined. At Blackwell's Island, the young girls were thrown into cells with prostitutes, sex perverts, and criminals.[17]

A magistrate summed up the prevailing attitude of the courts in these words: "You have no right to picket. . . . Every time you go down there you will get what is coming to you and I shall not interfere." Regardless of the evidence, or lack of it, the girls were usually convicted. When prosecutors failed to substantiate their charge that Nennie Bloom had assaulted a forelady, Magistrate Joseph Corrigan fined her $10 for disorderly conduct and stated that if more strikers appeared before him, he would send them to the workhouse. Another magistrate declared bluntly that while "the higher courts have held that strikers had the right to employ pickets and call names," he personally would forbid the right to picket. Still another magistrate told a group of bruised and bleeding girls: "You are on strike against God and nature, whose prime law is that man shall earn his bread in the sweat of his brow." Members of the WTUL cabled this remark to George Bernard Shaw, who replied: "Delightful. Medieval America is always in the most intimate personal confidence of the Almighty."[18]

The cruel treatment of the female strikers failed to dampen their spirit. "There never was anything like it," one union official declared in amazement. "An equal number of men never would hold together under what these girls are enduring."[19] It was precisely because women, who were not expected to take either their jobs or unionism seriously, were such militant strikers that the press expressed such amazement and devoted so much space to the waistmakers' uprising. The New York Women's Trade Union League, in its role as liaison between the strikers and the public, capitalized on the fact that the majority of the strikers were women. Members circulated detailed reports of police attacks on peaceful pickets, kept a careful tally of arrests, and described the callousness of police magistrates who sentenced young women to several weeks of hard labor for offenses as minor as yelling "scab" at strikebreakers. The league volunteered legal services in police courts, provided witnesses for arrested strikers, cross-examined those who testified, raised $29,000 in bail, and acted as a complainant at police headquarters. On December 6 the league established a strike headquarters, encouraging women who had been arrested to come in and report their experiences in detail. From these reports they drew up rules for pickets designed to minimize the chances of arrest. League members distributed copies of the "rules" to all strikers.[20]

League members also organized workingwomen's marches and rallies. On December 3 a group of ten thousand striking waistmakers, carrying banners that read "Peaceful Picketing is the Right of Every Woman," marched four abreast to City Hall to protest to Mayor McClellan against the abuse they had received at the hands of his "cossacks." Three league women—Ida Rauh, Mary Dreier, and Helen Marot—along with a representative group of strikers, handed the petition to the mayor and described to him their own experiences and those of other workingwomen at the hands of "New York's finest." The mayor assured the committee that he would take up the matter with the police commissioner.[21]

Strike headquarters were at the league office, where the WTUL provided an information bureau, coordinated all activities, dispatched lecturers, defended pickets, revitalized the practically defunct Local No. 25, and helped lift the morale of the young demonstrators. WTUL members and strikers edited and sold a special issue of the *New York Call* and the *New York Journal,* in which appeals for contributions were interspersed with a dramatic history of the strike. League members spoke to civic groups and church organizations, with invariably enthusiastic results. After Rose Schneiderman delivered a short speech at the Manhattan Congregationalist Church, its members passed a resolution supporting the strikers and urging the public "to find out who are these mean manufacturers . . . that are grinding down the girls." Even the Consumers' League departed from its customary practice and gave public support to the waistmakers—the first such action since 1905, when it had supported the strike of the laundry starchers in Troy.[22]

Accompanied by a sixteen-year-old waistmaker who had spent thirty days in jail for picketing, Rose Schneiderman raised money lecturing in colleges and at parlor meetings in Massachusetts with the president of the Boston WTUL. The league's Vassar graduates took Schneiderman and Pauline Newman, a young waistmaker who had joined the league during the strike, to Poughkeepsie to speak to the college community. Under the league's auspices, young strikers spoke about their working conditions at clubs and women's colleges. At one widely publicized luncheon at the Colony Club, one young woman after another told of her experiences as trimmer, tucker, operator, or finisher. "I can trim the neatest waist in town," one young striker told the club women, "but I get only $6.50. . . . I support our family." Such testimony brought over

$20,000 in contributions from clubwomen and college students. In addition, as a result of the league publicity, dozens of students from Vassar, Bryn Mawr, Barnard, and Wellesley served as volunteer pickets.[23]

Anne Morgan, J. P. Morgan's niece, was one of the women who was deeply stirred by the description of the working and living conditions of the waistmakers. Although she had never before shown any interest in labor disputes or in the trade union movement, she appeared on the waistmaker's picket line soon after the strike began. She explained her interest in the strike to the *New York Times:*

> We can see from the general trade conditions how difficult it must be for these girls to get along. Of course, the consumer must be protected, but when you hear of a woman who presses forty dozen skirts for eight dollars a week, something must be wrong. And fifty-two hours a week seems little enough to ask. These conditions are terrible, and the girls must be helped to organize and to keep up their organizations, and if public opinion is on their side they will be able to do it.

The New York league immediately made Anne Morgan a temporary member of its Executive Board.[24]

Another new upper-class board member was Alva Belmont, widow of Oliver P. Belmont. A few days after the strike began, she appeared on a waistmakers' picket line and announced her support for the strikers. "It was my interest in women, in women everywhere and of every class, that drew my attention and sympathies first to the striking shirtwaist girls," she explained to the press. "Women the world over need protection and it is only through the united efforts of women that they will get it."[25] As president of the Political Equality League, one of the city's newer and more active suffrage organizations, Belmont repeatedly linked the suffrage cause and the strike. At a highly publicized appearance at Jefferson Market Courthouse, she made this clear:

> I have arrived at the conclusion that we would all be better off if we visited the night court more frequently. Conditions in the mismanaged social life of New York City are nowhere else so forcefully brought out. . . .
>
> There will be a different order of things when we have women judges on the bench. Let me assure you, too, that the time is not far away when we will have women judges. During those six hours I spent in that police court I saw enough to convince me and all who were with me beyond the smallest doubt of the absolute necessity for woman suffrage . . . and the direct influence of women over judges, jury and policemen.[26]

Alva Belmont arranged weekly suffragist motorcades in which rich suffrage supporters drove striking shirtwaist makers through the neighborhoods of the Lower East Side to publicize the struggle. In addition, she hired the Hippodrome for a huge "women's rally" and invited leading suffragists and trade unionists to speak. An audience of eight thousand, including suffragists, trade unionists, Socialists, and even anarchists, applauded wildly as Reverend John Howard Melish of Brooklyn; Rose Pastor Stokes, Socialist organizer and lecturer; and Dr. Anna Howard Shaw, Methodist preacher and president of the National American Woman Suffrage Association, pleaded for justice for the shirtwaist strikers.* Leonora O'Reilly, with tears streaming down her face, delivered a heartrending account of a young garment worker's life of toil and despair. Several young strikers narrated their experiences at the hands of the police, the magistrates, and the employers' hired thugs.[27]

On December 20 the strike spread to Philadelphia. Leaders of Local No. 25 had known for some time that New York manufacturers were sending materials to Philadelphia for completion. ILGWU officials visited Philadelphia in November and early December determined to halt the manufacture of goods destined for New York. However, the Philadelphia strike grew, basically, out of the same deplorable conditions that existed in New York. The conditions of the fifteen thousand waistmakers in Philadelphia were summed up in an interview with an eighteen-year-old waistmaker, who told a reporter for the *Public Ledger* that she had gone into the shops seven years earlier, then only eleven years old. When there was plenty of work, she could sometimes earn as much as $9 a week, but in the summer she could not average more than $3, and some weeks she made so little that she could barely pay her carfare. Then there were the petty exactions: 2 cents a week to pay for an outing sponsored by the proprietor every summer; 25 cents for a key to the closet; needles sold at four times what they cost; and the tyranny of some of the forewomen, who kept the girls at their machines all day long in the summertime, even when there was no work and they earned nothing. Excuses of illness made no difference: "She would keep you in if you were most dead."[28]

While only 3,500 of these workers belonged to the union, officials believed that the nonunion workers would join the walkout if they called a strike. And so, demanding union recognition, a nine-hour day, a fifty-hour week, and uniform wage scales, the Philadelphia dress and waistmakers walked out in a general strike.[29]

The Philadelphia strike followed much the same course as that in New York: the waistmakers faced "gorillas" and police brutality, and the magistrates of Philadelphia were eager to sentence pickets to the county prison. The Central Labor Union endorsed the strike, and many trade

---

*The National American Woman Suffrage Association itself, however, refused to endorse the shirtwaist strike. A few days before the Hippodrome rally, the organization issued a statement stressing that it "neither stands for labor organization nor against it." Dr. Shaw, the statement continued, would speak as an individual at the Hippodrome meeting, and not as the association's president (*New York Times,* Dec. 3, 1909).

unions supported it. Throughout their fight, moreover, the striking workers were given support by leading society women and progressive-minded college women.[30]

WTUL leaders Margaret Dreier Robins and Agnes Nestor hurried from Chicago to Philadelphia and opened an office in the heart of the factory district, where pickets could report and strikers could receive sandwiches and coffee. The youth and enthusiasm of the strikers amazed league members. Day in and day out, despite attacks by the "gorillas" and arrests by the police, they were on the picket lines. On January 14, 1910, when a severe snowstorm hit the city, "the pickets proved faithful to their duty."

Society and college women, some in caps and gowns, mingled with the waistmakers on picket lines, and as in New York the police, in rounding up pickets, arrested a number of the upper-class women. Among them was Martha Gruening, a graduate student at Bryn Mawr College, who patrolled the street carrying a placard demanding justice for union girls. Charged with inciting to riot, she explained to the magistrate that she visited the factory daily to determine whether the police were arresting workers unjustly. He exploded: "It is women of your class, not the actual strikers, who have stirred up all this strife. Had you and your kind kept out of this, it would have been over long ago." She was sent to prison with three shirtwaist strikers.[31] The Philadelphia newspapers strongly condemned Mayor John Rayburn's administration for its lack of courtesy to the upper-class women. But the police continued to arrest and arraign young Philadelphia society women. In one case, a prosecutor angrily charged a woman with perjury for overstating the property she put up for bail.[32]

On January 12, 1910, the Philadelphia *Public Ledger,* under the headline "Women of Social Distinction Give Aid to Strikers," noted that this marked a turning point in Philadelphia's labor history, since "this large and influential class heretofore have not shown concern in labor movements of any sort." The actions of Bryn Mawr students as pickets provoked the comment from an officer of the college that "our girls do not do that sort of thing, you know." But the growing list of arrested Bryn Mawr girls contradicted her denial.[33]

On January 13, the Pennsylvania Women's Suffrage Association endorsed a strike for the first time in its history by calling upon the manufacturers to recognize the shirtwaist workers' union. After the resolution was unanimously adopted, college students went through the audience attired in caps and gowns and passed collection baskets. Several hundred dollars was turned over to the strikers.[34]

These were not the only unusual features of the strike in Philadelphia. On January 15 the *Public Ledger* reported "an entirely new propaganda adopted by the striking girls." Instead of shouting at the girls still at work to join their ranks, thereby guaranteeing their arrest, the pickets offered them cards on which the following was printed: "You are doing little more than starving to death on the dollar-a-day wages that you are getting. Why not starve outside? Outside we have fresh air and starvation is not so deadly. Inside, if you don't starve to death, you will die of tuberculosis. Come on, get a little fresh air."

"It is wonderful to note the effect of the mixture of humor and philosophy," reported the *Public Ledger*. "Last night several workers saw the cards and prompted further by the meagerness of their purses, asked to be taken to the union headquarters." Among those who signed up and joined the picket lines were blacks and Italians.[35]

When Local No. 15's leaders disclosed that they would be willing to settle without achieving union recognition, they created an uproar among the strikers. The girls insisted on including the union shop in the settlement, and Agnes Nestor supported their stand. "This sounds like a trick to get you back," she told the pickets. "Don't go into this thing blindly. We have plenty of money and can afford to wait." The *Public Ledger* called this "bravado," pointing out that "the treasury of the union is admittedly empty," but conceded that the Philadelphia "girl strikers still support the demand for the union shop enthusiastically.[36]

With their production almost completely halted by the Philadelphia strike, the New York Manufacturers' Association was more inclined to seek a settlement. On December 23, employers and union officials agreed on a compromise. The employers conceded to the demands of the workers for shorter hours, higher wages, and prompt consideration of an entire list of grievances, but they refused to recognize the union or establish the closed or union shop. The work week would be reduced to fifty-two hours; there was to be no discrimination against union members; needles, thread, and appliances were to be supplied free by the employers, as far as practicable; equal work was to be given during the slow seasons; four paid holidays annually were to be granted; all shops were to establish wage committees; and all strikers were to be reemployed and no others hired until this was accomplished. The Manufacturers' Association agreed that it would give consideration to any communications from any source concerning violations of the agreement and that it would welcome conferences about any differences that could not be settled between the individual shop and its employees. But the president of the association said that the manufacturers insisted on an open shop and "from that stand we will not budge."[37]

On December 27, the negotiated settlement was submitted to a vote of all union members. Since many of the women working in nonassociation, independent shops had earlier gained full union recognition, it was hardly to be expected that the strikers in the association shops would settle for less. Addressing the strikers, Morris Hillquit, Socialist Party leader, reminded them that the crux of their demands was union recognition: "Collectively the waistmakers are strong, individually they are helpless and defenseless. If the employers were today to concede all the demands of the strikers, but be allowed to destroy or even the weaken the union, they could and would restore the old condition of servitude in their shops, within a very few weeks or months." It came as no surprise, therefore, that the strikers overwhelmingly disapproved of the proposed settlement.[38]

After the rejection, the strike dragged on. While the enthusiasm of the strikers continued at a high pitch, funds ran low, and many of the pickets were obliged to depend on the WTUL soup kitchen for their meals. Meanwhile, the arrests continued and so did the fines, which ate up what little remained of the strike fund. Illness kept many of the strikers confined to their beds, while those who still picketed continued to shiver without winter clothing. League members also continued to picket. Their fur hats and coats stood out in sharp contrast to the clothing of the waistmakers, but they too suffered during the terrible winter. Vassar graduate Violet Pike, for example, reported daily for either picket or court duty. "Her hands deep in her pockets, her beaver hat a bit to the side and an angelic smile on her red lips," she was described as truly the "bravest of the brave, day in and day out shivering from cold and at times drenched to the skin."[39]

The climax of the New York strike occurred on January 2, 1910, at Carnegie Hall. Originally, several members of the Political Equality Association, led by Anna Shaw and Alva Belmont, had proposed a sympathy strike of all women workers in the city. But when this did not materialize, the Carnegie Hall mass rally was organized.[40] The audience sat spellbound as speaker after speaker heaped accusations and recriminations upon the heads of New York's public officials. The sponsors had sold box seats to liberal clubs and organizations and netted a substantial amount for the strike fund. On the stage, in the front row, sat twenty strikers who had served sentences in the workhouse. The 350 young women who had been arrested by the police and fined by the magistrates filled the rest of the stage. Each girl wore a printed sash stating how the court had dealt with her, such as "Workhouse Prisoner" or "Arrested."

The high point of the evening came when Leonora O'Reilly introduced Rose Perr. No taller than the average ten-year-old girl, with her hair in a long braid, Perr stood before the enormous gathering and told, in simple words, the alarming story of her arrest. The police had taken her to court as a witness because she had asked a police captain to arrest a "gorilla" who had slapped her companion. At the courthouse, she was suddenly accused of having assaulted a scab. Without any evidence, the magistrate thereupon sentenced her to five days in the workhouse before she even had an opportunity to testify.

Hillquit praised the strikers for forming a powerful union practically overnight and fighting a gallant battle to maintain it. He declared that the strike had demonstrated how women permeated industry life and proved how absurd it was for any man to say that woman's place was in the home: "Let him remember the thirty thousand women strikers of one single industry in one city and let him remember that in the factories these women are treated with even less consideration than men." These women, he continued, had shown that they could fight for their rights with heroism. "Be of good cheer, your victory will be glorious," he closed to thunderous applause. At the conclusion of his speech, the audience unanimously adopted a resolution condemning "the conduct of the police in this case as an indefensible abuse of power" and denouncing the court actions against the strikers as examples of "a prejudiced and vindictive mind": "The office of Magistrate has been perverted into an instrument of persecution and oppression."[41]

Following the Carnegie Hall meeting, the State Bureau of Mediation attempted to resolve the remaining questions in dispute between the union and the association. While Local No. 25 was willing to discuss the open or closed shop, the manufacturers' association refused. Likewise, on January 11, the association rejected the union's proposal, transmitted through the State Mediation Commissioner, for arbitration hearings by the commission, which would include consideration of the closed shop.[42]

And so the strike dragged on through January and into February. As strike benefits dwindled, hunger and privation became urgent problems. Then, too, the rich women's commitment to the strikers began to waver after the strikers rejected the settlement offered by the association. The strikers were not disturbed when the *New York Times* reversed its earlier cautious endorsement of the union shop and justified its change on the ground that the proposed settlement met all the strikers' other demands. But when some settlement workers and many of the upper-class women voiced their disapproval of the strikers' decision, this did affect the morale of the women on the picket lines.[43]

Meanwhile, underlying conflicts began to surface between the Socialists in the strikers' ranks and the rich women supporters of the strike. Even before the January 2 meeting at Carnegie Hall, a contingent of strikers visited Alva Belmont's home asking for a discussion with her about her real purpose in supporting the strike. Belmont refused to see the strikers and asked the girls to submit their questions to her secretary. They handed her two provocative questions: "(1) Are you interested in strikers because they are possible suffragists or because they are workers in trouble? (2) Do you believe the interests of the employers and workers are identical or could ever be identical?"

The secretary, after delivering the questions, promptly returned to announce that Belmont was too busy to answer. When the strikers asked for a future meeting, the secretary responded with a curt "No."[44] Still, most Socialists among the strikers felt that although the interview indicated that Belmont harbored insincere motives, it was necessary to smooth over the differences between the opposing groups in order to present a united front before the press and the association.[45]

To make matters worse, the Socialists believed that non-Socialist negotiators were trying to sabotage the negotiations and force the workers into worthless contracts. They were especially bitter over the role played by Eva McDonald Valesh, who, acting in a semiofficial capacity as AFL organizer, involved herself in many of the negotiating sessions. "It makes me wild to see that woman [Valesh] in our midst," Theresa Malkiel wrote in her diary of the strike. "And I'm almost sure that we aren't going to succeed until we make an effort to shake these serpents."[46]

By the beginning of February, with the strikers' resources nearing depletion, and with the society women showing a growing coolness toward the struggle, the end was inevitable. The union was compelled to sign agreements with many of the larger shops without either recognition of the union or endorsement of the union shop. It was on this basis that the Triangle Waist Company settled with the strikers in the first week of February.

By the second week of February almost the entire trade had resumed operation, and those few strikers whose stubborn employers refused to sign straggled back to their shops without a contract. On February 15 officials of Local No. 25 declared the general strike at an end. The great uprising of the shirtwaist makers, which had begun with such fanfare, ended unceremoniously without any rejoicing.[47]

On February 6 the Philadelphia strike was settled through arbitration between Local No. 15 and the Philadelphia Manufacturers' Association. Under the terms of the settlement, each side nominated two members to a Board of Arbitration, and these four chose a fifth impartial member. In the settlement the employers were not permitted to make any charges for straps, needles, or any other part of the machines, unless they were willfully broken by the operator, and the hours of labor were reduced to fifty-two and a half per week. But both wages and the issue of the union shop remained to be arbitrated. The disappointed strikers, who had hoped for more, returned to their shops. But Agnes Nestor, before returning to Chicago, urged the waistmakers to "build up the union so that when the time comes to make another agreement, you will be in a position to get better terms."[48]

Nestor was either too polite or too cautious to add that the settlement was probably the best the Philadelphia women strikers could gain in view of the fact that, in addition to the opposition they faced from their employers and the police, they also had to overcome the lukewarm attitude of the male-dominated union leadership, the lack of enthusiasm of many of the male workers, and a similar lack of enthusiasm on the part of most of the male unions in the city. Not only did male cutters and markers in the shirtwaist shops not go on strike until four days after the walkout by the women began: they also returned to work three days before the women settled. The men believed that it was impossible to win the strike, but the women refused to relinquish their goals and finally settled with great reluctance on the basis of the negotiated terms. While a number of male unions in Philadelphia endorsed the strike, they gave it little more than verbal support. Only the Jewish cigarmakers' union and the United Hebrew Trades offered any concrete financial assistance to the striking union. Small wonder, then, that the shirtwaist workers were compelled to look to upper-class women for support.[49]

When the strikes in both New York and Philadelphia were over, the ILGWU was able to point with justifiable pride to definite gains made by the strikers. Women who had worked sixty or more hours a week before the strike in New York now had a guaranteed work week of fifty-two hours (fifty-two and a half hours in those Philadelphia shops that had settled with the union), and in New York they were to be paid time and a half for overtime work. Workers no longer had to pay for power and materials, and other petty impositions had also been eliminated. Most important, nearly twenty thousand had joined Local No. 25 and ten thousand had become members of Local No. 15 during the strike.[50]

But the strike settlement had obvious limitations, and the waistmakers' contracts were weak. Because many manufacturers had to make individual settlements with the union, and because each shop determined its own piece-rate scale, neither conditions nor grievance procedures were standardized. As Hillquit had predicted, the failure to win a union shop opened the door to attempts by employers to restore previous conditions. Within months, waistmakers were coming to the WTUL to report violations, and shop strikes were becoming increasingly common. Unfortunately, a number of union leaders, instead of blaming this on the weaknesses in the settlement, attributed it instead to "the main illness of our Jewish organization—strike fever."[51]

Some controversy developed over the role played by black women during the struggle. On January 20, 1910, in an editorial entitled "The Waistmakers' Strike," the New York *Age,* a black weekly, boasted that it had recruited "colored girls as ironers with the firms whose employees are now on strike." After reporting that it had been asked to reject strikebreaking advertisements, and instead, to "help induce these colored girls to join the union, and that we dissuade other colored girls from taking the places of those now on strike," it went on to assert: "We have refused these requests both on general and specific grounds."

What were these grounds? The *Age* maintained that before the strike, "Negro girls were not asked to join the union." This, it declared, was tantamount "practically to an exclusion from the union and the workshop." Moreover, it was safe to assume from past experience that prior to their walkout, the waistmakers would have demanded the immediate discharge of any black girls hired by the employers. Finally, the *Age* claimed, it had asked the "philanthropic sponsor" of the strikers—presumably the New York Women's Trade Union League—for assurances .that "the unions would admit Negro girls in the future without discrimination as to employment, should they refrain from taking the positions now open." Since it had received no such assurance, the *Age* asked its readers if it could "in sense and justice advise competent Negro girls, being idle and until now denied employment, to turn down this opportunity?" And it asked: "Why should Negro working girls pull white working girls' chestnuts out of the fire?"

According to the *Age*, the waistmakers' strike brought into the "clearest light the issue of the Negro and the union." Trade unions and trade unions alone, it declared, were responsible for aligning the black on the side of the capitalists, and it was to be hoped that they would learn the lesson from the waistmakers' strike that "the Negro will continue to be the pivot upon which future strikes will turn so long as labor will ignore his right to work and thwart his ambition to advance in the mechanical world. The friends and leaders of labor should consider the Negro in days of prosperity as well as in those of adversity."

It is undeniable that the *Age* raised a pertinent issue; indeed, blacks had registered similar complaints against AFL unions and the Railroad Brotherhoods for a number of years. But the controversy arose over the application of this issue to the waistmakers' strike. Margaret Dreier Robins, national president of the WTUL, immediately wrote to the *Survey* insisting that the union did have black members—*one* in New York and *two* in Philadelphia—and that in the latter city "two of the most devoted pickets are colored girls, for they have not only been able to persuade the girls of their own race and color to stand by their sisters, but have also been most successful in persuading the white girls to stand by them." A black woman in New York who had joined the strike early in the battle was not only welcomed, wrote Robins, but "she is now chairman of her shop committee, elected by white girls to that office."*[52]

*Evidently even the national WTUL caught the irony of answering the charge with evidence about *one* black member in New York and *two* in Philadelphia, for at the poststrike meeting of the National Executive Board, the organization passed a resolution pledging to do something about organizing black women. The entry in the minutes read:
"The question of the increasing practice of bringing in Negro workers as strike breakers and underbidders was discussed, and it was felt that action must be taken to organize the colored women workers, both for their own protection and for the protection of the white workers. In this discussion, the help given by the National to strikes in New York and Philadelphia, preventing several hundred colored girls being used as strikebreakers was referred to with great appreciation. It was moved and seconded that this Executive Board offer its services to the National Association for the Protection of Colored Women stating the very great desire of the League to cooperate with them in their efforts to protect the colored women workers through organization. Unanimously carried" (Minutes of the Executive Board Meeting of the NWTUL, May 21, 1910, NWTUL Papers, Library of Congress).

Elizabeth Dutcher, an officer of the New York WTUL, charged publicly that the *Age* had distorted the waistmakers' union's policy toward blacks. In a letter published in the *Horizon,* founded and edited by W. E. B. Du Bois, she wrote:

> In New York, colored girls are not only members of the union, but they have been prominent in the union. One colored girl has been secretary of her shop organization all through the strike and has been very frequently at the union headquarters doing responsible work. The editor should also know that meetings were held during the strike at the Fleet Street Methodist Memorial Church (colored) in Brooklyn and St. Marks Methodist Church in Manhattan and that in both, members of the Ladies Waist Makers Union said definitely and publicly that colored girls were not only eligible but welcome to membership.

The *Horizon* expressed its pleasure at the opportunity to publish Dutcher's letter and urged all black Americans to read and study it carefully, especially "those persons and editors who, some unwittingly, are assisting in the present insidious effort to make our people Ishmaelites in the world of labor, or as someone has put it, to make us 'Cossacks' of America."[53]

If there was controversy about the role of blacks, there was none concerning that of Italian women during the strike. Both contemporary and later accounts agree that young Italian women "not only refused to come out of the shops but also took the place of Jewish strikers." Despite the fact that they made up at least one-fourth of the labor force in the waist industry, only two thousand of the strikers were Italians. According to the league, most of the Italians who struck did not remain out until a settlement was reached but went back to work early. However, it should be added that the ILGWU had no Italian-speaking organizer and had to depend on English to inform Italian strikers of developments, and that the Italian and Jewish women strikers, divided as they were by the barrier of language, met separately—a situation that was hardly conducive to the maintenance of solidarity among the Italians.[54]

Whatever the reasons, the union's failure to bring and keep out most of the Italian workers was clearly a factor in the waistmakers' inability to win a complete victory. There was also the contention that the failure of Local No. 25's leaders to anticipate the strike and prepare adequate funds for it seriously hampered the struggle from its beginning right up to the final settlement. Finally, the point is also made that the waistmakers did not enjoy the full support of either the international or the labor movement as a whole because a large percentage of the strikers were women, while the union officials were men. A great strike of unorganized immigrant women "was hardly calculated to win the support of the American Federation of Labor."[55] Although Pauline Newman and Rose Schneiderman traveled throughout New York State appealing for assistance from local labor unions, they only raised $600 through this method.[56]

In view of all these handicaps, it could be argued that without the yeoman service provided by the Women's Trade Union League, with the support of middle-class and upper-class women, the waistmakers would not even have gained a limited victory. "Not the least memorable feature of the New York waistmakers' strike," the *Literary Digest* observed even before the strike was over, "has been the evidence it affords of woman's humanity to woman." The weekly endorsed the following comment of the *Brooklyn Standard Union:* "The earnestness with which many prominent women have joined hands with the girls is in marked contrast with the aloofness of men of wealth when there is a strike in which only men are involved. *There is reason to believe that if a complete victory is won the rich women who enlisted in the cause made it possible*" [emphasis added].[57]

Apart from the fact that "a complete victory" was not won, the statement contained elements of both fact and distortion. It is true that league members did appeal to upper-class women in the language of sisterhood, stressing the need for these women to demonstrate their solidarity with the strikers by coming down to the factory district and inspecting conditions there for themselves. More important, they insisted that the women should join their sisters on the picket lines and help the strike effort by boycotting nonunion waists. As the special strike edition of the *New York Call,* edited by league members, put it: "Now is the time for women in New York, Philadelphia, and in fact everywhere where American shirtwaists are worn, to rise in their might and demonstrate that with them bargain-hunting can be subordinated to principle and that they have said goodbye to the products of the sweatshop. . . . Friends, let us stop talking about sisterhood, and MAKE SISTERHOOD A FACT!"[58]

To a remarkable extent, the strike did just that. "Women [of the upper class]," wrote Helen Marot, "who came to act as witnesses of arrests around the factories ended by picketing side by side with the strikers."[59] Mary Durham, a league official, wrote to Agnes Nestor in February, 1910: "Isn't it good to see this sisterhood of women at last really demonstrated in the active interest of women of wealth and leisure? Good to see them take up some of the crying needs of their sister women who are out in the world of work struggling for a living."[60]

And yet there is no justification for the conclusion drawn by the *Literary Digest,* the *Brooklyn Standard Union,* and several other contemporary observers (along with some later historians) that it was the "rich women" who made victory for the shirtwaist workers "possible." It was the female garment workers themselves—their militancy and endurance in manning the picket lines in frigid weather and in sustaining beatings, arrests, and imprisonment—and not the supportive activities of what

Rose Schneiderman called the "Mink Brigade" that made victory possible. The press even exaggerated the effect of the financial contributions of the upper-class women, through the league. Since the strike cost $100,000, it is clear that the league's contributions, which totaled $20,000, could not have financed it. Indeed, in its report dealing with the strike, the WTUL pointed out: "It is untrue to state, as has been stated, that the League financed and led the strike. The strike was organized and led by the Union."[61]

As we shall see, the exhibition of sisterhood that had united upper- and working-class women during the strike proved to be both exceptional and short-lived. But the Women's Trade Union League continued and was strengthened by the strike. Despite all the controversy provoked by its activities, they did help to attract workingwomen to the organization. The strike also brought to the fore a number of able and intelligent workingwomen who became active participants in both the ILGWU and the WTUL. Clara Lemlich, famous for her Cooper Union speech, Pauline Newman, and Mollie Schepps, an American-born dressmaker, joined the league during the strike and soon became members of its Executive Board. The composition of the league's organizing committees reflected the increased proportion of workers in the organization. In the years before 1909, most of the WTUL's standing trade committees were headed by allies; by 1910, all of them were led by workingwomen. Moreover, the league's major organizers in the years following the strike included Rose Schneiderman, Pauline Newman, Melinda Scott, Rose Sashon (another young waistmaker who joined the league during the strike), and Mollie Schepps. All of them were workingwomen.[62]

In truth, the shirtwaist strike appeared to have heralded the New York league's real initiation into the labor movement. During most of the strike, Local No. 25—in contrast to the attitude of the ILGWU officials—had treated the league as an equal partner and had solicited its assistance and advice in formulating strategy and settlements. In recognition of the league's service and as a guarantee of future cooperation, the union elected Rose Schneiderman to its Executive Board. Nor was this new acceptance limited to the waistmakers' union. When Leonora O'Reilly attended the New York State Federation of Labor convention in the summer of 1910, she noted that the delegates greeted her warmly and were very much interested in the league's work. In addition, the president of the Workingmen's Federation of the State of New York publicly praised the work of the league, and the president of the Boston Central Labor Union expressed the hope that it would be able to become a full-fledged member of the AFL. Even the *American Federationist* noted the league's existence and editorially applauded its achievements, while Gompers himself actually had friendly words for the league members and stated that the strike had demonstrated the practicality of unionism among women workers and "the capacity of those misused toilers to suffer, fight, and dare that justice might be done."[63]

Despite the strike's less-than-successful settlement, it marked a turning point in the history of the union movement among women workers, as well as in the union movement of the garment industry. The strike was both the largest and bitterest strike of women in the history of American labor struggles up to that time. During the eight weeks of preliminary skirmishing and the thirteen weeks of the general strike, the strikers had clearly demonstrated that workers who were regarded by leading officials of the AFL (and even by some of the ILGWU) as impossible to organize could be united in effective economic action. In this struggle, very young women, most of them recent immigrants, working primarily at an unskilled trade, were able to gain important concessions from their employers. Without either preparation or finances, the women had walked the picket lines through the rain and snow, remaining "solid" in spite of beatings, arrests, fines, and jailings. They had laid the foundation for future gains. Their conditions and struggles had gained the attention of middle-class and well-to-do individuals in New York, and their strike marked the first time these individuals were actively involved in championing the cause of the working masses. The strike pointed up for many New Yorkers the inadequacies of both their police department and the city's judicial system. It awakened many in the city to a new awareness of the problems facing workers in general and workingwomen in particular. "The great moral significance of the shirtwaist makers' strike," Morris Hillquit noted, "is that it helped awaken our dormant social conscience. The people of this city began to realize that society owes some duties to the toiling masses."[64]

Finally, the three months of picketing created a solidarity among the women workers and fostered a new awareness of what unity could achieve on the economic front. The strikers had gained the understanding that together they were a powerful force. As one woman phrased it: "This is not just a strike for self. Only by standing together can we get better conditions for all."[65]

Almost a quarter of a century later, an ILGWU veteran recalled that in the opening years of the century, "the waist and dress shops were the vilest and foulest industrial sores of New York and other big cities." And he went on: "Then came 1909. Then came the most heroic labor struggle in the history of the great city. Then came the beginnings of a strong and permanent organization in the needle trades. Then came the beginnings of decency in a vilely sweated industry."[66] These were true words. The impact of the women's strike in the waistmaking industry was a tremendous inspiration to the workers in the other branches of the industry and paved the way for the major advances in unionizing other garment workers. In years to come, thousands of workers would sing "The Uprising of the Twenty Thousand," the song dedicated to the waistmakers of 1909:

> In the black of the winter of nineteen nine,
> When we froze and bled on the picket line,
> We showed the world that women could fight
> And we rose and won with women's might.
>
> *Chorus:*
>   Hail! the waistmakers of nineteen nine,
>   Making their stand on the picket line,
>   Breaking the power of those who reign,
>   Pointing the way, smashing the chain.
>
> And we gave new courage to the men
> Who carried on in nineteen ten
> And shoulder to shoulder we'll win through,
> Led by the ILGWU.[67]

Two years after the "Uprising of the Twenty Thousand," the waistmakers' struggles played an important role in the establishment of International Women's Day. For it was the demonstration on March 8, 1908 in New York City of women workers in the needle trades that influenced Clara Zetkin at the International Socialist Congress in 1910 to move that the day of the demonstration of the American working women (March 8) become an International Women's Day, and that March 8 each year be dedicated to fighting for equal rights for all women in all countries. Under the leadership of Zetkin, the German Socialist Party woman spokesperson, the first International Women's Day celebration was held in Copenhagen that year.[68]

8

Repercussions of the
Garment Workers' Uprising

BARELY FIVE MONTHS after the shirtwaist makers had returned to work, another and more extensive general strike paralyzed the ladies' garment trade. In July, 1910, some sixty thousand workers employed in the cloak-and-suit branch of the industry left their workbenches en masse and marched to the picket lines.

In 1910 in New York City cloaks, suits, and shirts were manufactured in about fifteen hundred shops employing approximately sixty thousand workers, of whom about forty thousand were Jewish and ten to twenty thousand were Italian. After 1890, partly because legislation outlawing "homework" had virtually ended sweatshops, many small shops had sprung up. The newer clothing factories used lighter, better, and more specialized machinery run by steam or electricity. But even in these more modern factories, working conditions remained poor. Little provision had been made for adequate sanitary facilities; workers were still forced to buy their own sewing machines and to pay for repairs, oil, and thread; and inside subcontracting, which prevailed in most of the shops, created a chain of bosses whose common interest was in keeping wages down. In 1910 the average wage for operators was $15 to $18 a week, and for pressers, $14. Men worked for nine to nine and a half hours a day during the slack season and fourteen to sixteen hours a day when the shops were busy. In short, the cloakmaker's life, like that of the shirtwaist maker, was a bitter struggle for existence. This was especially true for the female workers, who held 10 percent of the jobs in this branch of the industry. They played a minor role in cloakmaking, working primarily as "helpers" in the finishing departments, and earned the woefully inadequate wage of $3 to $4 a week.[1]

Unlike the waistmakers' strike, which had been spontaneous and haphazard, the cloakmakers' strike in the summer of 1910 was carefully planned. Unlike Local No. 25's leaders, the cloakmakers' officers had anticipated the strike, had prepared adequate funds, and enjoyed the full support of the international union. Strike agitation had begun in August, 1908, and by the spring of 1909, about two thousand members had been recruited by the New York Joint Board of Cloak and Shirt Makers Unions. With the strike of the waistmakers, the movement for a general strike in the cloak and suit trade was ignited, and membership in the Joint Board soared. In July, 1910, a secret ballot on the general strike issue showed 18,777 for striking and 615 against, and a committee decided on the following set of demands: union recognition, the forty-eight-hour week, double pay for overtime work, and the abolition of subcontracting.[2]

When the strike call was issued on July 7, about sixty thousand cloakmakers, six thousand of them women, walked off their jobs. On this occasion the Italians, who constituted about a third of the labor force in the industry and who had been involved in all stages of planning and executing the strike, joined the Jewish workers.[3]

The cloakmakers began at once to negotiate with the smaller employers, who could not afford a long-drawn-out conflict and who rushed to arrange satisfactory agreements. But the larger manufacturers refused to yield to the demand for union recognition and the closed shop. A number of these larger cloak manufacturers thereupon formed the Cloak, Suit and Shirt Manufacturers' Protective Association and pledged not to bargain with the Cloakmakers' Union.[4]

Like the shirtwaist makers before them, the cloakmakers soon had to contend with the association's special policemen and thugs, in addition to the New York City police. All three groups joined forces in escorting strikebreakers into the struck shops. As in the shirtwaist makers' strike, too, magistrates regularly fined or sentenced pickets to the workhouse, while the police generally protected the thugs who were terrorizing the strikers. Moreover, the association obtained a limited temporary injunction restraining the union from coercing any worker into leaving his job through the use of "force, threat, fraud or intimidation." The strikers defied the injunction by mass picketing in the face of violence by the police and the special guards hired by the employers.[5]

Even though women workers made up a small minority of the strike force, they quickly assumed important positions in the strike organization. For example, Dora Landburg, who had grown up in the cloakmaking trade, enthusiastically directed the strike headquarters, coordinated the picketing, and dispatched aid to arrested strikers who requested bail.[6] In contrast to the shirtwaist strike, the WTUL played only a peripheral role in the cloakmakers' revolt, mainly because women constituted only a small percentage of the strikers. But John Dyche, the ILG-

WU's national secretary-treasurer, having learned something from the previous strike, requested help from the league and named Helen Marot and Leonora O'Reilly to the cloakmakers' strike committee. Every few days Marot visited the headquarters of the settlement committee, where the national officers sat in session. The union leaders appointed Marot and Rose Schneiderman to negotiate a settlement with those manufacturers who employed female alteration hands. League members formed a committee that raised money to distribute 209,000 quarts of milk to strikers' children.[7]

After mediation efforts by the State Bureau of Arbitration had failed (the association refused to enter into negotiations until the union agreed to abandon its demand for recognition and the closed shop),[8] A. Lincoln Filene, the Boston department store owner and a leading member of the Boston branch of the National Civic Federation, contacted Louis D. Brandeis and asked him to go to New York to help arrange a settlement of the strike. As counsel for the Boston cloak and suit manufacturers' association, Brandeis had helped to break a four-month general strike there in 1907 by obtaining injunctions against the union leaders.[9] Now he appeared in New York as a friend of labor but an enemy of the closed shop, one of the union's main demands. Under Brandeis' clever and persuasive maneuvering, Dyche and the majority of the strike committee agreed to eliminate the closed shop from the list of the union's basic demands. But the more radical of the union's executive officers, as well as the majority of the rank and file, declined to accept arbitration without some consideration of the closed-shop issue. In fact, the active personal intervention of Samuel Gompers was needed before indignant union leaders and members would agree to enter into a conference with the employers on July 28.[10]

The conference quickly came to an understanding on the specific grievances of the cloakmakers, but it could make no headway on the closed-shop issue. At this stage Brandeis put forward the formula of the "preferential union shop," which would bind an employer to give preference in hiring to any available union member while still permitting him to hire nonunion members and retain scabs. Brandeis did not invent the preferential union shop; the plan had been promulgated as a union demand in the 1892 strike of the AFL teamsters, scalemen, and packers in New Orleans.[11] Where the AFL was weak and fighting against an open-shop drive, it put forward the preferential union shop as a step toward the closed shop. By 1910, however, when the closed shop had been won in many contracts, acceptance of the preferential union shop represented a retreat.

Gompers, however, urged the union to accept the plan.[12] But with the *Jewish Daily Forward* denouncing the preferential shop as a "scab shop with honey," and with the *New York Call* urging the strikers to stick to their guns, Brandeis' maneuverings failed. The mass of the workers rejected his proposal, and on August 3 the union concluded all joint conferences and renounced all offers of peace and arbitration, declaring: "The rank and file of our organization demand the closed shop. There can be no compromise on that score and if we were to accept any compromise, the rank and file would not abide by our decision."[13]

So vigorously did the strikers oppose any retreat on the closed-shop issue that members of the strike committee who favored the preferential shop were actually threatened with violence.[14] But when the strike leadership, bowing to the determined opposition of the rank and file, rejected the agreement proposed by the association, Justice John W. Goff of the New York Supreme Court made the injunction against the strikers permanent. Goff labeled the strike a common-law civil conspiracy to obtain the closed shop and thereby to deprive nonunion men and women of the opportunity to work and drive them out of the industry. The police were authorized to disperse all pickets, peaceful or otherwise.[15] "For the first time in the history of labor disputes in the state," observes Graham Adams, Jr., "an injunction not only permanently restrained men from peaceful picketing but also forbade them to interfere in any way at all with those who wished to work."[16]

Even Julius Henry Cohen, the attorney for the manufacturers, described the injunction as "the strongest one ever handed down by an American court against trade unionism," and the New York *Evening Post,* which seldom favored the cause of labor in any strike, commented: "One need not be a sympathizer with trade-union policy as it reveals itself today in order to see that the latest injunction, if generally upheld, would seriously cripple such defensive powers as legitimately belong to organized labor."[17] Speaking for the AFL, Gompers called the decision another example of the "tyranny of the autocratic methods of concentrated capital and greed." The New York City Central Federated Union, in conjunction with the Socialist Party, organized a huge demonstration against this "judicial tyranny."[18]

Meanwhile, negotiations were continuing, and on September 2, the manufacturers presented a new proposal for a settlement with additional concessions. The strike committee, supported by only two hundred hastily assembled shop chairmen and with a minimum of debate, ratified the first collective bargaining agreement in the industry. No public announcement was made of the agreement, nor were any public assemblies held before the ratification.[19]

After nine weeks of bitter struggle, the "Protocol of Peace," as the agreement was called, won for the workers a fifty-hour week, bonus pay for overtime, ten legal holidays, free electric power installation for machines, no homework, weekly pay in cash rather than checks, limitations on overtime, a joint board of sanitary control to help clean up filthy shops, a committee for grievances and compulsory arbitration,* with no strike or lockout permitted before arbitration, and price settlements to be made in each shop by negotiation. As a concession, the manufacturers agreed to exert preference only between one union man and another: nonunion labor could be hired only when union help was unobtainable. The agreement also compelled employers to declare their belief in the union and in the ideal that all "who desire its benefits should share its burdens."[20] The settlement had tremendously important implications for unskilled women workers, since the agreement covered the wages and conditions of every worker in the trade, from skilled tailors to finishers.[21]

Despite these important gains, however, the settlement was a disappointment to many strikers, largely because it institutionalized the preferential union shop. Furthermore, unlike the usual collective bargaining agreement, the protocol had no time limit; it could be terminated by either side at will. Many rank-and-file workers also disapproved of the no-strike clause and the provision for compulsory arbitration.[22] Responding to this criticism, the union's official journal declared: "It is far better to strike for, and win recognition of our union, than an increase in wages, or decrease of hours, without the powerful organization needed to maintain the conditions once created. With such an organization, the possibilities of the future are unlimited."[23]

But events were soon to demonstrate that the union relied exclusively on the machinery of the Protocol and the good will of the employers to establish permanent industrial peace and failed to build a strong organization in order to enforce it. As a result, the employers were able to violate freely the terms of the Protocol.

The revolt in the garment trades next shifted to Chicago, where, on September 22, 1910, a small group of courageous women ignited the spark that led forty thousand unorganized clothing workers to strike. The uprising began when a few women employed in shop No. 5 of Hart, Schaffner & Marx, the largest clothing factory in the city, walked off the job when their piece rate was arbitrarily cut from 4 cents to 3¼ cents a pair. One of these girls was Bessie Abramowitz, an immigrant from Grodno, in White Russia, who had already been blacklisted in Chicago's clothing shops because of her militancy and was working at Hart, Schaffner & Marx under an assumed name. Under the leadership of Abramowitz and Annie Shapiro, twelve young women petitioned for a

---

*Minor grievances were to be submitted to a Committee of Grievances while important disputes were to be turned over to a permanent Board of Arbitration, whose decision was to be "final and conclusive."

return to the old rate. When this appeal was rejected, they struck and sought help from the United Garment Workers, which had a small, male-dominated local of clothing cutters within the Hart, Schaffner & Marx plant. The elite local had no interest in organizing young immigrant women, so the young strikers started to picket by themselves. At first they received little support from other workers in the plant, and it took three weeks of steady, day-by-day picketing by these fourteen determined strikers to convince the other workers that this was a serious effort to redress long-standing grievances of all workers. By the fourth week, other workers in the plant had begun to join the original fourteen women, and by mid-October almost eight thousand Hart, Schaffner & Marx workers had walked out. The walkout gradually spread to other manufacturing houses until the entire industry was paralyzed.[24]

With the United Garment Workers indifferent to their struggle, the strikers appealed to the Chicago Women's Trade Union League and the Chicago Federation of Labor for assistance. Both organizations responded instantly. However, the WTUL's National Executive Board had just established a policy requiring that any union requesting league assistance had to include two league members on its strike committee. Pressured by the strikers, the UGW leadership agreed to this stipulation.[25] Thereupon, the Chicago WTUL threw itself wholeheartedly into the strike. Members formed eleven separate committees to handle picketing, publicity, speakers, benefit meetings, public events, and relief. They established headquarters in the same building that housed the Chicago Federation of Labor offices.[26]

On November 2 the league held a formal breakfast and invited women strikers to attend and spell out their grievances. The strikers told of the low wages, the long hours, the inequities of the piecework system, and the unjust fines for damaged merchandise. They reported that the price of piecework had declined steadily. One young woman reported that she and her fellow workers received 12 cents for making a coat, including the pockets: "One week we would have to stitch single, and then the next week maybe we would have to stitch them narrow and then another week they would have to be wider. Of course, the change would make it take a longer time but they paid us the same." Other girls protested against the costly system of fines. At Hart, Schaffner & Marx, they reported, "any worker who damaged a pair of pants was made to buy them at the regular wholesale prices." If the canvas strips accidentally fell to the floor, the foremen fined the canvas makers 5 cents. Still others complained of the long workday. Some women complained about the petty tyrannies practiced by their foremen, who distributed work inequitably and used abusive and insulting language. A children's jacket maker explained that her foreman insisted that she carry a bundle of

350 pairs of sleeves to another room. Although she told him it was too heavy for her to lift from the floor, he insisted. When she lifted the bundle, she injured her back and was unable to work for several weeks.[27]

One of the original strikers explained why she and her colleagues had walked out:

> We started to work at seven-thirty and worked until six with three-quarters of an hour for lunch. Our wages were seven cents for a pair of pants, or one dollar for fourteen pairs. For that we made four pockets and one watch pocket, but they were always changing the style of the stitching and until we got the swing of the new style, we would lose time and money and we felt sore about it. One day the foreman told us the wages were cut to six cents a pair of pants and the new style had two watch pockets. We would not stand for that, so we got up and left.[28]

As in the New York strikes, the employers hired detectives and thugs and received the full support of the police. In fact, Chicago's police, long notorious for their brutality toward strikers, were even more barbarous than those in New York. By December, two of the strikers had been gunned down and killed by police bullets and many more had been injured by club-swinging members of the force. Arrests of strikers occurred daily, and members of the league's picket committee patrolled the streets in order to serve as witnesses for strikers arrested without cause. League members also joined the strikers' picket lines and reviewed the "Rules for Pickets" with the strikers each day.[29]

"Come, I want to introduce you to some of the girl strikers." So began an article in the *Chicago Daily Socialist* of November 21, 1910. The reporter, who had been invited to meet the strikers, continued:

> I met the girls. And such girls! One of them occupied the platform in front and her young strong voice rang out clear as a bell, penetrating every nook and corner of the great hall.
>
> Cheer after cheer went up from the three thousand strikers assembled there, as she urged the necessity of solidarity and the closed shop.
>
> These girls were the leaders of the strike and as pretty and sweet-voiced as any young women one could possibly meet anywhere. . . .
>
> They moved about among their men comrades gracefully, free and unaffected. Here was the perfect comradeship that had grown out of the sharing of work and struggles for better conditions.
>
> The men did not assume that chivalrous attitude of the gentleman, which oftentimes is but the thin coating of contempt, but consulted and advised with them as with those of their own sex.
>
> In fact, they appeared to consult the girls quite as often as the girls did them.

After forty thousand garment workers, ten thousand of them women, had walked off the job, the strikers received a crippling blow from their own union. Thomas Rickert, president of the United Garment Workers, was a conservative, old-line labor leader, interested in developing the union along craft lines. He was skeptical of the value of unskilled immigrants to the union and eager to come to terms with the employers. In November he announced an agreement with Hart, Schaffner & Marx, but it came short of what the strikers wanted and was unanimously rejected. Then league members and officials of the Chicago Federation of Labor learned that the UGW District No. 6's treasury was empty and that the union officers' offer to assist the strikers lacked any substance. In fact, the union had issued worthless vouchers for relief to over ten thousand people. Officials of the Chicago Federation of Labor, league leaders, and UGW officers then managed to raise $700 and proceeded to distribute $3 for each $5 voucher to the angry strikers.[30]

The strike revealed an extraordinary determination on the part of the strikers not to yield, in spite of cold, hunger, and the brutality of the thugs and police. A woman striker recalled that as she and her fellow workers were negotiating with their employer to call a halt to the strike, they heard a terrific noise: "We all rushed to the windows, and there we [saw] the police beating strikers—clubbing them on our account, and when we saw that we went out."[31]

On November 18 the Joint Conference Board, composed of strike leaders and representatives of the Chicago Federation of Labor, the WTUL, and the UGW, opened four commissary stores to distribute food to the strikers—four loaves of bread, one-half pound of coffee, one pound of beans, and two pounds of ham per family weekly. After Thanksgiving, herring and codfish replaced the meat allotment. To provide for these commissaries, which fed eleven thousand families each week, the league raised close to $70,000.[32]

On November 5 Rickert reached an agreement with Hart, Schaffner & Marx for arbitration of all issues without union recognition. Once again the workers rejected the proposal, and this time they made their hatred of the national officials so clear that Rickert had to leave the hall by a back door. Thousands of striking cutters, trimmers, and spongers resolved to "repudiate the action of . . . Thomas A. Rickert in signing any agreement without presenting the same for approval." Despite mounting violence against them (the final count was 374 strikers arrested and two killed), on December 8 the workers again rejected an agreement that would have sent them back to work without union recognition. It took another five weeks of hunger, cold, and violence before the workers of Hart, Schaffner & Marx, on January 14, 1911, reluctantly agreed to go back to work and refer all issues to an arbitration committee. But the other thirty thousand strikers maintained their ranks solidly until, on February 3, Rickert and his lieutenants, without consulting the strikers, the WTUL, or the officials of the Chicago Federation of Labor, declared the strike over.

Workers returned to their jobs without any agreement and with no method of adjusting the grievances that had driven them to strike. Those who had been the most militant of the pickets were not allowed to return to their former jobs. The twenty-five-year-old Sidney Hillman, Frank Rosenblum, Bessie Abramowitz (who later became Mrs. Hillman), and Sam Levin had risen to leadership among the workers during the strike, and they recorded that the great majority of the strikers "were forced to return to their old miserable conditions, through the back door; and happy were those who were taken back. Many... were victimized for months afterwards." Members of the WTUL and the Chicago Federation of Labor who had worked tirelessly for a just settlement felt as betrayed as the strikers themselves.[33]

Only the Hart, Schaffner & Marx workers operated under a contract as a result of the strike. This contract, drawn up by Clarence Darrow, the famous labor lawyer, who had volunteered his services in defense of the strikers, and company attorney Carl Meyer, is historically regarded as the first major victory in the annals of men's clothing workers' unionism. It established a minimum wage for various departments in the factory, a fifty-four-hour week, and time and a half for overtime. It also presaged future occupational safety and health measures by insisting that "all tailor shops be properly ventilated" and that "no sweeping of a character to raise dust in any of the shops be done during working hours." The agreement provided for overtime pay for extra work and initiated a permanent Board of Arbitration, composed of Darrow and Meyer, to hear and rule on future worker grievances.[34]

Despite its disheartening conclusion for most of the strikers, the Chicago strike brought new stature and vitality to efforts to organize garment workers. The Chicago workers learned to distrust the national leadership of the United Garment Workers, but they (and the leaders and members of the Chicago Federation of Labor) learned to appreciate and respect the contributions of the Women's Trade Union League. Indeed, the Chicago WTUL emerged from the struggle as "an essential element in the city's labor scene,"[35] while Margaret Robins' contributions to the negotiating commissions and the remarkable organizational skills and energy displayed by league members in operating the commissaries won wide acclaim throughout the nation. The strike also brought a new woman labor leader to the front. Following the strike, the league named Bessie Abramowitz organizer for the UGW and agreed to pay her salary.[36]

The Cleveland garment strike of 1911 followed the pattern that had emerged in New York and Chicago. Strikers—men and women alike—held out for ten long weeks to end low pay, unsanitary working conditions, inside subcontracting, and long and irregular hours. The strike began in June, when 4,000 men and 1,600 women walked off the job, demanding a fifty-hour week, abolition of charges for supplies and electricity, elimination of subcontracting, union recognition, and a permanent joint wage committee composed of worker representatives, outside arbitrators, and employers, for the purpose of establishing a uniform wage scale. As in New York and Chicago, union recognition became a crucial factor. Middle-class women again lent invaluable support, while WTUL organizers rushed to the scene to offer assistance.[37]

As in earlier strikes, too, the police came to the manufacturers' aid. But in Cleveland they were even more brutal than elsewhere. The *Cleveland Plain Dealer* described an attack of the police on the girl strikers: "They [the mounted police] galloped headlong at the crowd when they first appeared and the hundreds who blocked the street fled in terror. They swung their clubs when they reached the crowd and forced their way through, driving scores before them down the streets. Some girls who ran from them were chased for blocks." At one of the factories, forty-five women were arrested at one time. They promptly held a meeting in the prison and adopted resolutions condemning the police. As one observer noted: "Girls who maintain this fighting spirit in police cells are not going to be easily beaten." Pauline Newman, who had been sent to Cleveland by the ILGWU to help the strikers, reported that "the spirit manifested by the girl workers in Cleveland" was an "inspiration" to the entire labor movement.[38]

As in other strikes in the garment trade, young women assumed positions of leadership. Florence Shalor, a young Italian woman who supported her family with her job, served as secretary for the Italian strikers. Rebecca Saul, spokeswoman for the Jewish women strikers, ran strike headquarters every day from 5 A.M. to 10 or 11 P.M., coordinating the pickets and arranging for speakers to visit shop meetings. When Pauline Newman arrived in Cleveland, she was met at the train by fifty young women, who assured her that they were prepared to hold out in spite of increasing police violence and arrests. Secretary-Treasurer Dyche called on Margaret Robins for aid, and the WTUL leader visited the city to appeal to Cleveland's club women for their support of the strike. In addition, she organized a successful strikers' parade and a number of citizens meetings. Josephine Casey, another WTUL leader, also hurried to Cleveland to aid the strikers, while Gertrude Barnum toured the Midwest under ILGWU auspices, encouraging consumers and retailers to boycott Cleveland-made garments.[39]

Unfortunately, the strike failed. As it dragged on into October, the International's funds fell dangerously low, and the Cleveland manufacturers found New York and Chicago shops to fill their orders. In desperation, the ILGWU turned to the AFL Executive Council for assistance, pleading:

> For fourteen weeks the strikers have maintained their ranks unbroken. The strike has already cost over a quarter of a million dollars, almost all of which has been contributed by members and locals of the International Ladies' Garment Workers' Union. The Cleveland strikers are ready to keep up the fight until the principle of collective bargaining is recognized by the employers. Be prompt with your aid lest the employers starve us into submission.

But the AFL Executive Council remained deaf to the appeal. "And so," writes Elizabeth McCreesh, "despite the strikers' heroism and valuable support from sympathizers and union officials, organized manufacturers succeeded in halting the union movement among Cleveland's garment workers."[40]

Milwaukee's garment workers were more successful in their strike, for good reason. Of all the garment workers' strikes of the period, only the one in Milwaukee was not accompanied by police violence against pickets and unjustified arrests and imprisonment, largely because of the election of Emil Seidel, a Socialist, as mayor on the eve of the strike, which broke out late in November, 1910. The police chief, a holdover from the previous administration, ordered the customary police brutality toward the pickets, whereupon Mayor Seidel addressed an official letter to him:

> Complaints have been made here that disemployed citizens have recently been subjected to abusive epithets and rough handling by policemen. Whatever may be the basis of these complaints, I want it understood that no man on the police force has the right to interfere with a citizen who is not violating the law. I expect you, as Chief of Police, to make clear to the members of your department that as long as a citizen is within his legal rights, he should not be manhandled or insulted. Officers tolerating such tactics and patrolmen practicing them will be accountable. Hoping that reports referred to will, on investigation, prove to be exaggerated.

Apparently the police got the message. Deprived of their usual allies, the manufacturers settled on December 9 on the basis of a fifty-four hour week, time and a half for overtime, double pay for holidays, an open door to the employers (over the heads of foremen) for complaints of ill treatment, and the appointment of a committee representing workers and employers to discuss a new wage scale and the issue of union recognition.[41]

Most of the women workers who spearheaded the strike in the garment industries of New York, Chicago, Cleveland, and Milwaukee were of immigrant background. However, nonimmigrant women in the industry also demonstrated the willingness to fight for their rights and for unionism. All the women corset workers of Kalamazoo, Michigan, who struck in 1912 were born in the United States, and in this community of 35,000 inhabitants, fully half of the citizens belonged to families supported by one or more factory workers. After a spontaneous strike in 1911 to protest wage reductions, the strike leaders formed Local No. 82 of the ILGWU. Then in February, 1912, officials of the Kalamazoo Corset Company refused to renegotiate a contract with the union and discharged a number of women employees, accusing them of "disloyalty." Six hundred angry women workers declared a strike, demanding reinstatement of their discharged colleagues, a wage increase, and a reduction of the weekly work hours.[42]

Once the strike was under way, the women added new charges against their employers. They complained that the foremen awarded the more desirable jobs to those women who acquiesced to their sexual advances and neglected to collect charges from their favorites. Many girls signed affidavits describing unsanitary conditions, inadequate toilet facilities, and filthy communal drinking cups. Others testified to their supervisors' obsession with achieving sexual relations with the women workers: "The management of that concern is run by superintendents, some of them diseased and filthy, whose minds are occupied more with carnal pleasure than with the business of the firm."[*43]

Josephine Casey, Pauline Newman, and Gertrude Barnum of the ILGWU and Leonora O'Reilly of the WTUL came to Kalamazoo to assist the strikers. Shortly after Casey's arrival in the Michigan community, the police arrested and imprisoned her for leading pickets in the following prayer:

> Oh, God, Our Father, Who are generous... Our employer who has plenty has denied our request. He has misused the law to help him crush us.... Thou Who didst save Noah and his family, may it please Thee to save the girls now on strike from the wicked city of Sodom. Oh, help us to get a living wage.... Grant that we may win the strike... so that we may not need to cry often, "Lord deliver us from temptation."

Casey remained in jail for thirty-seven days and provided a model of heroism for women strikers of the period.[44]

The ILGWU called for a boycott of Kalamazoo goods, and organizers, WTUL members, and strikers traveled through neighboring states

---

*Similar charges were leveled against manufacturers and managers during the strike of women button makers in Muscatine, Iowa, which began on February 25, 1911, and lasted fifteen months. The strikers, members of Button Workers' Protective Union 12845, insisted that managers used their power to force sexual relations upon the women button makers. One manager, for example, maintained a "resting room" where women who gave "in to his devilish demands were reciprocated with a steady job. Those who did not comply with his wishes received discharge notices" (Pauline M. Newman, "The Strike of the Buttonworkers of Muscatine," *Progressive Woman*, April 1911, p. 12).

to publicize the union's case against the company. The prolonged strike and the boycott proved fatal to the corset company, which closed its doors permanently.[45] But the strike of Kalamazoo, like those of Cleveland and Chicago, brought new women workers to the fore as organizers and strike leaders, and they were to use the valuable experience they had gained in the struggles that lay ahead.

What of the waistmakers who had initiated the great revolts in the garment trade? In the last months of 1910 the waistmakers' shop agreements were nearing expiration, and it was clear that Local No. 25 was too weak to renew the agreements without considerable outside assistance. Consequently, the local asked for help from the representatives of the New York WTUL, the *Jewish Daily Forward,* the Central Federated Union, and the United Hebrew Trades. After studying the situation, the league persuaded the union to hire a new business manager "to systematize the organization of the union"; when the union agreed, the WTUL chose the manager and paid his salary.[46] However useful the assistance of the league was, it was hardly an ideal relationship when an outside organization could choose a union's leader and pay his salary.

Even with the outside assistance, Local No. 25 was too weak to hold its own. During the shirtwaist strike, 350 manufacturers had signed agreements with the union. A year later, many of these small contractors had either gone out of business or moved to new locations. Of the two hundred shops that remained, the union was able to renew agreements with 164. The large inside Manufacturers' Association shops remained totally unorganized.[47]

One of the largest firms that had resisted the union was the Triangle Shirtwaist Company, located near Washington Square. This was one of the factories about which the New York fire commissioner, in testifying before the State Factory Investigating Commission, had said: "I think that a great many of the fire escapes in buildings today are only put up to be called a fire escape. They are absolutely inadequate and absolutely useless."[48]

How inadequate and useless they were became a matter of history on Saturday, March 25, 1911. Sometime after 4:30 P.M. on that day, a crowd began to gather in front of the Asch Building, on the corner of Washington Place and Greene Street. The crowd had come together because there had been a muffled explosion, "like a big puff." At first, only small wisps of smoke could be seen coming out of an eighth-floor window. "But within a few moments," wrote New York *World* reporter James Cooper, who happened to be at the scene, "the entire eighth floor was spouting little jets of flame from the windows as if the floor was surrounded by a row of incandescent lights."

Suddenly something that looked like a bale of dark dress goods was hurled from an eighth-story window. "Somebody's in there, all right," exclaimed a spectator. "He's trying to save the best cloth." Cooper's account continued: "Then another seeming bundle of cloth came hurtling through the same window, but this time a breeze tossed open the cloth and from the crowd of five hundred persons came a cry of horror. The breeze disclosed the form of a girl shooting down to instant death."

So began the catastrophic Triangle fire. The company occupied the three upper stories of a ten-story building that was supposedly "fireproof," but it had only a single fire escape that ended five feet from the ground. The fire escape quickly collapsed. "As the fire-crazed vicitms were thrown by the collapse of the fire escape," noted the New York *Herald*, "several struck on the sharp-tipped palings. The body of one woman was found with several iron spikes driven entirely through it."

The many corpses found after the fire still bending over their sewing machines attested to the speed with which the blaze took its toll. Many victims did not even have time to leave their workbenches before the flames reached them. Most of the dead had expired within the first ten to fifteen minutes of the fire.

Other women, crazed with fear and pain, their hair and dresses aflame, made the terrible decision to jump. "They didn't want to jump," said one of the survivors. "They were afraid. They were saying their prayers first, and putting rags over their eyes so they could not see. They said it was better to be smashed than burned.... They wanted to be identified." Fifty-eight women who could not bring themselves to jump crawled into a cloakroom on the ninth floor, where they were later found burned to death, their faces raised toward a small window.

Before it was over, the Triangle fire had snuffed out the lives of 145 women, mostly immigrants. Many were the sole support of families either in America or in Europe. The Women's Trade Union League and the Shirtwaist Makers' Union, which handled the relief activities, estimated that the contributions of the slain workers to their households came to $45,000 a year.

All the conditions in the loft that made the tragedy inevitable—floors littered with flammable materials; narrow staircases in drafty, vertical wells; doors at the landings that opened inward if they opened at all (and one did not); the absence of sprinklers—had been called to the attention of the owners and employers many times, but nothing had been done about them. On the contrary, a Fire Department suggestion for the use of sprinklers had been rejected by a property owners' association on the ground that the cost amounted to "confiscation."

"I can show you 150 loft buildings far worse than this one," Fire Marshal William Beers told a New York *Evening Post* reporter after the fire. Of 1,463 factories in New York's garment industry, practically all had hall doors that opened inward instead of outward, as the law required; five hundred had only one fire escape, sixty had halls less than three feet wide, and fourteen had no fire escapes at all.

On Sunday, April 2, 1911, a memorial and protest meeting was held at the Metropolitan Opera House, under the auspices of the Women's Trade Union League. Workingpeople from the Lower East Side packed the galleries, while the orchestra, boxes, and balconies were filled with wealthy reformers. As Rose Schneiderman, instantly identified as the leader of the Triangle Shirtwaist strikers the year before, rose to speak, the galleries demanded that she be heard. Choking back tears, she began:

> I would be a traitor to those poor burned bodies if I were to talk good fellowship. We have tried you good people of the public and we have found you wanting.... The old inquisition had its rack and its thumb screw and its instruments of torture with iron teeth. We know what these things are today: the iron teeth are our necessities, the thumb screws are the high-powered and swift machinery close to which we must work, and the rack is here in the firetrap structures that will destroy us the minute they catch fire.... We have tried you citizens! We are trying you now and you have a couple of dollars for the sorrowing mothers... by the way of a charity gift. But every time the workers come out in the only way they know how to protest against conditions which are unbearable, the strong hand of the law is allowed to press down heavily upon us.... I can't talk fellowship to you who are gathered here. Too much blood has been spilled. I know from experience it is up to the working people to save themselves and the only way is through a strong working class movement.[49]

Sobered by Schneiderman's words, the meeting took the first steps that were to lead eventually to the formation of the New York Factory Investigation Commission, whose work will be discussed below.

On April 5, 1911, eighty thousand workingmen and -women marched up Fifth Avenue for four hours in a drenching rain, amid silent crowds numbering over a quarter of a million people, to attend the funeral of the victims. The faces of the marchers expressed better than any speeches their hatred of a system that showed more concern for improved machinery than for improved working conditions. But their anger reached a truly explosive stage months later when they learned that Isaac Harris and Max Blanck,, owners of the Triangle Company, tried for manslaughter in the first or second degree, had been found "not guilty." "It is one of those disheartening failures of justice which are all too common in this country," even the conservative New York *Tribune* conceded. The *New York Call* put it differently: "Capital can commit no crime when it is in pursuit of profits."[50]

Enraged by the callousness of the employers and their indifference to the safety and other needs of the workers, the waistmakers insisted on a second general strike. The leaders of local No. 25 were forced to accede to their demand. But the Women's Trade Union League disapproved of the plan. At the 1911 National Women's Trade Union League convention, Margaret Dreier Robins made the organization's position clear. The New York League was convinced, she said, that without "effective leadership," capable of "instructing the rank and file in the principles of trade unionsim and the best methods of getting practical results," a general strike would bring "untold suffering." Local No. 25's leadership, according to the league, was anything but "effective." Apart from the fact that they lacked "business sense or executive ability" and had no way of fighting the employers except with words when what was needed was "business methods," the men who managed Local No. 25—like those who led all ILGWU locals in the women's trades—still thought very little of women's ability to participate in trade union activities. Over 80 percent of the waistmakers' union's rank and file were female, yet men controlled the leadership and few women held positions of any responsibility within the organization. "Local 25's leaders regarded women as ignorant," notes Nancy Shrom Dye, "and had no interest in educating them to be serious trade unionists."[51]

When Local No. 25 called a second general strike in October, 1911, the league refused to endorse it and gave the strikers only minimal aid. In other words, the league had moved full circle from a position of cooperating with unions on the basis of the unions' policies to one of seeking to *determine* those policies, and, if its advice was not heeded, remaining aloof from the struggle or giving it only token support. The WTUL launched a concerted shop-by-shop campaign, concentrating its efforts on the American-born skilled workers in the uptown branch of the waist industry, After considerable effort, league organizer Melinda Scott managed to establish a small union of ladies' tailors, which later became ILGWU Local No. 38.[52]

In the spring and summer of 1912 the pessimism among league members over the future of immigrant women in the garment trades was dissolved by a tremendous struggle in which these very women were involved. Women fur workers had a major role in achieving a "great and remarkable victory" in this strike, in which the league itself played only a small part.[53]

In 1912 there were ten thousand workers in New York's fur manufacturing shops. About seven thousand of them were Jewish, most of them recent immigrants from eastern Europe. The remainder were Germans, Greeks, Italians, French-Canadians, English, Bohemians, Slovaks, and other nationalities. About three thousand were women, mainly finishers.[54] In April, 1904, the International Association of Fur Workers of the United States and Canada was organized, but the union's failure to organize the Jewish furriers led to its collapse and the surrender of its charter to the AFL early in 1911. At that point, the United Hebrew Trades initiated an organizing drive, and by the spring of 1912 three thousand of the ten thousand workers in the industry had been organized into three locals, which affiliated with the AFL. With its enlarged membership and with $3,000 in its treasury, the union felt prepared for a major struggle with the employers.[55]

The need for changes in the working conditions in the fur trade made the union confident that there would be a positive response to its call. The poverty-ridden life of immigrant workers in New York City was nowhere better illustrated than in the case of the fur workers. The cutters, the aristocrats of the trade, earned about $12 a week. Operators averaged only about $6, and finishers, all women, only $5. Most fur workers worked fifty-six to sixty hours a week, and some even longer, in filthy, disease-breeding sweatshops, usually located in ancient, broken-down wooden tenements or in basements. In one or two small rooms, without even a pretense of ventilation, about twenty fur workers would labor. Stairs, hallways, rooms, and closets were packed with dust-saturated fur pieces and cuttings. Stench and dust blanketed everything. Hair, dust, and poisonous dyes ate at the workers' eyes, noses, skin, and lungs as they toiled at the bench or machine.

In 1911 a New York State commission conducted an investigation of sanitary conditions in fur shops. A special panel of doctors examined the workers. Two out of every ten fur workers had tuberculosis, and another two had asthma. The fingers of many workers were rotted by dyes. The skin on their hands had turned black. The commission reported that eight out of every ten fur workers were suffering from occupational diseases.[56] Little wonder, then, that the newly formed union was confident that there would be an enthusiastic response to its strike call.

The union began its preparations for a general strike in the spring of 1912, quietly framing a set of demands, including union recognition, the closed shop, a nine-hour day (the fifty-four-hour week), paid holidays, the abolition of homework and subcontracting, and a union scale of wages. On June 14, 1912, union members were balloted on the strike issue; the final tabulation showed an overwhelming favorable majority—2,135 for a general strike and only 364 against. Two days later the union sent its demands to the manufacturers. On June 19 the two employers' associations—the Associated Fur Manufacturers and the Mutual Fur Protective Association (the latter comprising about three hundred employers)—rejected the union's demands. The fur manufacturers were resolved to oppose union recognition and the closed shop, and the MFPA determined "not to enter into any contract, agreement or secret understanding that shall or may conflict with the principle of the open shop."[57]

On June 20 the strike call was distributed in the fur market. As was the custom in all garment strikes of the period, the strike bulletin was printed in red and was known as the *Red Special*. Calling on the fur workers to "Arise to Battle," the *Red Special* declared: "Victory is positive.... The general strike starts today (June 20th) at 10 a.m. No one shall remain at work. Leave your shops as one man." Seven thousand fur workers in forty shops responded to the union's call. On the second day, 8,500 workers—three-quarters of them Jewish and two thousand of them women—were out from five hundred shops. By the end of the first week, the strike was general in fact as well as in name. Only members of the German Furriers' Union remained at work until the fifth week, at which time they, too, joined the strike. With 9,000 workers out, the trade was completely paralyzed.[58]

With the entire trade at a standstill, the union leaders expected a brief, triumphant struggle, but it soon became evident that the fur workers were in for a long and bitter battle. Although some small employers settled with the union during the first three weeks of the strike, the two employers' associations were determined to fight to the end, convinced that they could win by starving out the workers. The manufacturers simply closed their shops for three weeks, announcing that on July 8 the shops would open for all workers to return under the old conditions.

There was some justification for the employers' confidence. After the first three weeks of the strike, the union's financial resources were approaching the vanishing point, and many of the strikers were faced with starvation and eviction. But the women pickets marched around the buildings that housed the fur shops, carrying signs in Yiddish and English that read: "Masters! Starvation is your weapon. We are used to starving. We will fight on 'til victory!"[59]

As July 8 approached, the eyes of all New York were on the furriers. Would their ranks break? Nine thousand strikers gave the answer that morning as they walked the picket lines. Every shop remained empty. The strikers had won the first test.

Nine times during the next ten weeks, the employers repeated their announcement that the shops would reopen. Each time, the strikers kept the shops closed by their militant demonstrations.

As in all of the garment strikes, except the one in Milwaukee, the fur employers unleashed gangsters against the workers, and the police protected the strikebreakers by clubbing and arresting the pickets. More than 800 strikers were arrested, including 250 women; 54 strikers, 40 of them women, received workhouse sentences; and 215, over 60 of whom were women, suffered serious injuries at the hands of the thugs. But the furriers remained steadfast. The union was compelled to issue an appeal to all sympathetic groups for funds. An aid committee was elected by the United Hebrew Trades, with Rose Blank, a member of the Women's Trade Union League and its delegate to the UHT, as chairperson.[60]

Over $20,000 was raised through the *Jewish Daily Forward*. The

Cloakmakers' Union, which had received contributions from the fur workers during its own great strike, contributed $20,000, and the capmakers, $1,500. Special strike issues of the *Forward* and the *New York Call,* tag day collections, house-to-house canvassing, picnics, and theater benefits netted additional funds.* Lodges of fraternal organizations contributed $1,000. Other AFL unions raised another $1,000. But not one cent of the $60,000 raised and spent by the union in the course of the strike came from the national AFL. When Morris Shamroth, a member of the strike committee, went to the AFL Executive Council in Washington seeking financial assistance, Gompers sent him back with the message: "Tell the strikers to let the world know they are hungry and keep up the fight."[61]

The chairperson of the two thousand women strikers was Russian-born Esther Polansky. She was so militant in helping to organize the union that she was selected a member of the strike arrangements committee and then as head of the women strikers. As chairperson, she won additional fame by her own example, "because she herself never stopped considering when it was necessary to take down a shop or go up to a place where scabs worked. She never stopped before any danger. This the workers appreciated so much that not only did she win their admiration but also their willingness to sacrifice if she ordered them to do so."[62]

Toward the end of August, when the strike had been on for the better part of two months, negotiations finally got under way between the union and employer representatives. On August 22, at a specially arranged meeting of the strikers, the terms of a proposed settlement were read and explained. The strikers were granted nearly all their demands, including union recognition; only the closed shop and the demand for a half day on Saturday throughout the year were omitted from the proposed agreement. The work week was to include a half day on Saturday during the first eight months of the year, but a full day on Saturday for the remaining four months.

Socialist Meyer London, the strikers' legal adviser, was cheered when he urged them to stick to their demands. So, too, was Samuel Gompers, who said: "Since you have rebelled, which is a sign that you no longer want to stand for it, stay out and keep up your fight until your employers yield to your demands." The strikers overlooked the callous advice he had given them when they appealed for financial assistance. They then affirmed by unanimous vote that they would not return to their jobs unless the employers granted them the half-holiday on Saturday all year round, instead of simply for the first eight months.

Two weeks later, in the thirteenth week of the strike, victory was won.

---

*Tag days were days on which contributions were solicited, with each donor being given a tag to wear.

On September 8 the manufacturers acceded to the strikers' demand for the Saturday half holiday. "The Fighting Furriers" also obtained a forty-nine-hour week; overtime work only during the busy season, at time and a half; ten paid holidays; the banning of homework; wages to be paid weekly and in cash; a permanent Board of Arbitration and a Joint Board of Sanitary Control; a standing conference committee to settle all disputes, with five from each side and with an eleventh and deciding member to be named jointly by both sides—*and union recognition*. The agreement was to last for two years.[63]

"The power of unity and solidarity triumphed over the power of money, the power of police attacks and hunger and want," declared the *Jewish Daily Forward* in hailing the victory. It was a historic agreement, the best thus far achieved in the revolt of the garment workers and the first collective agreement in an industry in which there was not yet even a national union, for the AFL charter to the International Fur Workers of the United States and Canada was not to be issued until July 1, 1913.[64]

During the opening weeks of 1913, the New York garment workers in both the men's and women's branches were participating in tremendous labor uprisings. At one time more than 150,000 workers in the trade were on strike—men's tailors, white-goods workers, kimono and wrapper makers, and shirtwaist makers. "The local needle industries," exclaimed the *New York Call* in some astonishment on January 13, 1913, "have been practically paralyzed by one of the most gigantic and general uprisings which Greater New York has ever witnessed."

That same day one of the greatest parades in the history of the city occurred, as thousands upon thousands—estimates varied from 25,000 to 80,000—of strikers in the men's and boys' garment industry marched in Manhattan and Brooklyn to protest the brutality of police and hired thugs and to demonstrate their solidarity. The line of march in the Manhattan parade extended for more than thirty blocks and included strikers from about eight hundred workshops and factories. "One of the remarkable features of the parade," noted the *New York Times*, "was the number of nationalities represented. Workers from fifteen countries were pointed out, and they all marched shoulder to shoulder, seemingly on the best of terms." It then went on to add: "Fully a third of the marchers were women. Some of these were girls ranging in age from 16 to 20 years." But there were also "older women, whose bent backs told of years spent over sewing machines."

On the reviewing stand in Union Square were the speakers, and reporters noted that there was considerable anticipation expressed about the speech to be made by Rose Pastor Stokes, a Jewish workingwoman from the Cleveland ghetto who had married a millionaire but continued to devote her life to improving the conditions of the laboring class and furthering the cause of the Socialist Party.* In her speech Stokes encouraged the strikers to persevere in their demands and to swear not to return to work until the union had been recognized. The time had come, she said, when the employers "must recognize the rights of labor, whether they wanted to or not."[65]

The action of the men's tailors was the only garment strike in which men constituted the majority of the strikers, but its course was to have great importance for the future of women workers in the industry. As was the case in Chicago, these workers remained unorganized because of the indifference of the United Garment Workers leadership to the needs of the Jewish and Italian immigrant workers. When the UGW leaders at last realized that these workers, inspired by the struggles of the waistmakers, cloakmakers, and furriers, were ready to fight, they perceived that they had to give at least token support and indicated a willingness to go along. On November 15, 1912, after a series of organizational meetings, the New York District Council of the union issued a call for "a general strike of the entire clothing industry of Greater New York," and predicted that out of it "a mighty tailors' union will be built up."[66]

The tailors voted 35,786 for and only 2,322 against the general strike, to begin on December 30. By the end of the first week, it was conceded that more than 100,000 workers were on strike in the largest of all the struggles in the garment trades that had begun with the shirtwaist strike in 1909. Of the 100,000 strikers, fully one-third were women, the majority of them Jewish or Italian, with Poles, Russians, Lithuanians, Greeks, Germans, Czechs, and other nationalities making up the rest.†

On January 6, 1913, the union announced the beginning of mass picketing, headed by a picketing committee of ten thousand strikers, to secure a general 20 percent wage increase, a forty-eight-hour week,

---

*Stokes was born Rose Harriet Wieslander on July 18, 1879, in Augusto, Russian Poland. She took the name "Pastor" from her stepfather. In the autumn of 1890, Rose settled with her family in Cleveland. She worked wrapping cigars, in a shirtwaist factory, and selling ladies' bonnets in a department store. A letter she wrote to the *New York Jewish Daily News* in July, 1901, on conditions of factory workers led to her being offered a job as assistant to the editor of that paper's English section. In July, 1903, the *News* assigned her to interview James Graham Phelps Stokes, a wealthy resident of the University Settlement House. They fell in love and were married on her 26th birthday, in 1905. At her request, the word "obey" was omitted from the marriage ceremony. In July, 1906, the couple formally joined the Socialist Party.

†The militancy of the Italians aroused admiration in the Jewish press. "The vitality of the Italian workers," reported the *Jewish Daily Forward* on January 6, 1913, "was wonderful, their energy is simply incredible, their devotion exceeds everything." On January 11, the *Forward* urged Jewish workers not to "fall behind their Italian brothers" in militancy, and then quickly added "sisters," observing that Italian women were among the most militant of the strikers.

union recognition, extra pay for overtime, electric power for machines, abolition of tenement house work, and improved sanitary conditions in the shops. The significance of the last demand is indicated by the fact that Frances Perkins, executive secretary of the Committee of Safety (and in 1933 selected to be the first woman Secretary of Labor), described the workshops and factories of the clothing industry as "fire and death traps." She added, "The lessons of the Triangle fire have not been learned by the employers."[67]

The workers did not have sufficient funds to provide sustenance for themselves and their families during New York's bitter winter. They faced daily the savagery of strikebreakers, thugs, and police. One report read: "Blood flowed freely, skulls were cracked, ribs were broken, eyes blackened, teeth knocked out and many persons were otherwise wounded in a brutal assault on the garment strikers and pickets, not by the hired thugs and gangsters, but by the Cossacks, who comprise a part of the New York City police force." As in past strikes, the judiciary did what it could for the manufacturers, and when the strikers defied state Supreme Court injunctions outlawing peaceful picketing, hundreds of them were arrested.[68]

The strikers' militancy, combined with mounting support from the public and from the labor and socialist movements, forced individual firms to settle. On January 21 the Clothing Contractors' Association, speaking for itself and for the United Merchants' and Manufacturers' Association, agreed to enter into a conference with the UGW for the purpose of devising a means of settling the strike. At this point UGW President Thomas Rickert stepped into the situation and, as he had previously done in Chicago, disregarded both the strike leadership and the workers and accepted an agreement to end the strike. The strike leaders, bitter over this sellout, rejected the settlement. On the last day of February, the three largest associations of clothing manufacturers submitted a proposal for settling the strike, and Rickert again ignored both the strike committee and the strikers and promptly accepted the offer. Under this latest proposal, the workers were to return to their jobs immediately, pending an impartial investigation into the issue of reducing hours; the tailors were to obtain a general wage increase of $1 per week, with a proportional raise for pieceworkers; sanitary conditions would be somewhat improved; subcontracting would be abolished; and there was to be no discrimination in the reemployment of the strikers. Even though there was not a word about union recognition in any form, the UGW officially proclaimed the walkout at an end.[69]

With their struggle already weakened, the strikers were set back still further when the *Jewish Daily Forward* suddenly reversed itself, lined up with Rickert, and urged the strikers to accept the settlement and return to their jobs. Then, on March 7, Mayor Gaynor, acting with Rickert's express approval, ordered the police to disperse all remaining pickets. The strike faltered, and, on March 11, it ended. While the persistence and militancy of the workers produced a better agreement than either of the proposals accepted by Rickert—the workweek was reduced to fifty-three hours up to January, 1914, and to fifty-two hours thereafter for all but cutters, who were to enjoy a fifty-hour week to January, 1914, and not more than forty-eight hours thereafter, along with a small wage increase—it was the only one of the garment strikes in which the final settlement did not contain at least some form of union recognition.[70]

However, the strike did encourage a number of workers in the trade to organize, and the underhanded, strikebreaking tactics of the UGW officials were to have important repercussions. Three days after the strike ended, Isaac A. Hourwich wrote in the *New Review,* a left-wing Socialist monthly: "The work of building up a permanent organization of the tailors must now begin. If they are to profit by the lesson of this strike, they must rid themselves of boss rule (by Rickert and his henchmen)—if need be, by cutting loose from the national organization."[71] As a matter of fact the strike paved the way for 1914 rupture in the UGW and the resulting formation of the Amalgamated Clothing Workers of America, bringing with it a brighter future for all workers in the men's clothing trade, including women workers.

Meanwhile, the ladies' garment industry was the scene of a series of militant revolts, including a walkout by the white-goods workers— teenagers who worked in the worst garment shops at the most tedious tasks and who were described by one WTUL observer as "the youngest, the most ignorant, the poorest and most unskilled group of women workers who ever went on strike in this country."[72] Most of these young women earned a meager $20 a month for attaching ribbons to corset covers. On this wage, they barely survived. Sadie Aronovitch paid $3 a month for a sheet and the right to half a bed. Twenty-five cents a day went for food: coffee and a roll for breakfast, a sandwich for lunch, and a dinner served in a basement café. This left her $9 for clothing, amusements, and supplemental payments to her family.

Adding to the tribulations of their dreadful living standard were the daily abuses at the factory. An irate girl complained: "The foreman insults the girls and says hard bad words to them if they don't save the pins. Fines, fines, fines all the time. Ten cents if you lose a screw. You must make a hundred yards of ticking to pay for the screw and then you have nothing to eat. In my place five girls get $10 a week. All the others get between four and five."[73]

A group of two hundred workers had been organized into White Goods Workers' Union, Local No. 62, several years earlier by league members, but the union had failed to grow. However, the league was still involved with the small union through Rose Schneiderman, in her capacity as East Side organizer. Throughout 1911 and 1912, Schneiderman, Samuel Ellstein, whom the ILGWU had appointed as part-time manager of Local No. 62, and Samuel Shore of Philadelphia, who replaced him, asked the ILGWU and the New York WTUL Strike Council to fund a full-time organizer and support a general strike. The international office, faced with similar requests from small unions in the other women's trades, and unwilling to risk large sums of money on these trades while it was preoccupied with the struggle to maintain the cloakmakers' Protocol, refused.[74] The league, on the other hand, paid Rose Schneiderman to devote herself exclusively to the organization of the white-goods trade; however, the Strike Council was reluctant to support a move for a general strike, despite Schneiderman's argument that only a general strike could bring about widespread organization and give the union the members and the treasury it needed to enforce union wages and conditions. She also stressed that the women in the union, impressed by the general strikes in the waist and cloak trades and frightened by the Triangle fire, were agitating for a general strike.[75]

But the Strike Council remained adamant. Schneiderman was told that shop-by-shop organizing, while not as spectacular as a general strike, would produce better results in the long run. Women who joined the union could be thoroughly instructed in trade union principles and could learn to participate in union affairs. As Helen Marot put it, "The business of the League . . . is to bring women into places of responsibility in the organization of their trade." In a general strike, she maintained, men would dominate the situation and the "women would have no place and power and probably mostly no voice."[76]

The members of the league gradually relented in their opposition to a general strike, and finally the Strike Council pledged it modest financial support. Late in 1912 the international, too, authorized a general strike in the white-goods industry. On January 6, 1913, approximately seven thousand white-goods workers—nearly half the workers in the trade—answered the strike call. They asked for a 20 percent increase in wages; a flat fifty-four-hour week; abolition of child labor, of the fining system, and of subcontracting; recognition of the union; and a closed shop.[77]

On the eve of the strike, Shore, Schneiderman, and union leaders Lena Gasson, Florence Zuckerman, Mollie Lifschitz, and Mary Goff spent the night in a vigil in the ramshackle building that served as union headquarters, while WTUL members readied the designated meeting halls and prepared to organize the pickets under Schneiderman's supervision. By noon of the day of the strike, strikers had jammed the halls and eagerly paid the $1 initiation fee to join the union.[78]

Once on the picket lines, the strikers encountered the usual indignities and brutalities. The police carried out their usual indiscriminate arrests, and the employers' thugs beat up the young pickets. When WTUL members who accompanied strikers on picket duty issued public protests, the bosses adopted a new tactic. Into the battle came the gangsters' "molls." They filled their pocketbooks with stones, and when a skirmish began, they swung their loaded bags against the pickets' heads. They also carried concealed scissors, and at an opportune moment they would cut the strikers' long braided hair. In addition, they dogged the strikers' steps, keeping up a steady barrage of obscenities and urging them to join their ranks, with promises of easy money and good times.[79]

But the picket lines held fast, and as the fifteen-year-old girls walked the lines, they sang the "Song of the White Goods Workers" to buoy their spirits:

> At last all New York's White Goods toilers,
>   Just dropped the life of Slavery,
> And went to join the "Golden Soil"
>   Of the Union's Bravery.
>
> Now we're all doing our duties,
>   The spell of slavery to break,
> And the Boss's wife shall pawn the rubies
>   To get herself a Union Cake.
>
> We're getting beaten by policemen,
>   With their heavy clubs of hickory,
> But we'll fight as hard as we can
>   To win "Strong Union Victory."[80]

These plucky teenagers did not hesitate to tell their persecutors that they would fight back, and fight back they did. When one boss ordered a scab to hit a young picketer, the striking girl shrugged off the blow. "[I] gave the boss such a smash with my umbrella that it flew into two pieces. He was so surprised he fell down. . . . I was arrested, but I was so little and he so big and fat, the Judge said "Go on home," and he let me off. And from that day he [the boss] found out he was fighting with someone who wasn't afraid."[81]

The brutalities they faced taught the strikers many lessons. One picket told interviewers that when she had lived in Russia, she believed Americans had liberty, "but now I know the workers must fight for liberty in this country, too. It's the same fight everywhere. In Russia it is the Czar. In America it is the boss and the boss's money. Money is God in America."[82] The strike experience also awakened a great union spirit in the girls. One declared: "I think the union is like a mother and father and its children. I'd give my whole life for the union." Another said: "You know if we had to go back [to work] without the union I would die. My heart and soul is just with the union. I makes you feel so big instead of like a piece of dirt in the world." Still another confessed: "I eat two meals a day and wear my clothes until they fall off me, but I wouldn't be a scab."[83]

As in the great uprising of 1909–1910, prominent society women took up the strikers' cause—although not this time in association with the WTUL—marching on the picket lines, holding benefit functions, assisting in police court, posting bond, and generally focusing public attention on the strikers' plight and their bravery. These women developed an enormous admiration for the white-goods workers' courage and determination. Theodore Roosevelt paid a whirlwind visit to the strike scene and announced his shock over the working conditions and the treatment the "future mothers of America" had received during the strike. Fola LaFollette, daughter of the Progressive Senator from Wisconsin, picketed with the strikers, along with students from Barnard and Wellesley. Victor Berger, the Socialist congressman from Milwaukee, called for a federal investigation into clothing industry conditions. And New York City Mayor William Gaynor warned employers against the use of strong-arm methods. After league members and their striking colleagues had brought twenty-five cases of false arrest before Police Commissioner William Baker, Baker changed a number of officers and reprimanded others for their treatment of the young strikers.[84]

Although the union put the league in charge of strike publicity, the WTUL did not make the same concerted effort for the white-goods strikers as it had in the shirtwaist strike. The league contributed only $1,000 to the union's strike fund and raised only $6,000 in contributions. Also in contrast to its behavior during the waistmakers' strike, the league kept itself aloof from the union's leaders. The WTUL had come to view these leaders as almost as great enemies of the women strikers as the bosses were. "Before we are members of a union, we let our employers decide just what we are worth," Helen Marot declared. "No trading of bosses will solve our problems. The purpose of a strike is to get rid of bosses."[85]

The tendency of the league members to view the struggle as one that would lead only to a change of masters undoubtedly had an effect on the nature of the final settlement. The agreement specified improvements in working conditions: hours were reduced from sixty a week to fifty-two; charges for power and materials were abolished; subcontracting was ended in the association shops; there were pay increases for both salaried workers and pieceworkers, extra pay for overtime, and four annual legal holidays with pay. In addition, the contract established a wage floor: no worker was to work for less than $5 a week. While the manufacturers refused to agree to a closed shop, they did consent to negotiate with shop chairpersons whenever a disagreement occurred. The workers had hoped for a closed shop, and at one point during the six-week strike the workers had voted to continue the struggle until such an agreement could be reached. However, the association members would only accept the preferential union shop, in which union members would be given preference in hiring. While many girls raised violent objections to the settlement, claiming that it should have at least included a protocol agreement, the majority eventually voted, at an emotion-filled mass meeting, to accept the contract.[86]

The ten-member Executive Board of Local 62, elected directly after the strike settlement, included nine women. While Samuel Shore continued as manager, Mollie Lifschitz also stayed on as financial secretary, and at the request of the IGLWU officials, Rose Schneiderman served on the Grievance Board that was established by the settlement.[87]

The women of the Wrapper, Kimono, and House Dress Workers' Union, Local No. 41, walked out on January 8, 1913, and a week later, the leaders of Dress and Waistmakers' Union, Local 25, issued a call for their second general strike. The waistmakers' walkout, involving 25,000 waist- and dressmakers, ended three days later, on January 18, with the acceptance of a protocol for the industry that provided for new wage scales, a fifty-hour week, improved sanitary conditions, union recognition, and the establishment of arbitration boards to deal with workers' grievances.[88] The strike of the Wrapper, Kimono, and House Dress Workers' Union lasted longer. Amid desperate personal sacrifices, the women strikers refused to accept any agreement that did not provide for union recognition. On February 13, 1913, the manufacturers' association, feeling the pressure of public support for the strikers, signed a "Protocol of Peace" with Local No. 41.[89]

Two weeks later, the upsurge in the garment trade spread to Boston, where women workers in the children's dressmaking industry walked out, along with Boston's dress- and waistmakers. With the assistance of Boston's Women's Trade Union League, both strikes were won. On March 15, 1913, representatives of the manufacturers' association signed a protocol agreement with Local No. 49, the Boston dressmakers' union, and the ILGWU. In addition to the usual protocol terms, this accord included provisions for a $5 minimum wage, the establishment of a wage scale board to investigate costs and wages, and the employment of experts to decide on equitable wages.[90]

By the middle of March, 1913, every branch of the ladies' garment industry in the most important center of that industry—New York City—had contractual relations with the ILGWU that were based more or less on the cloakmakers' protocol of 1910, and similar agreements were being signed in Boston and other centers. By year's end, these trade agreements covered 90 percent of the international's membership in an industry in which women virtually monopolized the jobs. The wave of strikes that women had waged in the various branches of the women's garment industry had won thousands of new members for the union, and by 1913 the ILGWU ranked as the third-largest AFL affiliate, boasting ninety thousand members and the second largest enrollment of women. In fact, women constituted over 50 percent of the International's membership. Moreover, women were becoming active in the union leadership as well. Women strike veterans were traveling around the country as organizers, helping other women strikers, and awakening union consciousness in otherwise apathetic regions. Other militant women unionists accepted office in their locals, attended national conventions, assumed numerous speaking and publishing duties, led demonstrations, and sat on arbitration boards.

At the 1913 convention of the National Women's Trade Union League, Rose Schneiderman triumphantly cited the gains that workers in the women's clothing industry had made over the years since the uprising of the waistmakers. She pointed out that in September, 1909, just a few months before the shirtwaist strike, approximately 3,000 women belonged to unions in the garment trades. A year later, 16,716 women were enrolled as members. By September, 1913, New York State trade union records listed 63,872 women as members of New York City unions in the needle trades. Moreover, at least 60,000 women had gained a nine-hour day and a half holiday on Saturday. They earned at least 20 percent more than they had in the years before the general strikes, and they had established reasonably stable unions to which they could turn for assistance.

At the AFL convention in November, 1914, delegates appeared from two factions of the United Garment Workers, each claiming to represent the union. One faction, headed by Lager and Rickert, the UGW's top leaders, were enthusiastic advocates of Samuel Gompers' "pure and simple unionism." They ran the union on business principles and carried this concept so far that they made a private business of selling the union label, even to firms that operated with nonunion workers and ran their shops and factories as they pleased. Frowning upon strikes and depending on the union label for their bargaining strength, the UGW leaders placed their main reliance on workers who lived in small communities and worked in large factories manufacturing overalls.

The other faction of the UGW was made up of tailors and operators who worked in the large urban shops. A great majority of these workers were of immigrant origin, most frequently Yiddish-speaking eastern Europeans. These members of the UGW called for a new unionism that combined industrial unionism, class-consciousness, and socialism. They bitterly resented the corrupt, class-collaborationist policies of the national and local officials and their intimate relationship with the manufacturers. They also resented the fact that a minority of the membership—the overall makers—were being used by the autocratic leaders as a means of maintaining their domination of the union.

Ignoring the fact that the anti-Rickert faction at the 1914 convention represented the great majority of the men's clothing workers, the AFL's Credential Committee seated Rickert and his followers. The insurgents met in special convention in New York from December 25 to 28, 1914, and formed the "Amalgamated Clothing Workers of America." The union then represented forty thousand workers in the United States and Canada, a substantial number of whom were women.[91]

9

The Wobblies and
the Woman Worker

THE HEADLINE in the *Cincinnati Post* of January 9, 1905, fairly shrieked: "To SUPPLANT THE AFL, INTERNATIONAL LABOR ORGANIZATION LAUNCHED ALONG SOCIALISTIC AND INDUSTRIAL LINES." The story that followed described a "secret conference" held in Chicago for the purpose of launching a trade union movement that would consist of "one great industrial union, embracing all industries, founded upon the class struggle, and conducted in harmony with the recognition of the irrepressible conflict between the capitalist class and the working class."

The organization whose imminent birth was heralded on the *Post*'s front page was the Industrial Workers of the World (IWW). It came into being in 1905 because many progressive-minded elements in the labor and socialist movements were convinced that industrial unionism was superior to craft unionism in the struggle against the highly integrated organizations of employers; that it was impossible to convert the conservative American Federation of Labor into an organization that could achieve real benefits for the majority of workingmen and -women; and that existing industrially organized and radical organizations were ineffective in building a movement that would organize and unite the entire working class. In the eyes of these elements, there was a clear need for a new organization of labor that "would correspond to modern industrial conditions and through which they [the working people] might finally secure complete emancipation from wage slavery for all workers."[1]

The *Industrial Union Manifesto,* drawn up at the Chicago Conference of Industrial Unionists on January 2, 1905, stated the ideology of the new organization:

Universal economic evils afflicting the working class can be eradicated only by a universal working class movement. . . . A movement to fulfill these conditions must consist of one great industrial union embracing all industries—providing for craft autonomy locally, industrial autonomy internationally, and working class unity generally.

It must be founded on the class struggle, and its general administration must be conducted in harmony with the recognition of the irrepressible conflict between the capitalist and the working class.

It should be established as the economic organization of the working class without affiliation with any political party.

All workers who agreed with these principles were invited to meet in Chicago on June 27, 1905, "for the purpose of forming an organization of the working class along the lines worked out in the Manifesto."[2] An executive committee was appointed to help promote the meeting.

Although Mother Jones was one of the signers of the *Manifesto,* the executive committee was all-male. However, the founding convention of the IWW had twelve female delegates, including Mother Jones, Lucy Parsons (the widow of the Haymarket martyr), Emma F. Langdon of Denver Typographical Union No. 49, and Luella Twining, delegate of Federal Union No. 252 of the American Labor Union,[3] an industrial union movement active mainly in the West and one of the immediate predecessors of the IWW.[4] On Mother Jones' nomination, Langdon was appointed assistant secretary of the conference, and Twining served as presiding officer during the closing-day speeches. Parsons, who was named to the committee in charge of seeing that the minutes of the convention were printed, was the only one of the twelve who addressed the convention at some length. She spoke on June 29 and declared:

> I have taken the floor because no other woman has responded, and I feel that it would not be out of place for me to say in my poor way a few words about this movement.
>
> We, the women of this country, have no ballot, even if we wished to use it, and the only way that we can be represented is to take a man to represent us. You men have made such a mess of it in representing us that we have not much confidence in asking you; and I for one feel very backward in asking the men to represent me. We have no ballot, but we have our labor....
>
> We are the slaves of slaves. We are exploited more ruthlessly than men. Wherever wages are to be reduced, the capitalist class uses women to reduce them, and if there is anything that you men should do in the future, it is to organize the women.

Although Parsons mentioned the ballot, she made it clear as she continued that she opposed political action and saw the solution for labor solely through economic action.

> I believe that if every man and every woman who works, or who toils in the mines, the mills, the workshops, the fields, the factories, and the farms in our broad America should decide in their minds that they shall have that which of right belongs to them, and that no idler shall live upon their toil,

and when your new organization, your economic organization, shall declare as man to man and woman to woman, as brothers and sisters, that you are determined that you will possess these things, then there is no army that is large enough to overcome you, for you yourselves constitute the army.

Later in the convention Parsons spoke again, advocating revolutionary strikes such as were being waged that year by the Russian workers, who had already initiated the first Russian revolution by a general strike. "You men and women," Lucy Parsons told the delegates, "should be imbued with the spirit that is now displayed in far-off Russia and far-off Siberia, where we thought the spark of manhood and womanhood had been crushed out of them. Let us take example from them." Parsons also made a rousing speech at the convention's conclusion, urging the delegates to move on to the industrial areas of the nation, organizing the entire working class along the lines of industrial unionism, and to pay special attention to the long-neglected and especially exploited workingwomen.[5]

In comparison with the AFL, the IWW convention represented some important advances for women. It was not until 1907 that a woman (Agnes Nestor of the International Glove Workers' Union) presided over an AFL convention.[6] And the IWW motto, "An Injury to One Is the Concern of All" (a modification of the Knights of Labor slogan, "An Injury to One Is an Injury to All"), and the emphasis in the constitution barring exclusion of the unskilled—a very large section of the American working class—held out a real promise for workingwomen. In a statement that was to be restated and reprinted throughout the IWW's history, the Literature and Press Committee reported "to all working people" that "in this industrial union there is room for and no bar against any worker on account of race, sex, creed, or color, and an earnest invitation is extended to every worker to enroll him or herself a member of this union."[7]

In content this statement differs little from some of the AFL's utterances. The IWW, however, backed up its statement with concrete action. Initiation fees and dues were kept very low in order to make membership more readily available to the masses of low-paid, unskilled workers. During the debate, it was made clear that the delegates had the underpaid female workers very much in mind when they adopted this policy. One delegate argued for low initiation fees and dues by stating that they were necessary because "it is the women . . . that are the lowest paid," and noted that "there are women who are working for $3.60 a week—grown women!"[8]

The second convention lowered dues for women members even further, while maintaining the existing rates for men. While it could be argued that this was demeaning to the female sex, Paul Brissenden, one of the earliest historians of the IWW, was closer to the truth when he called the action evidence that the IWW favored feminine participation and was determined not to discriminate against women workers as the AFL and other labor organizations had done.[9]

At this same convention a heated debate took place over the appropriate term to be used in addressing general union meetings. The phrase "fellow worker" was finally agreed upon, as it "may be considered of the neuter gender, and applied to the masculine or feminine, as you chose, and . . . the committee deems that so far as the male members of the organization are concerned, they will never be lacking at any time in courtesy toward a lady."[10]

By setting forth their attitude toward workingwomen early, the founders of the new industrial union movement cleared the way for women to play an active role in it. Lillian Forberg, who had been a delegate to the first convention, was a member of Chicago's General Advisory Board as well as of the local Executive Board, and was cited for her activity as agitator and organizer among Chicago's textile workers. The IWW also cited a Mrs. Orr as being an extremely able secretary of Chicago Local No. 85.[11]

In 1909 the General Executive Board voted Ester Niemien "voluntary organizer's credentials" and assured that her expenses would be paid. The Portland IWW branch reported: "We have placed a lady organizer on the list (Miss Nina Wood) and believe she is going to do very effective work."[12] And in 1909, too, Elizabeth Gurley Flynn, the "rebel girl" of Joe Hill's song and the outstanding woman in the history of the IWW,* became a member of the General Executive Board, a position no woman had ever occupied in the AFL, or its successor organization, the AFL-CIO until 1980.[13] Thus, early in its history, the IWW employed women as organizers and union officials and soon accorded them representation in the highest body of the organization.

Elizabeth Gurley Flynn, born in 1890, was named after the family doctor, Elizabeth Kent. Annie Gurley Flynn, Elizabeth's mother, was an advocate of equal rights for women, and it was considered somewhat scandalous that she had her four children delivered and cared for by women physicians. She had been a member of the Knights of Labor in Concord, New Hampshire, before her marriage and continued to work as a tailoress after her marriage, helping to support the family. Tom Flynn, Elizabeth's father, was an Irish rebel who, although he was a competent engineer, was so absorbed in socialist pursuits that he kept losing jobs. As Elizabeth grew up, she met Irish revolutionists, feminists, socialists, and anarchists. One of her teachers, she wrote, instructed her

---

*Joe Hill, whose full name was Joseph Hillstrom, was an immigrant from Sweden and the most famous of the IWW songwriters. He wrote "The Rebel Girl" and dedicated it to Elizabeth Gurley Flynn while he was in a Utah prison awaiting execution on a murder charge. Joe Hill was executed in 1915.

so thoroughly in the Bill of Rights that "I have been defending it ever since."

Elizabeth won a gold medal in her grammar school debating society for urging that women should have the vote. By the age of fifteen she was insisting in public speeches that full freedom for women was impossible under capitalism and that the government should undertake financial support for all children, so that women could bear them without becoming dependent on men. Her maiden public speech, delivered on January 31, 1906, at the Harlem Socialist Club, was entitled "What Socialism Will Do for Women." Flynn discussed how socialism would bring about the abolition of prostitution, the economic independence of women, the social care of children, and the right of all women to an education, to participate in government, and to enter the arts, sciences, and professions.[14]

Flynn was arrested for the first time at sixteen, along with her father, for blocking traffic and speaking without a permit. At the trial her lawyer proclaimed her the "coming Socialist woman orator of America." Pardoned, she immediately returned to the soapbox.

Elizabeth Gurley Flynn joined the IWW in 1906 as a member of the mixed Local No. 179 in New York City. As a woman and a minor, she was exempt from the otherwise strictly enforced requirement that membership was for wage laborers only. Her first strike experience was during the summer of 1907 with the Bridgeport (Connecticut) Tube Mill workers. In that year, George B. McClellan, mayor of New York City, had boasted in describing his constituency: "There are Russian Socialists and Jewish Socialists and German Socialists. But, thank God! there are no Irish Socialists!" Thereupon James Connolly,* Tom Flynn, his daughters, Elizabeth and Kathie, and others formed the Irish Socialist Federation. Annie Gurley Flynn sewed a large green and white banner with the Irish slogan "Fag an Bealach" (Clear the Way) in a field of harps and shamrocks. In Connolly's view, the federation was formed not out of national sentiment but in estimation of the needs of a socialist movement growing in a cosmopolitan environment.[15]

Fifteen-year-old Kathie Flynn became secretary of the Irish Socialist Federation, and Elizabeth left New York to barnstorm the country for the IWW. The *Industrial Union Bulletin* wrote about a speech she delivered in Duluth, Minnesota, in November, 1907: "Elizabeth Gurley Flynn is nothing if not in earnest. Socialist fervor seems to emanate from her expressive eyes, and even from her red dress. She is a girl with a 'mission', with a big 'M.'" The Los Angeles *Times*, under the heading, "Most

---

*James Connolly, who was later martyred during the Easter uprising in 1916 in Ireland, was then living in New York, publishing the *Harp* to publicize the struggle for Irish freedom and organizing on the docks for the IWW. It was through Connolly that Elizabeth Gurley Flynn learned of the work of the IWW.

Bloodthirsty of Agitators are the She-Dogs of Anarchy," wrote of her speech in that city:

> E. G. Flynn is said to be only 17, but her power of speech has won her spellbound audiences all over the eastern cities and now the same thing is operating in the west. Never has she advised violence. But the teachings of the young girl are so intensely radical, and her demand for action so vehement that she is assured of a royal welcome from any audience of extremists.[16]

Gurley, as she was called, soon discovered that IWW members took seriously the admonition that all male members "will never be lacking at any time in courtesy toward a lady." She said she felt as safe among them "as in God's pocket."[17]

The Wobblies, as IWW members were known, were constantly seeking to convince women to join Flynn and carry the message of industrial unionism to the exploited workers. IWW publications carried frequent advertisements for "men and women to actually work in the industries and there organize the slaves."[18] In the main, the Wobblies dismissed the argument that women workers were impossible to organize, attributing their distrust for unionism entirely to their bad experience with the AFL. One IWW woman organizer blamed lack of agitation for the failure to organize women sufficiently. She not only called upon the IWW male organizers to make a special effort to recruit women, but also urged women to "organize themselves with our brothers into one great wage earners' army in the industrial field."[19]

In contrast to almost every other labor organization so far in American history, the IWW made an active effort to organize the Chinese, Japanese, and Mexican workers. In a leaflet entitled *To Colored Workingmen and Women* the IWW pointed out: "If you are a wage worker, you are welcome in the IWW halls, no matter what your color. By this you may see that the IWW is not a white man's union, not a black man's union, not a red or yellow man's union, but a working man's union. All the working class in one big union." Even in the deepest South, the IWW raised the banner of "No Race, No Creed, No Color" and united black and white workers in a common struggle on the basis of complete equality—without once establishing a Jim Crow local in the process.[20]

Wobbly writers pointed to the particular degradation of women, with their rock-bottom wage scales, and emphasized that this required "a special effort to organize the women workers." They also noted the restrictionist policies of the AFL, pointing out that each craft union "has its own means of limiting membership, by apprenticeship systems, initiation fees, closed books, and age, color, and even sex restrictions." To be sure, in time of strikes, the AFL unions did not "fail to appeal to the women for support—though when these women appeal for admittance on the same basis as men, they are told 'nothing doing.'" Thus, when the

AFL Drivers' Union of Stockton, California, went on strike, the laundry women refused to handle any scab work, and the AFL union won its demands. But later, when the girls struck for an eight-hour day and higher wages, "the men who belonged to the Drivers' Union all stayed on the job, scabbing on the girls, whose wages were $5.75 per week, scarcely enough to exist on." One had but to contrast this with the IWW policy and practice, the Wobbly writers said, to see the tremendous difference.[21]

The IWW repeatedly emphasized that women were in industrial life to stay: "They cannot be driven back to the home. . . . They are part of the army of labor." There was only one thing to be done: "Organize them with the men, just as they work with the men." In the IWW's concept, women were not personally responsible for any damaging effect their presence might have on wages and working conditions. Even more than men, they were victims of capitalist exploitation, "slaves" in the industrial system, and their exploited condition made their unionization even more vital. The IWW conceded that there were special problems in organizing women workers, but it rejected the old craft union cry that "women won't organize and strike" as merely an excuse for doing nothing or for barring women from the labor movement. The answer was "to encourage them wherever possible by granting them equal opportunities, duties, and privileges, even to the holding of executive office."

Male workers were urged: "Don't fight against woman labor; women find it necessary to work. They do not work because they enjoy making some corporation 'rich beyond the dreams of avarice!' They work because they have got to make a living." The advice continued: "Do not blame the women; blame the system. And do not be content with that! Educate, agitate, and organize for the purpose of improving conditions and changing the system."[22]

Yet the Wobblies also contradicted themselves on the question of women workers. If healthy men were jobless while women and children worked, the boss, not the women, should be blamed for the situation; but the solution was to organize the men and put the women where they belong, in the home.[23] But what about the assertion that women were in industry to stay? This statement, they said, meant only that young, unmarried women would always enter industry, providing a substantial, if shifting, element in the labor force. Of course they should be organized, for "the factory girl of today is the helpful and encouraging wife of the union man of tomorrow." The case of the married woman was entirely different. While it might be justifiable, even desirable, for the young, unattached female to enter the labor market, the Wobblies viewed with horror the thought of woman "leaving her home and children unprotected and uncared for during the working hours." (They did not appear to have considered any solution in the form of day care centers for children.) It was important, then, that they be eliminated from the work force.[24]

This was too much for one female member, who, signing herself "A Woman Toiler," wrote to the IWW press:

> Fellow Worker Man Toiler: You say you want us girls to keep out of the factory and mill so you can get more pay, then you can marry some of us and give us a decent home. Now, that is just what we are trying to escape; being obliged to marry you for a home. And aren't you a little inconsistent? You tell us to get into the IWW, an organization for wage workers only. We haven't heard of any Household Drudge's Union, not even in the IWW. Going from the factory back into the home means only a change in the form of servitude, a change for the worse for the woman. The best thing that ever happened to woman was when she was compelled to leave the narrow limits of the home and enter into the industrial life of the world. This is the only road to our freedom, and to BE FREE there is not anything to be desired more than that. . . . So we will stay in the factory, mill, or store and organize with you in the IWW for ownership of the industries, so we can provide ourselves with decent homes, then if we marry you, it will be because we love you so well we can't get along without you, and not to give you a chance to pay our bills, like we do now.[25]

Wherever possible, wives who were not directly involved in industry were organized into women's auxiliaries. Their existence appears to go back as far as 1906, when the *Industrial Worker* announced the formation of a women's labor auxiliary union in Muskogee, Oklahoma, and praised the work of the auxiliary for its efforts in defense of Moyer, Haywood, and Pettibone.* In addition, IWW agitators, in spite of considerable male opposition, especially among the newer immigrants, encouraged strikers' wives to attend strike meetings and to march on the picket lines. Thus involved, the women would be less inclined to call for a return to work.[26]

But the IWW never resolved the question of whether or not the wives of workers were eligible for membership. In 1908 a San Francisco housewife asked: "(1) Is a married woman of the working class a chattel slave or a wage slave? (2) Has she the right to belong to a mixed local of the IWW?"

She asked these questions, she continued, "because objection has been raised by some members of the Denver local to the effect that a married woman, a housekeeper, has no right to belong to a working-man's organization." Some Wobblies, she complained, even asserted

---

*The Moyer, Haywood, Pettibone case, one of the worst frameups in American history, flowed from the arrest of the three men, all active in both the Western Federation of Miners and the IWW, on a charge of murder of Frank Steunenberg, former governor of Idaho, on December 30, 1905. They were acquitted.

that these women "have no grievance against the capitalist class, therefore we have no place in the union. Our grievance is against our husbands, if we are dissatisfied with our condition." With this, the writer
disagreed vehemently:

> I believe the married woman of the working class is no parasite or exploiter.
> She is a social producer. In order to sustain herself, she has to sell her labor
> power, either in the factory, directly to the capitalist, or at home, indirectly,
> by serving the wage slave, her husband, thus keeping him in working condi-
> tion through cooking, washing, and general housekeeping.
>
> For being a mother and a housekeeper are two different functions. One is
> her maternal, and the other is her industrial function in society. I believe the
> wage slave's wife has got a right to belong to a mixed local. I think it should
> be encouraging for working men to see women enter their ranks and, shoul-
> der to shoulder, fight for economic freedom.
>
> Civilization denies us the right of expressing our political opinion at the
> ballot box. Will the economic organization, the IWW our only hope, exclude
> us and deny us the right to record our discontent against the capitalist sys-
> tem?

The editor replied that he could see no reason why a married woman
could not belong to a mixed local, but he had no idea what would become of the housewives when the mixed local developed enough members in the various industries to divide into industrial unions: "It is a
matter to which the next convention will give attention."[27] The next
convention, however, ignored the issue.

In some IWW circles, wives were regarded as the "ball and chain." In
the West, IWW literature proclaimed that the migratory worker, usually
a young, unmarried male, was "the finest specimen of American manhood . . . the leaven of the revolutionary labor movement," around
whom would be built a militant nucleus for revolutionary industrial
unionism. "The nomadic worker of the west embodies the very spirit of
the IWW," a writer rhapsodized in *Solidarity*. "Unlike the factory slave
of the Atlantic seaboard and the central states, he is most emphatically
not 'afraid of his job'. No wife and family cumber him. The worker of
the east, oppressed by the fear of want for wife and babies, dare not
venture much."

This contradictory attitude toward wives and children convinced
some observers that there were two IWWs—one in the West and one in
the East. To some extent, this was true. The average Western member of
the IWW was younger than his Eastern counterpart. He was likely to be
unmarried, or at least without binding family ties. The Western members were born in the United States, for the most part, while the Eastern
members were mostly foreign-born. Those Westerners who were of foreign birth were likely to have preserved old-country ties and characteristics. The Westerners were mainly men, while women were an important

element among the semiskilled and unskilled factory workers of the East.[28]

But the similarities were greater than the differences, and the attitude expressed about wives and children in IWW literature more frequently emphasized the importance of their role in helping to build the industrial union movement than the "ball and chain" concept. As a matter of fact, the same paper might contain both notions in consecutive issues. Thus, the *Industrial Worker,* which frequently extolled the migratory worker because he was free of family ties, also carried articles stressing the point that the low wages and wandering life style migrant workers had to endure robbed them of a normal family life: "The workers as a class are homeless. Part of the men are forced into a migratory life, going from place to place in search of work and are 'hoboes'; while the women, those who should be the wives of the hoboes are slaving in the mills or are in the [red light] district."[29]

The plight of the prostitute was a favorite theme of the IWW press. A "girl out of work" summed up the Wobbly theory on this social problem: "I'm out upon the town, because my fact'ry has shut down. In times like this, in this here land, it seems there ain't no real demand for girls except in this one trade." Unmarried women were on the street because they did not earn enough and because men did not make enough money to put them into the home as wives. *Solidarity,* the IWW's official organ on the East Coast, proclaimed that "Poverty is the Principal Cause, Direct and Indirect, of Prostitution." It concluded with a plea for unionization: "Our sisters and daughters have to sell their bodies in order to live—why? Because you and your likes didn't organize so you could make enough to place the woman where she belongs—in the home."[30]

"Employment Agencies Promote White Slave Traffic," headlined the *Industrial Worker,* as it angrily pointed out that even girls seeking honest work ran the risk of falling into vice through procurers posing as employment agencies. Charitable institutions, like the YWCA, also came under fire for making it possible for some women to survive on inadequate wages and thereby depressing pay scales for the rest. Then there were what the Wobblies termed "Sex-Subsidized Industries," which encouraged prostitution by paying men too little to support wives. Some turned to prostitutes, and women who could have been workers' wives were forced into prostitution to support themselves. "It is plain every industry is receiving a subsidy from either repression of sexual desires or their expression for commercial purposes."[31] The editor of the *Industrial Worker* came up with an intriguing and rather original suggestion: "For women I would indeed set a minimum wage. Roughly it would be this: go on the street and inquire the maximum earnings of the white slaves, then say to the boss: 'If this is the worth of a woman's body in iniquity, you must pay it for the use of that body in your shop.' "[32]

In all the considerable IWW literature relating to marriage and the family, there is little criticism of the traditional institution of marriage. Occasionally, the Wobbly press printed attacks on monogamous marriage, usually in the form of reprints from socialist journals, like George Bernard Shaw's "The Marriage Mart," but IWW papers rarely criticized marriage themselves or offered alternatives to it. It would appear that the IWW's image of a worker's utopia included a family in which the male worker was so well paid that he could return at night to the embrace of his wife and children and a well-cared-for home. Even the farm migrant received literature depicting him as wooing and winning the farmer's daughter and building a respectable family life—all through the power of industrial unionism.[33]

Viewing large families as providing "more slaves for the boss," the IWW endorsed birth control within marriage and condemned the attacks on the planned parenthood movement. "Ignorance and large families go hand in hand," the *Industrial Worker* explained. "Many women are 'stuffed' with the 'dope' that it is God's will to have all the children possible. If God wants them, he should have sense enough to tell them where to find employment and where to decently live."[34] It discussed and praised the labor organizations in Sweden, which disseminated birth control information among the workers, and it gave continuous support to the efforts of Margaret Sanger, the birth control pioneer, who was both a Socialist and an active supporter of the IWW in several key strikes.*[35] Gurley Flynn tells of an incident in the Paterson strike that illustrates the IWW attitude and the reaction of workingwomen and the wives of workers:

> We had a women's meeting, too, in Paterson at which Haywood, Tresca, and I spoke.... Tresca made some remarks about shorter hours, people being less tired, having more time to spend together and jokingly he said: "More babies." The audience of tired working wives did not cheer this suggestion. "No, Carlo," interrupted Haywood, "we believe in birth control... fewer babies well cared for." The women started to laugh and applaud.[36]

The attitude of major Wobbly figures toward marriage is revealing. Most IWW leaders led at least outwardly respectable lives. "Big Bill" Haywood was married, and although he and his wife, Nevada Jane, were estranged after 1903, Haywood provided materially for her until her death in 1920. Although he had a succession of love affairs, he managed

*IWW leaders, however, did not agree with Margaret Sanger as she became more and more fixed in her idea that birth control information was the key to all social problems. Flynn argued with her that while her work was very important, economic exploitation and not large families was the fundamental cause of poverty. But Sanger did not agree. (See Noel B. Gerson, *The Crusader* [New York, 1971], pp. 187–88.) However, for an IWW view closer to the Sanger position, see "Birth Control Economics," *Solidarity*, July 29, 1916.

to keep them from both his enemies and the public. During the last month of his life, Haywood legally married the Russian woman who had been his companion during his final years in the Soviet Union.[37]

Vincent St. John was also married, as was Ralph Chaplin, apparently very happily.[38] Joe Hill, according to his own testimony, died "for a woman's honor." He refused to reveal the name of the married woman he cited as his alibi the night of the robbery and murder for which he was convicted. He insisted that he had received his wound in a dispute with her husband, and that concern for her reputation kept him from disclosing her name.[39] Whatever one may think of Hill's judgment, it was in keeping with his great interest in enrolling women in the industrial union movement and his hope to "establish a kind of social good fellowship between the male and female workers." His songs frequently referred to the need to organize women workers "in the OBU (One Big Union)," as in the case of "What We Want":

> We want all the workers in the world to organize
> Into one great big union grand....
> We want the sailor and the tailor and the lumberjacks.
> And all the cooks and laundry girls,
> We want the guy who dives for pearls,
> The pretty maid that's making curls....
> We want the tinner and the skinner and the chambermaid....
> And all the factory girls and clerks,
> Yes, we want everyone that works,
> In one union grand.[40]

In January, 1908, during a speaking tour, Elizabeth Gurley Flynn met and fell in love with Jack Archibald Jones, a Wobbly organizer from Bovey, Minnesota. Their married life was brief and hectic: two years and three months, and most of that time they saw little of each other. Flynn was busy organizing and was arrested several times while agitating for free speech in Missoula, Montana, and Spokane. Jones, too, was in jail during part of the marriage.

The couple had two children. The first was born prematurely and died within a few hours—probably as a result of the harsh conditions Flynn had to endure while pregnant in a Spokane jail. When she became pregnant again, Jones demanded that she settle down to domesticity. This might have been a reasonable enough demand to make of a wife at that time, but it came with poor grace from a husband who had not shown enough marital concern previously to visit his wife in jail or to attend her two trials during this period. At any rate, by the time the second child was born, Flynn had had enough of Jones and the couple separated permanently. She later explained that continuing the marriage to Jones would have restricted her ambitions: "I wanted to speak and write, to travel, to meet people, to see places, to organize for the IWW. I saw no reason why I, as a woman, should give up my work for his. I knew by now I could make more of a contribution to the labor movement than he could. . . . But it wasn't easy in 1910."

However, it was made easier by her mother's assistance, for Annie raised Elizabeth's son while she resumed her speaking career. Although she did not remain on close terms with Jones, who pursued an eccentric political career, she was a character witness for him when his second wife died in an accident during their honeymoon. "He never killed *me,*" Flynn told questioners, "and he had plenty of provocation!"

The real love of Elizabeth Gurley Flynn's life was Carlo Tresca, whom she met when they worked together during the 1912 Lawrence strike. Tresca was a prominent anarchist and editor of the newspapers *Il Proletario* and *Il Martello.* "He was then a tall, slender, handsome man in his mid-thirties and I was deeply in love with him," Flynn recalled. They lived together for thirteen tempestuous years, although Flynn and Jones were not officially divorced until 1920. "This," she wrote, "was according to our code at that time—not to remain with someone you did not love, but to honestly and openly avow a real attachment."[41]

A relentless "jawsmith" (as IWW speakers and organizers were called), a tireless fund raiser, and a frequent contributor to the IWW and Socialist press, Elizabeth Gurley Flynn, a Wobbly paper concluded, "was indefatigable as a worker for the cause" throughout her long and remarkably useful life.[42]

Charming, eloquent, and beautiful, Flynn was loved by workers wherever she went. The Lawrence strikers were moved to sing in 1912:

> In the old picket line, in the old picket line,
> We'll put Mr. Lowe* in overalls
> And swear off drinking wine,
> Then Gurley Flynn will be the boss,
> Oh, gee, won't this be fine
> The strikers will wear diamonds in the good
> old picket line.[43]

Flynn tried to change some of the Wobbly attitudes and practices toward women, but she did accept their basic tenet that the problems of women could not be separated from those of the working class. She also shared the IWW's hostility toward socially prominent women becoming involved in strikes of working-class women. "So far as the Mrs. Belmonts and Miss Morgans from their high pedestal mix in labor battles and respectabilize them, so far do they weaken the revolutionary fibre of the workers."[44] Flynn emphasized that " 'The queen of the parlor' has no

*Arthur Lowe was manager of the Lancaster Mills Corporation and one of its largest stockholders.

interest in common with 'the maid of the kitchen,' the wife of the department store owner shows no sisterly concern for the 17-year-old girl
who finds prostitution the only door to avoid becoming a $5-a-week
clerk."[45] She did not formally oppose the woman suffrage movement
and insisted that women had every right to vote. She even had praise for
the militancy of Socialist women in the struggle for the vote.* But like
the IWW as a whole, Flynn considered the vote largely irrelevant and of
little importance to working-class women. The "vote will not free
women," she insisted, advising them to "find their power at the point of
production where they work." She considered the woman suffrage
movement dominated by "rich faddists," and complained that working-
class women were "made the tail of a suffrage kite in the hands of
women of the very class driving the girls to lives of misery and shame."[46]
Charles Ashleigh justified IWW opposition to woman suffrage by the
curious argument that even though middle-class women were not the
equals of men of their class, working-class women were. Therefore, they
already had what middle-class women hoped to achieve by the vote:

> The woman wage-worker and the wife of the wage-worker are the victims of
> industrial exploitation, not of suffrage inequality. They are robbed in the
> mill, factory or shop, where they, or their breadwinners, work. The woman
> worker lives by the same method as the male worker; by the sale of her
> labor-power to the boss. She is robbed, as the male worker is robbed, by the
> master appropriating the large portion of the product of her labor. She is
> robbed WHERE the male worker is robbed; on the INDUSTRIAL FIELD. She
> should fight for better conditions WHERE the most enlightened of the male
> workers, in ever-increasing numbers, are fighting: on the INDUSTRIAL FIELD.
> The woman wage-worker is not concerned in a sex war; she is concerned
> in a CLASS WAR. The boss enslaves men, women and children in the same way:
> by the exploitation of their labor power. On the industrial field, the woman
> worker has the same power as the man: she has the power of WITHDRAWING
> HER LABOR-POWER FROM INDUSTRY.[47]

There is no evidence that any Wobbly theoretician bothered to ask
workingwomen if they needed the vote to end their subordinate position
in society or if they felt they enjoyed the same economic power as male
workers. They certainly did not receive equal pay for equal work or
share opportunities to rise into the better-paying jobs. In short, it was a
vast oversimplification to say that women workers had the same eco-

*Most Wobblies especially admired the militant tactics and spirit of women suffragists in
England who went to jail for their principles and refused an offer of pardon if it
compromised their struggle. "They were just like the IWW boys," exulted *Solidarity*, (Dec.
2, 9, 1911). In 1916, the *Industrial Worker* declared that American suffragists were using
direct-action tactics in their fight for the ballot, and wondered why "if the women are to
use direct action, they do not use it to get for themselves something of value" (July 15,
1916).

nomic power as men to redress their grievances, and to conclude that they therefore did not need any political power.

Flynn did not accept the argument that under IWW leadership women were equal to men inside the class struggle. On the contrary, she emphasized that the IWW should become more sensitive to women's needs, make demands based on these needs, recruit more women into the organization, and eradicate the male chauvinism that prevented women from active participation. On this past point, she was quite specific. "I know a local," she wrote, "where members forbid their wives speaking to an IWW woman, 'because they'd get queer ideas'! I heard a member forbid his wife, who had worked nine hours in a mill, from coming to a meeting, 'because she'd do better to clean the house'! When I suggested an able woman as secretary of a local, several men said, 'Oh, that's a man's job! She couldn't throw a drunk out!'" Or she would describe the problem she faced when she gave lectures about birth control:

> I am besieged by women for information on this subject, and this opens up another avenue of assault upon the system, yet whenever the subject is selected by a local it is always amazing how few IWW workers bring their women folk to the meeting. It is time they realized that the IWW stands for a larger program than more wages and shorter hours, and the industrial freedom we all aspire to will be the foundation upon which a different world for men and women will be reached.

Even among revolutionists in the IWW, she heard the charge that women were "backward," "impossible to organize," "over-emotional, prone to take advantage of their sex, eager to marry and then submerged in a family, are intensely selfish for 'me and mine,' lack a sense of solidarity, are slaves to style and disinclined to serious and continuous study...."

> Nearly every charge could be made against some men and does not apply to all women; yet it unfortunately fits many women for obvious reasons. It is well to remember that we are dealing with the sex that have been denied all social rights since early primitive times, segregated to domestic life up to a comparatively recent date, and denied access to institutions of learning up to a half a century ago. Religion, home and child-bearing were their prescribed spheres. Marriage was their career and to be an old maid a lifelong disgrace. Their right to life depended on their sex attraction and the hideous inroads upon the moral integrity of women, produced by economic dependence, are deep and subtle. Loveless marriages, household drudgery, acceptance of loathsome familiarities, unwelcome child-bearing, were and are far more general than admitted by moralists, and have marred the mind, body, and spirit of women.

She therefore insisted that the IWW must "adapt our propaganda to the special needs of women" and that special kinds of organization suited to the conditions of women's lives had to be developed if the IWW were to have lasting success in organizing women workers. Unfortunately, "some of our male members are prone to underestimate this vital need and assert that the principles of the IWW are alike for all, which we grant with certain reservations." IWW literature had to be translated for foreigners, simplified for illiterates, and published with technical phrases for various industrial groups. The Western locals called for a paper written in the style "peculiar to their district." Similarly, IWW literature and organizing tactics had to be specially directed toward women, "based on their mental attitudes adapted to their environment and the problems it creates."[48] Nothing, however, came of this suggestion, or from a proposal by Frank Little in 1916 that "a special literature be created for women workers, that space for articles concerning female workers be provided in our papers, and that a league for women, with lecturers, be formed to carry on a special agitation for the benefit of women."*[49]

In December, 1914, Joe Hill wrote that in the West, the IWW had "created a kind of one-legged, freakish animal of a union" because of its predominantly male membership. He recommended that the IWW's female organizers be used "*exclusively* for building up of a strong organization among the female workers."[50] Although *Solidarity* featured this letter and endorsed the suggestion, little was done to put it into effect.[51] When female organizers, acting more or less on their own, did organize women workers, they were not enthusiastically welcomed by the Western Wobblies and even had to combat male chauvinism among IWW leaders, in addition to the opposition of employers.

The experience of Jane Street, a radical Colorado domestic worker, founder and secretary of Denver's Domestic Workers' Industrial Union, IWW, Local No. 113, illustrates this last point. She was determined to build a union of revolutionary housemaids who "don't believe in mistresses or servants. They would do away with caste altogether. They believe in removing the degradation from domestic service by teaching their employers to look upon the hands that feed them and wash for them, and scrub for them with respect or fear and humility."[52] By March 19, 1916, after three months of intensive organizing, she had succeeded in

---

*This was not the first time such a proposal had been put to the IWW. The August 3, 1907, issue of the *Industrial Union Bulletin* contained an article by Sophie Beldner that said, "Women are a little behind, and a greater amount of energy is needed to call them to action." She proposed that "a literature fund be established in one of the industrial centers where there are enough active women to take the initiative to carry out this plan." In the meantime, IWW women would contribute articles to the *Bulletin* "bearing on the question of industrial unionism and working class emancipation," and the best articles would be published "in leaflet form with the sanction of the general administration of the IWW. That, in my opinion, would be the only means by which we could reach the women in factory and at home, and make out of them a powerful factor in the onward march of the working class."

gathering enough maids to hold a secret mass meeting, where they spoke of their grievances and formulated the demands they would work for in the future: $12 a week, no work on Sundays, shorter hours, and better treatment.

Domestic servants, an isolated and diverse group, could not use the traditional strike techniques. To meet their particular needs, Street developed a new organizing technique, which she outlined in a letter to Mrs. Elmer F. Buse, a "fellow worker" who was planning to organize domestics in Tulsa. (Buse never received the letter, since it was intercepted by the Post Office before it reached its destination and was forwarded to the Justice Department during the government's campaign to prosecute the IWW out of existence.)[53] Street wrote:

> My method was very tedious. I worked at housework for three months, collecting names all the while. When I was off a job I rented a room and put an ad in the paper for a housemaid. Sometimes I used a box number and sometimes I used my address. The ad was worded something like this, "Wanted, Housemaid for private family, $30, eight hours daily."
>
> I would write them letters afterwards and have them call and see me. If they came direct, I would usually have another ad in the same paper, advertising for a situation and using my telephone number. I would have enough answers to supply the applicants. Sometimes I would engage myself to as many as 25 jobs in one day, promising to call the next day to everyone that phoned. I would collect the information secured in this way. If any girl wanted any of the jobs, she could go out and say they called her up the day before.
>
> I secured 300 names in this way. I had never mentioned the IWW to any of them, for I expected them to be prejudiced, which did not prove the case. I picked out 100 of the most promising of the names and sent them invitations to attend a meeting. There were about thirty-five who came. Thirteen of the thirty-five signed the application for a charter. Thirteen out of three hundred in three months time! So don't get discouraged.

At the end of a year, Street had succeeded in personally interviewing about 1,500 or 2,000 women, "telling them about the IWW and making them more rebellious, and placing probably over 1,000 in jobs." However, only 155 had signed up with the IWW, "only about 83 of whom we can actually call members." Since a great many women left town or simply drifted away, it was impossible to develop a larger, more permanent membership. Nevertheless, the *Denver Post* published cartoons depicting Wobbly maids as demanding and obtaining better conditions from recalcitrant employers.

The secret of the domestic union's strength lay not in the number of its members but in the operation of its employment office. The new union planned to build a card file of all the jobs for domestic workers in Denver and to make this information available to anyone looking for domestic work. By acting as its own employment bureau it would drive the "sharks"—employment agencies that thrived on exploiting workers—out of business. It would also make it impossible for recalcitrant employers to get help unless they met the union's demands. And it would start a union boardinghouse that would serve as an organizing center, where women could stay and leave their baggage while they looked for work. Jane Street told each maid: "You have one great advantage over your mistress. She must have you in her house. She won't wash her own dishes. You can get your rights by working on the individual woman."[54] She explained further to her Tulsa "fellow worker":

> If a girl decides to shorten hours on the job by refusing to work afternoons, or refuses to attend the furnace or to use the vacuum, etc., as a rule her employer does not fire her until she secures another girl. She calls up an employment shark and asks for a girl. With the union office in operation, no girl arrives, the shark's business having been crippled. The employer advertises in the paper. We catch her ad and send our girl who refuses to do the same thing as the other girl. If you have a union of only four girls and you can get them consecutively on the same job, you soon have job control. The nerve-wracked, lazy society woman is not hard to conquer.[55]

The union initially met with great success. Its list of jobs grew from three hundred in March to two thousand in May and six thousand in November.[56] When someone advertised for a maid in the paper, dozens of "union maids" would answer and demand the same wages until the prospective mistress was convinced that that was the going rate. The union even had its own song, "The Maids' Defiance":

> We've answered all your door bells and we've washed your dirty kids,
> For lo, these many years we've done as we were bid,
> But we're going to fight for freedom and for our rights we'll stand.
> And we're going to stick together in one big Union band.
>
> *Chorus:*
>   It's a long day for housemaid Mary, it's a long day's hard toil
>   It's a burden too hard to carry, so our mistress' schemes we'll foil.
>   For we're out for a shorter day this summer
>   Or we'll fix old Denver town.
>
> 2.
> We've washed your dirty linen and we've cooked your daily foods;
> We've eaten in your kitchens, and we've stood your ugly moods.
> But now we've joined the Union and are organized to stay,
> The cooks and maids and chauffeurs, in one grand array.
>
> *(Repeat Chorus):*[57]

And in case words were not enough to bring the mistresses to terms, there was always the threat of sabotage—a favorite IWW weapon, although more often discussed in theory than utilized in practice. "It is almost uncanny the way dishes slip out of that girl's hands," wrote a "Union maid" in an article entitled "Housemaids' Union Plots Revenge." "Picture father putting on his favorite soft shirt to find that the new laundress 'sabotaged' it by using plenty of starch."[58]

So, Jane Street explained, with only a "handful of girls," the Denver Domestic Workers' Industrial Union had "got results. We actually have POWER to do things. We have raised wages, shortened hours, bettered conditions in hundreds of places.* This is not merely a statement. It is a fact that is registered not only in black and white on the cards in our files in the office, but in the flesh and blood of the girls on the job."[59]

As the union grew stronger, it met ever-increasing opposition, and its enemies united to destroy it. These included the rich women of Denver, the YWCA, and, of course, the employment sharks whose business the union had crippled.[60] After intimidation of members had failed to weaken the union, the antiunion coalition hit upon a device that was more effective. They knew that one of the union's great sources of power was its card file of information on employers, which enabled it to function as an employment agency. On November 11, 1916, *Solidarity* carried the following devastating report under the heading, "Denver Housemaids' List Stolen":

> The robbery occurred in the early morning when Secretary Jane Street had stepped out of the office for a few minutes to go to the washroom on the floor above. Fellow Worker Street had been sleeping in the headquarters at night with a "gatt" under her pillow and a section of gas pipe within each reach guarding against just such an occurrence. She locked the door when leaving and upon her return found the list gone with the exception of a few cards scattered over the floor that the thief had apparently been in too great haste to pick up.

The loss of the card file was a serious setback, but the union did not go under. However, Street herself was charging male Wobblies in Denver with having done the union "more harm than any other enemy, the women of Capital Hall, the employment sharks and the YWCA combined. They have cut us off from donations from outside locals, slandered this local and myself and from one end of the country to the other, tried to disrupt us from within by going among the girls and stirring up trouble." The final blow was their refusal to grant the domestic workers' union a charter and then persuading national IWW headquarters not to charter the local. Moreover, whenever Street assisted domestic workers from other cities in forming locals, the same opposition developed

---

*David M. Katzman, however, believes that this success "had but a limited effect on the Denver servant market," even though Street's employment bureau was a unique feature. (*Seven Days A Week: Women and Domestic Service in Industrializing Services*, New York, 1978, p. 235.)

among male Wobblies. Sadly, but still hopefully, Street concluded her letter to the Tulsa "fellow worker":

> I am so sorry to tell you of these things—you who are so full of hope and faith and spirit for the revolution. I have tried to keep out of this letter the bitterness that surges up in me. But when one looks upon the slavery on all sides that enchains the workers—these women workers sentenced to hard labor and solitary confinment on their prison jobs in the homes of the rich—and these very men who forget their IWW principles in their opposition to us—when we look about us, we soon see that the Method of Emancipation that we advocate is greater than any or all of us and that the great principles and ideals that we stand for can completely overshadow the frailties of human nature.
>
> Stick to your domestic workers' union, fellow worker, stick to it with all the persistence and ardor that there is in you. Every day some sign of success will thrill your blood and urge you on! Keep on with the work.... Your success will spur on the girls here.
>
> Yours for industrial freedom. Yours for a speedy abolition of domestic slavery.[61]

Despite the theft of the card file and the problems with IWW male chauvinists, the union was growing stronger every day and had moved into new offices. The movement was also spreading outside Denver. By June, 1916, domestic workers in Salt Lake City had organized, followed by Duluth, Chicago, Cleveland, and Seattle.[62] But all these unions of domestic workers vanished when the entire Industrial Workers of the World came under brutal oppression at the hands of the federal government, which utilized the Espionage Act during World War I to destroy an organization employers were eager to see eliminated. The attack on the IWW was especially repressive in the West, and the maids' union in that area went under along with many other IWW organizations.[63]

Not all Western Wobblies were as hostile to women workers and their needs as those in Denver. The special exploitation of women migrant workers in California agriculture was a catalytic agent in the IWW's extensive efforts to organize these workers. In the great Wheatland Hops field strike in August, 1913, along with the demands for higher wages and other improvements, the IWW emphasized that men be assigned to help women with heavy sacks and that separate toilets be installed for women.[64]

Still, there is ample evidence that in quite a few respects, IWW ideology with respect to women workers differed little from that of the AFL. Like the federation, the One Big Union accepted the traditional and idealized conceptions of woman's role as mother and wife. Like the AFL members, too, not a few Wobblies looked down on and/or resented efforts by women workers to deal with their special needs and problems. Moreover, while the IWW preached that women were entitled to "equal opportunities, duties and privileges even to the holding of executive office," few women ever achieved positions in the Wobbly high command.

Flynn did recognize the weaknesses of the IWW in dealing with the special needs and problems of women workers and did try on a few occasions to push the Wobblies in the direction of meeting those needs. But she ran into the inevitable contradiction in the IWW's view that both sexes were equal in the class struggle, and this view weakened her efforts to achieve a special approach to women workers. In "The IWW Call to Women," published in 1915, Flynn put it this way:

> To us, society moves in grooves of class, not sex. Sex distinctions affect us insignificantly. . . . It is to those women who are wage earners, or wives of workers, that the IWW appeals. We see no basis in fact for feminist mutual interest, no evidence of natural "sex conflict," nor any possibility—nor present desirability—of solidarity between women alone. The success of our program will benefit workers, regardless of sex, and injure all who, without effort, draw profits for a livelihood. . . . The sisterhood of women, like the brotherhood of man, is a hollow sham to labor. Behind all its smug hypocrisy and sickly sentimentality loom the sinister outlines of the class war.[65]

Flynn failed to realize that unless class solidarity was accompanied by the eradication of male-supremacist tendencies in every aspect of the movement, the women workers might find that the IWW, despite its proclamations and resolutions, was not much different from the traditional labor organizations as far as they were concerned.

Yet the fact remains that in many important respects, the IWW approach to and treatment of the woman worker differed radically from that of the AFL. Unlike most other labor organizations of its time, and even many today, the IWW was not content merely to lament the status of working-class women in industrial society but set out to organize the women, who formed a substantial proportion of the unskilled workers and factory operatives. As we shall now see, their participation and militant activity could and did make the difference between success and failure in strikes.

10

The Lawrence Strike

THE CHARACTER of the working population in Lawrence's textile mills had undergone a distinct change in the nearly seven decades between the founding of the city in 1845 and the great strike of 1912. Until the 1880s, the dominant elements in the textile factories were native Americans, English, Irish, Scottish, and French-Canadians, and many of them were skilled workers. With the technological advances of the 1880s, the skilled personnel were rapidly displaced, and Italians, Greeks, Portuguese, Russians, Poles, Lithuanians, Syrians, and Armenians took their places. By 1912 the newcomers had become the predominant groups in the textile mills of Lawrence. Within a one-mile radius of the mill district, twenty-five different nationalities lived, speaking half a hundred different languages. The largest ethnic group in the city was Italian.[1]

The U.S. Bureau of Labor Statistics made a study of the weekly payroll reports from seven mills in Lawrence about seven weeks before the strike. It covered 21,922 workers (excluding overseers and clerks)— about two-thirds of the total number in the mills on the eve of the strike. The average rate per hour of 16,578 operatives, skilled and unskilled, in the four woolen and worsted mills was 16 cents, and the average amount earned for the week under study was $8.75. These wages included premiums or bonuses! But 59.8 percent of the operatives in the woolen mills earned less than 15 cents an hour, and 14 percent of those in the cotton mills made less than 12 cents. Almost one-third—33.2 percent—of both woolen and cotton operatives received less than $7 a week. The study reports were based on earnings during a week when the mills were running full-time. But none of the mills worked full-time throughout the year. Although the Bureau of Labor Statistics declared that it could not ascertain the amount of unemployment, it conceded that there was a serious curtailment of earnings due to lost time, and concluded that the $8.75 and $8.78 average wages for the week under study were far too high for an annual average.[2]

The Lawrence textile industry was a "family industry"—but this pleasant-sounding phrase had a deadly meaning for the workers. To keep the family alive, husbands, wives, and children worked in the mills. Even if the wife stayed at home to care for her young children, she was compelled to contribute to the family's income, by taking care of a neighbor's children for money, by doing another family's washing for a fee, or by taking in boarders or lodgers. Lodgers or boarders were an economic necessity for the majority of the immigrant households. They usually paid $3 or $3.50 per month for lodging and the use of the kitchen stove.

The prevalence of boarders and lodgers certainly destroyed any possibility of privacy, and, even though it eased the financial burden of the family, in many cases making survival posible, it also increased the burden of work for the woman of the house. She was often responsible for the cooking and laundry for the additional household members— sometimes in addition to working in the mills. Of 123 Italian families studied, 77 had boarders or lodgers, and in 34 of these 77 households, the wife of the head of the household also worked in the mills.[3]

The labor law of Massachusetts, passed as recently as 1909, stated that no child under fourteen years of age, and no child under sixteen who was unable to read and write "legibly simple sentences in the English language," should be employed in any factory, workshop, or mercantile establishment.[4] But as far as Lawrence was concerned, the law might never have been passed. On the eve of the strike in 1912, half the children in Lawrence between the ages of fourteen and eighteen were employed in the mills, and 11.5 percent of the textile workers were boys and girls under eighteen. If the earnings of the women were pitifully small, those of the children were even lower. Testimony before a congressional committee revealed that the youngsters earned $7 and $5, or even less, per week when the mills were running full time![5]

According to the U.S. Bureau of Labor, the average work week in the Lawrence mills was fifty-six hours. But 21.6 percent of the workers worked more than fifty-six hours, and none of the workers was paid more than the regular scale for overtime.[6] While the demand for a shorter work week was not an important issue in the strike—a fact that is hardly surprising, since with hourly rates as low as they were, the workers needed a longer week, not a shorter one, to earn enough to stay alive—one of the strikers' demands was for double pay for all overtime work.

Various complaints were voiced by workers appearing as witnesses at congressional hearings. Chief among their grievances were the premium, or bonus, system, a speedup plan designed to obtain the highest possible production from each worker;* the practice of holding back a week's wages on all new workers, thus imposing a heavy burden on them during the first two weeks of employment; and docking workers, especially children, one hour's pay for coming in five or ten minutes late, and if the lateness was repeated three times, firing them. Workers also complained that the tap water supplied by the mills was usually so warm, because of numerous steampipes, that they were forced to buy cold drinking water at a weekly charge of 10 cents in order to quench their thirst. And all witnesses expressed severe indignation at the tyrannical attitude of the foremen in their dealings with the workers. The overseers insisted that the women workers have sex with them as a condition of holding their jobs, swore at the men, women, and children indiscriminately, insulted the foreign-born workers, calling them "ignorant Dagoes and Hunkies," and in general treated them as if they were "dumb cattle."[7]

Lawrence had two dubious distinctions. It was one of the most congested cities in the nation, with 33,700 people dwelling in less than one-thirteenth of the city's area—the slum where nearly all the mill workers lived. And the infant mortality rate was one of the highest of all the industrial cities of the nation. In 1910, of the 1,524 deaths in Lawrence, 711, or 46.6 percent, were of children under six years old. Indeed, in that year, the death total in Lawrence was exceeded, according to the U.S. Census Bureau, by only six cities out of the forty selected. (Of the six, three others—Lowell, Fall River, and New Bedford—were also textile centers.) "A considerable number of boys and girls die within the first two or three years after beginning work," a medical examiner studying health conditions in the Lawrence mills wrote. "Thirty-six out of every hundred of all men and women who work in the mill die before or by the time they are 25 years of age."[8]

Foul tenements, poor diet, and lack of warm clothing were important factors in the high number of deaths. "Ironically enough," notes one student of conditions in Lawrence, "in the greatest woolen center in the country the producers of suits could not afford the price, which was prohibitive to them, nor could the women who made the cotton dresses pay $3.00 for them.... As for overcoats, they were out of the question,

---

*The premium system provided for a bonus to the worker whose output exceeded some fixed standard or for regular attendance. In the latter case, any worker who had not missed more than one day during a four-week period received a premium. But a worker could produce extra cloth for three weeks and then fall sick during the fourth and last week of the bonus period and he or she would lose the premium. If a machine broke down, a not uncommon occurrence, the record of regular production would be marred, and the premium for the entire four-week period would go by the board. (*See* Hearings on Strike at Lawrence, Mass., 62nd Congress, 1st Session, *House Document No. 671,* Washington, D.C., 1912, pp. 114–16.)

and to the spectator, it appeared that most of the workers of Lawrence wore sweaters beneath their suits or dresses."[9]

These, then, were the conditions that led to the great upheaval of the New England and other textile workers in 1912-1913—for conditions were no better in the other mill centers. But the spark that set off the explosion was the cut in wages for all workers following the passage of the fifty-four-hour law for women and for children under eighteen years of age. The law, adopted by the state legislature in 1911 as a result of pressure from organized labor in Massachusetts, was scheduled to go into effect on January 1, 1912. But the companies refused to pay the same wages for the shorter week as for the previous fifty-six-hour week, and since they applied the new law to all workers—male and female—it meant a reduction in pay for the workers. The corporations scoffed at the idea that the workers—separated into numerous crafts and twenty-five nationalities, speaking at least forty-five different languages, with fewer than 2,500 union members among the 30,000 mill workers, and even these divided between the United Textile Workers of America, AFL, and Local No. 20, IWW—could even consider a general strike, much less stage one.[10]

The Italian, Polish, and Lithuanian workers met on January 10 and 11 and voted to strike if their pay envelopes on January 12 showed any reduction. On the next afternoon, when it was clear that the mill owners had cut the wages, the general walkout began at the Everett Cotton Mill. The weavers, nearly all of them Polish women, stopped their looms. Officials attempted to explain the reduction in pay, but the women replied, "Not enough money," and left the mill. When the Italian workers in the Washington Mill opened their pay envelopes, they found that their weekly earnings had been reduced by an amount equivalent to two hours' work, or, as the workers put it. by "four loaves of bread."

The wages of these men and women were already at the starvation point. Suddenly, all the years of suffering from lack of food, miserable housing, inadequate clothing, poor health, and the tyranny of the foremen came to a head and erupted in an outburst of rage against the machines, the symbols of the bosses' repression. The workers ran from room to room, stopping the motors, cutting the belts, tearing the cloth, breaking the electric lights, and dragging the other operatives from the looms. Within half an hour, the work at the mill came to a standstill.

With the Washington Mill silenced, the unorganized strikers, many of them women, closed down mill after mill, waving American and Italian flags and shouting, "Better to starve fighting than to starve working"—which was soon to become the battle cry of the general strike. Repulsed by the police at several mills, they finally halted their attacks. But by Saturday night, January 13, an estimated twenty thousand textile workers had left their machines. By Monday night, January 15, Lawrence was an armed camp. Police and militia guarded the mills throughout the night.[11] The Battle of Lawrence, one of the epic struggles between capital and labor in American history, was on!

Since the AFL United Textile Workers would have nothing to do with the unskilled, immigrant workers in Lawrence, the strikers called on the IWW for help, and "the IWW came on feet of lightning."[12] Joseph J. Ettor, accompanied by Arturo Giovannitti, editor of *Il Proletario* and secretary of the Italian Socialist Federation, came immediately, and on January 13, under Ettor's leadership, the spontaneous outburst quickly gave way to a methodical strike organization rarely paralleled in the annals of the American labor movement. On January 15, pickets turned out en masse before each of the mills. This was the beginning of a daily practice that continued until the end of the strike. Never before had there been picketing on the scale employed in Lawrence. Indeed, it was the picket line that made the Lawrence strike a milestone in the history of American labor struggles. Every striker took his or her place on the picket lines, including those who, at first, joined the walkout reluctantly.[13] To get around the prohibition by city authorities against gathering in front of the mills, the strike committee, representing each of the different nationalities, developed the ingenious strategy of the moving picket line. Day after day, for twenty-four hours a day, long lines of pickets moved in an endless chain around the mill district to discourage strikebreakers. Each picket wore a white ribbon or card that said, "Don't Be a Scab." No one could get through the lines without being accosted. What is more, the chain did not violate the law because the strikers did not mass in front of the mills.[14]

The McKees Rocks and Hammond strikes had already demonstrated the militancy of foreign-born women, and the Lawrence strike fully corroborated it. The women strikers themselves and the wives of male strikers trod the frozen streets alongside the men and often occupied the front ranks in demonstrations and parades. Expectant mothers and women with babes in their arms marched with the others, carrying signs reading: "We Want Bread and Roses, Too." This slogan inspired one of the great songs of the Lawrence strike, which has since come to symbolize women workers and their struggles:

> As we come marching, marching
>   In the beauty of the day
> A million darkened kitchens,
>   A thousand mill lofts gray,
> Are touched with all the radiance
>   That a sudden sun discloses
> For the people hear us singing:
>   "Bread and Roses! Bread and Roses!"
>
> As we come marching, marching,
>   We battle too for men

For they are women's children,
  And we mother them again.
Our lives shall not be sweated
  From birth until life closes.
Hearts starve as well as bodies;
  Give us bread but give us roses!

As we come marching, marching,
  Unnumbered women dead
Go crying through our singing
  Their ancient cry for bread.
Small art and love and beauty
  Their drudging spirits knew
Yes, it is bread we fight for—
  But we fight for roses, too.

As we come marching, marching,
  We bring the greater days.
The rising of the women
  Means the rising of the race.
No more the drudge and idler—
  Ten that toil where one reposes,
But a sharing of life's glories:
  Bread and Roses, Bread and Roses![15]

As the brutality of the police intensified, the women strikers and the workers' wives volunteered to lead the picket lines in an attempt to discourage police attacks. But chivalry in Lawrence did not extend to strikes of the mill women, who were often terribly beaten and then arrested. In fact, more women than men appear to have been arrested for intimidating scabs while picketing. Even when they had enough money with them, they refused to pay their fines and chose rather to go to jail. As soon as they were released from jail, they were back on the picket lines. "The women pickets were very active today and very few scabs entered the mills," read a fairly typical report from Lawrence. Most reporters agreed that the women proved themselves fiercer and more courageous than the men.[16]

On Monday evening, January 29, Anna LaPizza, a thirty-four-year-old Italian woman, was on her way to visit friends and passed through a gathering of about a thousand strikers. She was shot through the heart and killed. Even though nineteen witnesses testified that they had seen a soldier murder LaPizza, Ettor and Giovannitti were arrested, indicted for murder, imprisoned, and removed from the strike leadership.[17]

William D. ("Big Bill") Haywood, with Elizabeth Gurley Flynn, took over
the leadership.

Impressed by the "active and efficient" women strikers, Haywood
told how "the women caught a policeman in the middle of the bridge
and stripped off all his uniform, pants and all. They were about to throw
him into the icy river, when other policemen rushed in and saved him
from the chilly ducking."[18] The police, Judge Mahoney of the Police
Court, and the other authorities of Lawrence also testified to the activity
and efficiency of the women strikers. On February 28, while considering
the case of Mary Yuganis, who had been arrested for violating a city
ordinance by obstructing a sidewalk, Judge Mahoney warned that while
it was hard for the police to arrest women and children, disorder had to
be prevented and the arrests would continue. He went on to charge that
it was all a "game," and that the men strikers were simply putting the
women in the front ranks in order to hamper the police from preventing
disorders. One woman delegate to the strike committee protested, saying: "I want to say to the press that the women strikers are not being
egged on by anyone or forced to go upon the picket line, as Judge
Mahoney has said, but that we go there because that is but duty. We are
not listening to anyone skulking in the background, as the judge has
stated, and if we did, we would have gone into the mills long ago."[19] But
the Lawrence authorities refused to retract the charge. The district attorney declared in court that the strike committee was made up of cowards who sent their women onto the picket line. He considered this
grossly unfair, since "one policeman can handle ten men, while it takes
ten policemen to handle one woman." The AFL, too. accused the IWW
of putting women on the front line, to which Flynn responded: "The
IWW has been accused of putting the women in the front. The truth is,
the IWW does not keep them in the back and they go to the front."[20]

As the police became more brutal, women strikers responded with
spontaneous street demonstrations. Fred Beal, then a young striker,
describes one occasion:

> One day, after the militia was called, thousands of us strikers marched to
> Union Street again. In the front ranks, a girl carried a large American flag.
> When we arrived at the junction of Canal and Union Streets, we were met by
> a formidable line of militia boys, with rifles and attached bayonets. They
> would not let us proceed.
>
> An officer on horseback gave orders: "Port Arms! Disperse the crowd!"
>
> Whereupon the militia, boys between the ages seventeen to twenty, guns
> leveled waist-high, moved toward the crowd. Their bayonets glistened in the
> sunlight. On and on they moved. The strikers in front could not move
> because of the pressing of the crowd behind them. It looked as if the murder
> of Anna LaPizza would be multiplied many times. And then the girl with the

American flag stepped forward. With a quick motion, she wrapped the Stars and Stripes around her body and defied the militia to make a hole in Old Glory.

The officer on horseback permitted us to proceed and there was no further trouble.[21]

In the course of the strike, and with Wobbly encouragement, leaders began to develop from the rank and file, especially among the women. Three women were elected to the Strike Committee—Rosa Cardello, Josephine Liss, and Annie Welzenbach. Welzenbach, a highly skilled worker, did invisible reweaving, repairing tiny holes in the cloth. Her husband was also a skilled worker and, as Lawrence workers went, the family was relatively well off. But Annie had started to work at the age of fourteen and knew well what the conditions were for the mass of the workers. She told a reporter: "I have been getting madder and madder for years at the way they talked to these poor Italians and Lithuanians." Completely dedicated to the strike, she led the parade down Essex Street day after day and was elected to the ten-member negotiating committee. She was instrumental in winning the support of the skilled workers for the strike. She also showed her concern for the unskilled workers when, in a conversation with President Wood of the American Woolen Company in Boston, she told him not to consider her needs and those of the other skilled workers as much as the needs of the poorly paid women. She then delivered a lecture to him on the slavery imposed by the premium system and described how poorly the people of Lawrence ate.[22]

Many young mill women traveled to other towns to try to raise funds for the strike. Meanwhile, on the picket line, their sisters were beating back every attempt of the companies to break the strike by introducing scabs. "Man Intimidated by Women Pickets," "Woman Fined $20 for Assaulting an Officer," "Jeannie Radsiarlowitz Convicted of Intimidating Man," "Annie Rogers Arrested for Molesting Soldiers," "Annie Welzenbach and Her Two Sisters Routed from Bed and Dragged Down to Police Headquarters for Intimidation"—these were typical headlines in the *Lawrence Evening Tribune* during the strike. Even the *Tribune*, which ordinarily maligned the strikers, was moved to protest when the Lawrence police were issued orders to strike women on the arms and breasts and men on the head.[23]

The IWW understood that the women were the key to winning the strike, and special efforts were made to help them with their problems. Special women's meetings were held, at which Flynn spoke about the unique oppression facing women workers and the obstacles facing the wives of workingmen, particularly immigrants:

The women worked in the mills for lower pay and in addition had all the housework and care of the children. The old-world attitude of man as the "lord and master" was strong. At the end of the day's work—or, now, of strike duty—the man went home and sat at ease while his wife did all the work preparing the meal, cleaning the house, etc. There was considerable opposition to women going to meetings and marching on the picket line. We resolutely set out to combat these notions. The women wanted to picket. They were strikers as well as wives and were valiant fighters. We knew that to leave them at home alone, isolated from the strike activity, a prey to worry, affected by the complaints of tradespeople, landlords, priests and ministers, was dangerous to the strike.... We did not attack their religious ideas in any way but we said boldly that priests and ministers should stick to their religion and not interfere in a workers' struggle for better conditions, unless they wanted to help. We pointed out that if the workers had more money, they would spend it in Lawrence—even put more money in the church collections. The women laughed and told it to the priests and ministers the next Sunday.[24]

Women were able to vote on all strike decisions. Rosa Cardello, Josephine Liss, Carrie Hanson, and Mary Bateman were cited for their "bravery and practical helpfulness."[25] But it was Elizabeth Gurley Flynn who came to symbolize the leadership that women could exercise. Labor reporter Mary Heaton Vorse wrote:

When Elizabeth Gurley Flynn spoke, the excitement of the crowd became a visible thing. She stood there, young, with her Irish blue eyes, her face magnolia white and her cloud of black hair, the picture of a youthful revolutionary girl leader. She stirred them, lifted them up in her appeal for solidarity. Then at the end of the meeting, they sang. It was as though a spurt of flame had gone through the audience; something stirring and powerful, a feeling which has made the liberation of people possible, something beautiful and strong had swept through the people and welded them together, singing.[26]

Vorse called Flynn "the spirit of the strike," and recalled later:

There was ceaseless work for her that winter. Speaking, sitting with the strike committee, going to visit the prisoners in jail and endlessly raising money. Speaking, speaking, speaking, taking trains only to run back to the town that was ramparted by prison-like mills before which soldiers with fixed bayonets paced all day long.... Every strike meeting was memorable—the morning meetings, in a building quite a way from the center of things, owned by someone sympathetic to the strikers, the only place they were permitted to assemble. The soup kitchen was out here and here groceries were also distributed and the striking women came from far and near. They would wait around for a word with Gurley or Big Bill. In the midst of this excitement Elizabeth moved, calm and tranquil. For off the platform she was a very quiet person. It was as though she reserved her tremendous energy for speaking.[27]

"Speaking, speaking, speaking." Flynn had to employ a new method of speaking to the men and women of forty-five different nationalities. While the IWW organizers had interpreters, they had no way of knowing whether the interpreters were telling the strikers to stay out or go back to work. Haywood thereupon decided that the organizers would have to speak English in a way that could be understood by the strikers. "Now listen here," he told Flynn, "you speak to these workers . . . in the same kind of English that their children who are in primary school would speak to them and they would understand that." "Well," she recalled later, "that's not easy—to speak to them in primary school English. Well, we learned how to do it. The only trouble is with me it kind of stuck."[28]

Flynn was also responsible for fund raising and for support work outside of Lawrence. Flynn and Haywood organized special schools for children during the strike to offset the instructions they were getting in school, which was "directed at driving a wedge between the school children and the striking parents. . . . Some teachers called the strikers lazy, said they should go back to work or 'back where they came from.'" We attempted to counteract all this at our children's meetings," Flynn noted. "The parents were pathetically grateful to us as their children began to show real respect for them and their struggles."[29]

Flynn also took charge of what came to be called the "Lawrence Children's Crusade," probably the most publicized episode connected with the strike. From the beginning of the battle, the Italians had considered sending their children to the homes of Italian Socialist Federation members in other cities. Both French and Italian unions had used this tactic many times in strikes in Europe, but it had rarely been employed in the United States. The majority of the strikers voted to support the Italian workers' proposal for the exodus. Flynn arranged for the transportation; she placed children from four to fourteen years of age in suitable homes provided by Socialist women in New York and other cities but turned down "publicity seekers," such as the wealthy Mrs. O. H. P. Belmont, for not "having the interests of the strikers at heart."[30]

The exodus of the children eased the relief burden while it also attracted enormous sympathy for the strikers' cause. The pitiful, emaciated condition of the children as they paraded, inadequately clothed, in the bitter winter weather down New York's Fifth Avenue stamped Lawrence as a city of starvation wages and aroused great resentment against the mill owners.[31] Nevertheless, the antilabor press attacked the Children's Crusade as an inhuman practice and as a threat against the sanctity of the home. "It must be stopped," the Boston American, a Hearst paper, demanded in an editorial.

The mill owners, disturbed by the unfavorable publicity created by the crusade, determined to put an end to further departures.[32] A statement issued by the chief of police proclaimed: "There will be no more children leaving Lawrence until we are satisfied that the police cannot stop their going."[33] As the children were assembling at the Lawrence railroad station on February 24, the police sought to block them from boarding the cars that would carry them to Philadelphia. A member of the Philadelphia Women's Committee testified under oath that policemen "closed in on us with their clubs, beating right and left with no thought of the children who then were in desperate danger of being trampled to death. The mothers and the children were thus hurled in a mass and bodily dragged to a military truck and even clubbed, irrespective of the cries of the panic-stricken mothers and children."[34] Fifteen children and eight adults, including pregnant mothers, were arrested, clubbed, thrust into patrol wagons, and taken to the police station.[35]

As the nation's press headlined the news of the police brutality, a wave of protests swept the nation and even carried over to Europe. Petitions poured into Congress demanding an investigation of the Lawrence strike. Socialist Congressman Victor R. Berger urged quick action on a resolution he had previously introduced calling for an investigation of the strike. A congressional investigation was undertaken, along with one by the U.S. Commissioner of Labor.[36]

On the same day that the children were beaten and arrested at the railway station, the women strikers launched their first major independent offensive in the streets. Part of the plan probably was to draw police and troops away from the railway station. The offensive was organized the day before by a pregnant Italian woman at a meeting where Haywood was to speak. "Big Bill" lifted her onto a table and she spoke in broken English:

> Men, woman: I come to speak to you. I been speaking to others. Just now tomorrow morning all women come see me half past four at Syrian Church. Tonight no sleep. You meet me at half past four, no sleep tonight.
>
> You all come with me. We go tell folks no go to work. Men all stay home, all men and boys stay home. Just now all woman and girl come with me. Soldier he hurt man. Soldier he no hurt woman. He no hurt me. Me got big belly. She too [pointing to one of her friends], she got big belly too. Soldier no hurt me. Soldier he got mother.

A scene of incredible enthusiasm swept the fifteen hundred strikers who heard her, many of them in tears. "Big Bill" had to leave the hall without making his speech; the Italian woman had said everything that had to be said.[37]

Unfortunately, her optimism proved to be unfounded. The troops attacked the women demonstrators, beating and arresting them. The speaker herself miscarried. Congressional investigators looked into the tragedy, and Mrs. William Howard Taft, wife of the president of the United States, was reported to have rushed from the room in distress when the beating of the pregnant women was described. Chief of Police Sullivan gave a casual, matter-of-fact explanation of what had happened:

There were times when we had difficulty in keeping these women from getting in the patrol wagon to be arrested; they were martyrs, heroines; they wanted to be held up, they wanted to be brought to the police station and charged with an assault and interfering with people; lots of them had money in their pockets, but they would not pay fines and would not accept bail; they wanted to be sent to jail. Now, on that Monday morning, a great many people were arrested—that is, these women, for assaulting workers were going to the mills—and they were brought to the police station and locked up.[38]

And that was that! But the strikers presented their point of view in a letter to the governor of Massachusetts, in which they explained:

Since the federal investigation is on, women thought they were secure in walking on the streets and that their constitutional rights were guaranteed. Peaceful women went to a meeting on March first, on a Friday. Returning home, about 15 of them were suddenly surrounded by 50 or more Metropolitan police officers. There had been no provocation, no shouting even or any noise. These women were assaulted and clubbed, and an officer in blue, leaning out of a window of city hall, urged them on in their fiendish, savage attacks. Breaking into two divisions, they would not allow the women to escape. . . . Not until one of the women, Bertha F. Carosse, 151 Elm Street, was beaten into insensibility did the thugs in uniform desist. The beaten woman was carried unconscious to a hospital and pregnant with new life; this was blown into eternity by the fiendish beating and was born dead, murdered in a mother's womb by the clubs of hired murder of the law that you have so recklessly overridden and abridged. . . . We will remember, we will never forget and never forgive.[39]

The strikers remained united behind their strike committee. After eight weeks without a break in the strikers' ranks, the mill owners began to negotiate with the strike committee. First they offered a 5 percent increase in wages; then 7 percent; then 7½. All were rejected. On March 12 the negotiating committee came back from their meeting with an offer of 25 percent increases for the lowest-paid workers, with a decreasing of increases for higher-paid workers. The premium system was not abolished, but all workers would now get time and a quarter for overtime work, and the companies promised no discrimination against strikers.

On March 14 twenty thousand strikers voted unanimously to accept the offer and go back to work. They vowed to keep their organization intact and concluded, as always, by singing the "Internationale": "The earth shall rise on new foundations. We have been naught, we shall be all!"

The settlement was a great victory for the Lawrence workers and for the IWW. By the end of the strike, more than ten thousand Lawrence textile workers were members of the IWW, fully 60 percent of them women. More than 90 percent of these new members were Italians, Portuguese, Poles, Lithuanians, Syrians, French, and Belgians. Most of them had been in the United States for less than three years, and nearly all had been considered "unorganizable" because they were women and immigrants from southern and eastern Europe.[40]

In an article entitled "The Women of Lawrence," the *Industrial Worker* gave the chief credit for the unprecedented victory to the bravery and enthusiasm of the women strikers and the strikers' wives.[41] It was a fully merited tribute. On many occasions, these women had taken over the picket lines, refusing to shrink before police troop brutality. They had prepared the food in the soup kitchens and had organized the Children's Crusade to provide adequate care for the children, while also making it easier for themselves to attend to their strike duties. They had fought together with the men, but they had often made their own decisions.

The IWW understood very well that the strike could not be won without the full participation of the women, and the Wobblies paid special attention to the women's needs. It was a correct decision. The special women's meetings organized by Flynn and Haywood enabled them to stand up to their husbands and other male coworkers who disapproved of their participation. During the entire strike, women were considered to be equal to men, and as workers, they served on all committees, picketed actively, initiated tactics, and not only did everything the men strikers did but also performed some duties that men were not prepared to do. It was their own idea that women strikers should not furnish bail or pay fines but stay in jail instead.[42]

The women used the skills they had developed in their roles as wives and mothers to help sustain the strike. They made food available through the soup kitchens. They sacrificed being with their children so that they could participate more actively in the struggle. As one reporter wrote after witnessing the beating of women and children at the Lawrence station: "I saw something of the weeping mothers and knew what a sacrifice some of them had made upon the altar of the general cause. It was what they gave to aid the struggle."[43]

The Lawrence strike gave these women a new sense of power. They were able to vote as equals with men in all strike decisions. They assumed positions of authority and leadership by participating in all committees and speaking and picketing in public. They led the picket lines and faced arrest and jail, even after the police used force and violence against them. The determination and militancy of the women strikers were decisive in the final victory.

In the end, the success of the Lawrence strike was achieved as a result of the solidarity of the workers against an enormous campaign on the part of the mill owners, the city, and the state to defeat the strikers. In the process, the workers gained a new sense of unity. As Mary Heaton Vorse put it:

> Young girls had executive positions. Men and women . . . have developed a larger social consciousness. . . . Almost every day for weeks people of every

one of these nations have gone to their crowded meetings and listened to the
speakers and have discussed these questions afterward, and in the morning
the women have resumed their duty on the picket lines and the working
together for what they believed was the common good.[44]

The women of Lawrence disproved many of the assumptions about
the role women could play in the labor movement. For one thing, the
majority of the immigrant women working in Lawrence were not "temporary" participants in the labor force but workers whose wages were an
integral part of the family income. For another, women, in particular,
proved during the strike that they were capable of assuming leadership
and acting in new roles in addition to the ones traditionally assigned to
them.

Unfortunately, however, the gains for the workers of Lawrence were
short-lived. After the trial and acquittal of Ettor and Giovannitti, which
was accompanied by a good deal of mass agitation and a one-day political
strike, the main IWW organizers left town. The mill owners then initiated a two-year campaign of retaliation and union-busting that had
three prongs: "God and Country" (a campaign designed to split those
born in the United States from the foreign-born workers), massive
blacklisting of activists, and a forced depression in the textile industry.
The American Woolen Company, the largest in Lawrence, announced
that it was moving south because it could not pay such high wages. By
January, 1915, there were fifteen thousand workers walking the streets
of Lawrence looking for work as the local depression became a national
disaster.

The employers' offensive was mainly responsible for the loss in IWW
membership in Lawrence. Still, it cannot be denied that the IWW's policies contributed to accelerating this decline. Because it was primarily
interested in unionizing during strikes, it failed to build a strong permanent union, and it left the workers without strong leadership. These
weaknesses resulted in precisely the same outcome in Little Falls, New
York, where there was no powerful employers' offensive after the strike
victory but where the IWW membership also declined disastrously after
a great upsurge.[45]

11

The Industrial Scene in World War I

WITH THE DECLARATION of war by the United States against the Central Powers (Germany and her allies) on April 6, 1917, and the nation's entrance into the world conflict, its industrial life underwent a profound change. There was a tremendous increase in war orders, and the military and industrial demands for labor accelerated at a rapid pace. Writing in the *American Labor Legislation Review* shortly after the armistice, Margaret A. Hobbes commented that the conflict's "most essential by-product was the recognition of the woman worker as an essential factor in industry."[1] Yet this recognition was slow in coming, and women did not immediately replace men to any great extent. Indeed, when war broke out, many people argued that there were enough men either too old or too young to fight to fill the gap created in industry. "The men of the country at a crisis can run it alone," one maintained. "we don't need the women."[2] Charles E. Knoeppel, the well-known industrial engineer, agreed; he insisted late in 1917: "Industry is not yet ready for women. There is a great deal of unemployment among men, more than necessary. Get the lounge lizards and loafers first."[3]

Even the government echoed these sentiments. For several months after the declaration of war, the Department of Labor maintained that no additional women workers were needed, since there were sufficient men available. "Plenty of Work for Men," Department spokespeople emphasized. There is no doubt that the opposition of trade union leaders to the employment of women influenced this policy. As John L. Gernon, First Deputy Commissioner of the New York State Industrial Commission, noted in 1918, even though two thousand women had already replaced men in New York State, "there was much opposition by the unions, so that some of the women were dismissed and others not employed."[4]

In *Women's Work in War Time*, published several months after the declaration of war, Irving Bullard pointed out that for every man in the trenches, twenty workers were required to provide the supplies for carrying on the war. He therefore insisted that women must immediately be recruited to fill the gaps created by the disappearance of male hands.[5] The Merchants Association of New York agreed that women workers were not yet being sufficiently utilized. In a report it declared:

> Careful investigation has failed to reveal that there has as yet been very much substitution of female employees. This does not mean that women are not used extensively in industry, for women have been regularly employed in a great many lines of manufacturing, and form a more important element in our labor supply than is usually thought. But they are not as yet generally substituting for men.

Of sixty employers questioned, only thirty-five employed female workers more extensively than before, while fifteen reported that they used them in positions that were always filled by women to some extent, and the remainder used "women to only a slight extent."[6]

But the situation soon changed dramatically. In the fall of 1917 the U.S. Employment Service launched a campaign to replace men with women in every position that a woman was capable of filling. Even without this government prodding, many employers were being forced to recruit women as not only conscription but also the sharp decline in European immigration dried up the available pools of male workers.

The first draft took place on July 20, 1917, and resulted in 1,347,000 men being called to the colors. Employers tried to fill these places with experienced female workers, and when they were unable to, they turned to recruiting campaigns to mobilize the so-called wageless women for war work.

The figures on the number of women employed in various categories of industries from before the first draft to after the second tell the story graphically:[7]

| | WOMEN EMPLOYED PER 1,000 WAGE EARNERS | | |
Industries	Before the First Draft	After the First Draft	After the Second Draft
Iron and steel and their products	33	61	95
Chemicals and allied products	79	98	142
Automobile bodies and parts	21	44	114

More specifically, the Women's Bureau of the U.S. Department of Labor conducted a survey of 562 plants engaged in work in metal products other than iron and steel.* Before the first draft, the plants em-

---

*In the first years following the armistice, the Women's Bureau of the United States Department of Labor, under the direction of Mary Anderson, published several reports analyzing the position of women during the war period.

ployed a total of 14,402 women. After the first draft, there were 19,783 women as opposed to 113,061 men employed in 518 firms. After the second draft, the number of women had increased to 23,190, while the number of men had decreased to 106,618 and the number of firms employing women had risen to 558.[8]

Female labor, which had previously been valuable as an industrial and commercial resource, now became a national necessity, especially after the second draft. As millions of men left for training camps and for duty overseas and the need for war materials reached staggering proportions, armament manufacturers had to rely increasingly on women workers.

That more women were now working in industry was not so startling as the fact that they were engaged in so many, for them, untraditional occupations. In June, 1917, *World's Work* had predicted that women's war work "will not consist in putting on trousers or an unbecoming uniform and trying to do something that a man can do better." But it soon had to swallow its words. By the winter of 1917–1918, the YWCA reported: "Avenues of work heretofore unthought of for them [women] have opened up. Calls are coming in for positions all along lines previously held by men, be it business manager, elevator operator, or errand boy."[9] Yet this was just the beginning; soon dozens of articles in such magazines as *Living Age, Literary Digest, New Republic, Delineator, Scribner's,* and *Atlantic Monthly* were describing girls' and women's labor in, among other places, dirigible factories, machine shops, steel mills, oil refineries, railway repair sheds, and saddleries, while newspapers carried headlines like:

GIRL CONDUCTORS OPERATING STREET-CARS
STEEL MILLS WANT WOMEN
WOMEN PRINT LIBERTY BONDS IN U.S. BUREAU OF
ENGRAVING. ALL BUT PRESSWORK DONE BY FEMININE
LABOR
WOMEN MAKE GOOD SHINGLE PACKERS
WOMEN WORKING IN IDAHO MILLS

The last of these headlines was followed by a dispatch from Moscow, Idaho, that read:

Women are being employed in considerable numbers in the lumber mills at Potlach, in this country, where lumbermen are engaged in getting out airplane stock. They wear overalls, do a man's work and receive a man's wages, according to the mill men. . . . Employment of the women is declared to be due to shortage of help in preparing the white and yellow pine for airplane use.[10]

By 1918, overall-clad factory women were toting shells, unloading freight, painting huge steel tanks, breaking up scrap iron, or wielding pickaxes. On the trains, they were handling baggage, repairing tracks, operating bridges, and even running the engines. In the cities, they wore the uniforms of elevator operators, streetcar conductors, and postmen.* Girls and women who had never worked before and those who had previously worked in non-war trades were in aircraft and munitions plants, shipbuilding yards, and steel mills, operating lathes, drill presses, milling machines, and other machinery and hand tools. In addition, women continued as part of the labor force in the usual women-employing industries—textiles, clothing, food, and others.

Almost 10 million American women were to enter gainful employment before the armistice. At least 3 million of them were in factories, over one million of these directly concerned with war equipment; 100,000 operated long-distance and intracity transport; 250,000 fabricated textiles (including items from tents to uniforms); and at least 10,000 were forging metal products. Further, female hands would play an essential role in providing sufficient food, clothing, and housing to equip the 4 million men in service at domestic installations and on overseas battlefields.[11]

Women performed ably during the war, and industrial commentators generally stressed their reliability and efficiency as workers. In August, 1917, a committee of Detroit plant managers, having investigated the production record and "teachability" of female operatives, concluded: "Far from looking forward to the substitution of women for men with dismay, the manufacturer has every reason to welcome the opportunity as one of the blessings in disguise which the war has brought." The New York Merchants Association concurred:

> Employers have stated that women substitutes have proved to be superior to the men whose places they have taken in carrying light materials about shops, in picking and sorting materials, in operating automatic machinery, in light assembly, in winding coils, as drill hands, and as inspectors. In factories, they are proving successful as feeders of printing presses, operators of lathes, machinery-oilers and cleaners, time-keepers, checkers and delivery clerks. They have made satisfactory railroad gate-tenders, ticket-sellers, car-washers and cleaners. Thus, in nearly every industry they have entered, they are giving an excellent account of themselves.[12]

Traditional reports have stressed that women workers during World War I were able, by their contributions to the war effort and the capability they displayed, to break down the barriers that had previously kept them out of many industrial activities and to lay the foundation for more specialized jobs, increased wages, better working conditions, and a more competitive status in the labor market—in sum, that they managed to

---

*For an excellent collection of photographs depicting women in many aspects of industrial work during World War I, see *Prologue: The Journal of the National Archives* 5 (Winter 1973): 209–239.

change drastically the existing sex-segregated organization of work and the prejudices concerning women's appropriate work roles. Thus Mary Van Kleeck wrote that "industy, not feminism, opened the way" for women to enter new areas of the work experience, and that "the war appears to have released the power of women's industrial processes more effectively than all the preaching of economic independence during the past fifty years." And Theresa Wolfson commented: "'Women's sphere' bade fair to become a thing of the past. The old line 'motherhood occupations' gave way to jobs to be done by available help or 'hands.' Industry became quite sexless in ideology as well as reality."[13]

Recent studies, however, have challenged both the facts and the conclusion. They maintain that despite hopes to the contrary, World War I not only did not render "woman's sphere" and the "old line motherhood occupations" a "thing of the past" but actually had the opposite effect, strengthening the previous restrictions on women's work. Maurine Weiner Greenwald, a leading exponent of this latter school of thought, argues: "Some changes did occur during the war, but the *nature* of the changes followed lines established long before the second draft call of 1918 increased the number of women workers. The war merely accelerated former trends in women's work, in the composition of the female labor force, and in attitudes towards women as workers."[14]

We shall test these conflicting interpretations by studying two key industries. But before we do this, it would be well to grasp the significance of certain developments that were universal. First, it is important to remember that when the war broke out, there already existed a seasoned, well-trained army of women workers in manufacturing industries and an even larger female contingent in other wage-earning activities. Before the war, these women had long been in typically female jobs in factory, mill, and office and were accustomed to the discipline imposed by the daily tasks performed in modern industry. Women had also been employed in metal factories long before the war. They had been at work in the core rooms of foundries and had fed automatic presses in cartridge, hardware, brassware, tin can, and other metal factories. They had operated automatic machines in manufacturing needles, pins, and jewelry, and had used small drills and tended power screwdrivers, working on rifles, pistols, typewriters, and sewing machine parts—all before the war.* Years before the war, they had varnished and lacquered, wrapped and packed, and labeled manufacturers. Stamping, punching,

---

*Of twelve women welders at the Mt. Clare shops of the Baltimore & Ohio Railroad during the war, eleven had worked at typical female jobs before the war. One had run a power sewing machine, another had worked in a button factory, a third in a cigarette factory, and a fourth in a silk mill. Others had worked variously as timekeeper, telephone operator, cashier, spooler and spinner in a cotton mill, home dressmaker, and weaver, while two had worked in munitions factories (Florence Clark, Memo on Electric Welder, Mt. Clare shops, Baltimore & Ohio Railroad, Baltimore, 31 October 1918, RG 14 WSS File 66b, National Archives).

and drilling—perhaps even cutting or grinding—this was the extent of their opportunity to serve in the metal factories before the war.[15]

The war, of course, brought with it a rapid expansion in the number of women engaged in these repetitive occupations, as well as in general unskilled work. But an important new factor in the picture was that the emergency created by the labor shortage cleared the way for women's access to the "master machines" and the "key occupations" in many industries. In the iron and steel and other metal industries, for example, it opened the machine shop and the tool rooms to them and introduced them, even if only in limited numbers, into the steel works and rolling mills. Moreover, the war emergency forced the experiment of teaching women workers to read blueprints, to adjust their machines, to set up and to measure and mark their own work, and to be responsible for its quality and its quantity.

Yet having said all this, it is necessary to add that a number of important factors, stemming from the traditional prejudices concerning women's appropriate work roles, impeded the full development of these tendencies. We shall see a number of these factors at work in specific industries, but one general factor was that when the emerging labor shortage brought about the employment of women as skilled operators on machines, the private and public training institutions of the country had trained only an insignificant number of women for these tasks. The plans that did get under way for training women either were inadequate or were not started early enough to produce many material results before the armistice.[16]

As hundreds of thousands of women entered industry during the war years, the previous hostility of men in their trades magnified and expanded. While strong friendships developed between some male and female workers, in many plants, male workers openly expressed their antagonism toward the women and refused to help or even to work alongside them. As we shall see, many men in union shops also vented their displeasure by opposing women for union membership. A serious problem in both union and nonunion shops was the inadequate toilet facilities—a problem compounded by the rudeness of male employees, who, according to women workers, took every opportunity to watch them using the toilets. Another aspect of this problem stemmed from the custom of changing clothes in the factory. It was considered wasteful to work in one's street clothes, so operatives changed to old, shabby clothes, or to uniforms in factories that required them, before starting to work. Foremen often deliberately set up inadequate shelters so that the men could watch the women change clothing. One girl complained that "the brazen fellers stood round and stared, they wanted to see how I put them [the clothes] on." The men would often strip off their clothes where they worked, regardless of the embarrassment of their female coworkers. One women voiced a common complaint when she stated: "You have to walk through the room with your eyes shut." Men often expressed their contempt for women workers by leaving the doors to the toilets open when they used them in order to embarrass their female coworkers. All too often, inspectors for the Women's Bureau found that women, embarrassed by the fear of exposure to male employees or because of the inadequate separation between the women's toilets and the men's workrooms, simply avoided using the toilet for the entire eight-hour shift.[17]

Women working on night shifts reported that men harassed them by shouting obscenities at them as they traveled to and from work. At the Philadelphia Navy Yard night shift, the situation became so bad that police and Navy Yard orderlies had to escort women workers home.[18]

While many of the men's actions may have been due solely to carelessness, it is clear that the entrance of women into factories in such large numbers was often bitterly resented by the male workers. Some of their hostility stemmed from the charge that "women were not working on an equality with the men" while demanding the same pay, or that they were being given the more desirable jobs that men had been waiting for years to secure.* But most of it was rooted in pre-war work experience when women had on occasion been hired at lower wages and used as strikebreakers. Many men feared that large numbers of women would lead, in the short run, to lowering of the existing wage and other labor standards and, in the long run, to the discharge of men. Sometimes the discharge of men was also a short-run by-product, and it certainly did nothing to reduce the men's antagonism to the presence of women workers when they read that "in one factory 150 men were discharged, not one of whom had been drafted, and women put in their places, giving them from $3 to $4 a week less than ... the men." The men particularly resented what had come to be known in England as the "Sister Susie Menace." "Sister Susie" was the type of woman worker described as "possessed by the peculiarly infantile form of patriotism which prompts her to volunteer her services or underbid the self-supporting and family-supporting man and woman."[19] As in England,

---

*This was listed as the reason for objections by male postal workers to the introduction of women carriers and clerks. They drew up a statement declaring that "they want it thoroughly understood that they are not prejudiced against women because they are women, but they want them to work on exactly the same equality as the men and not to be given the desirable jobs which take years for a postoffice employee to get. Men, who have become flatfooted and are suffering with varicose veins and the like as a result of carrying mail, have in the past been given easier routes. Since the women have been employed, these routes have been taken away from the men who have acquired them by seniority and given to the women. . . . Postoffice officials, in an effort not to have women clerks working until midnight, have shifted around some of the men to the 'swing shift' from 3 o'clock to midnight, regardless of the fact that these men have spent years in working up to the day work" (*Seattle Union Record*, Aug. 7, 1918).

there were plenty of employers in the United States ready to oblige the "Sister Susies."

Still, it was not primarily because of their patriotism that women entering traditionally masculine pursuits rarely received the same pay as men for the same jobs. While some women felt this situation was warranted because men often did heavier work and supported families, many expressed justifiable anger over the discriminatory job classifications and wage differentials. Most women hired during the war were classified as helpers, even when they performed the same work as men. A Women's Bureau investigation of the Philadelphia Navy Yard sail loft disclosed a fairly typical situation: Detailed job descriptions discriminated against women, though there was no evidence of any real difference between male and female jobs. Women were helpers and sewing machine operators, while men were sailmakers, upholsterers, mattress makers, machinists, laborers, general helpers, and sewing machine operators. Men cut the material for life jackets with electric knives, while women stenciled the marks showing where the material was to be sewed and where it was to be quilted, even though this work required them to lift large metal stencils onto the material. Women also performed gluing, another job considered undesirable. As indicated above, both men and women worked as sewing machine operators. Women held the least desirable job—stuffing life jackets—which was shunned because it required close work with kapok filling that irritated the ears, nose, and throat. Men stitched the bottoms of the life jackets, a task considered too dirty for women, but the real reason it was reserved for men was that it paid better, since its description showed that it was no dirtier than such women's jobs as stenciling and stuffing. Although the sail loft foreman assured the government inspectors that men and women received the same rate of pay, there were real differences. Eighty-one percent of the men, as opposed to 52 percent of the women, received the maximum pay for sewing machine operators. Ninety-one percent of the men, compared with 84 percent of the women, received the maximum rate for helpers. While only 11 percent of the male sewing machine operators received the minimum rate, as many as 45 percent of the women did. Clear-cut divisions existed in the salaries of men and women performing the same jobs and between the different jobs performed by the sexes in the Navy Yard.[20]

Other war industries also reflected clear distinctions between men and women. Another government installation paid a minimum daily rate for women of $2 to $2.24, but for men it was $3.20—the same as the *maximum* daily rate for women. Investigation by the Women's Bureau revealed that six private firms with government contracts discriminated by sex in the wages they paid for identical work. In the Bethlehem Steel Company, women received 20 percent less than men. The Eddystone

Mounts Company paid women 33 cents and men 45 cents for the same work. In the Fox Gun Company, women received 26 cents and men 35 cents, and the International Fabrication Company paid women 22 cents and men 25 cents. The Fayette Company explained the variance in wages on the grounds that men could perform heavier tasks, yet an investigation by the Women's Bureau found no evidence of this difference.[21]

When the Pennsylvania Railroad controlled Philadelphia's railroad employees under the National Railroad Administration, it made clear distinctions between men's and women's work and pay.* A supervisor at a Philadelphia terminal refused to consider applications by females for the position of assistant locomotive dispatcher, even though women had previously worked on this job. When the Women's Bureau of the Railroad Administration investigated, they found no reason women could not hold this position except the supervisor's personal prejudice. The woman who had applied had seniority equal to the male applicants' and fitted the job description, yet she was dismissed from the position. Six other women were found to be eligible for the job but did not apply for fear of being rejected by the supervisor. There were other discriminations on the Pennsylvania. Women coach cleaners made 22 cents an hour while men made 25 cents. After a raise in September, 1918, women received 34 cents and men 37 cents. The rationale given by the railroad for this situation was that the men received higher wages because they carried buckets, cleaned toilets, and put up scaffolds for women when they cleaned outside the train. Yet observation of the jobs found no difference between the tasks performed by men and women. Women worked at jobs traditionally ascribed specifically to men.[22]

Early in 1918 an automobile supply company in Chicago whose men earned $20 a week paid female replacements only $12. An airplane factory on Long Island hired women for two-thirds of a man's wages. In the electrical trades, employers customarily paid women a boy's salary.[23]

The complex nature of the impact of the war on women is nowhere better illustrated than in the case of black women. On the one hand, the great demand for labor to fill positions in the countless industries that directly or indirectly played a role in amassing an arsenal for the war, together with the drastic curtailment of the flood of immigrants (the traditional source of unskilled industrial labor), opened up new opportunities for black women, as they did for black men. Indeed, for black women, the unique opening of industrial opportunity was the most important development of the war. Nevertheless, black women still felt the

*The federal government assumed direct control over America's private railroads from 1918 until 1920. The takeover was intended to establish an economically and militarily efficient, rationalized continental rail system.

impact of racism on top of sexism; they were consistently given the least desirable jobs in factories and shops and just as consistently received considerably lower wages than white women, even when they were doing the same work.

The Great Migration brought perhaps 300,000 to 400,000 blacks north within the space of five years, beginning in 1915. Especially from 1916 to 1918, black women, either with their families or alone, moved in substantial numbers, some to urban centers of the South, but most to cities of the North. (Between 1910 and 1920 the black population of Chicago increased by 65,000 or 148.2 percent; in Detroit, by 611.3 percent.) They moved for a variety of reasons, but a letter from a barely literate black woman of Biloxi, Mississippi, published in the *Chicago Defender,* the black weekly that encouraged the migration, spoke for many: "From a willen workin woman. I hope that you will healp me as I want to get out of this land of sufring I no there is som thing that I can do here there is nothing for me to do I may be able to get in some furm where I dont have to stand on my feet all day I dont no just whah but I hope the Lord will find a place now let me here from you all at once."[24]

For the first time, job opportunities opened for black women in the textile industry, traditionally the largest employer of women, but equally traditionally, only of white women. Even in the South the tradition was broken, at least for the time being. The *Norfolk Journal and Guide,* a black weekly, carried the following front-page headlines in its September 15, 1917, issue:

MILLS OPEN TO COLORED LABOR
Women Employed in Hosiery Mills of Elizabeth City Due to Scarcity of Labor
Opening of Labor Opportunity Heretofore Closed to Members of the Race.

"The Hosiery Mills of this city that have heretofore employed white help," the story continued, "on account of the scarcity of labor have opened their doors to Negro women and girls, as a result of which 12 young women went to work at Passage Hosiery and about 14 at the Lawrence St. Mill Monday." Northern mills also opened their doors to black women; following the lead of Northern industries, which sent labor agents south to recruit black men, textile concerns began to send agents who brought young black women north to work in the mills. Some idea of the demand for women workers that necessitated this new policy can be gleaned from the fact that in several Reading, Pennsylvania, hosiery factories, manufacturers advertised that they would install electrical loopers* in private homes, free of charge, for operation by

*A device for forming loops in the yarn.

women who, because of their household duties, found it impossible to seek work in the mills.[25]

"Negro women are leaving the kitchen and laundry for the workshop and factory," William M. Ashby, executive secretary of the New Jersey Welfare League, reported. The new employees filled "places made vacant by the shifting of Hungarian, Italian, and Jewish girls to the munitions plants."[26] A Mrs. L——, who worked as an entry clerk in a Chicago mail-order house, replacing a Jewish girl, explained to a Negro investigator that she "used to be a maid in a private family, but she says she wouldn't work in service again" for any money:

> I can save more when I'm in service, for of course you get room and board, but the other things you have to take—no place to entertain your friends but the kitchen, and going in and out of the back doors. I hated all that. Then, no matter how early you got through work, you could only go out one night a week—they almost make you a slave. But now you can do other work in Chicago and don't have to work in such places.

Miss T—— S——, twenty-two years old, who had formerly worked as a cook in Georgia, came north and, after working as a waitress in Chicago, obtained a job in a box factory. She told the investigator: "I'll never work in nobody's kitchen but my own any more. No, indeed! That's the one thing that makes me stick to this job. You do have some time to call your own, but when you're working in anybody's kitchen, well you're out of luck. You almost have to eat on the run; you never get any time off, and you have to work half the night usually."[27]

It is clear that the Great Migration and the First World War meant that black women were able, for the first time, to get out of domestic service—but not in all cities at once. For example, more than 80 percent of the jobs held by black women in Philadelphia before the Great Migration were in domestic service. Many of these women worked primarily as "day work" domestics, living in their own homes and going out several times a week. Only white women worked at the higher-paying, more regular, "in-service" types of jobs, where they received free room and board at the homes in which they worked. When white women left domestic service for factories during the war, these positions in domestic service became available to black women who had been born in the North. Meanwhile, Southern migrant women replaced them in their former positions as day workers. Thus, the first positions available to most black women as they entered Philadelphia from the South were still as domestics.* Only slowly did they enter a score of Philadelphia industries.[28]

---

*From May, 1915, to May, 1916, 1,232 of the 1,413 black females coming from the South to Philadelphia were placed by the Armstrong Assocation as domestics. From May, 1917, to April, 1918, 2,085 domestics were placed (*Annual Report of the Armstrong Association,* Philadelphia, 1917, pp. 12-13; 1918, pp. 6-7).

But black women did move out of domestic service. In 1918 Emma L. Shields, with the cooperation of the Bureau of Labor Statistics and the Division of Negro Economics, conducted an investigation for the Women's Bureau of the conditions under which black women worked. One hundred and fifty plants, distributed over the states of New York, Pennsylvania, Ohio, Illinois, Michigan, Indiana, Virginia, West Virginia, and North Carolina, were visited. Of the 28,520 workers employed in these plants, 11,812 were black women, or more than 40 percent of all the women workers.[29]

More than half the black women surveyed were engaged in the tobacco industry, doing the same tedious work they had been doing for years. But many were in occupations that had been closed to them before, and in a number of instances they were still holding their own. They had acquired confidence in themselves and a "footing," however insecure, in the American economy outside of domestic service. They were employed in metal industries, where they worked at drilling, polishing, punch-press operating, molding, welding, soldering, and filling parts of automobiles, stoves, hardware, and enamel products. They were employed in the textile industry, not only, as in the past, scrubbing floors and cleaning lint and cotton from machines, but also as operators. In the large meat-packing plants, black women had taken the place of men in cutting hogs' ears. As general laborers, they washed cans or dishes in bakeries, canneries, and food establishments; peeled or pitted fruit; sorted rags in rag and paper factories; picked nuts; and pressed clothes. In laundries, most of them did the hot and heavy work, but some were doing more skilled work, and black women were also beginning to sort, mark, and hand-iron as well as machine-iron. In the garment industry, some factories employed only black women, and a few were beginning to admit them to any position they were able to fill.

For the first time in American history, black women were found in considerable numbers operating machinery of various kinds. Many of these involved only simple operations or repetitive movements, but some required a degree of skill. A few black women were found working as typists, stenographers, clerks, and bookkeepers.[30]

But there was another side to the story. Investigations made it clear that the opportunity for more highly skilled jobs, when it was available for women at all, was the privilege of white women in practically every instance. In the stockyards, black women were the ones who had to work on wet, slippery floors in rooms where the air was unpleasantly odorous and where there were marked variations in temperature and humidity. In the peanut industry, theirs was the job of dragging weighty and cumbersome bags. In the tobacco industry, black women did the stripping—that is, pulling the rib out of the tobacco leaf—the lowest-paying and most numbing and monotonous work in the factory. Strippers sat on boxes and plants to protect their feet from the wet floor, but the general dampness and darkness of the basement rooms was both uncomfortable and unhealthy. Few white women performed this work, and those who did worked at machines rather than doing hand stripping. They received several dollars a week more as machine strippers than the black women did as hand strippers.[31]

In the laundries, black women received the dampest and least desirable positions. They worked at passing materials between two heated rollers into manglers, a damp, dangerous job in which the women stood in puddles of water or on leaky wooden platforms. In the textile factories, they labored for the lowest wages and in the mills that made the cheapest types of goods, like middy blouses, overalls, and housedresses.[32]

The fiction that blacks could endure heat better than whites was used to keep black women in the hottest jobs in the candy and glass factories and bakeries. In the glass factories their work consisted of opening and closing molds for hot glass and carrying the hot glass after it had been blown in ovens. In bakeries they could only clean, grease, and lift hot, heavy pots and pans.[33] Essentially, black women performed the hot and heavy tasks which were now being refused by white women.

The discrimination in wages from which white women generally suffered applied to an even greater degree to black women. In plants where white women were paid the same wage as men if they were able to do the job, black women doing exactly the same work were paid less. In many factories, black women's pay regularly started at least $1 per week less than whites simply because they were black. Invariably, too, black women replacing white women, even if they worked as well as their predecessors, would receive from $2.50 to $3 less per week—$7 instead of $10, or $10 instead of $12.50. Not only did black women start at a lower wage, but, as government investigators found, in many cases where white women received wage increases after a short period their black coworkers remained at the starting salaries even after months of satisfactory performance.[34] It was estimated that black women, while earning more money than ever before during the war years, still received only 10 to 60 percent as much as white women even when both did the same work.[35]

Wage discrimination was only part of the picture. Separate facilities were becoming the pattern of industrial life, even outside of the South. During Wilson's administration, the institution of segregated toilets, lunchroom facilities, and working areas in a number of federal departments paved the way for segregated facilities in war plants and arsenals, where sanitary provisions for white women were superior and black women were segregated into the least desirable washrooms, lunchrooms, and lockers.[36] When black women complained about men entering their toilets through their workroom, they were laughed at. In one case, the plant manager refused to open an outside entrance because "colored women would take everything they could lay their hands on—pillow cases, towels, etc."[37]

Bias against black women was apparent in all aspects of the work experience. In general, under the U.S. Railroad Administration, which controlled the railroads, the higher-paying railroad jobs traditionally held by men were, as they became open, available only to white women, while the lower-paying menial tasks were the only jobs available for black women. Black women usually cleaned railroad cars and followed after trackmen, picking up the debris they left behind. They were often well paid, sometimes receiving salaries up to $95 a month, but they remained in these positions and other menial posts. And even in menial work, there was discrimination. In one terminal of the Pennsylvania Railroad, three black women and one white woman worked as linen counters. The white woman counted only clean laundry in an airy room on the ground floor, while the three black women sorted soiled linen in a dark basement. Even in car cleaning, color lines were established. In the Long Island yards of the Long Island Railroad, black women were barred from cleaning dining cars and restricted to coaches.[38]

Employers' racist attitudes toward black women constituted the chief reason for the discrimination suffered by these women. Some employers acknowledged that the black women worked satisfactorily but defended their vicious exploitation by insisting that these women needed more training than white workers because they were mentally backward and less habituated to the factory routine. The most common complaint concerned their irregular attendance, although nothing was said about the extra discrimination these women were forced to endure, which made the work anything but attractive.[39]

The employers' attitude toward black women was all too often reinforced by the bigotry of the workers. In one Philadelphia plant, black women were dismissed because the white women refused to stay on the job with black coworkers. Employers often argued that a "better class of white women" would simply refuse to work if they hired blacks. Still, in one small candy factory in Philadelphia, not only were blacks and whites working side by side, but white women were found working under the direction of a black female supervisor. The manager acknowledged that the white women had objected strenuously, but they had finally agreed when he explained that the black woman was the only one who knew all the processes and that it was necessary to have someone who could teach the others.[40]

Bias against black women did not stop at the workplace. The Chicago YWCA pointed out that many black girls were brought up from the South to work in industry "without any preparation having been made to house them or give them amusements or recreations," and that often they had to live in boxcars.*[41] As more and more blacks poured into Northern cities, the problem grew more severe, especially as whites insisted that blacks remain confined to a narrow area. The black ghetto expanded rapidly in inhabitants but not in size, with the result that housing became a severe and critical concern. Then came the antiblack riots. In the East St. Louis (Illinois) race riot of July 2, 1917, at least fifty persons were killed and 240 buildings destroyed in the black ghetto; estimates of property damage ran as high as $1 million.[42]

During the first three hours of the rioting, black women and children were spared. However, as the rioting increased in fury, white women, some the coworkers of black women in local factories and plants, joined the mob and began to direct their assaults upon black women. The part they played was described in a contemporary press dispatch:

> Another of the innumerable brutal incidents of the night was the attack of a young colored woman. White men and women were among the assailants.
>
> "Let the women have her," was the cry among the men, and white women began tearing the garments from their victim.
>
> The woman's cry, "Please, please, I ain't done nothing," was stopped by a blow in the mouth with the club which a woman swung like a baseball bat. Another white woman seized the victim's hand and the blow was repeated. Fingers tore at her hair and her waist was stripped from her.
>
> "Now let's see how fast she can run," suggested a woman, as the woman broke loose. The women were loath to leave her alone, but after following her with their blows for a short distance, they stopped and she ran crying down the street.
>
> The women next tried to get an aged colored woman who was guarded by three militiamen. One of them wrestled with the soldier for his rifle and others succeeded in getting in a few blows.[43]

"It was awful," a black woman worker in East St. Louis wrote. "We lost everything but what we had on and that was very little."[44]

Throughout the war, public interest focused on munitions making, and there was a stream of pictures and stories showing women engaged in this work—assembling small metal parts, operating drill presses, running milling machines, and heroically making cartridges despite the danger of explosion. The attention paid to the munitions industry was not only due to the presence of women; it was also due to the recent rise of the industry itself. Up to the outbreak of World War I in Europe, the

*Housing for women workers during the war was scandalous, and not only for black women. "Whether the state, the city or the employer is going to advance the enterprise of housing war workers," a study of the situation in 1918 insisted, "the federal government ought to adopt a standard of housing for women to which all building projects should conform." No such standard existed (Signe K. Toksvig, "Houses for Women War Workers," *New Republic*, Jan. 19, 1918, p. 344).

American munitions industry was a small one. With the outbreak of the war in 1914 the munitions industry increased tremendously in size, and industrial plants changed from turning out products primarily for peacetime use to producing the guns and grenades, shells and shrapnel, bayonets and bolos, and "swords and spears" of modern warfare. With the entrance of the United States into the war, the government drafted the forces and equipment of the makers of iron and steel, hardware, farming implements, and other peacetime products into the ranks of "war industries" to produce "rifles by the million and cartridges by the billion, bombs by the boatload, and artillery by the acre."

The need to recruit women for positions in the industry ordinarily filled by men became daily more apparent after the United States entered the war. Of the men engaged in the production of munitions, approximately 30 percent were of the draft age. In addition, there were skilled men within the age limit who were producing machine tools and other essentials necessary for the manufacture of munitions. Even before April, 1917, the number of skilled men in these manufacturing operations had fallen short of meeting the demands. With the nation's entrance into the war and a further need for munitions, it became necessary to distribute these skilled specialists in various plants to permit them to supervise the speedy and efficient production of all types of munitions necessary for the successful prosecution of the war. This sudden drain on manpower, coming at a time of a great expansion in the explosives and munitions industry, made it inevitable that women would be called upon to fill positions as munitions workers, both in the plants that directly produced the armaments and in those that provided the tools necessary to perform this work.[45]

In urging a speedup in employment in the munitions industry, the government stressed that the industry would be performing a patriotic service by releasing men for labor that could not be performed as satisfactorily by women. It cited the example of the primer works* at a naval torpedo station, where even before the United States entered the war, men were released and had gone into the machine shops of the station, where they could do work that women were still not efficient in performing. On the other hand, women, it turned out, worked faster and more successfully in making the primer. This experiment in shifting groups where they were most proficient had proved very successful and was proposed as a guide to be used in all work for the nation's defense. What the government failed to add was that if men were shifted to do the skilled work, women would never have the opportunity to obtain experience as skilled workers. Secondly, it ignored the hazards of the work to

---

*After the cartridge case has been shaped, the "head" is fed with a small percussion cap, called the primer, a process that is also performed on a dial machine.

which women were being confined. In the case of the primer works, the primers had already been filled with fulminate of mercury, one of the most powerful explosives used, and the women were always afraid that the primers would explode in the machine if they were in any way defective.[46]

The press, too, ignored the hazards of such employment. "Women Excel in Fuse Plants," the *New York Times* reported cheerfully, while another paper fairly glowed as it declared: "Conditions of war work are better for women than conditions of peace work, since there is a predisposition to efficiency . . . which makes even the most careless employer keep his plant cleaner and tidier than a laundry or a tailor's workroom."[47] The *Ladies' Home Journal* was more candid. It conceded that as men were shifted to skilled work, women were more and more confined to the hazardous operations in the munitions industry. But, it concluded ruefully, it was all for the good of the cause: "Women workers must be willing here, as in England, to accept positions which, in ordinary times, they would not even consider, if the war's demands are to be met."[48]

In paying tribute to the contributions of women workers in the munitions industry, Benedict Crowell, Director of Munitions, was practically radiant as he declared that "fifty percent of the number of employees in our explosive plants were women who braved the dangers connected with this line of work and to which they had been entirely unaccustomed but whose perils were not unknown to them." They were "not unknown" to the employers either; just before the United States entered the war, an explosion destroyed the Canadian Car and Foundry Company plant in Kingsland, New Jersey, killing many workers. But the industrialists took no precautions against accidents or disease. In 1917, after a survey of conditions in metal plants throughout the country, Alice Hamilton (the nation's leading expert on industrial hygiene) found that the managers of the arms factories rarely screened machines, provided any safeguards against explosion, or protected workers from the ill effects of mercury, lead, and trinitrotoluene (TNT). Lead poisoning presented particular dangers for women, since it could permanently damage their reproductive organs.[49]

A survey made in fifteen states for the National League for Women's Service, the first systematic effort to determine the capabilities of women in all regions of the country, revealed that in 1918 there were 1,266,061 women engaged in industrial work directly or indirectly needed to prosecute the war. The number of women employed in the industries surveyed since the 1910 Census had increased an average of 20 percent. But in munitions the increase was much greater. In 1910 there were approximately 3,500 women engaged in the munitions industry; by January, 1918, there were 100,000. But the survey also revealed that the vast majority of women were confined to performing the simpler and lighter processes and work of a repetitive, deadening nature. The work requiring skill was reserved mainly for men.[50]

Gradually, the fields in which women were employed increased. At the Brown and Sharpe Manufacturing Company of Providence, Rhode Island, women began to run automatic and hand machines in the screw department and in the gear-cutting department. In addition to tending the machines, they began to work right from the blueprints, performing everything that was expected of an automatic gear-cutting operator. In other New England plants, women were reported to be working on Gleason bevel-gear generators, Fellows gear-shaping machines, bench filing, and inspection work. The Boss Nut Company, a large metal trade company in Chicago, employed women in every department except the punch press. In one of New York's largest automobile factories, which had lost nearly a thousand men to the armed forces, women, after some preliminary training, were operating drill presses and automatic screw machines. Similarly, Detroit's Packard Motor Company, engaged chiefly in the production of trucks and airplane engines for the government, had lost nearly a thousand men to the draft. They were replaced entirely by women, who were used at the inspecting bench and on drilling and milling machines.[51]

At the Sperry Gyroscope Company in Brooklyn, New York, a firm engaged extensively in supplying the military forces with compasses and altometers, women were employed in assembling parts and in the glass-bending processes. At the Otis Elevator Company in Yonkers, New York, women were employed in machine shops on jobs that had formerly been performed exclusively by men. The women worked at making small machine tools, in drilling, in electrical work, and in other departments.[52]

One of the most serious problems of war manufacturing involved optical glass. Optical glass differs from ordinary glass in that it must be clear, without striae, and there must be no straining in it resulting from the final stirring and cooling. It must also yield a high transmission of light. All the optical glass used in the United States prior to the outbreak of hostilities in Europe had been imported from abroad. The war cut off this source of supply, and in 1915, experiments in the making of optical glass were under way at five different plants, led by the Bausch and Lomb Optical Company in Rochester, New York. By November, 1918, Bausch and Lomb was producing 3,500 pairs of field glasses a week and manufacturing range finders for the artillery and infantry divisions. The company employed six thousand workers, the majority of them women, many of whom were doing the most delicate, skilled work in the production of optical glass.[53]

The greatest amount of substitution of women for men in industries

directly related to war work took place in drilling machine operations.*
Seventy-two firms in the machine trade reported that women satisfactorily performed the work formerly done by men, and the replacement rate
was one woman for one man. More than one thousand women took the
places of men in working materials into rods, tubes, sheets, and wires.
Nearly five hundred were employed as core makers, molders, and
machine operators. Some women were substituted in the drafting rooms
or in the toolrooms. About 33,000 of them worked in the machine shops
operating machines, inspecting, and doing other types of hand work.
Women were also engaged in soldering, and while this was not entirely
new work for some, it was for most. Moreover, nearly all firms reported
that they employed women in this type of work for the first time during
the war.[54]

The work of women inspectors involved the use of gauges and the
reading of micrometers, vernier calipers, and blueprints.† All reports
stressed that women proved to be excellent inspectors. Their delicate
touch, quick eyes, and nimble fingers proved of great advantage in de-
tecting imperfections in gears and in gauging finished parts.[55] It is significant that more than 70 percent of the firms employing women on
inspection work continued to do so after the cessation of hostilities.[56]

Reports on the quality and productivity of women workers as compared with their male predecessors varied. In an early report (December, 1917), the National Industrial Conference Board stated that
women were slow in acquiring an appreciation of the difference between
a drill and a sharp tool and absented themselves from work more frequently than did the men. Six months later the board reported that from
a survey of 131 metal establishments, it appeared that women usually
turned out more and better work than men, were more careful with
their tools, and were more punctual and dependable.[57]

In a Women's Bureau survey of women employed on lathes in place
of men, twenty-six firms rated women's output as lower than that of
men, and ten declared women to be definite failures, usually because of
the lack of sufficient strength and skill. On the other hand, forty-five

*Drilling involves cutting holes in metal pieces by means of a revolving pointed tool. In
order that the hole may be drilled at the correct point and be of exact dimension, it is
customary to have the center and circumference of each hole drawn and prick-punched
in the layout room before it goes to the drill operator. When many duplicate pieces must
be drilled, the manufacturer has a mold, called a jig, made, in which holes containing steel
bushings or hollow plugs are the exact counterpart of those desired in the material to be
drilled. By far the greatest amount of work done by women during World War I was in
such jig work. Drilling jigs is considered the easiest work in the machine shop (U.S.,
Department of Labor, Women's Bureau, Bulletin No. 12, Washington, D. C., 1920, p. 97).
†Calipers are used to determine the thickness or diameter of objects or the distance between surfaces.

firms reported women's output as equal to men's, and in twelve, their output exceeded that of men. In fact, in the Computing and Recording Machine Company of Dayton, Ohio, women who replaced men because of war exigencies proved, after a thorough training course, to be more productive on turret lathes, while on bench work they were able to match their skill with the men and produce an equal amount.

On presses, automatic as well as foot, women exceeded men in output. Three-quarters of the seventy-two firms reporting to the Women's Bureau said that women's output was on a par with or exceeded that of men. Figures on the output of men and women doing identical drilling under the same conditions were obtained from three firms turning out war orders. On drilling holes in three-inch trench mortar shells, women's output was 40 percent greater than men's. Two establishments reported on drilling oil holes in stem gears and other machine parts. In one, man averaged fifty oil holes per hour, whereas women averaged forty-seven. In the other, women averaged forty-six per hour and men forty-four.[58]

The Lincoln Motor Car Company found that while women were a little slower than men, this was offset by their conscientious attention to every detail. The result of this minute attention was that their percentage of waste was very low.[59]

In general, the Women's Bureau investigation revealed that about 83 percent of the firms that compared women's output to men's declared their production to be as good as or better than that of men. The *American Machinist* confirmed this conclusion when it printed the results of a test conducted by a comptometer manufacturer, which showed that the slowest woman operator equaled the best man's daily performance.[60] But what was probably the most extravagant praise of women as workers in the war industries came from the president of an Ohio metal goods plant:

> In reference to the occupations in which women have replaced men, the following may give you some idea of the diversity of the work. In the machine department, women became expert and got out much greater production in running turret lathes, punch presses, bench lathes, milling machines, drill presses, grinding machines, and engraving machines, and in addition to the operation of these machines, we taught them to grind their tools, to act as job setters, and to superintend some of the departments. In the inspection department, practically every inspector was a woman. In the assembly departments ... all were women, and they did better work and got out more production than men, whom we tried on the job at various times without success. We found, too, that we could place as much, if not more, dependence on women in coming to their work and remaining on the job, which accounts for our having the lowest turnover in help in any factory ever heard of, which was less than 4 percent per year. We taught women to

inspect tools and check them over according to the drawings after they came from the tool shop, in which department women became expert. In the optical department, most of the employees grinding lenses were women, who were remarkably successful in the work. In the assembling of lenses, we had none but women on the job, and you will find by inquiring at the Ordnance Department that our lenses and prisms were as fine as any in the world.[61]

Still, women's contribution to the nation's industrial productivity during the war was limited by the difficulties created by traditional prejudices. In some shops, experienced machinists were instructed to train women right at the machines, while in a few, such as the Brown and Sharpe Manufacturing Company of Providence, employers placed the newly employed women among the men who were told to instruct the new women. In some larger factories, so-called vestibule schools—usually set up in corridors or vestibules of the factory—gave special training. Public or private schools also opened a few training courses for women workers. A West Side YMCA advertisement in the *New York Times* of September 26, 1918, read:

AUTO SCHOOL FOR WOMEN

Woman's great opportunity during the war is to release a man for the front by taking his place at the wheel. Our training makes women fit for Red Cross and Government service, also for public taxi work, private chauffeur work, sales demonstration and for their own cars. . . .

Also special women's class in Mechanical Denistry and Watch Repairing, two well-paid, growing professions. Many openings now and more after the war.

The same page carried an advertisement for a factory (vestibule) school, which read:

YOUNG WOMEN
To take WAR TRAINING for PATRIOTIC WORK

Here is your opportunity to learn business in an essential war industry and earn a good salary while learning.

HIGH SCHOOL GRADUATES PREFERRED

who have a knowledge of chemistry or physics.

In one of the shop departments, making scientific apparatus for the Government, beginners receive 25¢ per hour to start. Those who show ability are raised within 60 days and earn from

$15.00 TO $18.00 PER WEEK OF 48 HOURS

Stopping work at noon on Saturday.

WESTERN ELECTRIC CO., INC.

GO WHERE YOU'RE NEEDED MOST—HELP BEAT THE KAISER

In the vestibule schools, working conditions were reproduced as nearly as possible so that women might acquire some skill before beginning regular work. The schools varied in size from the modest type set up in one corner of a large workroom, where about five women at a time were instructed in the fundamentals of their work, to establishments that passed 2,500 workers through an intensive course of training in three weeks.

A typical metal trades training school was equipped with facilities for training about thirty women at one time. In addition to the operation of the machine, arithmetic, blueprint reading, and the use of measuring instruments were taught. The length of the course varied from ten days to three weeks. The cost of training ranged from $40 to $200 for each new employee, depending on the amount of additional equipment needed for the instruction.[62]

It was found that women who had been trained at the schools were less self-conscious when they were put to work on a machine. One employer who had one thousand women on machine work said: "The training school equips women with confidence, thoroughness, knowledge, and speed."[63] In most factories, the training school method guaranteed greater output and efficiency.

But many firms simply refused to install special instruction courses in their plants on the ground that the working force was too small to permit this extra expense or that the processes were too simple to require class instruction. Then, of course, there were employers who argued that the working life of the average woman worker was too short and the turnover too great to warrant any additional expense. Of 562 munitions firms investigated by the Women's Bureau, only 30 reported that they had trained their women workers in vestibule schools during the war. Although hundreds of women were employed in Cincinnati in October, 1918, only three plants there had established schools to train new workers. It seems incredible that on October 25, 1918, barely a month before the armistice, the federal government was sharply criticizing the munitions manufacturers of Connecticut for having failed "to install training schools for women workers."[64]

The vast majority of the new women workers were trained by foremen, many of whom resented the introduction of women into their sections of the factory and did very little to aid them in mastering their work. In not a few instances, these foremen made it quite clear that they believed women were not mechanically minded and never would be able to match the skill of male mechanics. The foreman would use mechanical terms that were beyond the comprehension of the average woman worker, and when the women were too timid to ask for a simpler explanation, they gleefully pointed to this lack of understanding as proof that women were unable to do the work. They invariably failed to bring poorly executed work to the attention of the women workers, so that the women, unaware that their work was unsatisfactory, continued to make the same mistakes. The foremen could then point to this work as further proof of the incapability of women to perform this type of industrial activity.[65]

Here and there, foremen were found who were able to instruct women beginners successfully and to maintain satisfactory production. But all too often the deeply ingrained prejudice against women workers came quickly to the surface, impeding both the productivity of the women workers and their contribution to the war effort. Still, the *Ladies' Home Journal* saw one virtue in the situation: too much training would spoil those characteristics of women that endeared them to men, and at least the current practice guaranteed that the girls "who take to war work like ducks to water" would remain womanly, "cheerful and abounding in gay spirits."[66]

This study of women's wartime experiences in America's munitions and related industries, while by no means complete, certainly points up the way in which the war altered previous patterns of women's work without bringing about any fundamental changes. To a large extent, what happened there was a microcosm of women's employment generally during the war years.

Anyone reading the wartime popular press might easily have concluded that a tremendous shift away from the traditional occupations of women was occurring in the American railroad industry. The reports indicated that while there were still women clerks and stenographers, they were also "filling many other positions," acting in large numbers as "passenger agents, station agents, and agents' helpers, car checkers, car accountants, cashiers, core-makers in the foundry, as brass polishers in the finishing rooms, even as yardmasters." In short: "In many departments women are being employed where formerly the work was done exclusively by men. Some of the new employees have had experience, but most are new in railroad work, but are proving efficient."[67] So many women were depicted as working in so many phases of the railroad industry that it came as no surprise when H. F. Anderson, manager of the Missouri, Kansas & Texas Railroad, predicted that if the war lasted three years, "many railroads in this country will be operated largely by women."[68]

But the cold statistics in government reports went a long way toward puncturing the illusion created by such statements. They demonstrated that while the employment of women in large numbers in railroad service was another innovation of the war, the vast majority of these women were concentrated in the traditional female occupations. Women's employment increased from 61,162 in January, 1918, to 90,052 in October, 1920—a 67 percent increase for a thirty-four-month period. The number of women employees rose continually until October, 1918, when a total of 101,785 women were engaged in railroad work. This figure

represents a gain of approximately 321 percent over the 1917 employment level of 31,400 women.[69]

But most of the women railway workers performed clerical or semi-
clerical tasks. Of the 101,785 women employed on October 1, 1918, (the
date applicable to all the figures cited below), 72 percent (73,620)
worked as clerks of all kinds—stenographers, typists, comptometer operators, accountants, ticket sellers, and information agents. Only the last
two positions were totally new to women.[70] "Generally," Maurine
Greenwald notes in her study of women workers in the railroad industry, "women performed routine, unskilled, or semi-skilled office work of
the variety they had performed before the war. While a few women
obtained supervisory positions during the war through apprenticeship
in routine office work, women expert in low-level secretarial skills
tended to remain in such positions."[71]

The second-largest group of women wartime railway workers was
made up of the 5,600 women (5 percent of the total) who toiled in the
traditional female occupation of cleaning. Women worked as common
laborers in stations, offices, coaches, and Pullman cars. During the war,
the scope of this occupation widened somewhat to include work on scrap
docks and in freight transfer stations and supply departments. As relatively heavy labor, the latter positions paid correspondingly higher
wages.[72]

Personal service workers in dining rooms and kitchens as matrons,
janitresses, laundresses, and hospital nurses were the third-most-
numerous group of female railway employees. However, only 2.8 percent (2,830) of the railroad women were working in these traditional
female roles. Telephone and telegraph operators composed the fourth-
and fifth-most-numerous groups of women railway employees, with the
former numbering 2,613, or 2.6 percent, and the latter totaling 2,409, or
2.4 percent of women workers. The presence of women in railroad
telegraphy did mark an important breakthrough for women, for it had
formerly been an almost exclusively male occupation—but the women in
this field represented a very small percentage of the total, and even that
percentage only temporarily.[73]

All this does not mean that women were not be be found in many
new railroad positions. There were women turntable operators, packers
of journal boxes, and attendants in toolrooms and storerooms. Women
worked as level adjusters in signal towers, as checkers in freight houses,
as car clerks, as operators of bolt-threading and nut- and car-bearing
machines, of turret lathes, of angle-cock grinders, of hammers, and of
cranes. Other women became air-brake cleaners, repairers, and testers,
in addition to electrical welders, oxyacetylene cutters and welders, and
core makers.[74] But, as was the case in the munitions and related industries, the actual number employed in such positions was small. Of the

5,000 women in wartime shop work, 4,500 were common laborers. "These women," it has been pointed out, "had gained access to a new work place, but the type of work they performed there was mostly unskilled."[75]

Space limitations preclude an examination of other industries in which the number of women workers increased during World War I, but enough has already been presented to permit us to draw several conclusions. First, there was definitely an expansion in the number of women involved in a wide variety of industrial pursuits, and women were engaged in more types of industrial activities than ever before. But secondly, and of equal importance, it would seem that most of the wartime women workers had previously been employed, and that the war simply produced a shift of women workers from one type of work to another, while drawing only a minority of new women—especially black women—into the labor force as industrial workers.*

To satisfy the demands of an America that was actively pursuing the war, as well as furnishing the Allies with war materials, a substantial proportion of the country's industrial potential had been converted to war production. These industries experienced an enormous increase in women workers, but the increase was essentially the result of a labor turnover as these women sought new positions that would enable them to meet the rising cost of living.† The turnover was further stimulated by government war contracts, issued on a cost-plus basis, which induced employers to compete for labor, often pirating workers from other plants. Even government departments competed with one another for women workers: ordnance took women from aviation, and shell production took them from powder production.[76]

Recognizing that as a result of the extraordinary demand for labor in war industries, wages there were bound to rise, women flocked to the industrial centers where the government was letting large contracts for war work of various kinds. Since manufacturers who did not have such contracts could not compete with the wages being paid by those firms that had received cost-plus contracts, women workers in these industries

---

*According to information compiled by the Women Service Section of the Railroad Administration in 1919 on 1,500 female clerks in eleven offices throughout the country, about half of the clerks had formerly worked in offices and had chosen the railroads during the war in preference to performing similar work elsewhere. A little over one-eighth of the women clerks had entered the railroad industry during the war from manufacturing and service work in other industries, while only one-fifth of the women employed as railroad clerks during the war had never before worked (*Annual Report of W. G. McAdoo, Director General of Railroads, 1918*, Washington, D.C., 1919, pp. 77-79).

†According to the Bureau of Labor Statistics, the increase was more than 29 percent between August, 1915, and June, 1916, and by June, 1918, the increase reached 58 percent. By 1917 the inroads of rising costs had caused a 6 percent loss in real hourly earnings (*Monthly Labor Review* 6 (June 1918): 146; 10 (June 1920): 79).

tended to move toward the highest wages, thereby creating more of a labor turnover than an actual increase in the number of women workers. After the government revealed that many thousands of women workers in industries directly or indirectly associated with the war had formerly been employed in dressmaking, a spokesperson for the dressmaking industry complained that its firms were being forced out of existence by these developments:

> With so many opportunities open in other industries more directly con-
> nected with the war, many of our workers have left this trade for more
> congenial occupations, or for more pay. To those who have remained, it has
> been necessary from time to time to grant wage increases, though neither our
> percentage of profit nor any increased volume of business warranted any
> such action.[77]

Estimates of the number of women who entered manufacturing during the war period range from 1½ million to the War Department's estimate of 2½ million. Whatever the figure, there does not appear to be much dispute over the fact that these women came in great part from other gainful occupations, the percentage of those so doing being placed as high as 95 percent.[78] Great significance was attached to the purportedly large increase of women in industry during the years of their active participation in war-related work. Although accurate figures are not available—because of errors made in the 1910 Census, comparison with 1920 has become impossible—a 1944 study drew the tentative conclusion that the net additions to the female labor force during World War I "were probably of minor proportions."[79] More recent studies have confirmed this hypothesis.

For most women workers, the war industries offered the opportunity to do what they had done before, or, as in the case of black women in railroad and laundry work, an extension of their roles as domestics. Despite the repeated tributes paid to the efficiency of women workers in so many new industrial activities, their actual work experience reinforced existing stereotypes. All this is apart from the fact, with which we shall deal later, that for most women the industrial experience of the war years was, at best, only temporary and ended when the war was over.

Another popular fallacy associated with women workers during the war was that they were in industry either for patriotic motives or for "pin money." This theory was exploded by investigations that disclosed that 20 percent of the women, at most, were independent workers. The remaining 80 percent used their earnings as a necessary part of their family incomes. The primary reason for the entrance of young women was shown to be the "bankrupt condition of the working families."[80]

By the beginning of 1918 the *Seattle Union Record* had just about lost patience with the reports by employers of how efficient women workers were proving to be, how absolutely essential their contribution was to the war effort, and how well they had demonstrated that women were capable of doing whatever men workers had done before the war. It observed sharply: "Every trades unionist will be able to read between the lines and see just what kind of hot air these women are being fed up with. If women are satisfactorily filling men's positions in so many cases, they should be receiving just the same wages as the men would be receiving at this time, and it is up to organized labor to see that this is being done."[81]

We shall now see to what extent organized labor fulfilled this mission.

12

Women and the Trade Unions in World War I

"Another important problem also confronts us, that is the question of women's labor," President John F. Hart informed the locals and members of the Amalgamated Meat Cutters and Butcher Workmen shortly after America's entry into World War I. He revealed that the federal government had requested that national and international unions admit women where contracts included closed or union shops, and where the unions excluded women or blacks as a rule. The Amalgamated, Hart pointed out, had approved the request even though it had already opened its ranks to women. The federal government, he explained, was striving to employ as much female labor as possible to meet the war emergency, and women were actually being placed "in positions formerly occupied by men." Members of the Amalgamated already knew this from their own experience: "They are entering the ranks of the Butcher Workmen by the thousands. In the sausage departments, in the trimming departments, and in the sales departments, the women are doing the work and doing it equally as well as men ever performed, and are unfortunately doing it for a much lower wage." He had little doubt that when the war was over and the men returned from the trenches,

> these women will say, "we have demonstrated the fact that we could perform this labor equally as well as you and we now demand that we be continued in these positions, as we stepped into the breach when the necessities of the war called you men away and now we demand that you continue us in our positions." Hence, we will not only be met with a business depression, but a determined effort on the part of women to fill the positions which have, in the past, been filled by men.

According to Hart, there was only one intelligent answer to the problem: to adopt the federal government's proposal for "the organizing of the women workers." It was, of course, up to the various locals to reach their own decision on this vital issue, but, Hart warned:

246

Do not flatter yourselves for a moment that you are going to change conditions. The only hope we can see is to insist upon their being organized and receiving the same wage for the same work that the men receive. But we leave that for the locals and the membership to think over, assuring them that it is an important question and one that will greatly affect your future interests.[1]

Many international unions complied with the federal government's request that they open their ranks to women and blacks, and they did so by adopting the following statement: "It is understood that no objection shall be made to the employment of women or colored men if the necessity arises." Sometimes the words "for the duration of the emergency" were added, although usually it was understood that the "necessity" was only for the war period. But many of the unions that did comply did so with tongue in cheek. While they ostensibly supported the policies devised by the Wilson administration to ensure peak production and industrial peace, their executive officers and boards, in keeping with the principle of local autonomy, left the matter up to the locals. These local unions, in turn, pursued two different policies. In industries in which women continued to perform work traditionally associated with women and men performed work that was clearly differentiated from that of women, the local unions recruited women members in an effort to extend and strengthen collective bargaining. But in occupations where women were introduced for the first time during the war, some local unions endorsed the "necessity clause" approach and allowed women to join only for the duration of the crisis. In many cases, local unions not only refused to organize women workers but resisted their employment altogether. Their international leadership, in practically every case, defended those local unions that ignored the orders to follow a policy of equal admission—even for the duration of the emergency.[2]

Similar duplicity was revealed in the AFL's approach to women workers after America's entry into the war. The widely publicized Resolution No. 92, adopted at the thirty-eighth annual AFL convention in 1918, read:

WHEREAS, The American Federation of Labor stands for equal pay for equal work, believing that these women should receive the same wages as those received by the men whose places they have taken in order to help the prosecution of this war and the elimination of the hun; and

WHEREAS, We believe that the best interests of the labor movement demand that a strenuous and continuous effort be made to organize these women into the trade union bodies of their respective crafts, be it

RESOLVED, That we call upon the officers and organizers of the affiliated international and national unions to make every effort to bring these women into the organizations of their respective crafts to which the men, whose places they have taken, are members.[3]

Yet at the same time, the AFL was devoting considerably more energy to protecting males from female competition than to improving

248 Women and the American Labor Movement

the lot of workingwomen and organizing them "into the organizations of the respective crafts." Gompers had made it clear that his main concern as far as women workers were concerned was to protect male workers from female competition. In "Don't Sacrifice Womanhood," published in the *American Federationist* in the summer of 1917 and reprinted widely in the official journals of the city central labor councils, Gompers urged that labor take a firm stand against "laying tasks on women they are not able to bear." He conceded that "at least three civilian workers are necessary to maintain one soldier in the field," and that "there must be definite plans formulated to maintain a continuous supply of workers." But, he went on, this must not include the "hastening of women into employment for which they are not fitted." In fact, there was no need "to force women into industry now" but simply to conduct careful studies to determine when they might be needed. Unfortunately, he warned, a skillful campaign was under way "for rushing women into all kinds of employment," and (horror of horrors!):

> In Cleveland between 75 and 100 women are running Bradley hammers in one shop. Women are wiping engines in the running house at Akron, Ohio; many are running engines in the machine shops and doing other laborious work around large manufacturing plants. One woman has been employed by the B & O railroad as a shop hand; she packs journal boxes, which are on the axles of wheels and must be filled with waste and oil. Flag women have appeared on railroads. Women are employed in the foundry trade, in machine shops and munition plants. One lumber yard in Chicago is reported to be employing women to handle lumber.

What, Gompers asked, would become of American motherhood if this trend continued? Certainly the first requirement of the day was to have all women seeking employment obtain physicians' certificates testifying to their ability to do the type of work previously performed exclusively by men.[4]

Gompers urged each international union "in which there are many women members" to place his "Don't Sacrifice Womanhood" message "in the hands of the secretary of every local union of women wage earners throughout the country" in order to influence them not to abandon their traditional occupations and seek to enter those primarily suited for men.[5]

The October, 1917, issue of the *American Federationist* featured an article by Gompers urging that women be brought into factories slowly, with due regard for their fragile nature, and suggesting that a committee be formed to determine the jobs from which they should be excluded. Gompers sent copies of the article to international unions with large women's membership and urged them to furnish the AFL national office with evidence that, where there was no shortage of available men, employers were using women as a device "to hasten the dilution of skilled labor by unskilled." He conceded that there was a shortage "in a comparatively few instances," especially of "the highest skilled mechanics or others possessing technical knowledge," but he suggested that these positions should be filled "by systematic methods of distributing labor throughout the country" rather than by women trained for the purpose.[6]

In each statement he issued on women workers, Gompers made sure to include the phrase "when they do equal work with men they should receive equal pay." But he also made it clear that he supported the principle as a means of reducing female competition with men: "I believe that that proviso established and maintained would be a sufficient deterrent to any employer to unnecessarily bring women into industry."[7]

Gompers consistently stigmatized women as a threat to existing standards in wages and working conditions. Yet, as many AFL and independent union leaders pointed out, he himself was in the lead in calling upon labor to sacrifice everything, including hard-won standards, in the interest of winning the war. So blind was Gompers to the contributions of workingwomen to the war effort that even Women's Trade Union League leaders, for all their desire to maintain cordial relations with the AFL president, had to engage in some acrimonious conflicts with him. Despite repeated appeals from league leaders, he deferred action on a WTUL request that he appoint two women to the Labor Adjustment Committee of the Council of National Defense, and it took many such requests from the league, some of them harshly worded, before he agreed to create a subcommittee on women in industry. It was chaired by the wealthy Mrs. J. Borden Harriman, and no trade unionists were appointed to the committee until the WTUL protested. But Gompers made sure that the board was kept merely advisory in nature so that the women still had no actual power.[8] It would appear that all the concessions league leaders had made in order to cement relations from Gompers during the war produced only a meaningless concession from him.

As the war continued, AFL and WTUL leaders developed totally opposing views on the role workingwomen should play in the war effort. At a conference called by the New York league to discuss the maintenance of labor standards during the war, several AFL spokespersons insisted that the only way to achieve that objective was by preventing women from replacing men in occupations previously filled mainly by men, and they even took pride in the fact that their organizations had already achieved the dismissal of women in a number of such occupations. Thomas Rock, president of the Central Federated Union of New York, told the conference that "women would have the active support of organized labor" so long as they did not cooperate with "employers who are substituting women for men."

League representatives, on the other hand, argued that it was unpatriotic to speak of dismissing women from positions in which they were making valuable contributions to the war effort, and that the way to maintain standards was to unionize the women along with the men and seek the same standards for both.[9]

Across the country the same issue was debated before the Seattle Central Labor Council—on the same day that the council received a National WTUL request that it endorse the women's suffrage amendment before Congress. The council instructed its secretary to write to members of the Washington Congressional delegation urging them to vote for the measure (and employing the league's language) "as a means of increasing the power of working women to protect their economic interests by the ballot." Then the council proceeded to clash with a league spokesperson who supported the employment of women as streetcar conductors and mail carriers. Declaring that "employment of women in such laborious work would be little short of criminal," the council especially condemned the entrance of married women, "otherwise supported by their husbands," into industry.[10]

Although the Central Federated Union of New York and the Seattle Central Labor Council had been worlds apart in their approach to women workers before the war—the former having been one of the most conservative and the latter perhaps the most progressive of any on this issue—they now saw eye to eye when it came to the exclusion of women from occupations that had up to that time been monopolized by men.

"Female Labor Arouses Hostility and Apprehension in Union Ranks," declared *Current Opinion* in April, 1918, reporting that a conflict had emerged between the leaders of organized labor and of women's groups. While the AFL and most of its affiliated unions were emphasizing that there was no need for women workers to enter occupations traditionally held by men, WTUL leaders were stressing that America's entry into the war meant that "women will find new avenues of employment—industries formerly closed to them will open their doors, and they will be drawn from unimportant industries to those essential to our national existence." To the trade unionists, this development meant the inevitable lowering of wage scales, while league spokespersons rejected this gloomy forecast and argued that the answer lay in unionizing the new women workers and establishing the "same wage scale for women and men." Only in this way, they maintained, could men be sure that when they came back from military service, they would not find "that not only have their places been taken, but wages cut."[11]

Gompers rejected the league's argument and showed his anger over the refusal of the organization's leaders to accept the AFL's reasoning when he coldly dismissed an invitation to address the WTUL wartime convention. At his suggestion, the AFL similarly rejected a proposal

from woman unionists that the Executive Council be expanded to thirteen members, two of whom were to be women—an action that was
criticized by the Federal Council of Churches. The significance of the
absence of women on the Executive Council was pointed up when the
1918 AFL convention referred the resolution quoted above to the council for implementation. The resolution called "upon the officers and
organizers of the affiliated international and national unions to make
every effort to bring these women into the organizations of the respective crafts to which the men, whose places they have taken, are members." But the council confined itself to seeking opinions from the officers of all national and international unions as to the most effective way
of achieving the intent of the resolution. The replies satisfied the Executive Council that these unions were doing all that was necessary "to
safeguard and protect the rights of women wage workers and maintain
standards." It thereupon assured workingwomen that, together with
these unions, the AFL Executive Council "will make every effort to give
wholehearted support in the endeavor to organize the women workers
of America to bring them the full fruition of organized effort that they
may be accorded as a right, equal pay for equal work with men." Beneath
this pledge by the Executive Council was a similar one that, together with
the national and international unions, the council would organize and
protect the interests of "colored workers."[12]

The latter pledge was never kept. When World War I came to an end
on November 11, 1918, the AFL had done nothing but discuss the problem created by the influx of black workers into industry and adopt
resolutions, without creating any effective machinery to put them into
operation. During the war, the national and local unions had grown
rapidly, enrolling hundreds of thousands of new members; some even
tripled in size.* Few of these new members were black.[13]

Fewer still were black women. "Unions don't mean anything to
colored people," said a thirty-year-old black woman doing clerical work
in a Chicago mail-order establishment when asked by an investigator
what trade unionism meant to her and others like her. This did not
mean that black women did not understand the value of trade unionism.
A black Chicago hospital worker told an investigator that she had decided to become a nurse after she saw that nurses in her hospital had a
union and realized "just how much they can mean to people. They
usually make the employers do the right thing by the people; unless the
nurses asked too much, they got what they wanted." She decided to take

---

*The membership of the AFL increased from 2,072,702 in 1916 to 2,371,434 in 1917; to
2,726,478 in 1918; and to 3,260,168 in 1919. The Boilermakers grew in membership
from 31,200 in 1917 to 103,000 in 1920; the Machinists grew from 112,500 in 1917 to
330,800 in 1920; the Electricians from 41,500 in 1917 to 139,200 in 1920 (Selig Perlman
and Philip Taft, *History of Labor in the United States, 1896-1932* [New York, 1935], p. 410).

"nurse training" when "she saw "how square" the nurses were with each other, "and how the union made them pull together, regardless of whether or not they liked each other. . . . The unions . . . 'make you treat the other fellow right regardless how you feel toward him.'" She knew she would not be able to join the nurses' union because of her color, but she hoped to help organize black nurses when she completed her training.[14]

The Women's Trade Union League, which had made very little effort to organize black women before World War I, tried to make up for its past neglect as black women now replaced many white women who moved into better-paying defense jobs from the traditional women's trades. Articles and editorials in *Life and Labor* demanded equal opportunity and equal treatment for black females; blacks were appointed to various league positions and were granted scholarships to the league's labor school.[15] Appeals were directed to AFL unions to organize black women, and Mildred Rankin, a black social worker, was appointed to direct a national office of Colored Women Workers. But it all added up to very little. One reason was that the effort to unionize black women was inadequately supported because of financial problems. But the major obstacle was the same as that confronting black men: the racism of the AFL and most of its affiliated unions. With several "colored organizers," Rankin went to the Berkeley and Portsmouth areas of Virginia to try to organize black women there, most of whom were "cooks, day workers, home laundresses, nurse maids," in the hope of forming them into "Federal unions now until there should be enough locals to form a National." But the rebuffs that black male workers in the area were receiving from the AFL convinced her that the plan would get nowhere, and she abandoned the idea. She also evidently abandoned a WTUL plan to form "a colored Women's Trade Union League." It was "too late" for a segregated movement, she informed Margaret Dreier Robins.[16]

An effort by socially minded middle-class black women to organize and protect black workingwomen led to the formation of the Women Wage-Earners' Association, with Jeanette Carter as president, Julia F. Coleman as secretary, and Mary Church Terrell, one of the foremost black women of twentieth-century America,* as treasurer. The association, centered in the nation's capital, sought to unite black workingwo-

---

*Mary Church Terrell was born in Memphis at the end of the Civil War. Her mother had been educated in slavery, and her father, Robert R. Church, Sr., was the son of a pro-Union slaveowner who made a fortune in real estate. Mary was sent to the North for schooling at the age of six. After being graduated from Oberlin College, she taught in Wilberforce University and at a colored high school in Washington, D.C. She married Robert J. Terrell, a black graduate of Harvard University, who became a municipal judge in Washington, a position he occupied for twenty years. Active in work among black women, Mrs. Terrell was elected first president of the National Association of Colored Women. At the age of eighty-nine, she was still fighting Jim Crow in Washington.

men, with its "main object . . . to better the working hours and the housing and wage-earning conditions of our women in all lines of work."
Recognizing that it would be difficult to bring such women into existing
trade unions, the association hoped to achieve this goal by lectures that
would show them how to help themselves while the organization was
seeking to persuade the unions to change their policies.[17]

Supported by the black weekly the *Norfolk Journal and Guide,* domestic servants, housemaids, waitresses, nurses, and tobacco stemmers
jointly formed a branch of the Women Wage-Earners' Association and,
six hundred strong, demanded improvements in their conditions and
increases in their wages to meet the rising cost of living.[18] Three
hundred of them were tobacco stemmers employed by the American
Cigar Company, and they demanded an increase in wages from 70 cents
to $1.50 per day and recognition of the association as their bargaining
agent. When the company rejected the demands, the black women
struck on September 5, 1917.[19] The *Norfolk Journal and Guide* endorsed
the walkout and argued in an editorial:

> In view of the present living conditions, *The Journal and Guide* is of the
> opinion that there are justice and reason in the demand of the women. We
> do not believe that under present conditions any adult laborer, man or wo-
> man, can subsist upon much less than the factory women are asking. The
> average woman who works in the factory of the American Cigar Company
> has to provide every week for house rent, for food, fuel, clothing, insurance,
> Church dues and incidentals. The items will run about as follows:

> | | |
> |---|---:|
> | House rent | $1.00 |
> | Fuel | .75 |
> | Clothing | 1.00 |
> | Insurance | .25 |
> | Church dues | .25 |
> | Lodge dues | .25 |
> | Incidentals | .25 |
> | | $7.25 |

At $1.25 a day, the women would earn $6.87 a week, as the working time
at the factory is 5½ days. . . .

Even if a woman is married or has other working members in her family
her pro rata of house rent cannot fall below $1.00 per week, nor fuel
allowance less than 75¢ with slab wood selling at $8 per cord and coal at $9.50
per ton. . . . So in view of these conditions it appears to us that there are both
justice and reason in the demands that the striking tobacco stemmers are
making for a living wage.[20]

Simultaneously with the strike of the tobacco stemmers, the domestic
servants—including cooks, maids, waitresses, and laundresses—decided
jointly to ask for a minimum wage of $1 per day, with some

modifications in working time. At the same time, the oyster shuckers, most of them husbands and brothers of the tobacco stemmers, went on strike, demanding an increase in wages. "Labor unrest among the colored people of Norfolk has been literally brought home to every household in the city," cried the *Norfolk Ledger-Dispatch,* a white daily; the *Virginian-Pilot,* another white paper, reported more calmly: "Norfolk is experiencing an unusual situation in labor circles." But it added the ominous report, with its portent of impending force and intimidation:

> Local Police Busy
>
> C. G. Kizer, chief of the Norfolk police department, is also beginning to take a hand in the labor situation. He has detailed a special squad of plainclothes men for this particular duty. The squad is instructed, too, to prevent "loafing" among the colored men and women. All industrial "slackers" reported by them will find themselves in the position of defendents before the police justice.[21]

The police, the paper added, were also asking for a government investigation of the Women Wage-Earners' Association to determine if it was a device to interfere with the war effort. The enraged *Journal and Guide* editorialized:

> The police department was not sent out to round up and arrest as slackers and loafers the three thousand white men who quite work in the navy yard because an increase in pay was denied them. No government sleuths and legal sharps were sent down to pry into the charter provisions of the unions to which the men belong. . . . The women are asking for BREAD, why give them STONE?[22]

The appeal fell on deaf ears. The strikers were arrested as "slackers," while efforts to obtain support from the white trade unions of the city brought no response. By the first week of November not only were the strikes broken, but the Norfolk branch of the Women Wage-Earners' Association had disappeared.[23]

In the end, the association was no more successful than the Women's Trade Union League. When the National Association for the Advancement of Colored People and the National Urban League pointed to the fact that, of the millions of new workers brought into the trade unions during the war years, hardly any were black, they made it clear that their indictment included black women.[24]

The situation was better for white workingwomen. Whereas black women were excluded from nearly all unions, the relations of white women with organized labor were subject to fairly wide variations. Developments in the streetcar, railroad, telephone, and other industries illustrate these variations in their wartime relations with organized labor.

Conspicuous among the occupations which were opened to women at the time of our entry into the war was the work of conductor on street and elevated railways and subways. While women had been employed as ticket agents by various companies for many years, the woman streetcar conductor was a complete innovation, and about her employment in this capacity have centered much discussion and several bitter controversies.

So began a Women's Bureau publication of 1921 entitled "Controversies Regarding the Right of Women to Work as Conductors." As the reader pursued the subject, however, it became clear that the controversy boiled down to the simple, clear-cut issue:

> between the men on the one hand who wished to maintain the work of street car conductors as strictly men's work, and on the other hand the women who had proved that they could do the work well, and who were not ready to accept their exclusion from an occupation where the pay was good, and the hours and working conditions no more unsatisfactory than in many other occupations considered to come within the sphere of women's activities.[25]

The catalytic agent in the dispute was the Amalgamated Association of Street and Electric Railway Employees of America, affiliated with the AFL.

As the Women's Bureau publication makes clear, the urban transit industry was one of the industries normally dominated by male workers that expanded its work force to include women workers during World War I. During the 1890s horse-drawn trolleys had given way to the new electric trolleys and, following the depression years 1893–1897, urban streetcar companies were rapidly consolidated by merger or receivership in order to achieve more efficient operation. By 1900 many urban transit systems operated a combination of routes that included surface streetcars, elevated railroads, and subway trains. The urban transportation work force was clearly stratified by skill and sexual differentiation. Pay scales reflected this stratification and ostensibly denoted skill level, seniority, and ability. Motorman and conductor represented the highest skill levels, the most prestigious positions, and therefore the best-paid jobs on the streetcar or train systems. Below these positions were those of the clerks, track and section men, ticket sellers, cashiers, car barn workers, and car service workers, who cleaned and maintained the equipment. The jobs to which women had been admitted before World War I were those of ticket sellers, cashiers, and car cleaners. The jobs of motorman and conductor were classified as open only to males and were guarded jealously by a collective male egoism that extolled virility and physical stamina.[26]

During the last months of 1917, streetcar managers in the larger urban centers began to explore the possibility of recruiting women workers to fill vacancies on the applicant lists for the car crews, where women had not previously been employed, and to employ women as "extras" to replace motormen and conductors who volunteered or were drafted. Rumors of the impending employment of women brought an immediate protest from the organized workers of the industry, who were almost exclusively male.[27]

Slightly more than half of the workers in urban transportation were organized, and the major collective bargaining agent was the Amalgamated Association of Street and Railway Employees, whose president was William D. Mahon. The only other "organized" workers were those represented by company unions or employee representational plans.[28]

The Amalgamated Association was one of the national trade unions that responded affirmatively to the federal government's request that the unions admit women, and agreed at the national level to admit them as a "necessity." But its Executive Board adopted a two-faced policy on the issue. In May, 1918, it held that "the Association is unalterably opposed to the employment of women in the occupation as either motormen or conductors." The union was hostile not only to the immediate employment of women on the cars, but also to any protective legislation that would modify working conditions so as to open the positions to women workers. Streetcar managers who sought to employ women conductors, union officials held, did so with the express intention of holding down wages in order to maximize profits under the guise of wartime emergency conditions.[29]

Criticized for violating its own commitment to the government, the Amalgamated's Executive Board in August, 1918, recommended that women be hired and accepted by the locals "if it is necessary, during the period of the war." The board also established a number of restrictions to be followed where women were employed during the emergency. Female workers were to enter employment on the same basis as men, except that women were to take their places at the bottom of the "extras" seniority list, giving them the least seniority in the work force.* Women were to receive the same wages as men and enjoy the same working conditions. Where they were employed in a closed or union shop, they were to be given apprentice permits, which allowed them to work for ninety days without belonging to the union. The board also ruled that "when women do enter the service, they shall become members of the organization, being entitled to the same protection, benefits and conditions that men are entitled to, coming under the working conditions and provisions of the agreement in the same manner."[30]

But of all the unions that, on the surface, followed the labor policy of

---

*Four vertical seniority lists were established. A worker moved from the temporary to the permanent list as an "extra," and then from the temporary to the permanent "regular" seniority lists. The conductorettes started at the bottom of the temporary "extra" list (*Motorman and Conductor*, September 1918, p. 31).

the Wilson administration, the Amalgamated Association pursued the most treacherous policy. Locals simply disregarded the instructions of the Executive Board and did so with impunity. Indeed, the Executive Board defended them. Moreover, the Amalgamated Association even conducted a campaign against women conductors, or conductorettes, as they called themselves, in cities where it did not have collective bargaining agreements. The major argument circulated by the union was that the employment of women conductors was part of a concerted employer offensive to break the union where it had collective bargaining agreements and to keep it out where it did not, and to reduce wages across the board, while the nation was distracted by its involvement with the war. Placing women on the cars marked the beginning of industrial "squalor" on a nationwide scale and was "all part of the plan to oust car men from their jobs." The Amalgamated openly suggested that unless the employment of conductorettes was checked, workingmen would in due time be completely replaced by women.[31]

In this campaign against conductorettes, the Amalgamated Association received the cooperation of government agencies. James M. Lynch, member of the New York State Industrial Commission, claimed that the employment of female conductors on New York City's streetcars would lead to violence, and asked: "How do you think a man will feel who, unable to find a job, boards a car and is obliged to hand his nickel to a woman? That is the problem in a nutshell. There is dynamite in it."[32]

The Department of Labor cooperated with the Amalgamated Association by complying with its request to send an investigator to study the use of conductorettes on New York City's streetcars. The union then widely publicized the investigator's findings that "the operation of the street cars is one of the last occupations which women should be hired or forced into."[33] The Labor Department's report admitted that the women conductors in New York City (about 30 percent of the conductors employed by the New York Railway Company and 21.7 percent by the Brooklyn Rapid Transit Company) were receiving the same wages as men, but it charged that the employment of women "is responsible in a small part for the fact that wages of all employees of the operating department have not increased as rapidly as have wages in other industries." (What the "other industries" were was not detailed.) While conceding, too, the "comparative lightness" of the work, the report stressed the long hours and the necessity for the conductores to be constantly on their feet.[34]

"There is no more reason why a woman shouldn't stand on her feet than anyone else," a women conductor who had left "a sedentary place as a dressmaker" told a reporter. "Sitting all the time is not good for you; you don't exercise your muscles. Women don't have exercise enough, and if they had more they would have stronger children." (This last was in reply to the Amalgamated Association's lament that conductorettes were doomed to produce a string of weak children.[35]) The Amalgamated Association did not, or course, publicize such replies to the report.

Since the Labor Department investigation did not result in the dismissal of New York City conductorettes, the union next publicized reports that the women were engaging in "gross immorality" in the car barns at the end of their runs and were frequenting nearby saloons, returning to their cars "intoxicated": "Women conductors have been seen in these saloons at all hours of the day and night. Sometimes they have been alone, but on many occasions were accompanied by men." It was not uncommon, too, the reports went on, to find "the woman conductor and the motorman embracing during part of the run, letting the car find its own way."[36] It is a sad commentary that even the enlightened *Seattle Union Record* published these slanderous attacks on women conductors without any further investigation, even headlining them "Women Fail to Make Good as Conductors." Sadder still was its failure to publish the result of a grand jury investigation demanded by a number of trade unionists who shared the Amalgamated Association's hostility to the entrance of women into male-dominated occupations. The investigation found the women conductors to be "working earnestly and honestly in their new occupations to make a living."[37] Had the Amalgamated Association and the New York trade unionists spend an equal amount of time and money unionizing the women, the results might have been better for everyone concerned—except, of course, the transit companies.

It was the controversies over the women conductors in Detroit, Kansas City, and Cleveland—especially in Cleveland—that aroused the widest attention. At the beginning of August, 1918, the U.S. Employment Service announced a shortage of 36,000 skilled workers for northern Ohio. The Cleveland Street Railway Company (CSR) hired 190 women conductors at the end of the month, on the basis of an estimated shortage. The company's official explanation was that there were not sufficient male workers to fill the vacancies, and that the war emergency required the hiring of women. The women were given a short period of training and placed on the seniority list as "extras" to fill the car crews as needed.[38]

The employment of the women conductors was immediately challenged by the (male) membership of Local 268 of the Amalgamated Association. The union disputed the company's claim that male workers were unavailable and threatened to strike unless the women were dismissed. However, it agreed to a compromise under which the women would be allowed to continue on the job while the Department of Labor investigated the alleged shortage of male workers in the Cleveland area. Meanwhile, Local 268 not only refused to admit the women conductors into the union but rejected their participation in any discussion to determine their future. It was able to convince the Department of Labor to ignore the women as well. To round out the picture, the company also failed to consult the women with respect to their fate.

The Labor Department sent Henry B. Dielmann and Margaret Russanowska to Cleveland to confer with the company and Local 268 to determine the validity of the company's decision to hire women workers. After reviewing the company's hiring records and the records of its employment agencies, the investigators reported that there was no real shortage of male workers. It conceded that the turnover rate of the CSR's work force was high and that the dismissal of the women would cause a lowering of standards, since their replacements would not be of a high caliber. Nevertheless, the report concluded that the labor situation in Cleveland did not warrant the employment of the women. It recommended that they be dismissed and their places filled by male workers.[39]

Originally, the two investigators recommended that the women conductors be retained for the time being, since their release would have crippled an already inadequate transportation system. But three weeks later, on September 21, they reversed themselves and recommended termination of the conductorettes by November 1—a reversal that the *Cleveland News* termed a "minor mystery."[40] "The most logical explanation for the termination order," writes Ronald M. Benson in a study of the Cleveland controversy, "is that the union convinced the Department of Labor that the continued presence of the women on the street cars would lead to a serious disruption of service, possibly a city-wide walkout by the car men."[41]

The report issued by the Department of Labor was immediately challenged by the women themselves. At a mass meeting of all the women workers on the cars, the Association of Women Street Railway Employees was organized and Laura Prince elected president. An Executive Committee was chosen to speak for the women and to formulate a strategy to defend their jobs. The association appealed to Secretary of Labor William B. Wilson to prevent their dismissal "on the grounds that they are responding to the Government's call for women to seek employment in essential occupations." The women sought a hearing before the National War Labor Board.[42]

In a detailed statement to the public and the government, the association of women conductors pointed out that shortly after the declaration of war, the federal government had requested women to fill jobs in "essential occupations." The 190 women who answered the job notices of the CSR did so for patriotic as well as personal reasons. They were, they said, doing their "bit for victory." Secondly, the women blamed both the company and the union for their current plight. It was, they declared, illegal for the company and the union to agree to submit the issue to the arbitration of a government investigatory body, since the women had been excluded from any discussion of their own fate. The company had engaged the women to work and had clearly stipulated that the only grounds for their dismissal were "incompetency, insubordination, or other unsatisfactory service." But the charge brought against them by Local 268 was merely that they were "women", the company had publicly acknowledged that they were satisfactorily fulfilling their duties. The women also charged that their rights had been violated by the Department of Labor's recommendation for dismissal, especially their "constitutional right to work." The most rankling aspect of the whole controversy, they insisted, was the refusal of Local 268 to admit them to the union, which would have given them protection against arbitrary dismissal. But the union's approach to their request to join was that they had disregarded the contract between Local 268 and the company, under which no women could be employed, and that they had no right either to the job or to union membership.[43]

Women's groups found another aspect of the controversy in Cleveland irritating. The Executive Board of the Amalgamated Association boasted publicly that it had complied with the Wilson administration's request that women be organized for the war emergency and covered by the collective bargaining contracts, and the AFL Executive Council even pointed to the union in justifying its claim that the various national and international unions were making a real effort to organize women workers. But the Amalgamated stood behind Local 268 in Cleveland from the beginning of the dispute, reserving its criticism for the women conductors. As they moved to gather support for the conductorettes, women's groups were quick to point to this duplicity. The National Women's Trade Union League and local leagues, suffrage clubs, feminists within and without the labor movement, and men sympathetic to the women's cause eagerly lent their support to the women's association. The move to dismiss the Cleveland women workers was seen "as a crisis in the women's struggle for economic independence—a fight for the right to work, and their equal opportunity with men."[44]

The entrance of feminists and suffragists into the dispute infuriated the Amalgamated Association. After all, the union had supported the suffrage amendment[45] and felt that for it to become the target of attacks by feminists was hardly a reward for its support. However, it explained that its critics were not really the sound-minded advocates of women's rights: "This controversy has been taken advantage of by sensationalists, sentimentalists, anti-unionists, and low-wage advocates, who have shed oceans of tears over a 'denial of women's rights.'" This "distorted clamor" over women's rights was the work of the "half-baked equality chanter" and the "inexperienced social reformer," who, if the truth were known, did not come from the working class at all.[46]

As the November 1 deadline approached, Local 268 refused to

modify its demand that the women conductors be dismissed. Since it was not clear when the War Labor Board would reach its final decision, the local stepped up its pressure for the women's immediate removal, threatening to strike if they were not dismissed. When the deadline arrived without a decision from the board, Local 268 delivered an ultimatum to President John J. Stanley of the CSR: Fire the women or the union would halt the cars. The company delayed until November 29, when it was temporarily "taken off the hook" by an interlocutory order issued by the War Labor Board, restraining the company from dismissing the women until a decision was issued. On December 1 the union announced a partial walkout, and on the following day, service was interrupted on a limited number of cars. At 5 A.M. on December 3, all the men employed by the CRS—2,400 motormen and conductors—went out on strike, halting all service on all the cars.[47] Later that day, the War Labor Board released its findings and recommendations in the case and ordered the streetcar workers back to work.[48]

The board recommended that the company hire no more women for the car crews and that all the women conductors be dismissed within thirty days. The company was directed to "remove and displace the women that are now in its service as rapidly as possible." The board upheld the company's argument that the women had been hired under the "necessity clause," but stated that since the armistice of November 11, the emergency had ceased to exist. To moderate the anticipated outcry from the suffrage and women's trade union forces, the board issued an addendum to its ruling the next day, urging President Stanley to try to find jobs elsewhere in the company for the women dismissed from the car crews. The kind of jobs were not specified, so that the women were suddenly confronted with the threat of being demoted from ticket takers to cleaning women—or members of the unemployed.[49]

The NWTUL, the feminists, and the conductorettes' association all rejected the War Labor Board's recommendations, which they refused to consider binding. On December 21 the women filed a petition for a new hearing, charging that the board had heard only one major witness—the mayor of Cleveland—and had refused to meet with the women or their representatives. Its decision, the conductorettes' association argued, affirmed the narrowest antifemale viewpoint in trade union circles and if not reversed would threaten all the gains made by women workers during the war. The 1921 report on the conductorettes issued by the Women's Bureau drew special attention to this aspect of the ruling: "It seemed to be a very dangerous precedent to deny to women the right to work in any occupation for no other reason than that their dismissal was demanded by the men, and without giving the women a hearing so that they might present their case."[50]

The board took the petition under advisement, agreed to set a date for a rehearing early in March, 1919, and assured the women that they would be permitted to appear to argue their case. The company agreed not to dismiss the women until March 1, despite pressure from Local 268. The conductorettes' association then retained as its counsel Frank P. Walsh, one of the most respected labor lawyers in the country, a former chairman of both the Commission on Industrial Relations and the War Labor Board.

In preparation for the new hearing on the dismissal order, Walsh told the association that he would rely on it and its supporters to prepare the major arguments for the brief—in fact, he agreed to plead the case only if the women had "the matter fully prepared."[51] Laura Prince of the conductorettes and Rose Moriarty, office manager and secretary-treasurer of the Champion Stove Company of Cleveland, assumed the major responsibility for preparing the case, in cooperation with the Reconstruction Committee of the NWTUL, while 100,000 members of the Women Suffrage Clubs of Cleveland pledged their full support for the struggle to "make America safe for working women."[52] Joining the defense were Margaret Dreier Robins, Ethel M. Smith, Emma Steghagen, and Elizabeth Christman of the NWTUL, Mary Anderson and Mary Van Kleeck of the Woman-in-Industry Service, and Anna Howard Shaw of the National American Woman Suffrage Association. The simple principle that drew this formidable defense array together was the conviction "that a government that demands universal service from its citizens in time of war should provide universal employment at a living wage for its citizens in time of peace."[53]

Walsh's decision to represent the women drew the expected chorus of criticism from male unionists. John Fitzpatrick, president of the Chicago Federation of Labor, warned Walsh that the unions in Cleveland were "very hostile" to the news. A meeting of the city's business agents almost succeeded in passing a resolution declaring Walsh's action "unfair to labor." Fitzpatrick, however, expressed his personal support for Walsh and admitted that the women's case had its merits. After all, he conceded, labor's original representatives and alternates on the War Labor Board were all men and could hardly be expected to be sympathetic to the plight of the conductorettes, and the dismissal order fully demonstrated this.[54]

As we have seen previously, Fitzpatrick was a long-time champion of women workers,* and both he and Walsh had had fairly recent evidence of the contributions that workingwomen could make to organized labor. Both had been associated with the significant wartime strike in the

---

*See Philip S. Foner, *Women and the American Labor Movement: From Colonial Times to the Eve of World War I* (New York, 1978), pp. 301, 314.

Chicago stockyards—Fitzpatrick as a member of the union's organizing committee, headed by William Z. Foster, and Walsh as the union's legal representative—and they had seen the importance of recruiting women into the organizing drive. While the organizational drive, spearheaded by the Stockyards Labor Council, was under the leadership of the Chicago Federation of Labor, the organizing corps included an active body of members of the Chicago Women's Trade Union League. Moreover, Mary Anderson, an avid supporter of equal pay (one of the strike demands was for equal pay for men and women), had been recalled from Washington to direct WTUL unionization of the women. The successful recruitment of the women workers was a vital factor in the great victory in Chicago in April, 1918, and was followed by triumphs in nine Midwest producing centers.*[55]

The case prepared by Laura Prince, Rose Moriarty, and the feminist supporters of the women conductors emphasized the issues raised in the months during which the women had struggled to keep their jobs: (1) The conductorettes were efficient and capable workers in their own right, whose abilities were documented by the company's personnel records; (2) the women had tried to join the union, Local 268, which would have given them protection against arbitrary dismissal, but the union had refused to admit them; (3) the work of the conductors was "primarily a clerical job, at which they were seated," and it was therefore not a strenuous or hazardous occupation for women; (4) the real reason for their dismissal was the simple fact that they were women and that the male members of the union were prejudiced against them; (5) there were enough vacancies on the cars of the Cleveland Street Railway to accommodate both the women and the returning veterans, so there was no economic reason for dismissing them; (6) Local 268 had violated the War Labor Board's interlocutory order by striking against the women, so the union was in violation of the board's ruling; and (7) the armistice did not end the jurisdiction of the WLB, for the Labor Department's order to replace the women had been appealed before November, 1918, and the board was within its competency in ordering the company to retain the women on the cars.[56]

At the hearing Laura Prince and Rose Moriarty were the witnesses for the conductorettes, Dr. Shaw spoke for the sufragists, and Mary Van Kleeck submitted written testimony on behalf of the Woman-in-Industry Service. The War Labor Board issued its second decision in the case of March 17, 1919, reversing its position and overturning the original dismissal order. The sixty-four women who had been fired after March 1

*Black women, however, benefited little, since the combined efforts of the Urban League, the Chicago and Illinois Federations of Labor, and the Women's Trade Union League "accomplished little toward persuading unions to lower their color bars" (William M. Tuttle, Jr., *Race Riot: Chicago in the Summer of 1919* [New York, 1970], p. 180).

were ordered to be rehired, and their seniority rights and all benefits restored. They were not to be removed for any reason other than "just cause" and then only on an individual basis.

The board based its reversal order on two major considerations. First, the women's case had not been presented when the original order was issued, and therefore they had been denied a fair and impartial hearing. Secondly, the company had sufficient vacancies to keep the women conductors and still rehire male workers returning from military service. Since the women had accepted the jobs in good faith, every effort should be made to retain them.[57]

The women and their defenders were jubilant. "Wasn't it a great victory?"Rose Moriarty exclaimed to Frank Walsh. "And to think the opinion was rendered on St. Patrick's Day! I was so pleased at the combination that I have not gotten down to a normal state yet."[58]

The victory, however, proved to be of little consequence, or, as a *New York Times* headline phrased it, "Women's Victory Vain."[59] Local 268 simply refused to accept the reinstatement order, and President Stanley of the CSR announced that the War Labor Board's new ruling would not be recognized by the company; the women would not be rehired, and the union's objections to women on the car crews would stand. The company could not afford another strike,[60]

Elizabeth Christman and Ethel Smith of the NWTUL pleaded with Frank Walsh to telegraph President Mahon of the Amalgamated Association and to press the national union to demand that the local abide by the decision and urge the rehiring of the women and their admission into the union. Walsh did as requested, but the Amalgamated refused to consider such a proposal. Local 268 stood firm in its determination to strike if the women were rehired, and the company not only would not rehire the women but pledged to employ no women in the future. All the allies could find in the way of consolation was Ethel Smith's observation when she wrote Walsh: "It means a great deal in this fight to have established the principle of equal rights through a national agency, even should we fall short of success as to the actual reinstatement of the Cleveland women."[61] But the principles of prejudice and discrimination proved to be far stronger.[62]

A controversy involving conductorettes on the Detroit United Railway ended in a small victory for the women. The union agreement with the company permitted the company to accept any person who seemed fit, who would then receive a work permit from the union. If after ninety days of service the company found the applicant competent and no reasonable objection existed against his membership, he was admitted to the union. In accepting the employment of women under the "necessity clause" principle, the Detroit local of the Amalgamated agreed to give conductorettes permit cards. But when, after the ninety-day period, they asked for admission into the union, they were refused. After the Armistice, the union demanded the immediate dismissal of those conductorettes already on the job and refused to give permit cards to fifteen women who had been training and were ready to go on as regular conductors. The conductorettes appealed to the War Labor Board, which found, first, that there was a sufficient supply of male labor available and that therefore the necessity for employing women no longer existed. At the same time it upheld the plea of the conductorettes that they had been engaged in good faith, had performed their work in a satisfactory manner, had fulfilled all the terms of their contracts, and were being discharged only because a group of men refused to work with them. The union, the board ruled, "must be content with the continued employment of the women now with the company" as long as they wished to remain and must issue permits to the fifteen who were ready to work as conductorettes. Since the union did not challenge the board's decision, the Detroit conductorettes were able to work as long as they wished to, even though the union never did issue the work permits. But as far as the future was concerned, the board's decision and the union's male chauvinism, condoned by the company, effectively closed this field of work to women.[63]

Only in Kansas City were the conductorettes really successful. At first, the Kansas City local also threatened to strike if women were employed, but then it reversed itself, convinced that the only useful route for both men and women was through labor solidarity and equal treatment. The union men welcomed women into the local, and insisted that the guaranteed minimum pay of the women be raised to equal the guaranteed wage of the men. When the Kansas City Railways Company refused to accede, the conductorettes, supported by the men conductors, appealed to the War Labor Board. The Board directed that "women employees shall receive equal pay for the same work, and the guaranteed minimum for women shall be increased from $60 to $75 per month, as now obtains in the case of men." The Board's decision, Valerie J. Conner observes, "reflected the harmony between the sexes by granting absolute wage equality, in uncompromising and direct language which the board had never used before and would not use again. . . ."

It was Cleveland, however, and not Kansas City, that set the pattern for the conductorettes. President Mahon of the Amalgamated Association made this quite clear in a letter to the Women's Bureau on May 13, 1920: "The dispute that was raised by our organization was against women as conductors on surface and trolley cars. Our organization took the position that it was to fit place for a woman to work and has decided against them."[65]

Gertrude Barnum of the WTUL defended the union's conduct in the Cleveland case, justifying her stand with the hoariest of arguments. The men had good reason to believe, she intoned, that the women had started work as conductorettes as a "war fad" and were not interested in belonging to the union because they viewed their work as "only temporary." The male unionists were therefore perfectly justified in viewing them as a nuisance: "If received in the union, they would only 'mess things up' and then get out."[66]

Yet the evidence reveals that relationship between men and women workers during the war varied considerably from place to place and union to union. Where women were welcomed into unions, they accepted the invitation gladly and made important contributions to advancing the interests of both themselves and of men workers, and together they obtained better working conditions. Where they were confronted by union opposition, women defended their own special interests. In general, the war gave many women their first contact with highly organized, militant male workers. Too often, the opposition of these male workers and their unions led the women to consider trade unionism and sex discrimination as synonymous. But for many, the contact taught them the advantages of trade union protection, and they learned from their association with progressive-minded male unionists the value of being organized into strong collective-bargaining unions. By 1920, trade union membership was 8 percent female, and 6.6 percent of all workingwomen were organized—a fivefold increase in a decade.[67]

Unfortunately, one of the real tragedies of this period lay in the fact that during the demobilization and reconstruction following the war, women workers were unable to obtain the protection of the trade unions in new postwar jobs, and (with rare exceptions) the male unionists were indifferent to the efforts of the women workers to maintain the gains made during the war. The federal government, too, which had played a large part in the major gains won by workingwomen during the war, now joined with state and municipal governments in supporting the veterans, who demanded their former jobs. Together with the trade unions, all of them took up the cry, "The women must go."

And go they did. For most women workers were shut out of the work they had done so effectively during the war. A Reconstruction Conference of women workers held in Washington, D.C., in January, 1919, concluded: "We have got to fight our way in—men will not open wide the doors."[68]

13

The Women's Trade Union League in the 1920s

AT THE 1918 AFL CONVENTION, the entire issue of postwar reconstruction was placed in the hands of the Executive Council, which was to conduct an investigation of the problem of readjustment and report the fruits of its survey.[1] In late December, 1918, the report was presented to the public as the official AFL plan for postwar America. Of immediate interest to wage earners were the demands for an eight-hour day and the guaranteed right to all workers to organize.

But when it came to proposals dealing with women, the unskilled, and blacks—sections of the labor force that had mushroomed in numbers and problems during the war years—the report was woefully weak. All it proposed was that women, when doing men's work, should receive equal pay for equal work, and that unskilled workers should be entitled to a living wage. (No mention at all was made of black workers.) The only concern expressed over the possibility of postwar unemployment dealt with returning servicemen, who, it was stated, should be aided by the government in finding work, provided with sustenance while unemployed, and given the opportunity for easy and ready access to the land.[2]

On October 6, 1919, an Industrial Conference was convened by President Woodrow Wilson in the nation's capital. Of those chosen by the AFL Executive Council to represent labor at the conference, not only were all fifteen men, but even those men who headed unions made up predominantly or largely of women workers, such as the ILGWU, were notably missing from the list.* Not surprisingly, the problems facing women workers received little attention at the conference. The only

---

*Two women were present among the public group of twenty-five members: Ida Tarbell and Lillian Wald (*Survey*, Oct. 25, 1919, pp. 35–36).

specific proposal with respect to women workers was for "Equal Pay for
Women who are performing the same work as Men."†[3]

Once again, it remained for the National Women's Trade Union
League and its various branches to try to fill the vacuum as far as the
postwar needs of workingwomen were concerned. In at least one respect, the league was notably successful. In February, 1919, the New
York league sent the following telegram to New York City's congressional delegation: "New York Women's Trade Union League, membership 70,000 organized workers, respectfully insists continuation Wom-
en's Division, Labor Department. Necessary protection women workers
and standardization of labor conditions. Bureau has done splendid work
during war, but is more necessary to working women during reconstruction." Rose Schneiderman, president of the New York league, added
that there never was a time when the division was more needed, with the
work of reconstruction going on, and that the work of the division could
be the basis for legislative work for women.[4]

Largely as a result of league pressure and lobbying, the Women's
Bureau of the Department of Labor was established on a permanent
basis.[5] Thereafter, the league and the bureau worked closely together.
In fact, there was a frequent interchange of positions between officials of
the two groups. Mary Anderson, chief of the Women's Bureau, came to
Washington during World War I after years as an organizer for the
National WTUL, and throughout her career in government maintained
close contacts with the league. Mary Winslow retired from the Women's
Bureau to sit on the WTUL Executive Board. The league regularly
petitioned Congress for an increase in the bureau's appropriation, while
Mary Anderson and other members of the Bureau solicited funds for
the WTUL.

This relationship was no accident, for the league and the bureau had
similar problems. Both were small and poorly funded, neither was able
to compel industry to obey its recommendations or to force male-led
unions to treat women workers fairly, and neither became an effective
force during the 1920s for the solution of the problems of workingwomen. Officials of the bureau regularly charged that male unionists either
ignored or belittled the problems of women workers. While Mary Anderson and her colleagues were urging increased participation by
women in union affairs, she herself was instructing her staff to "keep at"
specific unions that discriminated blatantly against women. She complained to A. J. Berre, secretary of the AFL Metal Department, condemning the International Molders' Union for the practice of expelling
any member who instructed a woman in foundry work. Women would
continue to enter the trades, Anderson warned Berre, and men ought to
realize that they, too, would benefit from effective organization of their

†An eleven-point labor plan was introduced at the sessions, but the conference broke up
without having passed a single resolution.

female coworkers. The AFL officials were as deaf to complaints from the Women's Bureau as they had been and continued to be to similar pleas by the WTUL.

The two organizations shared still another characteristic in that they were both practically all white. The efforts of Mary Church Terrell, the prominent black social activist, to establish a Colored Women's Division within the Women's Bureau came to naught. Mary Anderson was cool to the idea, maintaining that "colored women in industry are not a very large factor." But bureau bulletins and census reports alike indicated that black women were indeed 'a large factor" in American industry.[6]

Although neither the WTUL nor the Women's Bureau was a radical organization, both were plagued by charges that they supported "subversive, socialist and communist ideas." Indeed, during the 1920s, conservative newspapers, manufacturers' associations, antifeminists, and, unofficially, the U.S. War Department, as well as a number of AFL union officials, charged the league and the Women's Bureau with cooperating "in an international socialist conspiracy to subvert American institutions as part of an international woman's plot to Bolshevize America." The Daughters of the American Revolution, through its *Woman Patriot* magazine, and Henry Ford, in his *Dearborn Independent,* denounced the league as part of the "Communist conspiracy," and these attacks were widely reprinted throughout the country and were even read into the *Congressional Record.* In New York, James P. Holland, president of the State Federation of Labor, attacked the league as "a tail to the Socialist kite."

Yet the only evidence ever presented to support these charges was the facts that the league's revised constitution of 1922 urged that war be banned and that women workers of all countries work closely together, that the league campaigned for the Child Labor Amendment to the Constitution, and that it joined with other liberal groups in establishing a women's Joint Constitutional Committee to act as a clearinghouse for legislative efforts and to lobby for reform legislation.

In 1924 the *Dearborn Independent* accused Mary Anderson of being a Communist tool, and the *Woman Patriot* charged the Women's Bureau with attempting, along with the WTUL, to "Bolshevize" the United States by destroying the family. That same year, Lucia Maxwell, librarian for the Chemical Warfare Section of the War Department, drew up a chart that listed both the WTUL and the Women's Bureau (along with other prominent women's organizations in the United States) as members of a vast conspiracy, which she called the "Spider Web." The War Department printed and distributed the "Spider Web" chart, and it was reprinted in the *Dearborn Independent* and as a pamphlet by the National Manufacturers' Association.[7]

One of the pieces of evidence of the "vast conspiracy" cited in the "Spider Web" was the fact that both the WTUL and the Women's Bureau were involved in the Summer School for Working Women in

Industry established at Bryn Mawr College in 1921 under the direction
of Dean Hilda Smith, a former social worker.* From the beginning,
Smith saw to it that the staff included someone with a labor point of view
and actual experience in industry. The choice was Agnes Nestor, president of the Chicago Women's Trade Union League. Mary Anderson
attended the organizational meeting as a representative of the Women's
Bureau and served on the faculty-selection and admissions committees.[8]

Half the members of the Summer School's board of directors were
labor leaders and the other half were college people. Among the former
were Emma Elliot of the Philadelphia United Textile Workers and
Pauline Newman and Freda Millar from the Philadelphia Women's
Trade Union League. This "fifty-fifty" representation was endorsed by
the student-workers, who also advocated the admission of black workingwomen as students. Both suggestions were approved over the initial
opposition of Dr. M. Carey Thomas, president of Bryn Mawr (which did
not admit black women) and herself one of the initiators of the Summer
School. The black women were admitted to the Summer School, but at
first they were segregated in a separate hall. The student-workers con-
sulted with Hilda Smith, and thereafter the black women were integrated with the rest of the student body.[9]

Bryn Mawr donated campus space for the summer sessions, and the
Women's Trade Union League conducted a vigorous fund-raising campaign to enable the women workers to leave their jobs for one or two
months in order to study. However, these scholarships provided only
minimal living expenses for the period of study. Employers often refused to grant students leaves of absence, so that many Summer School
participants had to quit their jobs in order to attend and then had to
search for work when they returned home.[10] Libby Corngold, a student
at the 1927 Bryn Mawr Summer School, described "a typical employer's
reaction" as her contribution to the 1927 student magazine of essays:

Employee: Mr. M., I would like to ask you to give me a leave of
absence for two months, which I would like to spend attending
school.
Employer: A leave of absence? In the time when the season has
started? What kind of school is this?
Employee: Bryn Mawr Summer School.
Employer: Oh. So you want to attend a school which teaches workers how best to fight the bosses.
Employee: Not at all. This school's aim is to enable workers to think
more clearly on problems they are confronted with.

*Another workers' school—Brookwood Labor College—was founded in 1921 with the assis-
tance of Rose Schneiderman, who served on its board of policymakers. The first resident
school for workers in the United States was coeducational, with a two-year program and
three-week summer institutes.

Employer: What for do you want education? Can't you stitch coats without having any? ... [11]

During the school's early years, its curriculum was structured along classical collegiate educational lines, but the league, the trade unions, and the students themselves insisted on including economic issues in the curriculum.[12] About one hundred workingwomen were educated annually during the eight-week summer course. Many were dedicated unionists, but even those who were not members of trade unions were ready to "do their bit for the cause of organized labor" by the time they left Bryn Mawr.*[13]

The women workers who attended Bryn Mawr Summer School became leaders in their communities when they returned home, and many of them were instrumental in establishing evening classes for workingwomen in their home communities. While a number of them encountered difficulties in obtaining leadership positions in male-dominated unions, others did have an important impact on the trade unions. For fifteen years the Bryn Mawr Summer School was a leadership center for workingwomen. This league-inspired institution also encouraged labor to undertake its own program for training women. An educational clearinghouse and guidance center known as the Workers' Education Bureau was established by unionists and social reformers in 1921 and soon became an adjunct of the AFL. By 1925 forty-one AFL union affiliates were supporting the bureau, and federation representatives controlled its Executive Committee.[14]

One of the national leaders in workers' education was a graduate of the first WTUL labor class in 1914. She was Fannia Cohn, who was appointed to the position of organizing secretary when the ILGWU established a General Education Committee in 1916. In 1918 she was appointed Educational Director of the ILGWU, serving on its General Executive Board from 1916 to 1928, and was the first female vice-president of a major international union. Working with the league and the Women's Bureau, Fannia Cohn helped promote awareness of the need for education of workers, especially women workers, throughout the labor and reform movements. Planning educational programs for local union members and their wives and publicizing workers' classes

---

*Ninety-eight workingwomen attended in 1922. They came from twenty-three states from Maine to the Pacific Coast. Thirty industries were represented, with the largest group from the clothing trades, of whom fourteen made men's garments and twelve ladies'. The textile group was next in size, with eleven. The remaining trades were scattered, with from one to six in number. There were thirty-four unionists among the students, representing fourteen unions. Eight were members of the United Garment Workers, seven from the Amalgamated Clothing Workers, six from the International Ladies' Garment Workers, two from the telephone operators' department of the International Brotherhood of Electrical Workers, one from the Glove Workers' Union, two from the Boot and Shoe Workers, and one each from the leather workers, millinery workers, capmakers, bookbinders, and federal employees (*Seattle Union Record*, July 15, 1922). The number of unionists increased each summer.

and college institutes, she insisted that the worker educational programs give special consideration to the talents and contributions of women workers. Unfortunately, it was easier to advance this idea in programs in which the league was an important force than in those controlled by male-dominated unions. "The labor movement," she wrote, "is guilty of not realizing the importance of placing the interest of women on the same basis as of men and until they will accept this, I am afraid the movement will be much hampered in its progress."[15]

Two prominent league women—Melinda Scott of the United Felt, Panama and Straw Hat Rimmers and Operators Union and Agnes Nestor of the International Glove Workers Union—were appointed members of the AFL-sponsored American Labor Mission to Europe to visit England and France in 1918 with messages of hope and encouragement for European workers.*[16] Despite league pleading, however, working-women were not represented when labor organizations of the Allied countries met in Paris in February, 1919, to formulate a program for postwar employment and to advise the Paris Peace Conference delegates on labor issues.[17] In fact, only Gompers represented the views of American labor at the Commission on International Labor Legislation. After calling President Wilson's attention to the absence of any representatives of female workers and receiving his agreement that they should have a voice, the WTUL sent Rose Schneiderman and Mary Anderson to Paris, at its own expense, as spokespersons for "100,000 organized women, members of the Women's Trade Union League in the United States."†
They brought with them a list of proposals that would assure recognition of the rights of workingwomen for inclusion in the peace treaty. These would have required that the Committee on International Labor Legislation present to the Versailles Conference demands for compulsory education of children up to the age of sixteen and part-time education up to eighteen years; abolition of child labor; an eight-hour day and a forty-four-hour week; no night work for women; one day's rest in seven; equal pay for equal work; equal opportunities for men and women in trade and technical training; social insurance against sickness, accidents, industrial disease, and unemployment; provision for old age; and pensions and maternity benefits. The full enfranchisement of women would also be urged so that they might have "political, legal and industrial equality,"

---

*Investigating working conditions, Scott and Nestor also discussed with European labor leaders the peace terms, efforts for democracy, and an effective International Federation of Labor (see *Woman's Labor Leader: An Autobiography of Agnes Nestor* [Rockford, Ill., 1954], pp. 184–223).

†Mary Anderson received leave as assistant director of the Woman-in-Industry Service to represent the WTUL in France (Mary Anderson as told to Mary Winslow, *Woman at Work: The Autobiography of Mary Anderson* [Minneapolis, 1951], p. 121). Anderson came home disillusioned with the lack of sincerity of male political and labor leaders but convinced that the time had come "for labor women everywhere to get together and work together" (ibid., p. 124).

as well as "the protection of motherhood and the guarantee to every child of the highest possible development."[18]

Arriving too late to present their program, Schneiderman and Anderson met with Colonel E. M. House and Professor James Shotwell of the American delegation. But the only specific concession made to women workers was the inclusion in the "Bill of Rights" incorporated into the Versailles Treaty of a provision calling for "equal pay for men and women."[19] The league was similarly unsuccessful in persuading President Wilson to require women delegates at the League of Nations' International Labor Organization. The ILO charter merely provided that at least one female adviser must be present for the discussion of issues affecting women. However, while in Paris, Schneiderman and Anderson explored with other women the possibility of an International Working Women's Conference, and the National Women's Trade Union League issued a call to women labor leaders in European countries to meet in Washington for such a conference. With expenses underwritten by chairperson Margaret Dreier Robins, the first International Congress of Working Women (as it was named) attracted fifty delegates from twelve countries and visitors from seven others.*

The league not only sponsored and underwrote the Congress; it also prepared a "Union Women's Labor Program" for consideration by the delegates. It was a comprehensive "Program of Social and Industrial Reconstruction" and called for many of the special legislative measures for women workers that had been brought to Paris, including an eight-hour day, a forty-four-hour workweek, equal pay for equal work, equal opportunities for trade and technical training, social insurance with maternity benefits, compulsory insurance against unemployment for men and women alike, and consideration of the payment of unemployment benefits to workers on strike. The program also called for freedom of speech, the press, and assembly and for public ownership of natural resources.[20]

Although it was called the "Union Women's Labor Program," few provisions in the league's reconstruction program dealt with either unionization or the labor movement. Almost every measure was either political or legislative in nature. The same could be said of the First International Congress of Working Women, which met in Washington, D.C., in late October and early November, 1919. In opening the Congress, Margaret Dreier Robins made a telling point when she noted:

> Women had no direct share in the terms of the Peace Treaty. It's a man-made peace. Women have had no direct share in the labor platform,

---

*Delegates attended from Great Britain, Poland, France, Sweden, Belgium, Norway, Argentina, Canada, Czechoslovakia, India, Cuba, Denmark, Japan, The Netherlands, Serbia, Spain, and Switzerland.

with its emphasis on the protection of women in industry rather than its emphasis on the participation of women in plans to protect themselves which is significant of the attitude of men, even in the labor movement, toward women.

The "labor platform" stressed at the Congress was geared entirely to legislation. Discussion of laws establishing a universal eight-hour day for workingwomen consumed several days' deliberation. This was followed by a discussion of the need for laws providing maternity benefits for workingwomen before, during, and after the birth of a child.

In none of these discussions was there any mention of either a role for the trade unions or the need for organizing workingwomen into unions. In fact, the only reference to this aspect of the situation came in a message to the Congress from "Representative Negro Women of the United States in behalf of Negro Women Laborers of the United States."* Noting that 2 million black women engaged in such pursuits warranted "representation in the Council," the message called attention to their absence from the Congress. Since black women were "very little organized in unions or other organizations," the message continued, they had "very limited means of making their wishes known, and of having their interests advanced through their own representatives":

> Therefore, we a group of Negro women, representing those two million of Negro women wage-earners, respectfully ask for your active cooperation in organizing the Negro women workers of the United States into unions, that they may have a share in bringing about industrial democracy and social order in the world.

Apart from applauding the appeal, however, the Congress did nothing about it.[21]

The refusal of the U.S. Senate to ratify the Versailles Treaty limited the effectiveness of the International Labor Organization, since its success was "linked to American participation in the League of Nations."[22]

---

*The "Memorial" was signed by Elizabeth C. Carter, Executive Worker, War Work Council, YWCA, and Honorary President, National Association of Colored Women's Clubs; Mamie R. Rosse, President, Conference Branch M., Missionary Society, Liberia, West Coast of Africa; Leilia Pendleton, Folder and Compositor, Washington, D.C.; A. G. Green, Community Secretary, Public School of D.C.; Eva A. Wright, Milliner, Ohio and Washington, D.C.; Mary Church Terrell, Honorary President, National Association of Colored Women's Clubs, Washington, D.C.; Nannie H. Burroughs, President, National Training School for Women and Girls, Washington, D.C.; Carrie Roscoe C. Bruce, Public Schools, Washington, D.C.; Caroline Clifford, Chairperson, Committee on Children's Work, NAACP, Washington, D.C.; Elizabeth Ross Haynes, Working Woman, Fisk University and Washington, D.C. ("Typed Proceedings of the First International Congress of Working Women, October 28 to November 5, 1919," November 4 session, pp. 32–33, National Women's Trade Union League Papers, Library of Congress). Another copy is in Records of the Women's Bureau, U.S. Department of Labor, R.G. 86, November, 1919, "International Conference File," National Archives.

This time, the National Women's Trade Union League tried to fill the gap by making the International Congress of Working Women a permanent association of women workers. In Geneva, in October, 1921, delegates were present from twelve nations, and they changed the name of the Congress to the International Federation of Working Women, adopted a constitution, and elected Margaret Dreier Robins of the National Women's Trade Union League as president.

The declared objective of the federation was "to unite organized women in order that they may resolve upon the means by which the standard of the life of the workers throughout the world may best be raised." This time, priority was given to trade unionism, and the federation's goal was, first, to "promote trade union organization among women," and then to develop an international policy that gave special consideration to the needs of women and children. Secondly, it was to examine all projects for legislation proposed by the International Labor Conference of the League of Nations; and finally, it was to promote the appointment of workingwomen to organizations affecting the welfare of workers. As far as membership was concerned, the federation was to consist of "national trade union organizations. containing women members, and affiliated to the International Federation of Trade Unions," but it would also admit workingwomen's organizations "accepting its aims and agreeing to work in the spirit and to follow the principles of the International Federation of Trade Unions."* In emphasizing that the federation would "promote trade union organization among women," its Constitutional Committee noted: "That means that it shall in every way possible help to get women into the trade unions, not to form new trade unions apart from those already in existence, but to help to strengthen those unions that there are."[23]

Upon assuming the presidency, Robins declared that the first task of workingwomen of the world was "to make war against war." "The first battle in that war," she continued, "is to stop increasing armaments. Aramaments breed war." She then cited winning "the right to our daily bread" as the first domestic task of women workers, and, after pointing out that unemployment cast its shadow over workers' homes everywhere, she declared vigorously that "either unemployment or capitalism must go. If competitive private industry cannot employ the able and willing workers, then is competitive private industry doomed." Robins then urged workingwomen to try direct political action as a means of achieving their goals: "When we are hungry and homeless and

*The International Federation of Trade Unions was established before World War I, but its activities were disrupted by the outbreak of the war. The Allied labor movements discontinued their dues payments, as did the AFL, in 1914. The IFTU was reorganized after the war at a meeting in Amsterdam in 1919. Gompers was one of three representatives elected by the AFL to attend the session.

idle or slaughtering our brothers or killing our sons, let us vote against the government without regard to party."[24]

In 1922 Robins resigned as president of the National Women's Trade Union League in order to devote more of her time and money to the International Federation of Working Women. She was succeeded by Maude O'Farrell Swartz, the first trade union president of the league. A native of Ireland, Swartz had become a proofreader and member of the Typographical Union shortly after arriving in the United States. She was drawn into the league by the suffrage movement, attended its organizers' school, taught workers' classes, and was branch secretary before her election as president. While her election was an indication that more trade union women were involved in the league's leadership, the truth is that it was turning increasingly to politics as a means of accomplishing its objectives. Thus, the New York WTUL united with the Consumers' League, the YWCA, and other reform organizations to form a Women's Joint Legislative Conference, chaired by the league's Mary E. Dreier, sister of Margaret Dreier Robins. Asserting that unions had failed to safeguard women, the coalition lobbied for protective legislation. It is no wonder that a member wrote unhappily following the eighth annual WTUL convention: "The purpose of the League, as I understand it, is to organize workers into trade union groups, and yet at the convention, little time was given to this question."[25]

As the year 1920 closed and the new decade got under way, the Women's Bureau of the Department of Labor reported that "many women are not included in the membership of the big international unions. More than 12,000 are found on the rolls of the International Association of Machinists, and there are many thousands in the Brotherhood of Railway Carmen." Furthermore, 8 percent of the trade union membership was now female, with 6.6 percent of workingwomen organized.[26] But events soon disclosed that further progress in organizing women into the AFL was to be exceedingly difficult. In February a conference of AFL international and national unions called upon the public to recognize and support "the right of the working people of the United States to organize into trade unions." Each union representative present appended his name to the document with the statement: "To the above declaration and appeal we pledge ourselves and those we represent." Among those signing the appeal and pledge were the president and another representative of the International Molders' Union and the president and secretary-treasurer of the Journeymen Barbers' International Union, both unions that expressly excluded women from membership.[27]

Samuel Gompers, Frank Morrison, and all the other members of the AFL Executive Council also signed the appeal on behalf of "the right of the working people of the United States to organize into trade unions."

Yet a few weeks later, Secretary Morrison wrote in answer to an inquiry: "The American Federation of Labor would have authority to issue charters to women members of a trade only where such course would be authorized by the international organization having jurisdiction."[28] How this operated was illustrated in the case of the women barbers of Seattle, who, denied membership in the Barbers' Union, asked the AFL for a separate charter and were refused because the Barbers' Union objected. As we have seen, the women barbers received a charter from the Seattle Labor Council. But other women workers who were excluded from international unions were not so fortunate. Writing in the June, 1921, issue of *Life and Labor,* Mabel W. Taylor, organizer for the Women's Trade Union League, reported from Grand Rapids, Michigan, where many women were employed in the manufacture of furniture, that efforts to organize these women had failed. In giving the reasons, she pointed out that the union had refused to take the women into its organization and that when the women tried to organize separately, they were refused a charter by the AFL. The men in the shops then tried to have the women discharged "by belittling the amount and quality of the work they do, and by making the girls feel that they are interlopers."[29]

Aroused by these developments, the Executive Board of the NWTUL appointed a committee to confer with the AFL Executive Council to discuss the issuance of charters to groups of women not admitted to membership in the international unions of their trade. The committee met with the Executive Council on August 23, 1921, but nothing came of the discussions other than the suggestion by Gompers that conferences be held with those internationals that excluded women.[30]

But the league was not willing to rely on vague promises. Instead, it met with a group of women delegates to the 1921 AFL convention and helped form the Women's Committee for Industrial Equality. A resolution was drawn up to amend the AFL constitution. Introduced by Delegate Ethel Haig, a tobacco worker, it read:

> Nothing in this constitution shall be construed as recognition of any right on the part of the American Federation of Labor, or any affiliated union, or of any officers of such union, to deny or abridge the right of workers to membership and to all the privileges of membership in the union of their trade or industry on account of sex; and women in a trade under the jurisdiction of a union which does not admit women to membership on the same terms as men shall not be denied a separate and direct charter from the American Federation of Labor for lack of consent of that union.

The amendment was deliberately drawn so as to avoid direct interference with "autonomy" by not making it mandatory for an international to accept women. But it did provide that if entrance into the AFL

278   WOMEN AND THE AMERICAN LABOR MOVEMENT

was closed to any group of women by an international union, then another door could be opened through which they might enter. The issue was therefore clear. Either the AFL would recognize and support the right of women to be organized and live up to its repeated and frequent declarations of support for the "organizing of all workers, regardless of sex," or it would again use the slightest possibility of infringing on "the autonomy of the internationals" as an excuse for excluding women.

The industrial equality amendment produced an interesting discussion, and a number of male delegates spoke out in its behalf. But the AFL leadership would have none of it. Claiming that exclusion was the result not of prejudice but of the fact that women were not suited for work in the trades that banned them, the committee on laws introduced a substitute resolution, which read: "Resolved, that the international and national organizations that do not admit women workers give early consideration to such admission." The convention then rejected a floor amendment calling upon the AFL itself to charter locals if affiliates prohibited female members, and it went on to accept the committee's resolution by a vote of 164 to 73. The meaninglessness of this resolution was indicated by the fact that two of the five internationals that had banned women from membership—the Barbers and the United Brotherhood of Carpenters—were not scheduled to hold their conventions until 1924, and another—the Molders' Union—had not even set the date for its next convention.* Moreover, the presidents of each of these three organizations informed the press that no consideration would be given to the subject of women workers by his union until its convention was held, and that there was little likelihood that it would receive consideration even then. And when, a few months later, the WTUL appealed directly to the AFL Executive Council to issue charters to women if they were excluded by affiliates, the proposal was rejected. The council claimed it had no authority unless it was authorized by the unions involved.[31]

But the Committee for Industrial Equality remained hopeful. It changed its name to the National Woman's Union and planned to fight for an even stronger resolution at the 1922 AFL convention.[32] At the convention, Mary V. Halas, fraternal delegate of the NWTUL, drew up a resolution calling upon the AFL Executive Council to issue charters directly to women in occupations in which the unions refused to admit women to membership. She then had Luther E. Seward, president of the National Federation of Federal Employees, introduce it. However, the

*The other two unions whose constitutions or bylaws barred women from membership were the Elastic Goring Weavers' Association and the Pattern Makers' League.

Committee on Laws reported a revised resolution to the convention. It opened with fulsome praise for the AFL as having "since its inception . . . done everything in its power to organize the women workers of the country and to obtain for them equal rights, political as well as economical." Since, it claimed, only a few international unions refused to admit women to membership, "due largely to the *nature* of their work," the revised resolution proposed that the Executive Council take up the subject with the trade unions involved and endeavor to reach an understanding "as to the issuance of Federal charters." The revised resolution was quickly adopted.

How little was to be gained by this approach became clear soon after the convention. The women barbers in Seattle applied to the AFL for a federal charter on the basis of the 1922 resolution. At first it was granted, but it was then recalled after a vehement protest by the International Barbers' Union. At that point, the whole procedure was abandoned.[33]

Thus, while women delegates were permitted to attend its conventions and to introduce resolutions calling for the unionization of women workers, the AFL did little concrete along these lines. It did seem that the federation was finally beginning to move in 1923, after the Supreme Court invalidated a District of Columbia minimum-wage law for women—a decision that will be discussed below. The AFL reacted by raising the need for a unionization drive among workingwomen. Asserting that "if they [women] cannot be protected by law, we should protect them by organization," Gompers invited forty-five unions to a national conference in February, 1924. At this conference, a discussion was held about the agencies that already existed to help the woman worker. In his presentation Gompers stated that although the WTUL rendered valuable service during strikes, it was "inadequate to the task" of organizational work, being "academic." Its mission, he declared, was primarily educational, and he practically proposed that it be dissolved. In its place, he suggested the establishment, under his direct supervision, of an AFL women's bureau that would include a female executive officer and that would lead a joint organizational campaign financed by member unions.

Less than three weeks later, Gompers sent his secretary, Florence Thorne, to Mary Anderson to find out "if the League could be persuaded to go out of business." A number of leaguers viewed the proposal of an AFL women's bureau as little more than a device to undermine the league, and the fact that it was supported by the Barbers' and Carpenters' Unions gave credence to these suspicions. Still, the league leadership was even prepared to abandon its organizational activities and act as a link between the trade union movement and the general public—provided that the AFL women's bureau actually got under way. In a letter to Gompers signed by its Executive Council, the league pledged its willingness to coordinate its efforts with those of the AFL. The letter concluded:

> The fact that there are, according to the Women's Bureau of the United States Department of Labor, 3,156,600 women working at trades which come within the jurisdiction of the national and international organizations affiliated to the American Federation of Labor, and that the records of the American Federation of Labor show no more than 200,000 of this number in the membership of the American Federation of Labor, is a telling comment upon the overwhelming difficulties besetting the task of the organization of women. We believe that the coordination of effort in this direction under an able woman executive is the most important step that could be taken, and we gladly pledge the resources and the machinery of the National Women's Trade Union League in aid of this undertaking.[34]

The proposed women's bureau, however, never became a reality. Of forty-five unions invited to the first meeting, only thirteen sent representatives, and they objected to a women's bureau as an infringement on trade union autonomy. After another conference, the plan was turned over to the AFL convention in August, 1924. In its report to the 1924 AFL convention, the Executive Council merely declared: "After considering the whole situation, the Council felt that because of the very few pledges of substantial support to a separate and distinctive movement confined to organizing women wage-earners, it was obvious that a general concerted action would be impracticable." The Executive Council then proposed the following as the only way in which the AFL could deal with the issue of organizing the unorganized woman worker: "That the Federation can promote the organization of women in industry by making available informational sources and material and by carrying on the educational work necessary to a better understanding of the problem of women in industry and the necessity for constructive action."

Ironically, by 1924, not only were the five international unions that barred women from membership still continuing the practice, but a number of other internationals publicly acknowledged that they officially opposed the admission of women. These included the Teamsters' and Chauffeurs' Union, the Brotherhood of Blacksmiths and Drop Forgers, and the United Mine Workers.[35]

Then, at its 1925 convention, the Executive Council authorized the new president, William Green, "to work out a plan" for the unionization of women workers. The plan provided that the various unions in a given locality should make a joint intensive drive to organize women under their jurisdictions. Each union was to supply its own organizers, its own techniques, and the particular literature necessary for its special trade problems.

The campaign was initiated in the summer of 1926 and centered in Newark, New Jersey, under the direction of the AFL's legislative agent and top organizer, Edward F. McGrady. But the campaign received only nominal support. An insight into the reasons for the failure is provided by McGrady's attitude. When he was approached by two experienced WTUL activists with an offer to assist in the drive, he informed them that "women could not be organized; women do not want to be organized; women had been organized at great trouble and expense, and their unions had not lasted." The offer to assist in the Newark campaign was coldly rejected. "Why don't you forget all this business," McGrady urged the WTUL-ers, "and leave the labor movement to men? It's too rough for women. Why don't you get married?" His parting shot was both typical and revealing: "If you want to organize women, you'll have to wait until the Federation gets around to it. We think the time isn't ripe yet. It will not be for another twenty-five or fifty years. The trouble with you two is that you are ahead of your time."

At the 1926 AFL convention, Green acknowledged that the campaign had failed and urged that organizing drives among women be abandoned in favor of an educational effort, with appeals to the internationals themselves to organize women. When Rose Schneiderman addressed the delegates in her new capacity as president of the WTUL, she said not a word of criticism of the abandonment of organizational work among women and pledged league support for the educational effort.*[36]

The truth is that the WTUL had some time earlier decided to stop pressing the issue of the exclusion of women from unions affiliated with the AFL and the failure of the federation to mount a meaningful organizing campaign among women workers. The league now believed that the woman worker faced a more dangerous assault than the one growing out of the hostility of AFL international unions, and that in combating this danger, the campaign to change the policies and practices of these unions toward women workers had to be shelved.[37]

The issue was protective legislation. In the beginning of the twentieth century, states began to enact laws regulating the conditions and hours of workers. The Supreme Court struck down legislation providing for maximum hours for workers on the ground that it denied workers the right to make their own contracts of employment. In *Muller* v. *Oregon* (1908), however, the Court sustained similar legislation applying only to women workers, asserting:

*Schneiderman succeeded Maude O'Farrell Swartz, who decided in 1926 not to run for reelection because of her activity in behalf of workmen's compensation and her assistance to the New York league. Rose Schneiderman remained president of the national organization from 1926 until it disbanded in 1950.

That woman's physical structure and the performance of maternal functions place her at a disadvantage is obvious. . . . The two sexes differ in structure of body, in the functions to be performed by each, in the amount of physical strength, in the capacity for long continued labor, particularly when done standing, the influence of vigorous health upon the future well-being of the race, the self-reliance which enables one to assert full rights and in the capacity to maintain the struggle for subsistence.[38]

After *Muller,* the enactment of protective legislation had increased, and organizations like the WTUL and the Consumers' League had devoted more and more of their time and energy to promoting the passage of such laws.

But now it was seen by some that the legislation cut with a double-edged sword. While it did protect women from many of the worst abuses of the early twentieth-century industrial system, some legislation also served to exclude women from certain occupations. As we have seen, several hundred female subway workers in Brooklyn lost their jobs when the legislature prohibited women from working at night in such occupations. For various groups of women workers, protective legislation often made it more difficult to compete with male employees in the job market.

During World War I, the Women's League for Equal Opportunity was formed in New York City to lobby against the night work law and the fifty-four-hour statute. It was soon joined by the Equal Rights League, made up of women printers. However, both organizations were small until after the war, when their ranks were swelled as women telegraphers, streetcar operators, and others who had been working in traditionally male occupations stood to lose their jobs by legislative action. After 1918 both organizations sent lobbyists to every legislative hearing urging the repeal of existing protective legislation and the defeat of any additional laws.[39]

The chief opponent of protective legislation, however, was the Congressional Union, the most militant American suffrage organization, which later changed its name to the National Woman's Party. In 1921 the NWP turned its major attention to a proposed equal rights amendment to the Constitution. The amendment was very simple. It read: "No political, civil or legal disabilities or inequalities on account of sex nor on account of marriage, unless applying equally to both sexes, shall exist within the United States or any territory thereof."

The National Women's Trade Union League immediately expressed concern that both the state and the U.S. Supreme courts, constantly on the lookout for loopholes in the social and economic legislation, would seize upon the words "disabilities" and "inequalities" as a pretext to declare unconstitutional special legislation in various states relating to women in industry, and would proceed to wipe out the special dispensations granted to women workers by law after years of ceaseless struggle. Protective enactments granting special working hours and conditions of labor for women were on the statute books of many states. What was now to become of these laws? the WTUL asked. Moreover, it was not simply the equal rights amendment that posed a threat; the National Woman's Party made it clear that it was prepared to launch a campaign both to eliminate such laws as were already on the statute books and to defeat any new protective legislation. As Alice Paul, the leading spokesperson for the NWP, put it:

> We looked into the laws and found how unfair they were—man-made laws setting forth how long women might work, where and under what conditions. In some instances, perhaps, women were the better for them. But I do not wholly concede even that. If the laws had not been made women would have been forced to organize and make the same agreements that men made. They would have made these agreements as a body of individuals contracting for themselves. There would have been no question of "thou shalt."
>
> Men are not going to make laws which will place women in a position of industrial competition with them. Hence eight-hour laws for women and minimum wages for women. . . .
>
> In times of unemployment will an employer hire a woman who has the minimum wage and eight-hour protection behind her or will he hire a man without these handicaps? Theoretically, it might sound fine, but, getting down to brass tacks, what effect will these laws have but to drive women out of the fields of individual effort and free contract?[40]

The immediate reaction of the NWTUL and its various state organizations was that while the professional women who made up the bulk of the National Woman's Party might not need the safeguards of special legislation, workingwomen did, and they would not be aided by a meaningless equality if the protective legislation they needed more than men were wiped out. In reply, the Women's League for Equal Opportunity and the Equal Rights League pointed out that they had actually preceded the National Woman's Party in opposing protective legislation and that they spoke for many working women.[41]

The WTUL launched a vigorous campaign to destroy the credibility of the women opponents of protective legislation. It insisted, first, that these organizations were not really working-class but were financed secretly by manufacturing interests; and, secondly, that at best, they represented an atypical faction of the female work force. Workingwomen who opposed protective legislation, the league argued, were those who competed directly with men for work—as skilled typesetters, telegraphers, and streetcar operators and in other occupations that traditionally belonged to men. Protective legislation placed such workers at a disadvantage in finding and keeping work. But most women workers needed

protective legislation and, the league insisted, were not handicapped in
their opportunities by such laws. And even if a few suffered, the vast
majority benefited.[42]

The league's conviction that most women workers did not oppose
protective legislation was substantiated to its satisfaction in 1927 when
the Consumers' League of New York found in a survey that four out of
five women questioned supported a law limiting a woman's working
hours to forty-eight a week.*[43] But the National Woman's Party repeatedly dismissed such evidence, and wherever the league and its allies
sought the passage of protective laws for women workers, NWP spokeswomen were bound to appear to argue against the laws and to lobby for
their defeat. The league occasionally stressed the importance of guard-
ing "the mothers of the race" in its arguments for special laws. In the
main, however, it emphasized the fact that women were not equal to men
in the work force. "These laws apply only to women," one league pamphlet stated; "because women's hours as a rule are longer than men's,
women's wages as a rule are lower than men's. Women's economic need
is therefore greater than men's." Moreover, under existing social and
economic conditions, women had no way of commanding a position of
equality in the workplace. As Ethel Smith, speaking for the WTUL, said:

> For one reason or another, women do not organize into labor bodies as
> effectively as men. They are, in a good many instances, just transients on the
> job. It is not life work with them. Because of that, their labor strength cannot
> be compared with men. They cannot go to employers and make agreements
> for themselves. To keep them from being exploited, different states passed
> labor legislation. The Minimum Wage law is one; the eight-hour day is
> another. Without these laws women might still be working life-killing hours
> at miserable wages.

The WTUL argued further that the whole theory of the equal rights
advocates, that repeal of the protective laws would enable women to
make arrangements with employers through direct negotiation and free
contract, was an illusion because it ignored the historic experience of the
league itself in organizing workingwomen. Only through collective action had labor been able to achieve its goals, and collective action was,
according to league spokespersons, more difficult to build among
women workers than among men. Nor were they likely to succeed in
securing legislation that would protect both men and women—the only
type of protective legislation the National Woman's Party approved—
since most of the protective legislation had been adopted in the first
place only because of the argument that such laws were needed to eliminate "conditions which are so threatening to our national life."[44]

---

*The Consumers' League surveyed 462 workingwomen in manufacturing and mercantile
establishments.

Although the arguments of the WTUL practically constituted a confession that it had failed to strengthen workingwomen's status through collective bargaining power and had to depend primarily on protective legislation,* the opposition to the National Woman's Party was buttressed by support from organized labor, especially the AFL. The position of organized labor was summed up in the following editorial in *Labor,* the national newspaper:

> The position of organized labor is that every law which discriminates against women should be repealed but that all laws which give them a better chance in the struggle for a living wage and decent working conditions should be retained and strengthened. . . .
>
> Employers' organizations like the National Manufacturers' Association will undoubtedly put their money and influence back of the National Woman's Party proposal to repeal all laws designed to protect working women. The employers know that women workers are not in as good position to resist the greed and injustice of employers as are men. Hence the need for special laws for women.
>
> The Women's Trade Union League and other organizations which are authorized to speak for working women will marshal the opposition, and they should receive the support of every right-minded citizen.[45]

The battle between the friends and foes of protective legislation for women was launched in earnest in 1923. The Women's Bureau of the Department of Labor called a conference on Women in Industry early in January, 1923, in Washington. Mary Anderson, the bureau's chief, invited Alice Paul, vice-president of the National Woman's Party, to attend. But when Paul asked for a place in the conference program, Anderson informed her that this was impossible because of the large number of organizations that had already been given places. Thereupon, the NWP and the Women's League for Equal Opportunity accused Anderson of allowing the presentation of only those views that supported the theory that workingwomen needed special legislation, and both organizations urged Congress to refuse funds for the conference. Congress, however, rejected their request, and the conference went forward without representatives of the two protesting organizations.[46]

Then, in February, 1923, the Senate Judiciary Committee held hearings on the Lucretia Mott, or equal rights, amendment. Fifteen women opponents of the amendment, representing more than a dozen national

---

*Fannia Cohn implied as much when she gave only reluctant support to protective legislation. She wrote: "I do not think the problem of working women could be solved in any other way than the problem of working men and that is through trade union organization, but considering that very few women are as yet organized into trade unions, it would be folly to agitate against protective legislation" (Fannia Cohn to Dr. Marion Phillips, 13 September 1927, Cohn Papers, Box 4).

organizations, spoke for two hours, arguing that the proposed measure, if adopted, would destroy the laws protecting women with respect to wages and hours of employment, and even mothers' pension laws.[47] Among the speakers who attacked the amendment were such veteran activists as Melinda Scott, Rose Schneiderman, Mary Van Kleeck, Agnes Nestor, Florence Kelley, and Nellie Swartz. Scott, representing the United Textile Workers, for which she was now a leading organizer, made a deep impression on the committee when she said:

> What if it should take longer to secure equal rights for women by dealing with discriminations separately? Would it not be better to take a little longer than to inflict upon millions of working women the sufferings that would be involved by destruction of the laws which now give them decent hours and working conditions? The working women are not so much concerned about property rights—they have no property. The National Woman's Party does not know what it is to work 10 or 12 hours a day in a factory; so they do not know what it means to lose an eight-hour-day or a nine-hour-day law. The working women do know, and that's why they are unanimously opposing this amendment.[48]

"We have worked for many years to get our labor laws for women, and we have had much litigation to establish them," declared Agnes Nestor. "We do not want to have to do that all over again, especially when all that this amendment purports to do can be done without incurring such consequences." Agnes Regan, secretary of the National Council of Catholic Women, followed with the argument that the amendment flew in the face of fact, sense, and philosophy:

> The physiological differences between men and women, besides the obvious ones, are so many, so deeply laid, and so persistent, that no law can wipe them out. Woman should have in law definite specific rights, as nature has conferred upon her definite specific duties. It is neither justifiable nor reasonable to level down these rights for the attainment of a purely theoretical identity.[49]

Three spokespersons for the National Woman's Party appeared at the hearing, but outnumbered as they were by the opponents, they refused to testify, pleading instead for a postponement. It was clear from the proceedings, however, and from the statements of the committee members that the amendment was, for the time being at least, dead.

It was not long, however, before the foes of protective legislation for women scored a major victory. On May 25, 1920, the Children's Hospital in Washington, D.C., petitioned the Supreme Court of the District of Columbia to set aside an award of the Minimum Wage Board fixing the lowest rates for women workers in hospitals and hotels at $16.50 per week. A major argument advanced by the hospital's counsel (and endorsed by the District Hotelmen's Association, which was supporting the hospital) was that the minimum-wage law for women workers had already compelled industry either to substitute men for women or to make the minimum the maximum rate, thus injuring instead of aiding its supposed beneficiaries. Florence Kelley brought Felix Frankfurter and Mary Dewson into the legal proceedings in support of the Minimum Wage Board's decision. The former served as co-counsel and the latter furnished evidence justifying the minimum-wage legislation. One of the telling points made by the defense was that various industrial surveys, especially that by the Federal Bureau of Labor Statistics in 1920, which covered the earnings of half a million women, revealed that, despite wartime wage increases, from one-quarter to one-third of the employees in such trades as cigar manufacturing, candymaking, and silk weaving received less than subsistence wages. The counsel for the District Board argued that minimum-wage laws were both necessary and effective in relieving the exploitation of women operatives.[50] The court ruled that the minimum-wage law was constitutional. The District Court of Appeals then rendered two decisions. The first, on July 6, 1921, upheld the constitutionality of the law by a vote of 2 to 1, but a year later the full court decided against the law by a similar vote. The case was then argued before the U.S. Supreme Court, which ruled on April 9, 1923, by five to three, against the constitutionality of the minimum-wage legislation. The court majority based its position on the right of private contract, insisting that while laws could be enforced to regulate working conditions, the employer and employee must be free of any restraint in determining between themselves what wages were acceptable. The court minority, on the other hand, contended that since there had been general acceptance of the fact that working conditions could be prescribed by lawmaking bodies, and since wages were but an extension of working conditions, it followed that wages were also a proper subject for legislation.

In his strong dissenting opinion, Justice Oliver Wendell Holmes wrote: "It will need more than the Nineteenth Amendment to convince me that there are no differences between men and women, or that legislation cannot take these differences into account. I should not hesitate to take them into account if I thought it necessary to sustain the act."

However, Justice George Sutherland, speaking for the majority, argued that the "ancient inequality of the sexes" had disappeared as far as the freedom of contract issue was concerned: "In view of the great—not to say revolutionary—changes which have taken place since the utterance, in the contractual, political, and civil status of women, culminating in the Nineteenth Amendment, it is not unreasonable to say that these differences have now reached the vanishing point." Minimum-wage laws for women, he went on, were thus "no longer necessary."[51]

The National Woman's Party enthusiastically endorsed the Court's decision. *Equal Rights*, the militant feminists' magazine, approvingly quoted Justice Sutherland's argument that women were as able to safeguard their health and morals as men were and declared:

> When one finds the Supreme Court of the United States beginning to realize that women should be accorded emancipation from the old doctrine that she must be given special protection or be subjected to special restraint in her contractual and civil relationships, one can feel that at last the world is beginning to realize that women are adult human beings.[52]

The NWTUL and the Consumers' League were both enraged by the decision and fearful of its consequences. At the time of the Supreme Court decision, fourteen states had minimum-wage laws for women. While the ruling did not repeal existing wage-fixing laws in these states, "a wholesale reduction of wages of women" in these fourteen states was "to be expected as a result of the Supreme Court decision," Ethel M. Smith, NWTUL legislative secretary, predicted. But the league did more than simply lament the decision. In response to its call, representatives of twenty-eight national organizations met in Washington on May 14, 1923, to study the effect of the court decision and decide on countermeasures.* President Samuel Gompers and Vice-President Matthew Woll of the AFL denounced the "usurpation of legislative and executive functions by the Judicial Branch of the Government" and declared themselves as favoring, as a solution, the enactment of a law requiring the concurrence of seven or eight of the nine justices to declare a law unconstitutional. Florence Kelley went even further, calling for limiting the review powers of the Court by either statute or Constitutional amendment.

But Elizabeth Christman and Rose Schneiderman, speaking for the WTUL, argued that judicial reform was at best a remote possibility and demanded, instead, a vigorous campaign to organize women into unions as the only realistic course. Schneiderman declared that women wage earners "needn't accept any wage cuts if they stand together like men for a single day." Women's work, she went on, was "just as valuable as men's"; it must be compensated as highly—and would be, if only women organized. Then she lashed out:

> The idea of always being a "poor working girl" is nonsense. There is no reason why a working girl should be poor. Men bakers, for instance, who are organized get good wages. Girls working in such a prosperous business as the candy industry get starvation wages because they are not organized. I want to say to the women in the District of Columbia, if they would organize, they would not only get the $16.50 a week formally guaranteed to them by law, but more.[53]

---

*An earlier meeting called by the Consumers' League on April 20, 1923, failed to produce a concrete program of action to undo the Court decision, and the conference sponsored by the NWTUL was an effort to achieve such a program.

However, the only concrete action taken by the conference was the appointment of a national committee representing the AFL and the two leading women's organizations* to "work out a comprehensive trade union program to combat the wage slashing that already is threatening 9 million women wage earners in the United States as a result of the Supreme Court decision."[54] But in November, 1923, the committee reported itself as "hopelessly deadlocked." For one thing, it was impossible to obtain agreement in favor of legislation checking the court, whether through simple legislative act or by constitutional amendment. Moreover, the pleas for organization of women workers in order to meet the problem had little effect on the AFL leadership.[55]

Meanwhile, the entire structure of minimum-wage laws for women was collapsing as state courts ruled such statutes invalid or state legislatures repealed them. Except in Massachusetts, those few laws that remained on the books became "dead letters" under the impact of the Supreme Court decision. By the end of 1923 it was estimated that women's wages in at least five of the states that had had minimum-wage laws had been reduced by one-third. New York State Industrial Commissioner Bernard I. Sheintag, after pointing out that the average weekly earnings of women in that state's factories were only half those of men workers, blamed the situation on the absence of "some form of minimum wage legislation that will help the thousands of women wage earners who are bravely battling to keep their heads above water."[56]

Thus, by 1923, all the effort that had gone into improving the status of women's labor through legislation appeared to have ended in failure. Most reformers, having put all their eggs into the legislative basket, now conceded that they were "baffled" and had nothing to hold out to workingwomen.[57]

The WTUL did score one victory in 1923, but it was not in the United States. In Vienna, at the Third Congress of the International Federation of Working Women, the delegates of the league obtained passage of a resolution favoring labor laws for women, irrespective of whether or not such laws applied to men. This action, the league announced from its Washington headquarters, was "a victory for the program advocated by American working women" and a defeat for "the National Woman's Party and its campaign to eliminate protective laws for working women."†[58]

---

*The committee consisted of Matthew Woll, Florence Kelley, general secretary of the National Consumers' League, and a representative of the NWTUL.

†An interesting aspect of the Vienna Congress was the discussion on the question of organization of women. Rose Schneiderman delivered a speech explaining "the difficulties to be encountered in America when organizing women." First, she emphasized that "they had all the nationalities there were in Europe," and that many women workers had originally been "peasant women" in "their own countries," without trade union experience. Another problem was the "fluctuation of their membership. Every five years they

But even this victory was short-lived. At its ninth biennial convention in June, 1924, the league voted to disaffiliate from the International Federation of Working Women, which it had been instrumental in creating. The reason lay in the IFWW's affiliation with the International Federation of Trade Unions (Amsterdam), the international organization of Socialists, as a women's committee within the International Federation. While the WTUL was unhappy over the proposed auxiliary status, the major reason for its disaffiliation was its desire to avoid antagonizing Gompers and other AFL leaders, who were completely opposed to any relations with an international Socialist organization. It is ironic that it was Rose Schneiderman, a former Socialist, who introduced the resolution for disaffiliation.*[59]

The continuing conflict between the WTUL and the NWP over protective legislation for women reached a climax in January, 1926, when the Women's Bureau of the U.S. Department of Labor sponsored a Women's Industrial Conference in Washington. At the very first session, the proceedings were almost disrupted by the conflict over protective legislation. When things had quieted down, Mary Van Kleeck of the Russell Sage Foundation presented the argument that employment and working conditions for women had steadily improved during the preceding fifty years as a result of protective laws. She was quickly answered by speakers for the National Woman's Party, led by Josephine Casey of Chicago, who argued that the "genesis of this so-called protective legislation was in the minds of men not wishing women as their competitors."[60]

In a message to the 350 women at the conference, President Coolidge voiced his support for protective legislation for women. He recalled with pleasure that while he was governor of Massachusetts, he had signed laws "to protect women in industry which I approved to safeguard and to protect the motherhood and potential motherhood of our State."†[61]

---

had a total change in the membership of their unions. Therefore, they had to continually teach the ABC's of trade unionism over again." Again, there were women's auxiliaries, but they "functioned more during strikes, when they came out and helped." After that, they did very little. "If they could get a mothers' movement started, that might be the answer to the question of retaining the girl after she was married." All told, it was not a very encouraging picture that Schneiderman painted ("Proceedings of the Third Congress of the International Federation of Working Women," Vienna, Aug. 28, 1923, typed copy, NWTUL Papers).

*Other resolutions adopted at the NWTUL convention demanded the curbing of the U.S. Supreme Court's power; the abolition of the injunction in labor disputes; the organization of black workers; a new trial for Sacco and Vanzetti, who were called innocent of the murder with which they were charged; support of anti-Fascist organizations; and opposition to the French occupation of the Ruhr. There was little discussion of the organization of women workers (*New York Times,* June 17, 1924).

†Both President Coolidge and Secretary of Labor James Davis based their advocacy of protective legislation and their opposition to the equal rights amendment to the Constitution not so much on the need for protecting workingwomen as on the preservation of traditional concepts of the female role—as a wife and mother in the home.

The message was greeted with delight by the friends of protective legislation, but it failed to disconcert the National Woman's Party and its allies. Three hundred women were mobilized for a march to the White House, where they left a petition contending that they were placed at a disadvantage in competing with men in the industrial world by the "so-called welfare laws for women": "We who are earning our living find ourselves hampered by laws that prevent us from offering our services to employers on an equal basis with men; by laws that prevent us from entering various occupations entirely; by laws that prevent us from continuing work after we are married."*[62]

With this petition, the National Woman's Party captured the headlines, but the proponents of protective legislation struck back immediately. Twenty-seven trade union women attending the conference presented Coolidge with a counterpetition expressing their full support for protective legislation for women:

> We regard such not as discrimination against women, but means toward an equal industrial footing for women and men. Generally speaking, the women-employing industries are the industries in which the longest hours prevail. The destruction of all legal limitations upon hours of work for women would have the effect of lengthening women's hours of labor, without affecting the hours of men, thereby increasing the present inequality between the hours of women and those of men.
>
> Furthermore, to take the position that there should be no labor laws for women which do not apply also to men is to say, in effect, that women's conditions of employment shall not be improved by law until legislatures are ready to enact similar laws for men—a time which, when current economic facts are faced, is clearly far in the future.†[63]

After considerable turmoil, the controversy over protective legislation ended with the adoption of a compromise resolution. The conference instructed the Women's Bureau to "make a comprehensive investigation of all the special laws regulating the employment of women, to determine their effects," and provided for an advisory committee to include equal representation of both sides of the controversy.‡[64]

---

*The petition was submitted in the name of the Industrial Council of the National Woman's Party and was signed by Mary A. Murray and Margaret Hinchey of New York, Josephine Casey of Chicago, and Myrtle Cain of Minneapolis. Hinchey called herself a victim of protective legislation, insisting that she had had a good job on the New York subway but had lost it when the bill regulating the hours of labor of women on railroads was passed by the legislature. Murray was president of the Women's League of the Brooklyn and Manhattan Transport Company (*New York Times*, Jan. 16, 17, 18, 1926).

†The delegation was led by Melinda Scott, representing the AFL, Sarah A. Conboy, representing the United Textile Workers of America, and Agnes Nestor, representing the NWTUL (ibid., Jan. 22, 1962).

‡Maude Younger, Doris Stevens, and Alice Paul of the Woman's Party were balanced by Sarah Conboy of the AFL, Mabel Leslie of the NWTUL, and Maude Wood Park of the National League of Women Voters.

Needless to say, the controversy carried over into the advisory committee. The NWP favored public hearings with testimony from workingwomen. The WTUL pressed for "a technical study by experts and by scientific methods," contending that genuine workingwomen would be afraid to testify at public hearings. After weeks of argument, the league representatives resigned from the Women's Bureau committee.[65]

Meanwhile, Women's Bureau agents investigated the effects of labor laws involving some 660,000 women workers in eleven states. Their extensively researched study concluded that, with few exceptions, labor laws did not constitute a handicap to women's economic advances. On the contrary, in states that had good laws for women workers, better conditions for women in industry existed. Moreover, only when they were protected by laws were women able to obtain economic rights and benefits already enjoyed by male workers. The Woman's Party dismissed the investigation as one that was tailored to provide precisely those conclusions, to which Mary Anderson replied that the members of the Woman's Party were "hysterical Feminists" and "over-articulate theoretical Feminists . . . talking about things and conditions entirely outside their own experience and knowledge."[66]

While all this was going on, a major battle was shaping up in New York State. For several years, the Joint Legislative Conference, which had been established in 1919 to coordinate efforts for new protective legislation and which was led and financed by the WTUL, had lobbied actively for a forty-eight-hour law, with the encouragement of Governor Alfred E. Smith. But every time the lobbyists traveled to Albany to plead for the passage of the bill, they found that their opposition included not only manufacturers, especially cannery owners, but also sopkespersons for the National Woman's Party and the Women's League for Equal Opportunity. As a result, the bill consistently failed to pass.[67]

Finally, in 1926, the Mastick-Shonk bill gained sufficient support from Republicans and Democrats in both houses to ensure passage. The watered-down proposal, applying only to women in factories and mercantile establishments, permitted women in these establishments to work up to ten hours a day as long as they did not exceed forty-eight hours in one week, except that they could work up to fifty-four hours a week for ten weeks of a calendar year.

Despite the limitations of the proposed law, the measure provoked a spirited contest. On February 16, 1926, a delegation of workers led by Mary A. Murray of the National Woman's Party Industrial Council called on Governor Smith to voice opposition to the proposed law. A petition signed by 897 workingwomen from all parts of New York State read in part:

We are united in the opinion that if the Mastick-Shonk bill is passed and the law is enforced, the result will be that in a great many industries women will lose their jobs and be replaced by men.

We wage-earners believe that to restrict by legislation the hours of the labor of women, but not those of men, perpetuates the idea that women are of a class apart in industry; who are classed with children and who only are to be allowed to work at special hours, under special supervision, and subject to special governmental regulations.[68]

The women favoring the forty-eight-hour law, led by Mary E. Dreier, chairperson of the Joint Legislative Conference, visited legislators and urged them not to accept the statements made against the bill as representing the views of workingwomen. They distributed copies of a letter by Marie Bonanno of Dressmakers' Union, Local 89, in which she answered the argument raised in the petition that "women would lose their jobs and be replaced by men" if the bill was passed:

Why do these women suppose that 80,000 trade union women in the State are supporting the Mastick-Shonk bill if, as they assert, it will throw them out of work? As a member of Dressmakers' Union, Local 89, I wish to protest against any such fallacious argument. The women in my union and the other trade union women in the State are self-supporting. Many of them have dependents. They are in favor of the 48-hour week bill as a means of improving their working conditions. They would scarcely continue to fight for this legislation year after year if it would throw them out of work.

The petition which these members of the National Woman's Party presented to Governor Smith was said to have the support of 897 working women in the State. That is a negligible number compared to the organized women who support the bill.[69]

This time, the WTUL and it allies were successful. The New York State legislature passed the Mastick-Shonk forty-eight-hour bill and Governor Smith swiftly signed it into law. On March 26, 1927, the New York WTUL celebrated the only victory it had scored thus far in the decade of the 1920s on the legislative front. Since 1909 the league had worked, in conjunction with the Joint Legislative Conference, for the passage of a variety of legislative measures. It had supported an eight-hour day, a minimum-wage law, and state maternity insurance. Of them, only the eight-hour statute had finally been enacted into law, and a weak law at that.[70]

But so much of the league's funds had been devoted to fighting the equal rights amendment and safeguarding protective legislation that little remained for organizational activity. In fact, the combination of these outlays with the reductions in contributions from its allies resulted in deficits in 1924, 1925, and 1926. To reduce expenditures, after 1926 conventions were held every three years instead of every two, and the budget for 1927 was reduced 30 percent.[71]

During the 1920s the WTUL came under sharp criticism for disregarding organizational activity, and the criticism came from within the organization as well as from without. Executive Secretary Elizabeth Christman pointed out to board members in 1925 that only two chapters out of twelve employed organizers, that only three even had budgets, and that league membership had declined to its lowest point. "It would be illuminating to know," Christman declared, "how great a contribution to the labor movement is represented in the above summary."[72]

Not very much, if one is to judge by the statistics. The 1930 Census revealed that of some 11 million women in industry, perhaps 250,000 were in trade unions, half of these in the garment industry. Of 471,000 female textile workers, only 20,000 were in unions in 1927. Of 72,000 women employed in iron and steel, only 105 were organized. "Overall," concludes William H. Chafe, "the labor movement had reached 1 out of every 9 male workers, but only 1 out of every 34 females."[73] And nearly all of them were white.*

In 1925 a study of the unionization of office workers pointed out:

There is little in the records of the American Federation of Labor Conventions from 1905 (when the first office workers union was represented) to the present to indicate aggressive action by the Federation for the organization of this group of workers. The files of the "American Federationist" [the AFL's official organ] from 1907 to 1924 contain no article specifically on the problem of organizing this group[74]

The only AFL union of office workers in 1925 was the Bookkeepers, Stenographers & Accountants' Union, with a total membership of 1654 in twenty-nine locals. Most of the members worked in offices of unions affiliated with the AFL.[75] The situation had not changed by the end of the decade.[76]

Economist Theresa Wolfson put the blame for this situation squarely

---

*Some black women who worked as maids for the Pullman Company were organized into the Brotherhood of Sleeping Car Porters after it was formed in August, 1925. A year later "The Marching Song of the Fighting Brotherhood" called the union "the hope of the Porters and Maids" (*Messenger*, August 1926, p. 223; Philip S. Foner, *Organized Labor and the Black Worker 1619–1973* [New York, 1974], pp. 176–82). The main activity of women in the Brotherhood, however, was in the Colored Women's Economic Council, organized by the porters' wives and women relatives. The council formed women's auxiliaries in various cities, which staged rallies, bazaars, picnics, and other types of fund-raising activities. Of particular importance was the help the auxiliaries gave the porters' families who had suffered because of Pullman dismissals. A. Philip Randolph, Brotherhood president, pointed out that "it will be impossible for the Organization to look out for them (the dismissed porters) so that some systematic provision will have to be made and the best possible method at present is to use the Ladies Auxiliary for this purpose" (A. Philip Randolph to M. P. Webster, 31 January 1926, Brotherhood of Sleeping Car Porters Papers, Chicago Historical Society). Mattie Mae Hatford, president of the Women's Economic Council of Los Angeles, assured the Brotherhood it "need never despair as long as the women stand ready and willing to lend assistance" (*Messenger*, December 1927, p. 15).

on the hostility of the AFL and its member unions to women workers. The evidence was there. Thus, while the entire August, 1929, issue of the *American Federationist* was dedicated to women, with the lead editorial stressing the principle that legislation was no substitute for union protection, leading AFL organizers were still asserting publicly that it would take from twenty-five to fifty years before a campaign to unionize the workingwomen could be even begun.[77]

Inevitably, the questions arose: "Must the millions of exploited women remain miserably underpaid and overworked until the AFL gets around to them—in twenty-five or fifty years?" And "Will the American labor movement become aware of the necessity of organizing these women?"[78] Neither the WTUL nor the AFL appeared to have any answers.

But a movement did exist which offered an answer. Under the leadership of William Z. Foster, the Trade Union Educational League (TUEL) was organized in the early 1920s. Foster emphasized the importance of organizing the trade union militants to battle for a progressive program within the AFL and the Railroad Brotherhoods. The TUEL united Communists and non-Communists to campaign within the trade unions for amalgamation of craft unions into industrial unions; organization of the unorganized workers, with special attention to women and blacks; a Labor Party; and a policy of recognition of, and peaceful relations with, Soviet Russia.

While not without limitations in their approach to the issue, the Communists were without question the most ardent proponents of sexual and racial equality in the labor movement. Communist women, working in the TUEL, won the support of many women who were not Communists, and together they fought the male-dominated union bureaucracies in the ILGWU, the International Fur Workers' Union, and the Amalgamated Clothing Workers. They also were active in the drive to organize the unorganized textile workers in Passaic, New Bedford, and Fall River.

The TUEL campaign won widespread support in hundreds of local unions, state and national conventions, and central labor councils. In fact, the sweep of support for the TUEL program brought a counteroffensive from trade union bureaucracies. On the false charge that the TUEL was a "dual union," a policy of expulsion of individual trade unionists and whole unions got under way. This expulsion policy compelled the TUEL to become the Trade Union Unity League (TUUL), which now sought to achieve organization of the unorganized through independent industrial unions. The first of these industrial unions was the National Textile Workers' Union, organized by two hundred and fifty delegates, fifty of them women, who met in New York City on September 22–23, 1928.

Although no delegate represented the South, the National Textile Workers' Union turned its attention first to organizing in that section of the country.[79]

14

The Great Depression

FOLLOWING WORLD WAR I there was a depression, in which women workers, particularly black women, were hard hit by unemployment. But by mid-1923 it was over. Soon, large numbers of the American people were engaged in speculation on an unprecedented scale.

Then, in October, 1929, the break in the stock market precipitated the deepest and most prolonged depression in American history.

President Herbert Hoover was confident that the stock market crash of Tuesday, October 29, 1929, was merely a temporary setback and that economic vitality would be quickly restored through the voluntary cooperation of businessmen. He continued to stress the theme "Prosperity is just around the corner."[1]

Meanwhile, the number of unemployed rose, from 3 million in 1930 to approximately 15 million (some placed it as high as 17 million) in 1933. Wages dropped 45 percent, and the percentage of the population living at or below the subsistence level rose from 40 percent in 1929 (the year of greatest prosperity) to 75 percent in 1932.[2]

Ruth Milkman has made the point that women were less affected by the economic crisis than men "because the occupations in which women were concentrated, occupations sex-typed 'female,' contracted less than those in which men were concentrated." Hence, "women enjoyed a measure of protection from unemployment in the Great Depression." On the other hand, Rose Wortis noted early in the depression that since most women were concentrated in the irregular, unskilled, and highly seasonal industries, "the increase of unemployment generally has greatly affected working women."[3]

The April, 1930, census found an unemployment rate of 4.7 percent for women and 7.1 percent for men.[4] As the depression deepened, however, the position of women grew relatively worse. In 1931 and 1932, and again in 1933, the Women's Bureau of the U.S. Department of Labor insisted that unemployment among women was more wide-spread than among young male workers and was increasing at a more rapid rate in many industries. In 1933 the Women's Bureau estimated that at least 2 million women were without jobs.[5]

State and city surveys supported these conclusions. The New York State Department of Labor reported in 1933 that three out of ten women workers were jobless. The same proportion was reported in Cleveland. In Atlanta, half of all the jobless in the winter of 1932 were women. Chicago's unemployed women made up about one-fifth of all the jobless in the city. In Buffalo, New York, unemployment among women rose from 25.4 percent in 1932 to 56.2 percent in 1933, although "the employment status of men shows a considerable improvement over 1932. Moreover, 27 percent of the women were employed only in part-time work." On the basis of the national and local studies, Grace Hutch-ins concluded that the number of jobless women in the autumn of 1933 was closer to 4 million than to the 2 million figure in the Women's Bureau report.[6]

The consequent competition for employment served to intensify male enmity toward workingwomen. In Woonsocket, Rhode Island, men in the spinning mills struck against the employment of women, and President A. Lawrence Lowell of Harvard admitted that he had fired scrubwomen earning 35 cents an hour and replaced them with men at 37 cents rather than pay the women the 2 cents more an hour specified by the Massachusetts Minimum Wage Commission as the legal pay for that class of work.[7] The nine-point program on unemployment adopted by the AFL at its 1931 convention bemoaned the "unfortunate trend of family life" and urged "preference of employment to those upon whom family or dependency rests." Asserting that men had been "crowded" out of their "birthright" because of the increased employment of women, the president of the Carnegie Institute of Technology proposed that 75 percent of the available jobs be reserved for males.[8]

"If you are a woman, you will understand what it means to work in the factory and keep house. I have been working, even when my hus-band had a job, in order to make ends meet. Now he is out of work since last October, and don't ask me how we get along on my miserable earn-ings. But without it we would starve."[9] So went a letter from a working wife in May, 1930. But married women in the labor force were the target of the sharpest male attacks, accused of "selfishly" choosing to work for "pin money" or for personal satisfaction instead of devoting themselves to their designated full-time role as housewives and mothers. With too few jobs to go around, some legislators and employers sought to deny work to married women whose husbands had jobs. Section 213 of the 1932 Federal Economy Act, for example, required that one spouse re-sign if both husband and wife worked for the federal government. This meant, technically, that it was up to both marriage partners to decide which one should resign. But a Women's Bureau analysis of the results of Section 213 showed that more than 75 percent of the spouses who did resign were women. Section 213 remained on the books until 1937.[10]

Dozens of state legislatures received bills discriminating openly against married women. Most of them tried to reduce unemployment by removing married women from jobs controlled by the state and making these positions available only to single women and to men, married or single. Many of these bills did not pass, and state supreme courts ruled others unconstitutional. However, executive orders restricted state employment of married women in Alabama, Idaho, Indiana, Pennsylvania, and Rhode Island. A National Education Association survey for 1930–1931 revealed that 77 percent of the fifteen hundred school systems surveyed refused to hire married women as teachers and 63 percent dismissed married women.[11]

Industry across the country joined the campaign, sometimes in response to public prodding. On the request of the City Council, rubber companies and department stores in Akron, Ohio, agreed to discharge women workers whose husbands were employed and to replace them with men.[12] The National Federation of Business and Professional Women's Clubs reported that a number of private employers, with public support, had arbitrarily dismissed married women. In 1931 all married women workers were released by the New England Telephone & Telegraph and the Northern Pacific companies. All told, the majority of the nation's public schools, 43 percent of its public utilities, and 13 percent of its department stores imposed a curb on the hiring of wives. A 1936 Gallup poll revealed that 82 percent of all Americans believed that a wife should not work if her husband held a job. In opposition to this trend, the Women's Bureau, the Women's Trade Union League, the League of Women Voters, the National Woman's Party, and the Business and Professional Women's Clubs argued that families depended on married women's work and insisted that all women had a right to work.[13]

Joining this opposition was the Communist Party of the United States. "Why are Communists opposed to dismissing married women from jobs in order to make room for the unemployed heads of families?" was one of the questions submitted to the *Daily Worker*. The answer went in part:

> Communists are opposed to driving married women out of industry because this is a reactionary move, not only against women, but against the entire working class. It is an attempt on the part of the capitalists to lower the living standards of the workers, since the men who replace the married women are taken on at the latter's wages, which are far below those of working men. The spread of this practice will thus depress the wage scales of all workers as these lowered wages become the standard. In addition, the practice of dismissing women is part of the fascist campaign to degrade women to being beasts of burden—tied down to children, cooking and the church—with no opportunities for social and cultural advancement. . . .
> It must be emphasized that 40 percent of all the women in industry are

married women. They do not merely work to make pin money.... The Women's Bureau of the Department of Labor admits that 90 percent of the married women who are in industry toil because they must supplement the meager earnings of their husbands and children. ...

The fight for the right of working women to maintain their jobs is the fight of the entire working class....It is the duty of every employed and unemployed worker to join in this fight.[14]

Some of these married workingwomen were women from middle-income families that had been pushed across the line into poverty by the Great Depression.[15] In many cases, either the wife worked or the family went hungry. The following statements by a group of women in Bangor, Maine, gives striking testimony of the married women's need to work:

"There are five in my family, none of whom other than myself is employed at present."

"As my husband's pay has been decreased considerably within the past year, it is absolutely necessary that I obtain some sort of employment."

"Married with two children and my husband is unemployed at present."

"Married and my husband has been out of work for one and one-half years, so I have been trying to find work."[16]

Some cities did not hestitate to exploit this need for their own purposes. In its "Boost Birmingham" circular, the Birmingham Industrial Board pointed to the presence of "white married females" in the district who were ready to work at any wages so as to support their families: "If the woman of the home is gainfully employed, she can carry on the burden of supporting the family until her husband can find work."[17]

Even before the Great Depression, the U.S. Department of Labor had pointed out, in a 1928 report, that the wages of women workers were one-half to one-fourth lower than those of male workers; that 60 percent of all women workers in industry received less than $14 a week; and that women workers were employed with so little concern for their safety that 15 percent of all cases that went before the Compensation Board in 1929 were initiated by women, a large number of whom were permanently disabled.[18]

With the sharpening of the crisis, the conditions of workingwomen became even worse. Work standards were abandoned and sweatshops revived. "During the present period of unemployment, no standards have been secure," the Women's Bureau lamented in 1933. "Even when upheld through legislation or by strong trade union organization, serious breakdowns have occurred. More and more employers are unable or unwilling to meet the overhead expenses necessary in operating a factory, and are giving the work out to be done in homes at shockingly low wages." Wages in factories for women were also "shockingly low."[19] A "Girl Worker" in a Philadelphia dress factory wrote in September, 1931: "Some weeks I can't make $5. Often on pay day I've gotten in my envelope $3. Imagine $3 for slaving all week."[20] Letters to the Women's Bureau told of "bodies just caving in with hunger," of finding "no help nowhere," of "working from 8 A.M. to 5:30 P.M. to make eight cents."[21] In Oakland, California, experienced women canners made 75 cents a day for seven hours' work, while less experienced women earned only 30 to 50 cents.[22] In one Fall River mill, a female employee received only 5 cents an hour, while the highest-paid women earned 15 cents for a total of $7.20 for a forty-eight-hour week. In a Georgia factory in 1933, 90 percent of the women were paid less than $2.95 for a full week's work. Women's Bureau agents found women sewers in Connecticut earning less than $4 a week for working fifteen hours a day. Southern Appalachian mountain women, working steadily at piecework rates on handmade blouses and quilts, averaged an annual income of $52, and Mexican-American women in Texas "sometimes received less than 5 cents a day." In San Antonio during the 1930's a Chicana worker laid off by a food processing plant spent long hours cracking and picking pecans in the shack where she lived. For a full week's work, she earned two dollars."[23]

In the summer of 1932 the Bryn Mawr Summer School for Women published *Women Workers in the Third Year of the Depression,* reporting the experiences of 109 workingwomen from seventeen states. Only ten had experienced no unemployment at all during the past year. Their median wages were $480 a year, a drop from $861 a year in 1928. One woman electrical worker at the summer school told a typical story. From the summer of 1931 to the summer of 1932, she had earned only $360— despite the fact that she had worked a full fifty-two weeks! While she averaged $6.92 a week, the company often paid her only $4 a week and still deducted $10 from her monthly paycheck for "relief work."[24]

Welfare workers in New York City reported the following as examples of wages in the city's sweatshops: (1) A woman crocheted hats for 40 cents a dozen and was able to make only two dozen per week; (2) An apron girl, paid 2½ cents per apron, earned 20 cents a day; (3) A slipper liner was paid 21 cents for every seventy-two pairs of slippers she lined, and if she turned out one sliper every forty-five seconds she could earn $1.05 in a nine-hour day; (4) A girl got half a cent for each pair of pants she threaded and sponged, making $2.78 a week.

Connecticut's state commissioner of labor said that some sweatshops in that state paid girls between 60 cents and $1.10 for a 55-hour week. In Detroit the Briggs Manufacturing Company paid women 4 cents an hour. The Hudson Motor Car Company in the same city called back a small-parts assembler and then kept her waiting three days for a half hour of work, forcing her to spend 60 cents in carfare to earn 28 cents.[25]

Black women felt the impact of the Great Depression earliest and bore its heaviest burdens. Most of the employed black women on the eve of the depression were still in domestic service or in the most menial occupations in shops and factories—82 to 91 percent in New Orleans, Atlanta, and San Antonio. Soon, however, white women, by now willing to take any kind of available job, began to replace black domestics, waitresses, and menial workers. The results were reflected in the statistics of the unemployed.* In April, 1931, 8 percent of the black women in the North were unemployed versus 5 percent of the white women. In Cleveland, where one-sixth of the white women were jobless, more than half the black women were unemployed. A few Southern cities showed the same pattern. In Houston the proportion of black women unemployed was twice that of whites. A U.S. Department of Labor study of the period from 1928 to 1931 in Bridgeport, Buffalo, Syracuse, and Philadelphia found that "the proportion of Negro women unemployed ordinarily was greater than their share in the total woman population or among those in gainful employment." In Pittsburgh, according the the Women's Bureau, over 50 percent of all black women were unemployed in January, 1931, as compared with 19.4 percent of all women workers there.[26]

A study of unemployment in Louisville, Kentucky, conducted by the State Department of Labor in the spring of 1933 found that a little over one-half of the black women, in contrast to less than one-fourth of the white women, were without jobs. More than three-fourths of the Negro women wage earners in the survey depended for their livelihood on domestic and personal service, but the depression had thrown 56 percent of these workers out of work. The study concluded that as the depression lengthened and deepened, and as large numbers of unemployed workers from other fields began to clamor for work, black workers would be pushed out of the more menial, lower-paying, hazardous jobs that were usually their lot. A black woman summed up one of the tragedies of the Depression in these words:

> I am a Negro working woman who has done all kinds of work, the dirtiest and the hardest. But when times got hard the boss told me I would have to hunt me a job. White women were ready to do the work. I walked from house to house, begging for something to do and could not even find washing or scrubbing.[27]

Those black women who did find work were exploited by having to work long hours in poor environments and at inadequate pay. While women workers in general were often forced into the most dangerous sectors of an industry without any concern for their protection, this was particularly true of black women, and the Women's Bureau reported an

---

*Since black women became discouraged, gave up their search for employment more quickly, and were no longer counted in the unemployment census, real unemployment among black women was probably greatly underestimated.

especially great increase in accidents among them during the depression.[28] And just as women earned less than men during the depression, black women earned less than white women. In cigar and cigarette factories, the median income for white women in 1930 was $16.30 per week but only $10.10 for black women. A survey of wages in Georgia in that same year revealed that 90 percent of the black women and 21 percent of the white women earned less than $10 a week; 35 percent of the black women and 10 percent of the white women earned less than $5 a week. At a bagging mill in Charleston in 1930, over six hundred black women earned an average of $4 a week for a ten- to twelve-hour day, and if they were five minutes late for work, 25 cents was deducted from these miserable wages. In an Atlanta laundry, black women earned $6.50 weekly for a workday that began at 7:15 A.M. and ended at 7 P.M.[29]

Although the Women's Bureau noted that the depression had "fallen with particular severity" on black women, it saw little hope of changing this situation, and it placed the blame for this on the black women themselves. Nothing would change, the bureau maintained, until black women could "prove themselves capable of developing skill and steady work habits." "The Negro woman, if she would advance, must first show that she is worthy of the opportunity," Mary Anderson told a Conference on Interracial Problems in Atlanta on March 17, 1933.[30] What "opportunity" she had in mind, in view of the disastrous contraction of jobs during the Great Depression, was not made clear, nor did she explain how black women could develop "steady work habits" when so many of them had no work whatsoever.

The gruesome impact of the Great Depression upon the lives of the jobless and their families was told graphically in the contemporary press. "Starving Mother Kills Self and Four Children," headlined a UP dispatch from Reesville, Delaware.[31] The *Bridgeport Post* carried an advertisement from Margaret Sabo, nineteen years old, with the notice: "$1,800 Buys Me for a Wife." She was auctioning herself off, the paper explained, because "her father, a factory worker, has been out of work, the family debts have piled up, and they face starvation."[32]

Here is a description of how families in Philadelphia "managed":

> One woman went along the docks and picked up vegetables that fell from wagons. Sometimes fish vendors gave her fish at the end of the day. On two different occasions, the family was without food for a day and a half.... Another family did not have food for two days. Then the husband went out and gathered dandelions and the family lived on them.[33]

The effects of the depression were also seen in the accounts of 1 to 2 million more or less permanent migrants riding the rails. Of the railriders, or hoboes, more than 145,000 were homeless girls and women who were roaming the country in search of work or food and shelter. During the fall of 1931, hundreds of homeless women were sleeping in Chicago's parks. "Some of these women are mothers and have their children with them as they lie on newspapers exposed to the night air," one reporter noted. Elizabeth Conkey, Chicago's Commissioner of Public Welfare, told the press that a major problem was that thieves often stole "the very coats which sleeping women have thrown about themselves on the park benches." Many of these women had "come to us at their wits' end and literally wringing their hands."[34]

By 1932 only one-quarter of the unemployed were receiving any form of relief. In New York City, families lucky enough to get relief "obtained an average grant of $2.39 per week; in most places, people got only a little food." Arthur M. Schlesinger, Jr., writes that in 1932 the "average relief stipend was about 50¢ a day—per family."[35]

In relief, however, just as on the job, the black family received less than the white. In one Southern city, where blacks constituted 25 percent of the population but 40 percent of the unemployed, unemployed blacks received only 25 percent of the relief funds. The nationwide average grocery allotment for a black family on home relief was estimated in 1932 as only $1.25 a week.[36]

Even these meager funds might not have been forthcoming from local and state governments had not black and white unemployed workers joined forces in a militant struggle for work and relief, mostly under the leadership of the Communist Party. The task of mobilizing the unemployed was undertaken first by the Trade Union Unity League (TUUL), formed in 1929 with William Z. Foster as secretary, after attempts by the left-wing militants to work within the AFL had resulted only in expulsions and frustrations. The Trade Union Educational League (TUEL) had been a propagandist and educational organization, whereas its successor aimed at organizing outside the federation while continuing to bore from within.[39]

The Trade Union Unity League was organized at a convention held in Cleveland from August 31 to September 3, 1929. Seventy-two of the 690 delegates were women, and two of them—Rose Wortis of the Needle Trades Workers' Industrial Union and Ann Burlak, a young organizer for the NTWU—were elected to the TUUL's national committee. In connection with the convention a Women's Conference was held, at which women from the needle trades, textiles, mining, electrical, auto, and other industries described the problems facing workingwomen and pointed out that one of the major tasks of the TUUL "will be to organize 8,500,000 women workers, still practically unorganized." The Women's Conference was chaired by Mary Voice, a black representative of a ladies' auxiliary of the National Miners' Union and one of seven delegates from the miners' auxiliaries. The TUUL announced that the unionization of women workers was indeed a key problem of American labor: "The trade union leaders have altogether failed to defend the interests of the women workers, barring them from the unions and discriminating against them in industry, as they have done against the youth, the Negroes and the foreign-born."

The new industrial union movement announced its program for recruiting women workers. This called for equal pay for equal work and the general raising of women workers' wages in keeping with the rise in the cost of living; a minimum wage for women workers in agriculture and domestic service; the establishment of a seven-hour day and a five-day week, with a six-hour day for harmful and strenuous occupations; a full month's holiday annually with full pay; the prohibition of night work, overtime, underground work, and work in particularly difficult and harmful occupations; maternity leave on full pay for eight weeks before and eight weeks after confinement for all women wage earners; and paid intervals of not less than half an hour for nursing mothers every three and a half hours during the working day in special rooms to be set aside for feeding their infants. It also called for the organization of nurseries "for the children of women workers at the cost of the employers and under the management of the workers and their organizations" and for the installation in factories of special dressing rooms, washrooms, showers, and a sufficient number of seats for the women workers and office employees. Finally, "all forms of social insurance against unemployment, old age, sickness, etc., shall cover not only the industrial women workers but all women working for wages."[38] To further this program, which was the most detailed and advanced for women workers ever adopted by an American labor organization, the TUUL established a National Women's Department, organized women's commissions in the trade unions, and held trade union conferences for women workers.

But the first task undertaken by the TUUL was that of organizing the unemployed. In conjunction with the Communist Party, the TUUL began early in the Great Depression to organize the jobless into groups that were known at first as Councils of the Unemployed and later as Unemployed Councils.[39] From the outset, the TUUL demanded that "all unemployed shall be entitled to unemployed benefits sufficient to secure the maintenance of their families and dependents during the whole period of unemployment. Women workers, moreover, shall be entitled to unemployment benefits to the same amount as that of male workers." Relief work had to be such that it could be performed by women "without danger to health," and unemployed women workers were "to have equal representation with male workers on all state, municipal and other bodies associated with providing for the unemployed." Finally, it should be made illegal for any employer "to dismiss expecting and nursing mothers."[40]

March 6, 1930, was designated as International Unemployment Day by Communist parties throughout the world. Under the slogan "Starve or Fight," the Unemployed Councils in the United States issued a call for a nationwide demonstration on that day. On March 6 hundreds of thousands of unemployed in some thirty cities and towns demonstrated in the largest series of unemployment demonstrations in U.S. history.[41] Women were actively involved in each demonstration and were victims of police attacks. A *New York World* reporter wrote of the violent clashes between police and demonstrators at New York City's Union Square, where between 60,000 and 100,000 were attacked by police:

> Demonstrators and bystanders were slugged and kicked, blackjacked and knocked down by mounted police in the frantic fifteen minutes that followed the policemen's charge on the straggling parade of placard carriers.... Women were struck in the face with blackjacks, and many of the women were kicked as they lay on the ground or hoisted to their feet and booked or slapped by the policemen.... One of the women fought savagely, howling curses, and a bluecoat seized her around the shoulders with one arm and punched her with his free hand. A detective ran up and while the policeman held her, crashed his blackjack into her face three times before a man dragged her away.[42]

The members of the Amalgamated Clothing Workers and the International Ladies' Garment Workers' Union had been warned not to participate in the demonstration, but a number of the women at Union Square were members of these unions, while many others belonged to the Needle Trades Workers' Industrial Union.[43]

On July 4 and 5, 1930, at a meeting in Chicago attended by 1,320 delegates, one-third of them women, a new national organization was established—the Unemployed Councils of the U.S.A. One of its aims was to fight for passage of an Unemployment Insurance Bill. It proposed that until regular employment was provided or received, all unemployed persons, "regardless of race, sex, color or creed," should be given the "regular average wages earned by them while employed, but in no case less than $25 per week, plus $5 for each dependent member of the unemployed worker's family." Another provision was that "women entitled to social insurance payment on account of maternity shall receive payment for four weeks prior to the date of giving birth and four weeks subsequent thereto."[44]

In addition to publicizing the Unemployment Insurance Bill, the Unemployed Councils conducted regular demonstrations in towns, cities, and state capitals. In most instances, the demands were similar: an end to evictions, improved relief in cash and in kind, state and federal aid, and special provisions such as winter and children's clothing. Demands for women included equal insurance of full wages for unemployed men and women workers; equal unemployment insurance for single and married women workers; no dismissal of married women; free municipal lodging houses for homeless unemployed women; free medical care for unemployed pregnant women; and free hospital care during confinement and two weeks thereafter for mother and child.[45]

These demands were advanced under such slogans as "Work or Wages!" "Fight, Don't Starve!" "We Want Jobs, Not Charity!" "We Want Bread!" "Armories and Public Buildings for the Unemployed!" "Give the Bankers Home Relief; We Want Jobs!" and "United We Eat!"[46]

Matilda Molina Tolly, a Mexican-American leader of the unemployed in Los Angeles, recalled:

> We would move the furniture and people's belongings back into the houses emptied by the eviction notices. The landlords had a hard time, since it cost them $30 for a notice after the third time. After three attempts, the landlord had to stop. When relief was cut in the Chicano community, we had a big black casket, symbolic of what would eventually happen to these workers. This we displayed for several days until the relief was restored.[47]

Sharp struggles against evictions also occurred in New York, Chicago, Detroit, and other cities. It is estimated that in New York City these tactics succeeded in restoring 77,000 evicted families to their homes.[48]

On March 7, 1932, at a demonstration of unemployed workers at the Ford Motor Company in Dearborn, Michigan, organized by the TUUL and the Detroit Unemployed Council, four unemployed marchers were killed by the police. When friends suggested to the mother of one of the slain workers, sixteen-year-old Joseph Bussell, that he be buried in his best suit and shoes, she replied: "No, old clothes are good enough to moulder in the ground. Better to send the new things to the Kentucky miners. They have more need of them now."[49]

In December, 1932, during the fourth winter of mass hunger, the second nationwide Hunger March on Washington was organized for the unemployed.* The New York District of the Needle Trades Workers' Industrial Union elected forty delegates, and Communist Ben Gold was chosen as leader of the Eastern Division. Following an enthusiastic send-off in the Bronx Coliseum, 1,200 Hunger Marchers, 400 of them women, left for Washington to present their demands to Congress for enactment of the Unemployment Insurance Bill:

> That a system of Federal Unemployment Insurance be immediately established by an Act of Congress and made immediately effective, guaranteeing full wages to all workers wholly or partly employed, through no fault of their own, for the entire period of unemployment.
> That Unemployment Insurance be paid to every unemployed worker,

*The first Hunger March on Washington was in December, 1931.

adult and youth, whether industrial or agricultural, office employees and all
other categories of wage labor, native or foreign born, citizen or non-citizen,
Negro and white, men and women, and without discrimination against any
race, color, age or political opinion. . . .[50]

On December 4, some three thousand marchers arrived at the out-
skirts of Washington, where they were met by police who conducted
them to an isolated street. There, the Hunger Marchers found themselves bottled up with a steep bank to their left, a freight yard to their
right, and in front of them, the police, backed up by machine guns and a
gas squad of seventy-six trained men. Twelve hundred policemen and
seven hundred deputized firemen, equipped with sawed-off rifles, submachine guns, and tear gas bombs, were kept at the ready in nearby
barracks.

For almost three days, the marchers were kept confined to that one
street. No one was allowed to communicate with them. Truckloads of
food, gathered by housewives associated with the Council of Working
Class Women of New York City, were turned back by the police. There
were neither water nor sanitary arrangements until the police finally
permitted the construction of a toilet. There were no cots and no beds,
although many sympathetic Washingtonians had offered their help.[51]

Meanwhile, screaming headlines were warned of riots and insurec-
tion. The *New York Times* wrote that many of the marchers were women,
and that "many of the women wore fur coats."[52] The New York *Daily
News* reported that the leaders of the Hunger March were enjoying
themselves in "a suite of rooms at the expensive Hotel Raleigh on
Pennsylvania Avenue in Washington, where comely Communist girls
lounge about like a Follies troupe in a tryout."[53] In fact many of the
women Hunger Marchers were suffering from malnutrition. Helen
Lynch, a graduate of the University of Michigan and a leader of the
Unemployed Council in New York City, took the few dollars given her
by the council and spent it on those who had no food at all.[54]

On December 6, having finally obtained a permit to parade through
Washington, the three thousand demonstrators marched into the city
down Pennsylvania Avenue. They were halted two blocks from the Capital except for two delegations of twenty-five each, one chaired by
William Reynolds and the other by Herbert Benjamin* and Ann Burlak.† The Reynolds group met with Vice-President Charles Curtis, who

*Herbert Benjamin, a militant Communist, was the national leader of the Unemployed
Councils.

†A Pennsylvania textile worker, Communist Ann Burlak organized for the National Textile
Workers' Union in the South, then was summoned to Atlanta to help in the battle of
black and white workers for unemployment relief. She was at a meeting in Atlanta in 1930
of black and white unemployed, held under Communist sponsorship, when it was invaded by the police. Burlak and five other organizers, black and white, were arrested, and

refused to allow Reynolds to read a statement but, after an exchange, promised to lay it before the Senate. The other committee met with House Speaker Garner, who made a vague promise to see what he could do about the demand for unemployment insurance. The delegations then returned to the waiting marchers, who retraced their route back to the camp. Then the Hunger Marchers began the long trek home.[55]

One of the returnees was Dorothy Day, who had traveled with the veteran labor reporter Mary Heaton Vorse. When they had arrived in Washington, Day and Vorse had been shocked to see the ragged group of men and women camped out in the streets of the city, surrounded by an army of police and troops armed with submachine guns, sawed-off rifles, tear gas bombs, nightsticks, and rubber hoses—all because they had dared "to petition their government to take measures so that they and their children might not starve to death." Dorothy Day, a Catholic, was also shocked because, while women's organizations, pacifist groups, Quakers, and a few other religious organizations supported the demands of the marchers, no official Catholic source did so. And she thought:

> Far dearer in the sight of God, perhaps, are these hungry ragged ones, than all those smug well-fed Christians who sit in their homes, or in fear of the Communist menace. . . . How little, how puny my work has been since becoming a Catholic. How self-centered, how ingrown, how lacking in a sense of community.[56]

Five months after she returned from Washington, Dorothy Day published the first issue of the *Catholic Worker*, a newspaper that has continued down to the present.*[57]

---

charged with insurrection under a statute enacted during the Civil War against newly-freed blacks—a law that carried the death penalty. The "Atlanta Six," as they were called, remained in jail for six months until bail was obtained. Burlak was the first to be released, and began a speaking tour sponsored by the ILD to raise funds for the other five. The "Atlanta Six" were never brought to trial.

After she was elected secretary of the National Textile Workers' Union in late 1930, Burlak organized mill workers in Pawtucket and Pequod, Rhode Island and Lawrence and Salem, Massachusetts, and soon became known as the "Red Flame." On March 6, 1979, Burlak spoke at a meeting in Providence, Rhode Island. The following day the headline in the Providence *Evening Bulletin* read: "'Red Flame' Is Still Burning Bright After 50 Years Fighting For Her Cause." (Interview with Ann Burlak Timeson, Jamaica Plain, Massachusetts, December 22, 1979.)

*Dorothy Day was born in Brooklyn, New York, in November, 1897, and, after graduating from the University of Illinois in 1916, she became a member of the Socialist Party. She was a columnist for the Socialist journals, the *New York Call*, the *Masses*, and the *Liberator*. She worked as a nurse in Kings County Hospital in Brooklyn, a script writer for Pathé Films in Hollywood, and after conversion to Catholicism, as a writer for the Catholic *Commonweal* magazine. In 1933 Day became the cofounder and copublisher (with Peter Mairn) of the *Catholic Worker* in New York City, and, in addition to helping organize workers, she founded St. Joseph's House of Hospitality and other houses and farms for the poor and homeless (see Dorothy Day, *From Union Square to Rome* [New York, 1938] and Neil Betten, "The Great Depression and the Activities of the Catholic Worker Movement," *Labor History* 12 (Spring, 1971):243-58.)

Two of the leaders of the national Hunger March in December, 1932, were blacks. As many as one-fourth of the marchers were black, and of these, half were women. Many blacks who participated in the Hunger Marches noted that the Communists were usually resolute in resisting the racial barriers set up by local authorities in the towns through which the marchers had to pass. "'No discrimination against Negro workers!' 'Equal relief for the Negro jobless!' These and similar slogans were displayed on banners carried by the marchers, both Negro and white."[58]

Blacks not only participated on an equal footing in the various unemployed councils but often assumed leadership. Three thousand workers, two-thirds of them black, including a line of children, marched in Birmingham under the leadership of the Unemployed Council, demanding work or relief. The children were reported to have sung:

> Empty is the cupboard, no pillow for the head,
> We are the hungry children who fight for milk and bread
> We are the workers' children who must, who must be fed.[59]

A black women employed in one of the tobacco plants of Winston-Salem, North Carolina recalled how, "during the period of the Hoover Depression, when people just did not have bread and meat," four or five people came into Winston-Salem, got a few whites and blacks together, and formed an unemployment league:

> They would go down to City Hall and the County Commissioners to put the pressure on these people to appeal for government help for food. It was nothing but the roughest of food, pinto beans, fatback meat, but it kept us from starving. My mother, along with a few others, was able to get some clothes for a few members of our family and was able to get a ton of coal and a load of wood every now and then.[60]

In Shreveport, Louisiana, unemployed blacks and whites demanded "work or food" and battled police who tried to arrest them. Of two thousand hunger marchers in the same city in 1931, five hundred were blacks, and one, a women, was chosen to present a petition to Congress for unemployment insurance. The *New York Times* of April 2, 1931, reported that on the previous day, more than fifty hunger marchers, of whom about forty were black and twenty-five women, had entered the Maryland House of Delegates at Annapolis and demanded a hearing on petitions for aid to the unemployed. Three of the marchers, one a black woman, were permitted to address the House. Their demands included the use of funds earmarked for a proposed new penitentiary and from state salaries above $2,000 for the establishment of an unemployment insurance program. By the fall of 1931, it was a common sight to see blacks appearing at the head of unemployed demonstrations at numerous state capitals.[61]

In July, 1932, a cutback of relief to fifteen thousand families in St. Louis (with the prospect that eight thousand more families would be affected) led to the "July Riot," in which fifteen thousand demonstrators, many of them black, participated. Organized by the Unemployed Councils of St. Louis, the demonstration was attacked by police wielding clubs and hurling tear gas. "Most of the opposition to the police," the *St. Louis Post-Dispatch* reported, "came from Negroes, including women, who backed away from the gas, but threw bricks picked up from a wrecked building across the street." Throughout the summer of 1932, unemployed black workers, men and women, were active in St. Louis, fighting against relief cuts.[62]

In January, 1933, six thousand workers of the Briggs Mack Avenue plant in Detroit, two thousand of them women, answered a strike call by the TUUL's Auto Workers' Union.* Six weeks later they were still picketing the plant. One of the women strikers, interviewed on the picket line, told the reporter:

> There is a law in Detroit which says that women are not permitted to work over 10 hours a day and not more than 54 hours per week. But we women worked 60 and sometimes more hours per week, and still did not earn more than $7 or $8 per week. Sometimes we got even as low as 4 cents per hour—sometimes 10 cents. We never knew what we were going to get. The efficiency men had that all figured out.

The women workers finaly gained substantial wage increases, a minimum wage of 30 cents an hour, pay for waiting time ("dead time"), and a forty-eight-hour week. These gains, the *Detroit Free Press* observed, were a reflection of the fact that "the women workers played a leading role in the strike."[63]

In the spring of 1933, St. Louis was the setting for a strike of women workers that aroused nationwide attention. This was the strike of the women nutpickers against starvation wages and discriminatory practices.

Pecans grown along the Mississippi Valley regions were shipped by boat to St. Louis, where the nuts were picked, sorted, weighed, and packed. There were sixteen pecan factories in St. Louis, employing some three thousand women to do the picking and sorting. Seven of these were owned by the R. E. Funsten Company, founded in 1895 by R. E. Funsten and headed in 1933 by his son, Eugene.

Between 85 and 90 percent of the labor force in the pecan industry

---

*For several years, the Auto Workers' Union had focused attention on "the plight of women," and its official organ, the *Auto Workers News*, ran a special Women's Column. "Girls must have a chance to earn a decent living," the union insisted, and it pointed out that "one of the demands of the Auto Workers Union must be: 'Equal pay for equal work'" (Roger R. Keeran, "Communist Influence in the Automobile Industry, 1920–1933: Paving the Way for an Industrial Union,"*Labor History* 20 [Spring 1979]: 217).

were black women. They worked nine hours a day, five and a half days a week, from 6:45 A.M. to 4:45 P.M., with forty-five minutes for lunch. The few white women, most of them of Polish extraction, worked from 7 A.M. to 4:30 P.M., with one hour for lunch. A handful of men, black and white, were employed as foremen, weighers, crackers, and dryers. The men also handled the packing and shipping of the nuts.

Seated at a table before a 25-pound bag of nuts, each women would use a knife to separate the meats from the shells. Unbroken halves were placed in one pile and broken pieces in another, and the shells were also kept so that upon completion everything could be weighed once more to make sure it all added up to 25 pounds. A cleaner operation, in which only white women were employed, was that of sorting. The dirty work was parceled out among the black women.[64]

The women worked under sweatshop conditions. Bathroom facilities were primitive, and despite the fact that this was a food industry, there were no health standards. Shelling the nuts caused a great deal of dust, which produced continual coughing, while the nutmeats produced permanent stains, so that it was necessary to wear an apron to prevent damage to clothes. The cost of aprons was deducted from the weekly wages.[65]

Black pickers were paid 3 cents a pound for halves and 2 cents for pieces. The white pickers received 2 cents more per pound. During the years 1931–1933, the women had had their wages cut five times. One black woman who had worked for Funsten for eighteen years had averaged $18 a week in 1918; in 1933, her top weekly pay was $4. Another received wages as low as 63 cents a week. A special investigator for the American Civil Liberties Union reported that black workers were earning from 75 cents to $2.50 per week, with an average of $1.30, while white women were getting from $2 to $5, with an average of $4. Almost all the women found it necessary to contribute to the support of other members of the family, but so low were the wages that about 60 percent were on relief rolls.[66]

In 1927 a spontaneous strike at the Funsten Company plant had ended in failure. No further activity occurred until March, 1933, when a Communist Party member, with two family members working at the company, established contact with a group of discontented women. They met in various homes to discuss the need to change the outrageous conditions in the plants. When about twenty women had been brought together and had asked for outside support, William Sentner, a local Communist leader and organizer for the Food Workers Industrial Union, an affiliate of the TUUL, was assigned to help the women organize.[67]

After several more meetings, the women themselves decided on the following demands: (1) an increase in wages to 10 cents for halves and 4 cents for pieces; (2) equal pay for black and white workers and an end to discriminatory practices against black workers; and (3) union recognition. A union shop local was established and an executive committee elected. Soon the union had one hundred members out of the two hundred employees at Funsten's west side plant, and a few more in other shops.[68]

On April 24, 1933, a committee of twelve was elected to present the demands to Eugene Funsten. The women waited three weeks for an answer, meanwhile extending their organization to other plants. On May 12, having heard nothing from the company and convinced that further delay would only weaken their forces, they decided to call a mass meeting to vote on a strike. The following day, a vote was taken in favor of a strike, but it was agreed that the original committee would again seek an answer to the demands. If they were accepted, all would return to work. If rejected, all would walk out. As the committee was about to leave with the demands, one of the leading black women called on the rest to join in prayer, saying: "Oh, Lord, give us strength to win our demands. Boss Funston does not treat us Negro women right. We made the first step. Oh Lord, you should take the second step and if we must strike, help us win the strike." When the demands were rejected, nine hundred workers walked out. On the second day, workers in two additional Funsten shops and two other factories—the Liberty Nut Company and the Central Pecan Company—joined the strike, bringing the total to fourteen hundred women.[69]

On the second day, too, most of the white women joined the strike, and picketing of the struck plants was conducted by both black and white workers. Blondie Rossen, a young Polish worker, was the strike leader of the white women, but the overall strike leader was Connie Smith, a middle-aged black woman. It was she who coined the strike slogan, "We demand ten and four," and who told the St. Louis press:

> We want to be paid on the basis of ten cents a pound for half nuts and four cents a pound for pieces. This would give us an average wage of about $6.00 or $7.00 a week. We think we are entitled to live as well as other folks live, and we should be entitled to a wage that will provide us with ample food and clothing.[70]

One shop after another was called out to join the strike. Each shop elected its own strike committee and its own captains for the picket line. Picketing began every morning at five and the women brought their husbands and children to march with them around the plants. They were joined by other St. Louis workers and by members of the Unemployed Councils and of the Communist Party. A central strike committee, a negotiating committee, and a relief committee were established. Food was collected from sympathetic workers, especially meat cutters and clothing and bakery workers, as well as businessmen, while a truckload of food came from the Workers' International Relief in Chicago. Twelve hundred women were fed daily.[71]

As the conditions under which the nutpickers worked were made public, the community responded generously to appeals from the strikers. On one occasion, two black and two white women strikers, accompanied by an attorney for the American Civil Liberties Union, met with the Social Justice Commission of St. Louis at Temple Israel to ask for assistance. The strikers had with them several unopened pay envelopes with wages covering four days' work. Of eight that were opened, two contained $2 and the other $1.50. The shocked members of the Social Justice Commission voted to support the strike.[72]

Rabbi Harold Isserman, a leader of the Social Justice Commission, accused the employers "who were underpaying their workers" of attempting "to discredit their strike by ascribing it to Communist agitation." "The nut pickers' strike," he declared, "was not inspired by Communists, but it was led by Communists. It was inspired by a wage scale which was un-American, and which did not make possible even the barest subsistence for the workers. If it had not been for Communist leaders this tragic condition would not have been brought to light."[73] The St. Louis *Argus,* the local black paper, agreed and added: "Their [the Communist Party's] insistence on the same pay for the same class of work among the workers, both white and black, can't but strike a popular chord in the minds of the colored people."[74]

On the fourth day of the strike, Eugene Funsten offered the workers a one-third increase in wages and assured the white women that they would gain even more if they returned to work. Pleading that higher wages would cause the company to operate at a loss, Funsten said that this was all that could be offered. The St. Louis *Argus,* however, pointed out that with "the present price of nut meat averaging forty cents per pound, it would not take the mind of Einstein to calculate the vast amount of profit the producer of this commodity would receive at these wages."[75] In an interview in 1976 with the then president of the Funsten Nut Company—by that time a division of Pet Milk—history student Myrna Fichtenbaum ascertained that the company had actually earned an annual profit of 10 percent during the Great Depression. "A few calculations indicate to us that the Funsten profit yearly must have been about $250,000."[76]

When the first offer was rejected, Funsten offered 75 cents per 25-pound box of shelled nuts, but this, too, was rejected by the strikers. He then began to import strikebreakers from outside the city, who were escorted into the plants by police in patrol wagons and taxis. The strikers reacted angrily, "smashing two police cars and taxicabs carrying strike breakers."* Fifteen women pickets and union organizer William Sentner

---

*About one hundred women strikers were arrested during the strike.

were arrested, and fifteen hundred women, black and white, marched to City Hall in protest. They asked Mayor Bernard Dickman to order the police to stop protecting strikebreakers and to protect the right of peaceful picketers. They also called on him to assist in ending the strike. The mayor responded by appointing a committee to assist the union in seeking a satisfactory solution to the walkout.[77]

On May 23, 1933, the central strike committee met in an all-day session with Funsten, his attorney, and the mayor's committee. The company offered 90 cents for a 25-pound box of unshelled nuts, the equivalent of 8 cents for halves and 4 cents for pieces, together with the abolition of any differential between white and black nutpickers and recognition of elected shop committees. The central strike committee voted to accept the offer and to recommend that the strikers do likewise. Mayor Dickman addressed the strikers, urging them to accept the company's offer, which, he pointed out, represented a 100 percent wage increase for the workers. The women strikers voted unanimously to accept the offer, and the strike at Funsten was ended. Within a few days, other, smaller concerns met the strikers' demands of "ten and four," a uniform scale of wages for black and white workers, and recognition of the elected strike committees.[78]

Eleven locals of the Food Workers' Industrial Union, with fourteen hundred members, were established during the strike. Each local was interracial, though black women made up the great majority of the members, and black and white women served together on shop committees. One hundred women, mostly black, joined the Communist Party. One of them wrote: "I am 42 years old, married. I have worked for the same company, Funsten Nut Co. of St. Louis, for the last 18 years. . . . I also belong to a fraternal organization, and to a church. Before the strike, I was earning $3.00 per week, after the strike and at present I am earning $9.00 per week."[79]

In the midst of the Great Depression, before Section 7(a) of the National Recovery Act stimulated an upsurge of unionization, fourteen hundred St. Louis women workers, most of them black, had the courage to challenge a powerful corporation and the city's power structure. In an era when wage differentials were an accepted way of life, the Funsten nutpickers demanded and won equal pay for equal work for black and white workers alike. Although white women were active in the struggle, it was the pivotal role of the black women that was responsible for the final victory.

The strike victory in St. Louis acted as a catalyst for other struggles. In Chicago, about a month later, sixteen hundred black and white women employed by the Sopkin Dress Manufacturing Company, inspired by the victory of the St. Louis nutpickers, went on strike against wages of only $3 to $4 for fifty-two hours a week and the jim-crowing of black women and girls in separate and unsanitary toilet facilities. Under the leadership of the Needle Trades Workers' Industrial Union the women tied up production in the company's four plants. After two weeks the strikers won their demands for 25 cents an hour for a forty-four-hour week, equal pay for equal work, and no discrimination between white and colored workers.[80]

The victory of the St. Louis nutpickers also stimulated strikes of workers in the men's clothing and ladies' garment industries in the summer of 1933. In August, 1933, moreover, the *St. Louis Post-Dispatch* reported that hundreds of laundry workers had joined the newly organized Laundry Workers' Union. "Eighty percent of these workers are women," it added, "and nearly half are Negroes. The immediate cause of unionization, as in the case of the Funsten nutpickers strike, is the complaint of starvation wages."[81]

The Great Depression all but curtailed the activities of the Women's Trade Union League. Publication of *Life and Labor* was temporarily suspended for lack of funds, and for the same reason the Executive Board met only six times between 1929 and 1936, conducting most of its business by mail. After 1929, no convention was held until 1936. Local leagues concentrated on easing the plight of unemployed women and on seeking relief for them,[82] while the national league devoted its attention mainly to securing legislation to outlaw sweatshops and opposing the equal rights amendment sponsored by the National Woman's Party. WTUL President Rose Schneiderman appeared before the Senate Judiciary Committee in January, 1930, and warned that enactment of the equal rights amendment would destroy all existing laws protecting women workers. Such laws, she insisted, were "as necessary in our modern industrial system as are traffic laws in the city streets."[83]

Schneiderman was a member of the New York league's Committee on Unattached Women and worked to secure home relief for these women. But little was accomplished; the Home Relief Bureau, the league reported, "still refuses to accept many cases of unattached women, on the ground that their funds are limited." The league also tried to help unemployed women through continuing-education classes in the evening, but here, too, it ran into difficulty. "Our plans for unemployment relief," the league reported sadly, "met a disastrous setback in the order of the Board of Education closing continuation school classes to adults."[84]

A leading objective of the league, Schneiderman emphasized in January, 1930, was the "organization of workers into trade unions." But late that same year, at a WTUL conference, Leo Wolman was openly pessimistic as to what the league could actually accomplish in that direction. He pointed to the "virtual bankruptcy of the American Federation of Labor, with a steady loss of membership," and concluded that the labor movement was "facing its most crucial test for survival."[85] Evidently the league shared Wolman's pessimism, for it reported: "Organization work in the best of times is difficult, [and] particularly now when every worker is holding on with all their might to a job no matter how bad that job may be. Some workers almost tremble with fear of losing the little earnings they can get out of it." In 1930, convinced that its objectives could be achieved only through legislation, the league moved its national headquarters to Washington.

The league was fortunate when a staunch and powerful supporter—Eleanor Roosevelt—arrived in Washington. Mrs. Roosevelt's association with the WTUL went back to 1919, when she had attended a tea for delegates to the International Congress of Working Women and had hosted a luncheon for some of the representatives. She became acquainted with Margaret Robins, Rose Schneiderman, Mary Anderson, Maud Swartz, and other league activists, and a few years later she joined the league. She became close friends with Schneiderman and Swartz and brought them to Hyde Park to meet Franklin D. Roosevelt, then recovering from his polio attack. Mrs. Roosevelt represented the league before the 1924 Democratic Platform Committee, raised money for its activities, and taught in its evening classes. When her husband was governor of New York State, she persuaded him to attend the twenty-fifth anniversary party of the league and to appoint Swartz, its fomer president, to the State Industrial Commission.[86]

Eleanor Roosevelt's activities on behalf of workingwomen did not stop with educational and financial activities. In 1926 she joined in the mass picketing by three hundred striking women paper box makers, and in 1930 she publicly endorsed the ILGWU strike of Fifth Avenue dress shops. "Mrs. Roosevelt, wife of the governor," commented the *New York Times*, "is noted for her sympathies toward organized labor, and especially toward women in industry."[87] With Roosevelt's inauguration as president of the United States on March 4, 1933, Eleanor Roosevelt, member of the Women's Trade Union League, had a new opportunity to display these sympathies.

On December 1, 1930, on a farm near Silver Spring, Maryland, death ended the career of "Mother" Jones, hundred-year-old veteran of scores of hard-fought labor battles. A special car was chartered for a funeral coach, and, accompanied by an escort of honor, "Mother" started on her final journey to Mount Olive, Illinois. In accordance with her wishes, she was buried alongside the graves of five of her "boys," who were killed by strikebreaking gunmen in 1898, in a plot in Mount Olive Cemetary owned by the United Mine Workers of America.[88]

The legendary Mary Harris "Mother" Jones was born in Cork, Ireland, on May 1, 1830. She was the daughter of an "Irish agitator" and construction worker, Richard Harris, and came to America at the age of five. Mary attended parochial and public schools, studying elementary education and dressmaking. In 1861 she accepted a teaching position in Memphis and married George Jones, "a staunch member of the Iron Moulders' Union" and organizer for the Knights of Labor in the Southern and Southwestern coalfields. In his extensive travels for the Knights, Jones was accompanied by his wife and their four children.

In 1867 a yellow fever epidemic swept western Tennessee and struck the Jones's Memphis home. All four children and their father died. To earn a living, Jones began a dressmaking business in Chicago. After the fire of 1871 she moved her shop to a building adjacent to the office of the Knights of Labor. By day she worked "for the aristocrats of Chicago," among whom she had ample opportunity to observe luxury and extravagance, while from her shop window she saw "the poor, shivering wretches, jobless and hungry." At night, she attended the rallies of the Knights of Labor.

Mother Jones took part in her first coal strike in 1882 in Hocking Valley, Ohio. But it was her immersion in the struggles of the United Mine Workers of America—then a rising, vigorous, rapidly growing union—that made a labor leader of her. Until she was nearly one hundred years old, Mother Jones was where the danger was greatest—crossing militia lines, spending weeks in damp prisons, incurring the wrath of governors, presidents, and coal operators—as she helped organize the United Mine Workers with the only tools she felt she needed: "convictions and a voice."* She led the miners in strikes such as those in Virginia in 1891; in Pennsylvania and West Virginia in 1897, 1900, and 1902; in Paint Creek and Cabin Creek, West Virginia, in 1912–1913; in Ludlow, Colorado, in 1913–1914; and in Kansas in 1921. She fought as hard against corrupt union leaders as she did against operators when she felt they were blocking progress.

Mother Jones was nationally renowned in both the labor and socialist movements. In 1894 she had helped J. A. Wayland establish the Socialist weekly, *Appeal to Reason*, and four years later she was a founding member, along with Eugene V. Debs, of the Socialist Democratic Party. She joined the Socialist Party of America as soon as it was founded in 1901. Two years later, the Philadelphia *North American* reported that "Socialists will travel distances to listen to Mother Jones speak, and after the meeting, deem it a great honor to be able to shake her hand."[89]

*Mother Jones' major speeches appear in Philip S. Foner, editor, *Mother Jones Speaks: Speeches, Testimony Before Congressional Committees, Articles, Letters* (New York, 1982).

15
The CIO, 1935–1940

AT THE 1933 AFL CONVENTION, Elizabeth Christman, speaking on behalf of the Women's Trade Union League, pleaded with the delegates to take immediate action to organize the 5 million women in industry—"the legions of women barbers, hairdressers, manicurists, bakery workers, retail clerks, electrical manufacturing employees, hotel and restaurant workers, and many others." She conceded that past efforts to organize these workers had not been successful but maintained that the labor movement was "faced with another opportunity that has sprung up like a mushroom growth at the birth of the Blue Eagle. Legions of unorganized workers are suddenly realizing that, without the backing of unions, they haven't the ghost of a chance to get justice under certain codes and in fighting 'chiselers.'" Women bore the brunt of the NRA's weaknesses, she declared, and they were especially eager to join the labor movement, given the chance to do so.

The following year did produce a considerable spurt in female membership of the clothing unions, but in other respects the situation had not changed much when the AFL met for its 1934 convention. The *AFL Rank and File Federationist,* issued by left-wing members of the federation, reminded the delegates that despite the organizing drives that followed the establishment of the NRA, the AFL "still counts less than 200,000 women among its members."* It continued:

*The *Federationist* pointed out that the only AFL unions with more than 5,000 women members were the Boot and Shoe Workers Union, 11,000; the Bookbinders Union, 6,000; the United Textile Workers, 10,000; the International Brotherhood of Electrical Workers, 14,000, mostly telephone operators; the Actors Union, 5,000; the Hotel & Restaurant Employees, 8,000; the Federal Employees, 11,000; and the American Federation of Teachers, 10,000. "Put these together with the clothing workers and the railway clerks, and the total number is still under 200,000" (*AFL Rank and File Federationist,* June 1934).

Officials of the old craft-unions have been too rigid, too much occupied with their own comfortable positions as high-salaried officers, to trouble themselves about the organization of the great masses of unskilled and semi-skilled workers. Most women are found in this vast body of semi-skilled.[2]

Many women were now in the mass-production industries, but the AFL policy of craft-exclusiveness was unsuited to the organization of these industries.* After the passage of the National Industrial Recovery Act in June, 1933, local industrial unions were formed all over the country, and they requested admission into the AFL. The federation, determined to maintain the principle of organization by crafts, issued "federal" charters to organizations of unskilled and semiskilled workers in rubber, auto, steel, electrical, and other mass-production industries. However, these were only temporary charters, regarded as a device for holding on to the newly organized industrial locals until a way could be found to divide them up among the various craft unions. Since many AFL leaders did not consider the unskilled workers worth organizing, they hoped that in the process these workers would fall by the wayside.

Disillusionment with the AFL's policy of "federal" unions spread rapidly among the new flock of unionists in the mass-production industries, and many of the organizations launched during the union boom of the early New Deal days disintegrated. At the 1933 AFL convention, the WTUL's Christman had offered an industrial union resolution in the course of her appeal for the organization of workingwomen, but it was not voted on. A year later, John L. Lewis of the United Mine Workers, who was now the leading champion of industrial unionism, argued vigorously that it offered the only suitable way to organize the mass-production industries.† A compromise resolution was adopted, which

---

*Christopher L. Tomlins challenges the traditional view that the AFL affiliates were unable to deal effectively with problems of industrial change. But he concedes: "The AFL unions proved powerless to organize workers in those industries where the labor force was predominantly semi-skilled or unskilled—as throughout most of mass production" ("AFL Unions in the 1930's: Their Performance in Historical Perspective," *Journal of American History* 65 [March 1979]: 1033).

†During his first decade as UMW president, Lewis' policies had reduced the UMW from a membership of 500,000 to 75,000. But with the enactment of the National Industrial Recovery Act in June, 1933, Lewis reversed his policies, ceased expelling his rivals and opposition forces, and mounted a major campaign to reunionize the coal industry. Before the end of the year, over 90 percent of the coal fields were organized. Lewis was not only convinced of the wisdom of industrial organization—the UMW was an industrial union—but he was anxious to organize the steel industry to ensure the survival of the recently organized unions in the captive mines of the large steel producers. He also feared the rise of fascism, and felt that only a strongly organized labor movement could defeat its growing influence in the United States. Hence he led the movement within the AFL for the organization of mass-production industries through industrial unionism (see Saul D. Alinsky, *John L. Lewis: An Unauthorized Biography* [New York, 1949], pp. 232–46).

appeared to accept the principle of industrial unions, but it contained a rider limiting the scope of such unions. It stated that there had been

> a change in the nature of the work performed by millions of workers in industries where it has been most difficult or impossible to organize into craft unions. . . . However, we consider it our duty to formulate policies which will fully protect the jurisdictional rights of all trade unions organized upon craft lines.[3]

The AFL leadership's refusal to alter the union structure to accommodate the needs of the vast majority of workers in the mass-production industries produced a heated battle at the 1935 convention. A majority of the Committee on Resolutions opposed the issuance of industrial charters covering the rubber, automobile, radio, and other industries. A minority, led by John L. Lewis, insisted that "in the great mass production industries . . . industrial organization is the only solution." When the industrial union resolution was voted down by the convention (1,820,000 to 1,090,000), the pro-industrial unionists met separately and launched the Committee for Industrial Organization to encourage the formation of industrial unions, which were to affiliate themselves with the AFL.[4]

The CIO, as the committee was immediately called, was composed of eight international unions: the United Mine Workers; the Amalgamated Clothing Workers of America; the International Ladies' Garment Workers' Union; the International Typographical Union; the Oil Field, Gas, Well & Refinery Workers; the United Hatters, Cap & Millinery Workers; the United Textile Workers of America; and the International Union of Mine, Mill & Smelter Workers. There were no specific references to women in the statements launching the CIO, but it was obvious that unionization along industrial lines, as advocated by the CIO, would require the cooperation and participation of women workers, many of whom were excluded from the craft unions. Also, two of the most powerful founding unions—the Amalgamated Clothing Workers and the ILGWU—represented industries that employed substantial numbers of women, and the growth of these unions since 1933, especially the ILGWU, indicated even to the most skeptical that women could indeed be unionized. Furthermore, John L. Lewis had long supported the Women's Trade Union League, had endorsed equal pay in the NRA codes, and had championed the Women's Bureau. In a *New York Times* interview shortly after the CIO was launched, Lewis committed the new movement to equal pay for "substantially the same work."[5] Finally, in March, 1935, the Trade Union Unity League officially dissolved and, in keeping with the Communist Party decision calling for working from within the existing trade unions, the TUUL militants, men and women alike, began to play an important role in the CIO. They emphasized the importance of "organizing working women into the industrial unions," and urged: "Our task today is to take up seriously the problem of organizing women workers in the industries. The men workers will never be able to establish real union conditions as long as the women remain unorganized."[6]

Although linked to the AFL, the Women's Trade Union League acknowledged publicly that the "new organization techniques" of the CIO held out a better future for workingwomen and pledged itself to assist any group appealing for help.[7] The Women's Bureau, for its part, adopted a public position of impartiality between the AFL and the CIO. Mary Anderson maintained that there was room in the labor movement for both craft and industrial unionism, but she conceded that craft union practices adversely affected women workers and left them in a weaker position than the men. She also insisted that "it is always dangerous for workers to be segregated into several different organizations with different dues and different initiation fees and separate contracts with the employers."[8]

In 1935 Congress passed and President Roosevelt signed the National Labor Relations Act (the Wagner Act). It gave workers the right to vote for the unions of their choice; outlawed certain unfair practices used by employers against unions; and created the National Labor Relations Board (NLRB), with power to enforce the act. Rigidly antiunion employers found ways to circumvent the law, but it did stimulate union growth by strengthening the hand of labor organizations in their campaign to unionize workers and secure contracts.

The Committee for Industrial Organization remained formally in the AFL until November, 1936, when the federation's convention confirmed the Executive Council's suspension of all international unions that had associated themselves with the CIO. Months before this, however, the CIO was already operating almost as an independent movement, ignoring the warnings and threats of AFL leaders and providing stimulus for the greatest labor upsurge in American history.[9]

In 1936–1937, under the personal leadership of John L. Lewis and with funds from the United Mine Workers and other CIO unions, a series of great organizing campaigns took place in the rubber, auto, and steel industries; among packinghouse and textile workers; in electrical, radio, mining, woodworking, shipbuilding, and communications; and among seamen, warehouse workers, and many others. Many of these campaigns did not involve women directly because they were not employed in the industries, but women played a crucial role, directly or indirectly, in the great unionizing drives under the CIO's leadership.

In January, 1936, 137 tire builders at the Goodyear Rubber Company in Akron, Ohio, "sat down" in protest against a layoff of seventy Goodyear workers. They were promptly fired, but within ten days, rubber workers at two other major companies—Firestone and Goodrich—sat down and occupied the factories day and night. Soon, the first major sit-down strike of the 1930s was converted into an outside strike at

Goodyear, and for five weeks, fourteen thousand workers picketed the company's plants.[10]

It became evident early in the strike that company agents were beginning to exert pressure upon the mothers, wives, daughters, and sisters of the strikers in order to break their morale. To help meet the problem, Rose Pesotta of the ILGWU was sent to Akron to work with other CIO organizers who were directing the strike.[11] She wrote later:

> From my first day in Akron, I saw that women would play a vital part in the strike, and perhaps even be a decisive factor in the settlement. True, women workers in the Goodyear factory were comparatively few.... But mothers, wives, daughters of the striking men were there—and we were getting important help, particularly in the commissary, from women employed in the Firestone and Goodrich plants.*[12]

Another letter from Akron added emphasis to Pesotta's point:

> I spent Monday at the headquarters of the striking rubber workers, working with the women in the kitchen, and when I left, I was filled with enthusiasm and confidence that the strikers were bound to win if they continued in the same spirit. I want to deal chiefly with the part the women are playing in the strike, as members of the Women's Auxiliary of the United Rubber Workers.
>
> All the work of feeding the pickets is in the hands of the women. Only the cooking is done by two men cooks. There are about five women helping in the kitchen with the preparation of food, between two and four making sandwiches, about six at the large restaurant counter, at which meals are served 24 hours a day, then there are dishwashers, checking and stock girls and the woman in charge.
>
> The work is divided into shifts of six hours, but many of the women do not even go home. They stay on with their men. The husbands and sons of most of these women are union men, but these women are no less determined to stick it out to a successful finish. As one woman put it: "We got them [the bosses] unawares this time, before they had a chance to prepare gas bombs and barbed wire against us, and if they call the militia against us, why we will stick it out all the same."
>
> "Is your husband on the picket line, too?" I asked the woman who was peeling potatoes next to me. "Indeed," was the proud reply, "my husband is on the picket line and so is my 19-year-old son...."
>
> No wonder the men are so enthusiastic and determined. They have the wholehearted support of fine, courageous women who are with them shoulder to shoulder in this struggle.[13]

The strike settlement provided for no discrimination against members of the United Rubber Workers; a thirty-six-hour week with six-hour shifts in the tire and tube division, and with the workweek not to exceed forty hours in all other departments; and the provision that union shop

---

*Twenty percent of the members of the Firestone local of the United Rubber Workers were women.

committees would have the right to deal with foremen. "Shoulder to shoulder with their men, the wives, daughters, and sisters of the strikers marched through the business district to the strike headquarters in a great victory parade," reported the *Akron Beacon Journal* on March 21, 1936. "Their joy was unbounded," Rose Pesotta recalled. "Not since Armistice Day in 1918 had there been such jubilation in Akron."[14]

The victory of the Akron rubber workers revealed the full power of the sit-down strike for the first time. The tactic of seizing possession of and holding great plants was not entirely unknown to the workers of the United States,* but nothing like what was about to occur in the mid-1930s had ever been seen before. In the sit-down strike, the workers found a formidable weapon with which to overcome the powerful resistance to unionization of the giant manufacturing corporations in rubber, auto, steel, electrical, and other basic industries.

The Akron victory had also demonstrated how much a women's auxiliary could contribute to winning a strike. Many male workers, however, were still unwilling to accept this truth. "Women's auxiliary," sneered a group of men in the Transport Workers' Union in New York City. "We don't need a women's auxiliary. They'll sit around like a sewing circle every week and get silly notions in their heads. Let 'em stay at home and cook our dinners. That's what women are good for." Then on January 23, 1936, while the members of the TWU were sitting in at the Williamsburgh (Brooklyn) powerhouse, demanding that the company meet their request for better working conditions, members of the union's women's auxiliary appeared by the score and threw a picket line around the plant. While the women were picketing all through the night, they also found time to make huge pots of coffee and sandwiches for their husbands inside. Two days later, the company granted the strikers' demands. Several months later, John L. Lewis, addressing the TWU convention, paused in his speech to pay tribute to the union's women's auxiliary for its splendid contribution to the union victory during the powerhouse sit-down.[15]

The headline in the September, 1956, issue of the *United Automobile Worker* read: "Ladies' Auxiliary Helped Build UAW." The union's official organ noted that "in the crucial strikes, the chips-down organizing drives, in nearly every historic struggle, the gals were there. They kept soup kitchens going around the clock, tended each others' kids so families wouldn't be neglected, passed out literature, formed protest committees, and even took a hand at keeping the picket lines intact." "Call the rolls of the historic struggles," the article continued, "and you name the places where the Auxiliaries helped carry the day."

---

*What was probably the first sit-down strike in the United States took place under IWW leadership in 1906 at the General Electric plant in Schenectady, New York, and lasted for sixty-five hours.

They certainly helped "carry the day" in the greatest of all the early UAW battles—the General Motors sit-down strike in Flint, Michigan.

On December 30, 1936, the auto workers at the Fisher 1 and Fisher 2 plants sat down. The strike eventually spread throughout the General Motors empire, affecting approximately 140,000 of the corporation's automotive employees and more than 50 percent of its plants, but the center of the conflict from the end of December was Flint. There, the Fisher Body plants produced bodies and parts on which three-fourths of GM's automotive production depended. The most significant of the union's official demands, which were submitted to GM on January 4, 1937, was the request that the UAW be recognized as the exclusive bargaining agency for all GM employees.[16]

The Women's Auxiliary was formed by about fifty women after a street dance on New Year's Eve in front of the worker-held Fisher Plant 2. The auxiliary supported the striking men. They fed the strikers daily, set up a first-aid station, where they nursed casualties, distributed literature, ran around-the-clock picket lines, and took charge of publicity. The women also ran a day care center for the children of striking mothers, established a welfare committee and a speaker's bureau, and visited wives who opposed the sit-down to try to convince them to support their husbands.[17]

The Women's Auxiliary organized dancing, representing all nationality groups, in front of the plants. They formed "living formations" or mass charades to describe phrases like "Solidarity Forever" or "Sole Collective Bargaining," and they sang their theme song to the tune of "Marching Through Georgia":

> The women got together and they formed a mighty throng,
> Every worker's wife and mom and sister will belong,
> They will fight beside the men to help the cause along,
> Shouting the Union forever.[18]

The strikers, in turn, serenaded the women with their own band. One of their most popular songs was written by Maurice Sugar, UAW counsel:

> When they tie a can to a union man
>   Sit down! Sit down!
> When they give him the sack, they'll take him back,
>   Sit down! Sit down!
>
> Sit down, just take a seat
> Sit down, and rest your feet
> Sit down, you've got 'em beat
> Sit down! Sit down![19]

The responsibility for feeding several thousand workers, both inside and outside the plants, was enormous. The union kitchen was headed by Dorothy Kraus, wife of Henry Kraus, the union's editor. One day's food supply included 500 pounds of meat, 100 pounds of potatoes, three hundred loaves of bread, 100 pounds of coffee, 200 pounds of sugar, 30 gallons of milk, and four cases of evaporated milk. Two hundred people, mostly women, prepared this food.[20]

On the afternoon of January 11, as workers were handing food in through the main gate of Fisher 2, company guards suddenly appeared and overpowered them. The workers quickly ran up a ladder to hoist the food to the second floor, but the guards hauled it down. At that moment, in 16-degree weather, the company turned off the heat. When other workers, alerted to this new development, moved to battle the company guards, the Flint police advanced on the auto workers, opening fire on them with tear gas bombs. News of this action brought more workers to the scene. Women pickets deposited their children at the union hall and raced to the plant.

In the midst of the police attacks, Genora Johnson, the wife of a union man who was inside the plant, took the microphone of the union sound truck and cried out to the police: "Cowards! Cowards! Shooting unarmed and defenseless men!" Then to the women in the crowd, she cried: "Women of Flint! This is your fight! Join the picket line and defend your jobs, your husbands' jobs and your children's homes!"

The police continued firing until they were out of tear gas.* By morning, "The Battle of Bulls Run" in which the strikers and their supporters routed the Flint police was over—the "bulls" (police) ran. Eight thousand workers massed in front of Fisher 2 to celebrate the victory, while thousands signed up in the UAW.[21]

On January 21, 1937, the *New York Times* announced the formation of a "new automotive strike organization, the Women's Emergency Brigade," composed of "women who have husbands, sons or brothers in the General Motors strike." "The leader," the *Times* continued, "is Mrs. Geora [sic] Johnson, a pretty, 23-year-old mother of two children."† Following "The Battle of Bulls Run," Genora Johnson organized the Women's Emergency Brigade as a vanguard detachment of the Women's Auxiliary. The organization's purpose, Johnson told reporters, was "to be on hand in any emergency and to stand by our husbands, brothers, and sons. We will form a picket line around the men, and if the police want to fire, then they'll just have to fire into us."[22]

Starting with 50 women, the Flint Brigade soon grew to 350 and

*They were turned down by the Detroit and Saginaw police departments when they asked for an additional supply for the simple reason that these departments had run out of supplies of tear gas (Henry Kraus, *The Many & The Few: A Chronicle of the Dynamic Auto Worker* [Los Angeles, 1947], p. 139).

†Genora Johnson, with her auto worker husband and father-in-law, Kermit and Carl Johnson, formed a Socialist Party local in Flint, Michigan, in the early 1930s (Sherna Gluck, "The Changing Nature of Women's Participation in the American Labor Movement, 1900–1940's: Case Studies from Oral History," (Paper delivered at the Southwest Labor History Conference, March 5, 1977), p. 12, based on interviews with Genora Johnson Dollinger).

became the model for similar "Emergency Brigades" in other auto cities. The "Emergency Brigades" were set up with military precision. Each had a "general" and five "captains," and each captain had ten "lieutenants." This made it possible to call together thousands of union women at a moment's notice. On almost equally short notice, the Women's Emergency Brigades could mobilize thousands of women at weak or embattled points. Their uniform consisted of colored berets and arm bands with "EB" on them. Each group had its own color. Flint's was red; Lansing's white, and Detroit's green. "If we go into battle, will we be armed?" Genora Johnson was asked. "Yes!" she replied, "with rolling pints, brooms, mops and anything we can get." The members of the brigade also began carrying long "two-by-fours," whittled down at one end for better use as weapons.[23]

Mary Heaton Vorse, who covered the sit-down strike as a reporter, described the members of the Emergency Brigades as "strikers' wives and mothers, normally 'homebodies,' mature women, the majority married." The women were "doing this because they have come to the conclusion it must be done if they and their children are to have a decent life." Vorse described the Flint Brigade in action:

> Down the hill presently came a procession, preceded by an American flag. The women's bright red caps showed dramatically in the dark crowd. They were singing *Hold the Fort*.
> To all the crowd there was something moving about seeing the women return to the picket line after having been gassed.... The crowd took up the song. The line of bright-capped women spread itself in front of the high gate.... Some of the men who had jumped over the gate went back.... At half past three in the morning, a dozen women of the Emergency Brigade were on duty in the first-aid room in Pengally Hall.[24]

The brigade was ready for action when the sit-downers seized several other General Motors plants late in January. Creating a disturbance, they lured the police to Chevrolet Plant 9 at Flint, so that male strikers could seize Plant 4, the key to the motor assembly division. When Plant 9 was tear-gassed, the Emergency Brigade broke windows in the plant so that the strikers could breathe. Later, setting up a line in front of Chevrolet 4, the Brigade dared the police to attack. Historian Sidney H. Fine described the scene:

> Outside the plant, city police sought to enter one of the gates shortly after 4:00 p.m., but a few Emergency Brigade members stood in front of the building with locked arms and ignored police orders to disperse. One of them defiantly told the police, "Nobody can get in except our men." Other Brigade members soon came marching down Chevrolet Avenue, a flag bearer at the head of the procession. On instructions from Genora Johnson, who was issuing commands from a sound car, they formed a revolving picket line in front of the plant. They picketed to the rhythm of such songs as "We Shall Not Be Moved," while the police looked on rather sheepishly.[25]

The UAW declared February 3 "Women's Day." Hundreds of women began arriving from Detroit, Toledo, Lansing, and Pontiac to join the Flint Women's Emergency Brigade. The women decided to demonstrate right in the heart of Flint, and seven thousand of them marched through the streets with their children, carrying signs reading: "We Stand by Our Heroes in the Plants," and "Our Daddies Fight for Us Little Tykes." The women marched to Fisher Plant 1 and joined thousands of pickets already there. Together, the men and women created "one of the most amazing labor demonstrations ever seen in America." Carrying clubs, stove pokers, crowbars, and lead pipes and wearing their bright-red berets, the members of the Emergency Brigade were cheered by the strikers inside the plant. "The rallying effect of the women's brigade is felt on every hand," wrote a reporter. "Whenever the brigade appears, the workers rush to the roofs and windows of the plants to cheer and applaud them." Rose Pesotta, who obtained clothing for the strikers and went into the plants to speak to them, was tremendously impressed by the work of the Brigade: "One saw the Women's Emergency Brigade on duty at all hours of day and night—sewing in the commissary, in the first-aid station, and on the picket lines, working always to keep up the morale of the strikers' families."[26]

Encouragement was also given to the sit-down strikers and their families by a number of prominent women who appeared in Flint. Dorothy Dix, Cornelia Bryce Pinchot, and Ellen Wilkinson, a Labor Party member of the British Parliament, met with the strikers and their wives. Wilkinson told them that she had been commissioned by the British workers before she left for the United States to be "sure to visit Flint and report on the American phase of the sit-in campaigns that are sweeping the industrial world everywhere."[*27] Margaret Cowl, a Communist Party leader, met with the strikers' wives and indicated to them how important the Women's Auxiliary and the Women's Emergency Brigade of the sit-down strike was in convincing male workers in the mass-production industries of the "significant role wives of the workers can play in the battle for decent working conditions, better wages and union organization."[28]

For forty-four days—from December 30, 1936, to February 11, 1937—the GM workers and their womenfolk fought the giant corporation in a great sit-down struggle. At 2:35 A.M. on February 11, Michigan Governor Frank Murphy announced that peace terms had been arranged. The agreement recognized the UAW as the collective bargaining agency for its members, and the company agreed not to interfere with the right of its employees to belong to that union.[†29]

---

*Sit-down strikes occurred in Poland, Yugoslavia, and France from the end of the First World War to the early 1930s (Joel Seidman, *Sit-Down*, Pamphlet, League for Industrial Democracy, March 1937, p. 13).

†The agreement also stipulated that the strikers would get their jobs back without dis-

Throughout the "Battle of the Century," the Women's Auxiliary and the Women's Emergency Brigade kept the morale and determination of the striking men high. But the experience also did something for the women themselves. They found that activity outside the home increased their self-respect. The wife of a Cadillac striker wrote: "I found a common understanding and unselfishness I'd never known. I'm living for the first time with a definite goal. I want a decent living for not only my family but for everyone. Just being a woman isn't enough any more. I want to be a human being."[30] Mary Heaton Vorse described the Flint women's release from the isolation of the private home:

> Women from different towns got up and talked about the many activities in which they were engaged, what they did for their children, of the classes formed, how their committees worked, how they made little plays about the episodes of the strike.
>
> The hall was packed with women, the men standing in a fringe at the back. The chairwoman of the meeting was in command. All of the women were finding in themselves new powers and new strength and they had found each other. . . .[31]

For many of these women, the union now became an important factor in their lives. "A new type of woman was born in the strike," one of the members of the Emergency Brigade wrote after the battle had ended. "Women who only yesterday were horrified at unionism, who felt inferior to the task of organizing, speaking, leading, have, as if overnight, become the spearhead in the battle of unionism."[32] Sidney H. Fine later speculated, after reading these statements, that the participation of the women in the strike was probably more important for them than for the men.[33]

At its convention in August, 1937, the United Auto Workers voted full support for all women's auxiliaries in recognition of the women's contribution in Flint.[34] Justly proud of their contribution, the Detroit City-Wide Committee of the Women's Auxiliary of the United Auto Workers published the first issue of their bulletin, *Women in Auto*. The mimeographed magazine was full of stories about the strike and of how the women had come to the support of the union. Violet Bagget, one of the Auxiliary members, told of her long years of ignorance as to what her husband was "up to." She wrote that she had heard stories about beer parties and wild times, and when her husband told her he was going to union meetings, she was suspicious and resentful. When the strike began and he left for the picket line, she went to the union hall "with war in her eye":

---

crimination, and that on February 16 the company was to begin collective bargaining with the UAW on its demands for a thirty-hour week, a six-hour day, time-and-a-half for overtime, minimum rates of pay to provide "an American standard of living," seniority rights, abolition of the piecework system of pay, and mutual agreement on the speed of the production lines.

At the kitchen, I was met by a lady in an apron instead of the red-painted girls I was looking for. After getting a look around at half a dozen others, all in work clothes, peeling potatoes and onions, I decided to wait a while and just see for myself what those reds were like. . . . This all happened a month ago and I'm still spending most of my time there working for the union with the rest of them.[35]

The Women's Emergency Brigade disbanded after the strike and did not issue any bulletin. But in 1978 the Women's Labor History Film Project told the story of the Brigade in a forty-five minute documentary entitled "With Babies and Banners: The Story of the Women's Emergency Brigade," directed by Lorraine Gray and produced by Anne Bohlen. The film opens with the song:

It was the women that were fighting
As the strike came to be
The men were at the windows
Of a sit-down factory.

The film combines archival footage with interviews with six brigade veterans reunited forty years after the the strike at the home of Delia Parrish, one of the brigaders.

Delia Parrish tells how the company and even some of her neighbors viewed the brigade:

They called us all sorts of names. They just thought that I was a genuine old Bolshevik or red or anything else. I didn't care, that didn't bother me at all because I knew what I was doing, and I knew the purpose I was doing it for. I wouldn't have cared if the whole red Russia would have been there, just to help us out. . . .

Genora Johnson, founder of the brigade, explained that in helping their husbands win the strike and improve working conditions in the plants, the wives were helping themselves and their children: "The man was so driven by the speedup in the factory that he came home unable to be a decent companion to either his wife or his children. And some wives had to take an awful lot of bad treatment from their husbands."[36]

In its first issue, the bulletin of the Detroit Women's Auxiliary, *Women in Auto,* paid tribute to another publication, *Women in Steel,* the monthly bulletin of the women's auxiliaries of the CIO's Steel Workers Organizing Committee. "In the name of our common determination to make wives, mothers, daughters and sweethearts of union men a real force in the American labor movement," said the auto women, "we greet you, women in Steel."[37]

When the SWOC merged with the Amalgamated Association of Iron, Steel & Tin Workers, after the latter had agreed to affiliate with the CIO, the wives and daughters of the steelworkers were organized into the Women's Auxiliary of the Amalgamated Association of Iron, Steel and Tin Workers of North America. The aim was to enable the women "to lend aid to the union in all possible ways," to help them to maintain the morale of the steelworkers, to educate the auxiliary members in the principles of trade unionism, and to weld them into a force for social betterment so that "by uniting with their men they can put an end to some of the miserable social conditions existing in their community."[38]

Women of the Auxiliary Lodge 5, Chicago, announced that they had unfurled their banner in solidarity with their men, and, in the achievement of their common goals, they said, "We are prepared to make all the necessary sacrifices."[39] They picketed with their striking husbands in North Chicago and were gassed and beaten. At the Memorial Day massacre (May 30, 1937) at Chicago's Republic Steel plant, women were at the head of the mass picket line when the police first fired into the unarmed demonstrators and then beat the wounded and others with their clubs. Four workers were killed, over eighty wounded. A *St. Louis Post-Dispatch* reporter described the Paramount film of the massacre, which was never released for public showing. He wrote of how women, as well as men, were attacked by the club-swinging polic :. He described a girl

> not more than five feet tall, who can hardly weigh more than 100 pounds. ... She is seen going down under a quick blow from a policeman's club delivered from behind. She gets up and staggers around. A few minutes later, she is shown being shoved into a patrol wagon, as blood cascades down her face and spreads over her clothing.[40]

A few weeks later, June 19 was proclaimed "Women's Day" by the striking steelworkers in Youngstown, Ohio. In front of the gates of Republic Steel, tear gas and shots were fired at female pickets, some of whom were accompanied by their children. Rushing from a union meeting, men joined the demonstration, and a general battle with the deputies followed. Two strikers were killed, and forty-two, several of them women, were injured. The following day, labor reporter Mary Heaton Vorse was herself wounded by gunshot. A year later, Mrs. Barbara Krepechak described to the Senate Committee on Civil Liberties what had happened to her. The scene, she said, had been completely peaceful when suddenly a police officer demanded that the picket line disperse. "God damn, I make you move," he growled. Almost immediately afterward, she was shot in the leg. Stella Kirin told how Captain Charles Richmond of the Youngstown police gave the order to fire tear gas: "We had no chance to move before he told his men to fire tear gas at us."[41]

Having proved themselves an effective weapon, the sit-down strikes rolled like a wave across the country. By March, 1937, the CIO felt it necessary to advise newspapers that "sit-down" should be spelled with a hyphen. A leading CIO official defined a sit-down as "a cessation of work with the men remaining at work."[42] This conscious or unconscious neglect of women sit-down strikers is surprising in view of the fact that in the two weeks after the GM victory at Flint, they were involved in the eighty-seven sit-downs in Detroit. "Sit-down strikes, chiefly involving women and young girls, are in progress in seven auto parts and other manufacturing plants here," wrote a reporter from Detroit in mid-Feburary, 1937. "Nearly 3,000 workers are participating. They include spring cushion making, automobile stamping, pie-making, cigar making and food products plants." The girls at Farm Crest Bakeries slept on pie and cake rests until they received the cots that had been used by the Flint sit-down strikers. One of the women strikers at a Detroit cigar factory wrote:

> Some of us sitting here are doing fancy knitting work. Others are playing cards. A few are in the "kitchen" making noodles. There is music and the younger girls, with gay cellophane ribbons in their hair, are dancing. We've got to pass the time away, because, like one worker said: "We're gonna stick it out until past Easter, if necessary." The auto victory showed us how.
> So we women are sitting down these days, more than 3,000 strong in this Detroit factory alone.
> It all sounds like a lark, doesn't it? . . . But we are serious, dead serious. Our wages, from eight to fourteen dollars per week, and hours, from nine to ten each day, keep us that way.[43]

"The great transformation of Detroit, one of the country's strongest open-shop centers, to a union town is under way," observed a reporter.[44] Symptomatic of the change was what was called "the strike of strikes— the sit-down of F. W. Woolworth girls" in two five-and-dime stores. Even though Detroit had become somewhat used to sit-down strikes, this event was flashed in blaring headlines: "Girls Sit Down in Loop Ten-Cent Store."[45] Two hundred girls had sat down at the height of the shopping rush on a Saturday afternoon. Most of them were in their teens, and their young voices created a sensation as they contrasted in song the wealth of Barbara Hutton, the millionaire Woolworth heiress, and their own conditions:

> Barbara Hutton has the dough, parlez-vous.
> Where she gets it, sure we know, parlez-vous.
> We slave at Woolworth's five-and dime.
> The pay we get is sure a crime.
> Hinkey dinkey parlez-vous.

And

> Barbara Hutton eats good mutton—
> The Woolworth workers, they get nuttin'.[46]

They were striking for a forty-eight hour week, a 10-cent-an-hour wage increase over their pay, which was as low as $10.44 a week, and the right to collective bargaining.

On the seventh day of the sit-down strike, they scored a clear victory: a 5-cent-an-hour increase in wages; union recognition; annual vacations with pay; no charge for laundering uniforms; and payment for half the time they had been on strike. The agreement covered forty Woolworth stores in Detroit and was "the first time in history that such action has affected the great five-and-dime chain."[47]

Other sit-down victories followed. "Forty-seven Detroit Sitdowns Won by Strikers" read one headline in the Detroit papers on March 7, 1937. "A New High in Action of Women on the Labor Front" read another.[48]

In New York City, sit-downs in Woolworth's, Grand's, and H. L. Green's 5-and-10-cent stores dominated the news for ten days in March, 1937.Blankets, cots, guitars, and food (including fish on Friday for Roman Catholics) were passed to the striking women. "You're making history," Clarissa Michelson, general organizer of Local 1250, Department Store Employees Union, told the strikers. "When we get through, there'll be no more working for $10 and $11 a week."[49] H. L. Green Company was the first to settle, after the sit-down had lasted thirteen days, signing a contract that provided for 10 percent wage increases for workers receiving less than $20 weekly; 5 percent for workers making more than $20; union recognition for all union members; one week's vacation pay for workers employed a full year and two weeks for those employed for two years; a minimum wage of $14.50 for apprentices and $15.60 for regulars; and an eight-hour day. The contract covered all thirteen Green stores in the city.[50]

Woolworth and Grand settled later. In the case of Woolworth, the New York police ousted the women sit-down strikers, but they picketed outside, and Woolworth signed an agreement with Local 1250 granting the forty-eight-hour week, a minimum wage of $15.60 (which meant an increase of more than $1), vacations with pay, and rest periods.[51]

When 250 women at the Pennstate Tobacco Company in Philadelphia sat down, the company threatened to move the shop and machinery. Thereupon, a group of women blocked the move by lying down in the doorway in front of a truck that had come to move the machines. After a four-week strike, the strikers won a preferential union shop, sanitary conditions, a 5 percent wage increase, and an agreement for future negotiations to settle other grievances.[52]

The general strike against all the hosiery mills in the Reading, Pennsylvania, area in March, 1937, also took the form of a sit-down. "The tide has turned," exulted the *Hosiery Worker*. "A new psychological element is introduced when a striker is inside rather than outside on the picket line. . . . We are going to win!" Many of the strikers were women, and other women, "wives of men on strike, organized auxiliaries after the Flint model and are providing hot meals to the strikers."[53] The strike ended on April 23 with a wage scale acceptable to the American Federation of Hosiery Workers, union recognition, the dues check-off,* and arbitration of disputes. It was the first collective bargaining agreement signed with major plants in the full-fashioned-hosiery industry.[54]

In American industry at large during 1937, there were 477 sitdown strikes, affecting over 300,000 workers. Many of them were women who adopted this technique in hospitals, drug companies, restaurants, and hotels, in addition to the industries already discussed. Stella Nowicki recalled a sit-down strike in a Chicago meatpacking plant precipitated when one of the women, "in putting meat into the chopper, got her fingers caught. There were no safety guards. Her fingers got into the hotdogs and they were chopped off. It was just horrible." After a meeting during their break, three militants including Nowicki, all Communists, called to the workers, "Sit, stop." "And we had a sit down. We just stopped working right inside the building, protesting the speed and the unsafe conditions. We thought that people's fingers shouldn't go into the machine. . . . The women got interested in the union." The company was forced to put in safety devices.†

In Congress, the conservatives attempted to condemn the sit-down as illegal, but they were only able to secure the passage of a concurrent resolution condemning both the sit-down and unfair practices by employers. The resolution did not carry the force of law, and it was not until 1939 that the sit-down was finally declared illegal by the Supreme Court. One of the last of the sit-down strikes was by eighteen hundred members of the Packinghouse Workers Organizing Committee (CIO), who closed down the Kansas City Armour packing plant in mid-September, 1938, when the company refused to pay for the time lost during a grievance committee meeting. Women's Auxiliary members kept the strike going by passing buckets of coffee and sandwiches over the fence to the twelve hundred men and six hundred women sitting down. After a few days, the company gave in.[55]

One of the most prominent of the new CIO unions to include large numbers of women did not grow by means of the sit-down. On March 21, 1936, in Buffalo, New York, fifty delegates representing federal locals and independent unions in the electrical and radio industries formed the United Electrical & Radio Workers of America, and urged the Committee for Industrial Organization to give them assistance and support. The preamble to the UE constitution pointed out that the organization's aim was to unite "all workers in our industry on an industrial basis, and rank and file control, regardless of craft, age, sex, nationality, race, creed or political belief." James B. Carey of the Philco local was

---

*The system by which dues or an equal amount is deducted from the paycheck.
†The company, however, fired the leaders of the sit-down strike, and Stella Nowicki was both fired and blacklisted.

elected president and Julius Emspak of Schenectady General Electric, secretary-treasurer.[56]

Just one month after its formation, the new industrial union won a victory at Philco involving eight thousand workers. The wage increase was 10 percent for all male workers and a special increase of 15 percent for all women workers. "The purpose of this demand is to close up the gap in wages between men and women workers," the union informed the press.[57]

The biggest strike in the summer of 1936 was the UE strike at the Radio Corporation of America plant in Camden, New Jersey. On June 23, after David Sarnoff, RCA president, had refused to negotiate with a committee of UE workers, six thousand employees at the plant, many of them women, went on strike for union recognition, wage increases to bring wages up to those in other Philadelphia-area radio-electrical plants, and the seven-hour day. Within a few days the number of strikers had grown to nine thousand, 60 percent of them women. The mass picket lines were attacked by the Camden police, state troopers, and strikebreaking thugs. It was estimated that RCA spent close to a quarter of a million dollars fighting the strike, and women were not spared in the brutal attacks on the strikers. One account in the press read:

> "The police broke my arm on the picket line this morning, but I still have another arm and two legs and I'm going to be back on the picket line this afternoon." A young girl—an RCA striker—was speaking. She had just come back from the hospital, her tightly-bandaged arm in a sling. . . . The girl's militancy is not exceptional.[58]

Another woman striker, who also had her arm in a sling, said:

> One of the scabs had a piece of lead pipe wrapped in a newspaper. He was aiming for my head, and I reached up to protect myself. It came down on my wrist instead, and broke the bone and tore a couple of ligaments. I've got to get injections for it to make the blood clot. . . .
> I'm twenty-five years old. Been married eight years and have my husband and my little girl to support. Some of us have eight kids to support on thirteen dollars a week. We've got 9,000 on the picket line and lots of support from other unions in town. Sure we're going to win.[59]

On July 21, 1936, after five bloody weeks, Sarnoff agreed to a National Labor Relations Board election and provided that the company would recognize the union if it received a majority vote as the sole collective bargaining agency of the workers. Strikers would be reemployed without discrimination, and RCA would pay "as high wages under as favorable hours and working conditions as prevail in Camden-Philadelphia manufacturing establishments engaged in similar classes of work." Even though the battle was not over, the union had won an important victory. Although the UE won the election and was certified as the sole bargaining agent on November 9, 1936, it was not until three years later that the UE won clear collective bargaining rights at RCA.[60]

In September, 1936, UE joined the CIO—the first organization to affiliate outside of the original AFL unions that had formed it. The UE's growth was spectacular—from 33,000 members in December, 1936, to approximately 120,000 by August 31, 1937. About 40 percent of these workers were women! By this time, the union's name had been expanded to the United Electrical, Radio & Machine Workers as a result of the admission of a group of machinist locals headed by James Matles, a young organizer who had been a leader of the TUUL's Sheet Metal Workers Industrial Union and was active after the TUUL was dissolved in the AFL's International Association of Machinists. Matles was elected the UE's director of organization.[61]

The first woman to hold office in a UE local was Peg Darin, recording secretary of Local 601 in East Pittsburgh. She was elected for the first time on June 5, 1935, and was reelected each year until 1940. A worker at Westinghouse, Darin had been a student at the Bryn Mawr Summer School for Women in 1933. On her return to Pittsburgh, she joined Local 202 of the Sheet Metal Workers Industrial Union, TUUL, and later became a member of an independent union—Local 1010 of the Electrical and Radio Workers, which became Local 601 of the UE.[62]

Local 601's constitution, ratified in November, 1936, contained a clause inserted at the insistence of its women members. Article XI, Section 5 read: "The term 'he' in this Constitution and By-laws shall mean any member of the local." Article II, Section 1 provided for a dues differential, with men paying $1 monthly dues and women 60 cents. This was intended to lessen the burden on women until their wages were raised.[63]

Women constituted about one-third of the eleven thousand workers at Westinghouse's East Pittsburgh plant. The motor division was made up predominantly of women; the switch-gear and generator divisions had about 50 percent women, and the factory service department had between 30 and 40 percent women. From late 1936 through the spring of 1937, Local 601 conducted an all-out organizing drive in which women played a major role. But the local did not assign women just to organize women. Peg Darin recalled, "They never said, 'Well, here, you go out and you organize women.' No, I don't think it was categorized that way. Rather—'Here's a shop; you go out and you do the best to win the hearts and minds of the people in that shop.'" However, Darin believed that women suffered special oppression in the plant and that a special appeal to them was necessary:

> Now, I think in the case of women in the shop, they certainly needed some special attention, because they were more exploited than even the men.

But to say, "You're a woman, therefore we're going to relegate you to organizing only women," why, that would be wrong. That would be a *division*. And when you're a union, you don't divide, you unite.

Why should I feel that because I'm a woman I can't appeal to the mind of a man? To join me, as a worker—not as a woman, but as a worker—who has the same problems. I identify with people that work in a shop not on the basis of their sex, but on the basis of the fact that they're working for a living the way I work for a living. Therefore we have to stay together if we're going to get anywhere.[64]

By April, 1937, Local 601 had signed up 7,200 out of the 11,000 workers and was recognized by the National Labor Relations Board as the sole bargaining agent for the East Pittsburgh plant. By 1940 Local 601 had 17,000 members and was the largest local in the UE.[65] Dozens of women workers were elected shop stewards, and Peg Darin, as recording secretary, was a member of the grievance committee that negotiated with management. The local's constitution provided for the formation of a Women's Committee and stated:

The duties of the Women's Committee shall be to plan activities which will interest the women who are working in the Westinghouse plants in the struggle for better wages and conditions by planning things such as suppers, card parties, bingoes, women's forums, home economics classes, and other affairs of interest to women. Members of this committee shall have the power to sit on all other standing committees and to offer suggestions so that the proper women's appeal shall be made in all affairs of this union.[66]

But the Women's Committee never confined itself to organizing "suppers, card parties, and bingoes." Instead, it rapidly developed into the Women's Conference—an all-women forum that dealt with the special problems women faced on the job. Local conferences were held at which women of different divisions met to discuss grievances. District-wide conferences for the same purpose followed, and women delegates proposed solutions, which were submitted to the local's grievance committee. In many cases, the special grievances of women workers were dealt with and the company had to make adjustments. As we shall see, the Women's Conference played the leading role in forcing Westinghouse to equalize the wages of men and women workers. However, the Women's Conference never directly challenged the company's policy of setting "men's jobs" and "women's jobs," and the union did not seek to open training in the trades to women so that they could enter skilled jobs. Still, according to Peg Darin, male supremacy was not a serious problem in Local 601. The women workers were well received by the men. Women organizers commanded the men's respect and were successful in organizing them as well as women. As recording secretary and as the only woman on the Executive Board, Peg Darin claimed she never felt slighted:

I have to say it. I was never made to feel, well, I always felt accepted. Now all of the other officers were men. I was never made to feel that my ideas were unacceptable or that I didn't know what I was talking about. I think I was respected by the officers of the union and, of course, by the rank and file.[67]

"In the AFL, women office workers were subcitizens. Today they have full citizenship 'in the CIO." Thus declared Lewis Merrill of the United Office & Professional Workers of America as he described the union's growth in membership from 8,600 at the time of its first convention in May, 1937, to 45,000 in the summer of 1938. After a year's existence as a CIO international, the UOPWA boasted seventy-seven locals in twenty-six states and Canada.[68]* When the union announced the appointment of Ann Berenholz as executive secretary of its newly formed Joint Council, the *CIO News* commented: "Miss Berenholz is said to be the first woman in the country to hold a position of this sort."[69] Under her leadership, the UOPWA opened a union school for women members in New York City. Included in the curriculum were classes in "The Most for Your Money," "Marriage and Its Problems," "Women in Society Today," and the role of women in the history of the American labor movement.†[70]

On November 4, 1938, the CIO met in Pittsburgh for its first constitutional convention. The constitutional convention voted to continue the CIO, and its name was changed to Congress of Industrial Organizations.

Largely as a result of CIO organizing drives, there were 800,000 women union members in 1940, a sevenfold increase in six years, as contrasted with a tripling of the number of organized males. From 1938 to 1940 alone, the number of women unionists increased from 500,000 to 800,000. To be sure, 800,000 was still only a small minority of the 11 million women workers. But 800,000 represented the largest union membership of women workers up to this time in American labor history.

---

*Susan Estabrook Kennedy argues that the CIO did not enter the clerical industry and makes no mention of the United Office & Professional Workers of America. In fact, she paints an almost completely negative portrait of the CIO, and leaves the impression that sofar as women workers were concerned, it did not really differ from the AFL. (*If All We Did Was To Weep At Home: A History of White Working-Class Women in America* [Bloomington and London, 1979], p. 178.)

†The present writer taught this last-named course at the union school for women members of the UOPWA, as well as a similar course for both women and men members of the UE, organized by Ruth Young, educational director of the union's New York–New Jersey sections.

16

Government and Industry in World War II

IN THE YEAR preceding the Japanese attack on Pearl Harbor and the U.S. Declaration of War against Japan, Germany, and Italy, comparatively few women were hired by defense plants, even though the war was on in Europe and American defense industries were tooling up. For one thing, there was still a large backlog of unemployed men on which the expanding industries could draw. (At the beginning of the war, there were over 5 million unemployed men; by the middle of 1943, only 600,000.) Moreover, there was discrimination against women based on traditional prejudice and the belief that they lacked mechanical ability, despite their proven skills in the manufacture of armaments in World War I.

During the months before the war, neither the government nor employers paid much attention to the potential of women workers. During this period, too, defense demands withdrew vital materials from other production areas and temporarily threw women out of jobs all over the country; 11,000 women in the Pennsylvania silk mills and 16,000 in hosier mills lost their employment as silk was diverted to war production. Over 30,000 in radio and 41,000 in auto manufacture were thrown out of work.

All this changed with Pearl Harbor. The increasing labor demands, coupled with the effects of the draft, compelled the hiring of women in great numbers. "The Margin Now Is Womanpower" was the title of an article in *Fortune* of February, 1943. Journalists and public officials alike argued that women held the key to American success in the war. As the Office of War Information pointed out, "Working is a woman's way in war time," and "America at war needs women at work."[2]

During the Great Depression, it will be remembered, much attention was devoted to convincing women that their place was in the home, not in the office or on the assembly line, where their presence might deny work to men supporting families. Now, government agencies and special wartime committees launched massive campaigns to convince women to enter new defense jobs or take up old positions abandoned by drafted men. The slogan now was that "housekeeping as usual ended in America on the day of Pearl Harbor."[3]

The message was not only that women were vital to victory over fascism but that they had a special stake in that victory. If the Nazis and Japanese were victorious, the appeal went, women would be enslaved; they would "sink to a sub-human level," and their position in society would be restricted to *"kinder, küche, kirche, and knipe"* (children, kitchen, church, and the brothel).[4] A woman in Nazi Germany had only one role: motherhood. Similarly, in Japan she was a "virtual pawn of the state."[5]

Great emphasis was placed on the theme that work was woman's patriotic duty. As a typical newspaper advertisement phrased it, "Women who have already responded to the call will tell you that their job in a war plant gives them a deep sense of satisfaction—that grand feeling that they are doing their *full part to help speed the day of victory.*"[6]

High wages provided another popular appeal. An OWI newspaper spot reminded women that "a production worker earns good pay."[7] An OWI Radio Bureau announcement to women advised: *"Save for the future while you take care of today.* You will earn money for the needs of today, as well as for the new homes, furnishings, vacations, and other things that will be available after the war."[8]

Actually, for most women, the need to maintain a decent standard of living was a more compelling reason to work. The majority of the women in war industry worked in order to live, to meet rising prices, and, in the case of servicemen's wives, to supplement the inadequate government allotment checks. The Women's Bureau's study of women workers in ten war-production areas revealed that the vast majority contributed at least 50 percent of their earnings toward the maintenance of a family group.[9]

For whatever reason,* women poured into the factories. Between 1940 and 1945, the number of women in the labor force expanded from less than 14 million to slightly more than 20 million. At the peak, in 1945, women made up 38 percent of the work force, as compared with 25 percent before the war.[10]

In Michigan, a key state for war production, the number of employed women rose from 391,600 in March, 1940, to 799,100 in November, 1943. In Detroit, the number of women employed in manufacturing rose from 44,000 in August, 1942, to 107,000 in February, 1943.[11]

---

*Love and marriage were also a by-product of work on the assembly line. The August, 1942, *Saturday Evening Post* carried a story about a young woman's experience at a national defense training school. Just as she has completed a course in riveting, her teacher tells her, "I love you, rivet knocker! How about you and me getting welded?" They both leave for the factory to help "lick them Japs" (Kermit Shelby, "Rivet Knocker," *Saturday Evening Post* 225 [August 1, 1942]: 23, 56.

Before the war, 85 percent of female labor was employed in the non-durable-goods industries: textiles, apparel, leather, food, and paper. With the war, an increasing number worked in the durable-goods industries: communications equipment, small-arms ammunition, electrical equipment, iron and steel, automobiles, professional and scientific equipment, rubber products, and weapons under 20 millimeters in size. Women became welders and shipbuilders; they built airplanes and produced ammunition; they made complicated electrical equipment and riveted the sides of tanks. From 1941 to 1945, "Rosie the Riveter" was a common sight. By the war's end, women had entered virtually every phase of industry and were working in almost all areas of manufacturing.[12]

As early as July 24, 1940, the Women's Bureau had predicted that the employment of women would skyrocket if the United States entered the war and had issued the first guidelines for the employment of women in defense industries: (1) the physical characteristics of the jobs must be adapted to suit women's physique; (2) care should be taken to assure the safety of women and to assure continuous production; (3) women required special protection where hazardous poisons were used; (4) women often required special lighting; (5) care should be taken to provide seats and clean and comfortable surroundings for the woman worker; (6) women should be encouraged to wear practical clothing for safety and comfort; (7) minimum wage standards should be adhered to, and the prevailing wage standards should be maintained; and (8) training programs should be provided for new workers.[13]

These recommendations were studied by other federal agencies, but by the spring of 1942, nothing much had been done to carry them out.[14] During the first year of the war, a series of agencies grappled with a number of problems, including those of women workers: the National Defense Advisory Commission (NDAC), the Office of Production Management (OPM), and the War Production Board (WPB). In April, 1942, the War Manpower Commission (WMC) was created, with Paul V. McNutt at its helm. Sidney Hillman, of the Amalgamated Clothing Workers, chaired the Labor Division of each of the first three boards. Although Mary Anderson, Women's Bureau director, expressed confidence that he would give the bureau an important voice in administration, all that she succeeded in persuading Hillman to do was to appoint a subcommittee on women's employment in the OPM. Chaired by Anderson, the subcommittee worked up a series of standards and policies to apply to the employment of women in war work. Its report was submitted in April, 1942, but its recommendations were promptly buried.[15]

Although the Women's Bureau worked actively for women's interests throughout the war, its influence was dwindling. The bureau continued to investigate ways to expand the use of women in industry, made suggestions on working conditions and community facilities, publicized women's needs and contributions, and serviced requests from women's groups, unions, and government agencies. Yet it played little role in the actual development of policy, and none at all in its enforcement.*[16]

A Women's Advisory Committee (WAC) was appointed by WMC Director McNutt in August, 1942, but it was only able to send an observer, not a voting member, to the War Manpower Commission. Suggestions for the recruitment, training, and employment of women brought before the WAC met with either indifference or perfunctory formal acceptance. By 1943 one member of the WAC had resigned in frustration; the others, in an attempted showdown with McNutt, insisted that they be given more power and consideration. McNutt's assurances that he would consult with them frequently turned out to be empty promises.[17] Meanwhile, WMC's operating arm, the U.S. Employment Service (USES), proved to be "poorly equipped for its wartime tasks"— among other reasons, because it was virtually powerless to compel modifications of hiring practices and unable to accelerate rapidly the entrance of women and minority groups into war industry.[18]

"Women," declared the *American Association of University Women's Journal* in the fall of 1942, "are conspicuous for their absence in important government posts."[19] At about the same time, representatives of thirteen major women's organizations drafted a statement to McNutt declaring that "incorporating the knowledge and contributions of women into policy-making groups has not yet been satisfactorily accomplished." Charlotte Carr, former Secretary of Labor and Industry of Pennsylvania, was finally named assistant to the deputy chairman of WMC, but she found herself without any duties and soon resigned. McNutt was not disturbed. Asked about problems of womanpower, he retorted tersely, "There aren't any." There was no need, in his judgment, "to cope with women workers as a separate entity." There was a manpower problem, "but womanpower is indistinguishable from it." Jobs were jobs, he maintained, whether they were held by women or men.[20]

On July 6, 1943, the Women's Advisory Committee sent a confidential statement to McNutt detailing its grievances. It "unreservedly" criticized the WMC's failure to develop an integrated program of recruiting, training, and utilizing women. The report noted that "there has been no concerted approach to evaluate and measure successful methods as opposed to those which have failed" and insisted that "there must be more specific recognition that women constitute the principal non-military manpower resource to meet the requirements of war and

---

*Women's Bureau members were convinced that Secretary of Labor Perkins was determined to eliminate the special functions of the bureau and consolidate it with the newly established Bureau of Labor Standards (Judith Anne Scalander, "The Women's Bureau, 1920–1950: Federal Reaction to Female Wage Earning" [Ph.D. diss., Duke University, 1977], p. 258).

supporting war production activities and to maintain an adequate civilian economy." Finally, it severely criticized the Commission for ignoring
the Women's Advisory Committee. To correct this situation, the women
demanded the naming of liaison personnel in all WMC divisions and the
appointment of an executive assistant to oversee the implementation of
WAC policies.[21]

In August, Executive Director Lawrence Appley responded to the
committee's charges. He promised to seek the WAC's advice in matters
relating to women and to keep the committee informed as to general
policy. He reported, however, the WMC's rejection of the committee's
concrete demands. The WMC would appoint no special personnel to
look after women's questions, and it refused to delay pressing matters
until the WAC's opinion could be secured. "The situation," Eleanor
Straub concludes, "remained virtually unchanged; WAC's recommendations continued to be ignored, its advice rarely sought."[22]

Essentially, then, the Women's Advisory Committee was little more
than a "publicity organ."[23] While it was able, by means of speeches, press
releases, and articles, to publicize the need for womanpower and the
problems of the workingwoman, it was not successful in either formulating policy for women or integrating women into policymaking positions.
In July, 1943, only eight of the 641 top officials in the war agencies were
women. Little wonder, then, that there was continued talk of the "cold-
shouldering of women . . . in the war effort."[24]

Thus, while women were being mobilized in greater numbers than
ever in industry, they had hardly any influence over manpower policy.
At no time did the War Manpower Commission give women more than
an advisory voice in decision making, and their advice was usually ignored. This indifference, in turn, adversely affected women workers in
such areas as equal pay, day care, providing proper training, and a
nondiscriminatory attitude on the part of employers, male workers, and
unions.[25] Years later, Mary Anderson recalled that during World War II
there was a "great tendency among government officials . . . to speak
about 'the people' as a whole, but when they spoke of 'the people,' they
meant the men."[26]

Despite the manpower emergency, many employers were reluctant
to use women, insisting that women were not the equal of men in factory
work, that they did not understand machinery, and that they were not
trainable. Finally, employers complained of the added costs of adjusting
equipment for use by women and of providing such facilities as separate
washrooms. In the absence of direct statutory authority to compel employers to employ women, government agencies were forced to use persuasion.

The Women's Bureau undertook a massive campaign to convince
industry of women's potential contribution to the production program.

Beginning with a survey of the aircraft industry in early 1941, the bureau undertook analyses of a number of major war industries in order to disprove the traditional views about women's industrial aptitudes and abilities. Women, the bureau was able to establish, could operate milling machines; single, multiple, and radial drills; light lathes and chucking machines; boring, threading, grinding, and buffing machines; and punch presses. Women could also be used as inspectors, welders, sheet metal workers, winders, and optical grinders and polishers and in countless other capacities. The bureau pointed out that the number of women employed in industry had doubled during World War I and that many of them were trained and engaged in the same types of work demanded in World War II. While conceding that the work in foundries might be too physically demanding for women to perform successfully, the bureau was convinced, as Mary Anderson pointed out to labor Secretary Perkins, that "at least half of the operations in each of the industries could easily be done by women."[27]

The War Department, the Civil Service Commission, and especially the War Manpower Commission pushed the case for the employment of women workers in many of what were ordinarily considered men's jobs. The results of these efforts varied by industry and by region. Having already opened their doors to women prior to the United States' entrance into the war, the industries that manufactured ammunition for small arms and artillery increased the hiring of women considerably after Pearl Harbor. Since many of the steps that went into the making of bullets, cartridges, and shells were simple, "requiring training of not more than a week," women could be easily utilized. By March, 1943, two-fifths of all the factory employees in the industry were women, while in the bagging plants, some processes were taken over entirely by women.[28]

Although the aircraft industry was almost entirely male before the war, by May, 1943, women constituted 45 percent of the workers in the West Coast aircraft plants, 33 percent in the Midwest, and 26 percent on the East Coast. Making airplanes, Paul McNutt told the press in the first week of May, 1943, was rapidly becoming a "woman's industry. In many warplane plants, 70 to 80 percent of the new employees being hired are women, and they are doing nearly all the jobs that used to be considered men's work." W. Gerard Tuttle, Director of Industrial Relations for Vultee Aircraft, one of the first aviation plants to hire women, supported McNutt's evaluation, declaring that experience had demonstrated that 80 percent of operations in that plant could be performed by women "without sacrificing efficiency." "The women's help is already making it possible to speed our national defense production through the building of better airplanes in less time than could be done without them," Tuttle added. Mary Robinson went even further, declaring flatly that the "spectacular development of aircraft production would have been impossible without the aid of women."[29]

The electrical products industry equaled aircraft manufacture in the employment of women, and even exceeded it in the ratio of women to men. In 1940 there were 101,201 women, or 27 percent of the industry; by 1944, there were over 350,000 women, or nearly half of the work force. In the manufacture of radio and communications equipment, women constituted three-fifths of the work force.[30]

The nation's shipyards also experienced a female invasion. Before the war, only two navy yards and no private firms had hired women for production; the handful of women in shipbuilding sewed flags and sail lofts. By 1943, women were working in nearly all naval and commercial yards, filling over two hundred different positions, and constituting approximately 15 percent of the industry's total labor force.[31] Women were engaged in arc welding and gas welding and in working at the layout of steel plates, operating lathes, drill presses, punch presses, grinders, and screw machines; they had also proved themselves to be especially good at wiring, soldering, and coil winding in the electrical shops.[32]

When the war broke out in Europe in 1939, there were only 36,000 women employed by the railroads; by March, 1943, the number had risen to 63,000.[33] Women were doing jobs usually performed by men—in the offices and shops, at the roundhouses, at ticket windows and information desks, in station and baggage-room work, as cleaners and oilers of engines, as turntable operators, as conductors, and at "dressing" the track. Still, when it was revealed in November, 1942, that the nation's Class I railroads employed only 6,000 women in nonclerical positions, it was noted that this showing was much poorer than that made by the railroads in World War I.[34]

In the steel industry, the only jobs women held within the mills before the war were the sorting and inspecting of tinplate. By late 1943 they were employed in almost every division of the industry.[35] However, less than 5 percent of them were assigned to the blast furnace section. In the main, they were employed on the labor gangs, in such occupations as crane operators, crane followers, laboratory aides, inspectors, "pumpmen," "controlmen," tenders of levers and valves, and general helpers in the maintenance division.[36]

A Women's Bureau study showed that women appeared to be replacing men more rapidly at machines than at any other kind of work. Before the war, fewer than one-fourth of the women workers were machine operators, yet half of the women substitutes were placed on machines formerly run by men. After the machine operators, the most important occupational groups from the standpoint of numbers of jobs formerly performed by men were assemblers and inspectors. One-fourth of the assemblers, inspectors, and service or maintenance work-

ers, about three out of ten storeroom clerks, well over half of the packers
and wrappers, and all of the solderers were women who had taken over
men's jobs.[37] In 1939 women made up less than one-half of one percent
of the total wage earners in the approximately two hundred plants making machine tools. By early 1943 the proportion was about 11 percent of
a considerably expanded work force.[38]

The labor shortage, noted the Bureau of Labor Statistics, "literally
forced employers to try out women in all industries and almost all
jobs."[39] However, the War Production Board reported an uneven development, with some plants using women in sizable numbers while
others still contended that they could not do the work. Consequently,
while the WPB reported some success in breaking down barriers against
the employment of women by mid-1943, it concluded that "the wide
variation in the employment of women wage earners among plants engaged in the same type of production and the negligible proportion of
women still prevailing in some product groups give evidence of the
possibilities of further use of women in the production of combat
material."[40]

One woman voiced a common complaint to Eleanor Roosevelt:
"When you ask American women to plan to work for this war, isn't it also
necessary that you ask American industrialists to make a place for
women of all ages?" Another woman expressed the same theme in a
letter to Secretary of Labor Perkins. "All this talk about jobs for all ages is
absurd. There are no more jobs for the older woman now than when,
eight and one-half years ago, I was widowed and started out to look for
work."[41] This was written in the summer of 1943!

These grievances were caused by the fact that employers set a
maximum age for women applicants considerably lower than the
maximum set for men. Helen Baker's survey of the defense industries in
the fall of 1941 revealed that thirty to thirty-five was the average
maximum age for women applicants. Despite labor supply problems,
many employers refused to consider women over forty for jobs. In a
study of 1944 census data, the Women's Bureau discovered that over
three-fourths of the women in the labor force were under forty-five
years of age, and that of the 6½ million who had entered the labor force
after Pearl Harbor, over 80 percent were under forty-five.[42]

Baker's 1941 survey found that few industries had policies against
the employment of married women.[43] Indeed, as more and more industries, school systems, banks, and insurance companies repealed their
bans against hiring married women, a large part of the increase in the
female labor force came from the ranks of the middle-class married
women—a group that in normal times had overwhelmingly been housewives. In 1943 the Women's Bureau concluded that there was "almost no
discrimination against married women working," and that in most cases

this applied to mothers as well as to those without children.[44] Actually, many firms now began to prefer married women on the ground that they were "more stable and dependable," and, as some employers put it quite frankly, "would be easier to remove from the labor force at the war's end."[45] Whatever the reason, easily one-half of the wartime additions to the female labor force were married women. In 1944 married women workers began outnumbering single women for the first time in American history.[46]

Because of their generally lower family incomes, in 1940 black women were gainfully employed at a ratio of one to three, while white women were employed at a ratio of one to five. More than 1½ million (1,542,273) black women above the age of fourteen years were employed in that year. But 70 percent of these women were in the service categories, and a large number (245,000) were involved in agriculture.[47]

The boom in industry seemed to hold out the prospect that black women, along with white women, would find work in defense production. But the color ban remained, and black women encountered the same discrimination that had checked the progress of their husbands and fathers. Even more, in fact. As sociologist Charles Johnson observed, "Of all classes of labor, the Negro woman is in the most marginal position."[48]

Although employers at aircraft factories began a drive to recruit white women, black women who applied were rarely hired, even if they had gone through government training programs to gain the required skills. "While we are in complete sympathy for the Negro," the president of North American Aviation declared frankly, "it is against company policy to employ them as aircraft workers or mechanics . . . regardless of their training. . . . There will be some jobs as janitors for Negroes."[49]

Such employment discrimination when the country was clamoring for labor, coupled with the discrimination against blacks in the armed forces, aroused more anger in the black community than ever before. In late 1940 and early 1941 the NAACP, the Committee for the Participation of Negroes in the National Defense, and the Allied Committees for National Defense held mass protest meetings, but the exclusion of blacks from defense industries continued. Walter White, A. Philip Randolph, and other black leaders could not even get an appointment to see President Roosevelt to plead for government action. In order to bring the power of the black masses into the picture, Randolph suggested that 10,000 Negroes march on Washington, D.C., under the slogan: "We loyal Negro American Citizens demand the right to work and fight for our country."[50]

Randolph's call for a March on Washington struck an immediate response in the black community. By the end of May, 1941, March on Washington Committees had opened headquarters in Harlem, in Brooklyn, New York, and in Washington, Pittsburgh, Detroit, Chicago, St. Louis, and San Francisco.

The militant challenge to racism represented by the March could not be ignored in Washington. Several attempts to persuade Randolph to call off the March failed, but on June 24, he agreed to do so. In exchange, Roosevelt issued an executive order reaffirming the "policy of the United States that there shall be no discrimination in the employment of workers in defense industries or Government because of race, creed, color, or national origin," and declaring it

> the duty of employers and of labor organizations, in furtherance of said policy, and of this order, to provide for the full and equitable participation of all workers in defense industries, without discrimination because of race, creed, color, or national origin; and it is hereby ordered as follows: All contracting agencies of the Government shall include in all defense contracts hereafter negotiated by them a provision obligating the contractor not to discriminate against any worker because of race, creed, color, or national origin.

Although there was some concern among black women over the failure to include "sex" along with "race, creed, color, or national origin," it was generally conceded that the prohibition of discrimination because of race and color took care of this problem.[51]

Thus was born the Fair Employment Practices Committee (FEPC). With the committee functioning, with the passage of fair-employment laws in a number of states and municipalities, with pressure from black organizations and the growing labor shortages, the door slowly began to open for the entrance of black women into industry. During the war period their employment rose from 1.5 million to 2.1 million—an increase of 40 percent, compared with a 51 percent increase for white women. But it was not just the percentage that was important. In 1940, 70 percent of the black female workers were in domestic service; by 1944 this figure had dropped to 45 percent. Only 6½ percent of the black female labor force had worked in industry in 1940; four years later, that percentage had tripled.[52] "Negro women," exulted the *Pittsburgh Courier*, a black weekly, on February 8, 1944, "are now to be found in every one of the key war industries. They are sharing, sometimes in small measure, the wartime advances made by all women. Today, because of the critical lack of manpower, age-old prejudices are beginning to crumble." In the opinion of another black newspaper, it was "the beginning of a real emancipation for Negro women."[53]

But the change was neither rapid nor easy. Until 1943 not a single black operator was to be found in the entire Bell Telephone System. Gloria Shepperson, probably the first, was hired in New Jersey that year, and to secure the position she had had to fight an antidiscrimination case. "The first major breakthrough in black female hiring in Detroit did not come until the end of 1942," notes Alan Clive, "when, after a vigorous campaign by black protest organizations, token numbers of black women began to work at Willow Run, Kelsey-Hayes, and Murray Body."[54] The situation in the steel industry was worse. In 1943 nineteen-year-old Frances Stanton, in order to support herself and her infant daughter while her husband served in the armed forces, asked for employment at the Clairton Steel works, in Pennsylvania. While the plant was hiring white women "every day in the week," it totally ignored her employment inquiry.[55] Another black woman, Mrs. William Scott, who had a son in the navy, expressed her dismay in a letter to President Roosevelt: "They don't seem to be hiring colored women in Washington County [Pennsylvania] at all. There are two plants close by, one, in Washington, that is Jessop Steel, and the one in Bridgeville, but they will hire the white girls but when the colored girls go there they always refuse them."*[56]

Thousands of black domestics abandoned their positions for more lucrative factory work, but they continued to face many obstacles. The vice-president of the Sharon Steel Corporation in Sharon, Pennsylvania, declared that the absence of black women in his plant was due to the fact that "women employees will not work with non-whites."[57] During an FEPC public hearing in St. Louis in August, 1944, five companies charged with discrimination similarly claimed that social custom, the lack of separate toilet facilities, and the resistance of white employees prevented them from hiring black women. Handicapped by inadequate funds and harassed by segregationist congressmen, the FEPC had been slow to act against such blatant discrimination. In this instance, the agency rejected the excuses and demanded an immediate change in hiring policies.†[58]

A story in the Baltimore Afro-American in April, 1945, a few months before the war ended, describes still another obstacle black women had to overcome. The story reported that the Naval Ordinance Plant in Macon, Georgia, had hired black women for the first time since it had

*Edna Barber who sought employment at the Acme Die and Machine Company in Apollo, Pennsylvania, only to discover that white women at the plant "did not care to work with colored women," wrote to President Roosevelt: "The colored soldiers are overseas fighting for the four freedoms just the same as white soldiers. Now why is the colored woman refused employment [?]" (Dennis Clark Dickerson, "Black Steelworkers in Western Pennsylvania, 1900–1950," Pennsylvania Heritage 4 [December, 1977]: 58.)

†One of the companies involved—Carter Carburetor Corporation—had been the target of black protests in the summer of 1942, when hundreds of black men and women, under the leadership of the March on Washington Committee, picketed the company's plant carrying signs that read: "Barring Negroes from war industries makes Axis propaganda," "Carter employs 3,000 people, not one Negro: Is that democracy?" and "Racial discrimination is sabotage" (St. Louis Star-Times, Aug. 28, 1942; St. Louis Post-Dispatch, Aug. 29, 1942).

opened in 1942, after a fight led by the Macon branch of the March on Washington Movement and aided by the FEPC. The women hired were members of the first class of black women trained at the Macon Vocational School, which had previously barred its doors to blacks. The FEPC ordered W. L. Shiver, manager of the local USES office, not to refer any more women workers to the plant until the applications of hundreds of colored women had been given fair consideration. Ninety percent of the plant's workers were women. The story concluded: "Chief opposition to employment of colored women did not come from either management or the employees, but from white local housewives, who feared lowering of the barriers would rob them of maids, cooks and nurses."[59]

Women, regardless of race, faced a variety of discriminatory practices. Industry upgraded and promoted them much more slowly than men, and throughout the war, they continued to be clustered in the least skilled, lowest-paying jobs.[60] Black women encountered the worst discrimination. A good deal of publicity was given to a letter from one electrical corporation, reprinted by the Women's Bureau, which claimed that the company employed "2,000 Negro women, the majority of whom have been added in the last six months," and that these women were "engaged in 45 separate and distinct classifications covering a rather wide range of skills." Included among their assignments were those of "bench hands in various kinds of partial and final assemblies, cable formers, clerks, inspectors, many kinds of machine operators, testers, and wiremen."[61] However, the FEPC's first report, covering the period between July, 1943, and December, 1944, noted that more than one-quarter of all cases docketed by the committee were brought by black women, and that many dealt with unfair treatment in job assignments.[62]

Once they were able to secure jobs in the industry, black women were invariably assigned to the dirtiest and most difficult jobs. In steel mills, for example, they were assigned to the sintering plants or to other jobs that were almost as difficult. The kind of work in the sintering plants may be seen from the following description:

> Jobs around a sintering plant are all dirty and chiefly of a labor grade. Everything in such a plant is covered with iron dust. The sintering plant salvages ore and blast furnace flue dust by mixing it with water and spreading it on moving conveyors that carry it under gas flames for baking into clinkery masses known as sinters which are charged back to the furnace.[63]

The physically exacting position of grinder in a steel mill was reserved for black women. When one black woman at the Crucible Steel plant in Midland, Pennsylvania, saw that white women were being assigned to lighter work as point girls, she complained. Her supervisor told her to accept grinding or no job at all. Likewise, when a black woman grinder at Carnegie Steel in Farrell, Pennsylvania, asked her foreman "if colored girls could get better jobs," the reply was that they simply were not "wanted" in other departments.[64]

Black women eventually constituted between 35 and 75 percent of the work force in certain small Detroit plants. But a study made after Detroit's major race riot in June, 1943, revealed that "only 3 percent of the women employed in defense work were Negro, and these were mainly in custodial positions." In the small Detroit plants, too, black women "remained concentrated in such low-wage positions as janitors, sweepers, and material handlers."[65]

Evaluating the employment situation in war industries nationally, the War Manpower Commission reported in October, 1943, that "the employment of Negro women is limited to a small number of firms in a few industries."[66]

For many women, white as well as black, work during the war years was their first job in industry, and they needed training. During World War I, only 35,754 persons had received war training; during World War II, the number approached 10 million, at a cost to the federal government of approximately $500,000.[67] However, it was not until the spring of 1942 that women became a significant part of the program. On October 9, 1940, Congress approved a supplemental training appropriation that required that "no trainee under the foregoing appropriations shall be discriminated against because of sex, race or color." Nevertheless, the Office of Education, which supervised industrial training, continued to operate on the principle that since industry was basically hiring men, training should be confined to them. As Commissioner of Education John W. Studebaker put it bluntly to Mary Anderson: "As soon as employers show an inclination to use women, training will be offered to them."[68]

Not until February, 1942, was the policy of restricting training to men revised. On February 10 the War Production Board announced the "immediate extension of defense training to women on a basis of equality with the training of men."[69] Still, on May 4, 1942, the *New Republic* complained: "We do not have a reservoir of trained women workers, nor do we have the necessary training programs even now."

But women's training was beginning to expand, and by August, 1942, women constituted over one-quarter of all trainees in the Vocational Training for War Production Workers (VTWPW) program.[70] Before the war was over, over a million women had been enrolled in the VTWPW and the Vocational Education for National Defense (VEND) programs, and they received instruction in virtually every field. In the Engineer, Science and Management War Training (ESMWT) courses, conducted in conjunction with a number of leading colleges and universities, a total of 282, 235 women were trained, mostly in production supervision, general engineering, and aeronautical engineering. A quarter of a million young women received industrial defense training from the National Youth Administration (NYA) before that agency's demise in 1943, while 160,000 women, mostly foreladies and supervisors, participated in the War Manpower Commission's "Training-Within-Industry" program."[71] Eleanor Straub estimates that "one-tenth of the women in the labor force at the war's peak may have received government-sponsored training."[72]

As a result of the various training programs, a great number of women received the fundamentals of industrial education. Moreover, many women entered apprenticeship programs, and by the end of 1944, women apprentices were at work in eighteen skilled areas, including cabinetmaking, printing, and carpentry.[73]

"Women who have learned new skills," a 1944 study concluded, "will have, naturally, a better chance than before since they will have 'two strings to their bow' where they formerly had only one."[74] However valid this conclusion may have been in terms of upgrading their work status, there is no question that for many women the training programs were most important in building their confidence as well as their new skills.[75]

The sudden entrance of thousands of women into industrial life raised many problems. In a good number of cases, workingwomen were called upon to do two jobs at once—taking care of a home and perhaps children with the husband and father in the armed services, and working outside the home eight hours a day. Housecleaning, washing, mending, meal planning and preparation, and buying clothing and food had to be done after a full day's work.[76] The women's absence from home during normal working hours complicated the problem. During 1943 the Women's Bureau surveyed thirty-seven war industry communities in an effort to find out how well they were meeting the needs of women workers. They found that such workers were often unable to get to the grocery store before dinner and thus missed a chance to get the "good buys." Similarly, they were often unable to cash checks, buy clothes, or even have their hair done because the banks and stores would be closed before they returned from work.[77]

The biggest problem for working mothers, then as now, was what to do about their children during the working day. The WMC's October, 1942, directive to recruit all women possible for war work recommended that mothers of young children be spared "until all other sources of labor supply have been exhausted." Even then, the commission insisted that the "first responsibility of women with young children in war, as in peace, is to give suitable care in their own homes to their children." Government agencies, social workers, educators, and politicians echoed this advice.[78]

But in July, 1943, the OPM estimated that the armed forces and munitions industries alone would require 4 million additional workers in the next twelve months. The only realistic reserve was housewives, many of them with dependent children. Indeed, the number of employed women with children under ten years of age increased from 833,000 in March, 1940, to 1,470,000 in February, 1944.[79] Many were mothers whose husbands were in the service and who worked to support their families. Many of their children were becoming known as "door key" children—children who wore the keys to their houses around their necks because their mothers were working and would not be at home when they got out of school.

Large-scale wartime migration made the problem even more acute. As defense plants were constructed, the populations in war-impact areas soared. Tents and shacks sprang up along the highways as workers moved in, but there were no provisions for child care. Cooperative nurseries, in which mothers pooled their labor, could not meet this problem. Some states set up an administrative structure for day care, but most were reluctant to finance group child care, which many legislators viewed as a federal responsibility. Even in states that took initial steps, no network of nursery centers could be organized without federal assistance.*[80]

During the depression, the WPA had introduced day care on a national basis by opening centers for the children of mothers receiving government assistance. But this was primarily a relief effort and was not designed to stimulate the employment of mothers. The WPA centers were closed to women who were regularly employed. However, shortly after Pearl Harbor, the WPA opened its centers to children of working mothers and to youngsters with parents in the armed forces. It continued to operate this expanded program until the agency was liquidated in April, 1943.[81]

Throughout 1941, various government agencies, including the U.S. Children's Bureau (USCB) and the Federal Works Agency (FWA), examined the day care question, and a Joint Planning Board explored the possibility of adapting the WPA's nursery school program to meet defense needs.[82] In February, 1942, the board received a favorable ruling from the Bureau of the Budget, which permitted the use of Lanham Act funds for the construction and maintenance of child-care centers for the children of working mothers. The Lanham Act permitted federal financing of various community facilities and services in defense-impacted areas. On the basis of the Budget Bureau's ruling, and over the opposition of Congressman Fritz Lanham himself, the Federal Works Agency took over the financing of day care centers. However, the first project did not win final certification until August 31, 1942.[83]

---

*Michigan, New York, California, Pennsylvania, Connecticut, and Washington were the only states that supplied limited funds for day care centers.

Washington eventually spent nearly $53 million for hundreds of day care centers, established primarily in major production areas. In addition, the Federal Works Agency took over 1,150 of the former WPA nurseries and supported them with Lanham Act funds. But 550 of the original WPA nurseries were not reopened because they were not in "war-impact areas" and could not be covered by Lanham Act money.[84]

Under the Lanham Act formula, local communities were urged to form committees to show their war manpower needs and the need for child-care centers. These committees then applied directly to Washington, where the FWA staff, headed by Florence Kerr, assistant WPA director, reviewed the applications and approved the funds. The FWA granted money directly to local agencies, usually school systems or public welfare departments, which administered the program. Local communities were asked to provide 50 percent of the operating funds through fees and local contributions, but the FWA paid for over half the cost if the need was particularly acute.[85]

The most popular type of facility was the day nursery for two- to five-year-old children. Practices varied from area to area, but most centers operated continuously for twelve hours, from 6:30 in the morning to 6:30 in the evening. They served three meals a day, offered organized recreation directed by nursery teachers and volunteers, and provided cots or beds for afternoon naps.[86]

The day care center program, however, had more than its share of critics and opponents. These included Secretary of Labor Frances Perkins, who opposed both working mothers and child care and wrote to Katherine F. Lenroot of the Children's Bureau in June, 1942: "What are you doing to prevent the spread of the day nursery system, which I regard as the most unfortunate reaction to the hysterical propaganda about recruiting women workers?"[87] The persistent view that mothers belonged in the home, taking care of their children, undoubtedly weakened the child-care program. In addition, the Children's Bureau, the Office of Education, and the Federal Security Administration all lined up against the FWA program because they were themselves seeking control of day care policy and funds. These agencies insisted that group child care, if it existed at all, should be financed by the individual states, not by the Federal Works Agency. Yet it was already abundantly clear that state governments, with a few exceptions, were reluctant to finance group child care, and that no network of nursery centers could be organized without federal assistance.[88]

The bureaucratic struggle came to a head when the contending parties clashed over a day care bill introduced into Congress by Senator Elbert Thomas of Utah. The Thomas bill gave the Children's Bureau and the Office of Education final jurisdiction over day care and placed the burden for initiative and funding upon the states. It proposed to operate child-care programs primarily through the state offices of education and child welfare.

Speaking for the FWA, Florence Kerr made a strong case for continuing the program already in existence and was supported by the CIO women's auxiliaries (whose activities on behalf of child-care centers are examined in the next chapter). She was also backed by black groups who opposed placing the administration of the program in the hands of state governments, particularly in the South, "where segregation has been imposed upon one segment of the population and where past experiences have shown the distribution of public funds to be grossly inequitable, and where the most glaring inequalities in provision are made for Negroes."[89]

Although it passed the Senate, the Thomas bill died in a House committee. The FWA's authority remained intact and its federal child-care program, financed by the Lanham Act, served 100,000 children nationally.[90] Yet this was only about one-tenth of those who were eligible. The weekly fees charged for day care were often as high as $5.50 or $6 per child, an impossible burden for women in service trades who were receiving "wages as low as $12 and $16 a week," and no small sum for the majority of other workingwomen.[91] With the lowering of child-care fees, more mothers did bring their children to day care centers. Others complained, however, that the centers could not accommodate mothers working on the second or third shifts and that centers were located in sections that were inconvenient for working mothers. It appears, too, that many working mothers rejected day care services because they preferred to have their children cared for by relatives, neighbors, or friends rather than by strangers in a nursery. When neighbors, friends, or relatives were also on the production line, the children often were not taken care of at all. The October, 1943, issue of *Parents* magazine reported an individual type of solution: two women, both with husbands overseas, shared a house and, since they worked different shifts at the plant, alternated in caring for the child of one of the women.[92]

None of the individual arrangements appears to have been a satisfactory answer to the problem. But the Women's Bureau's 1944–1945 survey reported that 92 percent of Detroit workingwomen with children under fourteen years of age testified that they had made some provision for regular care, with only 2 percent relying on day nurseries. When an interviewer asked a group of Detroit working mothers why they did not avail themselves of the local day care program, she received such replies as: "I wouldn't have a stranger"; "No one could do better than my mother"; and "The baby might catch a disease in a nursery."[93]

Federal funding was also indirectly responsible for financing the child-care facilities established by some private corporations. The Curtiss-Wright Corporation, which held federal war supply contracts in the aircraft industry worth $4 billion, paid for its Buffalo child-care facility with federal funds by setting up its program under a separate nonprofit corporation. The Kaiser Industries Corporation built several child-care centers for its women shipyard employees. The Swan Island Center and Oregonship Center, near Portland, Oregon, became internationally famous. They reached their peak enrollment in the summer of 1944, when Swan Island had 444 children and Oregonship 390 per day. The centers had special features, too, such as long and flexible hours of operation, a skilled and well-paid staff, close proximity to the point of production, so that shipyard workers had less commuting time, and provision for hot take-out meals. This last service enabled workingwomen to come off the shift and pick up their children without having to prepare food at home.[94]

Kaiser's child-care centers became so famous that the company boasted that there were "instances of parents taking positions in the yards so that children could be eligible for the centers." What it did not disclose, however, was that the centers "were entirely funded at public expense by the U.S. Maritime Commission." Even then, the shipyard mothers were charged weekly fees for use of the centers, thereby contributing still further to the corporation's profits.[95] Nevertheless, the women shipyard workers were eager to use the day care facilities.

On the eve of Pearl Harbor, forty-four states and the District of Columbia had laws regulating the number of hours women could work each day; eighteen of these set the limit at eight hours per day. Twenty-two states and the District of Columbia prohibited or penalized the employment of women for more than six days per week; seventeen states regulated their employment at night; and forty-six states prohibited night work in certain fields. Similarly, twenty-five states and the District of Columbia required by law that women be given meal and rest periods of specified lengths.[96]

Helen Baker's study of defense industries during the fall of 1941 revealed that two-thirds of the plants surveyed continued to operate on forty-hour-a-week schedules.[97] However, within three weeks after Pearl Harbor, women's eight-hour-day laws around the country came under fire for hindering the war effort. The upshot was a Department of Labor statement, drafted at a conference in March, 1942, which recommended a forty-eight-hour week, lunch and rest periods for women, and one day of rest in seven. By the summer of 1942 this recommendation had received the official approval of the Departments of Labor, War, the Navy, and Commerce, the Maritime Commission, the Public Service Commission, and the War Production Board.[98]

Provisions regarding night work for women were the next target. By March, 1942, the aircraft industry in California was protesting that the payment of time-and-a-half to women who worked the midnight shift made full operation impossible. When the California Wage Board decided not to rescind the regulation, WPB Chairman Donald Nelson argued that this decision would "seriously hamper war production" and urged the governor of California to "eliminate all restrictions on employment of women at night." After much prodding, the Wage Board finally suspended the time-and-a-half provision.[99]

A Women's Bureau investigation in April, 1942, revealed that all but five states had provided for exemptions from protective labor legislation for women for the duration. In these five states, women were permitted by law to work fifty-four hours a week. Moreover, Massachusetts was the only state that continued to prohibit night work without any procedures for securing exemptions. Although the Women's Trade Union League fought to prevent relaxation of protective legislation for women unless a war emergency was actually proved, in no state were requests for exemptions from either hours or night work regulations rejected. Mary Anderson was therefore able to assure the War Production Board that "there is little or no evidence that State labor laws for women are hampering war production."[100]

Although standards increasingly continued to be suspended after the spring of 1942, Eleanor Straub concludes that, unlike the situation in World War I, "the body of protective legislation for women survived the war pretty well." She cites, for example, the fact that in ordnance, women's weekly hours of work had averaged fifty-five in World War I but only forty-seven in World War II. Straub attributes this difference to government and union pressure on employers to maintain standards and to the fact that the experience in World War I had convinced most employers that long hours of work for women decreased rather than increased their productivity.[101]

A study of war plants during 1942 and 1943 tends to sustain Straub's conclusion. It revealed that the eight-hour day and forty-eight-hour week were predominant. In addition, three-quarters of the plants had retained thirty-minute lunch breaks, and more than half had scheduled rest periods for women.[102] But a Women's Bureau survey at the end of the war revealed that twenty-four states and the District of Columbia had changed their legislative labor standards during the war. The bureau concluded that the "breakdown to a considerable extent in labor legislation on hours, etc., due to relaxation in standards and law enforcement measures to meet war emergencies," was a wartime loss for women.[103] It was confident, however, that these changes, for the most part, were "a temporary concession to war needs" and that there was actually "little permanent change in the flexibility of laws regulating women's hours of employment."[104]

Women entering war industry were assured by the War, Navy, and

Labor Departments that government policy required "equal pay for equal work for women." But statements requiring observance of the equal pay policy were not self-enforcing, and manufacturers customarily placed women in the lowest-paid jobs and paid them less for the performance of work traditionally done by men.[105]

The issue of equal pay soon came before the National War Labor Board (NWLB), which had been set up to settle labor disputes that hindered the war effort. In an early case brought against General Motors, the United Automobile Workers and the United Electrical Workers charged the company with paying its new women employees less than men on comparable jobs, and argued that such differentials would promote "tremendous resistance toward the influx of women on the part of male workers in the plants."[106] Elizabeth Christman argued the case against the company for the Women's Bureau, which she served as a special agent during the war. She pointed out that her own investigation, made at the request of the UE, showed a 20-cent-per-hour differential between men and women and contended that

> women in the labor force cannot be expected to exhibit the necessary morale when discriminated against by wage cutting. It is also important to the morale of the men on the job as well as those leaving for military duty to be confident that existing wage structures will not be undermined in their absence.[107]

In late September, 1942, the board ruled against General Motors, asserting that where women did work of "the same quality and quantity" as male workers, differentials were discriminatory. Furthermore, the NWLB warned that "using slight or inconsequential changes in a job as a reason for setting up a wage differential against women employees" would not be tolerated.[108]

In November, 1942, the NWLB issued General Order 16, permitting companies to equalize male and female wage rates on a voluntary basis.[109] The edict against General Motors and General Order 16 were hailed by the Women's Bureau as "the most significant step" ever taken by the federal government on the equal pay issue, and one writer stated flatly that "the miracle of equal pay for equal work . . . has at last come to pass."[110]

But the voluntary aspect of the Board's General Order 16, together with qualifications later placed on the original GM decision, hampered the achievement of equal pay for equal work. The board refused to support the demands of women workers that their wages in one plant be raised to a level comparable with those of male workers doing similar jobs in other plants in the area. Then there was the issue of determining women's pay by the principle of "rate for the job" rather than simply "equal pay." In the absence of a rate for the job, for example, it was not

uncommon to find skilled women machine operators making less than
unskilled janitors in the same plant. In an important NWLB case in July,
1943, the UAW charged that the male-female job classifications used by
Bendix Aviation Corporation were artificial distinctions and should be
replaced by wage rates based on a content analysis of all jobs in the
plants. The NWLB, however, rejected the union's argument and maintained that this was not an equal pay issue. It stood by this interpretation
throughout the war. Not until November 29, 1945, several months after
the war's end, did the board unequivocally approve the principle of
equal pay for women where they performed the same jobs as men. In a
telegram to the General Electric and Westinghouse Electric companies,
the board stated that it approved "the principle of a single evaluation line
for all jobs in a plant regardless of whether the jobs are performed by
men or women."[111]

Under General Order 16, employers could equalize wages without
prior approval, but they were not required to do so. Equal pay was
compulsory only when the NWLB ruled on the issue in a specific disputed case brought before the board's attention. But when unions failed
to make equal pay part of the union contract, or when an industry was
not unionized, there was little official recourse available to women. For
that matter, even when unions won favorable NWLB rulings, employers
were able to evade or delay compliance. The Women's Bureau learned,
for example, that despite the landmark ruling in the General Motors
case in September, 1942, equal pay was not in effect in the plant in
question as late as May, 1943.[112]

Many women complained to the Women's Bureau that employers
were able to maintain the pay differential by such ruses as paying women
hourly rates on jobs for which men received higher piecework rates or
giving different titles to similar jobs and thus changing job classifications
from skilled to semiskilled. Bureau investigators substantiated these
complaints.[113] But Mary Anderson could only tell the complaining
women workers that it was "only where equal wage rates *are an issue*
between employer and employee—where there is a dispute about it—
that the Board will order equal pay. If the union does not ask for equal
wage rates for women, the Board will not order this practice even if the
women are paid less."[114]

Much of the Women's Bureau's time and energy during the war were
spent trying to persuade male union leaders that it was in their own
self-interest to demand equal pay for women workers. Elizabeth Christman, assisted by May Dagwell and Mary Johnson, former trade union
women on the bureau's staff, visited local unions in several cities, urging
them to insert equal wage provisions in their contracts. Mary Anderson
appealed to the "selfishness for their own preservation" of male union
leaders, arguing that if women did the same work with equal skill for

lower wages, employers would fire men and replace them with women.[115]

A number of unions were persuaded, but as we shall see, organized labor, with some notable exceptions, failed to mount a sustained campaign on the equal pay issue.

Several states passed equal pay laws for women during the war, but they did little to help women. Michigan's state law guaranteed women equal pay for "similar" work, but the law was "so vague that it was virtually unenforceable."[116] The Illinois law made it unlawful for employers to pay women less when they did work equal to men's, but variations in pay for persons covered by union contracts were exempted from the law. The law also made exceptions for seniority, experience, training, skill, ability, "and other reasonable classifications excepting difference in sex"—thereby offering enough loopholes for any employer to creep through. Finally, complaints against employers had to be brought through the courts, and the maximum penalty was only a $100 fine.[117]

The New York State equal pay law was scheduled to go into effect on July 1, 1944, but State Industrial Commissioner Edward Corsi viewed enforcement as "a post-war issue." "Remember," he explained, "this is a war year. There's comparatively little discrimination between men and women workers." Yet a state survey of 143 manufacturing plants and 56 nonmanufacturing plants in March, 1943, revealed that only 60 percent of the former and 63 percent of the latter paid the same entrance rates to men and women.*[118]

Women's Bureau surveys during the war years on the issue of equal pay reveal a mixed picture. In small-arms- and cannon-manufacturing establishments, machine tools, cane sugar refining, and most old-line industries, considerably less than half paid the same rates for women as for men, and differentials based on sex were widespread. On the other hand, in shipbuilding aircraft assembly and at army supply depots, women workers were normally compensated on the same basis as men.[119]

The same mixed picture applied to women's wages in general. For many women, wages rose during the war. In Michigan they rose $14.40 per week between October, 1942, and August, 1944, while male wages increased only an average of $9.90 per week during the same period. Still, the gap between men's and women's earnings remained—the

---

*Actually, there was the beginning of enforcement before the war ended. In June, 1945, the State Labor Department upheld the complaint of a woman employee against the Bently Stores Corporation in New York City. She charged that she received basic pay of $36 weekly as a saleswoman, while a male salesman received $50. The department also upheld the complaint of four women finishers against the Gotham Uniform Company. They proved that they received $27.50 a week as against $37.50 for men (*New York Times*, June 12, 1945).

weekly wage gap favoring males by $15.22, or more than $700 a year. In New York State, the average weekly earnings in 1941 were $36.60 for men and $19.74 for women. In 1944 the figures were $48.12 for men and $34.50 for women. Women's wages here, too, had increased, but the gap favoring males remained.*[120]

The greatest increase in women's wages occurred in the major war industries. But as Mary Anderson pointed out to a meeting of Catholic unionists, "for every woman wage earner in a war industry, there are approximately 6 women in non-war industries.... There are some women working in factories today making $50, $60, and $70 a week. But they are the few—not the many. The high wages are not general."[121] A woman's average weekly earnings in manufacturing were between $30.78 and $33.28 in 1944. But a study by the Illinois Department of Labor in 1944 showed that the average weekly wage for women in department and variety stores was $12.11; in retail apparel stores, $24.43; in restaurants, $19.44; and in laundry and dry cleaning establishments, $21.13. The starting rate for a telephone operator in Chicago in October, 1943, was $17 a week, increasing at regular intervals over a thirteen-year period to a maximum of $29 a week, with the average at $21. Yet the minimum expenses of living for an operator, it was proved, came to $25.74 a week.[122] With prices having risen 23.4 percent between January, 1941, and November, 1943, an overwhelming number of women workers were unable to meet necessary expenses of living.[123]

In December, 1941, the Division of Women in Industry of New York State's Department of Labor estimated that women who worked in that state needed $20 a week to maintain themselves at an adequate level of living and to protect their health. In 1943 the National Industrial Conference Board estimated that it required a minimum of $30 a week for the average man to live and work in an urban area. But in New York City, department store clerks earned about $23 per week, while wages for file clerks, switchboard operators, key punch operators, and typists averaged from $5 to $8 below the minimum required.[124]

---

*Average hourly earnings of male and female wage earners in a number of selected manufacturing industries, October, 1941, to August, 1944, reveal the same gap.

	MALES		FEMALES	
Industry	Oct. 1941	Aug. 1944	Oct. 1941	Aug. 1944
Agricultural implement	$ .938	$1.160	$.725	$ .920
Automobile	1.184	1.379	.801	1.159
Cotton (North)	.672	.851	.535	.680
Electrical manufacturing	.992	1.304	.671	.892
Wool	.783	.984	.635	.805
Foundries and machine shops	.912	1.251	.583	.955

(*Economic Record* 11 [December 1941]: 253: *Management Record,* October 1944, p. 299.)

In 1942 Elizabeth Christman of the Women's Bureau* told a conference of trade unionists and auxiliary members that "peacetime and wartime wages for women have a common denominator—women earn less than men."[125] At the end of the war, the International Labour Office's publication *The War and Women's Employment* revealed that the gap between men's and women's earnings had not narrowed during the war.[126]

---

*On February 16, 1942, Mary Anderson wrote to Rose Schneiderman, president of the National Women's Trade Union League: "The Secretary of Labor is very anxious to secure the services of Miss Christman and detail her to us for work among the trade unionists in behalf of women workers." Anderson, therefore, asked Schneiderman for the NWTUL to release Christman "to work in the Women's Bureau for the duration." The Women's Bureau was finding it necessary to increase its personnel, but it was especially important that its personnel "should be experienced in industry and particularly in those industries which are doing all-out war production. It is also necessary that they should have knowledge and understanding of the trade union movement, preferably should be a member of the movement and also have had experience in the last World War. Such a person is Elizabeth Christman." Schneiderman agreed fully, and indicated the League's willingness to release Christman. "I am most confident that Elizabeth Christman will do a grand job in that position because of her all-around knowledge, training and experience in the labor movement." (Mary Anderson to Rose Schneiderman, February 16, 1942; Rose Schneiderman to Mary Anderson, February 17, 1942, Mary Anderson Papers, Schlesinger Library, Radcliffe College.)

17

The Trade Unions in World War II

THE ENTRANCE of increasing numbers of women into the nation's shops and factories after Pearl Harbor posed a challenge to the trade unions: Would they respond by opening up their ranks to their newly arrived sisters in order to achieve the dual purpose of protecting workers' conditions and adding to their strength, both in numbers and militancy?

For a while, at least, the outlook for such a response did not seem bright. Early in 1942, Mary Anderson felt impelled to write, "Labor unions are the outstanding opponents to the employment of women."[1] She was referring to the fact that a major problem in recruiting women for war work was that of securing their admission into unions, for many war industries operated under closed-shop agreements, which precluded the employment of anyone without the union's consent.*

The Communists were among the first to grasp the importance of prompt and decisive action by the unions to welcome these new allies. As early as December 26, 1941, the *Daily Worker* urged the trade unions to act immediately to bring women into their ranks:

> The trade unions will find among these women workers the basis for a splendid strengthening of union membership. Such has been the experience with their sisters already at work. To draw these new shop workers immediately into the unions is a No. 1 job for the labor organizations. This is essential not only in order to safeguard labor standards and the workers' rights during this war. It is also imperative because by entering the trade unions, these women workers can be invaluable in the forwarding of the war effort.

Not surprisingly, the CIO affiliates posed the least difficulty in this

---

*Although a closed shop agreement has had different meanings at different stages in American labor history, it is generally understood as a shop in which only members of the union signing the agreement are allowed to obtain and retain employment.

respect, since the organization had always allowed women to become members. To be sure, it took a good deal of persuasion by Elizabeth Christman to convince the West Virginia United Mine Workers not to strike over the employment of women but rather to accept them into the union. Generally, however, the CIO unions opened their doors to women members during as before the war. In the AFL, as we have seen, many unions had denied admission to women before the war. Pressured by both the government and the women workers themselves, a number of these unions—the International Association of Machinists, the Molders and Foundry Workers, the Iron Shipbuilders and Helpers, the Ironworkers, and the Carpenters and Joiners—revised their admission policies after Pearl Harbor. However, even with five thousand women employed in welding and hundreds more scheduled to be hired, the International Brotherhood of Boilermakers, the most intransigent of the AFL unions, refused to halt is opposition to women members until the fall of 1942. "Women Are to Be Admitted to Ranks of Boilermakers," read the headline in *Labor* of September 22, 1942. The report began: "For the first time in the 62 years since the founding of the International Brotherhood of Boilermakers, women are being admitted into the ranks of the union . . . following a referendum in which a majority of nearly two-thirds of those who voted favored acceptance of the women." However, since the number of those who cast ballots for the proposal fell short of the two-thirds required to make the referendum binding, the Brotherhood's Executive Council declared that the decision to admit women would have to be submitted to the union's next convention for ratification. Meanwhile, the order became effective, and lodges throughout the nation were instructed by President J. A. Franklin "to take in the women on exactly the same basis as men."[2]

The growing acceptance of women in AFL unions that had previously barred them is perhaps most clearly illustrated in the case of the Amalgamated Street and Railway Employees Association. It will be remembered that during World War I, the Amalgamated refused to allow women into the union, but from the very beginning of World War II, women were accepted on the same basis as men. The Amalgamated told a special conference on womanpower convened by the Office of Defense Transportation (ODT) in March, 1943, that women were welcome into its ranks on the basis of equality, and that "if they can stand the street car business, we want them."[3]

The Railroad Brotherhoods, however, continued to oppose the admission of women and proved the most unyielding to government pressure. At the ODT conference the spokesperson for the Brotherhood of Railroad Trainmen declared that "women cannot work in all phases of train service. As a matter of fact, it is questionable whether they really fit in any part of the train service." The representative of the AFL's Railway Employees Department argued that women were unsuited for the jobs his union covered, and that in barring them, "we are only trying to protect them from the very heavy work women have been doing for generations in Europe." The Teamsters' representative reported that because of the shortage of labor in many branches of their trade, the national union had agreed to allow each local to admit women to membership if it so desired, but with the understanding that "each applicant shall be requested to sign a statement agreeing . . . that the local can withdraw their membership whenever, in its judgment, the emergency ceases." Moreover, no union sickness or death benefits would apply to the women unionists, and certain branches of trucking were to remain closed to women for the duration.[4] To Elizabeth Christman, who was present at the conference as secretary of the National Women's Trade Union League, these provisions represented "one of the finest pieces of sex discrimination that I have heard in a long time."[5]

By the war's end, all AFL and CIO unions had admitted women, and even the transportation brotherhoods had opened their doors at least a crack.* But while the national unions may have altered their policies, several local unions remained opposed to the admission of women. In August, 1942, the International Brotherhood of Boilermakers and Iron Shipbuilders' referendum on whether or not women should be admitted to the union was approved by the membership. Nevertheless, Local Union 104 voted to keep women out, and Local Union 568 took a similar stand by a vote of three to one. Both locals were in the Puget Sound defense areas.[6]

As far as black women were concerned, the doors of many unions still remained closed tight. The CIO, with many black members and a national commitment to job equality, attacked this discrimination. The AFL also opposed it in theory, but individual unions practiced it repeatedly. In June, 1942, *Fortune* magazine reported that nineteen international unions, ten of them affiliated with the AFL, practiced discrimination against black workers. Even when unions pledged nondiscrimination in their charters, they continued to employ subtle means to exclude blacks, often using the initiation oath for this purpose. As reported by *Fortune*:

> In certain places and industries, the congestion of war orders has been so heavy that discriminating unions could not totally obstruct Negro employment without endangering production and their own jobs. In some of these instances a peculiar device is used: the Negro is not accepted as a member, but purchases from the union a working permit—an interesting hybrid of tenant feudalism and industrial democracy.[7]

Early in 1942, Philip Murray, who had succeeded John L. Lewis as CIO president, appointed a committee to investigate opportunities for

---

*One union—the Brotherhood of Bookbinders—still had a separate women's organization.

black workers. This body, which evolved into the permanent Committee to Abolish Racial Discrimination, conducted a vast educational campaign, which included frank discussions of racial discrimination and other issues. While placing the blame for the exclusion of minority group workers mainly on employers, it did not exonerate unions: "Where closed shop contracts exist and the union makes selections and referrals to employers, responsibility must be placed on the union unless the employer himself refuses to accept the worker because of race or color." Even CIO local unions were criticized for not resolutely supporting the national policy against discrimination. The committee pointed out that after a decision was made to employ minority group workers, the union had to make certain that the seniority rights of minority workers were not violated, because "nothing destroys a worker's morale more completely than the knowledge that despite his proficiency and his experience, he cannot be assigned to a more responsible job because of his race."[8]

The committee's literature also dealt with certain stereotypes that contributed to racism among white workers. One of them went:

THE SOCIAL-EQUALITY TABOO

Common use of eating facilities frequently creates conflict which unions can guard against. In communities where restaurants, cafés, and other public eating places do not serve Negro patrons, there must be strong sentiment in favor of providing separate eating facilities in or near industrial plants. . . .

The position of the union in this respect should be firmly taken. It is not enough to point out that thousands of white people every day eat and enjoy food prepared by Negroes and other racial groups. It must be emphasized that separation or segregation of workers in any form is undemocratic and unnecessary. . . .

This was followed by a section on "Women Workers":

Opposition to the use of women workers is often as strong as the resistance to the employment of Negroes and other minority groups. The employment of Negro men and white women in the same shop is frequently considered undesirable by some employers. White women workers often object to the employment of Negro women. What is needed in dealing with this problem is a more wholesome attitude toward women workers irrespective of race.

When union leadership accepts responsibility for developing proper relations and conduct where women workers are concerned, there need be no fear of serious difficulties.

Strongest objections to mixing the sexes are raised over the issue that Negro men will molest white women workers. This has long been the fallacious argument used in the South to justify segregation, lynching, and other practices of exclusion of Negroes. Where Negro women work with white men, there is the same remote possibility, although it is seldom given serious consideration.

The section concluded with the observation that "union observance" of the principle of equality "regardless of race" would "destroy all fears of race friction because of the presence of women workers."[9]

The literature distributed by the CIO's Committee to Abolish Racial Discrimination represented a milestone in American labor history. Throughout the war, the CIO and its Committee to Abolish Racial Discrimination joined with black organizations in opposing the reduction of funds for FEPC against the combined opposition of Southern members of Congress, employers, and AFL unions.* The all-out support of the CIO was undoubtedly a key factor accounting for FEPC progress. This, in turn, was of great significance for black workers, for, despite the CIO's stand against discrimination, blacks could not rely totally on some CIO unions to lift the yoke of discrimination and frequently looked to the Fair Employment Practices Committee to solve the problem. Nevertheless, as the *Crisis,* official organ of the NAACP, declared in September, 1942: "Even the labor shortages of the war boom would not have opened the gates for the black worker, had he not had the protection of the pan-racial policy of the CIO."[10] To a lesser but still significant extent, this applied to the black woman worker as well.

Despite the varied obstacles they had to overcome, women's membership in unions skyrocketed during the war. On August 29, 1942, Mary Anderson wrote to Mrs. Raymond Robins: "The women are joining the unions. A year ago we had a little over one million organized into trade unions and now we have three million five hundred thousand." Six months later, on February 5, 1943, she returned to the theme:

> About a year and a half ago we had about 1,000,000 women organized—that means in the AFL, CIO and Railroad Brotherhoods. Now we have 3,500,000 organized. It is a wonderful increase in membership. Then, too, in many of the unions, and that is particularly true of the young unions that have young men officials who had gone to war, women have had to take their places. Some of the unions are running a training school for women as officials.

However, not all unions had changed, Anderson noted. The United Brotherhood of Carpenters and Joiners (AFL) at first had not taken in women at all; then it took them in as auxiliary members with no right of vote or participation in the national union's affairs. Only when women received the same pay as men were they eligible for membership. "The

---

*In addition to the national Committee to Abolish Racial Discrimination, ten CIO international and national unions established their own committees. They included the American Newspaper Guild; the International Union of Mine, Mill & Smelter Workers; the National Maritime Union; the Retail, Wholesale & Department Store Union; the United Automobile, Aircraft & Agricultural Implement Workers; the United Farm Equipment & Metal Workers; the United Gas, Coke & Chemical Workers; the United Packinghouse Workers; the United Public Workers; and the United Office & Professional Workers.

auxiliary women, of course, do not receive the same pay as men and I do not know whether the union is doing a thing about seeing the women receive the same pay, so that may bar them from membership. They are the same old union and so many of the AFL unions are just like that."[11]

Estimates of the exact increase in women's union membership varied. According to Elizabeth Christman, it increased from only 245,000 in 1940 to 3,000,000 in September, 1943. The Women's Bureau put the increase at from approximately 800,000 before the war to 3,500,000 at the end of 1944. Of this number, about 1,500,000 were in the CIO and 1,300,000 in theAFL. The rest were organized in independent unions. The total represented about 20 percent of the 18,600,000 women employed in all industries in October, 1944.[12]

Since unions rarely classified their membership records by sex, the number of women organized could only be estimated. Nevertheless, it is clear that the greatest increase in women union membership in American history had occurred. It was with good reason that *Labor* could state: "Unionism is no longer a man's world. Over 3,000,000 women workers now carry union cards."[13]

In 1944 eleven national unions reported more than 40,000 women members. The UAW and the UE, both CIO unions, had the largest number. Prior to the United States' entry into the war, the UAW had claimed about 15,000 women members in Detroit. In September, 1943, there were about 80,000, representing a 10 percent increase of the entire membership to about 25 percent. The UAW reported in December, 1944, that it had 250,000 to 300,000 women members; representing over one-fifth of its total membership. That same month, the UE estimated that about 250,000, or 40 percent of its members, were women.[14]

Large numbers of women joined the International Association of Machinists (AFL), the United Rubber Workers of America (CIO), the United Steel Workers of America (CIO), the Aluminum Workers of America (CIO), and the Marine & Shipbuilding Workers of America (CIO), in addition to unions composed predominantly of women, such as the United Office & Professional Workers (CIO) and the Retail, Wholesale & Department Store Employees' Union (CIO).[15]

Unlike the previous generation of workers, who had, in the main, joined unions voluntarily during the great organizing drives of the 1930s, women workers were required, through closed-shop, or union-shop, clauses, to join a union in order to keep their wartime jobs. Therefore, Secretary of Labor Frances Perkins, for one, was not greatly impressed by the statistics revealing the great increase in female union membership. As she explained to Eleanor Roosevelt:

> It is, of course, true that their membership in trade unions shows a great increase during this wartime emergency when they have been employed in

aircraft factories, shipyards, automobile factories, etc., where the union had previously established a closed shop contract. That means that in such cases a woman upon employment is obliged to join the union, and one does not know the extent to which they are either active in the union or are considered.[16]

The question arises: To what extent was the increase in female union membership during the war accompanied by a corresponding increase in women's activity in union affairs and by their advancement to positions of responsibility and importance in organized labor? Several surveys furnish information on which to base an answer to this question. For example, a partial list of women union officers compiled in 1941 by Elizabeth Christman showed two women as secretaries of national unions and eighteen as members of general executive boards. One woman was listed as secretary of a state federation of labor and twenty-seven as secretaries of central labor unions. At the 1944 convention of the United Federal Workers (CIO), Eleanor Nelson became the first woman to be elected president of a national union since Agnes Nestor of the International Glove Workers Union more than forty years earlier. Nelson, who had been one of the four women delegates to the CIO's First Constitutional Convention in 1938, was chosen as the first and only woman on the CIO's national executive board in 1941. The AFL had no woman on its Executive Council. Ruth Young, executive secretary of the UE's huge District 4, was elected to that national union's Executive Board in November, 1944.[17]

A National Women's Trade Union League survey in the fall of 1943 revealed that "while formerly few of the women who belonged to unions even came to meetings, they are now assuming an increasingly active part in union affairs." Old prejudices were breaking down because many men who had been union officials were now in the armed services. Although the picture varied from local to local and from trade to trade, so that there is no way of presenting an overall view of women's increasing role in union affairs, the league's survey revealed that there were "greater numbers of women shop stewards, committeewomen and field workers." Still, the league's survey concluded that few women "held high union posts."[18]

A New York Times survey in September, 1943, added further evidence that women were beginning to assume more responsible positions in the unions. The UE reported eighteen female local presidents and forty-six women on its international staff, and noted that of its national full-time organizers, 35 percent were women. For the first time in its history, Local 16 of the United Office & Professional Workers of America had a woman president. The Book & Magazine Guild of the same union was also headed by a woman. Four women were now on the UOPWA's

General Executive Board. Although women had made up 70 percent of the American Communications Association (CIO) for some time, only since the war had they begun to assume any real responsibility in the union's activities. Young girls were rapidly becoming shop stewards or committee members and were moving into other leadership positions as men left for the services. There were six women organizers where there had been none before the war.

The Hotel & Club Employees Union in New York City had nine paid women staff members, as well as a number of shop stewards and delegates. The president of the Bakery Sales Union was a woman, as was the manager of Local 2 of the Department Store Employees. Katherine Lewis, daughter of John L. Lewis, was chosen secretary-treasurer of District 50, UMW, made up of all miners in fields other than coal, and Jennie Matajas, manager of the Knit Goods Workers in San Francisco, represented the AFL on the National Women's Advisory Committee of the War Manpower Commission.

At the UAW's 1944 convention, at a time when women constituted over one-fifth of the union's total membership, there were only thirty women among the more than two thousand delegates present. However, the UAW pointed with pride to the case of Mrs. Herschel Davis, a drill press operator in an auto plant in Indiana. Davis joined Local 400 in 1941, was elected vice-president in 1943, and assumed the presidency when the incumbent was drafted. UAW Local 250 in New York City reported that its new women members were "playing an active part in the union" and in some cases were even "more enthusiastic" than the men. Women members were also active in UAW Detroit locals, especially "in child-care programs, consumer activities, nutritional programs and in plant feeding in Detroit industries."[19]

The *New York Times* concluded that its national survey indicated that "the number of important posts held by women in unions is increasing, especially in war industries, but slowly."[20]

Neither survey mentioned the situation in two unions with large women memberships: the International Ladies' Garment Workers' Union and the Amalgamated Clothing Workers. Women made up 75 percent of the membership of the ILGWU and about 50 percent of that of the ACW, but each of these unions in 1941 had only one woman member on its Executive Board, and the woman on the ILGWU board was not reelected at its 1944 convention. Their New York locals, among the largest in the world, had all men officers from the top committees down.

Pauline Newman served during the war as educational director of the ILGWU's health center, where two hundred physicians, nurses, and pharmacists staffed a clinic for women tailors. Gladys Dickason's contributions to the Amalgamated Clothing Workers as the union's director of research led to her election as vice-president in 1946.* But Rose Pesotta hit the mark when she wrote, upon resigning as vice-president of the ILGWU: "Ten years in office had made it clear to me that a lone woman vice-president could not adequately represent the women who now make up 85 percent of the International's membership of 305,000."[21]

In 1944 the Women's Bureau undertook a survey of the role of women in unions associated with Midwest war industries. Its findings, based on a survey of eighty-one locals in ninety-five war plants, were: (1) the majority of women were not active in unions, and (2) while in a third of the unions, women held committee assignments, and in nearly a half, they were union officers, in most cases, these positions were not the important ones, but rather those concerned with recreation and social affairs. Three-quarters of the unions reported that women's attendance at meetings was poor, but they frequently cited male attendance as being little better.[22]

About a year after the war's end, the Women's Bureau conducted a survey of sixty-nine unions. It found only thirteen in which women held national office and a similar number in which they filled lower-level posts.[23] From this we may conclude that while the number of union posts held by women had increased during the war period, the number of women in official positions was still relatively small compared with their membership. Few women actually advanced to positions of responsibility and importance. While they were no longer entirely invisible in union leadership, women were still a distinct minority.

As before the war, it was in the area of women's auxiliaries that women occupied the highest official positions. Several million women—wives, mothers, daughters, and sisters of trade union men— were enrolled in women's auxiliaries of the AFL, CIO, and railroad brotherhoods. Some 2,500,000 of them were members of the American Federation of Women's Auxiliaries of Labor (AFL). At its convention in St. Louis in June, 1942, resolutions were adopted pledging full support for the war and for the maintenance of labor standards in wartime. Plans were laid for the immediate organization of additional auxiliaries in locals, central labor bodies, and state federations in order to carry forward the war program.[24]

At its third annual conference in Detroit in November, 1941, the National Coordinating Committee of CIO Auxiliaries changed its name to the Congress of Women's Auxiliaries—CIO (CWA). Faye Stephenson, president of the UAW auxiliaries, was elected president of the CWA,

---

*Dickason was the union's director of research from 1935 to 1954. She held a Ph.D. in economics.

and Julia Katz, a member of the United Federal Workers auxiliary, was chosen national director; Eleanor Fowler of the Newspaper Guild auxiliary was elected secretary-treasurer.* The eighty-one delegates and alternates from sixty-five organizations laid down the objectives of the organization: (1) to coordinate the work of all affiliated auxiliaries on a national and international scale; (2) to further the program of the CIO; (3) to unite all wives, mothers, sisters, and daughters of CIO members into a militant organization regardless of age, nationality, race, creed, or political belief; (4) to pursue an aggressive policy of struggle to improve conditions; (5) to foster the organization of unorganized women by encouraging the education of women to the benefits of union labor; (6) to promote social and cultural activities; (7) to struggle to end child labor; and (8) to participate fully in civilian defense work and the strengthening of morale in the struggle against Hitlerism.

"Defeat Fascism if we are to preserve our liberties," was the concluding note of the five-day sessions, and the CIO promised to work unceasingly toward this goal:

> Our women's auxiliaries have won distinction in the onward march of the CIO for their aid in the organization of the unorganized. We must now distinguish ourselves in the onward march of the women of America to strengthen the defense of the nation by improving the living standards, the health and the morale of the people of the nation.

"We must be trained," declared the report adopted by the conference. "We must begin now to organize adequate nurseries and schools. And above all, we must protect the gains which we have helped organized labor win by assuring equal pay for equal work." The outstanding contribution women's auxiliaries had to make was concerned with "the maintenance and strengthening of the living standards of every community in which we exist." Auxiliary members had "important and extraordinary abilities" to offer the nation—"experience, courage and loyalty and the ability to work as a group."[25]

Directly after the formation of the Congress of Women's Auxiliaries came Pearl Harbor. "The declaration of war does not change our program," the Congress declared, "but it does intensify the need for rapid carrying out of our program."[26] On January 10, 1942, the Congress, by then embracing about 100,000 women, set February 2-9 as "Beat Hitler Week." Three aims were announced: (1) to back up the pledge of the CIO for the uninterrupted production of ships, planes, and tanks for the

---

*Members of the Executive Board were officers of the women's auxiliaries of the American Newspaper Guild, UE, UAW, the International Woodworkers, the United Transport Service Employees, the Federation of Architects, Engineers, Chemists & Technicians, the Transport Workers' Union, the National Maritime Union, and the International Union of Mine, Mill & Smelter Workers.

duration of the war* by preparing CIO women to be ready to take their places in industry when called upon; (2) to work for the fullest protection of the civilian population, with emphasis on adequate air-raid defenses, shelters, and warning signals, and to secure the enrollment of auxiliary members in civilian defense activities; and (3) to build the strongest possible morale in every community by guaranteeing adequate food, clothing, shelter, medical care, and protection against profiteering and by strengthening the trade unions.[27] The CWA favored the national registration of women for work in the nation's production program as a necessary part of the war effort, but it insisted that simply registering women "won't make it possible for them to go to work and make the best contribution in the necessary numbers." It called for a policy of "immediate extension of defense training to women on a basis of equality with men."[28] But even this was not enough. "Why don't women take jobs?" asked Eleanor Fowler, secretary-treasurer of the Congress, and she answered:

> Principally because they have responsibilities that make it very difficult for them to go to work. Many of them have children—and there isn't a community in the country now where adequate facilities exist for the care of the children of working mothers. That's just as true of school-age children as it is of youngsters under six.
>
> It means that unless greatly extended facilities are provided quickly with government funds available with a minimum of red tape, millions of women can't take jobs without constant worry over their children's welfare....

The CIO urged the government to follow the example of Great Britain in assuring "full financial responsibility for wartime nurseries."[29]

Delegates from some thirty international and council auxiliaries and about eighty local auxiliaries attended the second annual conference of the CIO's Congress of Women's Auxiliaries, held in Boston at the same time as the 1942 CIO convention. They heard President Faye Stephenson report:

> During the first year, the Congress of Women's Auxiliaries has mobilized the women to support the CIO program for extended rationing and effective enforcement of price control regulations. In the recent election campaigns, it stimulated auxiliaries in many parts of the country to campaign among women to register and vote for CIO-endorsed win-the-war candidates.

In addition, the growing need for women in war industry had increased the importance of women's auxiliaries as "schools for unionism

---

*After meeting with President Roosevelt on December 17, 1941, CIO leaders agreed to a no-strike pledge and promised "to promote and plan for ever-increased production." Philip Murray, CIO president, said that Hitler and the Axis threatened "all our civil liberties," and that labor must counter this threat with the slogan: "Work, Work, Work, Produce, Produce!" (*CIO News*, Dec. 25, 1941).

where wives, sisters, mothers, and daughters of union men are equipped for active union membership." By stimulating programs to provide child care and other community facilities, Stephenson declared, the auxiliaries would enable "women needed in industry to take jobs without sacrificing the welfare of their families." In short, "as the proportion of women in the ranks of labor increased, the importance of the CIO auxiliaries increases, too."[30]

Reports from various auxiliaries followed. "From war relief to improvement of the schools, from Red Cross Aid to aid in our community defense activities . . . on all these fronts you will find the Ladies' Auxiliary of the Furriers' Union," reported the delegate from the Furriers Joint Council of New York's auxiliary. The members most active in the auxiliary, it was reported, had found their lives had become enriched. Even the problems of the home had become easier to solve when the auxiliary members involved themselves in activity outside the home: "Joe's temper tantrums or Minnie's loss of appetite become easier to handle when you mix them up in your mind a little with worries about a First Aid Class." Auxiliary members had the satisfaction of knowing that "history is not leaving them behind chained to the stove and the pots."[31]

Addressing the delegates, Philip Murray declared: "The future of the CIO movement will substantially depend on the support that the organization is given by women in industry and on the part played by the leaders who have guided the course of your organization.... We are relying on your zeal and understanding to help us build a great labor organization." He urged every CIO local to encourage and lend "wholesome support" to the auxiliaries wherever they existed. To help in the development of larger and stronger auxiliaries, Murray announced, he had appointed a National CIO Auxiliary Committee to establish a close relationship between the CIO and its auxiliaries.[32]

By the summer of 1943, it seemed that the great growth in women's membership in unions had reduced the need for women's auxiliaries. "You might think," wrote Julia Katz, national director of the CIO's Congress of Women's Auxiliaries, "that a job in a shipyard and membership in a union of 28,000 men and women would make you forget about women's auxiliaries. Quite the opposite is true." She had been working as an acetylene burner in the Bethlehem-Fairfield shipyard in Baltimore and had joined Local 43 of the Industrial Union of Marine & Shipbuilding Workers of America. Before she had been in the shipyard very long, she had met scores of auxiliary "graduates" and learned "how true it is that the auxiliary is the school for unionism." How did these women now feel about auxiliaries when they were members of a powerful union to whom they could bring their problems? "Believe me, sister, we feel more strongly than ever that a union needs an auxiliary. We feel that because we, the women in these unions, need the help of auxiliaries." And she went on:

We support our union's effort to fight for conditions that will maintain our ability to produce. But seven days a week in the shipyard, eight hours of work plus from two to four hours daily, traveling to and from work; endless hours of household responsibilities, for most of us when we get home, and keeping in touch with community agencies leaves little time and energy for checking on grocers' prices and doing the other day-to-day tasks which are necessary to achieve the CIO program. Do you wonder we applaud the program of the CWA-CIO? Indeed, we regard every effort of the CWA-CIO and of our own auxiliary as a service in our behalf.[33]

The CIO clearly shared this view, for its official organ, the *CIO News*, added a weekly column, "Women's Corner," edited by Eleanor Fowler, secretary-treasurer of the Congress of Women's Auxiliaries.* Although it devoted some space to dress patterns and recipes, the column stressed the importance of organizing women rapidly into auxiliaries "in order to insure their union-mindedness when they enter industry." It reported that several CIO auxiliaries had established price-control committees to check ceiling prices in the stores and child-care programs for children whose parents were working in war industry; and that a number of international unions had gone on record as being in favor of strengthening the auxiliaries. Thus, the eighth annual UE convention in September, 1942, instructed the union's General Executive Board to launch a drive to organize women's auxiliaries—the goal was a membership that would equal at least 50 percent of the union's membership. The resolution added that "many a housewife and mother is taking her place in our unions as a good trade unionist because of her past association with a women's auxiliary."[34]

The "Women's Corner" regularly reprinted a weekly legislative letter issued by the CWA. In one of them, the congress wrote to the Judiciary Committee of the House and Senate expressing "the strongest possible opposition to the Equal Rights Amendment" on the ground that it would destroy many of the "hard-won rights of women" by abolishing those laws "which protected the economic physical and social conditions of women, but do not apply equally to men."[35] In another issue, the "Women's Corner" stressed the need for day care centers for children of working mothers and urged every member of every auxiliary to send an appeal to her own congressional representative to support such legislation, as well as to support a tax bill based on ability to pay: "That would mean higher profits taxes and high income taxes, closing of loopholes in tax legislation, like that which allows husbands and wives to make sepa-

---

*The *American Federationist,* official organ of the AFL, did not add a women's column during the war, but it did feature women engaged in industry on its cover in several issues, while articles and editorials called for unionization and equal pay. President William Green was reported as urging that "each defense area should plan for adequate day nurseries and nursery schools" (*American Federationist* 50 (September 1943): 102).

rate returns and so saves wealthy families some $300,000,000 a year, and higher gift and inheritance taxes."[36]

One issue of the "Women's Corner" carried the headline: "It Does Happen Here. Beg Women to Take War Jobs Yet Deny Them to Negroes." In that column, Eleanor Fowler reported that the CWA had gone on record that it would conduct an aggressive campaign to assure that the barriers against the employment of black women in war industries were totally abolished, and that its Executive Board had voted to ask President Roosevelt "to force employers to observe the official policy of the government banning racial discrimination in war industry." The need, it declared, was urgent:

> There's a new bomber plant in Cleveland. Over 60% of the employees are scheduled to be women—and they're talking of bringing women workers in from other areas. But Negro women who want jobs in Cleveland are still waiting. In Indianapolis, the papers carry urgent ads for women workers in war industry and Negro women applying for these jobs are turned away....
>
> Negro men give their lives to win the war against Hitlerism on the battle front. It is utterly unfair that their wives and sisters should be denied the opportunity to work for victory on the production front.[37]

Discrimination because of color was not the only form of discrimination attacked by the "Women's Corner." Fowler noted, too, that "employers set up all sorts of age, height, and weight requirements by which they will limit the women they will employ."[38]

In a number of communities, the auxiliaries of the AFL, the CIO, and the railroad brotherhoods worked together. They joined, for example, in sponsoring a civilian defense rally in Cleveland on February 21, 1942, at which Margaret Bondfield, the first woman cabinet member of Great Britain, spoke on "British Workers and the War."[39] In July, 1942, a conference was called by the Consumers' Division of the Office of Price Administration (OPA) at the request of the auxiliaries of the three labor federations. Delegates came to the conference from the AFL, CIO, and railroad brotherhood auxiliaries, as well as from the Women's Trade Union League and other groups. The conference emphasized the importance of women's representation on price and rationing boards. It urged the establishment of an official system of volunteer price wardens to see that ceilings were strictly enforced. It also urged training classes for women, funds for wartime day nurseries, and rent ceilings throughout the United States.[40]

Although unions were often (and sometimes justly) accused of indifference to the needs of the woman worker, in a number of areas they did prove to be valuable allies. Throughout the war they worked for the improvement of day care facilities, and at the war's end they urged that these facilities not be instantly dismantled. In hearings on the Federal Equal Pay Bill, the AFL, the CIO, and a number of individual labor organizations urged Congress to outlaw wage discrimination.[41]

In general, the CIO conventions were more sympathetic to the needs of women workers than were those of the AFL, repeatedly calling for women to have positions of responsibility and leadership in unions and advocating state equal pay legislation. At its 1944 convention, the CIO adopted a five-point program in relation to women in industry calling for (1) the extension of equal pay for equal work to all plants under CIO contract and the enactment by the states of a uniform law prohibiting discrimination against women employees in payment of wages; (2) provisions in collective bargaining agreements for adequate rest and lunch periods, maternity leave without loss of seniority, and the inclusion of maternity benefits in group insurance coverage; (3) further development of community activities for child-care centers, adequate housing, especially for migrant women workers, and proper and extensive recreational facilities; (4) the expansion of special educational programs for women by unions, to bring them into positions of greater responsibility and leadership; and (5) protection of women's employment rights through the seniority clauses of union contracts.

By way of contrast, the AFL, at its 1944 convention, confined itself to recommending that special attention be given to the organization of women, and that they be aided in obtaining agreements assuring them of equal pay for equal work.[42]

Throughout the war the CIO worked closely with the Women's Bureau. Resolution No. 37, passed by the 1944 convention, urged "full cooperation" with the bureau to safeguard and improve conditions of women workers. The CIO sent unpublished organization papers on the needs of employed women to the Women's Bureau for criticism and comment. Special divisions to consider the problems of women workers were set up by several CIO unions, including the International Fur & Leather Workers Union, the United Retail & Wholesale Employees of America, the United Office & Professional Workers of America, the United Packinghouse Workers of America, and the Textile Workers Union of America. At their request, the Women's Bureau kept close contact with these union groups, offering them bureau pamphlets, survey data, and the services of bureau field agents.[43]

Addressing the convention of the Congress of Women's Auxiliaries in November, 1942, Philip Murray pointed with pride to the fact that the CIO had made the establishment of equal pay for women workers one of its cardinal principles. "No contracts of the CIO are written today without such provision," he added.[44] While this was an exaggeration, it is true that many unions made equal pay the subject of contract negotiations. As early as 1941, AFL organizers in the California canning industry had negotiated equal pay contracts, and the CIO Steel Workers Organizing Committee eliminated wage differentials for 6,500 women that ranged from 5 cents to as much as 20 cents an hour. In 1941 the United Automobile Workers struck the Kelsey-Hayes Wheel Company machine gun plant in Detroit because women were paid only 85 cents an hour compared with $1 for men.*[45]

In its 1941 contract the UE won the right of equal work for women at the Westinghouse East Pittsburgh plant. Then, in renewing the national contract with the Westinghouse Company in 1942, the UE won an agreement that women placed in jobs performed by men before the United States' entry into the war would be paid at the same rate as men. Also, women were given a larger wage increase in order to reduce the differential between men and women that the corporation had long had in force.[46]

By the latter part of 1943, the UE had about 150 signed agreements, covering 600 factories, which included the "equal pay" clause. The United Rubber Workers included the clause in 142 of its agreements, while the UAW had about 50 agreements embodying the principle.[47] On May 20, 1943, eighty CIO union officials representing unions in Indiana, Illinois, Wisconsin, Minnesota, and Iowa called personally on government officials to express their concern "over unequal rates of pay accorded women in some war plants as compared with men doing the same work." Although conceding that they were motivated in part by a desire to protect men's wages, the delegation insisted that they were primarily concerned about meeting the needs of their women members through establishing the principle of equal pay for equal work.[48]

But the column, "Mostly for Women" in the *Wayne UE Victory News* of August 14, 1942, noted that the "equal pay for equal work" clause in the UE contract with Westinghouse had both advantages and shortcomings:

> The very fact that our contracts provide equal pay for equal work is an inducement for our women to bend every effort to produce more—produce for victory. Its effect will also be felt in the front lines of our armed forces. Our boys fighting to defeat Hitlerism—to protect our homes and our liberties—will fight with wholehearted vigor, knowing that their standard of living is being protected on the home front.
>
> Yet despite this great step forward, women still do not—even with the equal pay for equal work clause in the contracts—have complete equality. Differentials in wages still exist because jobs are still being designated as "men's jobs" and "women's jobs."
>
> A job is classified and then after it is classified by some superman com-

---

*In December, 1942, over thirteen thousand auto workers, members of Canada's largest union—Local 200, UAW-CIO—won a five-day strike for the principle of equal pay for equal work. The strike ended when the Ford Motor Company of Canada agreed to the principle of equal pay for women (*Labor*, Dec. 7, 1942).

plex, a decision is reached by the masterminds of industry as to whether this job is to be a man's job or a woman's job. If it is designated as a woman's job, a "W" is put next to the labor grade and "presto chango," the rate is reduced by 15 cents. Yet this company claims to classify the job and not the person! . . .

Women must have full and complete equality on the question of wages and job opportunities in the plants where they work. . . .[49]

On November 28, 1945, several months after the war's end, the War Labor Board, under pressure from the UE, approved the principle of "a single evaluation line for all jobs in a plant regardless of whether the jobs are performed by men or women." The board recommended that the General Electric and Westinghouse Electric corporations negotiate with the UE to devise a formula "for narrowing in the immediate future unreasonable wage rate differentials now existing between men's and women's jobs." The recommendation covered 110 plants of the two companies and 180,000 employees in more than 40 cities.*[50]

In the spring of 1944 the Women's Bureau released the results of a survey of union policies with respect to women members. The bureau found that while national unions had endorsed the principle of equal pay for equal work, most contracts were negotiated by local unions; hence, it was necessary to work with the locals "to safeguard women's interests" by the insertion of equal pay clauses in contracts. In some local unions this created no problem, since women's leadership ran as high as 80 to 90 percent and women were even in charge of the locals. It was easier, moreover, to achieve the goal in CIO unions than in those affiliated with the AFL, for CIO unions had actually "invited" women to join and play a more active role in the organization. In any event, on the basis of suggestions by women of both the AFL and CIO, the Women's Bureau recommended that six clauses be included in union contracts. Four are pertinent:

1. General: It is mutually agreed by the company and the union that no discrimination based on sex or marital status shall be practiced or permitted.
2. Wages: Wage rates established under this contract shall be set by the job, not by the sex of the worker. Wage rates and job classification shall be based on job content. The starting rate of pay shall be the same for all inexperienced workers, irrespective of sex.
3. Seniority: Women shall accumulate seniority in the same manner as

*James J. Matles, late secretary-treasurer of the UE, called the WLB order to GE and Westinghouse "a first breakthrough on this issue [of equal pay for equal work] in mass production industry" (James J. Matles and James Higgins, *Them and Us: Struggles of a Rank-and-File Union* [Englewood Cliffs, N.J., 1974], p. 138). Strangely, however, this informal history of the UE contains only one reference to women workers—that relating to the War Labor Board decision, and that is confined solely to Matles' comment quoted above. This is certainly a limited view of the achievements of the union, which, during World War II, was credited with "having done the best job among women" (*New York Times*, Sept. 30, 1943).

male employees, and shall have the same rights of promotion or transfer to other departments. If it becomes necessary to eliminate or curtail the work of any department in which women are employed, they shall be entitled to carry seniority to other departments. . . .

4. Maternity Leave: Pregnancy shall not be grounds for dismissal of any woman employee. Any woman employee who is pregnant shall, upon presentation of a doctor's certificate stating the probable date of her confinement, receive maternity leave of not less than six weeks before delivery and two months after delivery.*[51]

Neither at that time nor later did the Women's Bureau indicate just how many local unions incorporated these clauses into their contracts. However, in a survey of the Midwest war industry, the bureau found that four-fifths of the union contracts provided seniority protection "to men and women alike without mention of sex."[52]

A number of unions prevented employers from returning to the depression practice of discriminating against married women. When the upstate New York Telephone Company granted married women only temporary employee status, thus denying them fringe benefits offered to regular workers, the National Federation of Telephone Workers (NFTW) took the issue to the National War Labor Board. With the assistance of a brief from the Women's Bureau, the union argued that the company was practicing "discrimination of the most insidious type . . .[which] has a tendency, if unchecked, to spread and threaten the job security of all women workers." The NWLB, in a split decision, ruled that discrimination of this sort was inadmissible.[53]

In *American Labor from Defense to Reconversion*, Joel Seidman has noted that the mass entrance of women into organized labor "created a serious education problem for the union movement, particularly since so many of these women lacked prior experience in industry and had not participated in the struggles for union organization and recognition."[54] The two unions with the largest female membership—the UAW and the UE—displayed special vigor in this area. The UE began early in the war to hold special conferences for women members to discuss their problems and instituted training classes to prepare women for leadership in the union.[55] Ruth Young, membership activities director of UE's District 4 in the Greater New York area, expressed the union's position when she declared that "the destiny of our country depends on its working men and women, and the working women have a special stake. Under fascism, women suffer the most."[56]

After six months of effort, Young was able to convince the New York City Board of Education to train women factory workers for defense jobs. The program began with one thousand women who had an oppor-

---

*The two other clauses dealt with rest periods and lunch periods.

tunity to learn wiring and winding, assembling, spot welding, and light drill press work.[57] On January 17, 1942, a ten-week "Union Leadership Training Course for Women" got under way under Young's direction. The *UE News* explained: "Because this is the first course of its kind to be given anywhere, the *UE News* is reporting the classes to make the material available to the widest possible audience."*[58] Classes were held on such subjects as the role of women in American history, negotiations, grievance procedures, parliamentary procedure, and public speaking. The sixth session was taught by Julius Emspak, the UE secretary-treasurer, who contrasted old and new methods in protecting labor's interests and told the trainees:

> In the last war, there was an emergency which resulted in the influx of women in the shops. The employers took advantage of this to cut wages. This war is being waged under different conditions. Organized labor is stronger than it was. Particularly we are organized now in the mass production industries, which turn out war products. This was not true in the last war. This is why we are in a better position to protect conditions, to insure equal pay for equal work, and proper utilization of women's talents and capacities for production for victory.[59]

A number of union papers whose organizations had large women memberships reprinted the summaries of the leadership classes from the *UE News*. Thus, the *UCAPAWA News*, organ of the United Cannery, Agricultural, Packing & Allied Workers of America (CIO), introduced its reprint of one of the UE sessions as follows:

> UCAPAWA women have always been an important part of our Union—women who were not afraid to go out and organize their local, women who find time to take on duties as officers, shop stewards and as untitled rank and filers to help carry on Union work.
> Today, as the men march off to the front lines, important responsibilities fall increasingly on our women members. Sometimes these women find, even in UCAPAWA, men who still believe that women have no place in public affairs. And sometimes, too, they are hampered by their own feelings of modesty, that they "do not know how to speak up," that after all they are "only women" who cannot handle issues outside the home.
> Our answer to such views is to take a look at American history. We find that our country would not be what it is today if women had not fought for freedom and for a better way of life. Active women in the year 1943 are following a course deeply rooted in American history. Here is the story as told by Dr. Philip Foner, outstanding historian. (These talks, reported by Katherine Beecher, were loaned to us by the *UE News*).†[60]

---

*This may be a reference to the first course to train women for union leadership offered by a union during the war, for the Women's Trade Union League had been offering such courses for years prior to the war.

†The present writer also taught sessions on women in the American labor movement for the UE classes training women for union leadership.

As part of the UE's educational program, a song was composed to compete with "Rosie the Riveter" and "Women Behind the Man Behind the Gun." Entitled "Winnie the Welder," it added a dimension in its fourth verse that neither of the other two songs mentioned:

When Winnie first hired in,
The pay was pretty thin,
So she set out to get her chums awake.
Tho' many said, "You can't,"
She organized her plant,
And now the workers get a better break.
She heads their union now,
And fast is learning how,
At settling grievances she knows her stuff,
By settling them she soon removes
All discontent, and this improves
Production and armed strength at once—
(And you all know what Hitler wants)
He wants the heat turned off![61]

Like the UE, the UAW sought to develop local union programs to train women leaders. However, it was not until 1944 that the UAW established a separate Women's Bureau within its War Policy Division to deal with the special needs of its estimated 250,000 dues-paying female members. The union empowered the bureau, which was headed by Mildred Jeffreys, a veteran organizer in the clothing industry, to conduct an educational campaign, to provide consultants on contracts pertaining to women, and to publish a special bulletin for female members. In December, 1944, the UAW Women's Bureau held a conference for women unionists. Among other things, the conferees prodded the UAW International Executive Board to take more vigorous action on the equal pay issue.[62]

In 1941 the UAW removed Richard Deverall as head of the union's Education Department "because of his alleged fascist and anti-Semitic sympathies." He was replaced by William Levitt, a left-winger. Levitt removed many of Deverall's appointees and hired Communists and other left-wingers in their place. One of those he brought into the department was Elizabeth Hawes, a well-known writer on fashion and other feminine issues, to deal with women's problems.[63] As the first woman international representative in the Education Department, Hawes visited UAW locals from coast to coast "to help the women start to help themselves" in struggling for equal pay, seniority rights, improved cafeteria food, and other grievances. Among other things, Hawes helped women to organize petition drives demanding seats for women in work areas. "Where a real effort was made," Hawes reported, "seats were obtained—for men as well as women."[64]

The Communists and their allies in unions like the UE, UAW,

UCAPAWA, and others were particularly active in the pursuit of better conditions for women during the war. "It is a pressing necessity," Earl Browder, Communist Party leader, declared in 1942, "to abolish all existing remnants of inequality between men and women." Communists condemned those in the labor movement who maintained that nature had designed women to keep the home, and they criticized unions for failing to do more about the "scandalous situation that prevails in the handling of the special problems of women workers."[65] They demanded that the unions come out aggressively not only for the improvement of conditions for women workers on the job but also for measures not directly related to job conditions, such as improved child care and the availability of shopping and laundry facilities in war communities. There is little doubt that the major contributions made by unions like the UE and UAW to improve the status of their women members during the war were greatly influenced by the role of the Communists in these unions.*[66]

"To say we could accomplish nothing except by striking was a lie," Elizabeth Hawes observed. "We got things all the time by sheer mass pressure."[67] But strikes did occur during the war, and women union members participated in them and sometimes assumed the leadership. Probably the largest wartime women's strike was that of the telephone operators in 1944. It began in Dayton, Ohio, and was triggered by the company's practice of importing telephone operators from other states who worked side by side with local operators but received a higher wage. As Robert C. Pollock, president of the Ohio Federation of Telephone Workers (affiliated with the National Federation of Telephone Workers), told the press: "No union leader could conscientiously order a girl making $21 a week to work beside a girl making $39.25 for exactly the same work."[68] The Ohio Federation of Labor voted its full support for the strike, which began on November 17, 1944, in Dayton and spread overnight to Columbus, Toledo, Xenia, Tiffin, Findlay, and Wellesville. Akron, Canton, and Youngstown operators soon joined the burgeoning walkout, and before the first three days were over, some twenty-five cities were affected and roughly ten thousand telephone operators were out on strike, not only in Ohio, but in Washington, D.C., and Detroit as well. When the National War Labor Board agreed to take the matter out

---

*Communists in the UAW pressured for a maternity clause in union contracts, and toward the end of the war, the UAW prepared a maternity clause, which it tried to have included in every UAW contract. Closely following the maternity clause recommendations of the Women's Bureau, the UAW clause contained the provision that a woman worker, with her doctor's approval, might continue to work until two months prior to delivery. She was to receive a leave of absence because of the impending childbirth and could return to work on presentation of a physician's certificate. Since about a third of the UAW's 350,000 womem members were married, the maternity problem was particularly important (*New York Times*, Sept. 22, 1944).

of the hands of the regional board and promised a special national panel to consider the question "immediately," the union called off the strike on November 23. "Had the strike lasted another 48 hours," declared the *Telephone Worker*, "it is safe to say that over 200,000 telephone workers would have been idle and the nation's communication system would have been paralyzed."[69]

On June 17, 1943, in Winston-Salem, North Carolina, approximately two hundred black women in the stemming department of an R. J. Reynolds Tobacco Company plant sat down at their machines and refused to continue with their work. The immediate cause of the spontaneous strike was their anger over the death of an elderly black man who had been overworked and had been refused proper medical care by the company foreman.[70] The underlying cause was a lifetime of abuse, low wages, hard work, and intolerable working conditions. In January, 1941, the average straight-time earnings of Reynolds workers were 46 cents an hour. But many black women working in the stemmeries were paid by the pound rather than by the hour, and, in many cases, wages and job classifications were determined at the convenience of management and the whims of its foremen and supervisors. Robert Black, a worker at Reynolds, recalled:

> I can use my wife as an example, and this goes for thousands of women in the stemmeries. You went into the plant and they had nails up on the side of the wall. You pulled off your dress and hung it up. If you had a lunch, you put yours on a wooden bench with your shoes under your bench. Cockroaches and things were running over your food all during the time you were out there sweating and dying. Now when you came out of the plant, your head was saturated with dust. There was dust all over you and nowhere to wash. These women were so drenched with perspiration that when you took off your work dress and put on your street dress the perspiration would still come through your clothes.[71]

A six-day, fifty-hour week was normal. There were no vacations, no seniority, no paid holidays, and no sick leave. There was, however, plenty of sexual abuse and racial humiliation. The company foremen had unlimited power. "Some of them were no different from prison guards," a black woman in the stemmeries recalled, "and some were even worse."[72] Even the women's restroom and dressing room were not off limits:

> When you go to the restroom, you was timed. If you didn't come out at that time, you went to the desk. The foreman would come in the toilet, come in the dressing room, where the women were, come in there and you had your clothes off. He'd say, "You been in here long enough, if you ain't done, you won't get done."[73]

The heat, the dust, and the constant motion and roar of the machines all added to the discomfort. Leaning against the steel of the stemming machine "caused a lot of women to have operations; some could never produce children."[74]

Although the company tried to prevent news of the sit-down strike from spreading to other plants, truck drivers who moved the tobacco in and out of the plants passed the word. The next day, the other plants of R. J. Reynolds, the largest tobacco production facility in the world, were shut down.

In 1936 a report from Winston-Salem had noted that "the biggest proportion of labor here are women workers," and that "women workers get about $4.50 a week." It concluded: "The Reynolds Co. continually struggles to keep the workers from organizing in any kind of a union." But in 1941, several years after the AFL Tobacco Workers Union, which had segregated blacks and whites into separate locals, had thrown in the sponge and left Winston-Salem, a group of black workers called in organizers for UCAPAWA-CIO, soon to become the Food & Tobacco Workers, CIO. This group included Robert Black, Velma Hopkins, Theodozia Simpkins, and Miranda Smith. A Tobacco Workers Organizing Committee was formed, and Miranda Smith became its regional director.

The big union push did not really begin until the spontaneous strike in June, 1943. By the end of the weekend, almost eight thousand union cards had been signed by both black and white workers.[75]

The Reynolds workers elected leaders, who compiled a list of grievances from each department. On June 20 the Reynolds management agreed to meet with the workers' selected representatives. These men and women demanded a reduction in work loads, increases in wages, amnesty for all workers involved in the sit-downs, and recognition of the Organizing Committee. After failing to convince the workers' representatives to order the strikers back to work, Reynolds signed a statement agreeing to the demands and, most significantly, recognizing the Tobacco Workers Organizing Committee.[76]

However, the company refused to recognize UCAPAWA. At an election on the question of union recognition, held under the auspices of the National Labor Relations Board in the first week of August, the CIO won an overwhelming majority in Unit I—the leaf house workers. But in Unit II the "no union" forces won by a close vote: 2,856 to the CIO's 2,829, while the AFL's Tobacco Workers' International Union received 115 votes.[77] UCAPAWA quickly requested a runoff, and the Regional Director of the NLRB sustained the protest on the ground that the company had interfered with the voting process. A second election was ordered and held on December 16 and 17, 1943. This time, UCAPAWA triumphed by a large majority. The Reynolds Company was ordered by the NLRB to bargain collectively with the union.[78]

After the union called in the U.S. Conciliation Commission, company officials began to bargain seriously. On April 13, 1944, Local 22, UCAPAWA-CIO, gained official recognition as the union representing the production workers at Reynolds. Black workers, and particularly black women, had played the leading role in the victory. As Robert Black put it, "The black women made that union possible. We could never have beaten them [Reynolds] without them. It was the militancy among those black women. The women, well all of us had something to gain, but they had everything to gain."[79]

The union contract included an eight-hour day and a forty-hour week, with time-and-a-half for overtime, seniority rights, grievance procedures, and the reinstatement with full seniority of most of the workers fired for union activity. However, many important issues, such as wages, check-off, the union shop, vacation pay, and seniority for stewards, could not be agreed upon, and these issues went to the War Labor Board for arbitration.[80] In a series of NWLB rulings over the following months, most of the union's proposals were accepted. Paid vactions of one week for one year's service and two weeks for regular employees, as well as vacations for seasonal workers, were granted. Union security, dues check-off, a minimum-wage increase of 10 cents an hour and increases of 1 cent to 20 cents to the lowest-paid workers, and top seniority for union stewards were all ordered by the War Labor Board. The wage increases were retroactive to the contract-signing date of April 24, 1944.[81]

Along with the wage increases, the reduction in working hours, and the union security came the establishment of basic human rights. One black woman, active in the union drive, put it succinctly: "I wasn't nothing but dirt down there before, but now they really respect me."[82]

In the summer of 1944, Local 22 set up an Education Committee with a full-time director. Classes in union history, union contracts, health, reading and writing, public speaking, home management, and municipal government were offered at the union hall. A radio program was broadcast each Saturday in which community issues were discussed and various union members presented their views. A Political Action Committee was formed to register people to vote and give courses on the state and federal constitutions. Many committee members went from door to door in voter registration drives, and by election time, seven thousand new voters had been registered in Winston-Salem.[83]

Although Local 22's membership was predominantly black and the union operated in a highly segregated social system, the workers understood the importance of black-white unity. In the preamble to the union's constitution, they pledged themselves "to build our organization democratically on an industrial basis without regard for craft, age, sex, race, color, nationality, religion or political beliefs."[84] In December, 1944, members of Local 22, including such militant women as Velma

Hopkins, Miranda Smith, Theodozia Simpkins, Viola Brown, and Christine Gardner, traveled to the national convention of the Food, Tobacco & Agricultural Workers Union (formerly UCAPAWA) to exchange experiences and strategy with other union members.[85] They were to use this knowledge, along with what they had already gained locally, in the great postwar struggles waged by Local 22.

Despite improving attitudes, the relations between unions and women workers during the war years were not always harmonious. Working women still suffered injustices, many of which were either deliberately overlooked or even encouraged by the unions. A Women's Bureau agent reported that "union contracts often openly discriminate against women in such matters as wage rates and seniority rights; or, if the contract does not discriminate, it fails to call for equality so that discrimination results in practice." Indeed, the Women's Bureau concluded that despite wartime gains and modifications, union contracts remained generally "inadequate for women."[86] The attainment of equal pay for equal work was dependent upon union support, but too often local unions failed to raise the issue with the company or the NWLB. Moreover, many unions circumvented equal pay by negotiating differentials under a job classification system or by accepting lesser wages for women when they worked in a shop separate from men. The Women's Bureau study of Midwest unions revealed that while half of the contracts called for equal pay, differentials were often allowed to continue.[87] A January, 1944, report by the agency charged that "local unions have used women's wage rates as a pawn to be sacrificed in favor of other seemingly more important objectives. . . . It is still not the rule that union contracts simply call for the job rates for all workers."[88]

Seniority rights also created a problem, particularly with the transportation unions. Union contracts specified that the heaviest and dirtiest work would be given to new employees, while the lighter and easier jobs were secured only after many years of service.[89] This situation made it difficult to employ women in the industry, and the Office of Defense Transportation suggested that the practice be suspended during the war. In July, 1943, Otto Beyer, director of the ODT's Transport Personnel Division, suggested the use of separate seniority lists classifying women as temporary employees in order to facilitate their placement in jobs they could handle.[90] Mary Anderson and Frances Perkins reluctantly agreed to the idea, but the Management-Labor Policy Committee of the War Manpower Commission refused to interfere with union practices. Thus, the unions were able to use seniority to restrict the employment of women.[91]

Some unions failed to grant women full union status and benefits or allowed the admission of women into the union only for the duration of the war. The Carpenters & Joiners granted full status only to those women who directly replaced men, forcing all other women in the industry to accept a nonvoting auxiliary status.[92] The Milwaukee Brewery Workers Union required women to pay dues, yet barred them from meetings and granted them no permanent status.[93] While national unions generally agreed to the principle of equality, the locals often reacted differently. When questioned by a Women's Bureau agent as to why the District 44 branch of the International Association of Machinists did not observe the national policy of admitting women to membership, the district chairman replied that the "'Dear Sirs and Brothers' do not see eye to eye with the Grand Lodge on this question."[94]

The key to women's problems with unions was the failure of the war emergency to erase the old fears and suspicions that unions harbored about women workers. Many rank-and-file union members were opposed to the employment of women in the persistent irrational belief that, regardless of the wartime emergency and their own financial need, they still belonged in the home and bringing them into industry would result in lowered pay scales. There was still a strong belief that unions could best help women by focusing on their husbands or future husbands—that is, on male workers. Unions often thought of women as merely "until" workers: "They are always working until they get married, until they have a baby, until the house is paid off. . . ."[95]

Complaints were voiced to Women's Bureau agents that women were hard to interest in the union programs, that they were willing to work for lower pay than men, and that they accepted the advantages of union membership but did not respect picket lines.[96] In 1943, at a conference of the New York Women's Trade Union League, UAW President R. J. Thomas criticized women for accepting the benefits but not the responsibilities of union membership. Describing the fight made by the UAW to put equal pay for equal work through the War Labor Board, of which he was a member, he asked: "Do you know not one woman has ever appeared before the War Labor Board to argue on that question? It was done by men, and that is a woman's problem."*

---

*Thomas obviously had not paid any attention when May McKernan, a delegate to the 1942 UAW convention, told her fellow unionists: "I should not like for the brothers to forget that when the subject of women comes up, they shouldn't say, 'Well, that's the woman's problem.' We are tired of men saying, 'Well, that's the woman's problem.'" Interestingly, Thomas opened his 1944 annual report to a union one-fifth female in membership with the customary salutation: "Dear Sirs and Brothers" (Alan Clive, "Women Workers in World War II: Michigan as a Test Case," *Labor History* 20 [Winter 1979]: 55). Clive points out that Thomas' description of the equal pay issue as "a woman's problem" overlooked the fact that "much hung on the issue: the pay of thousands of returning veterans who might be forced to accept a 'woman's wage' in order to reclaim jobs temporarily held by women; and the ability of the UAW to convince its members that it could win critical tests against management" (ibid.).

Thomas also criticized the attitude of women at Ford's Willow Run plant, where they made up 35 percent of the union. He complained that after the union had fought for years to gain an average rate of $1.14 an hour, "these women call me a pirate because they have to pay dues. They say they don't get service. And they don't even know why they're getting $1.14 an hour."[97] He threatened that unless women started carrying their own weight in unions, there would be no place for them in industry after the war.

In response, the Women's Bureau warned that the disappearance of women was improbable; more likely, the agency claimed, women workers would become disenchanted with unions and pose a special danger to them in the postwar years.[98] But even during the war there was evidence of such disenchantment. In 1943 *Fortune* magazine sponsored a survey of women's attitudes toward labor unions, conducting 2,700 face-to-face interviews with women from twenty to thirty-four years of age. A key question read:

> Which of these kinds of places would you personally rather work in?
> a. A place where there is no union and everyone deals directly with her boss/foreman.
> b. A place where there is a union of only company employees, but no national union.
> c. A place where there is a strong national union, but nonunion people can also work.
> d. A place where everyone must belong to a national union.

Almost half of the women questioned (44 percent) preferred no union. About 17 percent opted for a company union, 15 percent had no opinion on the question, 14 percent advocated a closed shop, and 12 percent endorsed strong national unions, but without the closed shop.[99]

Women who opposed unions attributed their opposition to a feeling that men were not interested in their problems, a dislike for union-sanctioned wage differentials, and the unions' disregard of "women's grievances." They accused labor leaders of failing to understand or care about their problems, needs, and goals. They resented the union practice of blocking women from traditionally male positions and treating them as second-class workers. Unions, they felt, were either insensitive or indifferent to the needs and aspirations of women workers, especially those who were married, and over 75 percent of the women entering the wartime labor force were married. Many unions shrugged off such issues as maternity leaves, child-care centers, and time off for mothers to care for their families when illness struck. To the male-dominated world of organized labor, such issues were "frills," but to women workers, they were centrally related to health, child neglect, juvenile delinquency, and family relationships. Women also resented the fact that union leaders openly declared that they favored higher wages for women workers only in order to maintain high wage levels for the returning veterans. They also complained that they were invisible in the union leadership.[100]

"Masculine opposition to women in industry is collapsing," Mary Anderson told a victory conference of women in industry sponsored by the Chicago Industrial Union Council (CIO) in February, 1943.[101] Privately, however, she was more cautious. "Sometimes we think we have gone an awful ways, and we have, but we have to go quite a bit more before we get real justice," she wrote to Mrs. Raymond Robins.[102] To a great extent, Anderson's evaluations summed up the impact of the war on women workers and the trade unions. By no means did the war settle problems between unions and women workers, but some permanent gains were made. Many trade unionists came to accept women in both the work force and the union movement. The war period offered the first real opportunity for great numbers of women and unions to come into contact with and gain some understanding of their common problems. For the first time, too, many trade union leaders began to bargain collectively for such female demands as rest periods, clean washrooms, day care centers, and maternity leaves, as well as wages, hours, and working conditions.

With what results? Following her tour of the country on behalf of the International Education Department of the UAW, Elizabeth Hawes presented her findings. "Do Women Workers Get an Even Break?" she asked. No, she replied, pointing out that equality with men remained just a promise. In a large number of cases, women industrial workers, thanks to the War Labor Board ruling, had succeeded in obtaining equal pay for doing work identical to that done by a large number of men in plants in which they were employed. But in some cases, the board had ruled that no matter how efficient women might be, it was right for them to be paid less for the same work if the man were doing their work in another shop:

> All over the nation since the beginning of the war, jobs formerly performed by one man have been broken down into their component parts to make a series of simpler jobs for new employees. Most of these jobs are now being done by women industrial workers. If you add up the total amount paid for all the simple jobs, you will usually find the total job, now performed by several women, is costing less in wages than it did when done by one man.
>
> And so, all over America, you will find women who know they are not receiving wages equal to men's and men in management and labor who recognize this. As for the right of a woman industrial worker to a better job or to any available job she can do in case of lay-off, in accordance with the seniority rules of her plant, the discriminations are as rife as in the matter of wages.

Yet Hawes conceded that great advances had been made during the war. The top leaders of all the unions had tried to compel the union locals to abolish all separate seniority clauses and female wage classifications in union contracts. Where union pressure had been sufficient, management had responded: "It was the United Automobile Workers and the United Electrical Workers, two CIO unions, which pushed through the WLB ruling which made equal pay for equal work a principle and in many places a reality." State and federal governments had also responded to pressure, with some states passing equal pay laws and others making "an honest effort" to enforce existing laws that prevented women from lifting heavy weights, providing adequate restroom facilities and rest periods, and so forth.

But more important was the fact that industrial women workers were themselves "beginning to break a silence centuries long—a silence characteristic of the chattel slaves they once were." Out of the war had emerged, for the first time in American history, a mass movement of women trade unionists—3 million strong—and a large number of the clearest-thinking and most outspoken women leaders the country had ever produced. "So far known primarily to the labor movement," Hawes declared, "these are the women who find time not only to keep up their responsibilities as wives and mothers and production workers, but also to organize women industrial workers and teach them how, through united union and political action, they can get an even break."[103]

The "Mostly for Women" column in the August 14, 1942, issue of the *Wayne UE Victory News* came out boldly for a far-reaching change in the status of women in America after the war: "Women must have full and complete equality on the question of wages and job opportunities in the plants where they work. They must emerge from this war with complete and absolute right to work at any job for which they are fitted."[104] But it soon became clear that the issue was not so much whether women would be able to work at jobs for which they were suited as it was whether they would be able to work at all.

When production cutbacks got under way, women were severed from employment at a rate much higher than that of men. In 1944, with the Allied victory in view and the war emergency drawing to a close, the first cutbacks began to be felt. In Detroit's Hoover Company, 85 percent of the workers laid off were women; at the Metal Stamping job shop, 98 percent of the layoffs were of women; at American Brake and Block, 90 percent; and at American Leather Products, Asbestos Manufacturing, and Baker Roulang Company, all the layoffs were of women. Across the nation, similar patterns emerged. In Wilkes-Barre, Pennsylvania, two-thirds of the workers laid off from an ordnance plant were women; in Nashville, almost all the workers laid off were women; in Indiana, over half the 11,700 workers laid off from the Evansville Ordnance Plant were women. Nearly 58 percent of the employees laid off at Twin Cities Ordnance in Minneapolis–St. Paul were women.[105]

Thus, even before VE Day, separation rates for women were consistently higher than those for males. A War Production Board report noted that nationally, between November, 1943, and February, 1944, nearly 5 percent of all women workers were separated from their jobs, while only 2 percent of the male workers were so affected.[106] In fact, by February, 1945, the *New York Times* was already referring to "the rise and fall of women in wartime industry."[107]

During the spring and summer of 1945, and especially after VJ Day, women were severed from employment at a rate approximately double that of men, and not many women were being hired in new jobs. For every hundred men laid off in May, 1945, seventy-three were hired; for every hundred women laid off, only sixty-three were hired. And few of these were black women. "A great deal of discrimination is being shown Negro women in the openings which are available," one survey concluded. "About the only jobs they are being permitted to fill are in the service industries."[108]

The U.S. Employment Service reported that women across the country were being forced to take severe pay cuts to find employment after the war plants closed. Women who had averaged 85 to 90 cents an hour were now being offered jobs at 45 to 50 cents an hour. Most of the women who had performed complex machine operations in wartime were now working at other sorts of jobs, most commonly "women's" positions, such as packers and wrappers.[109]

There were, of course, women who returned home willingly, but many did not. Some also fought back. "Waving placards which proclaimed that 'the hand that rocked the cradle can build tractors, too,'" went a report from Detroit on November 8, 1945, "about 150 women, displaced from their wartime jobs, threw up a picket line today at the Highland Park plant of the Ford Motor Company." The pickets, members of Local 400, UAW, carried signs reading "How Come No Work for Women?," "Ford Hires New Help. We Walk the Street," and "Stop Discrimination Because of Sex." The pickets told reporters that they had established the picket line after they had been laid off and their jobs had been taken by new male employees without seniority. Ford officials, for their part, explained that "women were not being hired at the plant at the present time because the manufacture of tractors was too heavy for such help." But the women pickets noted that management was shifting work assignments to give women heavy-lifting jobs as a method of ridding itself of unwanted women.* John G. Carney, president of Local 400, told reporters that fewer than 300 women were now employed at the Highland Park plant, as compared with a wartime peak of 5,849. He

---

*A government survey of conditions in Michigan in September, 1945, reported that this practice was fairly widespread (Sheila Tobias and Lisa Anderson, "Whatever Happened to 'Rosie the Riveter'?" *Ms.* 1 [June 1973]: 96).

was on his way to Washington, he added, to put the problem of these women members before the UAW international Executive Board.[110]

Nothing came of Carney's visit. The fact is that women received little help from the labor movement in meeting the problems of reconversion. At their 1944 conventions, both the AFL and the CIO did take up the question of women in industry, but neither dealt with the issue of postwar employment for women workers. The only reference to the question was in the CIO's call for protection of women's employment through the seniority clauses of union contracts. Neither the AFL's "Postwar Program," adopted on April 12, 1944, nor the federation's postwar planning committee dealt with the problems of reconversion as they affected the woman worker. The CIO reemployment plan, adopted at its 1944 convention, was also silent on this issue. Unions in the maritime, meatpacking, farm equipment, automobile and aircraft, textile, electrical and radio, metal mining, shipbuilding, and other industries offered detailed plans concerning reconversion and postwar employment. Pamphlets dealing with these issues were published, such as *Jobs After the War*, released by the United Farm Equipment Workers, *Program on Postwar Jobs for Shipbuilding*, published by the Industrial Union of Marine & Shipbuilding Workers, and *The UAW-CIO Postwar Plan* of the United Auto Workers. But the only solution offered to meet the postwar job needs of women workers lay in the achievement of full production and full employment through government intervention.[111]

For black women, who felt the impact of reconversion from war to civilian production even more severely than did white women, the outlook was even more grim. The Women's Bureau noted that "Negro women's wartime performance has provided proof that, given the training, they can succeed in any type of work that women can do." But the FEPC decided that all this was beside the point: "It is safe to predict that unless there is full employment or the continuance of present nondiscrimination, there will be much individual displacement of colored workers. Negro women, because of their present marginal status in industrial employment, will suffer most."[112]

The issue of reconversion and the woman worker was dealt with only at special conferences called by the labor movement. In January, 1944, the CIO Political Action Committee sponsored a Conference on Full Employment, headed by Dorothy Bellanca of the Amalgamated Clothing Workers, Ruth Young of the UE, and Jeannette Brown, executive secretary of the National Council of Negro Women. The conference called for adequate employment for women after the war, equal pay, child care, and the total integration of women into unions. In the resolution on postwar employment, it was declared that since great numbers of women then in war production might be expected to remain in industry, equal opportunity for postwar jobs should be offered them, with training and retraining facilities for reconversion purposes. The resolution also stressed the principle of equal pay for equal work by women and at the same time voiced vigorous opposition to the equal rights amendment pending in Congress as a "pernicious scheme to deprive women of hard-earned legislative gains and to prevent them from achieving, through legislation to safeguard working women, real equality."[113] Unfortunately, the resolution remained on paper.

The UAW also held conferences on the question of postwar employment for its women members, but UAW Vice-President Walter P. Reuther revealed how little the union had to offer them. On the one hand, he warned that "industry must not be allowed to settle the employment problem by chaining women to kitchen sinks." On the other hand, he warned the women that they could expect no "special privilege" to enable them to hold on to their jobs. The answer to women's postwar job problems, Reuther stressed, "lay not in special privileges but in creation of 60,000,000 peacetime jobs in America." He urged the women to fight for a full-employment economy by getting behind legislation in Congress for full employment. But he said nothing about what the union would do for its women members if such legislation was not enacted.

Joseph Velosky, director of the UAW Veterans Department, told the Women's Conference that the industry was planning to allow returning veterans to take the place of women regardless of seniority. He warned that the UAW would not allow the cry of war service to be used as a weapon to destroy women's seniority rights in any battle for jobs during reconversion. "We will not let employers use the veteran as a tool or wedge," he pledged.[114]

But how the union would solve the problem when the Selective Service Act guaranteed the veteran's right to reclaim his old job was not made clear. The fact is that the majority of UAW women members had not built up enough seniority by the end of the war to enable them to hold on to their jobs by means of seniority. Even a UAW leader admitted that those who did have the necessary seniority "were not being given the support they deserved in terms of union readiness to protect their seniority status."

In areas where unions had allowed women to work only for the duration or had established separate seniority lists for men and women, the seniority provision did not offer much protection. In Kenosha, Wisconsin, UAW Local 72 had negotiated an agreement with the Nash-Kelvinator Corporation allowing the employment of married women whose husbands were working or who had other means of support but specifying that such women were to be laid off first.[115]

In cases where employers and unions were ready and willing to remove women from the labor force, they used subtle ways of getting around seniority. Women workers were placed on midnight shifts with-

out regard to seniority in order to force them to quit, and work assignments were "shuffled" so that when layoffs came, the only jobs open to
women were heavy ones that they could not do. In the automobile industry as a whole, most contracts had stipulated that wartime shifts were
purely temporary. Consequently, the women faced a return to the sewing and trim departments and "wholesale layoffs."[116]

Even labor's reliance on a full-employment bill to protect women
came to nothing. The bill, in its original form, specifically excluded those
with "full-time housekeeping responsibilities" from the guarantee "of
sufficient employment opportunities." The bill's sponsor defended this
provision on the grounds that the measure was not "intended to take
housewives out of the homes and put them into industry or other employment."[117] Ironically, in its final form, the bill did not promise "full
employment" to anyone, and the exclusion of housewives was totally
unnecessary.

Women members felt that their unions had not done enough for
them, and many blamed it on the total domination of the unions by
men.* But some male members insisted that even more should be done
to get women out of their industry. As late as 1949 an irate male UAW
member complained: "Local 76 is doing nothing about getting rid of 15
women who persist in hanging on to their jobs at GM Parts Division
while veterans with children are being laid off. It's about time these
women realized that the war is over, and that they should stay home and
tend to their knitting."[118]

In her study of women workers and the UAW in the post-World War
II period, Nancy Gabin notes: "During the reconversion process and
continuing well into the post-war period, women complained of discrimination in layoffs and in job grading, but the male leadership and
membership of the UAW, in the main, did not respond with sympathy
or concern. Women discovered that management was not alone in want-
ing to exclude them from post-war jobs as a variety of jointly negotiated
contract clauses served to deny them the benefits that industrial organization was supposed to offer." Gabin lists three types of discrimination
sanctioned by various union and management agreements. They were:

> First of all, local agreements prohibiting the employment of married
> women and providing for the discharge of single women who married. Sec-
> ondly, agreements providing for unequal hiring-in rates for men and women
> and unequal wage rates on similar jobs discriminated against single and
> married women. Thirdly, women, under some agreements, were not permit-

*Shortly after VJ Day, a group of women picketed UAW headquarters in Detroit, demand-
ing that the Women's Bureau within the union be upgraded, that an all-female staff be
provided for the bureau, and that female representation be increased on the staffs of
other UAW divisions (Alan Clive, "Women Workers in World War II: Michigan as a Test
Case," *Labor History* 20 [Winter 1979]: 69–70n).

ted to exercise seniority rights equal to those of men in transfers and lay-offs.[119]

Although the number of women in the labor force dropped from a high of 19 million in 1944 to less than 17 million in 1946, it never sank to prewar levels, as had been the case following World War I. By 1947 the percentage of working women not only exceeded the 1940 level but continued to increase, as did the percentage of married women workers. Indeed, after World War II, the woman who worked was more often than not married and over thirty-five.[120]

Thus, after World War II, there was no reversion to the prewar female employment picture. Nor was there a reversion to the prewar trade union approach to the woman worker. Only one union—the Boilermakers—resumed its prewar practice of excluding women from membership.

Unfortunately, only five years after the war ended, in the midst of the "Cold War," eleven progressive unions, with almost a million members, were expelled from the CIO as "Communist-dominated" (as, fourteen years earlier, the CIO had itself been expelled from the AFL). Among the unions expelled were several of the "pace-setters for the whole trade union movement" in terms of wage scales and conditions won and in terms of sexual and racial equality. This is not to say that women members were fully represented at conventions and in positions of leadership, even in these progressive unions. But in general, these unions, with the UE in the leadership, had been the most conscientious in the labor movement in conducting major campaigns to eliminate discrimination in women's rates of pay and had been the most sensitive to sexism in their ranks. They were the unions, too, that had fought longest and hardest for the employment, upgrading, and representation of blacks in trade union offices.

The largest union expelled from the CIO was the UE, the third largest union in the organization. Long a leading champion of full equality for women workers, the UE continued to battle to eliminate discrimination in women's rates, and often succeeded in having jobs held by women reclassified to make the lowest rate for women equal to the common labor rate. The UE established a Fair Practices Committee to fight sexism and racism, and in a pamphlet entitled *UE Fights for Women's Rights* the committee signaled out the basic economic exploitation of women workers as the key to the oppression of women.[121]

18

1199

In 1952 a study of the American labor movement contended that the Women's Trade Union League was mistaken in its belief that most of its functions had been assumed by the unions and that the attitude of male union leaders had undergone a fundamental change. The AFL, the study argued, still did nothing to encourage the unionization of women other than to exhort its affiliates to provide special organizational programs for them and to include equal pay in collective bargaining agreements. The CIO showed a greater awareness of the needs of women workers, but it was reflected primarily in convention resolutions favoring equal promotional and seniority rights, maternity leaves in contracts, and support for a "Women's Status" bill that would commit the nation to an antidiscrimination policy by prohibiting sex bias in federal law.* But not much had been done to implement the resolutions, and several CIO leaders had voiced the view that pressing for the unionization of women might subject them to the charge of being "Communist-dominated." Although the study, under the auspices of the Labor Research Association, paid tribute to the left-wing unions for their efforts to organize women workers and to achieve equality for their women members, the main conclusion was grim: "The labor movement in 1952 is still run by men who have failed to provide the forces to organize women workers."[1]

The announcement early in 1955 of the merger of the AFL and CIO raised some hopes for a real breakthrough in the acceptance of women workers. Although leaders of women's organizations had long since learned to discount promises from top male labor leaders, there was an element in the statement of AFL President George Meany on the eve of

*The bill allowed exceptions, however, on the grounds of biological differences and social function.

the merger that could not be dismissed lightly. Meany, who had become president upon William Green's death in 1952, declared that

> the person who is unorganized because of a racial bar or discrimination of any kind is a threat to the conditions of those who are organized. Anyone who is underpaid, who has substandard conditions, threatens the situation of those in the unions.... The merger would mean more effective means to attain a fair employment practices bill on a national scale, and in attempts to assure civil rights in other fields.[2]

Meany's statement was itself the product of changes in the composition of the labor force that were having an important impact on the trade unions. Most of the new employees in Southern manufacturing plants since the war were nonunion women, and the phenomenal postwar growth of white-collar and service industries, both largely female, had pointed up the increasing importance of women in the labor force. In fact, in 1956, for the first time in American history, white-collar workers outnumbered blue-collar workers. The AFL had scored some successes in organizing white-collar workers, but overall, efforts to organize this work force had failed. It was becoming clear to many labor leaders that unless these workers were organized, the newly merged federation would soon represent only a small minority of the American workers.[3]

The AFL-CIO therefore insisted that unions were essential to the "advancement" and "human dignity" of women, and it urged its affiliates to include maternity leave provisions in collective bargaining agreements, to seek the cooperation of local communities and governmental agencies in the establishment of child-care facilities, and to include full participation of women in union affairs. The merged federation even looked to the federal government for assistance in protecting the rights of women workers, suggesting increased appropriations for the Women's Bureau and advocating additional protective legislation for women.[4]

But traditional attitudes prevented the action needed to change the picture. In 1957 President Meany expressed pride in the fact that women held two hundred full-time administrative positions, hundreds of regional offices, and thousands of local presidencies in the AFL-CIO. Aside from the fact that the evidence did not support this assertion, it was pointed out that even if it were true, this was still inadequate representation. Meany gave as the reason the usual union method of promoting from within, a system that lessened the opportunities for women, who were relatively new to the union movement. But what about a union like the ILGWU, where women were not only not "new" but constituted the vast majority of the membership? Even a champion of that union was compelled to comment that it should be "a source of concern" that in a union "four-fifths of whose members are women," the leadership had been for so many years almost completely male and that only one woman was then on the twenty-three-member General Executive Board, "which consists of the top executive officers and twenty-one vice-presidents."[5]

In at least one respect, the AFL-CIO marked a retreat from the CIO. For several years, Eleanor Nelson, president of the United Federal Workers, had sat on the CIO's National Executive Board. But no woman sat on the AFL-CIO's Executive Council.

In terms of the organization of industries employing large numbers of women, the AFL-CIO accomplished little more than the two major federations had before the merger. The only success scored in the South was the organization of the chambermaids, waitresses, housemen, and bellmen in Miami's luxury hotels in the course of a twenty-one-month strike and the expenditure of $2 million. In the Southern textile industry, the results were different. The largest strike in the twenty-four-year history of the Textile Workers Union of America began in 1959, when the Harriet-Henderson mills in North Carolina refused to temper its insistence on the right to veto union requests for arbitration. Despite large numbers of militant pickets, led by women, the plant reopened with scab labor under the protection of the police. After two and a half years marked by violence against the strikers,* and the expenditure of over $15 million, the strike was officially called off by a defeated and demoralized union. Only 90 of the 1,038 striking workers were rehired.[6]

Soon, the old cry began to be heard at AFL-CIO conventions that women were traditionally very difficult to organize and that money spent in attempting to unionize women was money wasted. "Let's face the fact," one male trade unionist said bluntly, "women are, in the main unorganizable. They are more emotional than men and they simply lack the necessary staying power to build effective unions."[7]

But just as these words were being uttered, two unions were demonstrating that the workers who were called "unorganizable" could be successfully organized. One of them was Local (later District) 65 of the Retail, Wholesale & Department Store Union. Beginning life as an organization for Jewish dry goods workers on Manhattan's Lower East Side, Local 65 participated in the great organizing drives of the 1930s and, through mergers with other locals, such as the shoe salesman and an organization of the city's textile workers, had increased its membership to about ten thousand. About 60 percent of the members were women, and while the union was headed by two men—Arthur Osman and David Livingston—a number of women, including Esther Letz, Molly Genser, and Ann Kravitz, occupied positions of leadership in the union.

District 65 began a drive to organize black and Puerto Rican workers employed in the lowest wage brackets. The union fought not only to increase the earnings of these workers, many of whom were women, but

*Boyd Payton, regional director of the TWUA and a Presbyterian elder, was beaten in his hotel room; his assailants were never found. However, Payton was convicted of conspiracy to damage the company's property and sentenced to six to ten years on the testimony of a paid hoodlum secretly employed by the state bureau of investigation (F. Ray Marshall, *Labor in the South* [Cambridge, Mass., 1967] p. 212).

also for an opportunity for them to advance to better positions in the "front office" and not to be confined for the rest of their working lives to jobs as stock and shipping clerks. The union made significant progress, and in the course of the campaign, it received the support of New York's black and Puerto Rican communities.[8] In the course of the campaign, too, Morris Doswell and Cleveland Robinson, two black workers, were appointed organizers of the union. Robinson later became vice-president.

The number of women members increased with the formation of the Distributive, Processing & Office Workers of America, whose driving force was Local 65. The new union took over many of the locals of the Food, Tobacco, Agricultural & Allied Workers and the United Office & Professional Workers when these unions collapsed in the face of continuous government prosecution and CIO and AFL raids. One of the locals of the new union was Local 22 in Winston-Salem, and its tradition of women's leadership was carried on in the Distributive, Processing & Office Workers of America.[9]

The other union that gave the lie to the old cry that women workers could not be organized was Local 1199. Strangely enough, this union, which now has 100,000 members in eighteen states, mostly women, had its origins in a local of Jewish pharmacists and drug clerks, originally organized in 1932 in the Bronx. In 1959, Local 1199, Retail Drug Employees, undertook the monumental task of unionizing workers in the voluntary hospitals of New York City. The majority of these employees called "the most needy and neglected group of workers in New York City,"[10] were black and Puerto Rican women. By April, 1979, an analysis of trade unions and women workers could state: "The most aggressive organizer among women workers is probably District 1199 of the National Union of Health Care and Hospital Employees. Its membership is over 70% female and, unlike other unions that organize women, 1199's membership is mostly third world—Blacks and Hispanics."[11]

In 1850 the New York Commission on Hospital Care described the city's hospitals as "dirty, unventilated, and contaminated with infection" and observed that the nurses, other than those of the religious orders, "were women who could get no other employment and were willing to include menial tasks with nursing." Another report said: "If patients were victims, so, too, were the hospital workers. Looked down upon by their society and their times, they were forced to work in institutions under the most miserable conditions. There were few if any rewards for the long hours and distressing conditions of their work."[12]

In the early hospitals, trained nurses were unknown. Women were hired without any education in the care of the sick and usually without any education at all. The men employed to attend male patients (women did not take care of men) had no better training. The main qualification for a nursing job was strength. Despite this, "the nurse," said an 1872 report of conditions at New York's Bellevue Hospital, "whose wages are $16 a month, seemed kind, willing and obliging."[13]

Nursing training was introduced in 1873, but for many years hospitals staffed their wards with nursing students, thereby saving money, while most graduate nurses went into the more lucrative field of private-duty nursing. As the number of hospitals increased and the technology involved in hospital care expanded during the twentieth century, what was originally a service provided by a physician with a nurse as helper became the work of a large and specialized staff. This, in turn, was broken down into several skilled, professional workers, such as nurses, dieticians, social workers, laboratory and X-ray technicians, physical therapists, and a corps of nonprofessional, unskilled workers who did the cooking, housekeeping, and assorted menial tasks.[14]

Unfortunately, while the demands on hospital workers increased, their low pay and abominable working conditions persisted. The first known attempts to organize hospital workers took place in San Francisco in the spring of 1919. The issues were shorter hours and improved working conditions. That same year, a similar attempt was made in New York. In September, 1919, the hospital attendants, whose occupation was described as "one of the most backward in the ranks of professional labor," were reported to have "decided to organize and to start propaganda showing up the degrading conditions under which they work." The workday was described as twelve hours long, the wages $36 a month, the meals "often unwholesome," and the conditions of work "dangerous, the men being constantly exposed to virulent diseases."[15] Later that same year, in an organizing leaflet, the union stated: "The work of the hospital attendant is as difficult and as tiresome, if not more, than work in any other trade. He takes care of 36 patients, attends to all their needs and does not get a minute of rest during his work. Besides that he is in danger of contracting the various diseases."[16]

In 1933 an effort was made to get the New York State legislature to extend the existing eight-hour law to include thousands of nurses, attendants, and others in mental hospitals (who were working "12 hours a day in stretches of 25 consecutive days, under the most arduous conditions"), and to prevent a proposed reduction in the pay of state employees working in hospitals, under which "wages ranging from $80 to $40 a month . . . would be reduced from 10 to 25 percent. Any such slash as this in wages barely meeting a livable standard seems nothing short of criminal,"[17] the pamphlet continued. The plea fell on deaf ears.

In 1936, after the general strike and labor upsurge in San Francisco, the Building Service Employees Union, AFL, launched the first large union drive in hospitals in that city, organizing the engine room, laundry, and dietary employees, as well as nurses' aides and orderlies in three San Francisco hospitals. Union recognition quickly spread to other hospitals in the Bay Area. "In San Francisco, most of the major hospitals have had union contracts for many years," a survey of the union status in hospitals reported in 1959.[18]

In general, the CIO paid little attention to hospital workers, but individuals working in hospitals, swept up by the enthusiasm engendered by the CIO's unionizing drives, themselves began organizing their coworkers. One such spontaneous organizer was Elliott Godoff, who was later to play a major role in the early organization of hospital workers by 1199. A pharmacist at Brooklyn's Israel Zion Hospital (now the Maimonides Medical Center), Godoff organized maintenance and laundry workers into the Hospital Employees Union, Local 171 of the State, County & Municipal Workers (CIO). In March, 1937, members of the union staged the first hospital sit-in strike in the United States, for union recognition and a 25 percent increase in wages. The police invaded the hospital grounds, broke up the strike, and arrested the strikers. The unionists were charged in court with violating the Penal Law, Section 1810, which referred to safety in hospitals. The strike failed.

In 1938 Godoff left his hospital job to become a full-time hospital union organizer, starting out with Local 128 of the State, County & Municipal Workers. In 1946 Local 128 became Local 444 of the United Public Workers of America. By the late 1940s, Local 444 represented several thousand workers in New York municipal hospitals and in several voluntary hospitals. However, it will be recalled that the United Public Workers was expelled from the CIO during the post–World War II cold-war witch hunts. In 1952, having lost many of its members, the UPWA local merged with Teamsters Local 237, and the drive to organize the municipal hospital workers continued.[19]

A number of unions made overtures in the direction of organizing nurses, but little was achieved. Only a few nurses, mainly those in the Minneapolis–St. Paul area,* belonged to local unions of hospital employees. In 1937 the American Nurses Association assured nurses that they did not need unions and that "in their professional associations, nurses have the instruments best fitted and equipped to improve every phase of their working and professional lives." A year later, the ANA urged its state affiliates to deal with such problems among their members as the situation demanded. The national association was to act as a policymaking and advisory body.

However, under pressure from its members after the California Association had gained a collective bargaining agreement, the ANA did adopt an Economic Security Program in 1946, at the same time assuring its members that collective bargaining was "not to be confused with labor

---

*The union in this area (the Building Service Employees, AFL) also covered hospital service workers.

unionism." Through this program, it informed nurses that it could secure for them "protection and improvement of their economic security—reasonable and satisfactory conditions of employment. . . ." But strikes were to be avoided at all costs. In 1950 the association adopted a no-strike policy on the grounds that nurses' responsibilities included not doing anything that might jeopardize the patients' welfare. By 1950 only two state nurses' associations, in California and Minnesota, had achieved collective bargaining agreements with hospitals.[20]

In 1959 the vast majority of New York City's hospitals—more than eighty-five—fell into the category known as "voluntary." (The other categories are proprietary hospitals, run privately and for profit, and city and state hospitals.) Voluntary hospitals are institutions that, by the nature of their organization and charters, must operate without profit. They are exempt from taxes and from the jurisdiction of minimum-wage laws and other measures designed to provide such worker benefits as disability and unemployment insurance. The average wage at one large voluntary hospital was as low as $21 a week.[21] With one exception, the voluntary hospitals were completely unorganized.

There were several reasons for the slow penetration of trade unionism into the voluntary hospitals. Most of the workers were women and poor—two conditions guaranteed not to attract most union organizers. As David R. Denton observes in his unpublished study "The Union Movement in American Hospitals, 1846–1976":

> Most American trade unions have always been reluctant to become involved in organizing female, minority, and other underprivileged workers, in part because of simple prejudice, but also because workers with such limited employment opportunities have had little upon which to build an effective bargaining position.[22]

By the 1950s the ethnic composition of the nonprofessional staffs in the hospitals had changed from Irish, German, Greek, and Italian immigrants to black and Puerto Rican workers—the former largely as a result of the population shift from the South after World War II.

Hospital workers were not only excluded from the social legislation of the New Deal that provided unemployment insurance, disability benefits, and minimum-wage protection. They were also excluded from the protection of the National Labor Relations Act, which provided collective bargaining rights for other workers, and from most of the state labor laws that recognized the right of workers to belong to unions of their own choosing. There were also laws against strikes of hospital workers. In fact, it was considered unthinkable that a hospital worker might desert his or her "calling" and leave helpless patients to join a picket line. Since the major voluntary hospitals were directed by wealthy trustees with tremendous influence in both the political arena and the media, they constituted an even more formidable foe, many unions believed, than ordinary employers.

With most long-established unions convinced that the workers at the voluntary hospitals were "unorganizable," their conditions continued to deteriorate.[23] Most workers in New York's voluntary hsopitals earned between $32 and $36 for a six-day, forty-eight-hour week. Laboratory technicians with Ph. Ds made $60 a week. There was no job security and there was little chance for advancement. Overtime without any extra pay was common. Many of the workers were so poor that they needed supplementary relief from the Welfare Department to feed, clothe, and house their families. As has been pointed out, they were barred by state law from collective bargaining, were not covered by laws guaranteeing either minimum wages or unemployment compensation, and, even though they worked in hospitals, they themselves had neither Blue Cross nor sick-pay insurance. "We were caring for sick people," Doris Turner, a black dietary worker, recalled, "but we couldn't afford to be sick. If you took time off to be sick, you'd be fired."

And, she added, there were also racism and sexism. She trained a white woman who made more per week than she did, and "they had a dining room that was set aside for the men to eat in and the men got free meals. Women weren't allowed in it." There was also "a little eatery in the hospital where you got better food than the cafeteria. Doctors and nurses, all white, of course, went there, but it was an unwritten law that blacks couldn't."[24]

Some of the philanthropists and businessmen who sat on the hospital boards contributed to the civil rights movement, but their interest in the welfare of poor people stopped at the entrance to the hospitals. Unions, they claimed, were not necessary either for the good of the hospital workers or for the proper administration of the institutions. On the contrary, they would constitute a threat to the functioning of the hospitals, for a strike or walkout would endanger the lives of the patients. They agreed wholeheartedly with Republican Senator Carl Curtis of Nebraska, who opposed the extension of minimum-wage coverage to workers in voluntary hospitals with these words: "I think of these charitable, nonprofit hospitals which seek to hold down their labor costs in order that their funds may reach more needy people.... Many employees serve as a labor of love, as a matter of dedication, yet they must receive and do receive some wages."[25]

On October 13, 1958, a *New York Times* editorial pointed out the important functions and services that the voluntary hospitals provided to the people of New York and urged their generous financial support. Two days later, in a letter to the editor, Leon J. Davis, president of Local 1199, Retail Drug Employees Union, AFL-CIO, after praising the services rendered by the voluntary hospitals, went on to add: "Under the theory that these hospitals are being subsidized by philanthropy, all kinds of reasoning is put forth why the hospitals cannot afford to pay a living wage. It appears that the biggest philanthropists are the workers who can least afford the luxury of subsidizing the hospitals."[26]

Founded in 1932, under the leadership of drug clerk Davis, as the Pharmacist Union of Greater New York, in 1936 it became Local 1199, Retail Drug Employees Union, a part of the Retail, Wholesale & Department Store Union, AFL. By 1958 Local 1199 encompassed six thousand pharmacists, porters, clerks, and other drugstore workers. Although it was relatively small and financially weak, the union had a long record of success in its organizing campaigns and an equally long record of opposition to discrimination. In 1936 it conducted a seven-week strike for the right of black pharmacists to work in Harlem stores, and with the backing of Harlem residents and community leaders, it won the struggle.

The first Local 1199 contract with a voluntary hospital was with the Maimonides Hospital of Brooklyn. However, as indicated above, the workers at Maimonides had been organized since the 1930s and were affiliated with the City Employees Union, Local 237 of the International Brotherhood of Teamsters. When the workers voted to move to Local 1199, Maimonides became the only voluntary hospital in New York City that had recognized the union at the time that the hospital organizing campaign began in 1958.

In the summer of 1958, Local 1199 decided to organize Montefiore Hospital. Montefiore was chosen almost by accident. A black porter at the hospital happened to compare his wages and conditions with those of a relative who worked as a porter in a Bronx pharmacy. The unorganized hospital porter was receiving $36 for a forty-four-hour week; the drugstore porter, who worked in an 1199-unionized pharmacy, was earning $72 for forty hours and, further, was covered by an employer-financed pension plan and health and welfare protection. Shocked by what he had learned, the Montefiore porter assembled a group of his coworkers, who went to 1199 and asked for help in organizing.[27]

Convinced that the time was ripe for organization of workers in the voluntary hospitals, Davis assigned Elliott Godoff, who had come to 1199 from the Teamsters in 1957 and had almost a quarter century of experience in organizing hospital workers, to sign up the Montefiore workers. Theodore Mitchell, a drugstore porter who had become the union's first black organizer, was assigned to work with Godoff.[28]

After several months, six hundred of some eight hundred workers at the hospital had joined the union. Citing average wages of $34 to $38 a week in most classifications, with laboratory technicians getting from $50 to $55, Local 1199 urged the hospital's management to sit down to discuss this and other problems that the workers had raised. Management, however, refused. With the employees of voluntary hospitals excluded from any labor legislation, the hospital had no obligation to negotiate. After petitions, telegrams, and delegations had failed to budge the trustees, the union, in November, 1958, threatened to strike. Facing a walkout of close to 90 percent of its nonprofessional employees, Montefiore agreed to recognize Local 1199 pending a certification election, and in December, 1958, the workers voted overwhelmingly for the union. Shortly thereafter, the details of the contract between Local 1199 and Montefiore Hospital were made public.

The contract covered 883 dietary and maintenance workers, nurses' aides, laundry, X-ray and laboratory technicians, housekeepers, office employees, and registered pharmacists. The pact, ratified unanimously, went into effect as of January 1, 1959, and was to run until July 1, 1961. It provided for across-the-board raises of $30 a month, with regular additional increases of up to $5 a month for every worker, depending on the category. The workweek was set at forty hours, five days a week, with time-and-a-half for overtime work. Sick leave with pay was guaranteed up to ten days a year, and a $10,000 fund was set up to provide disability benefits after a worker's sick leave was exhausted; it was to be jointly administered by the union and hospital management. Job security through a grievance system, with arbitration by an impartial person if the parties disagreed, seniority, maintenance-of-membership, and dues checkoff rounded out the historic contract.[29]

But more important even than the contract provisions was the fact that the union was able to negotiate a contract with the hospital. This had a truly electrifying effect on workers in voluntary hospitals throughout the city.

Davis and his colleagues recognized early on that a crucial factor in the organization of the nonprofessional workers in New York City's voluntary hospitals, the majority of whom were black and Hispanic women, was the need for a working coalition between the union and the civil rights movement. Local 1199 brought good credentials to such a coalition. In 1956 the union had solicited funds from its membership in support of the Montgomery, Alabama, bus boycott. In the process, the union established a friendship with Martin Luther King, Jr., leader of the boycott, which was to continue until King's assassination in 1968. On more than one occasion, King called Local 1199 "my favorite union."

Thus, when the organizational drive in the hospitals moved into high gear in 1959—two years before the first-sit-ins in the South—1199, after consultation with A. Philip Randolph and the Reverend A. J. Muste, was able to arrange for the assignment of Bayard Rustin, whose experience included a combination of activities in both the pacifist and civil rights movements, on a full-time basis to assist the union in establishing roots in the black and Puerto Rican communities as a prerequisite for the organizational effort in the hospitals.[30]

Even as the contract with Montefiore was being negotiated, Local 1199 was organizing workers in other voluntary hospitals all over the city. A reporter who attended a meeting of fifty workers from Lenox Hill Hospital described what took place. A Local 1199 organizer reported that Lenox Hill, with a total of six hundred workers, had two hundred signed up with the union, and he asked how the workers viewed the prospects for getting a majority:

> A Negro lady from the nurses' aides' department spoke up to say: "We're doing pretty good in our department, but a lotta people are afraid—they think they're gonna be fired. And some of the nurses told the girls they shouldn't join a union because then the hospital would be like a 'business.'"
>
> The others hooted, and one voice raised above the rest to say, "It's all right for the nurses to talk, they get plenty and they don't want us to get it."
>
> A lady from the kitchen staff raised her hand and reported that "the ladies in the cafeteria say they get paid mostly by tips and the union can't help them. One of the supervisors said the union can't help us, we'll still have to work no matter what the union does. Well, all I know is when I see those people making $32 a week I'm ready to join *anything*."[31]

On February 4, 1958, Leon Davis announced that the organizing drive had "brought 6,000 new members into Local 1199 in one month."[32] By that time the union had rolled up majorities in four hospitals and claimed to be reaching the same goal in several others. Davis sent letters to the directors of Mount Sinai and Beth David in Manhattan, the Jewish Hospital in Brooklyn, and the Bronx Hospital, announcing that the union had reached a majority there and requesting recognition and contract negotiations. He also announced that the union was approaching majority status at Knickerbocker, Lenox Hill, and Flower–Fifth Avenue Hospitals.[33]

The union demanded elections at seven hospitals. But the trustees, confident that the exemption of voluntary hospitals from collective bargaining legislation made their position impregnable, insisted that "nonprofit hospitals are no place for unionization."[34] When the *New York Times,* in a supportive editorial entitled "Unions for Hospital Workers," asked why hospital workers should be expected to accept wages lower than those offered in private employment, Dr. Henry N. Pratt, director of New York Hospital, replied: "There is no compulsion to work for a hospital," and insisted that "our hospital wages compare favorably with those in some industries."* Leon Davis promptly fired back the question: "Which industries pay as low as voluntary hospitals?"[35] There was no answer.

---

*The *Times* editorial infuriated the trustee of the city's voluntary hospitals, who demanded a meeting with the newspaper's editorial board (interview with District 1199 Executive Secretary Moe Foner).

After fruitless efforts to budge the hospital trustees, Local 1199 held strike votes among the workers at each of seven hospitals. The voting took place on the sidewalk outside each hospital, with workers casting secret ballots in portable voting booths. The results were a pro-strike majority of 2,258 to 95. No date was set for the strike, but the *New York Times* urged the hospital boards and administrators to take the results of the vote seriously.[36]

It was all in vain. Instead of sitting down and talking with the union, hospital officials tried to split the workers by playing on the racial composition of the pro-union workers. "You don't want to strike with all those Negroes and Puerto Ricans, do you?" white kitchen workers at Lenox Hill were asked. One replied: "If they're good enough to eat with and work with, they're good enough to strike with."[37]

On May 8, 1959, 3,500 workers at six voluntary hospitals—nurses' aides, orderlies, porters, elevator operators, kitchen workers, and other "housekeeping" employees, the majority of them women, and 85 to 90 percent of them black or Puerto Rican—walked off their jobs. In defiance of a State Supreme Court order, picket lines were thrown up at Mount Sinai, Beth Israel, Flower–Fifth Avenue, Brooklyn Jewish, Bronx, and Beth David Hospitals. The next day, the workers at Lenox Hill Hospital joined the walkout.

The leaders of 1199 perceived early in the strike that their only chance for success lay in rallying the public behind "*la cruzada*" (the crusade), as the city's Spanish-language newspaper, *El Diario*, referred to the hospital campaign. In spite of the militancy and determination of the strikers, the fact was that they represented services that could be replaced, at least temporarily. The professional and technical workers—to say nothing of the nurses—were not part of the strike, and theirs were the kind of skills that the hospitals would have found it impossible to supplant. This factor, combined with the awesome power of the hospital boards, made it imperative that the union arouse public opinion to demand a settlement. The union used every possible means to bring the pressure of prominent public figures, like Eleanor Roosevelt and Herbert H. Lehman, and the media to compel the hospital managements to yield.*

As the strike continued, hospital officials increased their efforts to intimidate the strikers into quitting the picket line and returning to work—but they failed. Interviewing the pickets during the third week of the strike, A. H. Raskin, then the *New York Times* labor reporter, wrote:

---

*The effectiveness of this campaign to rally public opinion behind the strike was recognized by the prestigious American Public Relations Association when it gave its 1959 award to 1199 Executive Secretary Moe Foner for his role in conducting the union's media and public relations during the strike.

They seem determined to carry on indefinitely. They say they are tired of being "philanthropists" subsidizing the hospitals with their labor. One girl picket said: "Whenever we feel disheartened, we can always take out the stub of our last paycheck and get new heart for picketing." She pulled out her own and showed that it came to $27 in weekly take-home....

Financial hardship has been a part of their life for so long that the prospect of higher pay is less of a goal for many than the pivotal issue of union recognition. They feel for the first time that they "belong"—and this groping for human dignity through group recognition is more important than more cash.[38]

This was particularly true for the women who had to endure sexist as well as racist exploitation. Small wonder that they were the most militant of the strikers. A typical press report read:

Two women strikers at Mount Sinai Hospital were arrested yesterday and charged with disorderly conduct and felonious assault. The two, Paula Colon, 21 years old, of 830 E. 179th Street, The Bronx, and Heida Viera, 23, of 60 East 104th Street, were held in $500 bail for a hearing Friday.

A patrolman, George Ackerman, said he was pushed and kicked by the two women after he had escorted an unidentified woman employee a safe distance past the picket line. A third woman, Irma Colon, sister of Paula, was charged with disorderly conduct and paroled until a hearing June 22.[39]

For forty-six days, these workers stayed out, battling the police and arrests. As it progressed, the strike increasingly reminded New Yorkers of the struggles that had "swept the mass production industries in the early years of the New Deal."[40] Certainly, not since the New Deal had New York City's labor movement become so deeply involved in a workers' struggle.

Decisive in this development was the role played by New York City Central Labor Council President Harry Van Arsdale, who had only recently been elected to head the merged labor organization in the city. Van Arsdale saw the hospital strike as a means of uniting all sections of the city's labor movement behind an effort in behalf of the lowest paid, most exploited workers. With his roots in the building trades section of the labor movement, he was able to persuade even the more conservative union leaders to throw their support behind this crusade.* At his urging, the building trades unions stopped work on new construction at Beth Israel Hospital. Van Arsdale himself was indefatigable during this period. Since the hospital boards would not sit down with the 1199 officials, it was Van Arsdale and his colleagues in the Central Labor Council who met with them for long hours at City Hall, seeking a settlement of the strike. Invariably. after such marathon sessions, he would

---

*New York City unions contributed $134,000 in support of the strike.

make the rounds of the picket lines, driven by an aide on a motor bike, encouraging the strikers. As one song that grew out of the strike put it:

We saw his motor bike
Up and down the strike,
And we felt fine.[41]

When Van Arsdale led seven hundred unionists, many of them labor leaders, to join the pickets at Beth Israel Hospital, the *New York Times* commented with some surprise: "Union chiefs who long ago retired their marching shoes in favor of taxicabs or Cadillacs have taken their place on the picket line beside the Negro and Puerto Rican strikers." Even the most "business-like exponents of business unionism," it noted, were caught up in "an emotional tide unknown since the sit-down days of the Thirties," adding that AFL-CIO President George Meany, too, had wired his full support and urged the strikers to "March on to Victory." Furthermore, the *Times* went on, unions that had traditionally closed their doors to blacks and Puerto Ricans had rallied to the support of the strikers. "Many of these unions," it declared, "are recognizing the need for reassessing their own benighted policies."[42]

Events were to demonstrate that the *Times* was being overoptimistic, but the Transport Workers president, Mike Quill, was correct when he told the strikers, in the course of assuring them that they would have the help of his union "until you win": "This strike represents a revival of the old spirit of unionism that sparked the labor movement and made it strong."[43]

The strike also marked the receding of the anti-Communist influence in the labor movement,* for a number of commentators noted that widespread labor support was being given to Local 1199, a union generally viewed as "so far to the left in its political orientation" as to convince the traditional labor leaders that it was "Communist-led." But as Raskin explained, "What pushed these reservations into the discard was the shock that most outside unionists felt on learning that the bulk of the strikers had been receiving wages of $32 to $38 a week, with no job security, overtime pay or grievance procedure."[44]

What also pushed it "into the discard" was the awareness on the part of both New York and national labor leaders that in the black and Puerto Rican communities the labor movement was more often viewed as an ally than a foe of racism,[45] and that the composition of the strikers made this struggle one in which organized labor might effectively counteract this view. Indeed, the strike marked the early stage of a civil rights–labor alliance, which was to grow in intensity during the next decade. Local

---

*The publication of the Association of Catholic Trade Unionists (ACTU), formerly a leading redbaiting journal, praised Local 1199 for leading the drive against miserable wages in the hospitals.

1199's deliberate efforts to enlist the support of the black and Puerto Rican communities now began to bear fruit. Black and Puerto Rican leaders rallied to the support of the strikers. "Your effort to organize the voluntary hospital workers," Thurgood Marshall, noted NAACP leader and later Supreme Court justice, told Local 1199, "could well be one of the most important organizing campaigns this city has ever seen. It is typical of the old tradition of labor—organizing workers, winning community support, getting done a tough job that needs doing." Congressman and clergyman Adam Clayton Powell personally led members of his congregation to the Mount Sinai Hospital picket line and shared a street meeting in Harlem with Leon Davis. Joseph Overton, president of the New York NAACP, expressed gratitude to Local 1199 for its efforts on behalf of New Yorkers of "Latin American and African descent" and for gaining for them "their just due for their labors."[46]

On June 22, 1959, the bitterly fought forty-six-day strike came to an end.* Although a justice of the New York State Supreme Court told the hospital managements that their refusal to recognize the union was "an echo of the nineteenth century,"[47] he could not budge them. To the end, management refused to grant union recognition, agreeing only to accept impartial grievance machinery and arbitration through outside representatives of the workers' choosing. Management also agreed to include the provision: "There shall be no discrimination against any employee because he joins or remains a member of any union or because he has presented a grievance under the grievance procedure." The agreement also included a minimum wage of $1 an hour, wage increases of $5 a week, a forty-hour week, time-and-a-half for overtime, seniority rules, job grades, and rate changes.

The settlement was known as the "PAC Agreement" because the Permanent Administrative Committee was established under the pact. The PAC was a body of citizens, half of whom represented management and the other half the public. None of them had any connection with the

---

*This was not the only strike of hospital workers in 1959. That same year, after the New York City hospital strike, the American Federation of State, County & Municipal Employees (AFSCME) launched a drive to organize the nonprofessional workers at Chicago's Mount Sinai Hospital. Seventy percent of the workers were women and 80 percent of them black. A strike for union recognition, begun in August, 1959, lasted six months and ended without union recognition but with a wage increase and some improvement in conditions. Unlike the situation in New York, the strikers did not have wide support from either the labor movement or the public. Although the shoe workers, jewelry workers, and packinghouse workers aided the strikers, the Teamsters crossed the picket line throughout the strike to make deliveries. "Volunteers and high unemployment in Chicago at the time because of a concurrent steel strike made it easy for hospitals to replace the workers" (Susan Reverby, "Hospital Organizing in the 1950's: An Interview with Lillian Roberts," *Signs* 1 [Summer 1976]: 1054. See also Robert B. McKersie and Montague Brown, "Nonprofessional Hospital Workers and a Union Organizing Drive," *Quarterly Journal of Economics* 77 [August 1953]: 372–404).

labor movement. Confident that under such an arrangement it could continue to dominate the scene, the Hospital Association agreed to accept the PAC, and thirty-seven hospitals signed the statement agreeing to the establishment of the grievance machinery.[48]

The agreement, Davis told the workers as they voted to accept the settlement, provided only "backdoor recognition" of the union. But, he assured them, "We'll be in the front door before long."[49] However, they had first to confront hospital managements that were determined to negate whatever concessions the strikers had wrung from them. For one thing, they rehired the strikers one by one, in some cases over a period of six or seven weeks. For another, the majority of the hospitals that had signed the statement accepting the machinery for reviewing wages and grievances soon made it clear that they had no intention of abiding by the terms. In September, 1959, the union reported that only in the hospitals in which the workers were organized were the provisions in effect. Even in those hospitals that were living up to the terms of the settlement, "there was no way for the union to resolve anything directly with management."[50]

In February, 1960, the union charged publicly that the hospitals had failed to abide by the terms of the settlement. With the exception of Mount Sinai, Davis told a press conference, the institutions had failed to establish equitable wage schedules. "Grievance procedures, where they exist, are a farce. They are specifically designed to obstruct rather than resolve workers' complaints in a fair and impartial manner."[51]

If the trustees believed that Local 1199 would become so discouraged that it would abandon the hospital field, they soon learned otherwise. Early in 1960 the union changed its name. It was still Local 1199 of the Retail, Wholesale & Department Store Union. But the local now called itself the "Drug & Hospital Union" instead of the "Retail Drug Employees' Union." The change, the press conceded, indicated "a lasting commitment to organize nonprofessional hospital workers."[52]

The May, 1960, issue of the *Drug & Hospital News,* the official publication of the union, carried a headline, addressed to the hospitals, which read: "No-Strike Pledge If You Sign. Sure Strike If You Don't." In the story that followed, Leon Davis indicated that he was sending letters to all the hospitals in which the union had a majority of the workers and that he would demand immediate contract negotiations. The workers would meet within two or three weeks to hear the answers. If the demand was rejected, strike votes would be taken among union members employed in the institutions.

No strike materialized in 1960. Instead, on June 30 a new settlement was signed after nearly three weeks of conferences conducted under the auspices of New York City Mayor Robert F. Wagner. Although once again there was no union recognition, the new peace plan streamlined the grievance machinery established under the 1959 accord. The chief change permitted recourse to mediation as well as arbitration if individual disputes arising out of dismissals or out of the application of hospital rules could not be resolved through direct negotiations. Moreover, to offset union complaints about the composition of the administrative committee—set up in the original plan to review wages, working conditions, and personnel practices annually—the committee was now to consist solely of public members instead of, as previously, six hospital trustees and six public representatives. The union's role in the handling of grievances would continue to be confined to the final stage.[53]

In announcing the terms of the new pact, the union advised its members not to claim "victory."[54] It informed them that Local 1199 was determined to win the fight for union recognition and that only when this was achieved would there be a real victory. But the hospital trustees were equally determined that there would be no union recognition, and they used their political influence, which was considerable, to make certain that the state legislature would not remove the exemption of voluntary hospitals from the state law.

In June, 1962, the management of Beth-El Hospital, in Brooklyn tried to use the device of adopting the "PAC" formula to avert an election, and the nonprofessional workers at the hospital went out on strike. They were later joined by the workers at the Manhattan Eye, Ear and Throat Hospital, who also struck for union recognition and higher wages. Leon Davis was jailed for thirty days for "contempt of court" because he refused to call off the strikes.[55]

Later that month, about fifty black and Puerto Rican community civic and religious leaders met at the offices of A. Philip Randolph, president of the Brotherhood of Sleeping Car Porters, to organize support for the striking hospital workers. The Committee for Justice to Hospital Workers, which emerged from the meeting, pledged to organize wide support in the black and Puerto Rican communities until the hospital workers "get what they are struggling for." Cochaired by Randolph and Joseph Monserrat, national director of the Migration Division of the Puerto Rican Department of Labor, and with Bayard Rustin playing a key organizational role, the committee grew to 235 black and Puerto Rican leaders, including Roy Wilkins, national secretary of the NAACP, James Farmer, head of the Congress of Racial Equality (CORE), Whitney Young, Jr., executive secretary of the National Urban League, James Baldwin, the noted black novelist, the Reverend Martin Luther King, Jr., the outstanding figure in the developing civil rights revolution, and Judge Emilio Nuñez, a leader of the Puerto Rican community.[56] In a letter to the *New York Times* supporting the hospital strike, Randolph, Monserrat, and Baldwin wrote:

> As leaders of the Negro and Puerto Rican communities, we believe that
> the hospital strikes symbolize in most dramatic form the second-class citizen-

ship status and sweatshop wages of all minority group workers in our city.
The hospitals' refusal to agree to such a simple request as a secret ballot
election and the elementary right of union representation is unreasonable,
unjust and cruel. Such refusal constitutes nothing less than a determination
to perpetuate involuntary servitude among the minority group workers at
the bottom of the economic ladder....

We want also to protest strongly the continued persecution of Local 1199
president Leon J. Davis for his valiant leadership in seeking to bring a measure of dignity and self-respect to these terribly victimized workers.[57]

By the "continued persecution" of Davis, the writers were referring to
the fact that he had been ordered back to jail, this time for six months,
for refusing to call off the strike at Beth-El Hospital.

In this struggle, too, Central Labor Council President Harry Van
Arsdale played a decisive role. Under his leadership, the city labor
movement united in condemning the persecution of Davis. Van Arsdale
himself led the top officials of many of the city's largest unions in open
defiance of the court order enjoining the strike and all picketing by
joining one thousand 1199'ers in a mass picketing demonstration at
Beth-El Hospital in Brooklyn.[58]

On July 15, A. Philip Randolph, on behalf of the Committee for
Justice to Hospital Workers, announced a "Prayer Pilgrimage" to be held
a week later and to be followed by a march of blacks and Puerto Ricans to
join the pickets at the Manhattan Eye, Ear and Throat Hospital. At the
same time, Randolph stressed that for the first time, New York's one
million blacks and 700,000 Puerto Ricans were joining forces, united by
a common interest in the hospital strikes. He warned the authorities that
refusal to grant the hospital workers the right to belong to a union of
their own choice had seriously exacerbated racial tensions in the city.
While the state and city governments were doing nothing to provide
legislation to correct this injustice, a group of "self-perpetuating trustees" was insisting on maintaining "archaic and outmoded labor
policies," which were causing "hardships to the patients, the employees,
and the public at large." Since nearly 90 percent of the employees were
black or Puerto Rican, it was hardly surprising that the members of the
black and Puerto Rican communities were convinced that they were the
special target of discrimination. Small wonder, too, that tensions in the
city were "worsening ... and becoming more explosive."[59]

The "explosive" situation became even more tense when the union
threatened eleven more walkouts for higher wages and union recognition by July 31. At this point, Governor Nelson Rockefeller decided to
intervene. He promised to recommend to the legislature the passage of a
law granting collective bargaining recognition to the workers in voluntary hospitals, provided that the union called off the strikes then in
progress and abandoned the threat to call out eleven more hospitals. In
the words of the *New York Times,* Rockefeller promised "for ill-paid

hospital workers collective bargaining rights which workers in most other industries have had for more than a quarter of a century.["][60]

After sixty-two days, on the basis of Rockefeller's assurance, the union called off the strikes at Beth-El and Manhattan Eye, Ear and Throat hospitals. Hailing the settlement as "historic," Martin Luther King, Jr., said that the pledge to bring about legislation assuring collective bargaining rights for voluntary hospital workers "marks a significant breakthrough for these exploited workers and opens the road to union organization, higher living standards, and first-class citizenship for them and their families." However, King always understood that more was involved in the struggle of the hospital workers than union recognition: "It is part and parcel of the larger fight in our community against discrimination and exploitation, against slums, against juvenile delinquency, against drug addiction—against all forms of degradation that result from poverty and human misery. It is a fight for human rights and human dignity."[61]

On July 22, 1962, a cross section of New York's black and white communities heard addresses by twenty-one speakers, including Socialist leader Norman Thomas, Roy Wilkins, David Livingston, Malcolm X, Bayard Rustin, Father George B. Ford, Representative William Fitts Ryan, A. Philip Randolph, and Leon Davis. Martin Luther King, Jr.'s, message came in the form of a telegram, since he was then involved in a great civil rights struggle in the South. "I am fully confident," King wrote, "that your historic organizing crusade will be successful in eliminating poverty wages and winning decent standards in Local 1199 contracts, and I bid you Godspeed as you move upwards and onwards." In his first and only public expression in support of a union, Malcolm X praised 1199 but added a word of warning:

> Don't select anybody to speak for you who is compromising or who is afraid of upsetting the *status quo* or the apple cart of those people who are running City Hall or sitting in Albany or sitting in the White House. As Leon Davis has already proven, you don't get a job done unless you show the man that you're not afraid to go to jail. If you aren't willing to pay that price, then you don't need the rewards or benefits that go along with it.

NAACP Executive Secretary Roy Wilkins struck the same theme when he declared: "Nobody gives you anything. You have to agitate, educate and sometimes you have to bludgeon people into giving you what is rightfully yours. The hospital workers have given New York an inspiration." Leon Davis was hailed as a man who had "given the labor movement a new sense of mission and consecration for the cause of the man lowest down."[62] And the woman, too!

By the beginning of May, 1963, the state legislature had passed and Governor Rockefeller had signed the law extending collective bargaining rights to hospital workers, but limiting its geographical coverage to

New York City. On May 8, over two thousand 1199'ers rallied in Manhattan Center to celebrate their hard-earned victory.

With the way cleared for them to organize into 1199, thousands of hospital workers signed up. One after another, the workers voted in elections for 1199, and the voluntary hospitals recognized the union as the collective bargaining agent for nonmedical employees following the elections. A few weeks after the legislature had amended the state labor law to cover hospital workers, the *New York Times* described Local 1199 as "the nation's largest organization of hospital workers, with contracts covering 8,500 employees at 24 voluntary hospitals."[63]

During the 1959 and 1962 strikes the technical and professional hospital workers, including many social workers, had remained on the job, enabling the hospitals to operate. In 1964 a campaign was launched to bring these staffs into 1199. The drive began with the formation of 1199's Guild of Professional, Technical and Clerical Employees, directed by Jesse Olson, a former pharmacist and one of the 1959 strike leaders. The resulting successful unionization of the technical and professional workers in the voluntary hospitals not only brought them the benefits of union membership but also "immeasurably strengthened the bargaining position of all other workers in the hospitals."[64]

By 1965, Local 1199 had scored a number of important achievements. Hospital union membership had grown from five or six thousand in 1959 to thirty thousand. Wages had more than doubled, and health and medical coverage for workers and their families had been won in union contracts. Workers and their dependents could be assured of hospitalization, surgical benefits, medical care in both their home and the doctor's office, an optical plan, disability pay of two-thirds of their salary up to $75 a week, diagnostic services including X-ray and laboratory work, maternity benefits, and life insurance up to $4,000. They enjoyed paid vacations (including four weeks after ten years' service), sick leave of twelve days a year, and the forty-hour-week (and in a number of contracts, the thirty-five-hour week), with time-and-a-half for overtime. There were three days' funeral leave in the event of death in a worker's immediate family, and, to top it off, two days' matrimonial leave.[65]

On March 23, 1968, three weeks before his assassination, Dr. Martin Luther King, Jr., told an 1199 rally: "You have provided concrete and visible proof that when black and white workers unite in a democratic organization like Local 1199, they can move mountains."[66] One of the "mountains" was moved shortly afterward. In full-page advertisements in leading New York newspapers, Local 1199 announced a "Hospital Crisis" and informed the public:

> We care for the patients, clean the rooms and prepare the food. Yet we cannot support our families on the wages we are paid. Most of us are black or Puerto Rican. But all of us are poor. And we've had enough of that....[67]

On July 1, 1199'ers triumphantly celebrated a new agreement, in which 21,000 workers who had been earning from $70 to $76 a week were to receive an average of $88 a week immediately and $100 a year later. (Most of these workers had been earning $32 a week less than ten years before.) In addition, for the first time the union agreement included a provision for a pension, with employers paying 5 percent of the gross payroll into a pension fund. For the first time, too, a job-training and job-upgrading program was included, under which employers were to pay 1 percent of the gross payroll into a fund, to be administered jointly by the union and management, to subsidize workers while they trained for better jobs.[68]

Local 1199's spectacular 1968 success in winning a $100-per-week minimum for nonprofessional voluntary hospital workers in New York City, climaxing a decade of dramatic progress in its organizing efforts, sent shock waves through the unorganized hospital and health-care communities throughout the nation—both labor and management. In October, 1968, the union announced the formation of the National Organizing Committee of Hospital and Nursing Home Employees, with Coretta Scott King as honorary chairperson. Immediately, Local 1199B was organized to represent the hospital workers in Charleston, South Carolina, and, after a strike which lasted 113 days—during which 1199 and the Southern Christian Leadership Conference united to carry on the struggle—the workers at the Medical College Hospital won a $1.60 pay floor, and wage boosts of 30 to 70 cents an hour. They also won the establishment of a credit union, and a grievance procedure in which the union could represent them.

The national growth of 1199 can be said to have begun in earnest after the Charleston strike. Local 1199E won an election to represent fifteen hundred service employees, mostly black women, at the Johns Hopkins Medical Center in Baltimore. In the contract the workers in the lowest category, who had been earning $1.60 an hour, received a minimum wage of $100 per week plus fringe benefits which included health insurance, an increase in paid holidays, and an employer-financed pension plan.

Other victories, although not so sweeping in scope, soon followed in Philadelphia, where Local 119C won elections, and in Pittsburgh, Durham (N.C.), and Connecticut. At a three-day conference in New York in December, 1969, the National Union of Hospital and Health Care Employees was founded. Headed by Leon Davis, with Elliott Godoff as executive vice-president and Moe Foner as executive secretary, the new union had two women on its Executive Board of seventeen: Doris Turner, secretary, and Mary Ann Moultrie, a vice-president. Including New York-based Local 1199, the national union at its birth had approximately fifty thousand members—more than many international unions in the AFL–CIO.[69]

19
La Huelga

At the AFL-CIO's December, 1961, convention the delegates were addressed by Maria Moreno, a Chicana farm laborer in the citrus groves of Tulare County, California. Moreno described the near-starvation conditions that she and her twelve children faced, of meals made up entirely of boiled greens or soup made from potato peelings, and of a nineteen-year-old son who passed up this pitiful fare so that his younger brothers and sisters could have more.[1]

Maria Moreno was the spokeswoman for the most helpless and deprived labor force in the country—the agricultural workers. Like the hospital workers, they were excluded from nearly all legislation that guarantees the rights of workers and establishes collective bargaining machinery in industry. Farm workers were still treated as if they had no rights under the law. They were excluded from coverage of the Taft-Hartley Labor-Management Relations Act of 1947 and the jurisdiction of the National Labor Relations Board. Like the hospital workers until 1959, they had never been effectively organized.[2]

After the failure of unionizing campaigns in the 1930s, virtually no one in the labor movement thought that farm workers could be organized. Added to their legal disabilities were those caused by the way agricultural labor was recruited and housed. For crops like melons or lettuce, which are highly seasonal, workers were usually not employed directly by the grower at all but by labor contractors, who recruited them through publicly operated offices or simply hired them off the streets of the "skid row" sections of town at dawn and loaded them into trucks or old school buses for the trip to the fields. For longer or more distant jobs, the workers were lodged in camps located on company property, which were inaccessible except with the owner's permission or by trespassing. Organizers could not approach the agricultural workers at work or afterward, since the camp was often their only home. They were usually disfranchised and thus politically powerless, while the growers had great political influence at all levels.

Adding to the powerlessness of the farm workers was the fact that many were Chicanos (Mexican-Americans), the so-called "wetbacks" (Mexican nationals who came to work in the fields illegally, supposedly by swimming across the Rio Grande, although the term applies to anyone who enters illegally from Mexico) *braceros* (Mexican national contract workers imported by the growers legally), and Filipinos. The three nationalities were kept separated and thus disunited.

Table raisins and wine grapes are California's most valuable crops and require the largest number of workers at the peak of the season— 76,650, or 25 percent of the total seasonal and year-round hired labor. Grape production, however, relies in part on comparatively stable, fairly permanent, semiskilled labor, since the workers must prune the vines in the winter, then girdle the trunks of the vines to prevent sap from returning to the roots, thin the "berries" in the spring, strip the leaves, and toss the cane to expose the bunches of grapes—all before the harvest. Moreover, the grapes have to be continually sprayed throughout the growing season. Since the demands of the modern grape industry require a large force for up to nine months of the year, thousands of grape workers make their permanent homes in small towns throughout the San Joaquin, Sacramento, Imperial, and Santa Clara valleys, where the bulk of the grapevines are located.[3]

In late 1964, Congress ended the *bracero* program, but Public Law 414, the McCarran Immigration Act, allowed limited numbers of *braceros* to be used in harvesting as long as they did not depress the prevailing wage pattern. During the summer of 1965, the first harvest after the end of the *bracero* program, the Department of Labor announced that *braceros* would be authorized for hiring by the growers only if the workers in the county for which they were requested were making $1.45 an hour—20 cents more than the prevailing wage in California. Radio stations throughout the agricultural valleys of California announced that $1.45 was the minimum that had to be paid before *braceros* could be used under Public Law 414.

Many farm workers interpreted these radio broadcasts and various newspaper reports to the same effect as meaning that they were now to be paid $1.45 an hour. In actuality, however, there was no minimum wage for farm workers. The minimum applied only to those counties for which *braceros* could be authorized.[4] This misunderstanding provided the catalyst for the Delano strike, which began in September, 1965. When it was over, five years later, unionization had come for farm laborers, the last unorganized industry in the United States.

The Delano strike actually began in Coachella, several hundred miles to the south. In 1960 the Agricultural Workers Organizing Committee (AWOC), AFL-CIO, and the United Packinghouse Workers of America had carried on a large organizing strike among Filipino workers in Coachella. (Filipino crews who lived and worked primarily in the Delano area had gone to Coachella to work before the Delano operations started.) The 1960 strike had been defeated by the refusal of the United States government to remove *braceros*, as required by law, and by the use of hundreds of armed and deputized ranchers to intimidate the strikers.[5]

In September, 1965, the Filipinos struck again, this time for $1.45 an hour, and called in the AWOC to help them. This time they were successful. The unity of the Filipino grape cutters, combined with the labor shortage caused by the changeover to non-*bracero* labor, forced the growers to pay the 20-cent-an-hour raise. While they did not sign a contract, the Filipinos returned to work.[6]

On September 8, 1965, the AWOC led the Filipino workers in a strike against the Delano growers for a contract covering wages of $1.45 an hour and 25 cents a box and improvements in working hours and working conditions. Many Mexican-Americans were crossing the picket lines, so strike leader Larry Itliong went to Cesar Chavez of the National Farm Workers Association (NFWA) and urged him to help take the Mexican-Americans out on strike. While Chavez felt that his NFWA was not prepared for such an extensive strike, he agreed to cooperate. Thousands of leaflets were handed out calling Mexican-American workers to a meeting to vote on a strike. On September 16 the NFWA joined the strike, which quickly spread to thirty-four Delano growers. As it spread, it also made the Spanish word for strike (*huelga*) part of the nation's vocabulary.[7]

The National Farm Workers Association was formed in Fresno in September, 1962, at a convention attended by about three hundred delegates—practically the entire membership. It was organized primarily by Cesar Chavez, but the first person Chavez called upon to work with him in organizing the Mexican-American farm workers into a union was Dolores Huerta. The two had first met in 1955 at a meeting of the Community Service Organization (CSO), a Chicano movement that had been started with the assistance of Saul Alinsky of Chicago, then the best known community organizer in the United States. They were introduced by Fred Ross, who was working with Saul Alinsky. Ross had discovered Chavez working in a lumber mill and brought him into the CSO to organize in the Mexican-American *barrio*, or community.

Chavez was born on an eighty-acre farm near Yuma, Arizona, where his Mexican-American parents tried to scratch out a living from the arid desert earth. The farm failed in the depression, and when Cesar was ten, the family packed everything it owned into a decrepit automobile and headed for California. There they began the circuit familiar to every migrant worker in California, working each crop in its turn: asparagus, grapes, beets, potatoes, beans, and plums. Cesar Chavez worked at picking, hoeing, thinning, leafing, digging, and pruning, until he went to work in a lumber mill. When he went over to work for the CSO, he proved to be an exceptional organizer, establishing some thirty-six branches among Mexican-Americans in California and a few in Arizona.

Dolores Huerta was born into a farm workers' family that had turned to running a small hotel in Stockton. She had earned a teacher's credentials from Stockton College, but instead of teaching she did Catholic charity work and joined the CSO after meeting Ross. She was sent to Sacramento, the state capital, as a full-time lobbyist for the CSO to pressure the legislature for disability insurance, unemployment insurance, and minimum-wage bills for farm workers. Although she was instrumental in securing the passage of bills that extended social insurance coverage and liberalized welfare benefits to farm workers and aliens, Huerta was convinced that legislation "could not solve the real problem" of Mexican-Americans. She was convinced that these workers, mired in poverty, could never escape through the CSO's strategy of pressure-group politics. What they needed was a union.

At approximately the same time, Cesar Chavez was reaching the same conclusion. By 1962 Chavez had presented the CSO with an ambitious program, which, if followed, would lead to the unionization of farm workers. When this program was rejected, he left the organization. The AFL-CIO's AWOC offered Chavez an organizing job, but he insisted on building his own organization and started to work at organizing in the fields. While his wife worked in the fields to support their family of eight children, Chavez organized small meetings of workers sympathetic to the idea of a union of agricultural laborers. Dolores Huerta, who had had some previous experience with the AWOC in Stockton, also left the CSO to join Chavez in organizing a new union.[8]

When Dolores Huerta began organizing, she had six children and was pregnant with a seventh. Barely five feet tall, she looked so frail that many believed she would quickly collapse under the strain. Then, too, she was accused of not taking sufficient care of her children. As she recalled:

> Everybody used to lay these guilt trips on me, about what a bad mother I was, neglecting my children. My own relatives were the hardest, especially when my kids were small. I had six and one on the way when I started—and I was driving around Stockton with all those little babies in the car, the different diaper changes for each one. It's always hard, not just because you're a woman but because it's hard to really make that commitment. It's in your own head. I'm sure my own life was better because of my involvement. I was able to go through a lot of very serious personal problems and survive them because I had something else to think about. Otherwise, I might have gotten engulfed in my difficulties and, I think, I probably would have gone under....[9]

When the National Farm Workers Association was formed, Chavez,

Huerta, and their colleagues deliberately called it an association, not a union. On the basis of their previous experience with ineffective organizers and lost strikes, farm workers, they thought, did not trust unions. In addition, they felt that not calling it a union might deflect grower repression. They hoped that in time the NFWA might become a union, but only after a solid foundation had been laid.[10]

The foundation was laid during the Delano grape strike. Although the only strong areas of the NFWA were Porterville, Earlimart (near Delano), and Delano itself, the members played an important role when the great strike came, while Chavez took over the leadership of the struggle. Picketing began at dawn, when workers moved out into the fields. The pickets carried NFWA banners with the union's symbol—a black Aztec eagle on a red flag, with the single word "HUELGA." At one location, two miles outside of Delano, a dozen young men who made up the pickets were described by a reporter as marching "slowly and with great dignity, while a stout and forceful·young woman addressed the fields across the road in Spanish through a portable loud-hailer."[11]

As the NFWA and AWOC pickets pulled crews out, the growers simply trucked in loads of scab workers from Texas and Mexico. But support for La Causa, as the struggle of the farm workers was being called, was growing. In 1966 a Senate Investigating Committee studying migrant labor came to Delano and held hearings in the local high school. This not only gave striking grape workers a national forum, but it also transformed Senator Robert Kennedy into their national champion. In addition, Bishop Hugh Donahue, speaking for all California's Roman Catholic bishops, voiced to the Senate Committee the Church's support of the right of farm workers to organize. Moreover, unions like the UAW, the Amalgamated Clothing Workers, and the Packinghouse Workers rallied behind the striking grape workers. Ann Draper of the Amalgamated Clothing Workers' union label department was particularly involved in support of the strike. "All through the grape strike she organized support caravans of food and helped guide trade unionists from many unions to the farm-labor strike. At union conventions, including the 1965 AFL-CIO meeting in San Francisco, she allied herself with other farm-labor movement supporters to win backing for the grape strike."[12]

But even with this strong clerical support, and even with the help of large unions, the Student Non-Violent Coordinating Committee (SNCC), and the Congress of Racial Equality (CORE), the strike did not appear to be effective. It was then that Cesar Chavez called for a nationwide consumer boycott, first against Schenley Industries, which owned a large ranch in Delano, then against DiGiorgio products (S & W Foods and Treesweet), then against the 11,000-acre Giumarra vineyards, and finally against all California grapes. Because the farm workers were not covered by federal labor laws such as the Landrum-Griffin Act, they remained unaffected by sections of the legislation that made use of the secondary boycott illegal.

Hundreds of farm workers, some with their wives, were dispatched to urban centers all over the country (and even into Canada) to promote and organize the boycott. Later, Dolores Huerta, who was sent to New York to direct the boycott in that city, told interviewers: "There were no ground rules. I thought, 11 million people in New York, and I have to persuade them to stop buying grapes. Well, I didn't do it alone. When you need people, they come to you. You find a way."[13]

She certainly did. "In New York City, in the dead of winter," wrote a reporter who followed her about, "she led boycott picketlines of farm workers and others and rallied union men and women to the farm workers' cause. Union officials, including some of the most conservative, gasped as she spoke out at meetings in a most forthright manner while rank and filers cheered her words as representative of the deep desires of all of the poor, not just those who toiled in the fields."[14]

The boycott spread the word of La Huelga—as the strike in the grape fields was commonly known—across the nation and into Canada, and for the first time, trade unionists in New York, Cleveland, Toronto, Chicago, Houston, and other cities met farm workers firsthand. They learned about the oppression of those who picked the grapes, lettuce, and other farm products. "A new consciousness of the Chicano in the United States was born as a result of the Huelga—especially in the trade-union movement," notes a reporter who covered the strike.[15]

Meanwhile, a merger of the NFWA and the AWOC had been consummated, under the leadership of Cesar Chavez. Instead of being given the status of a national or international union, the new organization was given the status of an organizing committee under the Executive Council of the AFL-CIO and was called the United Farm Workers Organizing Committee, AFL-CIO. However, it was able to form directly affiliated locals which were given relative autonomy, as in any international union.[16]

"The first table grapes bearing a union label—a fierce black eagle in a white circle on a red flag—were shipped to market this week," read a dispatch from Delano, California, dated May 30, 1970. The grapes came from seven growers who, unable to withstand the effects of the boycott any longer, had signed contracts with the UFWOC. Then on July 29, 1970, twenty-six Delano growers, led by the huge Giumarra Company, filed into the UFWOC's hiring hall to sign the contracts that ended the bitter five-year grape strike. Under the contract negotiated by Dolores Huerta, workers were to receive $1.75 an hour, a raise of 10 cents, plus a 25-cent bonus for each box picked. The following year, the rate would go up to $1.90. In addition, the growers would contribute 10 cents an hour to a health and welfare plan and 2 cents an hour to an economic development fund to be used for low-cost housing and the retraining of workers displaced by automation. The growers agreed not to use certain pesticides, including DDT, in the vineyards and to accept a union hiring hall. The UFWOC announced that the grape strike, six weeks short of its fifth anniversary, had been ended.[17] It was the greatest victory in the history of farm labor organizing.

Although most of farm workers' jobs were not sex-determined, traditionally pruning operations in the grape fields had been limited to men. But in 1971 the men, acting on the union's suggestion, taught their wives the intricacies of pruning. During the 1971–1972 season, the union sent out all workers regardless of sex to all available jobs, including pruning. This ended antiwoman bias in the fields.[18] Women picked, pruned, and packed in the fields, canneries, and sheds, side by side with the men. And they built their union together. When the United Farm Workers (AFL-CIO) was organized in 1974 with Cesar Chavez as president, Dolores Huerta was elected first vice-president, and women were involved in every aspect of union leadership. In 1977 Jessica Govea, who had worked on the UFW staff for eleven years, was elected to the Executive Board. Of the six men on the Executive Board, three were Chicanos, one was Filipino, one was white, and one black.[19]

When Dolores Huerta was asked how it had happened "that in the very culture from which the word '*machismo*' derives, the women have more visible, vocal and real power of decision than women elsewhere," she explained that this had not come about immediately or easily. While "the union had made a conscious effort to involve women, give them every chance for leadership, . . . the men did not always want it." In the beginning, at the first meeting, there were only men. This changed, but "the attitude did not disappear." "There is an undercurrent of discrimination against women in our own organization," she pointed out, "even though Cesar goes out of his way to see that women have leadership positions. Cesar always felt strongly about women in the movement."* Yet "a certain discrimination still exists. Cesar—and other men—treat us differently. Cesar's stricter with the women, he demands more of us. But the more I think of it, the more I am convinced that the women have

---

*In this connection, the recollection of Jessie Lopez de la Cruz is interesting: "One night in 1962 there was a knock at the door and there were three men. One of them was Cesar Chavez. And the next thing I knew, they were sitting around our table talking about a union. I made coffee. Arnold [her husband] had already told me about a union for the farm workers. He was attending their meetings in Fresno, but I didn't. I'd either stay home or stay outside in the car. But then Cesar said, 'The women have to be involved. They're the ones working out in the fields with their husbands. If you can take the women out to the fields, you can certainly take them to meetings.' So I sat up straight and said to myself, '*That's* what I want!'" ("My Life: Jessie Lopez de la Cruz as told to Ellen Cantarow," *Radical America* 12 (November–December, 1978): 34–35.) Later, Jessie Lopez de la Cruz became the first woman organizer working for the union out in the fields. As she explained: "There have been Dolores Huerta and others, but they were in cities organizing the people, and I was the first woman farmworker organizer out in the fields." (*Ibid.*, p. 35.) A full interview with Jessie de la Cruz appears in Ellen Cantarow, *Moving the Mountain: Women Working for Social Change* (New York, 1979).

gotten stronger because he expects so much of us. You could even say it's gotten lopsided ... women are stronger than men." Women, she explained, were especially effective on the picket line, with "more staying power," and the union's nonviolent ideology was influenced by this: "One of the reasons our union *is* non-violent is that we want our women and children involved, and we stay non-violent because of the women and children."[20]

In the process of the union's bitter struggles, the men had abandoned a good deal of their former opposition to women's activity and leadership roles. This emerged clearly during the union's struggle for survival against the combined efforts of the lettuce and grape growers and the Teamsters to destroy the UFW by forcing the workers to accept "sweetheart" contracts. The women led the picketing against the growers who had repudiated the contracts with the UFW and signed with the Teamsters, and the Teamsters attacked their picket lines. In one instance, the women were attacked by men wielding 2 × 4 boards, hoping to provoke a riot, while fifty policemen were waiting with patrol wagons to arrest the women if they fought back. "I was in charge of the line," Dolores Huerta recalled. "We made the men go to the back and placed the women in front. The Teamsters beat our arms but they couldn't provoke the riot they wanted, and we didn't give in. The police stood there, watched us get beaten; the DA wouldn't even let us sign a complaint. But we had gained a lot of respect from our men." "Excluding women," she continued, "protecting them, keeping women at home, that's the middle-class way. Poor people's movements have always had whole families on the line, ready to move at a moment's notice, with more courage, because that's all we had. It's a class, not an ethnic thing."[21]

With its members having little education or training, the UFW had to teach them the professional skills it needed. Indeed, Marie Sabadado, who directed the Robert F. Kennedy Farm Workers Medical Plan, Helen Chavez, Cesar's wife, who headed the Credit Union, and Dolores Huerta, the chief negotiator, all taught themselves.[22] Until Huerta was put in charge of negotiating the first contract, she had never seen a contract. "I talked to labor people, I got scores of contracts and studied them for a week and a half," she explained, "so I knew something when I came to the workers. ... I did all the negotiations myself for about five years. Women should remember this: be resourceful, you can do anything, whether you have experience or not." Women were especially effective as union negotiators, she maintained, because they had "a lot of patience," had "no big ego trips to overcome," and were "more tenacious." "It unnerves the growers to negotiate with us. Cesar always wanted to have an *all-woman* negotiating team."[23]

They were certainly "tenacious." Maximina de la Cruz and her husband, Juan, were born in Mexico around 1910 and entered the United

States on the *bracero* program to pick crops in Texas and New Mexico. In 1960 they moved with their son to the San Joaquin Valley. Both joined the union during the first strike in 1965. In the summer of 1973, while picketing growers who had signed with the Teamsters, Juan de la Cruz was killed by a rifle fired into the picket line from a truck. Maximina was observing the thirty-day mourning period when two interviewers came to her home. She told them of the changes the UFW had made in their lives and said bitterly but firmly:

> We *know* the growers. They want to go back to the old days the way it was before we had a union, when we got a dollar an hour, no toilets or water in the fields, no rest periods, and they could kick you out without any pay for not picking fast enough. A whole family earned less than one union man today. They fought us hard and dirty each time, but we didn't give in. We won't.... I'll be back at work in the fields, but not until the union gets its contracts back. I might have to wait a while but I know people will understand and help us win back our union. I'm proud to be a woman here.[24]

The UFW was then in the midst of its second national boycott, and on December 27, 1974, Dolores Huerta, who had been coordinating the boycott in New York, told an audience of farm workers and AFL-CIO supporters: "Victory is at hand!"[25]

Victory came, but not all at once. The Teamsters were forced to bow out of the agricultural field, and the growers slowly signed new contracts with the UFW. At its third constitutional convention, held in August, 1977, some 850 delegates attended, representing 60,000 farm workers. The UFW then had over seventy contracts, covering about 30,000 workers, almost all of them in California. (In 1975, the year of the previous convention, the union had had about fifteen contracts.) The other 30,000 workers represented by the delegates worked at ranches where the union had won representation elections but the growers had not yet signed contracts. They included the Giumarra Company and other San Joaquin growers.[26]

With an estimated two million farm workers in the country—200,000 in California alone—there was still a great deal to be done. But the UFW had survived and was growing slowly and steadily. Unionization of farm workers was at last permanent, and organization was spreading. The women of La Causa had seen to that.

On September 12, 1970, workers at the Farah Manufacturing Company in San Antonio, Texas, one of the largest manufacturers of men's and boys' pants in the United States, staged a parade to voice their support for the Amalgamated Clothing Workers of America.* At one

---

*A decade earlier women in the Tex-son clothing plant in San Antonio, members of the ILGWU, had won a strike against an attempt to cut their wages. "Mother is on Strike," a film made from TV news footage of the strike, was produced by the ILGWU.

point in the demonstration, Rosa Flores, a Farah worker and, like 85 percent of the workers employed by the company, a Chicana, raised her fist and shouted, *"Viva la huelga!"* ("Long live the strike!"). At that instant, the camera caught her. Her picture was printed on thousands· of posters, and Rosa Flores became known throughout thê country (and even abroad) as the Farah strike "poster girl." The poster itself carried the words: *"Viva La Huelga*—Don't Buy Farah Pants."[27] The boycott was so tremendous in scope that one paper was compelled to comment: "The massive support for the Farah boycott recalls that won by the mostly Chicano farmworkers during the table grape boycott of the 1960's."[28]

Farah operated nine plants in the Southwest and two in Mexico. It was the largest employer in El Paso, Texas, with 14 percent of the labor force—nearly six thousand workers—at its four plants. Ninety-five percent of the nine thousand workers in Farah's nine plants were Chicano, and 85 percent were women.[29]

Willie Farah, president of the company, boasted that he had "a paternalistic attitude" toward his workers and that he provided "a standard wage scale, free medical service, a retirement fund, transportation to work, and inexpensive meals in company cafeterias." "What more could employees want?" he asked.[30]

The workers at Farah told another story. Wages were low, starting at $1.70 an hour, and for many this remained the top wage. The average take-home pay was $69 a week. Raises were based on favoritism, and women with several years on the job were still being paid minimum wages. Those who were willing to date their "Anglo" supervisors were given preferential treatment, while others were subjected to harassment. There was no job security and no grievance procedure. No workers had ever been retired. Instead, to eliminate any retirement benefits, they were fired when they approached the retirement age. Health and safety regulations were practically nonexistent. Because of faulty equipment, accidents were common. Needles often snapped off the sewing machines, piercing the fingers (and at times even the eyes) of the seamstresses. When a woman left the plant to have a baby, she lost her seniority. There was no maternity insurance.[31]

In 1969 the workers began a union drive to affiliate with the Amalgamated Clothing Workers. Rosa Flores, the "poster girl," was one of the first Farah workers in San Antonio to sign a union card and one of the first to wear an organizing-committee button while at work. She told a reporter that she had been employed at Farah for about a year, cutting back pockets on pants. She was earning $1.80 an hour and producing about sixty bundles a day. Then management insisted that she raise her production, assuring her that she would get extra pay if she produced more. She went from sixty to seventy, then to eighty and eighty-five bundles a day, and finally she hit ninety bundles. But there was no pay raise. "That started me to thinking," she said. "I didn't like what I saw in the shop. They treated people like machines. They pushed you around to get you to produce more. And they didn't even pay you for it. So I decided to join the union."[32]

Others reached the same conclusion. As organizing spread through the Farah plants, the company harassed and fired union sympathizers. Despite these tactics, support for the union grew, and in October, 1970, the workers in the cutting department at the Gateway plant in El Paso voted to affiliate with the ACWA. The company refused to recognize the election, and more workers were fired.[33]

The Farah strike began in San Antonio, Texas, on May 3, 1972, when six workers were illegally fired for union activity. Workers walked off the job, and as news of the firing spread, Farah workers in El Paso and Victoria, Texas, and in Juarez, Mexico, joined the strike. In all, three thousand workers went out in protest against the firings. But as Margaret Quesada, one of the strike leaders, pointed out:

> We walked out because of the way we were treated, the low wages, constant speed-up, and few, if any, fringe benefits. After three years, my wages rose only to $1.90 an hour. If we asked for a raise, they would tell us to boost our quota, but either the quota was impossible to meet at the speed we could maintain or there was not enough work to fill the bigger quota.[34]

During the first week of the strike at Farah's El Paso plant, guards used attack dogs to menace the picket lines, and on May 24, 1972, police arrested nearly 125 workers under a state law (later declared unconstitutional) prohibiting mass picketing. Many workers were arrested in the middle of the night and jailed on $400 bond. At one point, there were more than 150 women strikers in the El Paso jail. Determined to maintain cheap labor as El Paso's major resource, the city administration gave its full support to Farah.[35]

Five months later, the union filed an "unfair labor practices" complaint with the National Labor Relations Board, charging that the company:

> Threatened and intimidated, by the use of guard dogs, striking employees who were then engaged in peaceful picketing at the plant.
>
> Discharged workers known to be union supporters and refused to rehire them for their former or equivalent jobs.
>
> Maintained close surveillance of various workers to intimidate them and prevent them from supporting or being sympathetic to the union.
>
> Curtailed all talking among employees during working time.
>
> Threatened the workers with "harsh treatment" if they became active in union affairs.[36]

Skyrocketing unemployment on both sides of the border, but particularly in Juarez, made it easy for Farah to replace strikers from the ranks of the jobless. Newspapers and unions in Juarez did support the strike, and a number of workers at Farah's plant in the Mexican city joined the strikers, but 50 percent unemployment in Mexico made it difficult to fight strikebreaking. At the same time, many workers employed by Farah in the United States were reluctant to join the strike for fear they would lose their jobs permanently and be unable to find other work.[37]

The strikers received $30 a week in strike benefits from the union, but because state laws in Texas and New Mexico denied unemployment compensation to striking workers, the strikers faced increasing financial hardships as the months wore on. Food stamps helped a great deal,* and women who could find work elsewhere did so, but if their new employers discovered that they were Farah strikers, they were usually fired.[38]

The ACWA sent organizers to El Paso, disbursed weekly strike benefits, helped organize a nationwide boycott of Farah pants, conducted classes, and produced and distributed a twenty-one-minute color film, *The People vs. Willie Farah*, in which women strikers told an interviewer, "You're always afraid at Farah." One scene showed "Fortress Farah," with the barbed wire, the high chain-link fences, and the guards with dogs. The Catholic Church endorsed the strike and permitted the strikers to meet in local church buildings. Workers from other plants in El Paso and across the country lent support to the strikers. A Citizens Committee for Justice to Farah Strikers included leading citizens, and the labor division was headed by the United Farm Workers president, Cesar Chavez, and its vice-president, Dolores Huerta.

The boycott was especially effective. The national AFL-CIO and unions like the United Farm Workers, Maritime, Teamsters, Meatcutters, Fur and Leather, District 1199, and the UAW—to mention but a few—came out in support of the boycott. Support also came from textile workers in England and other parts of Europe. The Hong Kong Textile Workers Union sent back unfinished products from Farah's plant. The Swedish labor publication *Bekladnads Folket* featured "Viva La Huelga" on its cover and called on its readers to show their "solidarity by not buying Farah trousers." The boycott became fully international with the endorsement of the International Federation of Textile Workers Unions.[39]

"Adopt a Farah Striker's Family," AFL-CIO President George Meany appealed to all affiliated unions and their locals, urging them to contribute $100 a month for each "adopted" family for the duration of the strike.[40] But for all the support that came from the unions and the

---

*Strikers in Juarez, Mexico, received $30 a week and an extra $45 a month because they could not get food stamps.

public, it was the Chicana women strikers who carried the strike forward
in the face of enormous hardships and difficulties. In fact, the strike was
a pivotal experience for the women involved. They began to do things
they had never imagined it was possible for women to do: walking picket
lines, speaking at meetings and rallies, and traveling across the country
to promote the boycott. Some of the most active strikers formed a group,
which they named Unidad para Siempre ("Unity Forever") to carry the
strike on to victory.

The strike experience changed the lives of many of the women.
During the strike, they made their own decisions and began to question
their old attitudes. "For years I wouldn't do anything without asking my
husband's permission," one striker told a reporter. "I see myself now,
and I think, good grief, married 19 years and having to ask to buy a pair
of underwear! During the strike it started changing. I began to stand up
for myself, and I began to feel that I should be accepted for the person I
am."[41]

In February, 1974, Judge Walter H. Maloney of the NLRB handed
down one of the strongest rebukes in NLRB history, denouncing the
Farah Manufacturing Company for its glaring and repeated violations of
federal labor law. Citing the company's continued abuse of its workers
and its unlawful antiunion practices, Judge Maloney ordered Farah to
reinstate six workers illegally fired and to rehire all those who had gone
on strike in 1972 to protest the firings. Maloney also ordered Farah to
halt immediately the practice of firing or discriminating against employees who presented grievances or engaged in strike activities; discouraging workers from joining the ACWA or any other union; and
harassing or coercing employees from exercising their basic rights under
the labor act.[42]

Up to this point, Farah had refused to sit down in a single negotiating
session with the striking Amalgamated Clothing Workers. His company,
Farah insisted, would never be unionized. But the drop of nearly $20
million in sales since the boycott of Farah products began and the fact
that Farah stock had dropped from $30 to $10 a share, climaxed by the
sharp rebuke from Judge Maloney, prompted Farah to change his mind.
On February 24, 1974, a contract was ratified, and the strike and boycott
of almost twenty-two months ended with full recognition of the union,
wage increases, a health and dental plan, job security, and many other
benefits.[43]

ACWA President Murray H. Finley hailed the victory and said that it
would not only help the cause of social justice for Mexican-Americans
but would also begin to change the political complexion of the Southwest. "This successful struggle," he declared, "now enables Mexican-
Americans in the Southwest to enter the mainstream of American
life—political as well as economic."[44] But in El Paso, the jubilant

Chicanas were telling reporters that the strike experience had already changed their lives. In the words of one woman striker:

> I believe in fighting for our rights, and for women's rights. . . . When I walked out of that company way back then, it was like I had taken a weight off my back. And I began to realize, "Why did I put up with it all these years? Why didn't I try for something else?" Now I want to stay here and help people to help themselves.[45]

The Farah strike and boycott were part of a general uprising of minority women workers, which had also made itself felt among the agricultural workers of Delano, California, and the hospital workers of Charleston, South Carolina. It was seen, too, in the six-month strike of nearly a thousand textile workers employed by the Oneita Knitting Mills at the company's two plants in the small rural towns of Andrews and Lane, South Carolina, in 1973. Some 85 percent of the workers at Oneita were women and 75 percent were black.

Oneita Mills operated in Utica, New York, from 1874 until 1948, when it fled upstate New York, with its unions and relatively high wages, and relocated in the South. In 1948 the Textile Workers Union of America (TWUA) had ten thousand members in Utica, the original home of Oneita. In 1973 it had barely four hundred members.[46]

In the early 1960s the ILGWU won an election, conducted by the NLRB, to represent Oneita's workers and struck for a period of eight months. On the advice of the NLRB, the workers returned to their jobs while negotiations continued. But without a union dues checkoff, the workers stopped paying dues regularly, and the union was broken.[47]

At the time of this strike, the workers were almost exclusively poor whites, with only two blacks—both janitors. But when most of the white workers got jobs elsewhere, Oneita began to hire black workers. This was a tendency throughout the textile industry of South Carolina. The percentage of black workers leaped from about 3 percent in 1960 to nearly 25 percent in 1973. The influx of heavy manufacturing industries had opened up more skilled jobs for white workers, leaving the lower-paying jobs in the textile industry for black workers, and especially black women.[48]

Many of the black families in the part of South Carolina where Oneita's two plants were located earned their living by sharecropping tobacco. At first, wages of $1.60 an hour, or a little more than $3,000 a year, seemed high to black women formerly paid $4 a day for picking tobacco. But Carmela McCutcheon, a strike leader, declared: "Working conditions in the mill are like the nineteenth century."[49]

Workers at Oneita had no seniority, no protection from layoffs, no pensions, no medical benefits, and no safety protection. As McCutcheon pointed out:

In the knitting department, as far as safety is concerned, there's practically none. No safety program is set up. The machines used to knit cloth are machines which require a great deal of oil. When you apply oil to the machine it runs off the machine onto the floor and there's no one to get it up. If you walk by and slip on this oil, you just slip and hurt yourself. There's no fire protection around. There's no fire extinguisher or anything like that. There's no health insurance. . . .

And the lint! After we work an eight-hour shift, when we walk out, we look like a bale of cotton.

They don't have any fans or anything to suck up this lint. It's all around in the air. And as a matter of fact in the sewing department you breathe this lint in your throat. Every so often I use oil just to let it glide on down. They don't have any facilities and they're not trying to do anything about the problem either.[50]

The "Carolina Cotton Mill Song" put it in verse:

Oh, I love to get into my clean bed
With its sheets so fair and white,
And when I am in my clean bed
I sleep through most of the night,

And my dreams are hardly troubled
By the worrying of my mind
For the workers who die of the brown lung
In the mills of Caroline.

Chorus:
Oh, the mystical people,
They think they are wise,
With the smooth on their faces
And stars in their eyes,
But the truths of this system are spoken and sung
By the workers who bear the brown lung.[51]

Since most of the workers were women, many found it necessary to pay for child care, and with weekly wages averaging less than $50, they were hard pressed to make ends meet.[52] Their homes reflected this condition. Many lived in unpainted shacks, heated in the winter by pot-bellied stoves, where families were cramped into two rooms. The homes were inheritances from the days when most of the workers were share-roppers in nearby plantations.[53]

In hiring black women workers, Oneita was confident that it had acquired a docile work force. But already black workers, with the experience of the civil rights struggle behind them, had taken the lead in recent organizing drives in the Carolinas. On November 19, 1971, workers at the two principal Oneita plants voted overwhelmingly in an NLRB-supervised election to be represented by the Textile Workers Union of

America. Then, for the next fourteen months, a committee of Oneita workers met at least once a month to negotiate a contract with several company representatives, although it became clear six months after the talks began that Oneita Mills had no intention of signing a union contract. In September, 1972, Oneita was cited by the NLRB for unfair labor practices for its refusal to bargain in good faith.[54]

On January 15, 1973, a year after the NLRB had certified the TWUA as the winner of representation elections in both plants, nearly a thousand workers failed to report to their machines in Andrews and Lane. About 70 percent of the workers in both plants were on strike, forcing Oneita to cut back to one operational shift.[55]

In 1973 a textile strike in the South was a very difficult undertaking, and the situation of the Oneita strikers was exacerbated by the fact that they were fighting for union recognition. As we have seen, every attempt to organize the Southern textile industry, whether by the Communists, the AFL, the CIO, or the AFL-CIO, had failed. Asked why, in view of the history of past failure, she had gone on strike, Mary Lee Middleton explained: "What can you do for your family on $1.60 per hour? When these kids get sick, I can't afford a doctor. We live on rice and biscuits, and I'd like to give them a piece of meat now and then. This strike is for my babies, and I'm not going back until we win a decent contract."[56]

On February 24, 1973, a "March for Justice" by Oneita strikers and local trade unionists moved down the main street of Andrews to protest the company's unfair labor practices and its refusal to bargain in good faith with the union. One thousand marchers, black and white, women and men, participated. They held aloft banners proclaiming "All the Way with TWUA" and "We will March Until We Get a Contract." The marchers sang:

> The union is behind us,
> We shall not be moved—
> The union is behind us,
> We shall not be moved.
> We're marching for our children,
> We shall not be moved.
> We're marching for our children,
> We shall not be moved.

"Contract, Contract, what we need is a good contract and we won't go back until we get a good contract," scores of black women shouted as they marched. Suddenly, a loud cheer went up from the marchers. Delegations of recently organized unions from Charleston, led by Local 1199B of the Drug and Hospital Workers Union, had arrived to march in support of the Oneita strikers. More cheers rose when TWUA General Secretary-Treasurer William DuChessi announced that the AFL-

CIO had launched a nationwide boycott of all Oneita products under the K-Mart, J. C. Penney, Sears, and Montgomery Ward labels.

Television camera crews from Florence and Charleston, South Carolina, reporters from four area newspapers, and the Associated Press covered the march and the rally at the City Hall. Thousands of South Carolinians and other Americans saw pictures of black women and white women marching together, supported by black and white men.[57]

The Oneita strikers stayed out for six months while the TWUA and the AFL-CIO gave them financial support and promoted the national boycott of Oneita products. Even though it was more difficult to enforce this boycott than it had been to enforce the grape and Farah boycotts, since the Oneita goods were sold under different labels, it did have an effect on the company. But the main factor was the militancy of the black women and the respect they gained from white workers. On June 10, 1973, after the strike had lasted six months, Oneita Knitting Mills signed a contract recognizing the TWUA as the bargaining agent for all of its workers. This was the first union contract won in the South in over a decade. Said one white striker to a reporter: "It was real necessary for the white and black to stick together, but what really made the difference this time was that the black women were so together and so strong. They carried the strike to victory."[58]

One reporter explained the victory somewhat similarly. "Eighty-five percent of the Oneita strikers were women," he wrote, "and 75 percent of the plant employees were black. Black women were the vast majority of the strikers and black women are the angriest, most militant and courageous in the working class because they felt the lash of exploitation and racist abuse even more than black men."[59]

"The Oneita victory has provided a major shot in the arm to our organizing staff," reported *Textile Labor,* the TWUA's official organ. In three months following the Oneita victory, the TWUA had won twenty of its last twenty-one representational elections in the South. However, the workers in these mills had not yet secured a union contract, and as the history of unionism in the South illustrated only too well, winning a contract was the most difficult part of the struggle. For ten years, J. P. Stevens, operating a chain of some sixty mills in the South, had been defying court decisions, several by the Supreme Court, ordering it to bargain with the TWUA. The Supreme Court had even held the high officials of J. P. Stevens in contempt of court—but still no contract.[60]

"A victory against J. P. Stevens," commented a labor reporter, "would be equal to the victory against General Motors in 1937 and open the South to wide-scale unionism. In the light of the new situation in the South, as is so well illustrated in the Oneita victory, it is time to concentrate the kind of strength that it takes to topple Stevens."[61]

On August 31, 1974, following more than a decade of defeats, the

TWUA won its first election over J. P. Stevens in Roanoke Rapids, a North Carolina mill town of fifteen thousand. In 1965, the TWUA had lost a tense election at Roanoke Rapids, and its 1974 victory was hailed by Wilbur Hobby, president of North Carolina's AFL-CIO, as signifying "a new day in Dixie. J. P. Stevens first, the textile industry second, and then the whole South."[62]

A labor reporter conceded the significance of the victory but urged caution: "It is hard to overestimate the significance of Roanoke Rapids, though it should be kept in mind that while a battle was won, the fight continues."[63] What was the explanation for the stunning victory at Roanoke Rapids? This was the question asked by many observers at the time. The most logical and acceptable explanation came from a labor reporter who wrote:

> The work force at Roanoke Rapids, like that at Oneita, South Carolina, changed. The changes generally favored the union.... In 1965, the work force was overwhelmingly white. Since then, many blacks, especially black women, have entered the textile industry and Roanoke Rapids was no exception. As a result, some 40 percent of the voters in Wednesday's election were black, and union officials said that their strong support for the union was a major factor in the TWUA victory.[64]

The failure of Stevens' race-baiting tactics also played an important part in the victory. White mill hands got handbills and circulars picturing white women and black men at union meetings, and Stevens sent its Roanoke Rapids employees an antiunion letter predicting that if the union won, blacks would "dominate and control" the union. But one reporter who visited Roanoke Rapids was so impressed by the unity of black and white mill workers that he predicted that "black and white mill hands no longer will turn on each other." As an example, he pointed to the experience of Crystal Lee Jordan, a white mill woman who played an important role in the organizing drive. "The first union meeting Crystal Lee Jordan went to in Roanoke Rapids," wrote the reporter, "was in a black church, and there were about 10 whites and 70 blacks attending." Crystal Lee Jordan was informed that she was dismissed and that the police were on the way. Here is what happened then:

> Crystal Lee returned to her work table to pick up her purse. Suddenly she pulled out a sheet of cardboard, and with her black marker lettered on it, "UNION." She climbed on her table and slowly began to turn, holding the sign high so the side hemmers, terry hemmers, terry cutters and packers could see what she had written....
> Later that night, Chief Beale would take Crystal Lee to jail, book her on disorderly-conduct charges, and the union organizers would come to bail her out.[65]

The story of Crystal Lee Jordan reached millions in the United States and abroad when it was used as the basis for the film *Norma Rae*, with Sally Field acting in the title role, for which she won an Academy Award as best actress.*

In the victories at Delano, at Farah Manufacturing, and at Oneita, brown and black women played crucial roles. At about the same time, white women were playing a similar role in helping the striking miners in Harlan win the first major United Mine Workers organizing victory in east Kentucky since the 1930s.

In the 1960s, a rank-and-file movement emerged in the UMW to challenge the dictatorship of Tony Boyle. Under Boyle's leadership the union did little organizing, and it made health and safety demands on the companies only when it was forced to do so. In 1969 the Farmington mine in West Virginia blew up, and seventy-eight miners were killed. The mine had been inspected sixteen times before and had been shown to be dangerous, but the coal operators simply asked for more extensions, and the Boyle administration did nothing.

The battle over mine safety became a leading issue in the rank-and-file miners' movement, and women were active in the struggle. They were elected leaders of the Disabled Miners and Widows of Southern West Virginia and also played leading roles in the Black Lung Association. Widows picketed mines in an effort to muster support for the Coal Mine Health and Safety Act.

In 1969 Joseph "Jock" Yablonsky broke with the Boyle machine and ran for president on a reform platform. When Yablonsky, his wife, and his daughter were murdered at the bidding of Boyle and his henchmen, the miners rose up in revolt and a great rank-and-file movement—Miners for Democracy—developed. Arnold Miller, who had spent twenty-six years in the mines and had fought for the movement against black-lung disease, was selected as the Miners for Democracy candidate for president, and he defeated Boyle, ending his dictatorship of the UMW.[66]

Part of the platform on which Miller was elected was to organize the unorganized. In June, 1973, the first evidence of the campaign came when the miners at the Brookside mine in Harlan, Kentucky, voted 113 to 55 to become part of the UMW. The company was owned by the giant Duke Power Company, the nation's sixth-largest utility. The company refused to recognize the union, and a bitter strike began on July 27, 1973, which soon brought back memories of "Bloody Harlan" of the 1930s. Scabs were brought in and protected by state police and deputy

---

*Crystal Lee Jordan is a real-life documentary film written by Gloria Steinem and produced by Joan Shigehawa for KERA-TV Dallas/Fort Worth, in association with *Ms.* magazine. It runs for sixteen minutes.

sheriffs. The 160 men on strike fought back and were beaten, arrested, and jailed.[67]

A few months after the strike began, a headline in the New York Times read: "Coal Miners Started the Strike—Then Their Wives Took Over."[68] The Brookside Women's Club was launched on November 4, 1973, by the wives, mothers, and sisters of the striking miners and the widows and wives of retired miners in the area after an injunction was issued limiting the strikers to two pickets at each mine entrance. "You can't keep scabs out with just two pickets," said the women, so they organized and went out to help the strikers.[69] As the scabs were brought in, the Brookside Women's Club began fighting them. They even beat up a state trooper and threw themselves in front of the scabs' cars so they could not cross the picket lines. Groups of women were arrested for violating the judge's new order that no more than six persons could picket at one time. When they went to jail, they took their children with them so that welfare officials could not place them in foster homes.[70]

The Brookside club women did other things, too. For Thanksgiving they cooked turkeys in a big hall where everybody had Thanksgiving dinner together. They formed study groups, started to issue a newspaper, and also helped other miners in their struggles. "When they vote for the UMW to come into a mine," Gussie Mills, a club member, told a reporter, "we're going there—all of us women. If the men that come out with us ain't got no jobs or anything, why we want to be able to support them to stay out in the strike. We've already been up to Highsplint, Kentucky. We went there to protest that they drawed guns on the men."[71]

The women were quite vocal as to why they were fighting to help their men win the UMW contract. It provided, among other things, for free hospitalization, a $5,000 death benefit to widows of working members, a $2,000 death benefit to widows of pensioners, pensions of $150 a month to members who had worked twenty years in the coal industry and were fifty-five years of age, two weeks' paid vacation, nine paid holidays, and a $120 Christmas bonus. Compared with these benefits, the Southern Labor Union, a "company-oriented" organization, offered "drops in the bucket."[72]

A New York Times reporter who visited the homes of the Brookside Women's Club members was appalled by what she saw. They were "a collection of company-owned shacks" with no indoor plumbing, and with water supplied by an outdoor spigot half a block away. "Recently, the Harlan County Health Department found this water to be 'highly contaminated' with fecal bacteria."[73]

On August 29, 1974, the thirteen-month strike against the Duke Power Company ended in victory. A contract was signed granting the conditions demanded by the miners and, above all, recognition of the

UMW as the sole collective bargaining agent representing the Brookside miners. At long last, the union had come to "Bloody Harlan." The jubilant miners made it clear that along with the $100 a week in strike benefits each worker received from the UMW, "the women have been the main reason that the strikers have been able to hold out so long." Mickey Messer, president of the Brookside local, was convinced that the "women's presence" kept the battle more peaceful, even though one striker was killed and several wounded. "After they [the women] beat up a few scabs, it kind of made them [the scabs] ashamed to come back."[74] "Although women on labor picket lines are nothing new," went one press report, "this is believed to be the first time in coal union history that women are so actively involved in a strike."[75] In the light of the role played by miners' wives in coal union strikes during the era of Mother Jones and the National Miners' Union, one may question the accuracy of this judgment, although it is certainly true that rarely had women in coal acted so effectively as a collective group.* In one respect, however, the activities of the women in the Brookside mine strike did mark a real "first." For the first time, such activities were fully revealed on film and brought to audiences around the world. The film is Barbara Kopple's *Harlan County, USA,* which won an Academy Award for the best documentary in 1976.†[76]

Harlan County, USA certainly makes it clear that without the women the strike would never have been won. The film intertwines the history of the miners' past struggles with the 1973 strike. The older men and women share their experiences of the 1930s with the miners of the 1970s. Florence Reece, the miner's wife during the 1931 strike in Harlan, is shown during one of her many visits to Brookside from her present home in Tennessee. In a quavering voice, Reece sings her song, the most popular of all miners' songs, "Which Side Are You On?"[77]

"It makes my blood boil," a woman veteran of the Harlan County thugs of the 1930s told an interviewer the morning after the "gun thugs" had shot up the home of the president of the local miners' union. And she ended furiously: "If I get shot, I get shot. They can't shoot the union out of me." Little wonder that the audience at the New York Film Festival, where *Harlan County, USA* was first shown, stood up and cheered.

---

*Seventy-year-old Minnie Lunsford, senior member of the Brookside Women's Club, recalled the days of "Bloody Harlan" during the 1930s and made the point that women did not picket then. "Women back in those days," she said, "wanted what we want—the benefits, the hospital card, the vacation pay—but they just weren't as glib. And back in those days, women just couldn't get out of the house" (*New York Times,* May 15, 1974). But contemporary reports indicate that the miners' wives did picket.

†In one interview, Kopple indicated that part of the film showing the opposition of the husbands to the women's participation was edited out. "The women really had to force their way into participating in the strike," said one of the women leaders in this scene (*Guardian,* Nov. 3, 1976).

As "The Brookside Strike Which Side Are You On?," written to the tune of Florence Reece's 1931 song* so tersely but effectively put it:

The miners down at Brookside
Are a courageous bunch of men.
And with their women by their sides,
Each has the strength of ten.[78]

Six years after the Duke Power Company signed the first union contract in Harlan, Kentucky, a similar breakthrough occurred in a Southern state. On October 19, 1980, workers at ten J. P. Stevens & Co. plants overwhelmingly approved a contract with the nation's second-largest textile firm and its first-largest anti-union company, marking a milestone in seventeen years of efforts to organize the Southern-based industry. About 700 workers from seven plants met in the auditorium of Roanoke Rapids Junior–Senior High School and leaped to their feet and yelled their approval when Clyde E. Bush, international representative of the Amalgamated Clothing and Textile Workers Union, asked if they approved the two-and-a-half-year pact. Later that evening, the three other unionized Stevens' plants in High Point, North Carolina, Boylston, Alabama, and Allendale, South Carolina, also voted enthusiastically in favor of accepting the new agreement. The contract gave workers a 19 percent retroactive pay increase already granted at nonunion Stevens plants, but as Ben Ketter, a thirty-year Stevens employee, noted: "It is a breakthrough for the South."

Interviewed in Burlington, North Carolina, where she was making a public appearance for the Amalgamated Clothing and Textile Workers Union that hired her to tell her story and enlist support for the union-led boycott of Stevens products, Crystal Lee Sutton, the real-life "Norma Rae," declared: "I sort of feel like running out in the street and shouting. I've waited a long time for this day. Today makes it all worthwhile."[79]

*For the story of the National Miners' Union and the events that led to the writing of Florence Reece's song, see Philip S. Foner, *Women and the American Labor Movement: From World War I to the Present* (New York, 1980), pp. 244–55.

20

The Coalition of
Labor Union Women

ORIGINALLY, between 600 and 800 delegates were expected in Chicago for the founding convention of the Coalition of Labor Union Women. A few months before the gathering, however, registration reached 1,500, and by conference time, the attendance had swelled to over 3,200 women. Participants came either as delegates from their unions or as individual trade union members. Over fifty unions from more than forty states were represented. Among the union signs that decorated the conference hall were those of the UE, IUE, UAW, Teamsters, Retail Clerks, ILGWU, ACWA, Meat Cutters, AFT, IAM, Department Store Employees, CWA, Flight Attendants, Grain Millers, AFSCME, AFTRA, Hotel & Restaurant Employees, SEIU, Farm Workers, Steelworkers, District 1199, District 65, and the Newspaper Guild. More than fifty representatives of UE locals participated in the conference, in addition to others who were members of UE organizing committees at unorganized shops in the Midwest. Thirty delegates came from the Newspaper Guild. Amalgamated Clothing Workers' women from every section of the union attended, 160 strong. "They reflected," said Joyce D. Miller, leader of the ACWA delegation, "the make-up of a larger coalition. All ages, cultures, races and geographical areas were represented."[1]

Most of the delegates were new to this type of event. When the delegates were asked at the opening plenary session how many were attending such a conference for the first time, well over half raised their hands. Most of the participants were white, but 20 to 25 percent were black and a few were Asian, Chicana, or other minority women.[2]

Opening the convention, Addie Wyatt hailed the huge turnout and said, "People ask, 'Why are union women getting it together?' I say, 'Women everywhere else are doing it. It's time we did it.'" The slogan "You've come a long way baby," she declared, "isn't quite true," and she cited statistics showing that the average woman who worked full-time and year-round made two-thirds of what the average man made. Wyatt called this "a crime, and a violent one." "We've given so much and settled for so little," she told the opening session as she recounted the inequalities that characterized the life of the workingwoman.[3]

The UAW's Olga Madar followed and expressed solidarity with others in the women's movement. Union women, she said, "were the first women's libbers," but after their successful fights for equal pay, for single, unified seniority lists, and for other forms of equality, they had not moved into other areas. "The women's movement gave an impetus to our moving ahead," she declared, and she praised the National Women's Political Caucus, the Women's Equity Action League, and the National Organization for Women. Trade union women, she said, did not agree with everything these organizations had done. When the women's movement started, many union women "had the same cultural hangups as the men over women having an equal role. But the women's movement has been helpful in making union women and blue-collar wives aware that there was blatant discrimination against women just because they were females."

"One result of this meeting," Madar continued, "is that fewer and fewer union women will be saying 'We are not women's libbers.' By coming here, they have proved that they are." She was confident that the other elements in the women's movement would be "delighted" to have the trade union women join in the fight, bringing with them the organizing skills they had acquired in their unions.[4]

No one present disputed Madar's enthusiastic praise of the women's liberation movement. Nor was there any debate at the convention over such issues associated with that movement as birth control, abortion, marriage, and the family. But a conflict did arise early in the conference over whether the coalition should support the United Farm Workers in its dispute with the Teamsters. The National Planning Committee tried to forestall a public fight at the conference by including in the Proposed Structure and Guidelines, Item 14, which read: "National CLUW and area CLUW chapters shall not be involved in issues or activities which a union involved identifies as related to a jurisdictional dispute." This rule would have kept off the floor all resolutions dealing with the struggles of the United Farm Workers, but the delegates, with almost complete unanimity, refused to accept this position. Teamster rank-and-filers rose and voiced solidarity with the Farm Workers' struggle, asking, along with many others, that CLUW go on record as being in support of the Farm Workers.

At a plenary session, the delegates voted to suspend the rules of the conference to allow themselves to deal with this proposal. Then, by an overwhelming majority, they voted to reject Item 14 in its entirety. The announcement of the vote was greeted by cries of "Viva la huelga!" However, support for the United Farm Workers in the form of an official resolution never materialized. While resolutions in support of the union emerged from almost every workshop, they were left to the incoming Executive Board to deal with, on the ground that there was "not enough time."[5]

"We have a message for George Meany. We have a message for Leonard Woodcock. We have a message for Frank Fitzsimmons. You can tell them we didn't come here to swap recipes."[6] These words of Myra Wolfgang, a vice-president of the Hotel & Restaurant Employees Union, typified the mood of the convention.* The delegates had come primarily to adopt a Statement of Purpose and set up an organization structure. Hammered out in long discussions, the Statement of Purpose outlined four basic areas of special concern:

1. *Organizing Unorganized Women:* "The Coalition of Labor Union Women seeks to promote unionism and to encourage unions to be more aggressive in their efforts to bring unorganized women under collective bargaining agreements, particularly in the areas where there are large numbers of unorganized and/or minority women." It would do this not on its own, but "within our intra, inter, and emerging union structures. . . ."

2. *Affirmative Action in the Workplace:* "Employers continue to profit by dividing workers on sexual, racial and age lines. . . . The power of unions must increasingly be brought to bear, through the process of collective bargaining, to correct these inequities. . . . We seek to educate and inspire our union brothers to help achieve affirmative action in the work place."

3. *Political Action and Legislation:* "It is imperative that union women through action programs of the Coalition, become more active participants in the political and legislative process of our unions. . . ."

4. *Participation of Women Within Their Unions:* "The Coalition seeks to inspire and educate union women to insure and strengthen our participation, to encourage our leadership and our movement in all areas. The Coalition supports the formation of women's committees and women's caucuses within labor unions at all levels, whenever necessary. Additionally, the Coalition will encourage democratic procedures in all unions."

Among other objectives to which the delegates committed themselves were urging unions to take positive action against sex discrimination in pay, hiring, job classifications, and promotion; support for legislation

---

*"We Didn't Come Here to Swap Recipes" was also the title of a documentary film of CLUW's founding convention produced by Community Access Television Productions (CATV), a nonprofit educational group based in Santa Cruz, California. A highlight of the film is the joint appearance of a member of the United Farm Workers, Josephine Flores, and Teamster Union member Clara Day, a black woman, espressing their determination not to allow themselves or the convention to be split, and the tremendous support given them by the convention.

providing adequate child-care facilities, a "livable" minimum wage, improved maternity and pension benefits, improved health and safety laws, and better enforcement of these laws; working for ratification of the ERA; and support for legislation to provide for both sexes the protection of statutes originally aimed at protecting women. Such protections included maximum-hours legislation, breaks in the workday, and the seating of workers on the job.[7] Thus, in calling for approval of the ERA, then before the state legislatures for ratification, the conference urged that it be supplemented by "an extension of truly protective legislation for all workers." This took into consideration the concern expressed by some women attending the conference that enactment of the ERA would result in elimination of still-needed protective legislation.

In addition, the conference declared: "We recognize that our struggle goes beyond the borders of this nation and seek to line up with our working brothers and sisters throughout the world through concrete action of international workers' solidarity."[8]

The Statement of Purpose did not mention family planning, birth control, or abortion. What the statement did do was raise the need for making the trade unions instruments to fight for the rights of all workingwomen by creating a base for organizing unorganized women, by attacking the special problems faced by women who worked, by involving women more fully in policymaking positions, and by generally improving the position of workingwomen through their unions and through political action and legislation.

The officers elected were Olga Madar, president; Addie Wyatt, national vice-president; Joyce Miller, East Coast vice-president; Clara Day of the Teamsters, Midwest vice-president; Dana Dunham of the CWA, Southern vice-president; Elinor Glenn, West Coast vice-president; Linda Tarr-Whelan of AFSCME, secretary; and Gloria Johnson of IUE, treasurer. A National Coordinating Committee was chosen, consisting of representatives named by participating national unions. Each major international union was to be represented by one to four representatives on the NCC. A Steering Committee of seventeen was to be elected by the national organization.

Membership in CLUW, based upon individual application, was open to all current and retired members of bona fide national or international unions engaged in collective bargaining who agreed with the Statement of Purpose, "*whether or not the particular local has recognition as a collective bargaining agent.*"[9]

In closing the convention, Addie Wyatt told the delegates that the gathering had crowded into two days a program "to right the wrongs of centuries." Women workers in the United States, she continued, were determined to join with the rest of the labor movement to build the unions, to organize the unorganized, especially women, to stop big business from dividing workers on racial and sexual lines, and to fight for full employment, for adequate child-care, for maternity and pension benefits, and for equal work. Then she reiterated one of the conference's main themes: "We *are* the unions. We are telling our unions that we are ready, available and capable to fight the fight. I still believe the union is the most viable and available channel through which we can win our goals."[10]

The *New York Times* correspondent reported from Chicago "a great deal of dissatisfaction expressed by many rank-and-filers" over what they described as "heavy-handed tactics by conference organizers in running the plenary and workshop sessions."[11] On the other hand, Lily Dias of UE Local 204 in Taunton, Massachusetts, summed up the view of most of the delegates when she called the gathering "fantastic." "Think what this will mean for the future of the working woman, or the young people coming up," she told a reporter. "This will go down in history and I hope I will live long enough to see what effects it will have."[12]

In general, the reaction to the founding convention of the CLUW was an amalgam of these viewpoints. "Welcome CLUW," editorialized the *Guardian*, "one of the most important new organizations to be formed in a long time." Millions of workingwomen were being increasingly pressed by economic necessity and miserable working conditions, it went on. They were seeking new ways to fight, "and CLUW can help them." At the same time, the CLUW could have an important influence on male workers, in "helping to overcome sexist attitudes and other manifestations of male supremacy ideology." The CLUW could also bring a "crucial and decisive new element to the women's movement. While nearly all the demands put forward by the largely middle-class women's movement have directly benefited working women, still, the movement until now has lacked a sector of women rooted in the labor movement." Nevertheless, the *Guardian* viewed CLUW as dominated by a "reformist leadership" and warned against allowing it to become "a bureaucratic top-down organization." In order for it to become a mass-based fighting organization for women," it was essential that rank-and-file women, particularly women of the oppressed nationalities, "transform CLUW by their active participation in it."[13]

Georgia Henning, a member of the Commission on Women's Equality of the Communist Party, who attended the Chicago conference as a delegate from the Social Service Employees Union, Local 371 of AFSCME in New York, felt that despite "many problems at the convention, not the least of which was the bureaucratic handling of many questions by the leadership, the women who founded CLUW came through a major test with flying colors." However, if CLUW was to become an important part of the struggle for democratic rights and rank-and-file control of the unions, "then the voice of women in the shops must grow, must be well-organized and must clearly lead the struggle."[14]

Most commentators pointed out that CLUW was building on the

basis of a long tradition of women's labor struggles. CLUW President Olga Madar told the 1974 convention of the Amalgamated Clothing Workers that CLUW had emerged in part to revive "the activist example set by early female unionists who were the nation's 'first feminists.'"[15] Yet it was also clear that the coalition was a new type of organization. Despite the view of some observers that the coalition and the WTUL were similar, and despite the fact that some of the objectives of the two organizations were the same, the coalition was not a latter-day version of the WTUL.[16] The middle-class and upper-class women who were so important in the league were not eligible to become members of CLUW, and the league, as it developed, had paid less attention to unionizing activities and more to those in the political arena. Nor was CLUW a women's auxiliary, but rather an organization of women workers and trade unionists. And it was not the traditional women's committee. Essentially, CLUW was the first interunion organization formed by trade union women on their own initiative to push for their special needs within the labor movement and in society as a whole. It brought the women's movement into the trade unions, emphasizing in its "Statement of Purpose" that women, as women, shared a need to organize and fight for their collective interests.

Three crucial questions remained to be answered after CLUW's founding convention. Would the platform of the new organization be carried into effect or remain on paper? Would the trade unions give more than lip service to the platform? And would the rank and file be able to exercise any significant influence on the organization's activities and leadership? In the months following the convention, women unionists in many areas held meetings to form local chapters. By December, 1974, President Madar reported that "the acceptance of CLUW has been astounding." There were twenty-four local CLUW chapters across the country, in Seattle, San Francisco, Sacramento, Boston, Minneapolis, New York, Cleveland, Cincinnati, Houston, Washington, D.C., Atlanta, and elsewhere. Madar also reported that there were 2,500 dues-paying members of CLUW.[17]

In view of the large turnout at the founding convention, these membership figures hardly seemed "astounding." Indeed, charges were already being heard that membership growth was being curtailed by the unduly complicated certification procedures for new chapters, which required three meetings before a charter could be granted. One commentator wrote that while the CLUW leadership wished to see the organization grow, "they did not want to go as fast as many rank-and-file women union members do."[18]

The failure of the membership to grow rapidly was also attributed to bitter and intense fighting in a number of chapters between the extreme left and the moderate rank-and-file, coupled with the determination of the CLUW leadership to prevent the organization from being taken over by the leftists and used as a weapon against the existing trade union leadership.[19] But others emphasized that a major problem facing CLUW was that its formation coincided with the deepening of the 1974–1975 recession. In the *Congressional Record* of March 13, 1975, Senator Harrison Williams (Democrat-New Jersey) noted that "American working women . . . are among the hardest hit by the recessionary impact." As of February of that year, he noted, there were 29,700,000 workingwomen in the country. But "in the third quarter of last year, just five short months ago, there were 30,500,000 working women—a decrease of 800,000 women in the workforce. And women are continuing to lose jobs at an alarming rate. During the month of January alone, the number of working women dropped by 213,000." In February, 1975, the unemployment rate for white women was 7.6 percent; in February, 1974, it had been 4.7 percent. The new unemployment rate for black and other minority women was a staggering 10.9 percent, up from 7.9 percent in February, 1974.[20]

Women workers began to see their recently achieved employment gains in traditionally male occupations either reduced or eliminated by the recession. Early in 1974, seven hundred women were hired at the Ford Brook plant in Cleveland as part of the Ford Company's "affirmative action" program to compensate for prior discrimination against women in the plants. But as the recession hit the auto industry, six hundred of the seven hundred women hired at the plant, having little seniority, were laid off. In 1974 General Motors laid off nearly all of the 500 women who worked on the assembly lines at GM's Fremont, California, plant, and all 350 women hired since 1970 at its Linden, New Jersey, plant.[21] The effect of the sinking economy on women and minorities was summed up by the U.S. Commission on Civil Rights in its booklet *Last Hired, First Fired: Layoffs and Civil Rights:*

> The recent recession has had a critical impact on minorities and women. Many had only recently obtained their first promising jobs. Increasing numbers had begun to penetrate employment areas of great importance in our society, such as state and local government. Because they have not had time to acquire adequate seniority, however, minority members and women have been affected disproportionately by the personnel cutbacks occasioned by this recession, and much of their limited progress has thereby been obliterated.[22]

Despite its limited membership during its first year of existence, the CLUW and its various chapters were able to deal with a number of key issues confronting women workers. CLUW chapters organized workshops, seminars, and classes on labor education to encourage more women to become active in unions. In New York City, CLUW members aided organizing drives at the Putnam and Macmillan publishing houses and supported the strikers at Harper & Row and Macmillan. By endorsing the Mondale-Brademas bill, the CLUW contributed to the movement for a network of federally funded day care centers. The CLUW endorsed and participated in the May 17, 1975, March Against Racism in Boston, giving concrete aid to the NAACP's efforts to desegregate the Boston schools. The CLUW and its chapters also backed the Farm Workers' boycott of lettuce and Gallo wines.[23]

During this first year CLUW's National Coordinating Committee placed special emphasis on encouraging the appointment of more women, particularly minority women, to leadership and policymaking positions within local, state, national, and international union structures. Union women were urged to attend their local union meetings, to participate in their local union programs, to run for elective office, and to serve as delegates to policymaking conferences and conventions.[24]

But central to the CLUW's activity during the first year of its existence was the fight against unemployment. At the National Coordinating Committee meeting held in St. Louis on January 18–19, 1975, more than a hundred women unionists from over fifty-five international AFL-CIO unions, the UAW, and the Teamsters' Union adopted an action program to deal with the economic crisis. CLUW chapters were urged to participate in observances on March 8—International Women's Day—aimed at combating unemployment and stressing the need to cope with the "faltering economy." Other activities approved at the meeting included the CLUW's sponsorship of public hearings to be held during the last week of April in cities with high unemployment, to which legislators would be invited and at which the women could testify to the effects of the economic crisis on them and their families; mass lobbying efforts in Washington in mid-June, in solidarity with unions whose members were especially hard hit by layoffs, to influence legislators, the government, and private corporations to accept responsibility for a full-employment program; and support for the actions and proposals of the National Coalition Against Inflation and Unemployment.

Specific demands raised with respect to the need for jobs and relief were (1) a shorter work week without a cut in pay; (2) cost-of-living increases; (3) supplementary unemployment benefits, financed by employers, for the duration of layoffs; (4) no overtime during periods of mass unemployment; (5) no speedup or job harassment; (6) extension of unemployment insurance at two-thirds of gross pay, and continuation of food stamps for all who needed them at no increase in cost; (7) enforcement of the Full Employment Act of 1946 and other measures aimed at creating full employment for all, and extension of the Emergency Public Service Act to provide more public works jobs for the unemployed at union wages and under union conditions; and (8) opposition to budget cuts in programs for the people's needs and a cut in military spending in order to pay for these programs.

The St. Louis meeting also passed resolutions in favor of the

Kennedy-Corman National Health Bill; of legislation making January 15, the birthday of Martin Luther King, Jr., a national holiday; and of a proposed law against involuntary sterilization. Also passed in St. Louis was a resolution condemning the junta terror and imprisonment of women in Chile and demanding freedom for all political prisoners. But the main emphasis was on the need for jobs and relief.[25]

Nor did these resolutions remain on paper. On March 8, CLUW chapters across the nation took to the streets to conduct demonstrations highlighting CLUW's demand for "Jobs for All." CLUW also played a major role in the massive trade union demonstration in Washington, D.C., on April 26, which saw 65,000 workers rally to demand jobs. CLUW's participation contributed to the pressure that led the Industrial Union Department of the AFL-CIO to sponsor the rally.[26]

On May 23, 1975, in response to the call by National CLUW for local actions to fight the rising joblessness among the nation's 34 million workingwomen, the New York Coalition of Labor Union Women held a seven-hour hearing, led by Eleanor Tilson, New York CLUW president and vice-president of the United Storeworkers Union. "CLUW and the labor movement demand that people be put back to work," she said in her opening statement. "'Jobs Now' is our major demand," if not by private industry, then through Congressional action to create jobs. She and other speakers supporting CLUW's call for "full employment" emphasized the importance of HR 50, the "Equal Opportunity and Full Employment Act of 1975," sponsored by Representative Augustus Hawkins (Democrat-California). It declared that full employment was the responsibility of the government.

The difficult condition of workers in key New York industries where women were in the vast majority—men's and women's apparel, communications (telephone operators), and social services—were discussed. Joyce Miller described the "brutal impact" of the recession on employment in the apparel industry. She pointed out that one of the most important industries in the country, with more than a million workers, 80 percent of them women, had a higher rate of unemployment than any other industry. Between March, 1974, and March, 1975, 41,400 jobs had been lost in New York City alone. The jobless, she continued, averaged $65 a week on unemployment insurance.

> They are losing their homes and their cars, are forced to double up with others; and seek food stamps. When this insurance runs out, they will have to seek welfare. The ACWA, which was the first union to establish day care centers for its members, had been forced to shut the centers down when factories close.

In communications, Thelma James, a black telephone operator, testified, women were working four days a week. James, a mother and the head of a family, declared: "I am poor, I am a diligent worker. But I suffer from emphysema and there is no sick leave. My children wear second-hand clothing." She called for "jobs and dignity" for these workers and urged the CLUW to support their cause.

"I hope you'll continue the fight for full employment," declared Kathryn Graze, an unemployed member of the United Pulp and Paperworkers Union. She was six months pregnant, she told the panel, and had been laid off at Christmas. Her husband had been laid off in March. Both were on unemployment insurance. She had neither maternity nor pregnancy benefits and was no longer covered under the union's hospitalization plan.[27]

On November 15, 1975, Los Angeles CLUW conducted a panel discussion on "Affirmative Action: Hiring, Layoffs, Seniority and Dismissal." What made this discussion noteworthy was the inclusion of "seniority" among the factors involved in unemployment among workingwomen. To the worker in the factory, seniority was and is crucial. A worker's standing on the seniority roster, which is determined by the date of hire, decides whether, when layoffs come, he or she will be demoted or perhaps let go altogether. It also determines the prospects for advancement into more-skilled and higher-paying jobs. Naturally, a worker can be expected to defend seniority fiercely against any attempt to interfere with it. Still, it is difficult to ignore the fact that seniority has been used to promote discrimination, on the basis of both color and sex, since white male workers, having obtained their positions in most cases before both blacks and women, have the most jobs with seniority status.[28]

Although they conceded that the hard-won seniority rights had to be maintained as a defense against employers' arbitrariness and victimization, the progressive forces in the labor movement during the recession of 1974–1975 demanded that seniority must not be allowed to become a hard-and-fast rule, and that there should be some modification of it so that layoffs would not hit first and hardest at women and minority workers. Supported by feminist organizations, especially NOW, women and blacks who had been laid off because of low seniority brought suits against their companies, challenging the established seniority principle as discriminatory because they threatened jobs only recently won by groups long denied equal opportunity. Charlotte Casey, one of the five hundred women laid off at the General Motors assembly plant in Fremont, California, argued: "We feel that we were laid off not because of our fault. They weren't hiring women until 1968." She maintained that seniority "perpetuates discrimination because women as well as minorities are always at the bottom of the seniority list."

Although the women challenged GM's layoffs in a suit in federal court, they did not call for the firing of men but rather for a shared-work program, such as a reduced workday for all the workers: "We are making it clear that no men should be laid off in order to keep women in the plant. There's plenty of work for everyone."[29]

But the AFL-CIO Executive Council insisted that the seniority system was "a cornerstone of the American labor movement" and should under no circumstances be modified to any extent whatsoever. In a statement on seniority and layoffs adopted on May 6, 1975, the Executive Council made it clear that it opposed "forced work-sharing" or any other tampering with seniority. The only solution to the problems of layoffs of women and minority workers, it maintained, was "full employment."[30]

In an interview with the *New York Times*, CLUW President Olga Madar denied that "seniority perpetuates discriminatory patterns." CLUW, she declared, did not believe that "the seniority system correctly applied is responsible for affirmative action programs not being implemented." It was management that was responsible, she insisted, and workers "should not pay the penalty for discriminatory practices of management." The remedies, she added, should punish those who had discriminated, meaning the employers. "The real solution," she went on, "is to turn the economy around." "How?" asked the *Times* reporter. "By providing more public service and public service projects," Madar answered.[31]

But not all CLUW members accepted Madar's reasoning. "Let's face it, most of the gains we won in recent years have pretty much been wiped out," CLUW officer Maria Hernandez, an SEIU activist, argued at the November 15, 1975, CLUW Los Angeles panel discussion. "CLUW members," she insisted, "must fight in their own unions for the principle that future contracts with employers will give the union some degree of control over who's laid off. If we continue to give bosses the indiscriminate 'last hired, first fired' right, non-whites and women workers will never make it."[32]

But Dina Rodriguez, a steelworker, challenged this approach by reminding the women of CLUW that older white workers in her mill— men with years of seniority—feared that "minorities and women are out for their jobs." She warned that such fears, no matter how irrational, could be used by the employers to create sharp divisions among the workers and weaken the union so that it could protect neither the newly hired nor the older workers. She described an approach adopted by CLUW members in her mill that had positive results:

> We talked to these old steelworkers with years of seniority—and we told them we don't want to take their jobs away from them. We did get some good ideas, though. Some of the older men, with lots of seniority, say they could get laid off without it really hurting because they're eligible for Supplementary Unemployment Benefit money through the union in addition to regular unemployment insurance. And us new workers, we can't get that money. So if the union fought for it, they'd be laid off while we work to get the seniority

needed. We can do the same thing for new workers when they come in the future, without bumping people who earned their seniority.[33]

While the women attending the discussion were not in agreement as to how best to deal with the seniority issue, they did agree that "CLUW members have to push their unions to deal with this problem."[34] And a reporter who covered the meeting wrote: "For the Los Angeles CLUW chapter, seriously split in past months by numerous political squabbles, plus the mounting unemployment problem for women workers, the meeting was counted an important success and a hopeful sign of progress for the unique women's workers' organization."[35]

Although no national AFL-CIO official had spoken at CLUW's founding convention, the *AFL-CIO News* found the conference sufficiently newsworthy to carry a story about the gathering.[36] However, the first time the AFL-CIO confronted the existence of CLUW head on was at its San Francisco convention in October, 1975. A number of resolutions, one from the Industrial Union Department of the AFL-CIO, called for endorsement and support of the Coalition of Labor Union Women. But the delegates voted it down on the recommendation of the Resolutions Committee, which declared that "CLUW is clearly in the trade union tradition. . . . But formal endorsement, because of CLUW's structure, is not possible." That structural obstacle, it explained, arose from the fact that CLUW had members from outside the AFL-CIO, such as from the UAW and the Teamsters.[37]

However, the forces that had brought CLUW into existence were very much present at San Francisco. For the first time in the history of the AFL-CIO, both the federation's policy on women workers and the role of women in the labor movement were debated on the convention floor. From the inception of the AFL in 1881 and throughout the years since the merger of the AFL and CIO in 1955, there had never been a woman on the Executive Council. In 1975 the Executive Council had only two black union leaders, both of whom represented small unions.* This scandalous situation was discussed at the Illinois AFL-CIO's annual convention, held on September 23–25, 1975, and the delegates voted to call on the upcoming AFL-CIO convention to name both minority unionists from major affiliates and women representatives to the Executive Council.[38]

The following week, at San Francisco, the Illinois resolutions were introduced. One of them called for increased representation of women and minority members on the Executive Council. The second, calling attention to the tradition that each council member should be the president of an affiliated international union, asked that this rule be changed

---

*The two were A. Philip Randolph of the Brotherhood of Sleeping Car Porters and Willard S. Townsend of the United Transport Service Employees of America.

and called for the direct naming of minorities and women "from among the major affiliates," where minority and women workers were in the hundreds of thousands. The Resolutions Committee recommended that the proposals be referred to the Executive Council for further consideration, making quite clear its conviction that there was no need for a change, since "all members of the Executive Council represent all members of Federation affiliates and no single member of the Council or group of members represents any minority or class of members."[39]

Although the racial and sexual composition of the AFL-CIO Executive Council remained all-male and largely white, the issue had at least been brought to the attention of the delegates. (Of these 876 delegates, it should be added, only 23 were women and about an equal number were black.) Moreover, women unionists had gotten a foot in the door at San Francisco. That process began when the Communications Workers of America, a union with many women members, introduced a resolution amending the AFL-CIO constitution to establish a separate "Committee on Women." In rejecting the proposal, the Resolutions Committee offered the alternative proposal that the "responsibilities" of the Committee on Civil Rights be broadened to include "responsibility for women's rights," and that the committee's staff be expanded to include persons "knowledgeable on women." The change would thus "make explicit in the constitution what is now implicit."

Myra Wolfgang of the Hotel & Restaurant Employees (one of the twenty-three women delegates) was less than enthusiastic about the substitute proposal. "I do not totally believe that half a loaf is better than none," she said. She did accept the substitute as a "foot in the door," adding, however:

> Let me assure you gentlemen of the convention and the 22 women delegates that the foot that is in the door is not encased in a ballet slipper. It is a marching shoe and it intends to march jointly with the men of the labor movement to address itself to the problems of millions of unorganized women in this country.

Wolfgang urged women to attend the upcoming CLUW convention on December 6–7, 1975, in Detroit and added the hope that "this foot in the door may lead some day to a Woman's Department" so that the problems of workingwomen could be dealt with adequately inside the AFL-CIO.[40]

In the end, the AFL-CIO, at its 1975 convention, added the phrase, "because of race, creed, color, sex, national origin or ancestry" to the section outlining the antidiscrimination responsibilities of the AFL-CIO Committee on Civil Rights and expanded the committee's staff to include persons concerned with the rights of workingwomen. It also pledged a continued fight for women's rights in the workplace, urged stepped-up publicity for ratification of the ERA in the four states still needed for the required total of thirty-eight,* called for an end to wage differentials based on sex, urged all affiliates to "encourage full partici- pation of women in all union activity," and endorsed fully adequate child-care legislation. In addition to the abolition of wage differentials, the convention also called for continued emphasis on sickness and acci- dent benefits, for pregnancy and maternity leave, to be paid on the same basis as for any other disability, and the inclusion of men in state laws that protected only women.[41]

Despite the failure to endorse their organization, CLUW leaders ap- peared to view the 1975 AFL-CIO convention as a major step forward as far as workingwomen were concerned.[42] But the West Coast Conference for Working Women, held in San Francisco a few weeks after the AFL- CIO delegates left that city, was totally critical of the federation. In the conference's keynote address, Joyce Maupin, veteran trade unionist and Union WAGE leader, attacked the AFL-CIO leadership for continuing to exclude women from its Executive Council and for failing to initiate a single program at the convention for the organization of women work- ers. She cited examples of successful organizing outside of the official trade union structure and urged a thorough discussion of independence versus affiliation with the existing trade union structure.

Although all the delegates shared Maupin's criticism of the AFL-CIO convention for its failure to take steps to organize women, and many spoke out in favor of independent organizing, the majority did not favor the convention's taking a stand on this question. A number of the dele- gates would be attending the CLUW's convention in Detroit, and they urged that no action be taken before the events at that convention could be evaluated. This position was endorsed, and when members of the independent United Workers Union of Seattle asked to present a resolu- tion in favor of independent organizing, the overwhelming majority voted to table the proposal.[43]

CLUW's second convention, which was called to draft a constitution for the organization, was attended by 1,275 women unionists from sixty-three national unions and forty-five states. Reporters pointed out that this figure was down from the 3,200 at the founding convention, and that fewer black women were in attendance than in March, 1974. They also noted that there appeared to be little or no representation of Spanish-speaking women and that delegates from the United Farm Workers were conspicuously absent.[44] Evidently few contacts had been established with these women.

---

*The convention urged that the votes of legislators on ERA be used as one of the principal criteria for their endorsement by the Committee on Political Education (COPE) or by individual unions. However, the question of making ratification of ERA a condition for any state being considered as a site for a future AFL-CIO convention was left to the Executive Council.

Convention delegates heard Congresswoman Bella Abzug hail CLUW's efforts and predict that the coalition would "usher in a new era of equality for working women." "We have an enormous responsibility to help our nation fulfill its commitments to all of the people," she said, and she urged CLUW "to work toward adoption of National Health Security and child-care legislation." She concluded her speech with the hope that by the next CLUW convention, at least one international union would have elected a woman president.* Then, to a great roar of applause, she noted that while George Meany had greeted CLUW warmly, "no woman yet sits on the AFL-CIO Executive Council." Cheers also greeted Abzug when she called for cutbacks in the military budget to divert money instead to education, health, and welfare.[45]

Most of the first two days of the convention were spent on discussion and adoption of the constitution. Before the delegates met, Madar had sent to all CLUW members the proposed constitution, an agenda for the convention, and suggested rules, along with a warning directed against "the small minority of our members who have attempted to divert us from our goals." (Who this "minority" was was not spelled out, but the *New York Times* termed it the "far left" and others mentioned the Trotskyist International Socialists associated with the Socialist Workers Party, and also the October League.)[46] At the convention, a group of delegates handed out a series of proposed amendments to the constitution, which they insisted would "help democratize it."[47]

With one exception, the administration-recommended constitution was adopted. The sole exception was the proposal that CLUW chapters with fifty members be entitled to one representative on the National Executive Board, CLUW's leadership body, in place of the provision for representation of seventy-five or one-hundred-member chapters. A proposal calling for the admission of unorganized women was defeated, despite the contention of its advocates that only through a change in the membership requirement could CLUW make any progress toward organizing the 37 million unorganized women in the work force. Only one-quarter of the delegates supported the motion on broadening the membership. A larger vote, although still a minority, was cast for a compromise motion permitting membership for women who signed union cards during organizing drives.[48]

CLUW's newly adopted constitution continued the qualifications for membership that were already in existence. It set up a National Council of five top officers and a National Executive Board with proportional representation from unions, regions, and chapters. A yearly member-

---

*At the time of the CLUW convention, no woman held the presidency of any of the 105 AFL-CIO unions. Shortly thereafter, however, the Screen Actors Guild elected Kathleen Nolan as its president.

ship fee of $10 was established, ($5 for retirees who maintained their union membership), with $1 going into a special travel fund to help defray the expenses of National Executive Board members who had no sources for reimbursement and thereby, it was hoped, to increase their participation in meetings.

The incumbent national leadership was reelected: Olga Madar, who had retired as UAW vice-president, as president; Addie Wyatt as vice-president;* Gloria Johnson as treasurer; Joyce Miller as secretary, and Patsy Fryman of the CWA as recording secretary. Twelve CLUW regions were to elect fifteen regional representatives, who, along with the chapter representatives, would sit on the National Executive Board. An additional forty-five board members were to be elected by their union's CLUW members.[49]

At a breakfast session called a "Tribute to Unions," President Madar added to the list of CLUW's accomplishments its participation in International Women's Day on March 8, in demonstrations across the nation supporting CLUW's demand for jobs for all, and in the demonstration in Washington on April 26 for jobs. The main thrust of CLUW, Madar emphasized, must be the fight for jobs, and she presented a plan, which was overwhelmingly supported by the delegates, for a jobs-and-equality demonstration to be held in Atlanta on January 15, the anniversary of the birthday of the late Martin Luther King, Jr.

That proposal was the only new action plan to emerge from the convention. CLUW's existing program for dealing with the economic crisis was reaffirmed. This program pledged CLUW's support for the Hawkins Full Employment Bill, for a shorter work week with no loss in pay, for the National Coalition to Fight Inflation and Unemployment, and for the Full Employment Action Council.[50]

"The Death of CLUW," an article by Ann Withorn published in *Radical America,* summed up the reaction in many left circles to the second CLUW convention. Withorn called the gathering "a sorry affair," which had left the coalition as "the official Women's Auxiliary of the trade union bureaucracy." Although CLUW still existed as a paper organization, she proclaimed, it was actually "dead."[51]

All this was inevitable, the doomsayers insisted. From the beginning, CLUW was only an instrument to promote the interests of high-ranking women in the trade unions, who used the organization to serve their own needs and not those of rank-and-file women. The "women bureaucrats" had linked themselves to the increasingly accepted "women's movement" as a means of promoting their own interests, but they had no real concern with advancing "feminist goals." The leadership of CLUW nationally and in local areas had been made up largely of women union staff

---

*Shortly after the convention, *Time,* in its January 5, 1976, issue, designated Addie Wyatt as one of the nation's twelve "Women of the Year."

members, beholden to male union leaders for their jobs. Whenever the CLUW leadership met with opposition, the charge went, they resorted to the same tactics as those used by these male leaders in their own unions to stifle dissent. They redbaited, censured, expelled, or stifled chapters that challenged the leadership's policies and packed meetings with women sent in by trade union bureaucrats, especially those associated with Albert Shanker's American Federation of Teachers. The aim was "to confuse the issues and manipulate the meetings," and in many cases, they succeeded. On top of all this, there was the economic crisis. High unemployment among women workers had forced the seniority issue to the forefront, but CLUW's leadership was unwilling to antagonize the male trade union hierarchy, which refused to consider the idea of modifying the seniority system. Consequently, CLUW could not function as a real advocate for women workers on an issue that was becoming increasingly important. Little wonder, the critics of CLUW concluded, that the organization failed to grow, and had even lost members.[52]

Others were not so ready to bury the organization. They argued that the need for CLUW was even greater than it had been when it was first organized and insisted that to fulfill its purpose the coalition had to respond to the needs of rank-and-file women and become a militant presence in the trade union movement. *Labor Today* argued that CLUW's second convention was proof that it was moving in the right direction, and that the convention's message was that "union women are determined to continue the fight for their rights." While the new constitution restricted future convention participation to elected delegates, which would probably make it much smaller, opportunities still existed for the membership to influence the organization's future development. "An active CLUW membership," the publication went on, "can preserve the militant, progressive qualities of CLUW and make a great contribution to advancing women's rights within the union movement and strengthening the position of organized labor."[53]

CLUW leadership, however, was convinced that it was on the right track. Their view was shared by Barbara M. Wertheimer and Anne H. Nelson, who wrote in their 1975 work *Trade Union Women: A Study of Their Participation in New York City Locals* that "CLUW ... has inspired working women throughout the country" and had great significance for union women.[54] After its second convention, CLUW's activities were aimed mainly at stabilizing the organization and slowly building a framework for future progress. When Joyce Miller, by then a vice-president of the merged Amalgamated Clothing & Textile Workers Union, replaced Olga Madar as CLUW president at the third convention,* held on September 17 and 18, 1977, she told the eight hundred

*Other officers elected at the CLUW convention were: Executive Vice-President Addie Wyatt (Amalgamated Meat Cutters), First Vice-President Georgia McGee (AFSCME),

delegates, alternates, and guests from twenty-eight unions and twenty-one local chapters that CLUW's top priority would be to increase its membership and develop programs and activities for local groups.[55]

A CLUW legislative conference held in Washington before its third convention attracted wide attention because it was addressed by AFL-CIO President George Meany, who revealed to the union women that an economist had recently told a House committee that the minimum wage was so weighted toward women workers that the AFL-CIO president must be a "closet feminist" for supporting it. "If supporting a living wage for all workers makes me a feminist," Meany told the women, "move over, sisters; I've been called a lot worse." "Speaking for the AFL-CIO Executive Council," Meany went on, "let me express our sincere appreciation for the support CLUW and your officers have given in this year's legislative fights. We know that we can count on you. You've proven that CLUW is an organization working to benefit all working people."[56]

A. H. Raskin of the *New York Times* hailed Meany's presence at the CLUW legislative conference as clear evidence of "Growing Acceptance for the Coalition of Union Women." But Professor Harry Kelber of Empire State College in New York City warned that it was a mistake for CLUW "to depend on labor leaders like Meany," who were "more interested in controlling and inhibiting CLUW than in promoting its objectives."[57]

President Joyce Miller had a different opinion. During the fourth national (and first biennial) convention of the Coalition of Labor Union Women, held on September 13–16, 1979, in New York City, she told an interviewer that the AFL-CIO had responded affirmatively to CLUW's call for a boycott against states that had not ratified the ERA. "The Federation complied with our request to move its convention from Florida (one of the non-ratifying states)," she said, "and individual unions are following suit."[58]

Miller reported to the nearly twelve hundred women trade unionists who attended the convention that CLUW had 8,000 members from sixty different unions in twenty-six chapters. While this was still only a small fraction of the more than 5 million union women, it represented a noticeable increase over the 5,500 members when Miller had assumed the presidency two years earlier. CLUW's growth was also reflected in the increase in black participation in the convention and in the fact that Hispanic women were present in greater numbers than before. The Convention proceedings were interrupted on September 14 so that members

---

Second Vice-President Clara Day (Teamsters), Treasurer Gloria Johnson (IUE), Recording Secretary Patsy Fryman (CWA), and Corresponding Secretary Odessa Komer (UAW). Outgoing CLUW President Olga Madar was designated "president emerita."

could join the pickets of the Department Store Union in support of its organizing drive at Abraham & Straus, Brooklyn's leading department store, 80 percent of whose workers were women.[59]

Workshops preceded the formal convention sessions, and this writer attended the one on organizing the unorganized. The eloquence and keenness of the women unionists who described their organizing experiences were extremely impressive. The session enabled the women to share their experiences and learn from one another. While CLUW does no organizing on its own, it was clear from the discussion that its chapters have played a significant role in support of union-organizing drives.

Tom Donahue, assistant to George Meany, and William Lucy, president of the Coalition of Black Trade Unionists, brought greetings from labor to the CLUW delegates. Donahue praised CLUW's contribution to the "revitalization of the labor movement," and Lucy declared: "We stand shoulder to shoulder with you in the struggle to end sex harassment and to pass the ERA." Eleanor Holmes Norton, chairperson of the Equal Employment Opportunity Commission, Bella Abzug, and Representatives Barbara Mikulski (Democrat-Maryland) and Elizabeth Holtzman (Democrat-New York) were among the women who addressed the gathering.

The 450 voting delegates passed resolutions renewing their commitment to the passage of the ERA and calling for a national health bill and job, health, and safety legislation. This latter resolution cited the increasing number of workers who die of job-related conditions and pointed out that "many employers are discriminating against women workers under the guise of 'protecting' their health—to the point of forcing them to be sterilized," and that there is "increasing scientific evidence that job dangers to women and their unborn children are also dangers to men and, in turn, to their children." The resolution also called for a broader fight to strengthen job safety and health laws that benefit all workers, since "workers do not have a legal 'right to know' the identity and dangers of the chemicals and substances to which they are exposed on the job." The same resolution called attention to the "constant attacks in Congress and the states by corporations, employer associations, and their bought legislators, who claim that, at a time of obscene corporation profits, they cannot afford these life-saving measures." The convention then resolved that "CLUW calls on all its members and chapters to work in their unions, chapters and local COSH (Committees on Occupational Safety and Health) groups to present a strong and vocal front to preserve and strengthen federal job safety and health protection in OSHA (Occupational Safety and Health Act)" and "to call upon industry to fix the workplace not the worker and thereby make the workplace safe for women and men."

Another resolution focused on the need to preserve and improve health care facilities: "The National Coalition of Labor Union Women will support local community groups and labor organizations throughout the country which are working to maintain and improve health services and are protesting the closings of health programs or facilities until there is quality affordable health care throughout the country for all persons in the land."

Resolutions were passed calling for equal pay for equal work of comparable value, and for affirmative action, including the representation of women at all levels of union leadership. A resolution also supported the organization of workers without regard to their legal residence and advocated permanent amnesty for all undocumented workers then in the country. The convention decided to hold a 1980 conference on organizing the unorganized. This had been one of the demands that came out of the workshop on organizing the unorganized.

The convention rejected a proposal from past president Olga Madar that urged the delegates to condemn the NAACP for scheduling its convention in a state that had not yet ratified the ERA. Louise Smothers of the American Federation of Government Employees, head of CLUW's minority women's committee, urged rejection of the proposal. "Why are we making the NAACP an issue when we have not yet got the house of labor in order?" she asked. The convention accepted her view.

On the question of qualifications for membership, the delegates rejected a motion to permit labor attorneys to join. Along with labor educators and other supporters, they were permitted to join separate support groups called "CLUW Associates," which were authorized at the convention.

CLUW's current officers (elected for the period 1979–1981) are President Joyce Miller (ACTWU); Executive Vice-President Addie Wyatt of the United Food & Commercial Workers, a union resulting from the merger of the Retail Clerks International Union and the Amalgamated Meat Cutters; First Vice-President Georgia McGhee (AFSCME), Second Vice-President Clara Day (Teamsters); Treasurer Gloria Johnson (IUE); Corresponding Secretary Odessa Komer (UAW); Recording Secretary Patsy Fryman (CWA); and President Emerita Olga Madar (UAW). Two new vice-presidents are Pat Halpin of the AFT and Gwen Newton of the Office & Professional Employees International Union. Five of the national officers are black.[60]

One of the most interesting aspects of CLUW's first biennial convention was a series of interviews with the delegates that were published in the press. Marian Cika, an assembly-line worker at the GM van plant in Lordstown, Ohio, told how she had come to work at the plant when her husband became ill and could not work. She had been a hospital worker but had changed jobs because the family needed more money. After her husband died, she went on, "I couldn't get Social Security or his pension, because his company had moved out of town. I was left with the hospital bills and they threatened to foreclose the mortgage on the house." It was the UAW benefits that had saved her from disaster. "The union contract covered my house and most of the hospital bills. If it wasn't for the union, we wouldn't have gotten them [the benefits], the company wouldn't have paid them."

She also spoke of the personal satisfaction she had derived from her activities: "I'm involved in activity and CLUW . . . and I'm not lonely any more."

Cika said she supported affirmative action and spoke of an occasion when the company had come to her with an offer for advancement over a black woman on the line with eight years' seniority. "I declined to take the job," she told the reporter. Because they acted together, Cika said, the other woman got her rightful job and she got the next one. "If we fight together," she concluded, "we will win."[61]

Cika's story illustrated the truth of what CLUW President Miller told the delegates at the biennial convention: "Women will not achieve equality in the workplace without the collective strength of unions behind them."[62]

Three years after it had been pronounced "dead," CLUW still lives and continues to speak for women in the labor movement and for labor in the women's movement. It continues, too, to face the challenge of organizing the unorganized women workers, of helping women, especially minority women, to escape from the lower-paid female "job ghettos," and of achieving a greater voice for women in all levels of the labor movement.* Further, it seems clear that the Coalition of Labor Union Women is the only national organization of women capable of meeting this challenge.

---

*In the fall of 1979, the Coalition of Labor Union Women Center for Education and Research launched the study entitled, "The Empowerment of Union Women." This is an 18-month national monitoring and resource project addressing the limited roles of women in U.S. unions, and developing a series of policy recommendations for unions and union members. "We are going to be keeping a very close eye on the progress made by unions in their attempts to bring women into full leadership positions," CLUW president Joyce D. Miller noted in announcing the study. (*Daily World*, December 21, 1979.)

Early in 1980 the CLUW Task Force on Contract Language published *Effective Contract Language for Union Women*, a 32-page booklet designed to provide model language for labor-management contracts to protect women's rights in such areas as equal pay for comparable work, non-sexist language, pregnancy benefit clauses, maternity leave, child-care, and non-discrimination clauses.

21

The Current Scene
and Future Prospects

Between 1950 and 1975, the sexual composition of the U.S. labor force underwent a dramatic transformation. The proportion of workingwomen sixteen years of age and over who participated in the paid labor force increased from 34 to 46 percent. In 1975, women constituted 40 percent of all workers, compared with 30 percent in 1950. In 1949 the Department of Labor disclosed that for the first time in the history of the United States, there were more working than nonworking women. One authority has written: "This shift is the single most important change in the labor force in this century."[1]

The added legions of women that have entered the labor force are in the main married women. Gone is the old concept that the male head of the family is solely responsible for the family's support, as is the idea that the woman is at most a part-time contributor to the family's income. The inflation that has become a staple ingredient of our economy is compelling more women to work and to stay in jobs longer. As *Time* magazine put it in the summer of 1979: "For millions of Americans it is now the second income from a working wife that enables families to make ends meet." Not only were more women working, but many were even holding down two jobs to keep their families afloat. In 1948, about 1.3 million held more than one job, compared with less than half that number in 1970. Many of the women "moonlighters" were married.[2]

About one-eighth of all women workers (some 4.8 million) are minority members. The rate of their participation in the labor force is generally higher than that of white women. Thus, 49 percent of all minority women, as compared with 46 percent of all white women, were in the labor force in 1976, and women constituted almost 46 percent of all minority workers.[3]

When we examine the kinds of work women do, another shift becomes evident. Women are holding jobs in occupations that were formerly open only to men, and in a number of cases the numbers of women in these traditionally male occupations are becoming significant. Thus, by the end of May, 1977, of the 36.5 million women workers, almost 5.5 million were in blue-collar jobs.[4]

The entry of women into blue-collar work, of course, is not new. As we have seen, women by the thousands stepped into such jobs during World War II (as so many had done in the First World War), when the men went off to battle. They helped keep wartime production flowing, filling jobs such as precision machinists, welders, assemblers, and riveters, in defense plants, steel mills, shipyards, and aircraft factories. But at the war's end, with the men coming home and plants gearing for peacetime production, seniority asserted itself, and the women were phased out of the blue-collar jobs.

While some jobs remained open to women for the next quarter of a century, the better-paid trades in the crafts and assembly-line jobs remained essentially male territory. But by November, 1978, the *Wall Street Journal* was reporting that women across the country were breaking down the barriers against them in the traditionally male blue-collar occupations.[5]

Around the country, scores of groups were springing up to train women to fill blue-collar jobs and to fight for their employment in these occupations. Among them were Women's Enterprises of Boston, the All-Craft Center and Women in Trades in New York City, Women in Apprenticeship Programs in San Francisco, Mechanica in Seattle, Chicana Service Action in Los Angeles, Women Working in Construction in Washington, D.C., Skilled Jobs for Women in Madison, Wisconsin, and Better Jobs for Women in Denver. Their programs were operated by blue-collar workingwomen and funded by the federal government under the Comprehensive Employment and Training Act (CETA) of 1973. Most of them provided free counseling and placement services as well as workshops to prepare women for the examinations given by the various apprenticeship programs, which are generally conducted jointly by labor and management.[6]

One of the most highly publicized of these groups—the All-Craft Foundation, which operated the All-Craft Center in New York City— evolved from a contracting and home-improvement business known as Lady Carpenter Institute, Inc. Started in 1963, Lady Carpenter employed women to work as carpenters, traditionally a man's trade. In 1972, in response to women's interest in learning woodworking for both homemaking and possible future work opportunities, Lady Carpenter opened a school to teach them a working knowledge of power tools and building procedures. By 1978, six hundred women had finished the courses. Lady Carpenter Institute continued to function as a home improvement center, but the All-Craft Foundation was established to further the employment of women in the skilled blue-collar trades. The foundation offered free child care as well as training in the basics of carpentry, cabinetmaking, electrical work, and plumbing to women who qualified under the CETA program. The course runs five days a week for one month, with backup training for as long as the student needs it to perfect her skill. Graduates are either placed in jobs or hired by the Mothers and Daughters Construction Company, a profit-sharing company affiliated with All-Craft. Women who do not qualify for CETA help can attend the course at night and pay their tuition by bringing in jobs for Mothers and Daughters.[7]

Joyce Hartwell, director of the All-Craft Center, pointed out in March, 1979, that over 90 percent of the women coming to the Center were ADC mothers, women receiving welfare assistance through the Aid to Dependent Children program. The "All-Craft Center," Hartwell continued, "is planned for the economically disadvantaged women, the group of women who are least likely to survive."[8]

"Women in construction is not a new situation," observed a journal published by the Brotherhood of Carpenters and Joiners in February, 1976. "There have been women in construction all around the world. . . . But in the United States to see women swinging a hammer is different."[9] It soon became clear, however, that the United States was not going to remain "different" in this respect for long. In fact, Robert A. Georgine, president of the AFL-CIO Building & Construction Trades Department in Washington, D.C., in May, 1977, urged the construction trades "to devote special attention to women." In a letter to the officials of the department's 383 locals and 33 state councils, Georgine, a former chief executive of the International Union of Wood, Wire & Metal Lathers, noted: "Discrimination because of sex cannot be tolerated in the trade union movement any more than racial discrimination can be permitted." He made it clear that "quotas and 'instant journeymèn' schemes are unacceptable," and asked the unions to: publicize apprenticeship openings in the community, develop relationships on local and state levels with women's groups and other organizations as possible sources of apprenticeship applicants; and ask school counselors to tell female pupils about construction jobs.[10]

It is difficult to evaluate just how serious Georgine's plea was, but the response to it was quite clear. The *Chicago Daily News* reported in mid-July, 1977, that "breakthroughs are scarce" and that the Building & Construction Trades head was "still waiting for results."[11] At about the same time, Advocates for Women and Women in Construction put pressure on Secretary of Labor Ray Marshall to set a goal of giving women 40 percent of the places in federally registered apprenticeship programs. The organizations contended that this figure was justified by the fact that women made up 40 percent of the nation's labor force. In July, 1977, they filled just 2 percent of the available apprenticeship places.[12]

The women's organizations also asked the Labor Department to put an end to the ordeals women construction workers were forced to endure. They told of the obscene graffiti campaigns waged against women "hard hats" on the walls of the buildings on which they worked, of crude remarks, obscene gestures, and pranks played on those "who dared to venture into a world where once the only sign of a woman was the girlie pinup in the construction site shack." They told, too, of physical threats and physical violence.[13]

Responding to pressure from the women's movement, the Labor Department issued a series of regulations ordering companies with federal contracts of $10,000 or more to meet specific goals for hiring women in all construction craft jobs. The department rejected the demand for 40 percent of the places in apprenticeship programs as "absolutely impossible," but it did pledge to end the "near total exclusion" of women by the construction industry.[14]

The regulations, published in August, 1977, required federal contractors to set goals and timetables for the hiring of female bricklayers, carpenters, plasterers, painters, and other skilled craftspersons in the construction trades. Initially, the goals would be 3.1 percent women construction workers during the first year of the program, 5 percent in the second year, and 6.9 percent in the third year. The regulations, however, included a historic provision requiring contractors to "ensure and maintain a working environment free of harassment, intimidation and coercion."[15]

This time, women did not have long to wait for results. Shortly after the new regulations were announced, the Massachusetts State Building & Construction Trades Council of the AFL-CIO, the trade group for all construction unions, sponsored a federally funded program in three cities called the "Women in Construction Project." The thirty-two-week program aimed at recruiting card-carrying union members, and it offered pre-apprenticeship training to women in carpentry, electrical work, plumbing, and painting. It also offered physical training in pushing, pulling, and lifting materials, as well as vocational counseling. The latter activity was handled by Women's Enterprises of Boston.

Fred Hansen, secretary-treasurer of the Construction Trades Council, explained the reason for the "Women in Construction Project." He told a reporter that the unions were sponsoring the program because they realized that under the new federal regulations, women had to get into the trades, "so the best way to deal with women in construction is to have a lot to do with how they get in."[16]

The affirmative-action programs required of federal contractors did bring some women into the male-dominated construction trades, but other federal programs were less productive. Many CETA-funded programs have been cut as part of the general budget slashing; as a result, projects like All-Crafts Center have more candidates than funds to service them. Nor can these projects help women who are mired in low-

464 WOMEN AND THE AMERICAN LABOR MOVEMENT

paying clerical jobs and want to advance to the skilled trades, since in order to qualify for the training and job placement at the centers, a woman must meet the poverty-level income required by the CETA regulations.

The first fifty longshorewomen in New York City began work in February, 1979, after the New York Waterfront Commission granted them temporary permits to work on the docks. The women won their jobs through the efforts of NOW's Urban Woman Project. That group, seeking work for women in nontraditional jobs, contacted women when they heard of the temporary job openings. Interestingly enough, the first New York City women dockworkers were trained at the All-Crafts Center.[17]

During World War II, women made up 10 percent of the work force in steel. After V-J Day, however, they were systematically purged from what had suddenly become "unsuitable work"—in spite of the fact that the Civil Rights Act of 1964 prohibiting employment discrimination due to sex made it clearly illegal for the steel companies to refuse to hire women. It has only been since the 1974 "consent decree" instituting quotas, which resulted from a combination of mass pressure and legal action by black workers and women, that significant numbers of women have begun to make it through the steel mill gates. That decree called for 50 percent of new apprentices to be minority or female.[18]

Theresa D'Agostino, the first woman worker in her Chicago steel mill since World War II, wrote: "Black workers were among the first to sense the difficult position I was in and went out of their way to express their support." Later, white workers admitted to her that they had been wrong in opposing her entrance. "I was one of those guys who said women workers have no place in a steel mill," one of them told her, "but after working with you, well I feel you got a right to be here." And black steelworker Gloria Kelly, who worked at the Burns Harbor Works of Bethlehem Steel near Chicago, told a reporter:

> When we insisted on our right to promotion, we were often forced to do the work of two employees. We couldn't have made it at all if it hadn't been for the support and solidarity of a number of our brothers who recognized that discrimination against women was discrimination against them also.[19]

Those "brothers," like the steelwomen, were members of Local 6787 of the United Steel Workers of America (USWA). Elsewhere, steelwomen reported, the union leadership remained uneasy about the presence of women in the mills and did not think they were "really 'worth fighting for' because there were so few of us and our votes don't count so much." "We need a union leadership," declared Jackie Lavalle of USWA Local 188 at Jones & Loughlin Steel in Cleveland, "that is going to say to the company, 'the women are sister union members and we fight for them the same as we fight for our brother members.'"[20]

Steelwomen were active in support of reform candidate Ed Sadlowski's unsuccessful bid for the presidency of the union. Women's caucuses sprang up in the steel plants, taking up not only the questions of maternity leave, sanitary facilities, and probationary employees but also the entry of women into the crafts,* greater representation for them in the union itself, and sexual harassment. The women in District 31 in the Chicago-Gary area were in the leadership of this movement. "Why a Caucus?" *District 31 Women's Caucus USWA Bulletin* asked, and it answered:

> Women steelworkers from the Chicago and northwest Indiana areas started meeting each other for the first time in the District 31 Women's Caucus. We were struck by the fact that the problems which we faced in the work place—unjust firings during the probationary period; layoffs; lack of sanitary facilities on the job; harassment of pregnant workers and lack of maternity benefits; constant attempts by the companies to violate laws outlawing dangerous conditions; special barriers put in our paths for entering apprenticeship programs; and just plain harassment of women workers— these problems were almost the same everywhere.
>
> It is clear that the steel industry still has not accepted our presence in the mills and everything possible is being done to discourage and push us out. As women workers who need our jobs, we have little choice but to fight back—if we just "sit back" we're bound to be "sent back" (out the gate)....
>
> Women steelworkers need the full strength of our Union to deal with our problems, and our Union needs an active and involved membership to be strong. Our purpose is to activate and educate women steelworkers in our union....[21]

District 31 Women's Caucus called for the establishment by the international of a Department of Women's Affairs, the convening of a unionwide conference of women steelworkers and Women's Committees, on both district and local levels; more women and minorities at all leadership levels in the union; the expansion and enforcement of affirmative action programs, including pre-apprenticeship training to enable more union members to qualify for craft opportunities; and joint action by the USWA with other unions to take up the struggle for child care in both the legislative and collective bargaining areas. "These are goals," the caucus insisted, "not just for female USWA members, but for every single union member and leader."[22]

Formed in 1976, within two years the District 31 Women's Caucus had a hundred members pledged to carry on "the fight for full equality in the work place and in the union." When discriminatory firings of probationary women took place at the plant, the Women's Caucus compelled the local office of the Equal Employment Opportunities Commis-

---

*Under maintenance, the basic crafts were carpentry, painting, and so on. Other crafts were those of machinists and toolmakers.

sion to take action to put them back on the job. Conferences of women steel workers were held in three districts of the union: District 29 in Detroit; District 27 in Canton, Ohio; and District 31 in Chicago-Gary.[23]

District 31's Women's Caucus also supported the drive initiated by Sadlowski to organize the unorganized, noting:

> Of special interest to our Women's Caucus is the fact that many of the unorganized workers seeking representation in the USWA are women. Two plants currently being organized are Desa Industries in Forest Park and American Lock in South Chicago Heights. Desa is 85% women and American Lock, where a petition for union election has just been filed, has 200 women employees.[24]

Pressured by the women's caucuses, the leadership of the USWA came out forcefully for ratification of the Equal Rights Amendment. In July, 1978, both the international office and District 31 sent buses to the massive ERA demonstration in Washington, D.C. The steelworker contingent in this action was also noteworthy for the high level of participation of black women. "Black women," wrote a white woman steelworker, "have been emerging as especially outspoken and dedicated leaders, not only among the women but of the union over all."[25]

Also in response to pressure from the women's caucuses, the USWA took up the struggle against the challenge to affirmative action by Brian Weber, a white steelworker from Louisiana, who charged that his employer, Kaiser Aluminum, and his union, the USWA, were discriminating against whites when they jointly set up a training program that reserved half its openings for minorities.

The story began in 1973. Congress had recently put more teeth into Title VII of the 1964 Civil Rights Act, barring discrimination in employment. As a result, the Kaiser Aluminum Company faced numerous Title VII suits with potentially huge back-pay liabilities. In the area surrounding Kaiser's plant in Gramercy, Louisiana, where the Weber case originated, 39 percent of the work force was black, but there were only 5 blacks among the plant's 273 craft workers.

In early 1974 Kaiser and the USWA negotiated a collective bargaining agreement covering fifteen Kaiser plants throughout the country. The agreement created a craft-training program patterned after a nationwide steel industry plan approved by the courts. Fifty percent of those selected for the program were to be from minorities, and the trainees were to be selected on the basis of their relative seniority within their racial groups.

In 1974 Brian Weber, who had worked as a laboratory technician at Kaiser since 1968, applied for one of the nine new craft training positions and was turned down because some thirty-five whites had higher seniority. But even though he was low on the white list, Weber still had more seniority than two of the five blacks selected from the minority list. He promptly sued both Kaiser and the USWA, charging "reverse discrimination" against all white workers.

Both a federal district court and the Fifth Circuit Court of Appeals ruled in Weber's favor, holding that Kaiser could create a racial quota only if it admitted past discrimination against blacks. And even then, it could grant a preference only to the individual blacks who had been discriminated against in craft hiring. Therefore, the courts contended, the affirmative action plan was illegal, since employers could not be burdened with the responsibility of correcting general "societal discrimination."

In joint action, Kaiser, the USWA, and the U.S. government applied for and obtained Supreme Court review.[26]

Earlier, in the suit of Allan Bakke against the right of the University of California to set aside a segment of each medical school class for blacks and other "approved minorities," as part of a plan for affirmative action, many trade unions had remained silent, largely at the behest of the American Federation of Teachers (AFT), which filed an amicus curiae brief on behalf of Bakke and welcomed the Supreme Court decision in his favor.[27] But in the Weber case, the labor movement in general took an unequivocal position against the challenge to affirmative action and rejected Weber's "reverse discrimination" argument. The women's movement and women workers played a leading role in opposition to Weber, realizing that if the charge of "reverse discrimination" was sustained by the Supreme Court, it would sound the death knell to programs for the training and upgrading of women workers to qualify them for the higher-paying, more-skilled positions filled largely by white males.

Thus, on January 12, 1979, representatives of more than twenty-five major labor, civil rights, and women's groups met in Washington to form a common front in defense of affirmative action programs. In addition, the USWA joined eleven other international unions and the AFL-CIO in filing amicus curiae briefs before the Supreme Court. One such brief was filed on behalf of District 1199 of the National Union of Hospital and Health Care Employees. In supporting the goal of affirmative action, the 1199 brief reviewed the accomplishments of its Training and Upgrading Fund in assisting minority workers, mostly women, to advance into technical and professional hospital jobs.[28]

The Supreme Court, by a five-to-two decision handed down in June, 1979, rejected the "reverse discrimination" charge. Justice William Brennan, writing for the majority, found that Congress had "left employers and unions in the private sector free to take ... race-conscious steps to eliminate manifest racial imbalance in traditionally white job categories." Since the agreement had been adopted voluntarily and did not involve state action, said Brennan, the only issue before the court was whether Title VII of the Civil Rights Act—the fair-employment provision—forbade such a plan. The court majority concluded that it did not and commented that "it would be ironic indeed if a law triggered by a nation's concern over centuries of racial injustice were used to prevent voluntary private measures to overcome inequities."[29]

Although the women's movement and the steelwomen both praised the USWA leadership for its role in the Weber case,[30] they were still unhappy about the absence of women in the union's leadership. By 1978 women made up over 10 percent of the USWA's membership—the majority of them in nonbasic steel industries such as can manufacturing and fabricating. But there was not one woman on the union's International Executive Board, while the staff, numbering in the hundreds, had fewer than a dozen women. The situation at the local level was often the same.[31]

The first break occurred on April 26, 1979, when Alice Puerala, a long-time worker at U.S. Steel, was elected president of the 7,500-member Local 65 in Chicago. Running against two men, she polled a plurality of 1,205 votes to their 1,168 and 1,077. In an interview following her victory, the first woman to head a local union in the steel industry described how she had had to go to court to get a job as a products tester in the South Works mill in Chicago. She announced that she looked forward to improving the union as a fighting organization, declaring that "the grievance committees have to fight the company to get decent working conditions in the plants. Sanitary conditions need to be improved." Then she added:

I did not win as a woman. I campaigned as a candidate who would do something about the conditions in that plant that affect 7,500 people—men and women. . . .
People in the plant looked on me as a fighter. I think it demonstrates that the men in the plant will vote for someone who is going to fight for them, make the union work for them.[32]

Later, speaking to men and women steelworkers at a forum on affirmative action in Republic Steel's Local 1033 union hall—a forum cosponsored by the Women's Committee of Local 1033 and District 31 of the USWA—Puerala gave major credit for the gains of steelwomen to the struggles against discrimination initiated by the black steelworkers at the Fairfield, Alabama, plant of U.S. Steel: "White workers gained as well as blacks and women from the gains in that case. It takes struggle to win, and we never would have won anything if we had been quiet."[33]

No group of women workers could testify to the truth of this statement more convincingly than the women coal miners.

Although women have begun in recent years to establish themselves in many traditionally male jobs, perhaps the most startling change has been the presence of women in the underground coal mines. While a few women were reported to have worked in family-owned strip mines, the number of women in the mines in 1973 appears to have been close to zero. Five years later, it had increased to 2,000 women among the 200,000 coal miners in the United States—or 1 percent of the total—and the figure reached 2,574 in June, 1979. In June, 1980 it was 3,061.[34]

In this connection, August 1, 1974, was a historic day in western Pennsylvania. On that day, three women went to work at the Bethlehem Mine Corporation's Mine No. 51 in Ellsworth. One of the women was black—the first black woman miner in Pennsylvania history. A century-old state law had prohibited women from working in the mines, but it was superseded by federal laws against discrimination in employment. What was also overcome was the traditional superstition among male miners that women underground brought bad luck. Bethlehem Mines Corporation, a subsidiary of Bethlehem Steel, had been compelled to bow to federal regulations against discrimination in hiring on the basis of sex.[35]

Bethlehem, the first major concern to break with tradition and send women underground, by November, 1978, had become the largest employer of women miners in the United States, with women working underground in its mines in Kentucky, Pennsylvania, and West Virginia.[36]

Most of the women currently working in the mines got their jobs either as a result of lawsuits against the industry or through pressure from the federal government. In Kentucky, West Virginia, and Tennessee, more than a thousand lawsuits and complaints have been filed demanding that coal companies hire women. "We've seen a mushrooming of complaints in the last few years," declared Galin Martin of the Kentucky Commission on Human Rights in November, 1978. "Once women became aware of the possibility of jobs in the mines, they applied in droves."[37] Many of them were divorced, widowed, or the wives of disabled miners, and a large number of them provided the sole means of support for their families. Others were tired of trying to live on the wages offered women in the traditional women's jobs and were determined to raise their standard of living. "When I became a miner, I just about tripled my income," said one woman miner.[38]

Until the women themselves began to organize and put pressure on the federal government to take action, most of them were turned away by the companies. One such organized group was the Coal Employment Project, an Oak Ridge, Tennessee, group that represented a coalition of Appalachian women's groups aimed at increasing opportunities for women to work in the coal mines. In 1978, at its insistence, the Department of Labor began an investigation of 153 coal-mining companies for allegedly widespread discrimination against women and minorities. The Coal Employment Project also filed an administrative complaint with the Office of Contract Compliance Programs in Washington. The complaint cited statistics showing that 99.8 percent of all mines were all-male and 98 percent of all mining employees were men. It charged that the companies were violating an executive order prohibiting federal contractors from discriminating and sought an order requiring them to hire one woman for every three men in entry-level jobs until women constituted 20 percent of the work force.[39]

On November 25, 1978, the Consolidated Coal Company of Pittsburgh, which had been accused of discrimination because it had rejected seventy-eight qualified women who sought jobs as miners between 1972 and 1976, admitted that it had indeed been guilty of discrimination and agreed to pay $370,000 in reparations to these women. It also agreed to hire them as miners and to hire one inexperienced woman for each experienced man until the women comprised 32.8 percent of its work force.[40]

Even though laws prohibiting women from working underground have been invalidated by recent federal legislation against job discrimination, in many parts of the United States the companies still cite superstitions among male miners as a reason for refusing to hire women miners. However, one woman miner reported:

> I'll never forget our first day. The men all lined up on one side of the portal and we could hear them saying under their breaths, "It's bad luck, women in the mines." Then one day a few weeks later, a shuttle car operator didn't show up for work and the only one who could do the job was a woman. They put her on the shuttle car. We're getting to be indispensable.[41]

The hiring of women miners in different coal fields touched off a heated debate in the *United Mine Workers Journal*, the union's official organ. One miner's wife, arguing against women in the mines, wrote: "God never wanted them to be equal or HE would have made them so." Another miner's wife insisted that it was "immoral" for women to work underground. "There aren't even toilet facilities," she wrote indignantly.

On the other hand, a miner's wife from Indiana asked: "Why should a woman type for $20 a day when she'd rather be doing a more physical type of work and getting better paid, too?" And she added: "Not all of us have husbands willing and able to work. Ever hear of disabled men or widowed women, or, heaven forbid, divorced women?" Other correspondents pointed out that women in the coal fields had always played an outstanding role in the miners' struggles and that women miners could now make a great contribution to the building of a stronger and more effective United Mine Workers. Pam Schuble, a woman miner from Indiana, agreed and wrote to the *Journal:*

All readers should not be so concerned about the sex of brother or sister workers, but what kind of union member this person is going to be. Only if we are united will we remain the strongest union in the United States. . . . The new women in the mines must help their men maintain their powerful United Mine Workers of America.[42]

In July, 1977, the UMW reported that there were 858 women miners in the 277,00-member union.[43] It also seemed that some of the men wanted more women to join their ranks. After three years at a Bethlehem mine in West Virginia, Linda Triplett reported: "Women are now an accepted thing. In fact we've been encouraged to be active in the union by the men."[44]

In October, 1977, Mary Maynard became the first woman president in the history of the United Mine Workers. Maynard was elected president of UMW Local 1971 of Rum Creek, West Virginia. "Her new position," commented the *New York Times,* "points to the ease with which women in a decade have come to be accepted in a union that has an image of aggressive masculinity."[45] Mrs. Maynard was not a miner; she drove a 48-ton truck for the Pittston Coal Company, one of the companies that had bitterly resisted employing women as miners. In 1978, after only a year as a miner, Linda Triplett was nominated to run for vice-president of Local 4172 in northern West Virginia. "I ran against a man and I guess people felt I'd do a good job because they elected me," she told a reporter. When the local president took a foreman's job a month later, Triplett became the first woman local president in the UMW who was a miner. A year later, in 1979, another woman miner, Pauline Shine, was elected president of the local.[46]

Triplett and Shine were the first women delegates to a UMW convention, and they submitted a motion to the 1978 gathering urging that paid maternity leave be made a negotiating item in contract talks. The motion was adopted. Although they had wanted to raise other women-related issues at the convention, the two delegates refrained from doing so because of their belief that they should not push things too fast. "But I'd like to see some kind of day care system established in the coalfields," Shine, a divorced mother, declared. She added: "Working in the mines and being active in the union has given me a whole new slant on things. I used to do clerical work and I was a nurse's aide. But it didn't pay nearly as well as the mines. And getting active in the union has made me interested in politics generally." She had circulated a NOW petition for the ERA at her mine and had gotten 117 out of the 170 miners to sign it in less than three hours.[47]

Several Appalachian chapters of NOW have played a role in organizing coal-mining women and have joined forces with Coalmining Women's Support Team and the Association of Kentucky and Virginia Women Miners in dealing with a whole variety of discrimination issues.

The first National Conference of Women Coal Miners took place in
June, 1979, at West Virginia State College in Institute, West Virginia.
While there was some question about the property of having the conference funded in part by the John Whitney Foundation, whose Consolidated Coal Company had been forced to hire women miners, the objections were overcome by the realization of the importance of the gathering as a means of bringing women miners together and enabling them to
share their experiences. Under the slogan "Women Miners Can Dig It
Too," about sixty women miners from West Virginia, Virginia, Kentucky, Tennessee, Alabama, Pennsylvania, Illinois, New Mexico, and
Wyoming met to discuss their special problems. Discussion ranged from
the fact that women miners had to "drive home dirty" because the company did not provide a bathhouse, to the lack of child care for women
who worked rotating shifts and the problem of where to buy work shoes
in women's sizes. But the most spirited discussion took place in workshops on how the women had gotten their jobs, what they did in the
mines, and how they kept from getting hurt.

Women described how the coal companies had refused to hire them
and had been unwilling even to take their applications. "They stall you
for as long as four years, yet they keep on hiring men," declared Laurie
Thrasher, a miner at U.S. Steel's Concord mine in Birmingham,
Alabama. Finally, U.S. Steel had hired twenty women at the Concord
mine, and now women constituted about 2 percent of the company's
Alabama work force. The company had moved, Thrasher reported, "but
only because they don't want a judgment against them." Then Nancy
Mullins, a forty-year-old grandmother and miner's wife from
Craigsville, West Virginia, told the conference that she had received a
$13,000 settlement from the Pittson Coal Company as compensation for
damages caused by its having ignored her application to be a miner for
four years.

Once hired, women miners described how they had had to fight the
company to be trained and also had to resist the pressure for production
at the expense of safety.* The lack of bathhouses in which women could
clean up after a day's work in the coal dust was high on the list of

---

*On October 2, 1979, thirty-five-year-old Marilyn J. McCusker became the first woman to
be killed while working in a U.S. mine. Mrs. McCusker was a general laborer assigned to
work as a roof bolter at the Rushton Mining Company's deep mine near Osceola Mills,
Pennsylvania. She was running a bolting machine when the roof caved in.

Mrs. McCusker and three other women had sued the mine company in federal court
in 1977, charging sex discrimination. She was awarded a cash settlement and the job as
part of an out-of-court settlement. She had worked in the mine for two years before she
was killed by falling rocks (New York Times, Oct. 5, Nov. 8, 1979). The tragic incident was
also the subject of a moving article, "Called at Rushton," by Calvin Trillin in the New
Yorker magazine (Nov. 12, 1979), which portrays quite graphically the open hostility
displayed by the mine management toward McCusker and her women coworkers.

grievances. A number of women told how they had used the United Mine Workers contract to solve some of their problems. But as Connie Weiss, a woman miner from Virginia, pointed out: "If you don't know your rights, you can't fight for them."

The first National Conference of Women Coal Miners closed with the unanimous adoption of the following resolution:

> We are proud to be UMWA members and we support our union brothers and sisters 100 percent. We need a strong UMWA to defend our rights and protect our working conditions. We resolve to go back to our local unions and fight the companies for affirmative action, against Weber, and for ERA. A woman's place is in the UMWA.[48]

Returning from the National Conference, Linda Triplett told a reporter: "You're going to be hearing a lot from women miners."[49]

The fact that breakthroughs have taken place in nontraditional jobs* should not create the illusion that anything approaching equality for women has been achieved in any of the blue-collar occupations. Apart from the fact that many gains have been nullified by recurring economic recessions and the impact of the "last-hired, first-fired" practice, women are still very poorly represented in a great variety of blue-collar jobs, among which are those of electricians, mechanics, office machine and appliance repairers, telephone installers, meat cutters and butchers, and diesel truck drivers. The first and only woman railroad engineer in this country was hired in 1977 by the Burlington Northern Railroad.†[50]

The majority of women in the workplace are still what Louise Kapp Howe calls "pink-collar workers," holding jobs in such female-concentrated areas as typing, nursing, hairdressing, and sewing. Mrs. Howe points out quite convincingly that most of the women entering the job market today are landing in these "pink-collar ghettos." For example, between 1962 and 1974, the number of women cashiers increased from 82 to 88 percent of the total; bank tellers from 72 to 92 percent; and payroll clerks from 62 to 77 percent.[51]

Mrs. Howe's sobering statistical analysis demonstrates that women are as confined to poorly paid "female" jobs today, with many more of them in the salaried work force, as they were in the 1900s. The Carnegie Corporation underscored the truth of this conclusion when it pointed

---

*By U.S. Labor Department definition, a job is nontraditional if less than 25 percent of the people holding it are women.

†An interesting sidelight is provided in the October–November 1979 issue of *Tempo,* publication of the Fur, Leather & Machine Workers Joint Board of the United Food & Commercial Workers. It contains a letter from John Simmons, the union's chief steward at the Pocahontas Tanning Co. in West Virginia, who sent along a picture of the first women workers at the tannery, fourteen in all, and wrote: "The picture is of all the female workers. . . . One of them is the janitor and the other is the 'night watchwoman.' The women are working out real well and the company plans to hire three more soon."

out in a 1978 report on female discrimination: "The rate of occupational segregation by sex is exactly as great today as it was at the turn of the century, if not greater."[52]

A June, 1978, listing of the Census Classification system revealed that majorities of women workers existed in only 20 out of 441 occupations. Even more startling is the fact that one-quarter of all women workers worked in only five occupations—secretary-stenographer, household worker, bookkeeper, elementary school teacher, and waitress. Over all, women are heavily concentrated in the service sector, and within that sector, in the lower-paying jobs in each category. They make up nearly half of all workers in the retail trades and over 80 percent of all hospital workers. Sixty percent of all workingwomen are clerks, saleswomen, waitresses, or hairdressers.[53] The *Wall Street Journal* concluded its survey of "Women at Work" in the summer of 1978 with the observation: "The majority of women working today hold clerical jobs that provide few chances for advancement. And all of them earn, on the average, only about $6 for every $10 earned by men. That ratio has not changed much since 1955, when the government began keeping such data."[54]

Despite the passage of the Equal Pay Act in 1953, which mandated equal pay for equal work, the gap between women's and men's earnings has grown in the last two decades. The authors of *The Subtle Revolution: Women at Work*, published in September, 1979, note that on the average, women make just under 60 percent of what men make, down from 63 percent in 1956. One reason for the discrepancy, according to the study, is that many women entering the job market for the first time are placed in low-paying jobs. Another is the difference in job assignments. "In business concerns, for instance," the authors note, "personnel officers may routinely seek women for secretarial positions and men as management trainees."[55]

But the secretarial pool is not the only locale of the "female ghetto." Throughout industry, hundreds of jobs are filled only by women, while others—the better-paying jobs—are occupied solely by men. In the automobile industry, for example, despite the presence of a number of women on the assembly lines, most women are generally put in the lower-paying jobs, such as those of cutting or sewing. Similarly, in the textile mills, the loom fixers are men and the loom tenders are women. Their pay differential is considerable. In the J. P. Stevens mills, discrimination against women is particularly pronounced. A study by the National Women's Committee to Support J. P. Stevens Workers* concluded:

*Sponsored by the Coalition of Labor Union Women (CLUW), the National Organization of Women (NOW), and the National Assembly of Women Religious (NAWR), the National Women's Committee to Support J. P. Stevens Workers was formed early in 1978.

A breakdown of the company employment by sex and race shows that black men and women are concentrated in the lower-skilled blue-collar jobs, while white women are similarly restricted. While white women have greater access to white-collar jobs than blacks, the great majority (85%) of the white females in these jobs are in the office-clerical category. By contrast, 71% of the white men in white-collar jobs are classified as managerial, administrative, professional or technical. The great bulk of the white women in blue-collar jobs (98%) are in the semi-skilled and unskilled classifications, while 25% of the white men in these jobs are classified as skilled workers.[56]

What is it like for a woman to work for J. P. Stevens, the second-largest textile company in the United States, about half of whose 44,000 workers are female? "It's like being on the chain gang . . . except no guns. Just pressure. Pressure all the time," says Mildred Whitley, a Stevens worker in Roanoke Rapids, North Carolina. After twenty-six years at Stevens, Whitley had a radical mastectomy and asked to be placed on a lighter job. She reported: "My supervisor told me that I could go ask the welfare for help. He informed me that I could either run the job no matter what it did to me, I could quit, or else he would fire me. All they want is your blood and then they let you go."

Nor is Whitley's story unique. She and other Stevens employees describe company practices in *Testimony: Justice vs. J. P. Stevens*, a twenty-two-minute color film produced by the Citizens' Committee for Justice for J. P. Stevens Workers,* in connection with the nationwide consumer boycott of Stevens products conducted by the Amalgamated Clothing and Textile Workers Union (ACTWU) in its campaign to organize J. P. Stevens. The company has been found guilty of violating the National Labor Relations Act fifteen times and has been adjudged guilty of contempt by a federal court of appeals for its antiunion activities.

The film is made up mostly of individual testimonials from Stevens workers about safety conditions, racial discrimination, the health hazards of cotton dust, and the attempts by Stevens to defeat the union with a barrage of often illegal tactics. Maurine Hedgepeth, a Stevens worker with three children, testifies about having been illegally fired for "talkin' union." She began work in the mills in 1957. After appearing before the National Labor Relations Board in 1964, she went on pregnancy leave.

> In January, when my leave was up, they wouldn't give me my job back. They told us if any of us was goin' to get any work we would have to leave town to do it, because nobody would hire us. Stevens doesn't just fire you. They fire your whole family. It took four years and 21 days before I got my job back. I had to go all the way up through the courts.

---

*The film was produced by Harold Mayer and Lynne Rhodes Mayer, who also produced the film on the Farah strike.

The film emphasizes the unity of interests between black and white workers. In one scene, a group of workers are talking about company efforts to foster racial antagonisms. "Before the election, they tried to pit the blacks against the whites and the whites against the blacks anyway they could," says a white woman. "But they were just trying to get the white people not to join the union. It didn't work."

"And so a long, grinding battle is now under way," concludes *Testimony*. "It is too late for us that're sick," says Lucy Taylor, a victim of brown-lung disease from breathing cotton dust. "But for the people working in the plants, and for our children that're coming on after us, we ask you to help us. Boycott J. P. Stevens."*

This film is set mainly in Roanoke Rapids, where 3,500 workers voted in 1974 for representation by ACTWU. After five years of negotiations, the company, defying the U.S. government, still refuses to agree to a contract in Roanoke Rapids. Nevertheless, the union is the certified bargaining agent, and the company must notify it in advance of all firings, disciplinary actions, and other changes in wages and working conditions. The union has the right to examine certain company records and to negotiate these items. Although the grievance procedure lacks teeth because of the absence of a contract, the union has been able to force reinstatement of some women who were fired unjustly. Linda Blythe, a drawing hand† in the card room at the Patterson Plant in Roanoke Rapids, is one of the women who was reinstated after the union and Stevens had argued her case for twenty-eight days. She told a reporter:

> I used to be scared. The boss-man would take me into the office and talk to me about something and I'd start crying. I was so scared I'd just sit there and cry and they would keep right on yelling. Now I don't cry no more because I know I have somebody that will back me up and I know my rights.[57]

---

*Although overshadowed by the boycott against J. P. Stevens, the boycott against Miss Goldy chickens, marketed by Sanderson Farms, a chicken processing company in Laurel, Mississippi, merits attention. Authorized by the AFL-CIO, the boycott is in support of 200 women strikers, most of them black, who went on strike against Sanderson Farms in February, 1979. The strike was led by Local 882, International Chemical Workers Union, and began after negotiations failed to produce a new contract. In addition to demanding higher wages—most of the workers are paid about $3.15 an hour, five cents more than the current Federal minimum wage—the women, who unload and cut the chickens, demanded improved health and safety conditions, and an end to sexual harrassment by male bosses at the plant.

Leading the picket line of women strikers a year after the strike began, Gloria Jordan, vice president of Local 882, told a reporter: "We were slaves on that plantation, but we got tired of that, so we left that plantation. We did not have any dignity when we worked.... Now we are not making any wages, but I say we have our dignity." (*New York Times,* February 27, 1980.)

†A drawing hand operates a machine for drawing slivers of thread.

Already, it is clear, the union-organizing campaign is giving the women who work for J. P. Stevens courage and self-confidence. Further proof is the fact that within the space of a month, the union won the first two elections held in Stevens plants in five years—in High Point, North Carolina, and Allendale, South Carolina.*[58]

In the garment industry, women sew and men cut. More than seventy years after the historic garment struggles for union conditions began, many women, especially blacks and Hispanics, still sew in sweatshops. Both the federal government and the ILGWU have acknowledged that in New York City there are five hundred sweatshops where women work at machines sewing dresses in small, grimy dress factories. As the *New York Times* reported in September, 1979, the shops

> are situated in dank cellars and broiling lofts, in barricaded storefronts and back-alley garages, in dingy attics and rundown apartments. They exploit minorities and illegal aliens, paying wages below the Federal minimum of $2.90 an hour, often operating from sunrise to sunset but not paying for overtime and sending out cut fabric for illegal sewing at home. They prey on the fears of workers who worry about losing their jobs or being deported as illegal aliens.

One of the sweatshop workers told the *Times* reporter that some of the women were paid as little as 75 cents a dress. She herself took bundles home to sew so she could watch over her two young children while she worked:

> I pick up a bundle every week. They told me last week they would pay me $1.10 a dress. But when I took back 12 dresses, they said they couldn't pay me until later. They just keep you hanging. Then you do some more work because you hope you'll be paid if you do it. I need the money but it's very unfair the way they treat us.[59]

Over the past decade, California has developed a garment industry second in size only to that of New York. More than 100,000 workers are employed in the industry there, about 60 percent of the number in New York. Probably more than 80 percent of the garment workers in California are of Hispanic origin, and the majority have entered the United States without the necessary documents. For many years, union leaders in the United States ignored the flood of such "undocumented workers," and when they did begin to acknowledge their existence, they fought to have Congress enact legislation to prevent their hiring.

Meanwhile, the sweatshops spread throughout the entire California

---

*The 68-to-48 victory at a Stevens plant in High Point on October 1, 1979, giving the Amalgamated Clothing and Textile Workers Union the right to represent more than 115 employees, was actually the second clear-cut election won by a union in the sixteen-year struggle with Stevens. The first came in 1974 for the more than three thousand Stevens employees at seven plants in Roanoke Rapids, North Carolina (see above, pp. 472–74). At this writing, the union still had not negotiated a contract at Roanoke Rapids.

garment industry. In January, 1979, after an investigation of the industry, the California Division of Labor Enforcement reported that 999 of 1,083 manufacturers in Los Angeles were violating state minimum-wage and overtime laws, that 376 did not have workmen's compensation insurance, and that many others were violating child labor laws and other state statutes. In place of the $2.90 hourly minimum, the sweatshop workers were lucky to get $2. For many, the forty-hour week was extended to one of sixty to seventy hours.

During the 1940s the ILGWU had built a membership of over twenty thousand in Los Angeles. With the influx of undocumented workers, however, that number had dwindled to less than seven thousand by 1975. In that year, the ILGWU leadership decided to abandon its previous policy of shunning undocumented workers and set out to organize the estimated eighty thousand garment workers in Los Angeles, most of whom were undocumented women from Mexico. It was the first organizing effort by a major union among undocumented workers. As Philip Russo, the ILGWU's chief organizer in Los Angeles, noted, the union had decided to break from the labor movement's traditional "no-aliens" stance "after realizing it would have to represent illegal aliens if it was going to continue representing garment workers."[60]

By 1979, other unions had decided to adopt a similar policy. The United Farm Workers signed a contract specifically covering undocumented farm workers; the retail clerks' union began a drive to organize them in some occupations in California, and the state's garment industry's three unions—the ILGWU, ACTWU, and the United Garment Workers—have undertaken to organize undocumented workers as well.[61]

As of 1960, 35 percent of black women workers were still domestic servants, and only 9 percent had clerical jobs. But by 1974, some 25 percent of the black women who were in the labor force had clerical jobs, and the percentage of black women who were servants had fallen to 11 percent. In 1963, white women earned an average of 36 percent more than black women; by 1973, the difference was 12 percent, and by May, 1974, the gap had been reduced to only 7 percent.[62]

However, while the differences in occupational and wage levels between white and black women have narrowed, the combined effects of racism and sexism remain. Seventeen percent of black women are still private-household workers, and only 38 percent of them hold white-collar jobs (as compared with 60 percent of all women workers). Nationally, black women continue to be concentrated in low-paying jobs. Not surprisingly, the Women's Bureau's 1977 booklet *Women with Low Incomes* revealed that among black women who worked year round, 33 percent were below the poverty line.[63]

In *Pink Collar Workers*, Louise Kapp Howe, while pointing out that seemingly overwhelming obstacles block women from preparing for and securing advancement in rewarding, useful work, nevertheless warns against "attitudes of gloom and doom." She prescribes

> a full employment program that will mean adequate and decent opportunities for all people, college and non-college, outside the pink-collar zone should they want it, particularly in the crowded labor market coming up. Unionization, flexible hours, affirmative action, equal education, particularly equal vocational education, paid maternity leaves, quality child care, all the middle range issues women are now working on—a deeper understanding of how this economic system capitalizes on the conflicts of women in dual roles—and little things like chairs for store workers.[64]

But if there is one point that *Pink Collar Workers* makes loud and clear, it is that women need to organize in unions and to make the unions serve their needs.

There are over 11 million office workers in the United States, and 76 percent of them are women. One in every three workingwomen spends her day in an office, but less than 10 percent of the office workers are organized. Yet the need for unionization in this area is acute. The average pay for all clerical work is $8,128 a year, only slightly above the current poverty level of $6,800 for a nonfarm family of four—and many clerical workers earn even less. Karen Shaver, a twenty-six-year-old secretary and mother of two from Winston-Salem, North Carolina, who is separated from her husband, told the members of the President's Advisory Committee for Women in September, 1979, that she was barely able to make ends meet on her $6,800-a-year-net income.

"One-half of my salary alone pays for my day-care costs, which are $3,255.20 a year," Shaver said. "This leaves me no money for groceries, not to mention maintaining a home. This is the very reason why my parents have three boarders now—myself and my two children." Then, her voice growing angry, she said: "I'm here today to tell you that working women are tired of working for a living when half of the low pay we as secretaries receive pays for the day-care costs alone. We're tired of not being able to afford enough to eat at times and our children being fed bologna sandwiches and God knows what else."[65]

While union representation of white-collar workers has jumped over 50 percent in the past twenty years, the main increases so far have been among service workers, principally teachers and hospital workers. Among office workers, the great majority of those who belong to a union are government employees. With rare exceptions, the male-dominated, blue-collar-oriented leadership of the trade unions has been slow to organize female clerical workers. Union officials argue that such employees are traditionally hard to unionize, are too personally involved with their employers, and do not think of themselves as permanent employees. Because the turnover rate is high—an estimated 25 to

45 percent—the unionists argue that it is a temporary occupation, a stepping stone to either better things or marriage.

As a result, recent efforts to organize clerical workers have taken place largely independently of the established unions and have emerged directly out of the women's movement. Marge Albert, a pioneer in these efforts in New York City and an organizer for District 65, wrote in the *New York Times:*

> The beginning of the new spirit in offices came a few years ago (1969–70) when employers imposed dress codes that decreed we couldn't wear pants to work. Women rebelled. They petitioned, sent delegations to management or simply agreed that on a particular day they'd all wear pants. . . . Employers who thought their "girls" were immune to the subversive ideas of "feminism" found these women suddenly making demands—to be treated with respect, to earn more money, to define their duties, to advance and to get fringe benefits other workers enjoy.[66]

In Boston a group of several hundred women founded Nine to Five in 1973. The organization drew up an "Office Workers' Bill of Rights," demanding equal pay and promotion opportunities, detailed job descriptions, maternity benefits, overtime pay, and the right to refuse to do personal errands for the employer. Through leafleting, meetings, and speakouts, the organized surveys of working conditions, Nine to Five mobilized women in Boston's large publishing and insurance industries. It also filed sex discrimination suits, picketed target companies, and pressured government agencies for strict enforcement of antidiscrimination laws.[67]

In Chicago's Loop area, about three hundred women formed Women Employed (WE) because, explained one of its leaflets,

> we feel we are not receiving decent wages, our work is not respected and we don't have promotion opportunities. Many of us have tried individually to change the situation but have come to realize that only when women form a pressure group will real changes be possible. We discovered that women are 45 percent of the Loop labor force but earn only 25 percent of the wages.[68]

WE grew to more than a thousand dues-paying members in over a hundred worksites. It exposed the sexist hiring practices of major employers in Chicago, won $1 million in back-pay suits, forced major companies to develop affirmative action plans, pressured the government to investigate sex bias, and won a state regulation banning the sale of discriminatory insurance policies.[69]

On the West Coast, Union WAGE (Women Act to Gain Equality) continued to provide information, legal advice, and picketing support to women office workers who tried to organize their coworkers in the Bay Area. Across the Bay, women clerical workers organized their own caucuses in the Alameda County Employees Union.[70]

In New York City, over three hundred office workers held a conference in October, 1973, where they discussed their working conditions and formed a citywide group called Women Office Workers (WOW), which announced:

> Our labor supports New York City as the financial, administrative and communications capital of our country. We process the materials in corporate headquarters, bank and insurance companies, government offices and behind desks in publishing, advertising and the media. But despite our numbers and our importance, our wages are low. For Black and Puerto Rican women, wages are even lower.[71]

On April 21, 1976, Women Office Workers Day in New York City was marked by such traditional events as employers taking their secretaries to lunch and giving them gifts of roses. But it was also marked by a lunchtime rally featuring the reading of a Women Office Workers' Bill of Rights, including the right to organize on the job and the right to choose whether or not to do the personal work of employers. "We don't want a day of token recognition like Mother's Day," WOW's Pat Fitzgerald told the rally. "We want real improvements in our working lives all year round."[72]

Over a dozen independent organizations of office workers have sprung up in cities across the country. Among their contributions has been the encouragement of workingwomen to speak out and seek protection against sexual harassment by male supervisors. WOW has worked closely with the Working Women United Institute (WWUI) in revealing the extent of unwanted sexual advances in various occupations, especially among office workers, and the degree to which job security is dependent on how well the female employee satisfies the boss as a sex object rather than as a worker.

WOW has also expressed objection to the frequent requirement that women workers perform all kinds of personal services for their employers. In a survey of fifteen thousand office workers, WOW found that 57 percent felt that they were not treated with respect as office workers and 33 percent reported sexual abuse, including threats of dismissal if they failed to comply with their employers' advances. Unfortunately, WOW reported, male-dominated unions were unlikely to provide any support for the women so threatened, and in any case, the vast majority of the women workers were not members of unions.*

---

*The Association of Flight Attendants and the American Federation of State, County & Municipal Employees (AFSCME) are among the few unions actively struggling against the sexual harassment of their members. But they have not been notably successful. Fear of reprisals has prevented women from utilizing the grievance procedure, and arbitrators have often dismissed complaints for "lack of evidence." In October, 1975, the Screen Actors Guild set up a morals complaint bureau designed to arbitrate harassment charges, and later the guild wrote into its contract a prohibition against conducting job interviews outside the office (*Wall Street Journal*, Jan. 29, 1976).

Fortunately, pressure from organizations like WOW and the concern of Eleanor Holmes Norton, chairperson of the Equal Employment Opportunity Commission (EEOC), produced an important action to curb sexual harassment on the job. "Sexual Harassment At Work Outlawed," was a front-page headline in the *New York Times* of April 12, 1980. The day before, EEOC published regulations explicitly forbidding sexual harassment of employees by their supervisors. The rules, Eleanor Holmes Norton explained, applied to Federal, state and local government agencies and to private employers with 15 or more employees. The rules state that employers have an "affirmative duty" to prevent and eliminate sexual harassment, which may be "either physical or verbal in nature." The rules set forth three criteria for determining whether an action constitutes unlawful sexual harassment. "Unwelcome sexual advances" become illegal if the employee's submission is an explicit or implicit condition of employment, if the employee's response becomes a basis for employment decisions, or if the advance interferes with workers' performance, creating a hostile or "offensive" environment. Harassment on the basis of sex is declared a violation of Section 703 of Title VII of the Civil Rights Act of 1964, and to enforce the rules EEOC can ask for an award of back pay, resinstatment of an employee, promotion or other types of relief available under Title VII.

As the history of Title VII demonstrates, it will take more than rules to outlaw sexual harassment at work. But the EEOC action is an important step forward in dealing with a problem increasingly important for the increasing numbers of working women.

Nine to Five continued to exist and function as a separate organization. But it also took the initiative in 1975 in launching Local 925 of the Service Employees International Union (SEIU). SEIU was chosen after Nine to Five had approached ten different unions but found none of

---

On October 8, 1979, fourteen hundred members of Local 3-38, International Woodworkers of America (IWA), all but fifty male lumber workers, shut down three logging camps and five mills in Shelton, Washington, in support of a woman member of the union fired for refusing to drop charges of sexual harassment against the Simpson Lumber Company. During the strike seven women employed at Simpson signed affidavits reporting that during their hiring interviews they had been "asked to take off their blouses, asked if they wore a bra, asked if they would have sex with their supervisors and had to endure comments about their breasts." Local 3-38 President Jim Lowry told the press that "as male chauvinistic as our workers might be, even they don't tolerate that kind of interview process" (*Guardian,* November 21, 1979, p. 4; *In These Times,* Dec. 5–11, 1979, p. 5.)

In the cases that reached the federal courts, judges at first ruled that sexual harassment does not constitute discrimination under the meaning of the Civil Rights Act. However, in July, 1977, the U.S. Court of Appeals in Washington, D.C., held that sexual harassment by a woman's employer or supervisor constituted sex discrimination under Title VII of the 1964 Civil Rights Act. In April, 1978, a Denver workingwoman was reinstated in her job and awarded back pay by a federal judge on the ground of violation of the Civil Rights Act because she had been fired for refusing to have sex with her boss (*New York Times,* July 12, 1977, Apr. 6, 1978).

them willing to finance an organizing drive among clerical workers while also meeting Nine to Five's request for complete autonomy and sensitivity to women's issues. The SEIU, a half-million-member union, prides itself on the fact that "scores of women have helped shape the union's direction since its AFL charter in 1929," that the union has "encouraged a leadership role for women from the beginning," and that it has always taken a position in support of "women's issues." It welcomed Nine to Five's initiative and gave the new local complete control over how it conducted its organizing and the hiring and firing of staff. Local 925 also receives training programs, legal support, research, and other assistance from the SEIU's international office, which makes a sizable contribution to the local's budget as well.[74]

All three of Local 925's full-time organizers are women who were connected with Nine to Five. The women-led local organizes women office workers in the private sector. It scored a key victory in 1977 when it unionized the 160-worker Allyn & Bacon Company, a Boston publishing house, and negotiated a contract there. It has also organized workers at several day care centers, at some Boston-area libraries, and at legal service agencies. A major campaign was launched against the First National Bank of Boston in the spring of 1979.

"Most women we deal with," local president and founding member Jackie Ruff has noted, "have had no direct contact with unions before. There is a tradition of white-collar consciousness expressed in the feeling that unions are for blue-collar workers, not secretaries." Then, too, the sheer lack of time that women workers had to commit to a union organizing campaign has also held back union drives. "They are holding down two full-time jobs, one at work and one at home," Ruff pointed out. Many of the women the local's organizers encountered were middle-aged and often politically conservative. "But they're not conservative when it comes to their rights," Ruff added, and the local's experience showed that all the obstacles that traditionally held back the organization of women clerical workers could be overcome. Although it had only a little over 350 members in 1979, the SEIU was confident that by "combining the best of the labor movement and the best of the women's movement," Boston's Local 925 would become a major force in the organization of women office workers.[75]

In 1978 a major step toward reaching clerical workers for unionization was taken with the formation of Working Women, National Association of Office Workers. This is a national association with twelve loca¹ affiliated organizations including Nine to Five in Boston, Women Office Workers in New York, Women Working in Cleveland, and Women Organized for Employment in San Francisco. Working Women's headquarters are in Cleveland and its director is former Local 925 organizer Karen Nussbaum. Membership is about eight thousand, but prospects for future growth are encouraging. Local affiliates have been successful in winning discrimination suits, forcing changes in working conditions, and successfully challenging a number of carefully chosen employers on such issues as equal pay and promotions, partly by petitioning federal and state authorities to enforce existing equal employment statutes.[76]

Working Women has made the nation's banks a special target. About 1.25 million of some 2 million bank employees are women, and 85 percent of them are in low-paying, usually dead-end jobs. A campaign against the New England Merchants National Bank in Boston, resulted in the promotion of more than a dozen women to officer level and the equalization of pay for female employees in several job categories. The campaign has caused the federal government to undertake its first major investigation of sex discrimination in the banking industry.*[55]

President Nussbaum told an interviewer that her organization's experience shows that there is a broad potential for union organizing among clerical workers. She declared:

> One in every five workers is in the clerical sector, and 80 percent of them are women. Yet the average salary is $8,000 a year for women clericals and $12,000 for men. Some banks hire tellers at $115 a week—that's not much more than the minimum wage. It may take five to ten years, but eventually there's going to be a sweeping unionization of clericals.[78]

However, Nussbaum and other officers of Working Women concede that there are limits to what can be accomplished without the legal right to bargain and to win an enforceable contract. For this reason, some see the independent women's groups as "sort of half-way houses on the road to full unionization," as in the case of Nine to Five, which launched Local 925 of the SEIU.[79]

The possibilities of using the independent women's groups to reach many women who would initially be turned off by a traditional union have been recognized by a number of unions. The SEIU was the first to see the value of such an alliance and continues to work with the nation-

---

*The campaign to organize the nation's bank workers received a major impetus when the AFL-CIO Executive Council voted in the summer of 1979 to endorse a national boycott of the Seattle-First National Bank, based in Seattle, and urged all labor organizations, union members, and the general public to withdraw their funds from the bank until it agreed to recognize and bargain in good faith with Local 1182 of the United Food & Commercial Workers. The local had been chartered by the Retail Clerks International Union, a forerunner of the UFCW, when the largest independent union of bank workers, with 4,700 employees at 176 locations throughout the state, voted in 1978 to affiliate with the RCIU. Even though the National Labor Relations Board panel unanimously agreed that the affiliation vote was proper, the bank refused to bargain in good faith and was charged by the Labor Board with "unfair labor practices." As of this writing, over one hundred labor organizations in the state of Washington have withdrawn funds from the bank, but Seattle-First persists in its refusal to bargain and has appealed the NLRB decision to the U.S. Court of Appeals (UFCW *Action*, September 1979, p. 23).

wide movement of independent women's groups.[80] The Communications Workers of America has also begun to move in the same direction. The CWA started a program with Women Employed in Chicago which exists as an independent organization, in which WE will do the groundwork in organizing a number of workplaces, turning over to the union information on successful techniques and the names of women in specific organizations who might be interested in an organizing drive. The union would then undertake responsibility for the organization drive itself.

In July, 1979, the CWA allocated funds for the expansion of the project to include other workingwomen's groups around the country. "I don't know of any union that has really tried to get at these workers," Patsy Fryman, assistant to CWA President Glenn Watts and a CLUW officer, told the *New York Times*, "but we are sure going to try."[81]

Actually, several other unions have "tried" and are still trying "to get at these workers." The Teamsters were successful in organizing nineteen hundred clerical workers at the University of Chicago, a result that was hailed as "a major victory."[82] District 65, now of the UAW, has also made inroads among clerical workers at private universities. Beginning with its successful organizing at Barnard College in New York, in 1974, District 65 has organized workers on the campuses of Boston University, Union College, and Teachers' College of Columbia University. At Boston University, an antilabor administration provoked an organizational strike that united the teaching and clerical staffs, and District 65 was able to register an important victory in achieving its first contract there after another walkout just after Labor Day, 1979.[83]

In the publishing field, District 65 not only used the affiliation of the formerly independent Association of Harper & Row Employees as a jumping-off point for the organization of publishing houses—which has already brought it success at Prentice-Hall in New Jersey—but it has also organized the editors, writers, and clerical personnel at the *Village Voice* newspaper in New York City. With its affiliation to the UAW in June, 1979, District 65, whose membership was already one-half women and one-third minority employees, looks forward to new and even greater advances among women and minority workers, including the vast body of unorganized clerical employees.[84]

Although the Office and Professional Employees International Union (OPEIU) was organized in 1945, until recently, the AFL-CIO affiliate had been lethargic about organizing. It made a major breakthrough, however, when it succeeded in unionizing several large offices of Blue Cross–Blue Shield. The victory of OPEIU Local 29, a local of clerical workers, at Blue Cross in Oakland, California, was particularly noteworthy. In 1977, Local 29, headed by President Edith Withington, a long-time militant in the labor movement, won the election at Oakland

Blue Cross by the overwhelming vote of 747 to 141. However, it took a strike to gain a contract that included wage increases ranging between $80 and $200 per month, automatic raises, recognition of seniority, a grievance procedure, an extra holiday, and an end to subcontracting out certain kinds of work. The union also won a provision for an agency shop, which meant that every worker in the unit at Blue Cross had to pay union dues or their equivalent in fees to the union.

Commenting on the victory, President Withington declared:

> I think one of the reasons we won Blue Cross was that we came across with women—we were women out there handing out leaflets—men, too, but it wasn't a bunch of men trying to organize a bunch of women. We were not looking down at them. They were our sisters. And even though one didn't make an issue of women's rights *per se,* the fact remained that we were women. We are a union whose membership is predominantly women and whose leadership reflects it.

Since the Blue Cross victory, the local has been approached by clerical workers at other locations seeking help in organizing. Withington and her colleagues see "the organization of clericals—women mainly—as the coming thing in the labor movement."[85]

In addition to independent women's groups of clerical workers, already called "the nationwide 9 to 5 movement," independent organizing has also emerged among household workers, "the last frontier of labor organizing." According to Department of Labor statistics, 97 percent of the household workers in 1976 were women. Fifty-three percent were black, another 4 percent Spanish-speaking, and the remainder from a smattering of European, Asian, and Pacific cultures. Wages averaged $2,732 a year—less than the poverty level—and two-thirds of the workers earned under $2,000 a year. Household workers enjoy no fringe benefits, no sick pay, no paid vacations, no pensions, no health insurance, no overtime, no severance pay, and no workmen's compensation, and in twenty-nine states there is no unemployment compensation for these workers.[87]

The first group to attempt to combat these evils in recent years was the National Committee on Household Employment (NCHE), formed in 1964. By 1969 it was organizing janitors, caretakers, and gardeners, as well as cooks and governesses, into local self-help groups to improve working conditions. At its first national convention in 1971, NCHE sponsored the formation of the Household Technicians of America (HTA). By 1976 the union claimed eight hundred dues-paying members in thirty-one chapters from Ohio to Florida.

Both the NCHA and the HTA are seeking to bring household workers under contracts that spell out working conditions, duties, levels of pay, sick leave, hospitalization, extra pay for holiday work, retirement benefits, and the like. Both also urge household workers to pay their social security and unemployment compensation contributions, arguing that only in this way can they avoid being helpless when they cannot find jobs and are too old to work.[88]

In the same area, New York's Community & Social Agency Employees District 1707 of AFSCME succeeded in organizing about 2,500 employees of Selfhelp Community Services—mostly black and Hispanic women—who provide homemaking services for the homebound aged and disabled.[89] As of this writing, however, the union has not been able to conclude negotiations of a first contract covering these workers.

As indicated earlier, District 1199 of the National Union of Hospital & Health Care Employees has demonstrated on several occasions how the cooperation of the trade unions and civil rights organizations resulted in successful organizing of hospital workers, most of them black and Hispanic women. Similarly, the unity of the trade unions and the independent women's groups—or, as SEIU put it, "the best of the labor movement and the best of the women's movement"—offers a new potential for organizing vast members of unorganized workingwomen. And whatever the shortcomings of trade unions as far as women are concerned, it is clear that women who are union members are better off in terms of wages, benefits, and working conditions than the majority of women who are not.[90] Increasing the percentage of women workers who are union members is of importance to all workingwomen—but the organization of workingwomen is likewise of the utmost importance to the entire labor movement.

The composition of the labor force is shifting from the male-dominated, blue-collar manufacturing and mining industries to the service and clerical fields, which have long been considered "women's work." In 1975, jobs in the clerical, retail, hospital, and food service fields accounted for 44 percent of the work force, and they have also accounted for most of the new jobs created since then. "If organized labor is to survive, it has to move into these areas," says Gena Polk of the Teamsters' Union.[91]

The challenge to labor is also illustrated by the fact that women have accounted for almost half of the growth in total union membership between 1956 and 1976. Between 1976 and 1978, the number of women members of trade unions, according to the Department of Labor, increased by 455,000. In the latter year, some 6.7 million women were members of trade unions, including such organizations as the National Education Association.*[92] Whereas in 1970 women made up only 12

*According to the Labor Department's analysis, trade union membership for 1978 showed a decline in the percentage of workers organized. This decline has continued almost uninterrupted for two decades. In 1978 only 19.7 percent of the U.S. work force was in unions, while in 1960 the figure was 23.6 percent.

percent of the union members in the United States, by 1976 the figure was up to 20 percent, and as of 1977, according to the Department of Labor's Bureau of Labor Statistics, women accounted for 27.6 of the employed wage and salary workers in labor unions. However, the bureau is quick to point out that while women constitute 40.5 percent of the civilian labor force, "substantial numbers of workingwomen have not become union members."[93]

The study points out further that labor union membership continues, as in to the past, to be concentrated among blue-collar workers. But the majority of women today are employed in white-collar and service jobs, which, with notable exceptions, the unions have not tried to organize. The masses of women workers, unorganized and underpaid, are still locked into the same pattern of discrimination that they faced before World War I. Most are still segregated into "women's jobs," which, by definition, are ill-paid, dead-end, and without prestige. Many of the gains made by the women's movement in its legal attacks on job discrimination and in opening up new jobs have been eroded by the succession of economic crises. Women still carry the double burden of two full-time jobs, one at work and the other at home. On salaries kept lower than men's, many working mothers must bear the added burden of paying for child-care services.

Pointing up this situation, CLUW President Joyce Miller, in her keynote address to the organization's biennial convention on September 15, 1979, insisted: "Women will not achieve equality in the workplace without the collective strength of unions behind them."[94] Unfortunately, however, the trade union movement has not moved with either speed or enthusiasm to use its "collective strength" to organize the new masses of women workers or to fight for equal rights for those women who are already organized. The tradition of sex discrimination is still operative in too many unions, as it is on the job.

Nevertheless, it is also true that more and more unions are coming to understand that unless they do organize the women who are entering the work force in ever-increasing numbers, they will not survive. These unions are devoting more and more attention to sex discrimination. The American Federation of State, County & Municipal Employees (AFSCME), for example, has distributed to all its locals, councils, and members a pamphlet called *What About Sex Discrimination?* The publication notes that "a labor union must fight discrimination in two roles—as representatives for workers and as employers."* Unions, it continues, must do more than simply refrain from discrimination: "Unions must challenge the discriminatory practices of employers with whom they bargain." Again: "Unions have a responsibility to see that equal pay laws

*The reference is to staff members employed by the union.

are carried out for their membership, especially at the bargaining table."
The pamphlet includes "An Action Program," which offers the following suggestions "to assist locals and councils in fighting sex discrimination on behalf of the female employees they represent as well as their
own employees":

What to Look For:
1. Examine collective bargaining agreements and look for possible evidence
   of sex discrimination, such as:
   • Are females denied the same promotion and transfer rights as males?
   • Are women unable to return to their old jobs with no loss of seniority
     following childbirth?
   • Are pension plan benefits for women different than for male em-
     ployees?
2. Check the workplace, looking at every area of employment, for discrimi-
   nation in job situations, such as:
   • Are women paid less for substantially the same work as men?
   • Are certain jobs or departments all or nearly all male, while others are
     all or nearly all female? (Statistics may be strong evidence of discrimina-
     tion.)
   • Are most females hired in at a lower rate of pay than most males?
   • Are females denied training or promotion opportunities offered to
     males?[95]

There are other questions that are not asked in the pamphlet but are
equally relevant to the question "What About Sex Discrimination?":
   • Are women represented properly in local, regional, and national positions
     of leadership?
   • Is space devoted in local and national union papers and magazines to
     women workers and to discussions of "women's issues," such as child care,
     maternity leave, and equitable protection for all women under the nation's
     social security system?
   • Is the belief still strong among male members that women cannot be or-
     ganized, with the result that little is done by the local union to organize
     unorganized women?
   • Is the history and role of women in building the American labor move-
     ment, and the union itself, brought to the attention of all members, men
     and women alike?

In his pamphlet *Sexism in the Labor Movement*, Harry Kelber suggested
that in unions where women constituted a substantial part or an actual
majority of the membership, they should organize themselves into caucuses and insist on various measures to protect their rights. He proposed
that the following demands be included in the program:
   • Women must be adequately represented on the union's negotiating
     committee to guarantee that they get a fair deal at the bargaining table....
   • Women must have membership on shop and local union grievance
     committees and be given an active role in contract enforcement....

> • Women must have seats on the union's executive board and other policy-making committees. . . .
> • Women must be given a fair share of leadership positions in each shop or local union. . . .

Perhaps the most concrete proposal for dealing with the issues facing women workers, and one that could serve as a model for many trade unions, is the resolution "Support Full Equality for Women," adopted by the 44th UE International Convention in September, 1979. The union pledged to continue its fight for no rates below common labor for women and for equal pay for work of equal value; to support job-posting and job-training programs that would enhance women's skills and upgrade them into better-paying jobs; to fight to make companies live up to their legal obligation to treat disability due to pregnancy as they would any other disability; and to pay special attention to the elimination of conditions that would impair the ability of workers to have healthy children. The resolution continued:

> Our union supports the right of all women, if they so choose, to obtain safe, legal abortions, and we oppose cutbacks in Medicaid funding for abortions;
>
> UE also supports programs that guarantee quality pre- and post-natal care for all women, and develop safe and effective birth control devices that are readily accessible;
>
> Our union continues to fight for the equal treatment of women and men under the law by working for the ratification of the ERA, and by continuing to refuse to schedule meetings in any state which has not ratified the ERA;
>
> Our union supports Federal funding for quality, around-the-clock child care programs for the children of working parents, and for the provision of extra sick time for workers with small children;
>
> Our union continues its support of other organizations involved in the struggle to achieve full social and economic justice for all women workers, and that we encourage fuller participation of our members in the Coalition of Labor Union Women; and
>
> BE IT FINALLY RESOLVED, that UE intensify its efforts to encourage the full participation of women in all levels of the union and in their community.[97]

On the eve of the AFL-CIO's thirteenth biennial convention in November, 1979, President George Meany, eighty-five and ill since the previous spring, announced that he would not seek a new term. It was assumed that he would be replaced by AFL-CIO Secretary-Treasurer Lane Kirkland; Mim Kelber, former policy consultant for the National Advisory Committee for Women, observed pessimistically: "Whether Lane Kirkland will use his new authority to promote female representation on the [Executive] Council remains in question."[98] But in his first major action as AFL-CIO president, Kirkland announced an initiative to bring women (as well as blacks and Hispanic-Americans) into top leadership positions within the federation. Traditionally, only chief executive officers of major affiliated unions of the federation have been elected to the Executive Council. Noting that no major union was headed by a woman, Kirkland disclosed that a committee of the council had been appointed "to explore in depth, and with seriousness of purpose, ways and means" by which women and minorities could be brought into the council. He indicated, too, that while the size of the council could not officially be enlarged until the next convention in 1981, women and minority members might be named to the council on a nonvoting basis until then, if the committee so decided. The committee might also decide to waive the tradition of requiring council members be general officers in their unions.[99] Actually, under the federation's written constitution, any member in good standing of any union in good standing is eligible for election to the council.

On August 21, 1980, Joyce D. Miller, president of the Coalition of Labor Union Women, became the first female member of the AFL-CIO Executive Council. Two other actions taken about the same time by the AFL-CIO indicated that a significant shift in policy toward women workers may be taking place. For one thing, as the AFL-CIO ended its 1979 biennial convention, for the first time the delegates went beyond the traditional support of equal pay for equal work by men and women. Women's organizations had complained that women are traditionally pushed into jobs, such as secretarial work, that may require the same skills, training, and effort as "men's work," such as semiskilled factory work, but that pay considerably less. The women's organizations demanded that pay for such comparable work be equalized.* In an unprecedented action, the AFL-CIO convention voted to support measures to end disparities in wages of men and women engaged in comparable

*As far back as 1952, conferences sponsored and held by UE on women's problems raised a demand similar to the one calling for equal pay for comparable work. But this issue remained dormant until the 1970s. In part this was because of the belief that the issue would be solved by the Equal Pay Act of 1963, which made it illegal for employers to pay women lower wages for performing the same job as men, and Title VII of the Civil Rights Act of 1964, which made it illegal for employers to discriminate against workers because of their sex. This changed when, in the 1970s, the United States Labor Department revealed that, on the average, women earned 59 cents for every dollar earned by men—a figure that had not changed in forty years—and that some 80 percent of all employed women worked in relatively low-paid clerical and service jobs with limited opportunities for advancement. A Conference on Pay Equity was held in Washington, D.C., at the end of October, 1979; it was attended by trade unions, women's groups, and government agencies. The conference stressed the issue of "equal pay for work of equal value" or "equal pay for comparable work" as a means to intensify the struggle against employers who consistently underrated so-called women's jobs. The true value and skills and responsibilities of these jobs must be emphasized, the participants agreed, because the segregation of women in low-paying, dead-end jobs has become the major means of discrimination against workingwomen. "For the average woman who works—who is increasingly the average woman—I do believe this is the issue of the 1980's," declared Eleanor Holmes Norton, chairperson of the EEOC (*New York Times*, Oct. 26, Dec. 15, 1979; *UE News*, Dec. 3, 1979, p. 4).

work, and to take steps to see that this principle was adopted through economic, legislative, and administrative actions.[100]

Then on December 4, 1979, the *New York Times* announced: "The trade union movement is about to undertake a major drive to organize women workers." The need was clear, it continued, even to the top leaders of the AFL-CIO: "Currently only 6.5 million of the 41 million women workers in the United States belong to unions and the membership rate of women in trade unions is half that of men." All this preceded the report that Howard D. Samuel, president of the Industrial Union Department of the AFL-CIO, had announced at a news conference that his department would start immediately to hire women organizers to recruit women into unions. The department had no women on its organizing staff or among the organizers it "borrows" from affiliated unions, Samuel acknowledged, adding quickly that at least half of all new organizers hired would be women. One of the reasons for the relatively low participation rate of women in unions, Samuel continued, was that "few unions recognize that women have special problems, hopes and needs. We hope to get unions to take cognizance of these problems and take special measures to deal with them."

Joyce Miller, CLUW president, shared the news conference with Samuel, and together they announced that their organizations would stage a "first of its kind" conference in Washington on January 24, 1980, to develop a strategy and specific plans for organizing women workers. Samuel and Miller agreed that one of the key issues at the conference was "equal pay for comparable worth." Miller called it "the woman's issue of the 80's," and Samuel agreed. "This is because women are pushed into 'female ghettos' in the workplace, particularly into clerical work and jobs in service industries," he explained. Other issues would be pregnancy disability, child-care programs, and occupational safety and health protection for women. But the most immediate task was to expand female membership of the unions. In this connection, Miller praised the decision of the Industrial Union Department to hire women organizers. A major reason causing women to stay away from unions, Miller said, was "that the labor movement has been viewed as male-dominated."

In a joint statement, Samuel and Miller declared:

> It is increasingly obvious that with each passing year women are becoming a more important factor in the national workforce. Yet, few unions have devoted enough serious thought to designing appeals aimed at attracting these millions of wage earners into union ranks. . . .
> We believe that the exchange of ideas, experience and plans at the "first of its kind" CLUW–IUD conference will help pave the way to much greater union membership among women in the future, as well as increasing participation in the leadership of their union organizations.[101]

President Joyce Miller of CLUW and Elmer Chatak, Secretary-Treasurer of the AFL-CIO Industrial Union Department, co-chaired the "first of its kind" one-day meeting held in Washington, D.C., on January 23, 1980, to discuss ways to promote union membership among women workers. The hope of forging an alliance to bring more women into the labor movement drew about 200 participants including international union officers, organizing directors from IUD affiliates, national and regional CLUW officials, and representatives of Working Women.

Miller called the meeting a "kickoff" to CLUW's organizing program, which would include establishing permanent organizing committees in each of 22 CLUW chapters around the country. She emphasized that the increase of women in the work force in the past decade (to more than 40 million in 1980), "has intensified the need to organize female workers and give them a chance to escape from the lower paid 'female ghettoes.'" "Some 80 percent of all women who are working today are in those female job ghettoes," she added. Miller emphasized that the wage gap between men and women—with women earning on the average only 59 percent of the wages paid to men—can be closed "only through trade unions." "There is no greater road to equality than to be covered by a union contract," she concluded.

Chatak told the participants that the AFL-CIO's Industrial Union Department hoped to "establish a lasting, ongoing relationship" with the women's groups. He insisted that "trade union fundamentals are as good today as they ever were," but he warned that "our approach, our sensitivity to the special needs of women workers, our efforts to reach out to them as union members and potential union members . . . all of these need rethinking—and improvement."[102]

Talk is cheap, and talk alone cannot convince women workers that fundamental changes in the approach of organized labor to them is in the offing. However, the facts indicate that if action does not follow, the results will be disastrous for the labor movement in the face of decreasing union membership and increased determination of the corporations to resist further unionization.

In 1952 a woman worker at General Motors' AC Spark Plug division in Flint, Michigan, published an article entitled, "Listen Here, Union Brothers!" After describing the discrimination against women in her plant, which employed about ten thousand shop workers, most of them women, and the absence of female representation in the union's leadership, she tried to explain why women had not done more about the situation: "Because of years of company intimidation, because jobs are scarce, and mainly because of the division the company has been able to create between men and women, it has been difficult for women to tackle these questions. It is also twice as difficult for a workingwoman to become active in the union as for a man, because she has the responsibility of the home when she leaves the shop."

In her appeal to union brothers, the automobile worker concluded: "The myth that women are not militants will be shattered once the women organize together with the men around their specific problems and demands."[103]

A quarter of a century later, in an interview on the current relationship between women workers and the American labor movement, Addie Wyatt, international vice-president of the United Food & Commercial Workers International Union and vice-president, since its founding, of the Coalition of Labor Union Women—the highest-ranking black woman in the trade union movement—offered several shrewd observations that indicated how the situation had changed since 1952, how some of the problems of women workers were still the same, and how valid was the concluding appeal of the female auto worker. "Despite some setbacks," Wyatt declared, "women are making substantial gains in the labor movement, and in the attainment of leadership positions. This is of vital importance to all working people, because it is a way of strengthening the entire labor movement." Notwithstanding the many problems they face, she continued, many women workers were "engaging in more union activity because they see this as the way to increase democracy on the job through their participation in the union." There was also "an increased sensitivity in some unions to the need for taking special measures to ensure women's participation." Unions were learning that "women have tremendous leadership potential. They make fine meeting chairpersons, they make fine shop stewards, they make good officers— and when the union takes advantage of this potential, the union makes itself stronger and more effective."

Wyatt favored the organization by women union members of women's committees and their getting together between meetings to talk about issues that concern them. "In doing so," she maintained, "they will find strength in each other and the courage to press these issues in the union."

While relations between women and the American labor movement have been improving rapidly, Wyatt went on, much more still had to be done. "Until the labor movement makes time to discuss women's issues, their problems and their frustrations," she emphasized, "we're not going to have a labor movement that is truly serving the membership." One basic truth had to be stressed over and over:

> The active participation of the women strengthens the union, and that is a very vital force for progressive social and economic change. If we're going to have a strong labor movement, then it's in every union member's interest to see that everyone is fully involved. Women have brought very special strengths to every institution and organization in which they have been in-

volved. This is a strong tradition, and the labor movement has to draw from this tradition. It's very important that men recognize this and see the participation of women as a factor in building a strong labor movement.[104]

The history of women and the American labor movement offers concrete evidence of the validity of this counsel.

APPENDIX
Working Women's 1980 Platform

This Platform was put together by the Coalition of Labor Union Women, the Displaced Homemakers Network, Wider Opportunities for Women, and the National Commission on Working Women. In a joint statement issued on Labor Day these organizations said the objectives of the Platform was to send "an urgent message to the presidential candidates" and to "focus public attention on the concerns of working women."

These concerns must become the concerns of the entire labor movement. The rank and file should take the lead in building a campaign for implementation of the Working Women's Platform.

1. Recognition

Recognize, understand and value the strong tradition and increasing importance of women as workers in all aspects of social, political, and economic life in America.

In 1979, 52% of women in the United States worked outside the home.

Most women work because of economic need. Almost two-thirds of all women in the labor force in 1979 were single, widowed, divorced, or separated, or had husbands whose earnings were less than $10,000.

2. Minority Women

Recognize the special needs, concerns and problems of minority women workers who face both sexism and racism.

Minority women have the lowest median income in 1977, the median income of year-round full-time workers was $8.303 for minority women, $8,787 for white women, $11,053 for minority males, and $15,230 for white males.

In 1978, 39% of black families, 20% of Hispanic families, and 11% of white families were headed by women.

3. Job Options

Eliminate job segregation by sex.

Occupational segregation by sex is a major factor in the overall low status of women in the work force. 80% of the women in the work force are concentrated in low-paying clerical, sales, service, factory, and plant jobs.

Women are: 98% of all secretaries;
             95% of all private household workers;
less than   10% of all skilled workers;
less than   5% of all top managers.

4. Wages

Eliminate wage discrimination by sex.

In 1977, the annual median income of women working full-time was 59% that of men. This gap has widened in recent years. In 1955, the figure was 64%.

5. Education and Training

Eliminate sex-stereotyping and other barries to equity in all publicly funded educational, employment and training programs, and promote equal access to these programs.

6. Employment Programs

Expand and create special programs to improve employment opportunities for all women (including young women, women on welfare, ex-offenders, displaced homemakers, handicapped, older and minority women), providing them with career development, skills training (including nontraditional work), supportive services, and access to upwardly mobile jobs.

Such special programs are needed because:

women head 49% of all poor families;
women are 75% of those people living in poverty;
women are 90% of those receiving Aid to Families
   With Dependent Children;
women are 50% of the unemployed;
women are 66% of discouraged workers.

7. Enforcement

Enforce laws and regulations mandating equal employment opportunities for women.

8. Health and Safety

Promote healthy and safe working conditions.

When working conditions involve exposure to reproductive hazards for both women and men, women workers have been forced to choose between sterilization and job loss.

9. Sexual Harassment

Maintain work environments free of sexual harassment and intimidation.

According to several recent surveys, approximately 60–75% of the women questioned experienced sexual harassment on the job.

10. Dependent Care

Provide accessible, quality care for children and other dependents.

In 1978, 53% of all mothers with children under 18 years of age were in the labor force. 5.9 million working mothers in 1978 had children under 6.

Only 1.6 million licensed day care slots are available for 6.9 million children under 6 with working mothers.

11. Organizing

Support the organization of the millions of unorganized women workers, and strengthen the role and participation of women in labor unions.

In 1980, only 12% of women workers belonged to a labor union.

12. Homemaking

Recognize homemakers as an important segment of the country's labor force, and recognize unpaid labor in the home as a significant contribution to the national economy.

13. Benefits

Promote equitable benefits for women, including pensions, social security, paid maternity leave, health care and health insurance.

Only 20% of the women in the private labor force are covered by pensions, and only 10% of retired women workers receive a private pension.

14. Work Schedules

Promote alternative work schedules (including flex-time, part-time, compressed work week, and job sharing) with appropriate benefits.

In 1978, a survey estimated that flex-time was available to only 6% of the work force.

15. Public Policy

Promote the participation of women in the formulation and evaluation of public policy affecting employment.

As of June 1979, women comprised a mere 2.9% of the federal judiciary (543 judges, 16 women). No woman has ever sat on the U.S. Supreme Court.[*]

In 1978, women held approximately 8% of all public offices in the United States, though they comprised 53% of the voting population.

[*This demand was set forth before the appointment of Justice Sandra Day O'Connor to the United States Supreme Court by President Ronald Reagan. The Platform made no mention of the Equal Rights Amendment (ERA), but all of the organizations which united to formulate the Platform are dedicated to adoption of the Amendment, and will play a role in the new drive to secure its adoption since the ratification by the necessary number of states failed in the summer of 1982. On July 14, 1982, the Equal Rights Amendment was reintroduced in Congress and the campaign to secure its incorporation into the Constitution begun anew.]

SOURCE: This article appeared in substantially the same form in the October, 1980 edition of *Labor Today*, page 7. Most of the statistics herein are from the U.S. Department of Labor, Womens Bureau, and the Bureau of Labor Statistics.

Notes

Chapter 1: The First Trade Unions (pp. 1–17)

1. The only report of this strike was published in the *National Gazette* of Apr. 23, 1825, which did not indicate the outcome.
2. For a summary of the status of women in Jacksonian America, see Eleanor Flexner, *Century of Struggle* (Cambridge, Mass., 1959), chaps. 1–3.
3. BARBARA EHRENREICH AND DEEDRE ENGLISH, *Witches, Midwives & Nurses—A History of Women Healers* (Oyster Bay, N.Y., 1972); Gena Corea, *Women's Health Care* (New York, 1977), chaps. 3, 4.
4. GERDA LERNER, "The Lady and the Mill Girl: Changes in the Status of Women in the Age of Jackson," *American Studies Journal* 10 (Spring 1969): 2–3.
5. BARBARA WELTER, "The Cult of True Womanhood, 1820–1860," *American Quarterly* 18 (Summer 1966): 151–74; Barbara Welter, "Anti-Intellectualism and the American Woman: 1800–1860," *Mid-America* 48 (1966): 258–70; Carroll Smith Rosenberg, "The Hysterical Woman: Sex Roles and the Role Conflict in 19th Century America," *Social Research* 39 (Winter 1972): 655–56; Aileen S. Kraditor, *Up from the Pedestal: Selected Writings in the History of American Feminism* (Chicago, 1968), pp. 11–13.
6. LOUISE M. YOUNG, "Woman's Place in American Politics: The Historical Perspective," *Journal of Politics* 38 (August 1976): 295–335.
7. LINDA KERBER, "The Republican Mother: Women and the Enlightenment, An American Perspective," *American Quarterly* 28 (Summer 1976): 43–49.
8. T. S. ARTHUR, *The Lady at Home: or, Leaves from the Every-Day Book of an American Woman* (Philadelphia, 1847), pp. 177–78; Welter, "The Cult of True Womanhood," p. 163.
9. ANN DOUGLAS, *The Feminization of American Culture* (New York, 1977), chap. 1.

10. EGAL FELDMAN, "New York Men's Clothing Trade, 1800–1861" (Ph.D. diss., New York University, 1959), pp. 5–7, 35–37, 65–75; Helen Sumner, "History of Women in Industry in the United States," vol. 9 of U.S., Congress, Senate, *Report on Condition of Women and Child Wage Earners in the United States, Senate Document 645*, 61st Cong., 2d sess., 1910–1913, pp. 119–121.

11. SUMNER, "History of Women in Industry," p. 117.

12. MATTHEW CAREY, *Miscellaneous Pamphlets, No. 12*, quoted in ibid., pp. 127–28. Matthew Carey, *Appeal to the Wealthy of the Land*, quoted in Sumner, "History of Women in Industry," p. 132.

13. MATTHEW CAREY, *Select Excerpts*, quoted in Sumner, "History of Women in Industry," p. 132.

14. *Mechanics' Free Press*, Dec. 18, 1830.

15. CAREY, *Appeal to the Wealthy*, quoted in Sumner, "History of Women in Industry," pp. 131–32.

16. "A Working Woman," in *Working Man's Advocate* (Boston), reprinted in New York *Daily Sentinel*, Aug. 21, 1830.

17. "Report on Female Wages," Philadelphia, Mar. 25, 1829, cited in W. Elliot Brownlee and Mary M. Brownlee, *Women in the American Economy: A Documentary History, 1675 to 1929* (New Haven and London, 1976), p. 147.

18. CARROLL SMITH ROSENBERG, "Beauty, the Beast and the Militant Woman: A Case Study of Sex Roles and Social Stress in Jacksonian America," *American Quarterly* 23 (October 1971): 579.

19. New York *Daily Sentinel*, Aug. 28, 1830.

20. "M" in *ibid.*, Feb. 12, 1831.

21. Boston *Evening Transcript*, Feb. 22, 1831.

22. New York *Daily Sentinel*, Mar. 5, 1831.

23. *Ibid.*, June 12, 14, 16, 1831.

24. *Ibid.*, June 25, 1831.

25. *Ibid.*, July 22, 24, 26, 1831; *Working Man's Advocate*, Aug. 13, 1831.

26. New York *Daily Sentinel*, July 21, 1831.

27. Ibid., July 26, 1831.

28. *Baltimore Republican and Commercial Advertiser*, Sept. 14, 20, 30, Oct, 2, 3, 1833, cited in Andrews and Bliss, *Women in Trade Unions*, pp. 38–39.

29. *Baltimore Republican and Commercial Advertiser*, Sept. 14, 1835, cited in Andrews and Bliss, *Women in Trade Unions*, p. 39.

30. *Working Man's Advocate*, June 9, 17, 1835.

31. Ibid., June 23, 1835.

32. SUMNER, "History of Women in Industry," p. 125.

33. *Lynn Record*, Jan. 1, 1834; Andrews and Bliss, *Women in Trade Unions*, p. 41; Alan Dawley, *Class and Community: The Industrial Revolution in Lynn* (Cambridge, Mass., 1977), chap. 1.

34. SUMNER, "History of Women in Industry," p. 168.

35. ANDREWS AND BLISS, *Women in Trade Unions,* pp. 42–43.

36. *Lynn Record,* Jan. 8, 1834.

37. Ibid.

38. Ibid., Mar. 12, 1834; *The Man,* Mar. 12, 1834; *Boston Courier,* Mar. 11, 1834; Andrews and Bliss, *Women in Trade Unions,* p. 44.

39. *Pennsylvanian.* Mar. 25, 28, 1836.

40. *National Laborer,* Apr. 2, 1836.

41. *Pennsylvanian,* Apr. 1, 4, 1836; *National Laborer,* Apr. 16, 23, 30, June 6, 13, 1836.

42. *Baltimore Republican and Commercial Advertiser,* Sept. 14, 1833.

43. PHILIP S. FONER, ed., *The Democratic-Republican Societies. 1790–1800: A Documentary Sourcebook of Constitutions, Declarations, Addresses, Resolutions, and Toasts* (Westport, Conn., 1976), pp. 13, 104, 205, 220, 225, 227, 229, 230, 253, 309, 354, 392.

44. JOHN R. COMMONS and Associates, *History of Labour in the United States* (New York, 1918), 1:88–106; Foner, *History of the Labor Movement,* 1:60–68.

45. New York *Evening Post,* July 13, 1819.

46. *American Citizen* (New York), April 10, 1809. See also ibid., June 23, 1810.

47. *Mechanics' Free Press,* Apr. 2, 1831. See also issues of Apr. 9, 16, 23, 30, 1831.

48. See *Address to the People of Philadelpha in the Walnut Street Theatre on the Morning of the Fourth of July, Common Era 1829, and the Fifty-fourth Year of Independence by Frances Wright* (New York, 1829). For the events leading up to Wright's speech and its influence, *see* Philip S. Foner, ed., *We, the Other People: Alternative Declarations of Independence by Labor Groups, Farmers, Women's Rights Advocates, Socialists, and Blacks, 1829–1975* (Urbana, Ill.), pp. 3–6.

49. New York *Daily Sentinel,* Aug. 21, 1830.

50. *Working Man's Advocate,* Jan. 2, 1830. The proposal was made by Cornelius Camden Blatchly. David Harris calls Blatchly's essay, *Some Causes of Popular Poverty, Arising from the Enriching Nature of Interest, Investigated in Their Principles and Consequences* (published in 1817), "the first significant contribution to modern socialist theory in the United States," since Blatchly affirmed "both the right of those who work to receive the full product of their labor and the right of every person to his just share in the ownership of the common materials of the world which are in existence at the time he is born" (*Socialist Origins in the United States: American Forerunners of Marx, 1817–1832* [Assen, Holland, 1966], p. 10).

51. New York *Daily Sentinel,* Mar. 27, 1830: *Working Man's Advocate,* Apr. 12, 1834.

52. *National Laborer,* Apr. 16, 1836.

53. JOHN BORDEN, "The Association of Working People of New Castle, Delaware: The First Labor Party of Delaware" (Master's thesis, University of Delaware, 1927), pp. 54–55.

54. Ibid., p. 36; Foner, *History of the Labor Movement,* 1:126.

55. *Proceedings of the Government and Citizens of Philadelphia on the Reduction of the Hours of Labor, and Increase of Wages* (Boston, 1835), p. 9.

56. See, in this connection, Bettina Eileen Berch, "Industrialization and Working Women in the Nineteenth Century: England, France, and the United States" (Ph.D. diss., University of Wisconsin, Madison, 1976)," pp. 241–43.

57. *Mechanics' Free Press,* July 15, 1829.

58. Quoted in Berch, "Industrialization and Working Women," pp. 244–45.

59. "Report of the Committee on Female Labor to the National Trades' Union," *National Laborer,* Nov. 12, 1836, reprinted in John R. Commons, et al., eds., *A Documentary History of American Industrial Society* (Cleveland, 1910) 1: 291–93.

60. SETH LUTHER, *An Address on the Origin and Progress of Avarice, and Its Deleterious Effects on Human Happiness* (Boston, 1834), p. 3.

Chapter 2: Factory Women, Their Unions, and Their Struggles (pp. 18–50)

1. SAMUEL REZNECK, "The Social History of an American Depression, 1837–1843," *American Historical Review* 40 (July 1935): 663–67; Foner, *History of the Labor Movement,* 1:167–68.

2. FONER, *American Labor Songs of the Nineteenth Century* (Urbana, Ill., 1975), p. 45.

3. NORMAN J. WARE, *The Industrial Worker, 1840–1860* (Boston and New York, 1924), p. 74.

4. *Voice of Industry,* July 3, 1845.

5. There is no biographical sketch of either Huldah J. Stone or Mehitabel Eastman in any biographical collections on American women, not even in the three-volume *Notable American Women,* ed. Edward T. James, Janet Wilson James, and Paul S. Boyer (Cambridge, Mass., 1971). There is a sketch of Sarah G. Bagley in vol. 1, but a more complete one may be found in Madeline B. Stern, *We the Women: Career Firsts of Nineteenth-Century America* (New York, 1963), pp. 84–94. Strangely, Stern lists Sarah Bagley as "America's First Woman Telegrapher" (which she was), but not as what she also was, America's first women labor leader. For biographical discussions of Huldah J. Stone, Mehitabel Eastman, and Sarah G. Bagley, see Philip S. Foner, *The Factory Girls: A Collection of Writings on Life and Struggles in the New England Factories of the 1840's by the Factory Girls Themselves, and The Story, in Their Own Words, of the First Trade Unions of Women Workers in the United States* (Urbana, Ill., 1977).

6. FONER, *History of the Labor Movement,* 1:193.

7. HARRIET H. ROBINSON, *Loom and Spindle: Of Life Among the Early Mill Girls* (New York, 1898), pp. 62–63.

8. RAY GINGER, "Labor in a Massachusetts Cotton Mill, 1853–1860," *Business*

History Review 28 (March 1954): 67-91; Stephen Thernstrom, *Poverty and Progress* (Cambridge, Mass., 1964), pp. 126-31.

9. FONER, *American Labor Songs*, p. 66; Foner, *Factory Girls*, p. 25; Shlakman, "Economic History of a Factory Town: A study of Chicopee, Massachusetts," *Smith College Studies in History* 20 (Northampton, Mass., 1935): 135-36.

10. HANNAH JOSEPHSON, *The Golden Threads: New England's Mill Girls and Magnates* (New York, 1949), p. 281.

11. For the emergence of these magazines and excerpts from their contents, see Foner, *Factory Girls*, pp. 25-53. See also Bertha M. Stearns, "Early Factory Magazines in New England," *Journal of Economic and Business History* 2 (August 1930): 92-95.

12. WILLIAM SCORESBY, *American Factories and Their Female Operatives* (1845; reprint ed., New York, 1968), p. 88; *Old South Leaflets* 3, no. 151 (Boston, 1885); Charles Dickens, *American Notes* (New York, 1842), p. 77.

13. ORESTES S. BROWNSON, "The Laboring Classes," *Boston Quarterly Review* 3 (July 1840): 112-15; Ibid. (October 1840): 46; "A Factory Girl," *Lowell Offering* 1 (December 1840): 16-23; Foner, *Factory Girls*, pp. 27-28.

14. Published in *Working Man's Advocate*, Jan. 17, 1846.

15. ROBERT G. LAYER, "Wages, Earnings. and Output in Four Cotton Textile Companies in New England, 1825-1860" (Ph.D. diss., Harvard University, 1952), p. 176. A published summary of Layer's thesis is available as *Earnings of Cotton Mill Operatives, 1825-1914* (Cambridge, Mass., 1955).

16. *Lowell Offering* 3 (September 1840): 43, 284.

17. Ibid., 3 (October 1843): 56-57; Foner, *History of the Labor Movement*. p. 194; Lucy Larcom, *A New England Girlhood* (Boston, 1890), pp. 222-23; Gerda Lerner, "The Lady and the Mill Girl: Changes in the Status of Women in the Age of Jackson," *American Studies Journal* 10 (Spring 1969): 6-8.

18. WARE, *The Industrial Worker*, p. 121; *Voice of Industry*, July 3, 1845.

19. ALLAN MACDONALD, "Lowell: A Commercial Utopia," *New England Quarterly* 10 (March 1937): 44; *Awl* (Lynn), July 26, 1845; Foner, *History of the Labor Movement*, p. 198.

20. S.G.B., "Pleasures of Factory Life," *Lowell Offering* 1 (December 1840): 23-26; S.G.B., "Tales of Factory Life. No. 1," ibid., 3 (February 1842): 65-68; *Lowell Advertiser*, July 10, 1845; *Voice of Industry*, July 10, 1845.

21. *Voice of Industry*, July 17, 1845, Jan. 2, 1846; *Lowell Advertiser*, July 15, 26, 1845; Foner, *Factory Girls*, pp. 61-68.

22. FONER, *Factory Girls*, pp. 74-75; Stearns, "Early Factory Magazines," pp. 93-98.

23. *Voice of Industry*, May 8. 1846.

24. See "The Factory Girls Expose the 'Beauty of Factory Life,'" in Foner, *Factory Girls*, pp. 74-95, and "Operative" in ibid., p. 311.

25. *Factory Girls*, Jan. 15, 1845.

26. *Voice of Industry*, May 29, June 5, 10, 12, 1845; Andrews and Bliss, *Women in Trade Unions*, pp. 71-72.

27. *Voice of Industry,* Feb. 27, 1846. The constitution is also reproduced in Foner, *Factory Girls,* pp. 104–6.

28. *Voice of Industry,* Dec. 19, 26, 1845, Jan. 9, May 5, Nov. 13, 1846; *Young America,* Nov. 15, 1845.

29. *Voice of Industry,* Nov. 7, 1845.

30. Ibid., Sept. 5, 1845. See also *Working Man's Advocate,* Mar. 8, 1845.

31. FONER, *History of the Labor Movement,* 1:198; *Voice of Industry,* Nov. 7, 1845, Mar. 6, 13, 1845.

    For descriptions by Bagley, Stone, and Eastman of their speaking tours, see "Three Pioneer Woman Labor Leaders," in Foner, *Factory Girls,* pp. 159–211.

32. *Voice of Industry,* Jan. 9, 1846; "The Female Department of the *Voice of Industry,*" Foner, *Factory Girls,* pp. 42–56.

33. *Voice of Industry,* Feb. 20, 1846; "Factory Tracts No. 1," Boston Public Library, Rare Book Room; "The Factory Tracts," in Foner, *Factory Girls,* pp. 130–41.

34. *Voice of Industry,* Jan. 9, Apr. 17, Nov. 28, 1846.

35. Originally published in *Voice of Industry,* Nov. 7, 1845, and reprinted in "Factory Tracts No. 1," and in Foner, *Factory Girls,* pp. 138–40, and Foner, *American Labor Songs of the Nineteenth Century,* p. 59.

36. "Slavery, North and South," by a "Ten Hour Woman," in *Mechanic* (Fall River), Oct. 5. 1844, and *Manchester Operative,* reprinted in ibid., Nov. 2, 1844.

37. *Lowell Advertiser,* Feb. 10, 1845.

38. *Voice of Industry,* Sept. 25, 1845, Jan. 23, 1846. For these and other antislavery writings of the female operatives, see Foner, *Factory Girls,* pp. 275–79.

39. *Lowell Advertiser,* Feb. 10, 1845; *Voice of Industry,* Dec. 26, 1845.

40. FONER, *Factory Girls,* pp. 282–88.

41. ROBINSON, *Loom and Spindle,* p. 133. The article by "Ella" was entitled "Woman," and appeared in the *Lowell Offering* 2 (January 1841): 129–35; it is reprinted in Foner, *Factory Girls,* pp. 38–44.

42. *Lowell Offering* 2 (January 1841): 132–35; "Woman's Rights," in Foner, *Factory Girls,* pp. 293–323.

43. See *Lowell Offering,* December 1840, pp. 12–13; January 1841, pp. 125–29, and *Operatives' Magazine,* April 1841. pp. 12–14; March 1842, pp. 15–17.

44. *Factory Girls' Album,* Mar. 14, 1846, Feb. 15, 1847; *Voice of Industry,* Aug. 14, 1847; Foner *Factory Girls,* pp. 295–99.

45. *Factory Girls' Album,* Apr. 25, 1846; *Voice of Industry,* Apr. 2, 1847.

46. *Voice of Industry,* Jan. 22, 1847; Foner. *Factory Girls,* pp. 316–19.

47. See "Three Pioneer Women Labor Leaders," in Foner, *Factory Girls,* pp. 159–211.

48. *Voice of Industry,* July 13, 1847; Foner, *Factory Girls,* pp. 191–93.

49. *Voice of Industry,* July 13, Sept. 10, 1847; Foner, *Factory Girls,* pp. 192, 202.

50. *New Era of Industry,* Aug. 3, 1848.

51. For the ten-hour movement prior to 1840, see Foner, *History of the Labor Movement,* 1:102–3, 115–18, 130, 160, 163.

52. WARE, *The Industrial Worker,* pp. 129–30.

53. The arguments are presented in "The Demand for the Ten-Hour Day," Foner, *Factory Girls,* pp. 215–18.

54. *Voice of Industry,* Sept. 18, 1845; Foner, *Factory Girls,* pp. 180–81.

55. LAYER, "Wages, Earnings," pp. 496–503; *Voice of Industry,* Jan. 9, May 15, 1846.

56. JOHN R. COMMONS and ASSOCIATES, *History of Labour in the United States* (New York: 1918), 1:550–62; John R. Commons, et al., eds., *A Documentary History of American Industrial Society* (Cleveland, 1910), 8:23–25; Foner, *History of the Labor Movement,* 1:202.

57. For the petitions of 1842 and 1843 and the formation of the New England Workingmen's Association, see Foner, *History of the Labor Movement,* 1:202–7.

58. *Voice of Industry,* June 5, 1845. Bagley's speech is reprinted in Foner, *Factory Girls,* pp. 108–10.

59. *Voice of Industry,* Jan. 15, 1845; Massachusetts, House, *House of Representatives of the Commonwealth of Massachusetts During the Session of the General Court A.D. 1845,* no. 50 (Boston, 1845), pp. 1–5.

60. Massachusetts, House, General Court, *House Document no. 5,* 1845, pp. 1–6, 15–17. The full report is published in Foner, *Factory Girls,* pp. 236–42.

61. *Lowell Offering* 5 (April 1845): 96.

62. *Lowell Advertiser,* Sept. 2, 1845.

63. Ibid., Nov. 10, 1845; *Voice of Industry,* Nov. 28, 1845.

64. *Pittsburgh Journal* and *Pittsburgh Spirit of Liberty,* reprinted in *Young America,* Nov. 15, 1845.

65. New York *Tribune,* Oct. 31, 1845; *Young America,* Nov. 15, 1845; *Lowell Advertiser,* Dec. 13, 1845.

66. CHARLES E. PERSONS, *Labor Laws and Their Enforcement* (New York, 1911), p. 41; *Young America.* Dec. 27, 1846.

67. Massachusetts, Senate, General Court, *Senate Document No. 81,* 1846, pp. 19, 21.

68. *Voice of Industry,* Dec. 29, 1845; Apr. 10, Nov. 3, 1846; *Factory Girls' Album,* Sept. 2, 1846.

69. *Voice of Industry,* July 29, 1847.

70. *Manchester* (N.H.) *Democrat,* Aug. 22, 1847; Foner, *Factory Girls.* pp. 266–69.

71. FONER, *History of Labor Movement,* 1:211.

72. *Voice of Industry,* Oct. 30, 1847.

73. ALAN DAWLEY, *Class and Community: The Industrial Revolution in Lynn* (Cambridge, Mass., 1977), pp. 38–64.

74. *Newburyport Daily Herald*, Feb. 24, 1860; *Boston Advertiser*, Mar. 21, 1860; *Haverhill Gazette*, Feb. 24, 1860; *Lynn Weekly Reporter*, Apr. 7, 1860; New York *Herald*, Feb. 27, 1860; Massachusetts, Bureau of Statistics of Labor, *Eleventh Annual Report, 1880*, pp. 17–19; *Boston Traveller*, Feb. 25, 26, 1860.

75. *Lynn Weekly Reporter*, Jan. 21, 1860; Phillips Barry, "The Fall of the Pemberton Mill," *Bulletin of the Folksong of the North East* 3 (Fall 1931): 16–17.

76. *Boston Traveller*, Feb. 15, 1860; New York *Herald*, Feb. 26, 1860; *Lynn News*, Feb. 22, 1860.

77. *Boston Traveller*, Feb. 28, 1860; *Newburyport Daily Herald*, Feb. 29, 1860; *Lynn Weekly Reporter*, Mar. 3, 1860.

78. *Lynn Weekly Reporter*, Mar. 6, 1860; *New York Times*, Mar. 8, 1860.

79. *New York Times*, Mar. 8, 1860.

80. New York *Herald*, Feb. 27, Mar. 1, 1860.

81. *Newburyport Daily Herald*, Mar. 7, 1860; Foner, *History of the Labor Movement*, 1:243; *New York Times*, Mar. 7, 1860.

82. *Lynn News*, Mar. 7, 1860; *Lynn Weekly Reporter*, Mar. 10, 1860; *New York Times*, Mar. 7, 1860.

83. *Lynn Weekly Reporter*, Mar. 10, 1860.

84. Ibid., Mar. 12, 1860; *Lynn News*, Mar. 12, 1860.

85. *Lynn Weekly Reporter*, Mar. 24, 1860, Mar. 10, 17, 1860.

86. *Lynn News*, Mar. 21, 1860; *Lynn Weekly Reporter*, Mar. 10, 1860; *Boston Advertiser*, *Boston Courier*, *New York Times*, Mar. 8, 1860.

87. *Boston Bee*, Feb. 23, 1860; *Newburyport Daily Herald*, Feb. 29, 1860.

88. *Springfield Republican*, Mar. 2, 1860; *Newburyport Daily Herald*, Mar. 23, 1860; Dawley, *Class and Community*, p. 112.

89. *Lynn Weekly Reporter*, Apr. 7, 1860.

90. *Boston Courier*, Feb. 27, 28, 1860.

91. *Lynn News*, Mar. 7, 1860; John G. Nicolay and John Hay, eds., *Complete Works of Abraham Lincoln* (New York, 1905), 5:247–50; Foner, *History of the Labor Movement*, 1:292.

92. *Lynn Weekly Reporter*, Apr. 14, 21, 1860.

93. DAVID MONTGOMERY, *Beyond Equality: Labor and the Radical Republicans, 1862–1872* (New York, 1967), pp. 34–35.

94. U.S., Bureau of the Census, *Manufacturing of the United States in 1880 Compiled from the Original Sections of the Eighth Census*, 1865; U.S., Bureau of the Census, *Manufactures of the United States in 1870, A Compendium of the Ninth Census*, 1872; Ross K. Baker, "Entry of Women into Federal Job World—at a Price," *Smithsonian* 8 (July, 1977):83–85.

95. New York *Tribune*, Oct. 9, 14, 1863, Mar. 22, 1864; New York *Herald*, Nov. 14, 1863; Virginia Penny, *Five Hundred Employment Adapted to Women* (Philadelphia, 1868), pp. 190–93, 301–11, 331–34.

96. *Fincher's Trades' Review*, Nov. 21, 28, 1863, June 25, 1864.

97. New York *Sun*, Nov. 5, 11, 1863, Dec. 17, 1863; New York *Tribune*, Dec. 9, 1879, Jan. 19, 1881.

Chapter 3: The National Labor Union (pp. 51–69)

1. *Boston Daily Evening Voice*, Jan. 12, 1865.

2. *New York Times*, June 16, 1865; New York *Herald*, July 14, 1865.

3. *Boston Daily Evening Voice*, Aug. 9, 1865, Dec. 18, 1866.

4. *Leslie's Magazine*, July 22, 1865.

5. *Boston Daily Evening Voice*, Nov. 8, 1865.

6. ANDREWS AND BLISS, *Women in Trade Unions*, pp. 106–7.

7. EDITH ABBOTT, *Women in Industry* (New York, 1910), p. 236; Horace Greeley and others, *The Great Industries of the United States* (Hartford, Conn., 1870), pp. 540–42.

8. Quoted in Ruth Delzell, "1866—Laundry Workers Union, Troy, N.Y.," *Life and Labor* 2 (November 1912): 333.

9. NANCY DUCATTE, "The Shirt and Collar Industry and Kate Mullaney," Troy, N.Y., undated paper, p. 3. Copy in library of Trade Union Women's Studies, Cornell University, 7 East 43rd Street, New York, N.Y.

10. *Boston Daily Evening Voice*, Apr. 2, 12, 1866; *Rochester Union and American*, May 16, 1866; *New York Times*, Dec. 26, 1866.

11. *Jackson* (Miss.) *Daily Clarion*, June 24, 1866. I am indebted to Ken Lawrence of the Deep South People's History Project, Tougaloo, Mississippi, for furnishing me with a copy of this issue of the *Daily Clarion*. A brief excerpt from the petition appears in Ken Lawrence, "Mississippi's First Labor Union," Tougaloo, Mississippi, Deep South People's History Project, Freedom Information Service, 974, mimeographed pamphlet.

12. "Resolutions of the International Industrial Assembly of North America," in John R. Commons, et al., eds., *A Documentary History of American Industrial Society* (Cleveland, 1910), 9:123.

13. *Fincher's Trades' Review*, Sept. 10, 1864.

14. JAMES C. SYLVIS, *The Life, Speeches, Labors and Essays of William H. Sylvis, Late President of the Iron-Moulders International Union and also of the National Labor Union* (Philadelphia, 1872), pp. 120, 217–22, 398–400; Jonathan Grossman, *William Sylvis, Pioneer of American Labor, A Study of the Labor Movement During the Civil War* (New York, 1945), pp. 98–99, 226–28, 229–32, 257–60; David Montgomery, *Beyond Equality: Labor and the Radical Republicans, 1862–1872* (New York, 1967), p. 234; Foner, *History of the Labor Movement*, 1:421–23.

15. "Resolutions of the Founding Convention of the National Labor Union," in Commons, et al., eds., *Documentary History of American Industrial Society*, 9: 135; Foner, *History of the Labor Movement*, 1:384–85; *The Address of the National Labor Congress to the Workingmen of the United States* (Chicago, 1867).

16. ABBOTT, *Women in Industry,* pp. 192–93; Andrews and Bliss, *Women in Trade Unions,* pp. 91–92; *Workingman's Advocate,* Apr. 12, 19, 1867.

17. *Workingman's Advocate,* Apr. 26, 1867.

18. ANDREWS AND BLISS, *Women in Trade Unions,* pp. 95–96.

19. *Workingman's Advocate,* Aug. 24, 31, 1867.

20. Admittedly this is a simplified presentation of one of the most complex issues in the history of the women's rights movement.

21. PHILIP S. FONER, ed., *Frederick Douglass on Women's Rights* (Westport, Conn., 1976). pp. 30, 151, 184.

22. KATHERINE ANTHONY, *Susan B. Anthony: Her Personal History and Her Era* (New York, 1954), p. 215.

23. *Revolution,* July 2, 1868.

24. Ibid., Sept. 21, 1868.

25. Ibid., Sept. 28, 1868.

26. Ibid., Dec. 3, 1868.

27. SYLVIS, *Life, Speeches,* pp. 229–31.

28. ELLEN DUBOIS, "A New Life: The Development of an American Woman Suffrage Movement, 1860–1869," (Ph.D. diss., Northwestern University, 1975), p. 196.

29. FONER, *Frederick Douglass on Women's Rights,* pp. 33–35.

30. *Revolution,* Sept. 28, 1868.

31. *Workingman's Advocate,* Oct. 1, 8, 15, 1868.

32. *Revolution,* Sept. 7, 1868.

33. MONTGOMERY, *Beyond Equality,* p. 234.

34. New York *World,* Sept. 17, 23, 1868; New York *Tribune,* Sept. 23, 1868; *Revolution,* Sept. 21, 1868; Israel Kugler, "The Woman's Rights Movement and the National Labor Union (1866–1872)," (Ph.D. diss., New York University, 1954), p. 93; Dubois, "A New Life," pp. 206–8.

35. *Proceedings of the Second Session of the National Labor Congress in Convention Assembled at New York City, September 21, 1868* (Philadelphia, 1868), p. 4.

36. KARL MARX AND FREDERICK ENGELS, *Selected Correspondence, 1845–1895* (New York, 1935), p. 255.

37. *Proceedings of the Second Session of the National Labor Congress,* pp. 8–10.

38. Ibid., p. 39; Kugler, "Woman's Rights Movement," p. 94.

39. DUBOIS," A New Life," pp. 210–11.

40. *Revolution,* Oct. 1, 1868.

41. *Workingman's Advocate,* Mar. 6, 13, 20, 1869; Sylvis, *Life, Speeches,* pp. 221–22.

42. PHILIP S. FONER, *Organized Labor and the Black Worker, 1619–1973* (New York, 1974), pp. 23–24.

43. New York *World,* Aug. 17, 1869; *Workingman's Advocate,* Sept. 4, 1869; *Revolution,* Sept. 7, 1869.

44. *Workingman's Advocate*, Sept. 4, 1869.
45. New York *World*, Aug. 17, 1869; Kugler, "Woman's Rights Movement," p. 100; Montgomery, *Beyond Equality*, pp. 398-99.
46. DuBois, "A New Life," p. 272.
47. *Workingman's Advocate*, Sept. 4, 1869.
48. Kugler, "Woman's Rights Movement," p. 193.
49. *Revolution*, Sept. 7, 1869.
50. Foner, *Frederick Douglass on Women's Rights*, p. 30.
51. Parker Pillsbury in *Revolution*, Sept. 7, 1869.
52. *National Anti-Slavery Standard*, Nov. 30, 1869, and reprinted in Philip S. Foner and Ronald L. Lewis, eds., *The Black Worker: A Documentary History from Colonial Times to the Present*, (Philadelphia, 1978), 2:16-17.
53. *Proceedings of the Colored National Labor Convention Held in Washington, D.C., on December 6, 7, 8, 9, 10, 1869* (Washington, D.C., 1870), pp. 43-44, 55-58, and reprinted in Foner and Lewis, *The Black Worker*, pp. 36-39, 49-50. For the story of the Colored National Labor Union, see Foner, *Organized Labor and the Black Worker*, pp. 30-46.
54. *Revolution*, July 25, 1869.
55. DuBois, "A New Life," p. 203.
56. *Revolution*, Aug. 26, 1869.
57. *Workingman's Advocate*, Apr. 23, June 25, Aug. 27, 1870.
58. Andrews and Bliss, *Women in Trade Unions*, p. 88.
59. Foner, *History of the Labor Movement*, 1:387.
60. *New York Times*, Aug. 10, 1871.

Chapter 4: The Knights of Labor (pp. 70–97)

1. Terence V. Powderly, *Thirty Years of Labor, 1859-1889* (Columbus, 1890), pp. 534-35; Foner, *History of the Labor Movement*, 1:433-37.
2. Henry J. Browne, *The Catholic Church and the Knights of Labor* (Washington, D.C., 1949), pp. 58-64; Powderly, *Thirty Years of Labor*, pp. 252-57, 359-61.
3. U.S., Department of Labor, Women's Bureau, Bulletin No. 225, *Handbook of Facts on Women Workers*, 1948, p. 1; U.S., Department of Labor, Women's Bureau, Bulletin No. 218, *Women's Occupations through Seven Decades*, 1947), pp. 208-23.
4. Andrews and Bliss, *Women in Trade Unions*, pp. 113-16; Norman J. Ware, *The Labor Movement in the U.S.A., 1860-1895* (New York, 1929) pp. 88-89; Gerald Grob, *Workers and Utopia: A Study of Ideological Conflict in the American Labor Movement, 1865-1900* (Chicago, 1969), pp. 52-55; Philip S. Foner, *History of the Labor Movement in the United States 2* (New York, 1955): 61.
5. Charlie to Powderly, 25 April, 1887; Powderly to Will C. Bailey, 25 April 1887; John A. Forsythe to Powderly, 24 May 1884; Powderly to Forsythe, 28

May 1884, Terence V. Powderly Papers, Catholic University (hereafter cited as Powderly Papers).

6. ANDREWS AND BLISS, "Women in Trade Unions," pp. 115–16; Foner, *History of the Labor Movement*, 2:61–62; "Report of the General Instructor and Director of Woman's Work," *Proceedings of the General Assembly of the Knights of Labor, 1889*, pp. 4–5.

7. FONER, *History of the Labor Movement*, 2:62; *New York Times*, 8 Sept. 1882; Elizabeth S. Bryant to Powderly, 1 February 1883; Powderly to Bryant, 8 February 1883, Powderly Papers.

8. U.S., Congress, House, *Report No. 447*, 49th Cong., 2d sess., 1887, p. 85; Andrews and Bliss, *Women in Trade Unions*, pp. 130–32; Alan Dawley, *Class and Community: The Industrial Revolution in Lynn* (Cambridge, Mass., 1977), pp. 189–90.

9. *John Swinton's Paper*, Nov. 29, 1885, Jan. 3, 24, Feb. 28, Apr. 4, Apr. 11, 25, 1886.

10. CLAUDE GOLDIN, "Female Labor Force Participation: The Origin of Black and White Differences, 1870 and 1880," *Journal of Economic History* 37 (March 1977): 87–100.

11. PHILIP S. FONER, *Organized Labor and the Black Worker, 1619–1973* (New York, 1974), pp. 46–50; *Memphis Watchman*, reprinted in New York *Freeman*, Jan. 15, 1871, and in Cleveland *Gazette*, Jan. 22, 1887.

12. FONER, *Organized Labor and the Black Worker*, pp. 56–57; Sidney H. Kessler, "The Negro in the Knights of Labor" (Master's thesis, Columbia University, 1950), pp. 48–54; Kenneth Kann, "The Knights of Labor and the Southern Black Worker," *Labor History* 18 (Winter 1977): 54–55; Melton A. McLaurin, "The Racial Policies of the Knights of Labor and the Organization of Southern Black Workers," *Labor History* 17 (Fall 1976): 575–76; C. R. Alexander to Powderly, 14 October 1886, Powderly Papers.

13. FONER, *Organized Labor and the Black Worker*, pp. 53–55; McLaurin, "Racial Policies of the Knights of Labor," pp. 576–77; *Proceedings of the General Assembly of the Knights of Labor, 1887*, p. 1587; *Report of the International Council of Women Assembled by the National Woman Suffrage Association, Washington, D.C., U.S. of America. Mar. 25 to Apr. 1, 1888* (Washington, D.C., 1888), p. 155; *New York Times*, Sept. 8, 1883.

14. ANDREWS AND BLISS, p. 131; Foner, *History of the Labor Movement*, 2:62.

15. *Progress*, Mar. 26, 1885; *John Swinton's Paper*, June 5, Sept. 13, Oct. 11, 1885; Michael A. Gordon, "The Labor Boycott in New York City, 1880–1886," *Labor History* 16 (Spring 1975): 213–14.

16. *John Swinton's Paper*, Apr. 5, 1885.

17. MELECH EPSTEIN, *Jewish Labor in the U.S.A.: An Industrial, Political and Cultural History of the Jewish Labor Movement* (New York, 1950–53), 1:109; Louis Levine, *The Women Garment Workers*, (New York, 1924), pp. 32, 37–38; New York *Herald*, July 22, 28, 1883; New York *Tribune*, July 22, 1883; *New York Times*, July 22, 23, 28, Aug. 1, 2, 1883.

18. LIZZIE SWANK HOLMES, "Women Workers of Chicago." *American Federationist* 12 (August 1905): 508–9.

19. *Cohoes Daily News,* Mar. 12, 13, Apr. 15, May 14, June 16–17, July 20–23, Aug. 15–16, 1882; Daniel J. Walkowitz, "Working Class Women in the Gilded Age: Factory, Community, and Family Life among Cohoes, New York, Colton Workers," *Journal of Social History.* 5 (Summer, 1972): 486.

20. *New York Times,* Feb. 22, 1885; *Irish World,* Mar. 7, Apr. 4. 1885; Foner, *History of the Labor Movement,* 2:63; Gordon, "The Labor Boycott," p. 212.

21. *Yonkers Statesman,* Feb. 27, Mar. 6, May 15, 22, 1885; *John Swinton's Paper,* June 7, 1885.

22. *John Swinton's Paper,* May 24, 1885; Gordon, "The Labor Boycott," p. 213.

23. *Yonkers Statesman,* Aug. 22, 29, 1885; Foner, *History of the Labor Movement,* 2:64.

24. *New York Times,* June 6, 1886; *Journal of United Labor,* December 1883; *John Swinton's Paper,* Apr. 26, 1885; Gordon, "The Labor Boycott," p. 211; Foner, *History of the Labor Movement,* 2:64; David Montgomery, "Workers' Control of Machine Production in the 19th Century," *Labor History* 17 (Fall 1976): 500.

25. JAMES J. KENNEALLY, "Women and Trade Unions, 1870–1920: The Quandary of the Reformer," *Labor History* 14 (Winter 1973): 44; Powderly to Hayes, 22 December 1889, Powderly Papers.

26. Printed Circular marked "Received Nov 14, 1887," Powderly Papers.

27. *New York Times,* Aug. 31, 1886; *Journal of United Labor,* July 23, 1887; *Journal of the Knights of Labor,* quoted in Edward T. James, "More Corn, Less Hell? A Knights of Labor Glimpse of Mary Elizabeth Lease," *Labor History* 16 (Summer 1975): 408–9.

28. *Proceedings of the General Assembly of the Knights of Labor, 1886,* pp. 163-64, 287-89; Frances Willard, *Glimpses of Fifty Years* (Chicago, 1892), p. 523.

29. *Proceedings of the General Assembly of the Knights of Labor, 1886,* p. 952.

30. *Report of the International Council of Women,* p. 154; Andrews and Bliss, *Women in Trade Unions,* pp. 130-31; interview with Leonora M. Barry Lake in *St. Louis Post-Dispatch,* undated clipping in Leonora M. Barry Lake Folio, Sophia Smith Collection, Smith College Library.

31. Form 74, "Women's Work," File A1-38, Powderly Papers; *Proceedings of the General Assembly of the Knights of Labor, 1888,* p. 14.

32. *New London Telegraph,* Oct. 3, 1888, clipping in letter of L. M. Barry to Powderly, New London, Oct. 4, 1888, Powderly Papers.

33. LENORA M. BARRY to Powderly, 1 March 1888; Barry to Rev. Father McEnroe, 12 March 1888, copy in Powderly Papers; Foner, *History of the Labor Movement,* 2:65.

34. POWDERLY to Barry, 27 February; 23, 29 March; 25 July 1888, Powderly Papers.

35. *Report of the International Council of Women,* pp. 153-56; *Woman's Journal,* Apr. 7, 1888. Copies of several of Barry's speeches to suffrage and temperance conventions are in the Leonora M. Barry Lake Folio, Sophia Smith Collection, Smith College Library.

36. "Report of the General Investigator of Women's Work and Wages," *Proceedings of the General Assembly of the Knights of Labor, 1888*, pp. 9–10.

37. "Report of the General Investigator of Women's Work and Wages," *Proceedings of the General Assembly of the Knights of Labor, 1887*, pp. 1582–84.

38. Ibid., pp. 1581–82.

39. BARRY to Powderly. 15 November 1887. Powderly Papers.

40. *Proceedings of the General Assembly of the Knights of Labor, 1887*, p. 1585; ibid., *1888*, pp. 1, 4.

41. *Proceedings of the General Assembly of the Knights of Labor, 1888*, p. 1.

42. Ibid., p. 2.

43. Ibid., p. 14.

44. "Report of the General Investigator of Women's Work and Wages," *Proceedings of the General Assembly of the Knights of Labor, 1889*, pp. 1–2, 6.

45. BARRY to Powderly, 4 October 1888, 29 December 1888, Powderly Papers.

46. POWDERLY to Barry, 30 November 1889, Powderly Papers.

47. LEONORA BARRY LAKE to General Assembly, Nov. 10, 1890, *Proceedings of the General Assembly of the Knights of Labor, 1890*, p. 6.

48. Ibid., p. 162; Eleanor Flexner, *Century of Struggle* (Cambridge, Mass., 1959), p. 196.

49. FONER, *History of the Labor Movement*, 2:157–71.

50. *New York Times*, May 20. 1886.

51. *Troy Northern Budget*, May 19, 1886.

52. Ibid., May 22, 1886.

53. Ibid., May 20, 1886; *New York Times*, May 20, 21, 1886.

54. *Troy Northern Budget*, May 23, 1886.

55. Ibid., June 6, 1886.

56. Ibid., June 13, 1886.

57. *New York Times*, June 23, 1886.

58. *Troy Northern Budget*, June 25, 26, July 7, 9, 10, 1886.

59. FONER, *Organized Labor and the Black Worker*, pp. 59–61.

60. *New York Times*. Feb. 26, 1897; *Savannah Tribune*, Mar. 10, 1894; *Philadelphia Press*, June 3, 1894; Foner, *Organized Labor and the Black Worker*, pp. 62–63.

61. Chicago *Inter-Ocean*, June 2, 1894.

62. FONER, *Organized Labor and the Black Worker*, pp. 62–63.

63. FONER, *History of the Labor Movement*, 2:168–70.

64. *Journal of United Labor*, Feb. 25, 1885. Nov. 25, 1886, Apr. 30, Dec. 3, 1887, May 2, 9, 1889.

65. Quoted in Andrews and Bliss, *Women in Trade Unions*, p. 126.

66. *Irish World*, July 29, 1882.

67. Reprinted in *John Swinton's Paper*, Oct. 4, 1885.

68. CAROLYN DANIEL MCCREESH, "On the Picket Lines: Militant Women Cam-

paign to Organize Garment Workers, 1882–1917" (Ph.D. diss., University of Maryland, 1975), p. 49.

Chapter 5: The American Federation of Labor (pp. 98–119)

1. For the formation of the Federation of Organized Trades and Labor Unions, see Foner, *History of the Labor Movement,* 1:518-24. For the change to the American Federation of Labor, see Foner, *History of the Labor Movement,* 2:132-44.

2. FONER, *History of the Labor Movement,* 1:520-21.

3. *Proceedings of the Federation of Organized Trades and Labor Unions, 1882 Convention,* pp. 16, 19, 20, 23; Alice Henry, *Women and the Labor Movement* (New York, 1923), pp. 52-55.

4. *Proceedings of the Federation of Organized Trades and Labor Unions, 1883 Convention,* pp. 13, 15, 19.

5. *Proceedings of the Federation of Organized Trades and Labor Unions, 1885 Convention,* p. 16.

6. *Proceedings of the AFL Convention, 1887,* p. 9.

7. FONER, *History of the Labor Movement,* 2:189-90, Bernard Mandel, *Samuel Gompers, A Biography* (Yellow Springs, Ohio, 1963), pp. 43, 61-70.

8. MARY MEENIN to Chris Evans, 20 June 1892, American Federation of Labor Correspondence, American Federation of Labor Building (hereafter cited as AFL Correspondence).

9. RALPH SCHARNAU, "Elizabeth Morgan, Crusader for Labor Reform," *Labor History* 14 (Summer 1973): 340-41; Foner, *History of the Labor Movement.* 1:475-76.

10. The Illinois state certificate of incorporation, dated December 12, 1888, is in the Thomas J. Morgan Collection, Illinois Historical Survey, University of Illinois, Urbana, Ill.

11. Mrs. Thomas J. Morgan to Gompers, 12 November 1888, AFL Correspondence.

12. Copy of leaflet, "The Aims and Objects of Ladies' Federal Labor Union No. 2703") in AFL Correspondence; *Chicago Recorder,* July 29, 1894.

13. MRS. THOMAS J. MORGAN to Gompers, 20 August 1891, AFL Correspondence; *Chicago Tribune,* Feb. 21, Mar. 9, 1892; Scharnau, "Elizabeth Morgan," pp. 342-43; Ellen M. Ritter, "Elizabeth Morgan: Pioneer Female Labor Agitator," *Central States Speech Journal* 22 (Fall 1971): 242.

14. Quoted in Ritter, "Elizabeth Morgan," p. 243.

15. *Chicago Tribune,* Jan. 26, 1890.

16. The articles appeared in the *Times* between July 30 and August 17, 1888.

17. SCHARNAU, "Elizabeth Morgan," p. 342.

18. *Chicago Herald*, Nov. 3, 1888; *Chicago Times*, Nov. 3, 1888.

19. *Chicago Tribune*, Feb. 21, 25, 1892; *Chicago Herald*, Feb. 21, 25, 1892. Printed circular issued by the Illinois Women's Alliance, Mar. 1, 1893, in AFL Correspondence; Scharnau, "Elizabeth Morgan," pp. 343-44.

20. BESSIE LOUISE PIERCE, *A History of Chicago, 1871-1893* (New York, 1957): 294-95; Scharnau, "Elizabeth Morgan," pp. 344-45.

21. NANCY SCHROM DYE, "The Women's Trade Union League of New York, 1903-1920" (Ph.D. diss., University of Wisconsin, 1974), p. 40; McCreesh, "Picket Lines," pp. 53-56; Grace Dodge, ed., *Thoughts of Busy Girls, Who Have Little Time for Study, Yet Find Much Time for Thinking* (New York, 1892).

22. *The American Hebrew*, Oct. 26, 1888, and reprinted in Morris U. Schappes, "The Political Origins of the United Hebrew Trades, 1888," *Journal of Ethnic Studies* 5 (Spring 1977): 28.

23. EMILY BARROWS, "Trade Union Organization Among Women of Chicago" (Master's thesis, University of Chicago, 1927), pp. 43-44.

24. ALICE HAMILTON, *Exploring the Dangerous Trades: The Autobiography of Alice Hamilton* (Boston, 1953), p. 81.

25. The best study of the origins of the settlement house movement in the United States and its links with the labor movement is Allen F. Davis, *Spearheads for Reform: The Social Settlements and the Progressive Movement, 1890-1914* (New York, 1967). One should, however, also consult the works by settlement house residents such as Jane Addams, *Twenty Years at Hull House* (New York, 1910); Lillian Wald, *The House on Henry Street* (New York, 1915); Mary Simkhovitch, *Neighborhood: My Story of Greenwich House* (New York, 1938); Philip Davis, *And Crown Thy Good* (New York, 1952), and Robert S. Woods, ed., *The City Wilderness: A Settlement Study by the Residents of the South End Boston* (Boston, 1898).

26. BARROWS, "Trade Union Organization," pp. 43-44; Dorothy Rose Blumberg, *Florence Kelley: The Early Years* (New York, 1966), pp. 210-13. For Kelley's correspondence with Engels, see Dorothy Rose Blumberg, "'Dear Mr. Engels': Unpublished Letters, 1884-1894, of Florence Kelley (Wischnewetsky) to Friedrich Engels," *Labor History* 5 (Spring 1964): 105-28.

27. WILLIAM RHINELANDER STEWART, *The Philanthropic Work of Josephine Shaw Lowell* (New York, 1911), pp. 34-37, 357-58; Biographical Notes, "Leonora O'Reilly," undated biographical sketches, file 1, box 1, Leonora O'Reilly Papers, Schlesinger Library, Radcliffe College (hereafter cited as O'Reilly Papers).

28. IDA VAN ETTEN, *The Condition of Women Workers Under the Present Industrial System* (New York, 1890), p. 8; Jacob Andrew Lieberman, "Their Sisters' Keepers: The Women's Hours and Wages Movement in the United States, 1890-1902" (Ph.D. diss., Columbia University, 1971), p. 34; Maude Nathan, *Story of an Epoch-Making Movement* (New York, 1926). pp. 15-16.

29. ALLIS ROSENBERG WOLFE, "Women, Consumerism, and the National Consumers' League in the Progressive Era, 1900-1923," *Labor History* 16 (Summer 1975): 383.

30. New York Association of Working Girls Societies, "New York Association of Working Girls Societies," April 1893, pp. 5–8, copy in box 15, O'Reilly Papers.

31. IDA VAN ETTEN to Gompers, 2 February, 8 June 1891. AFL Correspondence.

32. *Proceedings of the AFL Convention, 1891*, pp. 26–27, 36.

33. HENRY V. JACKSON to Gompers 31 May 1891; John O'Rourke to Gompers, 2 July 1892, AFL Correspondence.

34. LENA ARDNER to Gompers, 23 March 1892; Julia Howard to Gompers, 24 March 1892, AFL Correspondence.

35. Copy of resolutions, dated Feb. 12, 1892, in AFL Correspondence.

36. *Troy Northern Budget,* Jan. 6, 11, 1891.

37. Ibid., Jan. 11, Feb. 1, 1891; *Troy Daily Times,* Jan. 7, 15, 29, 1891.

38. H. J. OGDEN to Gompers, 1 February 1891, AFL Correspondence.

39. DORA SULLIVAN to Gompers, 19 October 1891, AFL Correspondence; *Troy Northern Budget,* Nov. 20, 1891; *Troy Daily Times,* Nov. 23, 1891.

40. MABEL HURD WILLETT, *The Employment of Women in the Clothing Trade,* (New York, 1902), pp. 65, 184; Lillian Wald, *House on Henry Street,* pp. 204–6; McCreesh, "Picket Lines," pp. 66–67; Schappes, "United Hebrew Trades," pp. 15–23, 28.

41. *The Garment Worker* 1 (April 1893): 16–17; *Proceedings of the Third Annual Convention of the United Garment Workers* (Philadelphia, 1892), pp. 3–10; Chas. F. Reichers to Gompers, 26 June 1892, AFL Correspondence, McCreesh, "Picket Lines," pp. 68–70.

42. McCREESH, "Picket Lines," pp. 68–70.

43. JAMES P. HOOLEY to Gompers, 4 October 1891; Joan J. May to Gompers, 22 December 1891, AFL Correspondence.

44. MARY K. O'SULLIVAN, "Autobiography," manuscript in Schlesinger Library, Radcliffe College, Cambridge, Mass., pp. 1–67, 87–88, 98–99.

45. DORA SULLIVAN to Gompers, 19 October, 16 December 1891; 8 January, 18, 26 February, 17 March 1892; Mary E. Kenney to Gompers, Troy, 12 August 1892, AFL Correspondence; Gompers to Dora Sullivan, 4 May 1892; Gompers to AFL Executive Council, 17 November 1891; Gompers to Mamie Mahoney, 24 April 1894, Samuel Gompers Letter Books, Library of Congress.

46. KENNEY to Gompers, 18 May 1892, AFL Correspondence.

47. KENNEY to Gompers, 28 September 1892, AFL Correspondence.

48. MARY KENNEY O'SULLIVAN, "Autobiography," pp. 62–64; McCreesh, "Picket Lines," pp. 62, 69.

49. KENNEY to Gompers, 15 September 1892, AFL Correspondence.

50. GOMPERS to AFL Executive Council, 30 September 1892; Chris Evans to Gompers, 1 October 1892; John B. Lennon to Gompers, 1 October 1892, AFL Correspondence.

51. KENNEY to Gompers, 10 October 1892, AFL Correspondence; *Proceedings of the AFL Convention, 1892*, pp. 17, 30.

52. KENNEY to Gompers, 11 November, 8 December 1892, AFL Correspondence.

53. MRS. T. J. MORGAN to Gompers, 20 August 1891, AFL Correspondence.

54. RAY STANNARD BAKER, quoted in Leo Stein, ed., *Out of the Sweatshop: The Struggle for Industrial Democracy* (New York, 1977), pp. 88–89.

55. *Chicago Daily News*, Aug. 12, 1891; *Chicago Daily Tribune*, Aug. 12, 1891.

56. Chicago Trade and Labor Assembly, *The New Slavery: Investigation into the Sweating System as Applied to the Manufacture of Wearing Apparel, A Report Prepared by Mrs. Thomas J. Morgan* (Chicago, 1891), pp. 9–10, 18–19, 20, 23–24. For a good summary of the pamphlet, see Ritter, "Elizabeth Morgan," pp. 246–50.

57. MRS. T. J. MORGAN to Gompers, 9 June 1891, AFL Correspondence; *Rights of Labor*, Oct. 10, Nov. 17, 1891.

58. FLORENCE KELLEY to Henry Demarest Lloyd, 12 June 1891, letter quoted in Blumberg, *Florence Kelley*, p. 130.

59. MORGAN to Gompers, 7 April 1892, AFL Correspondence.

60. *Chicago Times*, Apr. 7, 1892.

61. EARL R. BEDNER, *A History of Labor Legislation in Illinois* (Chicago, 1929), pp. 153–54, 188, 262–64; Scharnau, "Elizabeth Morgan," pp. 346–48.

62. MORGAN to Gompers, 27 January, 21 February, 9 March 1892; 15 March, 2 August 1892, AFL Correspondence; *Chicago Daily Tribune*, Feb. 21, Mar. 9, 1892.

63. *Proceedings of the AFL Convention, 1894*, pp. 31, 45–46; Henry, *Women and the Labor Movement*, p. 54.

64. MORGAN to Gompers, 21 November 1892, AFL Correspondence.

65. JOHN F. O'SULLIVAN to Gompers, Boston, 26 December 1893, AFL Correspondence; Gompers to E. E. Pitt, 29 December 1893, Gompers Letter Books, Library of Congress.

66. Minutes of the Meeting of the AFL Executive Council, N.Y.C., Jan. 13, 1894, AFL Correspondence.

67. SAMUEL GOMPERS, *Seventy Years of Life and Labor* (New York, 1925), 1:482.

Chapter 6: The Women's Trade Union League (pp. 120–132)

1. ELEANOR FLEXNER, *Century of Struggle* (Cambridge, Mass., 1959), p. 169.

2. E. J. HUTCHINSON, *Women's Wages* (New York, 1919), pp. 151–54; Allen F. Davis, "The Women's Trade Union League: Origins and Organization," *Labor History* 5 (Winter 1964): 5; McCreesh, "Picket Lines," pp. 139–40.

3. BETTINA EILEEN BERCH, "Industrialization and Working Women in the

Nineteenth Century: England, France, and the United States" (Ph.D. diss., University of Wisconsin, Madison, 1976), pp. 297–98; Gladys Meyerand, "Women's Organizations," *Encyclopedia of the Social Sciences* (New York, 1935), 15:465; Benjamim Stolberg, *Tailors' Progress: The Story of a Famous Union and the Men Who Made It* (New York, 1946), p. 61.

4. DOROTHY ROSE BLUMBERG, "'Dear Mr. Engels': Unpublished Letters, 1884–1894, of Florence Kelley (Wischnewetsky) to Friedrich Engels," *Labor History* 5 (Spring 1964): 132.

5. *Annual Report of the National Consumers' League for 1903* (New York, 1903), pp. 6–8, 42–54. The National Consumers' League 12th Annual Report (for the year ending December 3, 1912) contains an Approved List of Factories.

6. *Proceedings of the AFL Convention, 1903,* pp. 22–23.

7. DOROTHY ROSE BLUMBERG, *Florence Kelley: The Making of a Social Pioneer* (New York, 1964), pp. 208–10.

8. PHILIP DAVIS, "The Social Settlement and the Trade Union," *Commons* 1 (April 1904): 142–47.

9. *Weekly Bulletin of the Clothing Trades,* Mar. 24, 1905, p. 2, reprinted in Nancy Schrom Dye, "Creating a Feminist Alliance: Sisterhood and Class Conflict in the New York Women's Trade Union League, 1903–1914," *Feminist Studies* 3 (1975): 25.

10. HELEN MAROT, *American Labor Unions* (New York, 1914), pp. 5–10.

11. *Report of the Industrial Commission on the Relations and Conditions of Capital and Labor Employed in Manufactures and General Business* (Washington, D.C., 1901) 7:60–62, 250.

12. *New York Times,* May 20, 21, 22, 1902; *Worker,* May 20, 1902.

13. IRVING HOWE, *World of Our Fathers* (New York, 1976), pp. 124–25, quoting *Jewish Daily Forward,* June 15, 1902.

14. ANNA STRUNSKY WALLING, ed., *William English Walling: A Symposium* (New York, 1938), pp. 4–8.

15. DAVIS, "Women's Trade Union League," 9–10n. For a general discussion of this interplay, see Arthur Mann, "British Social Thought and American Reformers," *Mississippi Valley Historical Review* 42 (March 1956): 682–92.

16. GLADYS BOONE, *The Women's Trade Union League in Great Britain and the United States of America* (New York, 1942), pp. 20–21.

17. *Women's Union Journal* 13 (1888): 68.

18. HAROLD GOLDMAN, *Emma Paterson* (London, 1974), p. 67.

19. YVONNE KAPP, *Eleanor Marx,* vol. 2, *The Crowded Years* (New York, 1978), p. 85.

20. CHARLES BOOTH, ed., *Labour and Life of the People,* vol. 1 (London, 1889), pp. 435–38; Sidney and Beatrice Webb, *The History of Trade Unionism, 1660–1920* (London, 1919), p. 402.

21. KAPP, *Eleanor Marx,* 2:382–83.

22. London *Times,* July 23, 1880. Also quoted in Lislotte Glage, "Clementine

Black: A Study in Social History and Literature" (Paper in preparation for Ph.D., University of Hannover), p. 22.

23. *Women's Trades Union Review* 1 (1891): 14.

24. BOONE, *Women's Trade Union Leagues,* pp. 24-25.

25. Biographical sketch of William English Walling in National Women's Trade Union League Papers, box 1, Library of Congress, Manuscripts Division (hereafter referred to as NWTUL Papers).

26. "Report of the Meeting Held to Organize the Women's Trade Union League," NWTUL Papers, box 1; Samuel Gompers, *Seventy Years of Life and Labor* (New York, 1925), 1:490.

27. "Report of Second Meeting Held to Organize the Women's Trade Union League," NWTUL Papers, box 1.

28. "Report of Third Meeting Held to Organize the Women's Trade Union League," NWTUL Papers, box 1.

29. Minutes of Annual Meeting of the NWTUL, Apr. 18, 1907, NWTUL Papers, box 1.

30. *Constitution of the National Women's Trade Union League of America Adopted in Faneuil Hall, Boston, November 17-19, 1903,* art. 3. The original is in NWTUL Papers, box 25.

31. WILLIAM ENGLISH WALLING to Leonora O'Reilly, 17 December 1903 (with notations in O'Reilly's handwriting), O'Reilly Papers; W. E. Walling to Mary McDowell, 25 November 1903, NWTUL Papers, box 1.

32. *Proceedings of the AFL Convention, 1903,* p. 249; *American Federationist* 10 (December 1903); Mary Kenney O'Sullivan to Alice Henry, n.d., NWTUL Papers, box 28.

33. DAVIS, "Women's Trade Union League," p. 12; "Report of the Annual Meeting, October 7, 1904," NWTUL Papers, box 2.

34. "Report of the Annual Meeting, October 7, 1904," NWTUL Papers, box 2.

35. PHILIP S. FONER, *History of the Labor Movement in the United States* (New York, 1964) 3:235-39.

36. Ibid., p. 230n.; *Annual Report of the Women's Trade Union League of New York, 1907-1908,* p. 5.

Chapter 7: The Waistmakers' Revolt (pp. 133-154)

1. PEARL GOODMAN AND ELIA UELAND, "The Shirtwaist Trade," *Journal of Political Economy* 18 (December 1910): 814-16; Louis Levine, *The Women's Garment Workers* (New York, 1924), pp. 144-48; William Mailly, "The Working Girls' Strike," *Independent* 67 (Dec. 23, 1909): 1416-20.

2. GOODMAN AND UELAND, "The Shirtwaist Trade," pp. 817, 819, 820-25; Woods Hutchinson, "The Hygienic Aspects of the Shirtwaist Strike," *Survey* 23 (Jan. 22, 1910): 541-50; Miriam F. Scott, "The Spirit of the Girl Strikers,"

Outlook 94 (Feb. 19, 1910): 394–95; McCreesh, "Picket Lines," pp. 163–64; Dye, "Women's Trade Union League" p. 160.

3. HUTCHINSON, "Hygienic Aspects," p. 547; Scott, "Spirit of the Girl Strikers," p. 394; Constance D. Leupp, "The Shirtwaist Strike," *Survey* 23 (Dec. 18, 1909): 383–86; Hyman Berman, "Era of the Protocol: A Chapter in the History of the International Ladies' Garment Workers' Union, 1910–1916" (Ph.D. diss., Columbia University, 1956), p. 72; *New York Call,* Dec. 16, 1909.

4. MCCREESH, "Picket Lines," pp. 162–63.

5. LEVINE, *Women's Garment Workers,* p. 149; *Proceedings of the Eighth Convention of the ILGWU, 1907* (New York, 1907), p. 30; *Report and Proceedings of the Ninth Convention of the International Ladies' Garment Workers' Union, 1908* (New York, 1908), p. 28; *New York Call,* Aug. 27, 1909; McCreesh, "Picket Lines," p. 166.

6. *New York Call,* Sept. 6, 8, 1909.

7. *New York Call,* Sept. 16, Oct. 12–20, 1909; Sue Ainsley Clark and Edith Wyatt, "The Shirtwaist Makers and Their Strike," *McClure's Magazine* 36 (November 1910): 70–86.

8. *New York Call,* Oct. 22, 1909.

9. BERMAN, "Era of the Protocol." pp. 78–79; *New York Call,* Nov. 25, 1909; *Souvenir History of the Ladies' Waist Makers' Union,* pamphlet in folder 56, n.d., National Women's Trade Union League of America Papers, Schlesinger Library, Radcliffe College, Cambridge, Mass., p. 11; (hereafter cited as NWTUL Papers). *Annual Report of the New York Women's Trade Union League, 1909–1910,* pp. 11–12; Mailly "Working Girls' Strike," p. 1417.

10. Secretary's Report, WTUL of NY, Nov. 11, 1909, WTUL of NY Papers; Dye, "Women's Trade Union League," p. 159.

11. New York *World,* Nov. 23, 1909; *New York Call,* Nov. 23, 1909; Levine, *Women's Garment Workers,* pp. 153–54; Leupp, "Shirtwaist Strike," pp. 383–86; Scott, "Spirit of the Girl Strikers," pp. 392–96; *Souvenir History,* p. 12.

12. MCCREESH, "Picket Lines," p. 171.

13. Secretary's Report, Women's Trade Union League of New York, Nov. 17, 1909, WTUL of NY Papers; Dyche, "Strike of the Ladies' Waist Makers of New York," p. 2.

14. MAILLY, "Working Girls' Strike," p. 1419; *New York Call,* Nov. 23, 26, 27, 1909; Charles S. Bernheimer, *The Shirt-Waist Strike: An Investigation Made for the Council and Head Worker of the University Settlement* (New York, 1910), pp. 3–5.

15. MAILLY, "Working Girls' Strike," p. 1419; *New York Call,* Nov. 26–28, 1909; *New York Times,* Dec. 28, 1909; Graham Adams, Jr., *Age of Industrial Violence, 1910–1915* (New York, 1966), p. 106.

16. LEUPP, "Shirtwaist Strike," p. 383; *Annual Report of the Women's Trade Union League of New York. 1909–1910,* p. 14.

17. *New York Call,* Dec. 23, 1909; *New York Times,* Jan. 3, 1910.

18. *New York Times,* Dec. 21, 24, 1909, Jan. 4, 6, 7, 1910; Leupp, "Shirtwaist

Strike," p. 384; *New York Call,* Nov. 25, 1909, Jan. 7, 1910; *Souvenir History,* pp. 13–14.

19. MARY CLARK BARNES, "The Strike of the Shirtwaist Makers," *World To-Day* 18 (March 1910): 267.

20. New York *World,* Dec. 4, 12, 1909; Dye, "Women's Trade Union League," p. 165; McCreesh, "Picket Lines," p. 173.

21. *Souvenir History,* pp. 14–15; *New York Call,* Dec. 4, 1909; Theresa Malkiel, *Diary of a Shirtwaist Striker* (New York, 1910), pp. 15, 20–21.

22. *New York Times,* Dec. 17, 1909; Dye, "Women's Trade Union League," pp. 165–66.

23. *New York Times,* Dec. 16, 1909; Minutes of the Regular Meeting of the Women's Trade Union League of New York, Feb. 7, 1910, WTUL of NY Papers; *Annual Report of the Women's Trade Union League of New York, 1909–1910,* p. 14.

24. *New York Times,* Dec. 14, 1909; *Annual Report of the Women's Trade Union League of New York, 1909–1910,* pp. 12–13; Minutes of the Executive Board of the WTUL of NY, Dec. 15, 1909, WTUL of NY Papers.

25. *New York Call,* Dec. 23, 1909; *New York Times,* Dec. 4, 1909.

26. *New York Times,* Dec. 21, 1909.

27. *New York Call,* Dec. 6, 1909; *New York Times,* Dec. 6, 1909; Malkiel. *Diary of a Shirtwaist Striker,* p. 23; *Souvenir History,* pp. 15–16.

28. *Philadelphia Public Ledger,* Feb. 5, 1910.

29. Ibid., Dec. 8, 9, 10, 20, 21, 1909; *Philadelphia Evening Bulletin,* Dec. 9, 10, 20, 21, 1909; McCreesh, "Picket Lines," pp. 174–75.

30. *Philadelphia Evening Bulletin,* Jan. 7, 11, 12, 13, 14, 17, Feb. 1, 5, 1910; *Philadelphia Public Ledger,* Jan. 7, 13, 15, 21, Feb. 3, 1910; Mary Durham to Agnes Nestor, 6 February 1910, Agnes Nestor Papers, Chicago Historical Society.

31. *Philadelphia Evening Bulletin,* Jan. 31, 1910.

32. *Philadelphia Public Ledger,* Jan. 15, 1910; McCreesh, "Picket Lines," p. 175.

33. *Philadelphia Evening Bulletin,* Jan. 11, 1910.

34. Ibid., Jan. 13, 1910.

35. *Philadelphia Public Ledger,* Jan. 15, 1910.

36. Ibid., Jan. 17, 20, 1910.

37. *New York Call,* Dec. 27, 28, 1909; *New York Times,* Dec. 28, 1909.

38. *New York Times,* Dec. 28, 1909; Levine, *Women's Garment Workers,* p. 164; Morris Hillquit, "Speech to the Striking Waist Makers," Jan. 2, 1910, Morris Hillquit Papers, State Historical Society of Wisconsin.

39. MALKIEL, *Diary of a Shirtwaist Striker,* p. 55.

40. *New York Times,* Jan. 3, 8, 1910; *New York Call,* Jan. 3, 1910.

41. *Souvenir History,* p. 20; Malkiel, *Diary of a Shirtwaist Striker,* pp. 58–60; *New York Call,* Jan. 3, 1910; Morris Hillquit, speech at Carnegie Hall, Jan. 2, 1910, Morris Hillquit Papers, State Historical Society of Wisconsin.

42. *New York Times,* Dec. 21, 25, 1909, Jan. 4, 5, 6, 11, 1910; Mary Brown Sumner, "The Spirit of the Strikers," *The Survey* 23 (Jan. 22, 1910: 550–55; *New York Call,* Jan. 4, 11, 12, 1910; New York Department of Labor, *Bulletin No. 43,* March 1910, pp. 35–43.

43. *New York Times,* Dec. 28, 1909; Bernheimer, *Shirt-Waist Strike,* pp. 9–10; *Survey* 23 (Jan. 15, 1910): 506.

44. *New York Call,* Dec. 12, 1909.

45. MALKIEL, *Diary of a Shirtwaist Striker,* p. 57.

46. Ibid., pp. 28, 45.

47. *New York Call,* Feb. 7, 15, 1910; McCreesh, "Picket Lines," p. 179.

48. *Philadelphia Public Ledger,* Feb. 7, 1910; *Philadelphia Evening Bulletin,* Feb. 8, 1910.

49. BARBARA MARY KLACZYNSKA, "Working Women in Philadelphia, 1900–1930" (Ph.D. diss., Temple University, 1975), pp. 240–41; *Philadelphia Evening Bulletin,* Jan. 18, 1910.

50. MIRIAM F. SCOTT, "What the Women Strikers Won," *Outlook* 95 (July 12, 1910): 480–88; John A. Dyche, *The Strike of the Ladies' Waist Makers* (New York, 1910), p. 2; Berman, "Era of the Protocol," p. 103.

51. MAX KATZMAN to Agnes Nestor, Philadelphia, 17 May 1910, Agnes Nestor Papers, Chicago Historical Society; *Proceedings of the Annual Convention of the ILGWU, 1912,* p. 69; Nancy Schrom Dye, "The Women's Trade Union League of New York, 1903–1920" (Ph.D. diss., University of Wisconsin, Madison, 1974), pp. 178–79.

52. *Survey* 23 (Jan. 29, 1910): 580–81, 620–21.

53. *Horizon* 5 (March 1910): 8–9.

54. Minutes of the Executive Board of the WTUL of NY, Feb. 16, 1910, WTUL of NY Papers, *Proceedings of the Third Biennial Convention of the NWTUL, 1911,* p. 19; Adriana Spadoni, "Italian Working Women in New York," *Colliers'* 44 (Mar. 23, 1912): 122; Frank Edwin Fenton, "Immigrants and Unions: A Case Study, Italians and American Labor, 1870–1920" (Ph.D. diss., Harvard University, 1957), p. 49; Dye, "Women's Trade Union League," p. 277.

55. DYE, "Women's Trade Union League," p. 170.

56. *Annual Report of the Women's Trade Union League of New York, 1909–1910,* p. 11.

57. "Rich and Poor in the Shirtwaist Strike," *Literary Digest,* Jan. 1, 1910, p. 6. Emphasis added.

58. *New York Call,* Dec. 29, 1909. Strike Edition.

59. HELEN MAROT, "A Woman's Strike—An Appreciation of the Shirtwaist Makers of New York." *Proceedings of the Academy of Political Science in the City of New York* (1910): 127–28; Dye, "Women's Trade Union League," p. 171.

60. MARY DURHAM to Agnes Nestor, 6 February 1910, Agnes Nestor Papers, Chicago Historical Society.

61. *Annual Report of the Women's Trade Union League of New York, 1909–1910,* p.

524 NOTES TO CHAPTER 8 (PP. 155–183)

11; Dye, "Women's Trade Union League," (p. 170) does give the impression that the league financed the strike.

62. *Annual Report of the Women's Trade Union League of New York, 1909–1910* and *1910–1911;* Dye, "Women's Trade Union League," pp. 172, 203.

63. Report of Summer Work of the WTUL of NY, Oct. 3, 1910, WTUL of NY Papers; Dye, "Women's Trade Union League," p. 172; "President's Address," pamphlet, 1910, p. 8, file 300, O'Reilly Papers; Samuel M. Gompers, "The Struggle in the Garment Trades—From Misery and Despondency to Betterment and Hope," *American Federationist* 20 (March 1913): 189–90; James J. Kenneally, "Women and Trade Unions, 1870–1920: The Quandary of the Reformer," *Labor History* 14 (Winter 1973): 48.

64. HILLQUIT, "Speech to the Striking Waist Makers," Jan. 2, 1910, Hillquit Papers.

65. *New York Call,* Feb. 6, 1910.

66. WILLIAM M. FEIGENBAUM, "Memories of 1909—The First Dress-Makers' Revolt," *Justice,* Sept. 1, 1933, p. 9.

67. Zilphia Horton Folk Music Collection. Tennessee State Library and Archives, Nashville, Tenn.

68. "Internationaler Frauentag," in *Clara Zetkin: Ausgewahlte Reden und Schriften* 1 (Berlin, 1957): 480.

Chapter 8: Repercussions of the Garment Workers' Uprising (pp. 155–183)

1. LOUIS LEVINE, *Women's Garment Workers* (New York, 1924), pp. 168; 176; Hyman Berman, "Era of the Protocol: A Chapter in the History of the International Ladies' Garment Workers' Union, 1910–1916" (Ph.D. diss., Columbia University, 1956), pp. 107–108; *New York Call,* July 8, 1910.

2. *Proceedings of the Tenth Annual Convention of the ILGWU, June 6–11, 1910,* pp. 47–48, 71–72; *New York Call,* June 30, 1910; *New York Times,* June 30, 1910; Levine, *Women's Garment Workers,* pp. 180–81.

3. *New York Call,* July 8, 1910; Levine, *Women's Garment Workers,* pp. 172, 181; *Union Labor Advocate* 11 (August 1910): 12; Frank Edwin Fenton, "Immigrants and Unions: A Case Study, Italians and American Labor," 1870–1920" (Ph.D. diss., Harvard University, 1957), pp. 496–97; *Proceedings of the Tenth Annual Convention of the ILGWU,* pp. 49, 57, 94.

4. *New York Call,* July 12, 1910; *New York Times,* July 12, 1910.

5. *New York Times,* July 21, Aug. 12, 13, 14, 1910.

6. *New York Call,* July 15, 1910; Levine, *Women's Garment Workers,* pp. 192–93.

7. HELEN MAROT, "Secretary's Report, July 20, 1910," WTUL of NY Papers. McCreesh, "Picket Lines," pp. 187–88.

8. *New York Call,* July 13, 21, 22, 1910; *New York Times,* July 13, 1910.

9. *Eighth Convention Report of the ILGWU, Report of the President,* pp. 5–6; Berman, "Era of the Protocol," pp. 48–49.

10. *New York Call,* July 28, 1910; Berman, "Era of the Protocol," pp. 126–28.

11. FONER, *History of the Labor Movement,* 2:200.

12. GOMPERS to Abraham Rosenberg, 4 August 1910, AFL Archives.

13. *New York Call,* July 30, Aug. 4, 1910; Levine, *Women's Garment Workers,* pp. 186–91.

14. *New York Times,* Aug. 28, 1900; *New York Call,* Aug. 27, 29, 1910.

15. *New York Times,* Aug. 28, 1910.

16. GRAHAM ADAMS, Jr., *Age of Industrial Violence, 1910–1915* (New York, 1966), pp. 115–16.

17. Reprinted in *Literary Digest,* Sept. 10, 1910, p. 372.

18. *New York Times,* Aug. 29, 31, 1910; *Weekly Bulletin of the Garment Trades* 10 (Sept. 2, 1910): 4.

19. BERMAN, "Era of the Protocol," p. 151; Melvyn Dubofsky, *When Workers Organize: New York City in the Progressive Era,* Amherst, Mass., 1968, pp. 187, 194–95.

20. *New York Call,* Sept. 3, 1910; "The Outcome of the Cloakmakers' Strike," *Outlook* 96 (Sept. 17, 1910): 99–101.

21. *New York Call,* July 4, 1910; Helen Marot, "A Moral in the Cloakmakers' Strike," *Outlook* 96 (Sept. 17, 1910): 99–101.

22. BERMAN, "Era of the Protocol," pp. 152–53; John Laslett, *Labor and the Left* (New York, 1957), chap. 4.

23. *The Ladies' Garment Worker* 1 (Nov. 1, 1910): 2.

24. *Official Report of the Strike Committee of the WTUL of Chicago,* p. 6; McCreesh, "Picket Lines," p. 189.

25. ROBERT NOREN, United Garment Workers, to Emma Stehagen, 9 October 1910, NWTUL Papers, Schlesinger Library, Radcliffe College, Cambridge, Mass.

26. *Official Report of the Strike Committee,* p. 6; McCreesh, "Picket Lines," pp. 189–90.

27. *Official Report of the Strike Committee,* p. 6; McCreesh, "Picket Lines," pp. 190–91; Mary Anderson and Mary N. Winslow, *Woman at Work* (Minneapolis, 1951), p. 38.

28. ANDERSON and Winslow, *Woman at Work,* pp. 38–39.

29. *Official Report of the Strike Committee,* pp. 10–11.

30. Ibid., pp. 13–14; Matthew Josephson, *Sidney Hillman, Statesman of American Labor* (New York, 1952), p. 54.

31. *Life and Labor,* February 1911, p. 52.

32. *Official Report of the Strike Committee,* pp. 15–17.

33. *Chicago Daily Socialist,* Oct. 22–28, 1910; Leo Wolman, et al., *The Clothing Workers of Chicago, 1910–1922* (Chicago, 1925), pp. 26–27; *New York Call,* Nov. 10, 1910; Josephson, *Sidney Hillman,* pp. 41–57.

34. ANNE S. RIVERA, "Clarence Darrow for the Amalgamated," *Advance,* May 1974, p. 12; Alice Henry, "The Hart, Schaffner & Marx Agreement," *Life and Labor* 2 (June 1912): 170–72.
35. MCCREESH, "Picket Lines," p. 194.
36. JOSEPHSON, *Sidney Hillman,* pp. 58–60.
37. *New York Call,* June 8, 1911; Levine, *Women's Garment Workers,* pp. 209–12.
38. *New York Call,* Aug. 6, 1911; *Life and Labor,* October 1911, p. 307; Margaret Dreier Robins to Members of the Executive Board, 4 August 1911, NWTUL Papers.
39. *Proceedings of the Eleventh Convention of the ILGWU, Toronto, 1912,* pp. 93–94.
40. MCCREESH, "Picket Lines," p. 196.
41. *Public,* Dec. 16, 1910, pp. 1187–88; *Milwaukee Leader,* Dec. 11, 1910.
42. Minutes of the Meetings of the National Executive Board of the NWTUL, Apr. 17, 18, 19, 1912, O'Reilly Papers; Pauline Newman, "The Story of the Corset Workers Strike in Kalamazoo, Michigan," clipping in O'Reilly Papers; McCreesh, "Picket Lines," pp. 199–200.
43. *Proceedings of the Eleventh Convention of the ILGWU, Toronto, 1912,* pp. 28–29; "Report of an Investigation of the Present Strike at the Kalamazoo Corset Company's Factory, April 17, 1912," O'Reilly Papers; McCreesh, "Picket Lines," p. 200.
44. "Report on an Investigation...": Leonora O'Reilly, "The Story of Kalamazoo," *Life and Labor* 2 (August 1912): 228–30.
45. *The Ladies' Garment Worker* 5 (October 1914): 87; McCreesh, "Picket Lines," pp. 200–201.
46. *New York Call,* Dec. 22, 1910; Secretary's Report of the WTUL of NY, Dec. 21, 1910, WTUL of NY Papers.
47. NANCY SCHROM DYE, "The Women's Trade Union League of New York, 1903–1920" (Ph.D. diss., University of Wisconsin, Madison, 1974), pp. 180–81.
48. New York, Factory Investigating Commission, *Preliminary Report,* 1915, 2:25, 331.
49. The discussion of the fire is based on reports in the New York *World,* Mar. 26–30, 1911; *New York Call,* Mar. 26–Apr. 8, 1911; New York *Herald,* Mar. 26–27, 1911, and the excellent account of Leo Stein, *The Triangle Fire* (New York, 1962).
50. New York *Tribune* and *New York Call,* reprinted in *Literary Digest,* Jan. 6, 1912, p. 6.
51. *Proceedings of the Third Biennial Convention of the NWTUL, 1911,* p. 18; Nancy Schrom Dye, "The Women's Trade Union League," p. 183.
52. *Proceedings of the ILGWU Convention,* 1912, pp. 53–58; Dye, "Women's Trade Union League," pp. 184–86.
53. *Life and Labor* 2 (December 1912): 357.
54. PHILIP S. FONER, *The Fur and Leather Workers Union* (Newark, N.J., 1950), p. 39.

55. Ibid., pp. 24–26.

56. Ibid., pp. 40–41.

57. Ibid., pp. 39–42; *New York Call,* June 15–22, 1912; *Jewish Daily Forward,* June 15–19, 1912.

58. FONER, *Fur and Leather Workers Union,* pp. 42–43.

59. Ibid., p. 44; *Jewish Daily Forward,* July 7–8, 1912; Rose Blank, "Strike of the Furriers," *Life and Labor* 2 (December 1912): 360–61.

60. FONER, *Fur and Leather Workers Union,* pp. 46–47; Blank, "Strike of the Furriers," p. 360.

61. Quoted in Foner, *Fur and Leather Workers Union,* p. 48.

62. BLANK, "Strike of the Furriers," p. 360.

63. FONER, *Fur and Leather Workers Union,* pp. 44–49; *New York Call,* Aug. 22, 24, 25, Sept. 7, 8, 1912.

64. *Jewish Daily Forward,* Sept. 9, 1912; Foner, *Fur and Leather Workers Union,* pp. 51–52.

65. *New York Call,* Jan. 14, 1913; "Uprising in the Needle Trades in New York," *Life and Labor* 2 (March 1913): 69–70; *New York Times,* Jan. 14, 1913.

66. HARRY BEST, *The Men's Garment Industry of New York and the Strike of 1913* (New York, 1913), pp. 14–15; *New York Call,* June 6, 1912; *Weekly Bulletin* 11 (May 31, 1912): 4; June 7, 1912, p. 4; 12 (Oct. 25, 1912): 1; *Garment Worker* 12 (Nov. 15, 1912): 1.

67. *New York Call,* Dec. 24, 30, 21, 1912; Jan. 5, 6–7, 8–12, 1913; *New York Times,* Jan. 8, 1913; *The Garment Worker* 12 (Jan. 17, 1913): 1; Best, *Men's Garment Industry,* pp. 16–18.

68. *New York Times,* Jan. 4, 1913; *New York Call,* Jan. 3, 14, 18, 23, 1913, and letter of A. Appelberg in ibid., Jan. 22, 1913; *Garment Worker* 12 (Jan. 17, 1913): 1.

69. *New York Call,* Jan. 1, 17, 22, 27, 28, 29, Feb. 3, 7, 10, Mar. 1, 1913; *New York Times,* Jan. 15, 21, 27, 1913; *Garment Worker* 12 (Jan. 24, 1913): 1; ibid. 12 (Jan. 31, 1913): 1–2; Best, *Men's Garment Industry,* p. 23; Letter Books, Feb. 10, 1913, Socialist Party: Local New York, Tamiment Institute Library, New York University.

70. BEST, "Men's Garment Industry," pp. 20–25; *Fiftieth Anniversary Souvenir History of the New York Joint Board of the Amalgamated Clothing Workers of America, 1914–1916* (New York, 1964), pp. 55–57; Dubofsky, *When Workers Organize,* pp. 79–82; *New York Call,* Mar. 9, 12, 13, 1913; *New York Times,* Mar. 2, 13, 1913; *Garment Worker* 12 (Mar. 14, 1913): 1–2; Algernon Lee Scrapbooks, Labor Struggles, 1913, Taminent Institute Library, New York University.

71. ISAAC A. HOURWICH, "The Garment Workers' Strike," *New Review* 1 (Mar. 15, 1913): 426–27.

72. MARTHA BENSLEY BRUERE, "The White Goods Workers Strike," *Life and Labor* 3 (March 1913): 73–75.

73. Ibid., p. 73; New York *World*, Mar. 2, 1913; McCreesh, "Picket Lines," pp. 219–20.

74. "The Unrest in the Garment Trades," *Ladies' Garment Worker*, December 1911, pp. 10–11; May 1912, pp. 7–8; *Proceedings of the ILGWU Convention, 1912*, pp. 78, 88–90; Dye, "Women's Trade Union League," p. 186.

75. ROSE SCHNEIDERMAN, "The White Goods Workers of New York: Their Struggle for Human Conditions," *Life and Labor* 3 (May 1913): 132; Minutes of the Strike Council of the WTUL of NY, Apr. 2, 1911, Sept. 26, 1912, WTUL of NY Papers; Dye, "Women's Trade Union League," p. 187.

76. Minutes of the Strike Council of the WTUL of NY, Apr. 2, 1911; Minutes of the Executive Board, Oct. 24, 1912; Secretary's Report of the WTUL of NY, Aug. 22, 1912, WTUL of NY Papers; "The Stress of the Seasons," *Survey* 29 (Mar. 8, 1913): 806; John A. Dyche, *Strike of the Ladies' Waist Makers, of New York*, New York, 1910, pp. 187–88.

77. *New York Call*, Jan. 7, 1913; "Uprising in the Needle Trades in New York," p. 69.

78. HARRY LANG, *"62," Biography of a Union*, (New York, 1940), pp. 93–99; Minutes of the Executive Board Meeting of Jan. 23, 1913, WTUL of NY Papers, Schneiderman, "White Goods Workers," p. 134.

79. LANG, *"62,"* pp. 101–5; McCreesh, "Picket Lines," p. 221.

80. "The Song of the White Goods Workers," original in NWTUL Papers, Schlesinger Library, Radcliffe College, Cambridge, Mass., and reprinted in McCreesh, "Picket Lines," p. 216.

81. New York *World*, Mar. 2, 1913.

82. Ibid.

83. LEVINE, *Women's Garment Workers*, p. 227; Lang, *"62,"* p. 111; Schneiderman, "White Goods Workers," p. 136.

84. Minutes of the Executive Board of the WTUL of NY, Jan. 23, 1913, WTUL of NY Papers; Helen Marot, "What Can a Union Do for Its Members?" *New York Call*, Jan. 27, 1913; Dye, "Women's Trade Union League," p. 189–90.

85. LEVINE, *Women's Garment Workers*, pp. 229–30; Lang, *"62,"* p. 131; Schneiderman, "White Goods Workers," p. 136; "Report of the New York League to the Biennial Convention of the National Women's Trade Union League," O'Reilly Papers.

Dye claims that the settlement did not mention either recognition or a preferential shop ("Women's Trade Union League," p. 190). But all other authorities include the preferential shop in the agreement.

86. McCREESH, "Picket Lines," p. 223.

87. *New York Call*, Jan. 16–19, 1913; *New York Times*, Jan. 19, 1913; Levine, *Women's Garment Workers*, pp. 223–26; Berman, "Era of the Protocol," pp. 165–72.

88. DUBOFSKY, *When Workers Organize*, pp. 83–87; Levine, *Women's Garment Workers*, pp. 226–28.

89. LEVINE, *Women's Garment Workers*, pp. 229–31; *Ladies' Garment Worker* 2 (August 1911): 14; McCreesh, "Picket Lines," pp. 225–26.

90. *New York Times*, Mar. 13–14, 1913; Berman, "Era of the Protocol," pp. 194–95; Levine, *Women's Garment Workers*, pp. 219, 235.

91. Charles Elbert Zaretz, *The Amalgamated Clothing Workers of America* (New York, 1934), pp. 73–90.

Chapter 9: The Wobblies and the Woman Worker (pp. 184–204)

1. *Proceedings of the First Convention of the Industrial Workers of the World*, New York, 1905, p. 82.

2. Ibid., pp. 3–6.

3. Ibid., pp. 610–14. Other female delegates were Isora Forberg, Evelyn Boehmann, Lilly Levenson, Mary E. Breckon, Rosa Sulway, Julie Mechanic, Mrs. E. C. Cogswell, and Bessie A. Hannan.

4. Originally called the Western Labor Union, its name was changed to American Labor Union in June, 1902. For the history of both the WLU and the ALU, see Foner, *History of the Labor Movement* 3:413–39.

5. *Proceedings, First Convention, IWW*, pp. 39, 167–73, 244–46, 248, 269; Philip S. Foner, *History of the Labor Movement in the United States*, vol. 4, *The Industrial Workers of the World, 1905-1917* (New York, 1965), pp. 34–36 (Hereafter cited as Foner, *IWW*.)

6. FONER, *History of the Labor Movement*, 3:231.

7. *Proceedings, First Convention, IWW*, pp. 520, 522.

8. Ibid., p. 462.

9. *Proceedings of the Second Annual Convention of the IWW*, Chicago, 1906, pp. 96–97; Paul Brissenden, *The IWW: A Study of American Syndicalism* (New York, 1920), p. 42.

10. *Proceedings, Second Convention, IWW*, p. 419.

11. "Minutes of the General Advisory Board," *Industrial Union Bulletin*, Mar. 30, 1907; "Minutes of the Local Executive Board," ibid., Jan. 10, 1907, Mar. 30, 1907, Aug. 17, 1907, Sept. 14, 1907, Nov. 9, 1907. See also "Debates in the Ghetto," ibid., May 4, 1907.

12. "General Executive Board," ibid., Nov. 9, 1907; "Still Growing in Portland," ibid., Mar. 30, 1907; "Call for Fifth Convention," *Industrial Worker*, Mar. 19, 1910.

13. ELIZABETH GURLEY FLYNN, *I Speak My Own Piece: Autobiography of "The Rebel Girl"* (New York, 1955), pp. 13–54; Rosalyn Fraad Baxandall, "Elizabeth Gurley Glynn: The Early Years," *Radical America* 8 (January–February 1975): 98.

14. Copy of speech in Elizabeth Gurley Flynn Papers, American Institute for Marxist Studies, New York City.

15. FLYNN, *I Speak My Own Piece*, p. 34: New York *World*, Aug. 23, 1906.

16. Los Angeles *Times*, Mar. 15, 1908.

17. BAXANDALL, "Flynn," p. 100.

18. See, for example, advertisement in *Industrial Worker*, May 20, 1910, p. 2.

19. *Industrial Union Bulletin*, Aug. 3, 1907.

20. *Industrial Worker*, Apr. 22, 1909; *Solidarity*, June 6, 1914; "To Colored Workingmen and Workingwomen," IWW leaflet, Elizabeth Gurley Flynn Collection, Wisconsin State Historical Society; *Voice of Labor*, reprinted in *Solidarity*, June 24, 1911; Foner, *IWW*, pp. 123, 125.

21. *Solidarity*, July 8, 1916.

22. ELIZABETH GURLEY FLYNN, "Women and Socialism," *Solidarity*, May 27, 1911; Foner, *IWW*, pp. 127–28. *One Big Union Monthly*, Sept. 1, 1919, p. 25.

23. ELIZABETH GURLEY FLYNN, "Women in Industry Should Organize," *Industrial Worker*, June 1, 1911. Similar is her article, "Women and Unionism," *Solidarity*, May 27, 1911.

24. *Solidarity*, Nov. 23, 1918.

25. "From a Woman Toiler," *Solidarity*, June 25, 1910.

26. *Industrial Worker*, March 1906, p. 6; August 1906, p. 10; Flynn, *I Speak My Own Piece*, p. 122.

27. SOPHIE VASILIO, "Women in the IWW," *Industrial Union Bulletin*, Apr. 25, 1908, and editor's reply in ibid.

28. *Solidarity*, Sept. 17, 1910; Foner, *IWW*, p. 120.

29. ERNEST GRIFFEATH, "On Free Love and the Home," *Industrial Worker*, June 5, 1913.

30. *Voice of the People*, July 30, 1914; Bill Boyd, "The Girl Out at Work," *Solidarity*, June 29, 1916, Feb. 5, 1921.

31. *Industrial Worker*, Apr. 3, 1913, Dec. 8, 1910, July 12, 1913; *Voice of the People*, Aug. 13, 1914.

32. *Industrial Worker*, Apr. 10, 1913.

33. *Solidarity*, Feb. 8, 1912; "Capitalist Morality," ibid., Sept. 3, 1910; Bill Lloyd, "The Wobbly and the Farmer's Daughter," *Solidarity*, Jan. 1, 1921.

34. "Large Families," *Industrial Worker*, June 1, 1911.

35. *Industrial Worker*, Sept. 28, 1911; "Family Limitation," *Voice of the People*, Nov. 1, 1914; Margaret Sanger, *Autobiography* (New York, 1938), p. 79.

36. FLYNN, *I Speak My Own Piece*, p. 152.

37. JOSEPH R. CONLIN. *Big Bill Haywood and the Radical Union Movement* (Syracuse, N.Y., 1969), pp. 106–7; Mabel Dodge Luahan, *Intimate Memoirs*, vol. 3, *Movers and Shakers* (New York, 1936), pp. 186–88.

38. FLYNN, *I Speak My Own Piece*, p. 84; Ralph Chaplin, *Wobbly: The Rough and Tumble Story of an American Radical* (Chicago, 1978), pp. 112–25.

39. PHILIP S. FONER, *The Case of Joe Hill* (New York, 1965), pp. 25–36.

40. JOYCE L. KORNBLUH, ed., *Rebel Voices: An IWW Anthology* (Ann Arbor, Mich., 1974), p. 138.

41. FLYNN, *I Speak My Own Piece*, pp. 54, 68, 75–77, 103, 108, 140, 323; Foner, *IWW*, pp. 188–89; Baxandall, "Flynn," pp. 102–3.

42. *One Big Union Monthly,* October 1919, p. 39; New York *Tribune,* Feb. 2, 1913; Foner, *IWW,* p. 149.

43. KORNBLUH, *Rebel Voices,* p. 180; Patrick Renshaw, *The Wobblies: The Story of Syndicalism in the United States* (New York, 1967), p. 11, Flynn, *I Speak My Own Piece,* p. 129; Benjamin H. Kizer, "Elizabeth Gurley Flynn," *Pacific Northwest Quarterly* 34 (July 1916): 110–12; Interview with Elizabeth Gurley Flynn, Jan. 31, 1964; *Daily World,* June 30, 1976.

44. *Solidarity.* Jan. 8, 15, 1910.

45. ELIZABETH GURLEY FLYNN, "IWW Call to Women," *Solidarity,* July 31, 1915.

46. *Solidarity,* May 27, 1911; June 28, 1911; Elizabeth Gurley Flynn in ibid., May 27, 1911, and in San Francisco *Bulletin,* Oct. 3, 1914, Elizabeth Gurley Flynn Collection, Wisconsin State Historical Society.

47. CHARLES ASHLEIGH, "Women in the IWW," *Industrial Union Bulletin,* Apr. 25, 1908.

48. ELIZABETH GURLEY FLYNN, "Problems Organizing Women," *Solidarity,* July 15, 1915.

49. "Tenth IWW Convention." *Solidarity,* Dec. 16, 1916.

50. *Solidarity,* Dec. 19, 1914.

51. FONER, *IWW,* pp. 128–29.

52. JANE STREET, "Denver's Rebel Housemaids," *Solidarity,* Apr. 1, 1916.

53. JANE STREET to Mrs. Elmer F. Buse (1917), original in Department of Justice, Record Group, File 1870-28, National Archives, Washington, D.C., and reprinted in Daniel T. Hobby, ed., "We Have Got Results: A Document on the Organization of Domestics in the Progressive Era," *Labor History* 17 (Winter 1976): 103–8.

54. "Housemaids Form Union in Denver," *Solidarity,* Apr. 1, 1916.

55. HOBBY, "We Have Got Results," pp. 104–5.

56. JANE STREET in *Solidarity,* Apr. 1, 1916.

57. *Solidarity,* May 6, 1916.

58. Ibid., Apr. 1, 1916.

59. HOBBY, "We Have Got Results," p. 105.

60. *Solidarity,* Apr. 8, 1916.

61. HOBBY, "We Have Got Results," p. 107.

62. *Solidarity,* Dec. 16, 1916.

63. FONER, *IWW,* pp. 557–58.

64. Ibid., pp. 2, 62–64.

65. FLYNN, "IWW Call to Women," *Solidarity,* July 31, 1915.

Chapter 10: The Lawrence Strike (pp. 205–218)

1. U.S., Congress, House, Hearings on Strike in Lawrence, Mass., *House Document No. 671,* 62d Cong., 1st sess., 1912, pp. 458, 460. Maurice B. Dergan, *History of Lawrence, Massachusetts* (Lawrence, Mass., 1924), p. 44; Donald B.

Cole, "Lawrence, Massachusetts: 1845–1912" (Ph.D. diss., Harvard University, 1956), p. 35; *Textile Manufacturers Journal,* Mar. 9, 1912, p. 4; Frank Edwin Fenton, "Immigrants and Unions: A Case Study, Italians and American Labor, 1870–1920" (Ph.D. diss., Harvard University, 1957), pp. 320–21.

2. U.S., Bureau of Labor, *Report on Strike of Textile Workers in Lawrence, Massachusetts in 1912,* pp. 19, 76–78; U.S., Department of Commerce and Labor, Bureau of the Census, *Census Monographs,* vol. 10, 1929; Paul F. Brissenden, *Earnings of Factory Workers, 1899 to 1927,* U.S., Bureau of the Census, monograph 10, 1929, pp. 45, 96, 104, 113, 114.

3. DONALD B. COLE, *Immigrant City: Lawrence, Massachusetts, 1845–1921* (Chapel Hill, N.C., 1963), pp. 101, 108, 109.

4. U.S., Congress, Senate, *Report on the Strike of the Textile Workers in Lawrence, Massachusetts in 1912. Senate Document No. 870,* 62d Cong., 2d sess., 1912, p. 204.

5. U.S., Bureau of Labor, *Report on Strike of Textile Workers,* pp. 19, 28, 71, 120, 160, 205; Lewis E. Palmer, "A Strike for Four Loaves of Bread," *Survey,* Feb. 3, 1912, pp. 1695–99.

6. U.S., Bureau of Labor, *Report on Strike of Textile Workers,* pp. 22, 88, 119.

7. U.S., Congress, House, *House Document No. 671,* pp. 114–15; *Solidarity,* Mar. 2, 1912; John B. McPherson, "The Lawrence Strike of 1912," *Bulletin of the National Association of Wool Manufacturers* 12 (1912): 236–37.

8. U.S., Bureau of Labor, *Report on Strike of Textile Workers,* pp. 191–204; Dr. Elizabeth Shapleigh, "Occupational Diseases in the Textile Industry," *New York Call,* Dec. 29, 1912.

9. IRVING J. LEVINE, "The Lawrence Strike" (Master's thesis, Columbia University, 1936), p. 35.

10. *Lawrence Evening Tribune,* Dec. 22, 23, 28, 1911; Jan. 4, 12, 1912.

11. FONER, *IWW,* pp. 306–11.

12. ELIZABETH GURLEY FLYNN, "Memories of the Industrial Workers of the World (IWW)," Occasional Paper No. 24 (1977), American Institute for Marxist Studies (New York, 1977), p. 9. The publication is a report of an address Flynn delivered at Northern Illinois University on November 8, 1962, less than two years before her death.

13. *Lawrence Evening Tribune,* Jan. 17, 1912.

14. *Lawrence Sun,* Jan. 14, 20, Feb. 24, 1912; U.S., Congress, House, *House Document No. 671,* pp. 294–95; Foner, *IWW,* pp. 321–22.

15. "Bread and Roses," by James Oppenheimer, in Joyce L. Kornbluh, ed., *Rebel Voices: An I.W.W. Anthology* (Ann Arbor, Mich., 1964), p. 196.

16. *New York Call,* Feb. 24, 1912; *Lawrence Evening Tribune,* Feb. 24, 1912; Dergan, *History of Lawrence,* p. 173.

17. U.S.. Congress, House, *House Document No. 671,* p. 249.

18. WILLIAM D. HAYWOOD, *Bill Haywood's Book: The Autobiography of William D. Haywood* (New York, 1929), p. 249.

19. *Lawrence Evening Tribune,* Feb. 28, 1912.

20. *Solidarity,* Mar. 2, 1912, July 31, 1915.

21. FRED BEALE, *Proletarian Journey* (New York, 1927), p. 44.

22. *Lawrence Evening Tribune*, Jan. 27, Feb. 16, 1912; Harry Emerson Fosdick, "After the Strike in Lawrence," *Outlook*, June 15, 1912, reprinted in *Solidarity*, July 6, 1912.

23. *Lawrence Evening Tribune*, Jan. 17, 22, Feb. 16, 19, 1912.

24. ELIZABETH GURLEY FLYNN, *I Speak My Own Piece: Autobiography of "The Rebel Girl"* (New York, 1955), p. 122.

25. JAMES P. HEATON, "The Legal Aftermath of the Lawrence Strike," *Survey* 28 (July 6, 1912): 509–10; Vida D. Scudder, "For Justice's Sake," ibid., Apr. 16, 1912, p. 77; Justus Ebert, *The Trial of a New Society* (Cleveland, 1913), p. 42.

26. MARY HEATON VORSE, *Footnote to Folly* (New York, 1935), pp. 13–14.

27. MARY HEATON VORSE, "Elizabeth Gurley Flynn," *Nation*, Feb. 17, 1926, pp. 175–76.

28. FLYNN, "Memories," p. 10.

29. FLYNN, *I Speak My Own Piece*, pp. 125–26.

30. FONER, *IWW*, p. 325.

31. *New York Call*, Mar. 6, 1912; *Lawrence Evening Tribune*, Feb. 10, 18, 1912; Margaret Sanger, *Autobiography* (New York, 1938), p. 81.

32. *New York Call*, Feb. 8, 1912; *Boston American*, Feb. 15, 18, 1912.

33. FONER, *IWW*, p. 326.

34. JOYCE L. KORNBLUH, ed., *Rebel Voices: An IWW Anthology* (Ann Arbor, Mich., 1964), p. 162; Rosalyn Fraad Baxandall, "Elizabeth Gurley Flynn: The Early Years," *Radical America* 8 (January–February 1975): 107.

35. U.S., Congress, House, *House Document No. 671*, pp. 201–8, 249–53, 301–9; *Lawrence Evening Tribune*, Feb. 24, 1912; *Lawrence Sun*, Feb. 25, 1912; *Solidarity*, Mar. 2, 1912; *New York Call*, Mar. 6, 1912.

36. *New York Call*, Feb. 25, 1912; *The Public*, Mar. 1, 1912, p. 202; *Congressional Record*, 62d Cong., 2d sess., pp. 2485–86.

37. LESLIE MARCY AND FREDERICK SUMNER BOYD, "One Big Union Wins," *International Socialist Review* 12 (April 1912): 625.

38. U.S., Congress, House, *House Document No. 671*, p. 302.

39. *Solidarity*, Mar. 16, 1912.

40. *Lawrence Sun*, Mar. 14–15, 1912; *New York Call*, Mar. 14–15, 1912; Foner, *IWW*, pp. 340–42.

41. *Industrial Worker*, July 25, 1912, p. 4.

42. LINDA STERNBERG, "Women Workers and the 1912 Textile Strike in Lawrence, Massachusetts," Paper, Division 3 Project, Hampshire College, Amherst, Mass., Apr. 28, 1975, pp. 74–76.

43. RAY STANNARD BAKER, "Revolutionary Strike," *American Magazine* 74 (May 1912): 30c.

44. MARY HEATON VORSE, "The Troubles at Lawrence," *Harper's Weekly* Mar. 16, 1912, p. 10.

45. STERNBERG, "Women Workers and the 1912 Textile Strike," 112–15.

Chapter 11: The Industrial Scene in World War I (pp. 219–245)

1. MARGARET A. HOBBS, "Wartime Employment of Women," *American Labor Legislation Review* 8 (1918): 332.

2. *Living Age* 285 (July 1917): 3.

3. *Industrial Management* 55 (1917): 351.

4. *New York Times*, Jan. 13, 1918.

5. IRVING W. BULLARD, *Women's Work in War Time* (Boston, 1917), p. 14.

6. *Annual Report of the New York Merchants' Association, 1917*, p. 17.

7. *New York Times*, July 20, 1918.

8. MARY VAN KLEECK AND MARY McDOWELL, "The New Position of Women in American Industry," U.S. Department of Labor, Women's Bureau, Bulletin No. 12 (Washington, D.C., 1920), p. 17.

9. *41st Annual Report of the Young Women's Christian Association*, (Chicago, 1917), p. 21.

10. *Seattle Union Record*, Jan. 12, Aug. 10, 24, Nov. 2, 1918.

11. W. T. GILMAN, "Women and Heavy War Work," *Scribner's Monthly* 65 (1918): 113–16; Hobbs, "Wartime Employment of Women," pp. 332–38; Dudley Harmon, "What Are These War Jobs for Women?" *Ladies' Home Journal* (November 1917) 31, 91–92; *New York Times*, Jan. 12, 17, 1918; Esther Norton, "Women in War Industries," *New Republic* 13, Dec. 15, 1917, pp. 179–81; Florence Kelley, "The War and Women Workers," *Survey* 39 (March 9, 1918): 628–31; Benedict Crowell and R. F. Wilson, *How America Went to War: The Armies of Industry* (New Haven, 1921), I:188, 259; II:530–31, 631; Van Kleeck and MacDowell, "New Position of Women in American Industry," pp. 11–93.

12. H. F. PORTER, "Detroit Plans Recruitment of Women for War Work," *Industrial Management* 55 (August 1917): 659; Alfred L. Smith, ed., "Increased Employment of Women in Industry During Wartime," *Annual Report of the New York Merchants' Association, 1917*, p. 10.

13. *Atlantic Monthly* 127 (October 1920): 250; Theresa Wolfson, *The Woman Worker and the Trade Unions* (New York, 1926), p. 29.

14. MAURINE WEINER GREENWALD, "Women Workers and World War I: The American Railroad Industry, A Case Study," *Journal of Social History* 9 (Winter 1975): 154.

15. U.S., Department of Commerce, Bureau of the Census, *Twelfth Census of the United States, 1900, Occupations*, IX:8–10; U.S., Department of Labor, Women's Bureau, *What Industry Means to Women Workers* (Washington, D.C., 1925), pp. 5–6.

16. VAN KLEECK AND MACDOWELL, "New Position of Women in American Industry," p. 13; Pauline Goodmark, "The Facts of Women in War Industries," *New Republic*, Dec. 29, 1917, p. 251; Sister M. Laurite Kroger, "Women in Industry During World War I" (Master's thesis, University of Cincinnati, 1950), pp. 23–26; Anna Center Schneiderman, "The Influence of the World War on Women in Industry" (Master's thesis, Columbia University, 1929), pp. 44–46; Tamah Veronica Jenkins, "Some Aspects of the Labor Movement with Special Emphasis on Women and Children; 1915–1919" (Master's thesis, Atlanta University, 1968), pp. 16–18.

17. FLORENCE KELLEY, *Wage Earning Women in War Time* (New York, 1920), pp. 264–69; "World War and Defense, 1910–1919—Survey of Certain Plants," typewritten report, Women's Bureau, War Department, Box 20, U.S. Department of Labor, National Archives.

18. BARBARA KLACZYNSKA, "Working Women in Philadelphia, 1900–1930" (Ph.D. dissertation, Temple University, 1975), p. 104.

19. *Seattle Union Record*, Aug. 18, Oct. 27, 1917.

20. Memo, 26 Apr. 1919, from Woman-in-Industry Service to Secretary of Navy RE: Philadelphia Naval Aircraft Factory, Women's Bureau, War Department, Box 20, U.S. Department of Labor, National Archives.

21. To Mary Van Kleeck, Director, Woman-in-Industry Service, from Helen Byrnes, Industrial Agent, Woman-in-Industry Service, Women's Bureau, War Department, Box 20, Folder 263, April 25, 1918; U.S., Department of Labor, Women's Bureau, War Department, "Wages of Work of Women in the United States Arsenal and Ordnance Plants Working for Government," typewritten report, Box 29, Folder 383, National Archives; Minutes of the Conference Between United States Government, Cloth Manufacturers and Cloth Weavers Union 72, typewritten report, pp. 41–42, U.S. Department of Labor, National Archives.

22. U.S., Railroad Administration, "Complaint 73, Pennsylvania Railroad—Assistant Locomotive Dispatcher," typewritten report, Box E-101, National Archives; U.S., Railroad Administration, "Discrimination in Rates of Pay; Women Coach Cleaners—West Philadelphia Yard," Box E-98, Folder 19V, National Archives.

23. U.S., Bureau of Labor Statistics, "Wartime Employment of Women," *Monthly Labor Review* 7 (October 1918): 193–218; Gordon Watkins, *Labor Problems and Labor Administration in the United States During the World War* (Urbana, Ill., 1919), pp. 72–75; "Where War Wages Do Not Reach," *Survey* 40 (June 22, 1918): 351–52.

24. U.S., Department of Labor, *Negro Migration in 1916–1917* (Washington, D.C., 1919), pp. 116–18; Emmett J. Scott, *Negro Migration During the War* (New York, 1920), pp. 25–26. The letter from the black woman in Biloxi, Mississippi, was reprinted in Emmett J. Scott, collector, "Letters from Negro Migrants, 1916–1918," *Journal of Negro History* 4 (July 1919): 296–319, and later reprinted in *America's Working Women*, compiled and edited by Rosalyn Baxandall, Linda Gordon, and Susan Reverby (New York, 1976), p. 133.

25. SCOTT, *Negro Migration During the War*, p. 55; *Textile World Journal* 53 (Nov. 24, 1917), p. 13.

26. Quoted in Nancy J. Weiss, *The National Urban League, 1910–1940* (New York, 1974), p. 98.

27. Chicago Commission on Race Relations, *The Negro in Chicago* (Chicago, 1922), pp. 385–87, 419–20, reprinted in Jerold S. Auerbach, *American Labor: The Twentieth Century* (Indianapolis, 1969), pp. 146–48.

28. "The Armstrong Association," *Opportunity* (August, 1923), p. 25; "Annual Reports of the Armstrong Association" (Philadelphia, 1917), pp. 12–13; 1918, pp. 6–7; Klaczynska, "Working Women in Philadelphia," pp. 53–55.

29. U.S., Department of Labor, Women's Bureau, *The Negro Woman Worker*, Bulletin No. 165 (Washington, D.C., 1938), p. 8.

30. Ibid., pp. 8–11; see also Alice S. Cheyney, "Negro Women in Industry," *Survey* 46 (Apr. 23, 1921): 119.

31. U.S., Department of Labor, Women's Bureau, Bulletin No. 100, Box 40, National Archives; Barbara Klaczynska, "Why Women Work: A Comparison of Various Groups—Philadelphia, 1910–1930," *Labor History* 17 (Winter 1976): 85–86.

32. Memo to Agnes Paterson from Mrs. Helen B. Irwin, March 3, 1919, Box 40, Women's Bureau, U.S. Department of Labor, National Archives.

33. KLACZYNSKA, "Why Women Work," p. 85.

34. CHEYNEY, "Negro Women in Industry," p. 119; U.S., Bureau of Labor Statistics, *Wages and Hours in Slaughtering and Meat Packing, 1917* (Washington, D.C., 1918), p. 1083; Memo to Agnes Paterson from Mrs. Helen B. Irwin.

35. JENKINS, "Some Aspects of the Labor Movement," p. 30.

36. PHILIP S. FONER, *Organized Labor and the Black Worker, 1619–1973* (New York, 1974), pp. 121–22.

37. U.S., Railroad Administration, "Unsanitary Conditions of Cleaning Yards Due to Use of Toilets by Cleaners," Complaint No. 81, typewritten report, Box E-101, Folder 260, National Archives; Klaczynska, "Working Women in Philadelphia," pp. 56–57.

38. U.S., Railroad Administration, Women's Service Section, Department of Labor Series 14, Folder 194—"Discrimination in Rates of Pay," Complaint Nos. 83, 81; U.S., Railroad Administration, "Unsanitary Conditions of Cleaning Yards"; Greenwald, "Women Workers in World War I," p. 168.

39. CHARLES WESLEY, *Negro Labor in the United States, 1850–1925* (New York, 1927), p. 262.

40. "Colored Women in Industry in Philadelphia," *Monthly Labor Review* 12 (May 1921): 1047.

41. Minutes of Meetings of the Board of Managers and the Executive Committee of the Young Women's Christian Association, December 13, 1917, cited in Abby Joan Parises, "A History of the Early Years of the Chicago YWCA: 1876–1918" (Master's thesis, Roosevelt University, 1975), p. 71.

42. ELLIOT M. RUDWICK, *Race Riot at East St. Louis, July 2, 1917* (Carbondale, Ill., 1964), pp. 4, 50, 52–53.

43. *Norfolk Journal and Guide*, July 7, 1917.

44. "Documents of the Race Riot at East St. Louis," introduction and notes by Robert Asher, *Journal of the Illinois State Historical Society* 65 (Autumn 1972): 328.

45. GLENN HARRIS, "Training Women for War Work," *American Machinist* 68 (Jan. 10, 1918): 47; Benedict Crowell, *Report of America's Munitions, 1917–1918* (Washington, D.C., 1919), p. 104.

46. AMY HEWES, *Women as Munition Makers—A Study of Conditions in Bridgeport, Conn.* (New York, 1917), p. 30; *New York Times*, Aug. 27, 1917.

47. *New York Times*, Jan. 7, 22, June 8, 14, 29, 1918; Rebecca West, "Mothering the Munitions-Maker," *New Republic*, Oct. 6, 1917, p. 266.

48. *Ladies' Home Journal* 34 (November 1917): 83.

49. CROWELL, *Report of America's Munitions*, p. 125; Crowell and Wilson, *How America Went to War*, I:187; Amy Hewes, "Women as Munition Makers," *Survey* 37 (Jan. 6, 1917): 381–85.

50. *New York Times*, Jan. 15, July 24, 1918; "Women in Munitions Work," *Outlook* 118 (Apr. 24, 1918): 682.

51. DAVID EARLL, "Our Experience with the Employment of Women," *American Machinist* 68 (Feb. 7, 1918): 240; M. E. Hoag, "Phenomenal Increase in Production," *American Machinist* 68 (Jan. 10, 1918): 46; *New York Times*, Dec. 2, 1917; "Women Employees of the Packard Motor Company," *American Machinist* 68 (July 11, 1918): 929.

52. *New York Times*, Dec. 17, 30, 1917.

53. CROWELL, *Report of America's Munitions*, p. 139.

54. VAN KLEECK AND MACDOWELL, *New Position of Women in American Industry*, pp. 94, 97, 100.

55. W. H. DIEFENDORF, "Women in the Gear Industry," *American Machinist* 68 (Oct. 3, 1918): 642.

56. VAN KLEECK AND MACDOWELL, *New Position of Women in American Industry*, pp. 97, 111.

57. *New York Times*, Dec. 17, 1917, July 24, 1918.

58. VAN KLEECK AND MACDOWELL, *New Position of Women in American Industry*, pp. 99, 112.

59. "Why We Are Replacing Men with Women," *Factory Magazine* 18 (1917): 313; V. B. Turner, "Women in the Mechanical Trades of the United States," *Monthly Labor Review* 7 (September 1918): 213.

60. VAN KLEECK AND MACDOWELL, *New Position of Women in American Industry*, p. 95; *American Machinist* 68 (January 1918): 451.

61. VAN KLEECK AND MACDOWELL, *New Position of Women in American Industry*, pp. 18–19.

62. "Women in Machine Shops," *American Machinist* 68 (May 2, 1918): 768; J. V. Hunter, "The Training of Women as Machine Operators," *American Machinist* 68 (Sept. 26, 1918): 565.

63. "Women in Industry," *Survey* 38 (Apr. 19, 1918): 112.

64. VAN KLEECK AND MACDOWELL, *New Position of Women in American Industry*, p. 761; W. A. Wall, "Employment of Women in Our Industries," *American Machinist* 68 (May 30, 1918): 910; "Using Women in Cincinnati Shops," *American Machinist* 68 (Oct. 31, 1918): 626; *New York Times*, Oct. 26, 1918.

65. VAN KLEECK AND MACDOWELL, *New Position of Women in American Industry*, pp. 133–35.

66. Ibid., pp. 135–36; *Ladies' Home Journal* 34 (September 1917): 32.

67. *New York Times*, May 1, 2, 1917; *Seattle Union Record*, Jan. 12, 1918.

68. *Butcher Workman*, July 1917, p. 15.

69. *Annual Report of Walter B. Hines, Director General of Railroads, 1919* (Washington, D.C., 1920), p. 61; Schneiderman, "Influence of the World War on Women in Industry," p. 12.

70. ELIZABETH KEMPER ADAMS, *Women Professional Workers* (Chatauqua, N.Y., 1921), pp. 233–35; Grace Coyle, *Present Trends in Clerical Occupations* (New York, 1928), pp. 11, 14, 33.

71. GREENWALD, "Women Workers and World War I," p. 156.

72. *Annual Report of W. G. McAdoo, Director General of Railroads, 1918* (Washington, D.C., 1919), p. 18.

73. Ibid., p. 73.

74. Ibid., p. 17.

75. GREENWALD, "Women Workers and World War I,", p. 157.

76. W. S. WOYTINSKY, et al., *Employment and Wages in the United States* (New York, 1953), pp. 179–82.

77. U.S., Employment Service, *Bulletin*, Aug. 6, 1918, p. 3; Chicago *Tribune*, Aug. 1, 1918; *New York Times*, Dec. 16, 1917, Mar. 6, 1918.

78. JOHN MAURICE CLARK, *The Costs of the World War to the American People* (New Haven, Conn., 1931), p. 45.

79. CLARENCE D. LONG, *The Labor Force in Wartime America*, Occasional Paper 14, National Bureau of Economic Research, New York, March 1944, p. 46.

80. C. E. PERSONS, "Women's Wages in the United States," *Quarterly Journal of Economics* 29 (Feb. 1915): 201–34; "Report of the New York City Health Department," *New York Times*, July 27, 1919.

81. *Seattle Union Record*, Jan. 12, 1918.

Chapter 12: Women and the Trade Unions in World War I (pp. 246–266)

1. *Butcher Workman*, May 1917.

2. *New Republic* June 4, 1919, pp. 202–3.

3. *Proceedings of the AFL Convention, 1918*, p. 38.

4. SAMUEL GOMPERS, "Don't Sacrifice Womanhood," *American Federationist* 24 (August 1917): 747–49; *Seattle Union Record*, Aug. 18, 1917. See also Samuel Gompers, "Women Workers in War Time," *American Federationist* 24 (September 1917): 747–49.

5. SAMUEL GOMPERS TO ANDREW WENNEIS, Secretary-Treasurer, International Fur Workers' Union, 22 May 1917, International Fur and Leather Workers' Union Archives.

6. "There Is No Shortage of Labor," *American Federationist* 24 (October 1917): 22–25.

7. SAMUEL GOMPERS TO ANDREW WENNEIS, Secretary-Treasurer, International Fur Workers' Union, 12 October 1917, International Fur and Leather Workers' Union Archives; *Seattle Union Record*, Aug. 18, 1917.

8. *Advance*, Apr. 27, 1917, p. 6; Marc Karson, *American Labor Unions and Politics, 1900–1918* (Carbondale, Ill., 1958), pp. 145–56.

9. *New York Times*, Jan. 13, 1918.

10. *Seattle Union Record*, Dec. 19, 1917, Feb. 16, 1918.

11. "Female Labor Arouses Hostility and Apprehension in Union Ranks," *Current Opinion*, April 1918, pp. 292–93. See also report of "Workingwomen in Wartime Conference," *New York Times*, Dec. 16, 1917.

12. *New York Times*, June 9, 1917; *Proceedings of the AFL Convention, 1918*, pp. 202, 219; *Proceedings of the AFL Convention, 1919*, pp. 188–89.

13. PHILIP S. FONER, *Organized Labor and the Black Worker, 1619–1973* (New York, 1974), pp. 136–43; John D. Finney, Jr., "A Study of Negro Labor During and After World War I" (Ph.D. diss., Georgetown University, 1957), pp. 146–88.

14. Chicago Commission on Race Relations, *The Negro in Chicago* (Chicago, 1922), p. 89, and reprinted in Jerold S. Auerbach, *American Labor: The Twentieth Century* (Indianapolis, 1969), p. 151.

15. *Life and Labor*, May, June, July, August 1918; *Proceedings of the Biennial Convention of the NWTUL, 1919*, pp. 14–17.

16. MILDRED RANKIN TO MARGARET DREIER ROBINS, 10 August 1918, Margaret Dreier Robins Papers, University of Florida Library, Gainesville, Florida, hereinafter cited as Robins Papers.

17. *Norfolk Journal and Guide*, Mar. 3, May 12, 1917.

18. *Norfolk Ledger-Dispatch*, Sept. 3, 1917.

19. Ibid., Sept. 6, 1917.

20. *Norfolk Journal and Guide*, Sept. 29, 1917.

21. *Norfolk Ledger-Dispatch*, Oct. 3, 1917; *Virginian-Pilot*, reprinted in *Norfolk Journal and Guide*, Oct. 5, 1917.

22. *Norfolk Journal and Guide*, Oct. 5, 1917.

23. *Norfolk Ledger-Dispatch*, Nov. 12, 13, 14, 1917.

24. FONER, *Organized Labor and the Black Worker*, p. 143; Finney, Jr., "Study of Negro Labor," pp. 189–90.

25. "Controversies Regarding the Right of Women to Work as Conductors," *Women Street Car Conductors and Ticket Agents* (Washington, D.C., 1921), pp. 2, 3.

26. U.S., Department of Commerce and Labor, Bureau of the Census, *Special Reports, Street and Electric Railways, 1902* (Washington, D.C., 1902), p. 79; U.S., Department of Commerce and Labor, Bureau of the Census, *Special Reports, Street and Electric Railways, 1907* (Washington, D.C., 1910), pp. 193, 201.

27. *Motorman and Conductor*, November 1917, p. 21; Leo Wolman, *The Growth of American Trade Unions, 1880-1923* (New York, 1924), p. 135.

28. *Monthly Labor Review* 7 (April 1918): 1030-32. For a biographical sketch of William D. Mahon, see Gary M. Fink, ed., *Biographical Dictionary of American Labor Leaders* (Westport, Conn., 1974), p. 227.

29. *Trade Union Leader*, May 25, Dec. 21, 1918.

30. *Motorman and Conductor*, September 1918, p. 31.

31. BENJAMIN M. SQUIRES, "Women Street Railway Employees," *Monthly Labor Review* 6 (May 1918): 1049-50; *Trade Union Leader*, Nov. 30, 1918.

32. *Trade Union Leader*, Apr. 27, 1918.

33. *New York Times*, May 5, 1918.

34. Ibid., May 10, 1918; Squires, "Women Street Railway Employees," pp. 1049-70.

35. *New York Times*, May 11, 1918.

36. Ibid., May 20, 1918; *Seattle Union Record*, Sept. 7, 1918.

37. *New York Times*, May 21, 1918.

38. *Life and Labor*, January 1919; p. 15; *Report of the Cleveland Railway Company for the Fiscal Year Ended December 31, 1918* (Cleveland, Ohio, Jan. 29, 1919).

39. Entry 4, National War Labor Board Docket #491, *Employees v. Cleveland Street Railway of Cleveland, Ohio*, Mar. 17, 1919, National Archives.

40. Ibid.

41. RONALD M. BENSON, "Searching for the Antecedents of Affirmative Action: The Case of the Cleveland Conductorettes in World War I" 1975 (Paper in possession of present writer), p. 5.

42. *New York Times*, Sept. 24, 1918; Entry 4. National War Labor Board Docket #491; *Cleveland Plain Dealer*, Dec. 7, 8, 12, 14, 1918; *Monthly Labor Review* 6 (June 1918): 55-57.

43. *Cleveland Plain Dealer*, Dec. 14, 1918; *Women Street Car Conductors and Ticket Agents*, p. 8.

44. *Life and Labor*, January 1919, p. 14; Benson, "Searching for Antecedents," pp. 8-9.

45. Benson, "Searching for Antecedents," p. 9.

46. *The Trade Union Leader*, Dec. 21, 1918.

47. *Cleveland Plain Dealer*, Dec. 3, 1918; *New York Times*, Dec. 4, 1918.

48. *Cleveland Plain Dealer*, Dec. 4, 1918; *New York Times*, Dec. 4, 1918.

49. *Woman Street Car Conductors and Ticket Agents*, p. 9.

50. Ibid.; Benson, "Searching for Antecedents," p. 11.

51. FRANK P. WALSH TO ETHEL SMITH, 2 December 1919, Frank P. Walsh Papers, New York Public Library, Manuscripts Division, hereinafter cited as Walsh Papers.

52. ROSE MORIARTY TO FRANK P. WALSH, 13 December 1918, Walsh Papers.

53. *Life and Labor*, March 1919, p. 52.

54. JOHN FITZPATRICK TO FRANK P. WALSH, December 26, 1918, Walsh Papers.

55. *Butcher Workman,* April 1918; David Brody, *The Butcher Workman: A Study of Unionization* (Cambridge, Mass., 1964), pp. 75–82.

56. *Life and Labor,* April 1919, p. 98; Benson, "Searching for Antecedents," pp. 13–14.

57. *New York Times,* Mar. 17, 1919; *Life and Labor,* April 1919, p. 98.

58. ROSE MORIARTY TO FRANK P. WALSH, 20 March 1919, telegram, Walsh Papers.

59. *New York Times,* Mar. 19, 1919.

60. *Cleveland Plain Dealer,* Mar. 19, 1919.

61. ELIZABETH CHRISTMAN AND ETHEL SMITH TO FRANK P. WALSH, 19 March 1919, telegram; Ethel Smith to Frank P. Walsh, 21 March 1919, Walsh Papers; Benson, "Searching for Antecedents," pp. 14–15.

62. *New York Times,* Mar. 19, 1919.

63. *Women Street Car Conductors and Ticket Agents,* pp. 11–12.

64. Ibid., pp. 13–14.

65. *Women Street Car Conductors,* p. 15.

66. *New York Times,* Mar. 30, 1919.

67. LEO WOLMAN, *The Growth of American Trade Unions,* 1880–1923 (New York, 1923), p. 162.

68. *Seattle Union Record,* Jan. 21, 1919.

Chapter 13: The Women's Trade Union League in the 1920s (pp. 267–295)

1. *Proceedings of the AFL Convention, 1918,* p. 236.

2. *Proceedings of the AFL Convention, 1919,* pp. 70–80.

3. *New York Times,* Sept. 23, Oct. 10, 1919; *Proceedings of the AFL Convention,* 1920, p. 81.

4. *New York Times,* Feb. 1, 1919.

5. JACOB ANDREW LIEBERMAN," "Their Sisters' Keepers: The Women's Hours and Wages Movement in the United States, 1890–1925" (Ph.D. diss., Columbia University, 1936), pp. 386–91.

6. JUDITH ANNE SCALANDER, "The Women's Bureau, 1920–1950: Federal Reaction to Female Wage Earning" (Ph.D. diss., Duke University, 1977), pp. 39–40.

7. Ibid., pp. 103–6, 168–72; *Labor,* Mar. 12, 1921.

8. *Seattle Union Record,* July 15, 1922.

9. BARBARA MARY KLACZYNSKA, "Working Women in Philadelphia, 1900–1930" (Ph.D. diss., Temple University, 1975), pp. 264–66; Manuscript autobiography of Hilda Smith, Schlesinger Library, Radcliffe College.

10. KLACZYNSKA, "Working Women in Philadelphia," pp. 267–68.

11. Copies of the Bryn Mawr mimeographed student magazines can be found in Hilda Smith Papers, Boxes 3, 4, Schlesinger Library, Radcliffe College.

12. KLACZYNSKA, "Working Women in Philadelphia," p. 268.

13. *Seattle Union Advocate,* Sept. 2, 1922.

14. HILDA SMITH autobiography.

15. KLACZYNSKA, "Working Women in Philadelphia," pp 270–71; Fannia Cohn to Helen

Norton, 9 February 1932, Fannia Cohn Papers, New York Public Library, Manuscript Division, Box 5.

16. AGNES NESTOR, *Woman's Labor Leader: An Autobiography of Agnes Nestor* (Rockford, Ill., 1954), pp. 184–88.

17. SAMUEL GOMPERS, *Seventy Years of Life and Labor* (New York, 1925), 2:483–84, 494, 510.

18. *New York Times*, Mar. 7, 1919.

19. Ibid., Mar. 30, 1919; Gompers, *Seventy Years of Life and Labor*, 2:483–84, 494, 510.

20. *New York Times*, Oct. 12, 1919.

21. This discussion is based on the typed "Proceedings of the First International Congress of Working Women, October 28–November 5, 1919," in the NWTUL Papers.

22. FRANK L. GRUBBS JR., "Organized Labor and the League to Enforce Peace," *Labor History* 14 (Spring 1973): 256.

23. *Proceedings of the First Biennial Congress, International Federation of Working Women, Geneva, Switzerland, October 22–24, 1921*, copy in NWTUL Papers; *Labor*, Nov. 19, 1921; Alice Henry, *Women and the Labor Movement* (New York, 1923), pp. 212–15.

24. *New York Times*, Oct. 18, 1921; *Labor*, Oct. 22, Nov. 19, 1921.

25. *New York Times*, Feb. 16, 1919; Letta Perkins, "Report of the Eighth Annual Convention," NWTUL Papers.

26. *Labor*, Dec. 25, 1920.

27. *American Federationist* 20 (March 1921): 122.

28. Ibid.

29. *Life and Labor*, June 1921, p. 32.

30. HENRY, *Women and the Labor Movement*, p. 102.

31. *Proceedings of the AFL Convention, 1921*, pp. 74, 85–88, 94–95.

32. KATHERINE FISHER, "Women Workers and the AFL," *New Republic*, Aug. 3, 1921, pp. 265–67.

33. *Proceedings of the AFL Convention, 1922*, pp. 101, 322–26; Theresa Wolfson, *The Woman Worker and the Trade Unions* (New York, 1926), pp. 68–69.

34. SCALANDER, "The Women's Bureau," pp. 108–9.

35. *Proceedings of the AFL Convention, 1924*, p. 49; Wolfson, *Woman Worker and the Trade Unions*, p. 71.

36. WOLFSON, *Woman Worker and the Trade Unions*, p. 75; *Proceedings of the AFL Convention, 1925*, pp. 131–32; 1926, pp. 80–84; Ann Washington Craton, "Organizing the Women Workers," *Nation*, Mar. 23, 1927, pp. 312–13.

37. *New York Times*, Aug. 15, 1924.

38. *Muller v. Oregon*, 208 US 412, 421–22.

39. ELIZABETH FAULKNER BAKER, *Protective Labor Legislation* (New York, 1925), pp. 222–23.

40. *New York Times*, Mar. 12, 1922; *Seattle Union Record*, Jan. 21, 1922.

41. BAKER, *Protective Labor Legislation*, pp. 242–44.

42. *Life and Labor*, January 1920, p. 60; May, 1920, p. 38; Nancy Schrom Dye, "The Women's Trade Union League of New York, 1903–1920" (Ph. D. diss., University of Wisconsin, Madison, 1974), pp. 431–33.

43. Consumers' League of New York, *The Forty-Eight Hour Law: Do Working Women Want It?* (New York, 1927), p. 5.

44. *Seattle Union Record*, Sept. 23, 1922.

45. *Labor,* Jan. 3, 1923. See also Samuel Gompers, "Equal Rights Law Will Hurt Women," ibid., Jan. 21, 1922.

46. *New York Times,* Jan. 11, 20, 1923; J. Stanley Lemons, *The Woman Citizen, Social Feminism in the 1920's* (Urbana, Ill., 1973), pp. 195-97.

47. *Labor,* Feb. 16, 1923.

48. Ibid., Feb. 16, 23, 1923.

49. Ibid., Feb. 16, 23, 30, 1923.

50. LIEBERMAN, "Their Sisters' Keepers," pp. 405-8; Florence Kelley, "The District of Columbia Minimum Wage," *Survey* 45 (Feb. 12, 1921): 702.

51. *Atkins* v. *Children's Hospital of the District of Columbia,* 261 US 525 (1923), 522-53; *New York Times,* Apr. 10, 1923.

52. "Minimum Wage Decision," *Equal Rights* 1 (April 1923): 14-15.

53. *New York Times,* May 16, 1923; *Labor,* May 26, 1923.

54. *Labor,* May 26, 1923.

55. *New York Times,* Nov. 14, 1923.

56. *Labor,* Apr. 14, 21, 28, Nov. 23, 1923.

57. *Lieberman,* "Their Sisters' Keepers," p. 432.

58. *Labor,* Aug. 25, 1923.

59. *New York Times,* June 17, 1924; Mary Anderson, as told to Mary Winslow, *Woman at Work: The Autobiography of Mary Anderson* (Minneapolis, 1951), p. 196.

60. *New York Times,* Jan. 21, 1926.

61. Ibid., Jan. 17, 1926.

62. Ibid., Jan. 18, 1926.

63. Ibid., Jan. 22, 1926.

64. Ibid.

65. Ibid., Feb. 14, 1926; *Annual Report of the Women's Trade Union League of New York, 1926-1927,* pp. 16, 18; U.S., Department of Labor, Women's Bureau, *The Effects of Labor Legislation on the Employment Opportunities of Women,* Bulletin No. 65 (Washington, D.C., 1928), pp. xv-xvi.

66. SCALANDER, "The Women's Bureau," pp. 201-2.

67. *New York Times,* Feb. 9, Mar. 17, 18, May 15, 18, 1925.

68. Ibid., Feb. 8, 17-18, 1926.

69. Ibid., Feb. 21, 1926.

70. Ibid., Mar. 27, 1927.

71. Ibid., Apr. 14, 1927.

72. Minutes of the Executive Board Meeting, Sept. 11-13, 1925, NWTUL Papers.

73. SCALANDER, "The Women's Bureau," p. 109; William Henry Chafe, The American Woman: Her Changing Social, Economic, and Political Roles, 1920-1970 (New York, 1972), p. 68.

74. LUCY P. CARNER, "Unionizing New York City Women Office Workers" (Master's thesis, Columbia University, 1925), p. 6.

75. Ibid., pp. 7-12.

76. *New York Times,* Jan. 12, 1930.

77. THERESA WOLFSON, "Trade Union Activities of Women," *Annals of the American Academy of Political and Social Science,* May, 1929, pp. 120-31.

78. Craton, "Organizing the Women Workers," p. 313.

79. For a detailed account of the activities of the Trade Union Educational League in the ILGWU, the Amalgamated Clothing Workers' Union, the International Fur Workers' Union, and the Passaic, New Bedford, and Fall River strikes, see Philip S. Foner, *Women and the American Labor Movement: From World War I to the Present* (New York, 1980), pp. 153–224.

Chapter 14: The Great Depression (pp. 296–317)

1. ARTHUR M. SCHLESINGER, JR., *The Crisis of the Old Order* (Boston, 1957), pp. 166, 207, 219.

2. PHILIP S. FONER, *Organized Labor and the Black Worker, 1619–1973* (New York, 1974), p. 189.

3. RUTH MILKMAN, "Women's Work and Economic Crises: Some Lessons of the Great Depression," *Review of Radical Political Economy* 8 (Spring 1976): 75–77 (emphasis in original); *Daily Worker*, Sept. 23, 1930.

4. U.S., Department of Commerce and Labor, Bureau of the Census, *Fifteenth Census of the United States, 1930, Unemployment* (Washington, D.C., 1930), 2:13–18.

5. U.S., Department of Labor, Women's Bureau, *Employment Fluctuations and Unemployment Among Women, 1928–1931*, Bulletin No. 113 (Washington, D.C., 1933), p. 24; U.S., Department of Labor, Women's Bureau, *Women Workers in the Third Year of the Depression*, Bulletin No. 103 (Washington, D.C., 1933), p. 10.

6. GRACE HUTCHINS, *Women Who Work* (New York, 1934), pp. 180–81.

7. *Life and Labor*, Mar. 30, 1930; *Labor*, Mar. 15, 1930.

8. *Proceedings of the AFL Convention, 1931*, pp. 119–21; *Labor*, Apr. 12, 1931.

9. *Daily Worker*, May 10, 1930.

10. U.S., Congress, *Congressional Record*, 75th Cong., 1st sess., June 1, 1937, pp. 6934–45.

11. Ibid.

12. *Daily Worker*, March 12, 1930.

13. LORINE PRUETTE, ed., *Women Workers Through the Depression: A Study of White Collar Employment Made by the American Woman's Association* (New York, 1934), p. 104; Valerie Kincade Oppenheimer, *The Female Labor Force in the United States: Demographic and Economic Factors Governing Its Growth and Changing Composition* (Berkeley, Cal., 1970), pp. 127–30; William Henry Chafe, *The American Woman: Her Changing Social, Economic, and Political Roles, 1920–1970* (New York, 1972), pp. 108–9.

14. ELSA JANE DIXLER, "The Woman Question: Women and the American Communist Party, 1929–1941" (Ph.D. diss., Yale University, 1974), pp. 204–5; *Daily Worker*, June 6, 1935.

15. WINIFRED D. WANDERSEE BOLIN, "The Economics of Middle-Income Family Life: Working Women During the Great Depression," *Journal of American History* 65 (June 1978): 60–64; U.S., Department of Commerce and Labor, Fifteenth Census of the United States, 1930, *Population* 5: *General Report on Occupations* (Washington, D.C., 1933), table 1, p. 272; U.S., Department of Labor and Commerce, Bureau of the Census, Sixteenth Census of the United States, 1940, *Population* 3: *The Labor Force; Industry, Employment, and Income*, part 1 (Washington, D.C., 1943), table 9, 26.

16. ELEANOR GEORGE Dow, "Working Women in Bangor" (Master's thesis, University of Maine, Orono, 1933), p. 151.

17. *Daily Worker*, Aug. 4, 1930.

18. *New York Times*, Sept. 4, 1928.

19. U.S., Department of Labor, Women's Bureau, *A Century of Industrial Change: Women at Work* (Washington, D.C., 1933), pp. 15–16.

20. *Daily Worker*, Sept. 5, 1931.

21. Letters to the Women's Bureau in "Women," "Secretary Perkins' General Subject File, 1933–1940," Records of the Secretaries of Labor, R.G. 174, National Archives; Judith Anne Scalander, "The Women's Bureau, 1920–1950: Federal Reaction to Female Wage Earning" (Ph.D. diss., Duke University, 1977), p. 223.

22. *Daily Worker*, Sept. 1, 1930, Oct. 6, 1932.

23. *Labor*, May 2, 1933; *Daily Worker*, June 4, 1933; Scalander, "The Women's Bureau," p. 230; Julia Kirk Blackwelder, "Women in the Workforce, Atlanta, New Orleans, and San Antonio, 1930 to 1940," *Journal of Urban History* 4 (May 1978): 331.

24. U.S., Department of Labor, Women's Bureau, Bulletin No. 103, pp. 3–5.

25. EDWARD ROBB ELLIS, "What the Depression Did to People," in Thomas R. Frazier, ed., *The Private Side of American History: Readings in Everyday Life* (New York, 1975) 2: 227.

26. FONER, *Organized Labor and the Black Worker*, p. 190; Blackwelder, "Women in the Workforce," p. 345; *New Leader*, Dec. 5, 1931; Philip Klein, *A Social Study of Pittsburgh: Community Problems and Social Services of Allegheny County* (New York, 1938), p. 279; Mary Elizabeth Pidgeon, *Employment Fluctuations and Unemployment of Women: Certain Indications from Various Sources, 1928–31* (Washington, D.C., 1933), p. 43; U.S., Department of Labor, Women's Bureau, Bulletin No. 113, pp. 24, 168–70.

27. JEAN COLLIER BROWN, *The Negro Woman Worker*, Women's Bureau, Bulletin No. 165 (Washington, D.C., 1938), pp. 1–4; *Southern Worker*, Feb. 14, 1931.

28. U.S., Department of Labor, Women's Bureau, *A Century of Industrial Change*, p. 13; *Daily Worker*, Apr. 14, 1931.

29. HUTCHINS, *Women Who Work*, p. 184; *Daily Worker*, Mar. 3, 1932; *Southern Worker*, Sept. 13, Oct. 25, 1930.

30. SCALANDER, "Women's Bureau," p. 42.

31. *Daily Worker*, Oct. 23, 1933.

32. *Bridgeport Post*, Mar. 19, 1930 and reprinted in *Daily Worker*, May 24, 1930.

33. BONNIE R. FOX, "Unemployment Relief in Philadelphia, 1930–1932: A Study of the Depression's Impact on Voluntarism," *Pennsylvania Magazine of History and Biography* 95 (January 1960): 102.

34. *Labor*, Sept. 29, 1931; *Daily Worker*, Dec. 1, 1931.

35. FRANCES FOX PIVEN AND RICHARD A. CLOWARD, *Regulating the Poor* (New York, 1971), p. 60; Schlesinger, *Crisis of the Old Order*, p. 263.

36. FONER, *Organized Labor and the Black Worker*, pp. 190–91.

37. WILLIAM Z. FOSTER, *From Bryan to Stalin* (New York, 1937), pp. 216–38; *Daily Worker*, Oct. 14, 1929.

38. *The Trade Union Unity League: Its Program, Structure, Methods and History* (New York, n.d.), pp. 26–27; *Daily Worker*, Sept. 6, Oct. 9, 1929.

39. DANIEL J. LEAB, "'United We Eat'": The Creation and Organization of the Unemployed Councils in 1930," *Labor History* 8 (Fall 1976): 299–300; Albert Prago, "The Organiza-

tion of the Unemployed and the Role of the Radicals, 1929–1935" (Ph.D. diss., American University, 1976), pp. 32–35; *New York Times*, Mar. 7, 1930; *Daily Worker*, Mar. 7–8, 1930.

40. *Daily Worker*, Oct. 15, 1929.

41. PRAGO, "Organization of the Unemployed," pp. 61–63; *New York Times*, Mar. 7, 1930; *Daily Worker*, Mar. 7–8, 1930.

42. *New York World*, Mar. 7, 1930.

43. *Daily Worker*, Mar. 7, 1930.

44. LEAB, "'United We Eat,'" pp. 300–310; Prago, *"Organization of the Unemployed," pp. 114–16; Daily Worker*, July 31, 1930.

45. *Daily Worker*, Dec. 1, 1931.

46. PRAGO, "Organization of the Unemployed," pp. 123–25.

47. Interview with Matilda Molina Tolly in the *World*, Mar. 9, 1974, Magazine Section.

48. PRAGO, "Organization of the Unemployed," p. 146.

49. ALEX BASKEY, "The Ford Hunger March—1932," *Labor History* 13 (Summer 1972) 348–49.

50. PRAGO, "Organization of the Unemployed," p. 155.

51. *Daily Worker*, Nov. 22, Dec. 4, 5, 6, 1932; *New York Times*, Nov. 30, Dec. 5, 6, 1932.

52. *New York Times*, Nov. 30, 1932.

53. Quoted in Malcolm Cowley, "King Mob and John Law," *New Republic*, Dec. 21, 1932, p. 146, and in Prago, "Organization of the Unemployed," p. 157.

54. OAKLEY C. JOHNSON, "Helen Lynch, Organizer of the Unemployed," *World*, Mar. 19, 1974; *Social Welfare*, Mar. 10, 1938, pp. 20–22.

55. *Washington Post*, Dec. 7, 8, 1932; Edward Dahlberg, "Hunger on the March," *Nation*, Dec. 28, 1932, p. 174; Prago, "Organization of the Unemployed," pp. 158–59.

56. DOROTHY DAY, *The Long Loneliness* (New York, 1952), pp. 232–34.

57. Ibid., pp. 265–68; "Dorothy Day and the Catholic Worker Movement," *America*, Nov. 11, 1972, pp. 18–22.

58. PRAGO, "Organization of the Unemployed," p. 161; Foner, *Organized Labor and the Black Worker*, p. 191; Elizabeth Lawson, *The Jobless Negro* (New York, 1933), p. 13.

59. ANGELO HERNDON, *Let Me Live* (New York, 1937), p. 93.

60. Quoted in Robert Korstad, "Local 22-FTA" (Paper in possession of the writer, 1977), p. 36.

61. *Baltimore Sun*, Apr. 2, 1931; *New York Times*, Apr. 2, 1931.

62. *St. Louis Post-Dispatch*, July 22, 23, 1932.

63. *Detroit Free Press*, Jan. 13, Feb. 14, Mar. 6, 28, 1933; *Daily Worker*, Mar. 6, 1933.

64. MYRNA FICHTENBAUM, "The Funsten Nut Strike, May, 1933" (Senior thesis, Department of History, St. Louis University, 1976), pp. 20, 21; Ralph Shaw, "St. Louis' Biggest Strike," *Labor Unity*, August 1933, pp. 122–23; *St. Louis Post-Dispatch*, May 18, 1933.

65. *St. Louis Post-Dispatch*, May 18, 1933.

66. FICHTENBAUM, "Funsten Nut Strike," pp. 23–24.

67. Ibid., pp. 25–26.

68. *St. Louis Post-Dispatch*, May 21, 1933; *Daily Worker*, June 1, 1933; Bill Gerbert, "The St. Louis Strike and the Chicago Needle Strike," *Communist* 12 (August 1933): 804; Fichtenbaum, "Funsten Nut Strike," pp. 24–28.

69. *St. Louis Post-Dispatch*, May 13, 14, 1933.
70. *St. Louis Star-Times*, May 24, 1933; Fichtenbaum, "Funsten Nut Strike," pp. 29–30.
71. *St. Louis Post-Dispatch*, May 19, 20, 1933; *Daily Worker*, June 1, 1933.
72. *St. Louis Post-Dispatch*, May 19, 20, 21, 1933; Fichtenbaum, "Funsten Nut Strike," pp. 30–31.
73. FICHTENBAUM, "Funsten Nut Strike," p. 49.
74. Reprinted in ibid., p. 51.
75. *St. Louis Argus*, May 26, 1933; Fichtenbaum, "Funsten Nut Strike," p. 32.
76. FICHTENBAUM, "Funsten Nut Strike," p. 32.
77. *St. Louis Post-Dispatch*, May 18, 19, 23, 24, 1933; *Daily Worker*, May 22, 23, 29, 1933.
78. *St. Louis Post-Dispatch*, May 24, 1933; Fichtenbaum, "Funsten Nut Strike," p. 34.
79. *Daily Worker*, May 29, 1933; Fichtenbaum, "Funsten Nut Strike," pp. 34–35; Hutchins, *Women Who Work*, p. 140.
80. *Daily Worker*, June 30, 1933; Bill Gerbert, "The St. Louis Strike and the Chicago Needle Strike," *Communist* 12 (August 1933): 803–5.
81. *St. Louis Post-Dispatch*, Aug. 9, 1933; Fichtenbaum, "Funsten Nut Strike," p. 57.
82. *Labor*, Dec. 20, 1932.
83. Ibid., Dec. 6, 1932.
84. Women's Trade Union League of New York, "Report of Work," September 13 to December 6, 1932, WTUL of N.Y. Papers, New York State Department of Labor Library.
85. Women's Trade Union League of New York, "Report of Organization Work" for October, 1932, WTUL of N.Y. Papers.
86. JOSEPH P. LASH, *Eleanor and Frank* (New York, 1971), pp. 128–32; Chafe, *American Woman*, pp. 32–34.
87. *New York Times*, Oct. 4, 1930.
88. *Labor*, Dec. 9, 1930.
89. This brief account of the life of Mother Jones is based on the following sources: Mary Field Parton, *The Autobiography of Mother Jones* (Chicago, 1925), pp. 8–9, 12–13, 30–49, 71–72, 76–77; Dale Featherling, *Mother Jones, the Miners' Angel* (Carbondale, Ill., 1971), pp. 50–67; Philadelphia *North American*, July 17, 1903.

Chapter 15: The CIO, 1935–1940 (pp. 318–337)

1. *Proceedings of the AFL Convention, 1933*, pp. 88–89; *New York Times*, Oct. 4, 1933.
2. GRACE HUTCHINS, "5,000,000 Women Workers Eligible for Trade Unions," *AFL Rank and File Federationist*, June 1934.
3. *Proceedings of the AFL Convention, 1934*, pp. 120–36.
4. JAMES O. MORRIS, *Conflict Within the AFL: A Study of Craft Versus Industrial Unionism, 1901–1908* (Ithaca, N.Y., 1938), pp. 212–13.

5. *New York Times,* Dec. 12, 1935.

6. ROSE WORTIS in *Daily Worker,* Mar. 3, 1936; Minutes of the Executive Board meeting, Dec. 18, 1936, WTUL of NY Papers.

7. *Daily Worker,* May 10, 1936.

8. MARY ANDERSON TO HARRY GODDARD LEACH, 17 March 1936, Mary Anderson Papers, Folder 27, Schlesinger Library, Radcliffe College; Judith Anne Scalander, "The Women's Bureau, 1920-1950: Federal Reaction to Female Wage Earning" (Ph.D. diss., Duke University, 1977), pp. 100-101.

9. RICHARD BOYER AND HERBERT M. MORAIS, *Labor's Untold Story* (New York, 1955), p. 293.

10. HAROLD S. ROBERTS, *The Rubber Workers* (New York, 1944), pp. 224-35; Irving Bernstein, *Turbulent Years: A History of the American Worker, 1933-1941* (Boston, 1970), pp. 589-97; Ruth McKenney, *Industrial Valley* (New York, 1939), pp. 219-36.

11. ROSE PESOTTA, *Bread Upon the Waters,* edited by John Nicholas Beffel (New York, 1944), pp. 195-204.

12. Ibid., pp. 211, 217.

13. R. K. in *Daily Worker,* Mar. 8, 1936.

14. PESOTTA, *Bread Upon the Waters,* p. 226.

15. *Daily Worker,* Jan. 2, 15, 24, 26, May 23, 1936, June 25, 1937.

16. HENRY KRAUS, *The Many and the Few: A Chronicle of the Dynamic Auto Workers* (Los Angeles, 1947), pp. 78-79; Sidney Fine, *Sit-Down: The General Motors Strike of 1936-1937* (Ann Arbor, Mich., 1969), pp. 121-50.

17. WALTER LINDER, *The Great Flint Sit-Down Strike Against GM, 1936-37: How Industrial Unionism Was Won* (Ann Arbor, Mich. 1970), p. 98.

18. FINE, *Sit-Down,* p. 200.

19. PESOTTA, *Bread Upon the Waters,* p. 239.

20. LINDER, *Great Flint Sit-Down Strike,* p. 101.

21. *Flint Auto Worker,* Jan. 12, 1937; Kraus, *Many and the Few,* p. 137; Fine, *Sit-Down,* pp. 6-7.

22. *New York Times,* Jan. 21, 1937.

23. *New Republic,* Feb. 17, 1937, pp. 38-39.

24. Ibid., p. 39; Mary Heaton Vorse, *Labor's New Millions* (New York, 1938), p. 77.

25. FINE, *Sit-Down,* p. 270.

26. MARY MACK, "The Emergency Brigade," *Sunday Worker,* May 14, 1937.

27. *Daily Worker,* Feb. 14, 1937.

28. Ibid.

29. FINE, *Sit-Down,* pp. 304-6.

30. VORSE, *Labor's New Millions,* pp. 80-81.

31. Ibid., pp. 85-86.

32. FINE, *Sit-Down,* p. 201.

33. Ibid.

34. *Proceedings of the Second Annual Convention of the International Union, United Automobile Workers of America, Milwaukee, Wisconsin, August 23 to 29, 1937,* pp. 252-53; Bill Gerbert, "The Convention of 400,000," *Communist 16 (October 1937): 899-900.*

35. *"Women in Auto," reprinted in Daily Worker,* Mar. 13, 1937.

36. The discussion is based on the script of the film.

37. *Daily Worker,* Mar. 13, 1937.

38. Ibid., Dec. 17, 1936.

39. Ibid., Feb. 28, 1937.

40. *St. Louis Post-Dispatch,* June 17, 1937; Boyer and Morais, *Labor's Untold Story,* pp. 304-5.

41. *New York Times,* June 19-20, 1937; *Daily Worker,* Aug. 6, 1938.

42. *New York Times,* Mar. 9, 1937.

43. GEORGE MORRIS in *Daily Worker,* Feb. 19, 1937; Detroit *Free Press,* Feb. 20, 1937; *Daily Worker,* Mar. 7, 1937.

44. LAWRENCE EMERY in ibid.

45. *Detroit Free Press,* Mar. 5, 1937.

46. Ibid., Mar. 7, 1937.

47. Ibid., Mar. 6, 1937; *Daily Worker,* Mar. 6, 1937.

48. *Detroit Free Press,* Mar. 7, 1937; *Daily Worker,* Feb. 28, 1937.

49. *New York Times,* Mar. 13-16, 937; *Daily Worker,* Mar. 15-16, 1937.

50. *New York Times,* Mar. 26, 1937; *Daily Worker,* Mar. 30, 1937.

51. *New York Times,* Apr. 1, 1937; *Daily Worker,* Apr. 1, 1937.

52. *Daily Worker,* July 30, Aug. 1, 10, 1937.

53. *Hosiery Worker,* Mar. 5, 1937; *Daily Worker,* Mar. 3, 1937.

54. *Reading Times,* Mar. 26, 1937; *Hosiery Worker,* Apr. 9, 30, 1937.

55. STELLA NOWICKI, "Back of the Yards," in Alice and Staughton Lynd, eds., *Rank and File: Personal Histories by Working Class Organizers* (Boston, 1973), pp. 67-68; Fine, *Sit-Down,* pp. 332-35; *Daily Worker,* Mar. 26, 1937, Sept. 15, 1938; *CIO News,* Sept. 17, 1938.

56. RONALD L. FILIPPELLI, "UE: The Formative Years, 1933-1937," *Labor History* 17 (Summer 1976): 365-66; *UE News,* Feb. 10, 1975, p. 4.

57. *Daily Worker,* Apr. 30, 1936.

58. Ibid., July 5, 1936; *New York Times,* June 24, 25, 1936.

59. Ibid., July 15, 1936.

60. BERNSTEIN, *Turbulent Years,* pp. 609-10.

61. FILIPPELLI, p. 368n.

62. LINDA NYDEN, "Women Electrical Workers at Westinghouse Electric Corporation's East Pittsburgh Plant, 1907-1954," (M.A. thesis, University of Pittsburgh, 1975), pp. 43-46.

63. Ibid., p. 56.

64. Ibid., p. 53.

65. Ibid.

66. Ibid., p. 57.

67. Ibid., p. 58.

68. *CIO News,* May 21, 1938.

69. Ibid., Apr. 23, 1938.

70. *Daily Worker,* Oct. 7, 1939.

Chapter 16: Government and Industry in World War II (pp. 338–361)

1. *New York Times*, June 12, 1940; U.S., Congress, *Congressional Record*, 77th Cong., 1st sess., Oct. 23, 1941, p. 8189.

2. "The Margin Now Is Womanpower," *Fortune*, February 1943, p. 101; Office of War Information (OWI), *Women in the War* (Washington, D.C., 1944), p. 2.

3. Susan B. Anthony II, *Out of the Kitchen—Into the War* (New York, 1943), p. 2.

4. Ibid., p. 4.

5. Helen Mosucki, "The Unhappiest Women in the World," *Saturday Evening Post*, July 8, 1944, p. 19; "Japan," *Life*, Sept. 18, 1944, p. 66.

6. Quoted in Eleanor Straub, "United States Government Policy Toward Civilian Women During World War II" (Ph.D. diss., Emory University, 1973), pp. 127-28. Hereinafter referred to as Straub dissertation.

7. Quoted in ibid., p. 128.

8. Fact Sheet No. 218, quoted in ibid., p. 129.

9. U.S., Department of Labor, Women's Bureau, *Women Workers in Ten Production Areas and Their Postwar Employment Plans*, Bulletin No. 209 (Washington, D.C., 1946), pp. 51, 53.

10. Mary Elizabeth Pidgeon, *Employment of Women in the Early Postwar Period*, Women's Bureau Bulletin No. 211 (Washington, D.C., 1946), pp. 4, 5, 8; National Manpower Council, *Womanpower* (New York, 1945), p. 157; *New York Times*, Apr. 29, 1945.

11. Alan Clive, "Woman Workers in World War II: Michigan as a Test Case," *Labor History* 20 (Winter 1979): 47; "Women at War," *Life*, June 5, 1944, p. 74.

12. Theresa Wolfson, "Aprons and Overalls in War," *Annals of the American Academy of Political and Social Science*, September, 1943, pp. 46-55.

13. Judith Anne Scalander, "The Women's Bureau, 1920-1950: Federal Reaction to Female Wage Earning" (Ph.D. diss., Duke University, 1977), pp. 256-57.

14. Straub dissertation, p. 130.

15. Ibid., pp. 249-51.

16. Scalander, "Women's Bureau," p. 258.

17. Eleanor Straub, "United States Government Policy Toward Civilian Women During World War II," *Prologue: The Journal of the National Archives* 5 (Winter 1973): 246-50.

18. Straub dissertation, p. 33.

19. *AAUW Journal* 36 (Fall 1942): 20.

20. Straub dissertation, pp. 52-53; *New York Times*, Feb. 14, 1943.

21. *Program and Administrative Program in Operation to Mobilize and Utilize Women for Wartime Employment, July 6, 1943*, pp. 2, 4, 5, 8, 11, 14-20, File "Women—Utilization of Women for War Production," Records of May Thompson Evans, RG 211, National Archives.

22. Straub dissertation, pp. 58-59.

23. Ibid., p. 59.

24. Anthony, *Out of the Kitchen*, pp. 179-80.

25. Straub, "United States Government Policy Toward Civilian Women During World War II," *Prologue* 5 (Winter 1973): 254.

26. MARY ANDERSON, AS TOLD TO MARY WINSLOW, *Woman at Work: The Autobiography of Mary Anderson* (Minneapolis, 1951), p. 64.

27. U.S., Department of Labor, Women's Bureau, Bulletins No. 189-2; 189-3; 189-4; 192-6; 192-8; 192-9 (Washington, D.C., 1942, 1944, 1945); Mary Anderson to Secretary of Labor Frances Perkins, 27 May 1942, File "Women's Bureau 1942," Secretary Perkins' General Subject File, 1940–1944, RG 174, National Archives.

28. STRAUB dissertation, pp. 169–70; Mary Robinson, "Women Workers in Two Wars," *Monthly Labor Review* 56 (October 1943): 657.

29. *Labor*, May 8, 15, 1943; Robinson, "Women Workers in Two Wars," p. 658.

30. ROBINSON, "Women Workers in Two Wars," p. 659.

31. ELEANOR V. KENNEDY, "Employing Women in Shipyards, 1942," *Monthly Labor Review* 56 (February 1943): 277.

32. WOLFSON, "Aprons and Overalls," p. 47.

33. STRAUB dissertation, pp. 60–62.

34. DOROTHY SELLS, "Women Workers in the Transportation Industry," *Monthly Labor Review* 56 (March 1943): 177.

35. ETHEL ERICKSON, *Women's Employment in the Making of Steel, 1943*, Women's Bureau Bulletin No. 192-5 (Washington, D.C., 1944), p. 3.

36. Ibid., p. 3.

37. *Women Workers in Some Expanding Wartime Industries*, Women's Bureau Bulletin No. 197 (Washington, D.C., 1943), p. 20.

38. DOROTHY NEWMAN AND MARTHA ZIEGLER, "Employment of Women in the Machine Tool Industry, 1942," *Women's Bureau Bulletin No. 192-4* (Washington, D.C., 1944), p. 1.

39. "War-Time Employment of Women in Manufacturing," *Monthly Labor Review* 57 (October 1943): 724.

40. *Employment of Women in War Work, May, 1943*, pp. 1, 2, 4, 8, 9, File 241.11, Policy Documentation File, RG 179, National Archives; Straub dissertation, p. 174.

41. ANNE R. SMITH TO MRS. ROOSEVELT, 19 November 1942, Personal Correspondence, Box 164, Eleanor Roosevelt Papers, Franklin Delano Roosevelt Library, Hyde Park, N.Y.; Charlotte E. Barrington to Frances Perkins, 4 August 1943, File, "Older Women," Accession 53-A-409, Box 11, RG 86, National Archives; Straub dissertation, p. 138.

42. HELEN BAKER, *Women in War Industries* (Princeton, N.J., 1942), p. 12.

43. Ibid., p. 19.

44. *Women Workers in Some Expanding Wartime Industries*, p. 13.

45. STRAUB dissertation, p. 178.

46. PIDGEON, *Employment of Women in the Early Postwar Period*, pp. 19–20.

47. KATHERINE BLOOD, *Negro Women War Workers*, Women's Bureau Bulletin No. 20 (Washington, D.C., 1945), pp. III, 2, 3; C. L. Golightly, "Background of Current Negro Employment," FEPC Records, 1944, p. 1, National Archives.

48. CHARLES S. JOHNSON AND ASSOCIATES, *To Stem This Tide* (Boston, 1943), p. 121.

49. HARVARD SITKOFF, "Racial Militancy and Interracial Violence in the Second World War," *Journal of American History* 58 (December 1971): 665; Neel A. Wynn, *The Afro-American and the Second World War* (New York, 1975), pp. 13–16.

50. PHILIP S. FONER, *Organized Labor and the Black Worker, 1619–1973* (New York, 1974), pp. 239–40.

51. *New York Times,* June 26, 1941; Herbert Garfinkel, *When Negroes March* (Glencoe, Ill, 1959), pp. 60, 85.

52. BLOOD, *Negro Women War Workers,* pp. 16–18.

53. WALTER R. CHIVERS, "Effects of the Present War Upon the Status of Negro Women," *Southern Frontier* 4 (December 1943): 1.

54. THOMAS R. BROOKS, *Communications Workers of America: The Story of a Union* (New York, 1977), p. 90n; Clive, "Women Workers in World War II," p. 52.

55. FRANCES STANTON TO FRANKLIN D. ROOSEVELT, 5 April 1943, Carnegie-Illinois File, FEPC Records, Regional Files, Region III, National Archives; Dennis Clark Dickerson, "Black Steelworkers in Western Pennsylvania During World War II" (Paper in writer's possession), p. 7.

56. MRS. WILLIAM J. SCOTT TO FRANKLIN D. ROOSEVELT, 22 April 1944, FEPC Records, Regional Files, Region III, Box 610, National Archives; Dickerson, "Black Steelworkers," p. 7.

57. National Malleable and Steel Casting Company File, FEPC Records, Region III, Box 612, National Archives; Dickerson, "Black Steelworkers," p. 8.

58. The hearings and decisions are in FEPC Legal Division, RG 228, National Archives, and are summarized in Straub dissertation, pp. 191–92.

59. *Baltimore Afro-American,* Apr. 28, 1945.

60. STRAUB dissertation, p. 181.

61. BLOOD, *Negro Women War Workers,* p. 21.

62. Fair Employment Practices Committee, *First Report* (Washington, D.C., 1945), p. 43.

63. CHESTER W. GREGORY, "The Black Woman in War Work, 1941–1945," *Northwest Journal of African and Black American Studies* 1 (Fall 1973): 23.

64. ETHEL M. COTTON File and Farrell & Sharon Penna. File, FEPC Records, Region III, Box 599, National Archives; Dickerson, "Black Steelworkers," p. 8.

65. AUGUST MEIER AND ELLIOTT RUDWICK, *Black Detroit and the Rise of the UAW* (New York, 1969), pp. 136–54; Harvard Sitkoff, "The Detroit Race Riot of 1943," *Michigan History* 53 (Fall 1969): 187; Clive, "Women Workers in World War II," p. 53.

66. *Developments in the Employment of Negroes in War Industries, October 16, 1943,* p. 5, File "5-3K," Classified General Records, Historical Analysis Section, RG 21, National Archives.

67. W. DANIEL MUSSER, "Vocational Training for War Production Workers, Final Report," Office of Education Bulletin No. 10 (Washington, D.C., 1946), pp. 4, 24; Straub dissertation, p. 213.

68. J. W. STUDEBAKER TO MARY ANDERSON, 29 October 1940, Container 1, Accession 56-A-284, RG 86, National Archives; Straub dissertation, p. 217.

69. War Production Board (WPB), "Policy Regarding Training of Women, February 10, 1942," File "8.c.1," Classified General Records, Historical Analysis Section, RG 211; National Archives; Straub dissertation, p. 221; "Women in War Work," *New Republic,* May 4, 1942, p. 593.

70. STRAUB dissertation, p. 222.

71. "Vocational Training, 1940–1944," *Monthly Labor Review* 59 (October 1944): 821; Straub dissertation, pp. 225–28.

72. STRAUB dissertation, p. 228.

73. Ibid., p. 224.

74. MARJORIE GRIFFIN, "Women in Industry: A Study of Their Places in the American

Economy as Influenced by World War II" (Honors thesis, Swarthmore College, October 1944), p. 41.

75. *Review of Radical Political Economy* 4 (Winter 1972): 23.

76. Letter of Mrs. Barbara W. Clapp in *New York Herald-Tribune*, Feb. 24, 1943.

77. *Community Services for Women War Workers*, Women's Bureau Special Bulletin No. 25 (Washington, D.C., 1943), pp. 2–3.

78. War Manpower Commission (WMC), Manual of Operations, Title III, Sections 2–4, "Recruitment, Training and Employment of Women Workers," Oct. 17, 1942, pp. 1–2, Reference Records, WAC, RG 211, National Archives; Straub dissertation, pp. 138, 260–61; William Henry Chafe, *The American Woman: Her Changing Social, Economic, and Political Roles, 1920–1970* (New York, 1972), pp. 163–64.

79. FRANCES E. MERRILL, *Social Problems on the Home Front* (New York, 1948), p. 157.

80. "The Problems of a Boom War-Industry Town," *Child Welfare League of America Bulletin*, October 1943, pp. 7–9; Clive, "Women Workers in World War II," p. 60; Howard Dratch, "The Politics of Child Care in the 1940's," *Science & Society* 38 (Summer 1974): 174.

81. KATHERINE CLOSE, "Day Care Up to Now," *Survey Mid-Monthly*, 79 (June 1943): 194–95.

82. U.S., Children's Bureau, *Proceedings of Conference on Day Care of Children of Working Mothers*, Children's Bureau Bulletin No. 281 (Washington, D.C., 1942), pp. 16–17, 74–75.

83. CHAFE, *American Woman*, pp. 165–66.

84. DRATCH, "Politics of Child Care," p. 178.

85. Ibid., p. 176.

86. *Day Care News*, April 1945, pp. 16–19.

87. FRANCES PERKINS TO KATHERINE LENROOT, 6 June 1942, File "Children's Bureau, 1942," Secretary Perkins' General Subject File, 1940–44, RG 174, National Archives; Straub dissertation, pp. 281, 282n.

88. ANTHONY, *Out of the Kitchen*, pp. 135–36.

89. U.S., Congress, Senate, Committee on Education and Labor, 78th Cong. 1st sess., 1942, pp. 34, 37, 78.

90. Ibid., p. 34.

91. STRAUB dissertation, pp. 288–89; Clive, "Women Workers in World War II," p. 65.

92. JANE LYNOTT CARROL, "Raising a Baby in Shifts," *Parents Magazine*, October 1943, pp. 20, 77–79.

93. U.S., Department of Labor Women's Bureau, Bulletin No. 209, pp. 55–56; Clive, "Women Workers in World War II," pp. 65–66.

94. DRATCH, "Politics of Child Care," pp. 196–98.

95. Ibid., pp. 198, 200.

96. U.S., Department of Labor, Women's Bureau, *State Labor Laws for Women with Wartime Modification, Part V: Explanation and Appraisal*, Bulletin No. 202-5 (Washington, D.C., 1946), pp. 1, 24; Straub dissertation, pp. 230–31.

97. HELEN BAKER, preliminary draft, "Women in Defense Industries," Feb. 2, 1942; pp. 11–12, enclosure memorandum Clara M. Berger to Miss Jay, 11 March 1942, File "Women's Bureau, 1942," Secretary Perkins' General Subject File, 1940–44, RG 174, National Archives; Straub dissertation, pp. 232–33.

98. U.S., Department of Labor, Women's Bureau, *Bulletin No. 197*, p. 14.

99. U.S., Department of Labor, Women's Bureau, Report, Mar. 6, 1942, File 241.11, Policy Documentation File, RG 179, National Archives; Donald Nelson to Elmer Olson, 12 March 1942, ibid.; Straub dissertation, pp. 235–36.

100. MARY ANDERSON TO THELMA MCKELVEY, 17 April 1942; Memo from Mary Anderson to Mary LaDame, 1 June 1943, "Women's Bureau, 1943," RG 211, National Archives; Straub dissertation, pp. 236–37; *New York Times*, Jan. 3, 1943.

101. STRAUB dissertation, pp. 237–38; Lester M. Pearlman, "Ordnance Workers in 1918 and 1943," *Monthly Labor Review* 57 (December 1943): 1074.

102. "Plant Practices for Women Factory Employees in Selected War Industry Plants— 1942 and 1943, June 1943," File "U.S.—Hours," Contains 7, Accession 54-A-78, RG 86, National Archives; Straub dissertation, p. 238.

103. MARY V. ROBINSON, Material for Miss Miller's Use in Talk to . . . , May 28, 1945, p. 9, File 213, Container 3, Accession 55-A-485, RG 86, National Archives; Straub dissertation, p. 230.

104. U.S., Department of Labor, Women's Bureau, *State Labor Laws for Women with Wartime Modifications, Part V*, pp. 36–39; Straub dissertation, p. 238.

105. File "U.S. Equal Rights—Equal Pay," Container 7, Accession 54-A-78, RG 86, National Archives; Straub dissertation, pp. 239–40.

106. NWLB Verbatim Transcript, General Motors Corporation and UAW, CIO and UEW, CIO, Case No. 2252, September 3, 1942, p. 61; Transcript of Hearings in Dispute Cases, 1942–1945, Headquarters Records, National War Labor Boad, RG 202, National Archives; Straub dissertation, pp. 240–41.

107. Press Release, 24 August 1942, p. 2, enclosure, Memo from Mary LaDame to Mary Anderson, 22 August 1942, Secretary Perkins' General Subject File, 1940–1944, RG 174, National Archives; Straub dissertation, p. 241.

108. Opinion of the Board, Sept. 26, 1942, pp. 1–2, Case No. 2252, Provisional File, Dispute Case Files, Headquarters Records, RG 202, National Archives; Straub dissertation, pp. 241–42.

109. File "Equal Pay Source Material Folder," Container 4, Accession 58-A-850, RG 86, National Archives; Straub dissertation, p. 242.

110. LAURA NELSON BAKER, *Wanted: Women in War Industry* (New York, 1943), p. 63.

111. ELLA J. POLINSKY, "NWLB Policy on Equal Pay for Equal Work for Women," Research and Statistics Report No. 32, September 1945, pp. 14–17, File "Equal Pay Source Material," Container 4, Accession 58-A-850, RG 86, National Archives; Straub dissertation, pp. 246–48; *New York Times*, Nov. 29, 1945.

112. Recommendations of the Women's Bureau on War Labor Board's "Equal Pay" Policy, August 14, 1943, p. 4, File "AA Work on Equal Pay, WLB & Other War," Container 3, Accession 68-A-3357, RG 86, National Archives; Straub dissertation, pp. 249–50.

113. ETHEL ERICKSON, Field Report (Confidential), December 18, 1942, Buick Jother Aircraft Engine Co., Melrose Park, Chicago, "Regional Field Offices File," Women's Bureau, National Archives.

114. MARY ANDERSON, "Women in War Work and the Equal Pay Issue," Speech to conference of Illinois and Wisconsin Women's Trade Union Leagues, Oct. 24, 1943, p. 4, File "Speeches 341-5-306-317," Container 7, Accession 53-A-409, RG 86, National Archives; Straub dissertation, p. 349.

115. U.S., Department of Labor, *Economic Indicators Relating to Equal Pay* (Washington, D.C., 1963); Judith Anne Scalander, "The Women's Bureau: 1920-1950: Federal Reaction to Female Wage Earning" (Ph.D. diss., Duke University, 1977), pp. 256–57.

116. Clive, "Women Workers in World War II," p. 53.

117. *CIO News*, Aug. 2, 1943.

118. *New York Times*, June 12, 1945.

119. MARGARET KAY ANDERSON, *Employment of Women in the Manufacture of Cannon and Small Arms in 1942*, Women's Bureau Bulletin No. 192-3, p. 30; Ethel Erickson, "Women's Employment in Aircraft Assembly Plants in 1942," Women's Bureau Bulletin No. 192-1 (Washington, D.C., 1942), pp. 22–24; Dorothy Newman, "Employing Women in Shipyards," Women's Bureau Bulletin No. 192-6 (Washington, D.C., 1944), pp. 31–32; Joan De Caux, *Employment of Women in Army Supply Depots in 1943*, Women's Bureau Bulletin No. 192-8 (Washington, D.C., 1944), p. 26; Joan De Caux, *Women's Wartime Jobs in Cane-Sugar Refineries*, Women's Bureau Bulletin No. 192-9 (Washington, D.C., 1945), p. iv; Newman and Ziegler, "Employment of Women in the Machine Tool Industry, 1942," p. 35; Straub dissertation, pp. 250–51.

120. CLIVE, "Women Workers in World War II," p. 54; Straub dissertation, p. 252.

121. Memo from Rachel F. Nysander to the Field, 8 April 1944, p. 2, File, "Regional General Memos, 1943–1947," Container 1, Accession 56-A-260, RG 86, National Archives.

122. U.S., Department of Labor, Women's Bureau, *Women's Wages in Wartime, November, 1944*, pp. 3, 4, File "Women (Miscellaneous) 1942–1945," WAC RG 211, National Archives; Brooks, pp. 78–79.

123. U.S., Congress, Senate, Committee on Education and Labor, *White Collar and Fixed Income Groups*, Report No. 1 on Sen. Res. 74 by the Subcommittee on Wartime Health and Education, 78th Cong., 1st sess. (1944), pp. vii, viii.

124. *PM*, Jan. 1, 1942; Elbert D. Thomas, "20,000,000 Forgotten Americans," *American Magazine* 127 (May 1944): 87–88.

125. ELIZABETH CHRISTMAN, "Women in War Industries," speech before Annual Interstate Conference of Women Trade Unionists and Auxiliary Members, Oct. 3, 1942, p. 4, File "Office," Records of Mary Brewster White, Information Service RG 211, National Archives; Straub dissertation, p. 258.

126. International Labour Office, *The War and Women's Employment* (Washington, D.C., 1945), p. 208.

Chapter 17: The Trade Unions in World War II (pp. 362–395)

1. MARY ANDERSON TO MRS. RAYMOND ROBINS, 4 March 1942, File 12, Anderson Papers.

2. "Admission of Women to Union Membership," *Monthly Labor Review* 55 (November 1942): 10006; Theresa Wolfson, "Aprons and Overalls in War," *Annals of the American Academy of Political and Social Science* 229 (September 1943): 54; *Labor*, Sept. 22, 1942.

3. Division of Transportation Personnel, Summary Report, Conference on Womanpower in Transportation, Office of Defense Transportation (ODT), Mar. 18, 19, 1943, p. 22, File "5-3 E," Classified General Records, Historical Analysis Section, RG 21, National Archives; Straub dissertation, p. 195.

4. Ibid., pp. 19–20, 25; Straub dissertation, pp. 195–96.

5. Ibid., p. 25.

6. KAREN SUE ANDERSON, "The Impact of World War II in the Puget Sound Area on the Status of Women and the Family" (Ph.D. diss., University of Washington, 1975), pp. 40–41.

7. *Fortune*, June 1942, p. 73.

8. CIO Committee to Abolish Racial Discrimination, *Working and Fighting Together: Regardless of Race, Creed, or National Origin* (Washington, D.C., 1943), pp. 5–7.

9. Ibid., pp. 14–16.

10. PHILIP S. FONER, *Organized Labor and the Black Worker, 1619–1973* (New York, 1974), p. 257.

11. MARY ANDERSON TO MRS. RAYMOND ROBINS, 29 August 1942, 6 February 1943, File 12, Anderson Papers.

12. U.S., Department of Labor, Women's Bureau, *Women's Stake in Unions*, Women's Bureau Union Series No. 5 (Washington, D.C., 1946); *New York Times*, Sept. 30, 1943; Wolfson, "Aprons and Overalls," p. 54.

13. *Labor*, May 24, 1946.

14. *New York Times*, Sept. 30, 1943.

15. Ibid.

16. FRANCES PERKINS TO ELEANOR ROOSEVELT, 18 February 1944, Correspondence with Government Departments, Box 915, Roosevelt Papers; Straub dissertation, p. 198.

17. GLADYS BOONE, *The Women's Trade Union Leagues in Great Britain and the United States* (New York, 1952), pp. 223–24.

18. *New York Times*, Sept. 20, 1943.

19. Ibid., Feb. 5, Sept. 30, 1943.

20. Ibid., Sept. 30, 1943.

21. *Labor Research Association, Labor and the War: Labor Fact Book 6* (New York, 1943), p. 62; Rose Pesotta, *Bread Upon the Waters,* edited by John Nicolas Beffel (New York, 1944), p. 234.

22. U.S., Department of Labor, Women's Bureau, "Women in Unions in a Mid-West War Industry Area," unpublished report, July 10, 1945, pp. 3, 8, 11, Container 1, Accession 56-A-50, RG 86, National Archives; Straub dissertation, pp. 198–99.

23. Memo from Elizabeth D. Bendam to Miss Williams, 19 December 1946, File "Union Questionnaire—1946," Container 19, Accession 55-A-556, RG 86, National Archives; Straub dissertation, p. 199.

24. *American Federationist* 49 (July 1942): 110–13.

25. *CIO News*, Nov. 24, 1941; *Daily Worker*, Nov. 24, 1941; *Pilot*, Dec. 5, 1941.

26. *CIO News*, Dec. 20, 1941.

27. *Daily Worker*, Jan. 11, 12, 1942.

28. *UE News*, Mar. 7, 1942.

29. *CIO News*, Nov. 9, 1942.

30. Ibid., Sept. 28, Nov. 9, 1942.

31. Ibid.; *Auxiliary News*, issued by the Ladies' Auxiliary, Furriers Joint Council, Jan. 22, 1942, vol. I, no. 3. Copy in author's possession.

32. *CIO News*, Nov. 9, 1942.

33. Ibid., Aug. 2, 1942.

34. Ibid., Sept. 21, 28, 1942.

35. Ibid., Mar. 2, 1943; *New York Times*, Mar. 7, 1943.

36. *CIO News*, June 12, 1942.

37. Ibid., May 31, 1942.

38. Ibid.

39. *UE News*, Mar. 7, 1942.

40. *Labor and the War: Labor Fact Book 6*, p. 64.

41. U.S., Congress, Senate, Committee on Education and Labor, *Equal Pay for Equal Work for Women*, Hearings on Sen. Res. 1178 before a subcommittee of the Senate Committee on Education and Labor, 79th Cong., 1st sess. (1945), pp. 121, 129, 161, 168; Straub dissertation, p. 204.

42. *New York Times*, Sept. 10, 1944.

43. "Correspondence Unions—Boxes 860–865," Women's Bureau, National Archives.

44. *CIO News*, Nov. 16, 1942.

45. U.S., Department of Labor, Women's Bureau, "Women in Unions in a Mid-West War Industry Area," unpublished report, July 10, 1945, p. 12, Container 1, Accession 56-A-50, RG 86, National Archives; Straub dissertation, p. 200.

46. LINDA NYDEN, "Women Electrical Workers at Westinghouse Electric Corporation's East Pittsburgh Plant, 1907–1954, pp. 60–61.

47. WOLFSON, "Aprons and Overalls," p. 54.

48. *New York Times*, May 21, 1943.

49. Quoted in Nyden, "Women Electrical Workers," pp. 63–64.

50. *New York Times*, Nov. 29, 1945.

51. Ibid., Apr. 8, 1944.

52. U.S., Department of Labor, Women's Bureau, "Women in Unions in a Mid-West War Industry Area"; Straub dissertation, p. 201.

53. Memo from Frieda S. Miller to George W. Taylor, 5 May 1945, File "AA Work on Equal Pay," WLB & Other War, Container 3, Accession 68-A-6357, RG 86, National Archives; Memorandum, Alice Angus to Miss Plunkett, 18 October 1945, File "National War Labor Cases 269," Container 1, Accession 56-A-284, RG 86, National Archives; Straub dissertation, p. 201.

54. JOEL SEIDMAN, *American Labor from Defense to Reconversion* (Chicago, 1953), p. 154.

55. GLADYS DICKASON, "Women in Labor Unions," *Annals of the American Academy of Political and Social Science*, May, 1947, 72; "Women in Unions in a Mid-West War Industry Area"; Straub dissertation, p. 202.

56. *Daily Worker*, Jan. 11, 1942.

57. Ibid.

58. *UE News*, Jan. 25, 1942.

59. Ibid., March 7, 1942.

60. *UCAPAWA News*, March 15, 1943.

61. "Winnie the Welder," lyrics by A. N. Towson, in *Program, Women to Win the War Conference*, Columbus, Ohio, December 13, 1942, File "Unions—Electrical Workers," Container 8, Accession 55-A-556, RG 86, National Archives; Straub dissertation, p. 203.

62. Local 50, UAW-CIO, *A Program for Willow Run, March 12, 1943*, File "Willow Run Federal Coordinating Committee," Records Relating to the Operation of the Area Offices, Detroit-Willow Run, RG 212, National Archives; Straub dissertation, p. 204; Clive, "Women Workers in World War II," p. 55.

63. ROGER R. KEERAN, "'Everything for Victory,' Communist Influence in the Auto Industry During World War II," *Science & Society* 43 (Spring, 1979): 4–5; Thomas E. Linton, *An Historical Examination of the Purposes and Practices of the Education Program of the United Automobile Workers of America, 1936–1959* (Ann Arbor, 1965), pp. 97–100.

64. ELIZABETH HAWES, *Hurry Up, Please, It's Time* (New York, 1949), pp. 15, 16, 39, 44, 133.

65. EARL BROWDER, *Victory—And After* (New York, 1942), p. 19; Elizabeth Gurley Flynn, "The New Role of Women in Industry," *Communist* (April 1943), p. 355.

66. KEERAN, "'Everything for Victory': Communist Influence in the Auto Industry During World War II," p. 6; Foner, *Organized Labor and the Black Worker*, pp. 256–57.

67. HAWES, *Hurry Up, Please*, p. 133.

68. THOMAS R. BROOKS, *Communications Workers of America: The Story of a Union* (New York, 1977), p. 82; *New York Times*, Nov. 22, 1944.

69. BROOKS, *Communications Workers*, pp. 82–84; Jack Barbash, *Unions and Telephones: The Story of the Communications Workers of America* (New York, 1953), pp. 41–42.

70. *FTA News*, July 15, 1943.

71. Quoted in Akosua Barthwell, "Trade Unionism in North Carolina: The Strike Against Reynolds Tobacco, 1947," American Institute for Marxist Studies Occasional Paper No. 21 (1977), p. 5.

72. ROBERT KORSTAD, "History of Local 22-FTA" (Paper in possession of the author, 1977), pp. 40–43; *FTA News*, July 15, 1943.

73. KORSTAD, "History of Local 22," p. 34.

74. Ibid.

75. *Daily Worker*, July 6, 1936; *FTA News*, July 15, 1943.

76. KORSTAD, "History of Local 22," p. 44.

77. *FTA News*, Aug. 1, Sept. 1, 1943.

78. *FTA News*, Jan. 1, 1944.

79. Quoted in Barthwell, "Trade Unionism in North Carolina," p. 10.

80. *FTA News*, Apr. 15, 1944.

81. Ibid., Sept. 1, 1944; Korstad, "History of Local 22," p. 52.

82. KORSTAD, "History of Local 22," pp. 52–53.

83. *FTA News*, Nov. 15, 1944; Korstad, "History of Local 22," pp. 53–54.

84. Quoted in Barthwell, "Trade Unionism in North Carolina, pp. 9–10.

85. KORSTAD, "History of Local 22," pp. 55–56.

86. Memo from Alice Angus to Miss Miller, 26 July 1944, File "Union Study, 1944," Container 19, Accession 55-A-556, National Archives; Memo from Elizabeth Christman to Miss Larrabee, April 1942, p. 2, File 213 Reports—Christman, Container 3, Accession 55-A-485, RG 86, National Archives; Straub dissertation, pp. 205, 208.

87. U.S., Department of Labor, Women's Bureau, "Women in Unions in a Mid-West War Industry Area"; Straub dissertation, p. 205.

88. "Women and the Unions, January 19, 1944," File "AA Work on Equal Pay, WLB & Other," Container 3, Accession 68-A-6357, RG 86, National Archives; Straub dissertation, p. 206.

89. U.S., Department of Labor, Women's Bureau, *Status of Women in Unions in War Plants*, Women's Bureau Union Series No. 1 (Washington, D.C., 1945); Straub dissertation, p. 206.

90. "Hire More Women, Improve Training, Railroads Urged to Meet Labor Shortage,"

Victory, Nov. 24, 1942, p. 6; Otto S. Beyer, "Restrictions on Employment of Women Resulting from Seniority Rules and Similar Provisions in Collective Bargaining Agreements, July 12, 1943," File "Seniority," Reference Records, File 115-3E, Classified General Records, Historical Analysis Section, RG 211, National Archives; Straub dissertation, p. 206.

91. Memo from Martha J. Ziegler to Frieda Miller, 14 December 1945, File "Ziegler 1945," Jan. 1 through June 1945, Container 10, Accession 65-A-1064, RG 86, National Archives; Straub dissertation, pp. 206-7.

92. MARY ANDERSON TO MRS. RAYMOND ROBINS, 6 February 1943, File 12, Anderson Papers.

93. Memo from Ziegler to Miller, 14 December 1945; Straub dissertation, p. 207.

94. Christman to Larrabee, April 1942; Straub dissertation, p. 208.

95. ELIZABETH FAULKNER BAKER, *Technology and Woman's Work* (New York and London, 1964), p. 370.

96. U.S., Department of Labor, Women's Bureau, "Women in Unions in a Mid-West War Industry Area"; Straub dissertation, p. 210.

97. *New York Times*, Oct. 24, 1943.

98. "Women and the Unions, January 19, 1944"; Straub dissertation, pp. 210-11.

99. *Fortune*, Aug. 12, 1943.

100. D'ANN CAMPBELL, "Women and Unions at War: The Challenge of the 1940's" (Paper in possession of the present writer).

101. *New York Times*, Feb. 15, 1943.

102. MARY ANDERSON TO MRS. RAYMOND ROBINS, 7 May 1942, File 12, Anderson Papers.

103. ELIZABETH HAWES, "Do Women Workers Get an Even Break?" *New York Times Sunday Magazine*, Nov. 19, 1944.

104. Quoted in Nyden, "Women Electrical Workers," p. 64.

105. SHEILA TOBIAS AND LISA ANDERSON, "Whatever Happened to 'Rosie the Riveter'?" *Ms.* 1 (June 1973): 93-96; "Women in Industry," *Monthly Labor Review* 58 (May 1944): 1031-32; "Effects of Layoffs on the Employment of Women at the Twin Cities Ordnance Plant, Minneapolis-St. Paul, Minnesota," Apr. 13, 1944, p. 1, File 7-4, General Correspondence, RG 244, National Archives; Straub dissertation, p. 336.

106. War Progress No. 193, May 27, 1944, p. 2, Unclassified General Records, Historical Analysis Section, RG 24, National Archives; Straub dissertation, p. 327.

107. *New York Times*, Feb. 10, 1945.

108. CLARA F. SCHLOSS AND ELLA JOAN POLINSKY, "Postwar Labor Turnover Among Factory Workers," *Monthly Labor Review* 54 (March 1947): 411; *New York Times*, Feb. 10, 1945; Campbell, "Women and Unions at War," p. 11.

109. "Baltimore Women Workers in the Postwar Period," unpublished report, n.d., p. 1, Container 7, Accession 55-A-556, RG 86, National Archives; Straub dissertation, pp. 347-48.

110. *New York Times*, Nov. 9, 1945.

111. *Labor Fact Book 7* (New York, 1945), pp. 97-102.

112. "Women at War," *Brown America*, November 1943, p. 5; Straub dissertation, pp. 192-93.

113. *New York Herald-Tribune*, Jan. 16, 1944.

114. *New York Times*, Dec. 9, 10, 1944; *United Automobile Worker*, Jan. 1, 1945.

115. "Seniority in the Automobile Industry, *Monthly Labor Review* 59 (September 1944): 473; Campbell, "Women and Unions at War," p. 12.

116. "Seniority in the Automobile Industry," p. 473.

117. U.S., Congress, Senate, Committee on Banking and Currency, *Full Employment Act of 1945*, Hearings on Sen. Res. 300 before a subcommittee of the Senate Committee on Banking and Currency, 79th Cong., 1st sess. (1945), p. 19; Straub dissertation, p. 318.

118. *Separate and Unequal: Discrimination Against Women Workers in World War 2: The UAW, 1944-1947*, Women's Work Project (Silver Spring, Md., 1978).

119. Nancy Gabin, "Women Workers and the UAW in the Post-World War II Period: 1945-1954," *Labor History* 21 (Winter 1979-80): 9-10, 18.

120. John Oppenheimer, *The Female Labor Force in the United States* (New York, 1947), pp. 6–19.

121. Philip S. Foner, *Women and the American Labor Movement: From World War I to the Present* (New York, 1980), pp. 394–416; Philip S. Foner, *Organized Labor and the Black Worker, 1619–1973* (New York, 1974), pp. 272–83; *UE Fights for Women Workers* (New York, 1953); *UE News*, July 1952.

Chapter 18: 1199 (pp. 396–416)

1. Labor Research Association, *Labor Fact Book 11* (New York, 1952), pp. 48-49.

2. *Freedom*, March 1955.

3. Gertrude Bancroft, *The American Labor Force: Its Growth and Changing Composition* (New York, 1958), pp. 120-22.

4. *Proceedings of the AFL-CIO Convention, 1955*, pp. 125-26; *1959*, pp. 64-68.

5. *Proceedings of the AFL-CIO Convention, 1957*, pp. 40-42; *Labor History* 9 (Summer 1968): 63-64.

6. F. Ray Marshall, *Labor in the South* (Cambridge, Mass., 1967), pp. 210-15.

7. *Proceedings of the AFL-CIO Convention, 1959*, pp. 116-17.

8. *Daily Worker*, May 4, 9, 1965; Philip S. Foner, *Organized Labor and the Black Worker, 1619-1973* (New York, 1974), pp. 287, 295, 313.

9. *Freedom*, November 1951.

10. Dan Wakefield in *Dissent* 6 (Winter 1959): 162.

11. Ben Bedell in *Guardian*, Apr. 4, 1979, p. 5.

12. William Cahn, "Working in Hospitals: Then and Now," *1199 Drug & Hospital News*, special issue, September 1976, p. 11.

13. Ibid., p. 9.

14. Ibid., p. 25; James O. Hepner, John M. Moyer, and Carl L. Westernhaus, *Personnel Administration and Labor Relations in Health Care Facilities* (St. Louis, 1969), pp. 9-29.

15. *New York Call*, Sept. 2, 1919; Cahn, "Working in Hospitals," p. 31.

16. Quoted in Cahn, "Working in Hospitals," p. 31.

17. Ibid.

18. Ibid.; *New York Times*, Mar. 26, 1959.

19. *Daily Worker*, Mar. 19, 26, 1937; *1199 Drug & Hospital News*, March 1975, p. 5.

20. David R. Denton, "The Union Movement in American Hospitals, 1846-1976" (Ph.D. dissertation, Boston University, 1976), pp. 110-15.

21. *New York Times*, Mar. 26, May 17, 1959.

22. DENTON, "Union Movement in American Hospitals," p. 62.

23. SUSAN REVERBY, "Hospital Organizing in the 1950's: An Interview with Lillian Roberts," *Signs* 1 (Summer 1976): 1053-54; Cahn, "Working in Hospitals," pp. 37-38.

24. CLAUDIA DREYFUS, "The Woman from 1199," *New York Daily News Magazine,* July 20, 1975 (reprinted in *1199 Drug & Hospital News,* September 1975); "Gloria Steinem Writes on Local 1199," *New York,* July 27, 1970 (reprinted by Local 1199).

25. CAHN, "Working in Hospitals," pp. 34-35.

26. *New York Times,* Oct. 15, 1958.

27. *New York Times,* Oct. 15, 1958, Mar. 26, 1959.

28. A. H. RASKIN, "A Union With 'Soul,'" *New York Times Magazine,* Mar. 22, 1970, p. 24.

29. *New York Times,* Feb. 27, Mar. 26, 1979; *1199 Drug & Hospital News,* Mar. 12, 1959.

30. Interview with District 1199 Executive Secretary Moe Foner.

31. DAN WAKEFIELD, "Victims of Charity," *Nation,* Mar. 14, 1959, p. 66.

32. *New York Times,* Feb. 5, 1959.

33. Ibid.

34. Ibid., Mar. 26, 1959.

35. Ibid., Mar. 7, 11, 13, 1959.

36. Ibid., Apr. 4, 1959; Marshall Dubin, "Twenty Years in the Hospitals," *1199 Drug & Hospital News,* January 1979, p. 15.

37. DORIS TURNER, quoted in "Gloria Steinem Writes on Local 1199."

38. *New York Times,* May 24, 1959.

39. Ibid., May 30, 1959.

40. Ibid., June 7, 1959.

41. HENRY FONER, "We're Just Wild About Harry," song written for the hospital workers' victory rally (Copy in present writer's possession).

42. Ibid., May 24, June 7, 1959.

43. Ibid., May 24, 1959.

44. Ibid.

45. FONER, *Organized Labor and the Black Worker,* pp. 328-32.

46. *Local 1199 Drug & Hospital News,* Mar. 12, 1959; *New York Times,* May 18, 25, 1959.

47. *New York Times,* June 23, 1959.

48. Ibid.

49. Ibid.

50. Quoted in Dan Wakefield, "Hospital Workers Knock at the Door."

51. *New York Times,* Feb. 20, 1960.

52. Ibid.

53. Ibid., July 1, 1960.

54. Ibid.

55. Ibid., June 30, 1960.

56. Ibid., June 30, July 1, 1962.

57. Ibid., July 14, 1962.

58. Ibid., June 29, July 13, 1962.

59. Ibid., July 16, 1962.

60. Ibid., July 18, 1962.

61. Ibid., July 21, 1962.
62. Ibid., July 23, 1962.
63. Ibid., May 13, 1963.
64. DENTON, "Union Movement in American Hospitals," p. 133; Leon J. Davis and Moe Foner, "Organization and Unionization of Health Workers in the United States: The Trade Union Perspective," *International Journal of Health Services* 5 (1975): 22.
65. *1199 Drug & Hospital News*, March 1965.
66. Quoted in Raskin, "A Union with 'Soul.'"
67. Reprinted in *1199 Drug & Hospital News*, July 1968.
68. *New York Times*, July 1, 2, 1968; *1199 Drug & Hospital News*, July 1968.
69. For the detailed story of the development of 1199 into a national union, see Philip S. Foner, *Women and the American Labor Movement: From World War I to the Present* (New York, 1980), pp. 438–55.

Chapter 19: La Huelga (pp. 417–438)

1. *Proceedings of the AFL-CIO Convention, 1961*, pp. 127–28.
2. STUART JAMIESON, *Labor Unionism in American Agriculture*, U.S. Department of Labor, Bureau of Labor Statistics, Bulletin No. 836 (Washington, D.C., 1945), pp. 234–35.
3. *Some Facts About California Agriculture*, University of California Agricultural Extension Service (Berkeley, 1968), pp. 20–35.
4. Ibid., pp. 74–80.
5. KEN BLUM, "The Delano Grape Strike," *International Socialist Journal* 5 (July 1968): 299–300.
6. "The Farm Workers' Struggle—The Delano Grape Strike" (United Farm Workers Organizing Committee, n.d.), mimeographed copy in possession of the present writer.
7. *New York Times*, Sept. 17–18, 1965.
8. ANN LOFTIS AND JACK BELDEN, *A Long Time Coming* (New York, 1976), pp. 117–21.
9. BARBARA L. BAER AND GLENNA MATHEWS, "The Women of the Boycott," *Nation*, Feb. 23, 1974, pp. 233–34.
10. LOFTIS AND BELDEN, *A Long Time Coming*, pp. 202–3.
11. EDGAR Z. FRIEDENBERG, "Another America," *New York Review of Books*, Mar. 3, 1966, p. 10.
12. *New York Times*, June 12, 13, 15, 1966; Ronald B. Taylor, "Huelga! The Boycott That Worked," *Nation*, Sept. 17, 1970, pp. 167–70; Sam Kushner, *The Road to Delano* (New York, 1975), p. 182.
13. BAER AND MATHEWS, "Women of the Boycott," pp. 237–38.
14. KUSHNER, *Road to Delano*, p. 170.
15. Ibid., p. 162.
16. LOFTIS AND BELDEN, *A Long Time Coming*, pp. 221–23.
17. *New York Times*, May 31, July 30, 31, 1970.
18. KUSHNER, *Road to Delano*, p. 201.
19. ELLEN ROSENZWEIG, "UFW Holds Third Convention," *Guardian*, Sept. 14, 1977, p. 5.
20. BAER AND MATHEWS, "Women of the Boycott," pp. 233–34.

21. Ibid., p. 234.

22. Ibid., p. 237.

23. Ibid.

24. Ibid., p. 236.

25. *Daily World*, Dec. 28, 1974.

26. ROSENZWEIG, "UFW Holds Third Convention," p. 5.

27. *Advance*, August 1972, p. 9.

28. *Guardian*, May 16, 1973, p. 15.

29. *El Paso Times*, May 4, 5, 1972.

30. *New York Times*, Feb. 4, 1974.

31. *El Paso Times*, May 12, 1972, June 16, 1973.

32. *Advance*, August 1972, p. 9.

33. *El Paso Times*, Oct. 14, 16, 1970.

34. *Guardian*, May 16, 1973, p. 5.

35. *Advance*, August 1972, p. 8; *El Paso Times*, Sept. 14, 1972; *New York Times*, Feb. 4, 1974.

36. *Advance*, October 1972, p. 6.

37. *Daily World*, May 18, 1973; *Advance*, October 1973, p. 6.

38. *Advance*, August 1972, pp. 8–9; October 1973, p. 6.

39. Ibid., August 1972, p. 8; October 1973, p. 6.

40. Ibid., August 1972, p. 8.

41. *In These Times*, Apr. 19–25, 1978, p. 19.

42. *Advance*, February 1974, p. 3.

43. *New York Times*, Feb. 25, 26, 1974; *Daily World*, Mar. 5, 1974.

44. *New York Times*, Feb. 27, 1974; *Daily World*, Feb. 27, 1974.

45. *In These Times*, Apr. 19–25, 1978, p. 19.

46. *Textile Labor*, June 1973, p. 6.

47. *Guardian*, Mar. 28, 1973, p. 9.

48. *New York Times*, Sept. 1, 1974.

49. *New York Times Magazine*, Aug. 5, 1973, p. 11.

50. *Guardian*, May 30, 1973, p. 5.

51. *Nation*, Mar. 27, 1976, pp. 356–57.

52. *Textile Labor*, March 1973, p. 4.

53. *Guardian*, May 28, 1973, p. 8.

54. *Daily World*, Sept. 20, 1973.

55. *New York Times*, Apr. 18, 1973.

56. *Guardian*, May 30, 1973, p. 8.

57. *Textile Labor*, April 1973, pp. 2–3, 21.

58. *Southern Patriot*, July 12, 1973, p. 12.

59. GEORGE MORRIS in *Daily World*, Aug. 14, 1973.

60. *Textile Labor*, September 1973, p. 12; Bruce Raynor in *Guardian*, Oct. 24, 1973, p. 7.

61. GEORGE MORRIS in *Daily World*, Aug. 14, 1973.

62. *New York Times*, Sept. 1, 1974.

63. ED McCONVILLE, "The Southern Textile War," *Nation*, Oct. 2, 1976, p. 295.

64. *New York Times*, Sept. 1, 1974.

65. HENRY P. LEIFERMANN, "The Unions Are Coming," *New York Times Magazine*, Aug. 5, 1973, p. 26.

66. *Miners' Voice*, November 1971, p. 7; Paul Nyden, "Miners for Democracy" (Ph.D. diss., Columbia University, 1973, pp. 28–40.

67. *New York Times*, July 30, Aug. 15, 17, 1973.

68. Ibid., May 15, 1974.

69. Interview with Gussie Mills, Brookside Women's Club, *Labor Today*, February 1974, p. 4.

70. *New York Times*, May 15, 1974.

71. Interview with Gussie Mills, *Labor Today*, February 1974, p. 11.

72. *New York Times*, May 15, 1974.

73. Ibid.

74. Ibid.

75. Ibid.

76. "Kopple Gets Things Done," *In These Times*, Feb. 2–8, 1977, p. 10; "The Making of *Harlan County, USA:* An Interview with Barbara Kopple" by Gail Pellet, *Radical America* 11 (March–April 1977): 36–37.

77. "The Making of *Harlan County, USA*," p. 40.

78. *Daily World*, Mar. 30, 1974.

79. San Francisco *Chronicle*, Oct. 20, 1980; *AFL–CIO News*, Oct. 25, 1980.

Chapter 20: The Coalition of Labor Union Women (pp. 439–459)

1. *UE News*, Apr. 8, 1974, p. 6; *Advance*, April 1974, p. 9.

2. *International Socialist Review* 36 (March 1975): 6.

3. *UE News*, Apr. 8, 1974, p. 6; *New York Times*, Mar. 25, 1974.

4. *New York Times*, Mar. 25, 1974.

5. *Chicago Sun-Times*, Mar. 25, 1974; *UE News*, Apr. 8, 1974, p. 7.

6. *Time*, May 6, 1974, p. 80.

7. *Statement of Purpose, Structure and Guidelines Adopted by Coalition of Labor Union Women Founding Conference, March 23–24, 1974* (Chicago, Illinois).

8. Ibid.

9. Ibid.; *Chicago Sun-Times*, Mar. 26, 27, 1974; *Advance*, April 1974, p. 9.; *UE News*, Apr. 8, 1974, p. 6.

10. *Labor Today*, July 1974, p. 11.

11. *New York Times*, Mar. 25, 1974.

12. *UE News*, Apr. 8, 1974. p. 7.

13. *Guardian*, Apr. 3, 1974.

14. *Daily World*, Apr. 27, 1974.

15. *Advance*, November 1974, p. 12.

16. For the view that the WTUL and CLUW were similar, see Patricia Cayo Sexton, "Workers (Female) Arise! On Founding the Coalition of Labor Union Women," *Dissent* 21 (Summer 1974): 384. For an opposing view, see William Henry Chafe, *Women and Equality: Changing Patterns in American Culture* (New York, 1977), pp. 125–26.

17. *Daily World*, Dec. 28, 1974.

18. ANN WITHORN, "The Death of CLUW," *Radical America* 10 (March–April 1976): 48–49; Madeline Provinzano in *Daily World*, Nov. 26, 1974.

19. WITHORN, "Death of CLUW," p. 49.

20. "Women Hit Hard by Recession," *Guardian*, Apr. 9, 1975, p. 8.

21. *Wall Street Journal*, Nov. 5, 1974.

22. *Last Hired First Fired: Layoffs and Civil Rights, A Report of the United States Commission on Civil Rights, February, 1977* (Washington, D.C., 1977), pp. 60–61.

23. *Daily World*, July 6, 1974; *Labor Today*, July 1975, p. 4.

24. *UE News*, Nov. 4, 1974, p. 5.

25. Ibid., Feb. 10, 1975, p. 4; *American Teacher*, February 1975, p. 16; *Daily World*, Jan. 29, 1975.

26. *New York Times*, Mar. 9, 1975; *Daily World*, Apr. 27, 1975.

27. *Daily World*, May 24, 1975.

28. PHILIP S. FONER, *Organized Labor and the Black Worker, 1619–1973* (New York, 1974), p. 427.

29. *Wall Street Journal*, Nov. 5, 1974; Renee Blakkan, "Women Challenge Seniority," *Guardian*, Nov. 27, 1974, p. 4.

30. *AFL-CIO News*, May 10, 1975.

31. *New York Times*, Mar. 6, 1975.

32. *People's World*, Nov. 22, 1975; *Daily World*, Dec. 9, 1975.

33. *Daily World*, Dec. 9, 1975.

34. Ibid.

35. ROB BAKER, "Women and Seniority," *People's World*, Nov. 22, 1975.

36. *AFL-CIO News*, Mar. 30, 1974.

37. *Proceedings of the AFL-CIO Convention, 1975*, pp. 120–21; *Daily World*, Oct. 15, 1975; *New York Times*, Oct. 15–16, 1975.

38. Chicago *Sun-Times*, Sept. 24, 26, 1975.

39. *Proceedings of the AFL-CIO Convention, 1975*, pp. 152–54.

40. Ibid., pp. 184–86; *New York Times*, Oct. 17, 1975.

41. *Proceedings of the AFL-CIO Convention, 1975*, pp. 342–46.

42. *AFL-CIO News*, Dec. 13, 1975.

43. *People's World*, Nov. 22, 1975.

44. BEN BEDELL, "CLUW: More of Same," *Guardian*, Dec. 13, 1975.

45. *AFL-CIO News*, Dec. 13, 1975; *New York Times*, Dec. 10, 1975; *Guardian*, Dec. 13, 1975.

46. *New York Times*, Dec. 11, 1975; Bedell, "CLUW," *Guardian*, Dec. 13, 1975.

47. *Daily World*, Dec. 10, 1975.

48. BEDELL, "CLUW," *Guardian*, Dec. 13, 1975; *Daily World*, Dec. 10, 1975.

49. *AFL-CIO News*, Dec. 13, 1975; *Labor Today*, February 1976, p. 2.

50. *Labor Today*, February 1976, p. 2; *Daily World*, Dec. 10, 1975.

51. ANN WITHORN, "Death of CLUW," pp. 47–51.

52. Ibid.; "CLUW Has Its Mysteries," *Majority Report*, reprinted in *Industrial Worker*, April

1975, p. 2; "Shankerism vs. CLUW," *Labor Today*, February 1975, p. 7 (letter from Kristine K. Osbakken, American Federation of Teachers, Philadelphia).

53. JANE FIELD, "Women in the Trade Unions: Reality, Need, Potential," *Daily World*, Dec. 4, 1975; *Labor Today*, February 1976, p. 2.

54. BARBARA M. WERTHEIMER AND ANNE H. NELSON, *Trade Union Women: A Study of Their Participation in New York Locals* (New York, 1975), p. 16.

55. *New York Times*, Sept. 20, 1977.

56. *AFL-CIO News*, Sept. 20, 1977.

57. Ibid.; Harry Kelber, *Sexism in the Labor Movement* (New York, 1978), p. 16.

58. *In These Times*, Oct. 3–9, 1974, p. 9.

59. *New York Times*, Sept. 15, 1979.

60. Ibid., Sept. 17, 1979; *Daily World*, Sept. 15, 16, 18, 1979; *Guardian*, Oct. 3, 1979, p. 8; *In These Times*, Oct. 3–9, 1979, p. 4.

61. VICTORIA MISSICK, "A Woman's Place Is in Her Union," *Daily World*, Sept. 27, 1979, p. 18.

62. *In These Times*, Oct. 3–9, 1979, p. 4.

Chapter 21: The Current Scene and Future Prospects (pp. 460–495)

1. MARGARET A. SIMERAL, "Women and the Reserve Army of Labor," *Insurgent Sociologist* 8 (Fall 1978): 164.

2. *Time*, Aug. 27, 1979, p. 24; *Wall Street Journal*, May 22, 1979; *AFL-CIO News*, July 14, 1979; *Daily World*, Aug. 1, 1979.

3. U.S., Department of Labor, Women's Bureau, *Women Workers Today* (Washington, D.C., 1976), p. 5.

4. *New York Times*, June 12, 1977.

5. *Wall Street Journal*, Nov. 13, 1978.

6. *New York Times*, Aug. 23, 1977.

7. *Women Working: Meet the "All-Craft Women,"* pamphlet (New York, 1978).

8. *Daily World*, Mar. 8, 1979.

9. *Hawaii Carpenter*, Feb. 20, 1976.

10. *AFL-CIO News*, May 20, 1977.

11. *Chicago Daily News*, July 11, 1977.

12. *New York Times*, July 15, 1977.

13. Ibid., Aug. 23, 1977.

14. Ibid., July 15, 1977.

15. *AFL-CIO News*, Aug. 20, 1977; *New York Times*, Aug. 23, 1977.

16. *Wall Street Journal*, Nov. 13, 1978.

17. *Daily World*, Sept. 27, 1978, Feb. 9, 1979.

18. *New York Times*, Apr. 12, 1974.

19. THERESA D'AGOSTINO, "A Woman of Steel," *Daily World*, Mar. 8, 1975.

20. *Labor Today*, March 1978, p. 3.

21. *District 31 Women's Caucus USWA Bulletin*, no. 5, copy in possession of present writer.

22. Ibid.

23. ANTONIA FIELD, "Notes by a Woman Steelworker," *Political Affairs* 57 (August 1978): 31.

24. *District 31 Women's Caucus USWA Bulletin*, No. 5.

25. FIELD, "Notes by a Woman Steelworker," pp. 30–31.

26. *AFL-CIO News*, Jan. 27, 1978.

27. KEN BODE, "Unions Divided," *New Republic*, Oct. 15, 1977, p. 20.

28. *New York Times*, Jan 13, 1979.

29. *AFL-CIO News*, June 30, 1979.

30. *District 31 Women's Caucus USWA Bulletin*, no. 9.

31. FIELD, "Notes by a Woman Steelworker," pp. 30–31.

32. *New York Times*, Apr. 27, 1979; *In These Times*, May 2–8, 16–22, 1979.

33. *Daily World*, Aug. 2, 1979.

34. Ibid., June 14, 1979, June 10, 1980.

35. Ibid., Aug. 24, 1974.

36. *Wall Street Journal*, Nov. 29, 1978.

37. BEN BEDELL, "Women Take Their Place in the Mines," *Guardian*, Nov. 29, 1978, p. 6.

38. *Wall Street Journal*, Nov. 29, 1978.

39. Ibid., Nov. 13, 1978.

40. *New York Times*, Nov. 26, 1978; *Daily World*, June 14, 1979.

41. TIM WHELLER, "Women in the Mines," *Daily World*, Dec. 29, 1977.

42. *United Mine Workers Journal*, June, July, August 1974, and quoted in Nancy Klein, "Women in the Mines," *Daily World*, Aug. 24, 1974.

43. *New York Times*, Oct. 9, 1977.

44. BEDELL, "Women Take Their Place in the Mines," p. 6.

45. *New York Times*, Oct. 9, 1977.

46. *Daily World*, June 4, 1979.

47. BEDELL, "Women Take Their Place in the Mines," p. 6.

48. LINDA MCMICHAELS, "Women Coal Miners Can Dig It Too," *Daily World*, June 14, 1979.

49. Ibid.

50. Ibid., Jan. 13, 1977.

51. LOUISE KAPP HOWE, *Pink Collar Workers: Inside the World of Women's Work* (New York, 1977), pp. 62–74.

52. Quoted in *Daily World*, June 23, 1978.

53. *New York Times*, June 15, 1978.

54. *Wall Street Journal*, Aug. 28, 1978.

55. ROBERT E. SMITH et al., *The Subtle Revolution: Women at Work* (New York, 1979), pp. 32–34.

56. Quoted in leaflet, *The Struggle Continues Against J. P. Stevens*, copy in possession of present writer.

57. *In These Times*, June 29–July 5, 1977, p. 7; Gretchen Donart, "Women Workers at J. P. Stevens," *Labor Unity*, March 1979, pp. 12–13.

58. *New York Times*, Nov. 3, 1979.

59. Ibid., Sept. 18, 1979.

60. *Daily World*, Feb. 25, 1975; *Guardian*, July 26, 1978; *New York Times*, June 3, 1979.

61. *New York Times,* June 3, 1970; *Daily World,* Sept. 15, 1979.

62. *New York Times,* May 14, 1974; Adele Simons, Ann Friedman, Margaret Dunkle, and Francine Blau, *Exploitation from 9 to 5* (Lexington, Mass., 1975), pp. 48, 54.

63. U.S., Department of Labor, Women's Bureau, *Women with Low Incomes* (Washington, D.C., 1977), pp. 32–34; *Daily World,* Feb. 15, 1978.

64. HOWE, *Pink Collar Workers,* pp. 288–93.

65. JEAN TEPPERMAN, "Organizing Office Workers," *Radical America* 4 (January–February 1976): 3–4; *New York Times,* Sept. 15, 1979.

66. Reprinted in *Guardian,* May 15, 1974, p. 7.

67. *New York Times,* July 9, 1979.

68. *Guardian,* Sept. 14, 1977.

69. *New York Times,* July 9, 1979.

70. TEPPERMAN, "Organizing Office Workers," p. 5.

71. *Guardian,* May 15, 1974, p. 7.

72. *New York Post,* Apr. 22, 1976.

73. *New York Times,* Oct. 25, 1977.

74. *SEIU: A Commitment to Women,* 1979 pamphlet in possession of present writer.

75. Ibid.,; Ben Bedell, "Clerical Workers on the Move," *Guardian,* Apr. 4, 1979, p. 5.

76. *New York Times,* July 9, 1979.

77. Ibid.; Bedell, "Clerical Workers on the Move," p. 5.

78. BEDELL, "Clerical Workers on the Move," p. 5.

79. *New York Times,* July 9, 1979.

80. *SEIU: A Commitment to Women.*

81. *New York Times,* July 9, 1979.

82. Ibid.

83. *Distributive Worker,* September 1979.

84. *New York Times,* June 4, 1979.

85. JUDY SHATTUCK, "Strong Woman, Strong Union," *Employee Press,* reprinted in *Daily World,* Apr. 8, 1978.

86. RON CHERNOW, "All in a Day's Work," *Mother Jones* 6 (August 1976): 11.

87. Ibid., pp. 11–16.

88. *Daily World,* July 26, 1977.

89. *Voice of 1707,* October 1978.

90. EDNA E. RAPHAEL, "Working Women and Their Membership in Labor Unions," *Monthly Labor Review* 97 (May 1974): 27.

91. *New York Times,* July 9, 1979.

92. *Daily World,* Sept. 21, 1979.

93. *New York Times,* July 9, Oct. 3, 1979; *Guardian,* Aug. 14, 1979.

94. *AFL-CIO News,* Sept. 22, 1979, p. 2.

95. AFSCME, *What About Sex Discrimination?* 1979. Copy in possession of present writer.

96. HARRY KELBER, *Sexism in the Labor Movement* (New York, 1978), p. 13.

97. *UE News,* Sept. 24, 1979.

98. MIM KELBER, "AFL-CIO—For Men Only," *Nation,* Nov. 17, 1979, p. 491.

99. *New York Times,* Nov. 21, 1979.

100. Ibid.; *AFL-CIO News,* Nov. 24, 1979, p. 6.

101. *New York Times,* Dec. 4, 1979; *AFL-CIO News,* Dec. 15, 1979, p. 7.

102. *New York Times,* Jan 25, 1980; *AFL-CIO News,* Feb. 2, 1980.

103. *March of Labor,* May, 1952, p. 12; Grace Hutchins, *Women Who Work* (New York, 1952), p. 71.

104. *Labor Today,* March 1977, p. 3.

Bibliography

Manuscript Collections

Amalgamated Clothing Workers Headquarters, New York City
American Clothing Workers Correspondence Files and Newspaper Clippings

American Federation of Labor Archives, American Federation of Labor Building, Washington, D.C.
American Federation of Labor Correspondence

American Institute for Marxist Studies, New York City

Boston Public Library, Rare Book Room
Factory Tracts No. 1

Catholic University of America, Washington, D.C.
Terence V. Powderly Papers

Chicago Historical Society
Mary E. McDowell Papers
Agnes Nestor Papers

Franklin D. Roosevelt Library, Hyde Park, New York
Eleanor Roosevelt Papers

Illinois Historical Society
Thomas J. Morgan Papers

International Fur and Leather Workers Union Headquarters, New York City
International Fur Workers Union Correspondence Files

Library of Congress, Manuscripts Division, Washington, D.C.
Sophonisba P. Breckenridge Papers
Samuel Gompers Letter-Books
National Women's Trade Union League Papers

Local 1199, Drug and Hospital Workers Union Headquarters, New York City
Local 1199 Files

National Archives, Washington, D.C.
  Carnegie–Illinois File 228, Regional Files, Region III
  Department of Justice, Record Group 60, File 1870–28
  Department of Labor Conciliation Service Papers
  Department of Labor Papers
  Fair Employment Practices Committee Papers
  FEPC Legal Division, Record Group 228
  National War Labor Board Papers, Record Group 86, Record Group 202
  Office of War Information, Bureau of Special Services, Record Group 44
  Records Relating to the Operation of the Area Offices, Detroit–Willow Run,
    Record Group 2121
  Unclassified General Records Historical Analysis Section, Record Group 21,
    Record Group 24, Record Group 211
  United States Railroad Administration Papers, Record Group 14
  Women's Bureau, Correspondence Unions, Record Group 174, Record
    Group 179
New York Public Library, Manuscripts Division
  Fannia Cohn Papers
  Frank P. Walsh Papers
New York State Labor Library, New York City
  Women's Trade Union League of New York Papers
Radcliffe College, Cambridge, Massachusetts, Arthur and Elizabeth Schlesinger
    Library on the History of Women in America
  Mary Anderson Papers
  Maude Nathan Scrapbooks
  National Women's Trade Union League of America Papers
  Leonora O'Reilly Papers
  Mary K. O'Sullivan, Manuscript Autobiography
  Harriet H. Robinson Papers
  Hilda Smith Papers
Smith College Library, Northampton, Massachusetts
  Mary Van Kleeck Papers
  Sophia Smith Collections
  Women in Trade Unions Collection: Leonora M. Barry Lake Folio
State Historical Society of Wisconsin, Madison
  Elizabeth Gurley Flynn Collection
  Morris Hillquit Papers
Tamiment Institute Library, New York University
  Eugene V. Debs Clipping Book
  Algernon Lee Scrap Books
  Rose Schneiderman Papers
  Socialist Party Letter Books
  Southern Tenant Farmers Union Papers, microfilm copies
Tennessee State Library and Archives, Nashville, Tennessee
  Zilphia Horton Folk Music Collection

University of Florida Library, Gainesville, Florida
  Margaret Dreier Robins Papers
University of Illinois, Illinois Historical Survey
  Thomas J. Morgan Collection
Wayne State University Library, Detroit, Michigan
  Matilda (Rabinowitz) Robbins Papers

Unpublished Theses, Dissertations, and Papers

ANDERSON, KAREN SUE, "The Impact of World War II in the Puget Sound Area on the Status of Women and the Family," Ph.D. diss., University of Washington, 1971.

BARROWS, EMILY, "Trade Union Organization Among Women of Chicago," M.A. thesis, University of Chicago, 1927.

BENSON, RONALD M. "Searching for the Antecedents of Affirmative Action: The Case of the Cleveland Conductorettes in World War I," Paper in possession of present writer.

BERCH, BETTINA EILEEN, "Industrialization and Working Women in the Nineteenth Century: England, France and the United States," Ph.D. diss., University of Wisconsin, Madison, 1976.

BERMAN, HYMAN, "Era of the Protocol: A Chapter of the History of the International Ladies' Garment Workers' Union, 1910–1916," Ph.D. diss., Columbia University, 1956.

BORDEN, JOHN, "The Association of Working People of New Castle, Delaware: The First Labor Party of Delaware," M.A. thesis, University of Delaware, 1927.

CAMPBELL, D'ANN, "Women and Unions at War: The Challenge of the 1940's," Paper in possession of present writer.

COLE, DONALD B., "Lawrence, Massachusetts, 1845–1912," Ph.D. diss., Harvard University, 1956.

DENTON, DAVID R., "The Union Movement in American Hospitals, 1846–1876," Ph.D. diss., Boston University, 1976.

DICKERSON, DENNIS CLARK, "Black Steelworkers in Western Pennsylvania During World War II," Paper in possession of present writer.

DuBois, ELLEN CAROL, "A New Life: The Development of an American Woman Suffrage Movement, 1860–1869," Ph.D. diss., Northwestern University, 1975.

DUCATTE, NANCY, "The Shirt and Collar Industry and Kate Mullaney, Troy, N.Y.," undated paper, Library of Trade Union Women's Studies, Cornell University, New York City.

FELDMAN, EGAL, "New York Men's Clothing Trade, 1800–1861," Ph.D. diss., New York University, 1959.

FENTON, EDWIN, "Immigrants and Unions: A Case Study of Italians and American Labor, 1870–1920," Ph.D. diss., Harvard University, 1957.

FICHTENBAUM, MYRNA, "The Funston Nut Strike, May, 1933," Senior thesis, Department of History, St. Louis University, 1976.

FINNEY, JOHN D., JR., "A Study of Negro Labor During and After World War I," Ph.D. diss., Georgetown University, 1957.

GLAGE, LISLOTTE, "Clementine Black: A Study in Social History and Literature," unpublished Paper, in preparation for Ph.D., University of Hannover, Germany.

GREENWALD, MAURINE WEINER, "Women, War, and Work: The Impact of World War I on Women Workers in the United States," Ph.D. diss., Brown University, 1977.

JENKINS, TAMAH VERONICA, "Some Aspects of the Labor Movement with Special Emphasis on Women and Children: 1915–1919," M.A. thesis, Atlanta University, 1968.

KORSTADT, ROBERT, "History of Local 22–FTA," Paper in possession of present writer.

KRIVY, LEONARD PHILIP, "American Organized Labor and the First World War, 1917–1918: A History of Labor Problems and the Development of a Government War Labor Program," Ph.D. diss., New York University, 1965.

KLACZYNSKA, BARBARA, "Working Women in Philadelphia, 1900–1930," Ph.D. diss., Temple University, 1975.

KROGER, SISTER M. LAURIE, "Women in Industry During World War I," M.A. thesis, University of Cincinnati, 1950.

LEVINE, IRVING J., "The Lawrence Strike," M.A. thesis, Columbia University, 1936.

LIEBERMAN, JACOB ANDREW, "Their Sisters Keepers: The Women's Hours and Wages Movement in the United States, 1890–1925," Ph.D. diss., Columbia University, 1971.

MCCREESH, CAROLYN DANIEL, "On the Picket Lines: Militant Women Campaign to Organize Garment Workers, 1882–1917," Ph.D. diss., University of Maryland, 1975.

NYDEN, LINDA, "Women Electrical Workers at Westinghouse Electric Corporation's East Pittsburgh Plant, 1907–1954," M.A. thesis, University of Pittsburgh, 1975.

NYDEN, PAUL, "Miners for Democracy," Ph.D. diss., Columbia University, 1973.

PRAGO, ALBERT, "The Organization of the Unemployed and the Role of the Radicals, 1929–1935," Ph.D. diss., American University, 1976.

ROSEN, DALE, "The Alabama Share Croppers' Union," Baccalaureate honors thesis, Radcliffe College, March, 1969.

SCALANDER, JUDITH ANNE, "The Women's Bureau, 1920–1950: Federal Reaction to Female Wage Earning," Ph.D. diss., Duke University, 1977.

SCHNEIDERMAN, ANNA CENTER, "The Influence of the World War on Women in Industry," M.A. thesis, Columbia University, 1929.

STEINBERG, LINDA, "Women Workers and the 1912 Textile Strike in Lawrence, Massachusetts," unpublished Paper, Division III Project, Hampshire College, Amherst, Mass., April 28, 1975.

STRAUB, ELEANOR, "United States Government Policy Toward Civilian Women During World War II," Ph.D. diss., Emory University, 1973.

Public Documents

Manufacturers of the United States in 1870: A Compendium of the Ninth Census, Washington, D.C., 1872.

New York, Factory Investigating Commission, *Preliminary Report of the Factory Investigating Commission, 1912,* Albany, 1912, 3 vols.

New York, Factory Investigating Commission, *Second Report of the Factory Investigating Commission, 1913.* Albany, 1913, 4 vols.

New York, Factory Investigating Commission, *Third Report of the Factory Investigating Commission, 1914,* Albany, 1914.

New York, Department of Labor, *Annual Reports,* 1902–1914.

Massachusetts, General Court, Senate, *Senate Document No. 81,* Boston, 1846.

Massachusetts, *House of Representatives of the Commonwealth of Massachusetts During the Session of the General Court,* A.D. 845, no. 50, Boston, 1845.

Massachusetts, Bureau of Statistics of Labor, *Eleventh Annual Report, 1880* ("Strikes in Massachusetts"), Boston, 1881.

U.S., Bureau of Labor Statistics, Handbook of American Trade Unions, *Bulletin 618,* Washington, D.C., 1936.

U.S., Congress, Commission on Industrial Relations, *Final Report and Testimony,* Washington, D.C., 1916, vol. 4.

U.S., Congress, *Report of the Industrial Commission on the Relations and Conditions of Capital and Labor Employed in Manufacturers and General Business,* Washington, D.C., 1901, vol. 7.

U.S., Congress, "Report on the Strike of the Textile Workers in Lawrence, Massachusetts," 62d Cong., 2d sess., *Senate Document No. 870,* Washington, D.C., 1912.

U.S., Congress, Senate, Committee on Banking and Currency, *Full Employment Act of 1945: Hearings on Sen. R. 300 Before the Subcommittee of the Senate Committee on Banking and Currency,* 79th Cong., 1st sess., Washington, D.C., 1945.

U.S., Congress, Senate, *United States Senate (Education and Labor) Committee, Report upon the Relations between Capital and Labor,* Washington, D.C., 1883, vol. 1.

U.S., Congress, Senate, Committee on Education and Labor, *Equal Pay for Equal Work for Women: Hearings on Sen. Res. 1178 Before a Subcommittee of the Senate Committee on Education and Labor*, 79th Cong., 1st sess., Washington, D.C., 1945.

U.S., Congress, Senate, Committee on Education and Labor, *Report No. 897*, Women's Division of the Department of Labor, 64th Cong., 2d sess., Washington, D.C., 1917.

U.S., Department of Commerce, Bureau of the Census, *Fifteenth Census of the United States, 1930: Unemployment*, Washington, D.C., vol. 2.

U.S., Department of Commerce and Labor, Bureau of the Census, *Special Reports, Street and Electric Railways, 1902*, Washington, D.C., 1902; *Street and Electric Railways, 1907*, Washington, D.C., 1907.

U.S., Department of Labor, Women's Bureau, *Women's Occupations through Seven Decades*, Bulletin No. 218, Washington, D.C., 1947.

U.S., Department of Labor, Women's Bureau, *Women's Occupations through Seven Decades*, Bulletin No. 218, Washington, D.C., 1947.

U.S., Department of Labor, Women's Bureau, *Handbook of Facts on Workers*, Bulletin No. 225, Washington, D.C., 1948.

Organizational Publications and Records

Amalgamated Clothing Workers of America, *Proceedings of the Second Biennial Convention*, Rochester, 1916.

American Federation of Labor, *Proceedings of the Convention*, 1887, 1888, 1891, 1892, 1893, 1898, 1908, 1912, 1913, 1916, 1922, 1924, 1925, 1929, 1931, 1933, 1934.

American Federation of Labor and Congress of Industrial Organizations, *Proceedings of the Convention, 1955, 1957, 1973, 1975*.

Cleveland Railway Company, *Report of the Cleveland Railway Company for the Fiscal Year Ended December 21, 1918. Submitted to the Stockholders on the Last Wednesday of January, 1919*, Cleveland, January 29, 1929.

Congress of Industrial Organizations, *Proceedings of the First Congress of Industrial Organizations, Held in the City of Pittsburgh, Pennsylvania, November 14–18, 1938, inclusive*.

Federation of Organized Trades and Labor Unions of the United States and Canada, *Proceedings of the Convention*, 1882, 1883.

Industrial Workers of the World, *Proceedings of the First Convention*, 1905.

United Automobile Workers, *Proceedings of the Second Annual Convention of the International Union, United Automobile Workers of America, Milwaukee, Wisconsin, August 23 to 29, 1937*.

Young Women's Christian Association, *Forty-first Annual Report*, Chicago, 1917.

Newspapers and Magazines

Advance (New York City)
AFL–CIO News (Washington, D.C.)
American Citizen (New York City)
Atlantic Monthly (Boston)
Boston Advertiser
Boston Bee
Boston Courier
Boston Daily Evening Voice
Boston Traveller
Chicago Herald
Chicago Times
Chicago Tribune
Cleveland Socialist
Cohoes Daily News (New York)
Factory Girls' Album (Exeter, N.H.)
Garment Worker (New York City)
Guardian (New York City)
Haverhill Gazette
Hawaiian Carpenter (Honolulu)
Horizon (Nashville)
Industrial Union Bulletin
Industrial Worker (Spokane)
International Socialist Review (New York City)
Irish World (New York City)
Jackson Daily Clarion
Jewish Daily Forward (New York City)
John Swinton's Paper (New York City)
Journal of United Labor
Labor (Washington, D.C.)
Ladies' Garment Worker (New York City)
Ladies Home Journal (New York City)
Living Age (New York City)
Milwaukee Leader
Motorman and Conductor (Washington, D.C.)
Nation, The (New York City)
New Leader (New York City)
New Republic (New York City)

New York Call

New York Daily Sentinel

New York Evening Post

New York Herald

New York Sun

New York Times

New York Tribune

New York World

Norfolk Journal and Guide

One Big Union Monthly

Pennsylvanian (Philadelphia)

Philadelphia Evening Bulletin

Philadelphia Public Ledger

Progress (New York City)

Reading Times

Revolution (New York City)

St. Louis Argus

St. Louis Post-Dispatch

St. Louis Star-Times

San Antonio Express

Seattle Union Record

Solidarity (New Castle, Pa.)

Southern Worker (Chattanooga)

Springfield Republican (Massachusetts)

Textile Labor (Lawrence)

Time (New York City)

Troy Northern Budget (New York)

Troy Daily Times (New York)

UE News (New York City)

Voice of Industry (Lowell)

Voice of the People (New Orleans)

Voice of 1707 (San Francisco)

Wall Street Journal (New York City)

Washington Post

Weekly Bulletin of the Garment Trades (New York City)

Woman's Journal (Boston)

Workingman's Advocate (Chicago)

Working Man's Advocate (New York City)

Yonkers Statesman (New York)

Young America (New York City)

Books

ABBOTT, EDITH, *Women in Industry*, New York, 1910.

ADAMS, ELIZABETH KEMPER, *Women Professional Workers*, Chatauqa, New York, 1921.

ADAMS, GRAHAM, JR., *Age of Industrial Violence, 1910–1915*, New York, 1966.

ADDAMS, JANE, *Twenty Years at Hull House*, New York, 1910.

ANDERSON, MARY, AND MARY N. WINSLOW, *Woman at Work: The Autobiography of Mary Anderson*, Minneapolis, 1951.

ANDREWS, JOHN B. AND HELEN BLISS, "History of Women in Trade Unions, 1825 to the Knights of Labor," *Senate Document 645*, 61st Cong., 2d sess., Washington, D.C., 1911, vol. 10.

ANTHONY, SUSAN B. II, *Out of the Kitchen—Into the War*, New York, 1943.

APTHEKER, HERBERT, ed., *A Documentary History of the Negro People in the United States, 1933–1945*, Secaucus, N.J., 1974.

ARTHUR, T. S., *The Lady at Home: or Leaves from the Every-Day Book of an American Woman*, Philadelphia, 1847.

ASHBAUGH, CAROLYN, *Lucy Parsons, American Revolutionary*, Chicago, 1976.

AUERBACH, JEROLD S., ed., *American Labor: The Twentieth Century*, Indianapolis, 1969.

BAKER, ELIZABETH FAULKNER, *Protective Labor Legislation with Special Reference to Women in the State of New York*, New York, 1925.

——, *Technology and Woman's Work*, New York and London, 1964.

BAKER, HELEN, *Women in War Industries*, Princeton, N.J., 1942.

BEALE, FRED, *Proletarian Journey*, New York, 1937.

BENDER, THOMAS, *Toward an Urban Visison: Ideas and Institutions in Nineteenth Century America*, Lexington, Ky., 1975.

BERNHEIMER, CHARLES S., *The Shirt-Waist Strike: An Investigation Made for the Council and Head Worker of the University Settlement*, New York, 1910.

BEST, HARRY, *The Men's Garment Industry of New York and the Strike if 1913*, New York, 1913.

BLUMBERG, DOROTHY ROSE, *Florence Kelley: The Making of a Social Pioneer*, New York, 1964.

BOONE, GLADYS, *The Women's Trade Union League in Great Britain and the United States of America*, New York, 1942.

BRISSENDEN, PAUL F., *The I.W.W.: A Study of American Syndicalism*, New York, 1920.

BROOKS, THOMAS R., *Communications Workers of America: The Story of a Union*, New York, 1977.

BROWNE, HENRY J., *The Catholic Church and the Knights of Labor*, Washington, D.C., 1949.

BROWNLEE, W. ELIOT AND MARY M. *Women in the American Economy: A Documentary History, 1675 to 1929*, New Haven and London, 1976.

BULLARD, IRVING W., *Women's Work in War Time*, Boston, 1917.

CHAFE, WILLIAM HENRY, *The American Woman: Her Changing Social, and Political Role*, New York, 1971.

——, *Woman and Equality*, New York, 1971.

CHAFEE, ZACHARIAH, JR., *Free Speech in the United States*, Cambridge, Mass., 1948.

CHAPLIN, RALPH, *Wobbly: The Rough and Tumble Story of an American Radical*, Chicago, 1948.

CHICAGO COMMISSION ON RACE RELATIONS, *The Negro in Chicago*, Chicago, 1922.

CLARKE, JOHN MAURICE, *The Costs of World War to the American People*, New Haven, Conn., 1931.

COCHRAN, BERT, *Labor and Communism*, Princeton, N.J., 1978.

COLE, DONALD B., *Immigrant City: Lawrence, Mass., 1845–1921*, Chapel Hill, 1963.

COMMONS, JOHN R., et al., *History of Labour in the United States*, New York, 1918, vols. 1 & 2; New York, 1935, vol. 3.

——, eds., *A Documentary History of American Industrial Society*, Cleveland, 1910, vol. 6.

CONLIN, JOSEPH R., *Big Bill Haywood and the Radical Union Movement*, Syracuse, N.Y., 1969.

COYLE, GRACE, *Present Trends in Clerical Occupations*, New York, 1928.

CROWELL, BENEDICT, *Report of America's Munitions, 1917–1918*, Washington, D.C., 1919.

——, AND R. F. WILSON, *How America Went to War: The Armies of Industry*, 2 vols., New Haven, 1921.

DAVIS, ALLEN F., *Spearheads for Reform: The Social Settlements and the Progressive Movement, 1890–1914*, New York, 1967.

DAVIS, PHILIP, *And Crown Thy Good*, New York, 1952.

DAWLEY, ALAN, *Class and Community: The Industrial Revolution in Lynn*, Cambridge, Mass., 1977.

DAY, DOROTHY, *The Long Loneliness*, New York, 1952.

DICKENS, CHARLES, *American Notes*, New York, 1842.

DOUGLAS, ANN, *The Feminization of American Culture*, New York, 1977.

DODGE, GRACE, ed., *Thoughts of Busy Girls Who Have Little Time for Study Yet Find Much Time for Thinking*, New York, 1892.

DUBOFSKY, MELVYN, *We Shall Be All: A History of the Industrial Workers of the World*, Chicago, 1969.

——, *When Workers Organize: New York City in the Progressive Era*, Amherst, Mass., 1968.

DYCHE, JOHN A., *Strike of the Ladies' Waist Makers, of New York*, New York, 1910.

EBERT, JUSTUS, *The Trial of a New Society*, Cleveland, 1913.

EHRENREICH, BARBARA, AND DEEDRE ENGLISH, *Witches, Midwives and Nurses: A History of Women Healers*, Oyster Bay, N.Y., 1972.

EISLER, BENITA, ed., *The Lowell Offering: Writings by New England Mill Women (1840–1845)*, Philadelphia and New York, 1978.

EPSTEIN, MELECH, *Jewish Labor in the U.S.A.: An Industrial, Political, and Cultural History of the Jewish Labor Movement*, 2 vols., New York, 1950–1953.

FEATHERLING, DALE, *Mother Jones, the Miners' Angel*, Carbondale, Ill., 1971.

FINE, SIDNEY, *Sit-Down: The General Motors Strike of 1936–1937*, Ann Arbor, Mich., 1969.

FINK, GARY M., ed., *Biographical Dictionary of American Labor Leaders*, Westport, Conn., 1974.

FLEXNER, ELEANOR, *Century of Struggle: The Women's Rights Movement in the United States*, Cambridge, Mass., 1959.

FLYNN, ELIZABETH GURLEY, *I Speak My Own Piece: Autobiography of the "Rebel Girl,"* New York, 1955.

FONER, PHILIP S., *American Labor Songs of the Nineteenth Century*, Urbana, Ill., 1975.

_____, *American Socialism and Black Americans: From the Age of Jackson to World War II*, Westport, Conn., 1977.

_____, *The Fur and Leather Workers Union*, Newark, N.J., 1950.

_____, *History of the Labor Movement in the United States*, New York, 1947, vol. 1; New York, 1955, vol. 2; New York, 1964, vol. 3; New York, 1965, vol. 4; New York, 1980, vol. 5.

_____, *Organized Labor and the Black Worker, 1619–1973*, New York, 1974.

_____, *Women and the American Labor Movement: From Colonial Times to the Eve of World War I*, New York, 1979; *From World War I to the Present*, New York, 1980.

_____, ed., *The Democratic-Republican Societies, 1790–1800: A Documentary Sourcebook of Constitutions, Declarations, Addresses, Resolutions, and Toasts*, Westport, Conn., 1976.

_____, *The Factory Girls: A Collection of Writings on Life and Struggles in the New England Factories of the 1840's by the Factory Girls Themselves, and the Story in Their Own Words of the First Trade Unions of Women Workers in the United States*, Urbana, Ill., 1977.

_____, *We, the Other People: Alternative Declarations of Independence by Labor Groups, Farmers, Women's Rights Advocates, Socialists, and Blacks, 1829–1975*, Urbana, Ill., 1976.

FONER, PHILIP S., AND RONALD L. LEWIS, eds., *The Black Worker: A Documentary History from Colonial Times to the Present*, Philadelphia, 1978, vol. 2.

FOSTER, WILLIAM Z., *From Bryan to Stalin*, New York, 1937.

GARFINKEL, HERBERT, *When Negroes March*, Glencoe, Ill., 1959.

GOLDMAN, HAROLD, *Emma Paterson*, London, 1974.

GOMPERS, SAMUEL, *Seventy Years of Life and Labor*, New York, 1925, vols. 1 & 2.

GROSSMAN, JONATHAN, *William Sylvis, Pioneer of American Labor: A Study of the Labor Movement during the Civil War*, New York, 1945.

GUTMAN, HERBERT, *Work, Culture, and Society in Industrializing America: Essays in Working-Class and Social History*, New York, 1977.

HAMILTON, ALICE, *Exploring the Dangerous Trades: The Autobiography of Alice Hamilton*, Boston, 1953.

HARRIS, DAVID, *Socialist Origins in the United States: American Forerunners of Marx, 1817–1832*, Assen, Holland, 1966.

HAYWOOD, WILLIAM D., *Bill Haywood's Book: The Autobiography of William D. Haywood*, New York, 1929.

HENRY, ALICE, *Women and the Labor Movement*, New York, 1923.

HEPNER, JAMES O., JOHN M. MOYER, AND CARL WENTERNHAUS, L., *Personnel Administration and Labor Relations in Health Care Facilities*, St. Louis, 1969.

HEWES, AMY, *Women as Munition Makers—A Study of Conditions in Bridgeport, Conn.*, New York, 1917.

HOWARD, DONALD S., *The WPA and Federal Relief Policy*, New York, 1943.

HOWE, IRVING, *World of Our Fathers*, New York, 1976.

HOWE, LOUISE KAPP, *Pink Collar Workers: Inside the World of Women's Work*, New York, 1977.

HUTCHINS, GRACE, *Women Who Work*, New York, 1934 and 1952.

HUTCHINSON, E. J., *Women's Wages*, New York, 1919.

JOHNSON, CHARLES S., AND ASSOCIATES, *To Stem This Tide*, Boston, 1943.

JOSEPHSON, HANNAH, *The Golden Threads: New England's Mill Girls and Magnates*, New York, 1949.

JOSEPHSON, MATTHEW, *Sidney Hillman, Statesman of American Labor*, New York, 1952.

KAPP, YVONNE, *Eleanor Marx: The Crowded Years*, New York, 1978.

KATZMAN, DONALD, *Seven Days a Week: Women and Domestic Service in Industrializing America*, New York, 1978.

KELLEY, FLORENCE, *Wage Earning Women in War Time*, New York, 1920.

KENNEDY, SUSAN ESTABROOK, *If All We Did Was to Weep at Home: A History of White Working-Class Women in America*, Bloomington and London, 1979.

KLEIN, PHILIP, *A Social Study of Pittsburgh Community Problems and Social Services of Allegheny County*, New York, 1938.

KORNBLUH, JOYCE L., ed., *Rebel Voices: An I.W.W. Anthology*, Ann Arbor, Mich., 1964.

KRADITOR, AILEEN S., ed., *Up From the Pedestal: Selected Writings in the Story of American Feminism*, Chicago, 1968.

KRAUS, HENRY, *The Many and the Few: A Chronicle of the Dynamic Auto Workers*, Los Angeles, 1947.

KUSHNER, SAM, *The Road to Delano*, New York, 1975.

LABOR RESEARCH ASSOCIATION, *Labor and the War: Labor Fact Book*, New York, 1943 (6), 1945 (7), 1950 (9), 1951 (10), 1952 (11).

LANG, HARRY, *"62," Biography of a Union*, New York, 1940.

LARCOM, LUCY, *A New England Childhood*, Boston, 1890.

LASH, JOSEPH, *Eleanor and Franklin*, New York, 1971.

LASLETT, JOHN M., *Labor and the Left*, New York, 1970.

LERNER, GERDA, ed., *Black Women in White America: A Documentary History*, New York, 1972.

_____, *The Female Experience: An American Documentary*, Indianapolis, 1977.

LOFTIS, ANN, AND JACK BELDEN, *A Long Time Coming*, New York, 1976.

LUAHAN, MABEL DODGE, *Intimate Memoirs*, New York, 1936, vol. 3.

LYND, ALICE AND STAUGHTON, *Rank and File: Personal Histories of Working Class Organizers*, Boston, 1973.

LYND, ROBERT S. AND HELEN M. *Middletown in Transition*, New York, 1937.

MCKENNEY, RUTH, *Industrial Valley*, New York, 1939.

MALKIEL, THERESA, *Diary of a Shirtwaist Striker*, New York, 1910.

MANDEL, BERNARD, *Samuel Gompers, A Biography*, Yellow Springs, Ohio, 1963.

MARTIN, GEORGE, *Madame Secretary: Frances Perkins*, Boston, 1976.

MARX, KARL, AND FREDERICK, ENGELS, *Selected Correspondence, 1845–1895*, New York, 1936.

MAROT, HELEN, *American Labor Unions*, New York, 1914.

MASON, LUCY RANDOLPH, *To Win These Rights: A Personal Story of the CYO in the South*, New York, 1952.

MEIER, AUGUST, AND ELLIOTT RUDWICK, *Black Detroit and the Rise of the UAW*, New York, 1969.

MERRILL, FRANCES E., *Social Problems on the Home Front*, New York, 1948.

MONTGOMERY, DAVID, *Beyond Equality: Labor and the Radical Republicans, 1862–1872*, New York, 1967.

MORRIS, JAMES O., *Conflict Within the AFL: A Study of Craft Versus Industrial Unionism, 1901–1928*, Ithaca, N.Y., 1938.

NATHAN, MAUDE, *Story of an Epoch-Making Movement*, New York, 1926.

NESTOR, AGNES, *Woman's Labor Leader: An Autobiography of Agnes Nestor*, Rockford, Ill., 1954.

OPPENHEIMER, JOHN, *The Female Labor Force in the United States*, New York, 1947.

PARTON, MARY FIELD, *Autobiography of Mother Jones*, Chicago, 1925.

PENNY, VIRGINIA, *Five Hundred Employments Adapted to Women*, Philadelphia, 1868.

PESOTTA, ROSE, *Bread Upon the Waters*, edited by John Nicholas Beffel, New York, 1944.

PIDGEON, MARY ELIZABETH, *Employment Fluctuations and Unemployment of Women: Certain Indications from Various Sources, 1928–1931*, Washington, D.C., 1933.

PIERCE, BESSIE LOUISE, *A History of Chicago, 1871–1893*, New York, 1957, vol. 3.

POWDERLY, TERENCE V., *Thirty Years of Labor, 1859–1889*, Columbus, Ohio, 1890.

PRUETTE, LORINE, ed., *Women Workers: Through the Depression. A Study of White Collar Employment Made by the American Woman's Association*, New York, 1934.

ROBERTS, HAROLD S., *The Rubber Workers*, New York, 1944.

RUDWICK, ELLIOTT M., *Race Riot at East St. Louis, July 2, 1917*, Carbondale, Ill., 1964.

SANGER, MARGARET, *Autobiography*, New York, 1938.

SCHLESINGER, ARTHUR M., JR., *The Crisis of the Old Order*, Boston, 1957.

SCHNEIDERMAN, ROSE, with Lucy Goldthwaite, *All for One*, New York, 1967.

SCOTT, EMMETT J., *Negro Migration During the War*, New York, 1920.

SEEGER, PETE, *The Incompleat Folksinger*, New York, 1972.

SEIDMAN, JOEL, *American Labor from Defense to Reconversion*, Chicago, 1953.

_____, *The Needle Trades*, New York, 1942.

SIMMONS, ADELE, ANN FRIEDMAN, MARGARET DIMBLE, AND FRANCINE BLAU, *Exploitation from 9 to 5*, Lexington, Mass., 1975.

SMITH, ROBERT E., et al., *The Subtle Revolution: Women At Work*, New York, 1979.

STEIN, LEO, *The Triangle Fire*, New York, 1962.

_____, ed., *Out of the Sweatshop: The Struggle for Industrial Democracy*, New York, 1977.

STEWART, WILLIAM RHINELANDER, *The Philanthropic Work of Josephine Shaw Lowell*, New York, 1911.

STOLBERG, BENJAMIN, *Tailors' Progress: The Story of a Famous Union and the Men Who Made It*, New York, 1946.

SYLVIS, JAMES C., *The Life, Speeches, Labors and Essays of William H. Sylvis, Late President of the Iron-Moulders International Union and also of the National Labor Union*, Philadelphia, 1872.

TENNANT, RICHARD B., *The American Cigarette Industry*, New Haven, 1950.

TAFT, PHILIP, *The AFL in the Time of Gompers*, New York, 1957.

THERNSTROM, STEPHEN, *Poverty and Progress*, Cambridge, Mass., 1964.

TRACHTENBERG, ALEXANDER, ed., *The American Labor Year Book, 1917–1918*, New York, 1918.

VORSE, MARY HEATON, *Footnote to Folly: Reminiscences of Mary Heaton Vorse*, New York, 1955.

_____, *Labor's New Millions*, New York, 1938.

WALD, LILLIAN, *The House on Henry Street*, New York, 1917.

WALLING, ANNA STRUNSKY, ed., *William English Walling: A Symposium*, New York, 1938.

WARE, CAROLINE F., *The Early New England Cotton Manufacture*, Boston, 1931.

WARE, NORMAN F., *The Industrial Worker, 1840–1860*, Boston and New York, 1924.

_____, *The Labor Movement in the U.S.A., 1860–1895*, New York, 1929.

WEBB, SIDNEY AND BEATRICE, *The History of Trade Unionism, 1660–1920*, London, 1919.

WERTHEIMER, BARBARA, *We Were There: The Story of Working Women in America*, New York, 1977.

_____, AND ANNE H. NELSON, *Trade Union Women: A History of Their Participation in New York Locals*, New York, 1975.

WILLARD, FRANCES, *Glimpses of Fifty Years*, Chicago, 1892.

WILLETT, MABEL HURD, *The Employment of Women in the Clothing Trade*, New York, 1902.

WOLFSON, THERESA, *The Woman Worker and the Trade Unions*, New York, 1926.

WOLMAN, LEO, *The Growth of American Trade Unions, 1880–1923*, New York, 1924.

WOODS, ROBERT S., ed., *The City Wilderness: A Settlement Study by the Residents and Associates of the South End*, Boston, 1898.

WYNN, NEEL A., *The Afro–American and the Second World War*, New York, 1975.

YELLEN, SAMUEL, *American Labor Struggles*, New York, 1919.

ZARETZ, CHARLES ELBERT, *The Amalgamated Clothing Workers of America*, New York, 1934.

Pamphlets, Bulletins, and Leaflets

Address of the National Labor Congress to the Workingmen of the United States, Chicago, 1867.

AFSCME, *What About Sex Discrimination?* N.p., 1979.

BARTHWELL, AKOSUA, "Trade Unionism in North Carolina: The Strike Against Reynolds Tobacco, 1947," American Institute for Marxist Studies, Occasional Paper, 1977.

Chicago Trade and Labor Assembly, *The New Slavery: Investigation into the Sweating System as Applied to the Manufacture of Wear-Apparel, A Report Prepared by Mr. Thomas J. Morgan*, Chicago, 1891.

CIO Committee to Abolish Racial Discrimination, *Working and Fighting Together: Regardless of Race, Creed, or National Origin*, Washington, D.C., 1943.

Constitution of the National Women's Trade Union League Adopted in Fanueil Hall, Boston, November 17–19, 1903, Boston, 1904.

Consumers' League of New York, *The Forty Eight-Hour Law: Do Working Women Want It?* New York, 1927.

District 31, Women's Caucus, USWAA, Bulletin No. 3, copy in possession of present writer.

FLYNN, ELIZABETH GURLEY, "Memories of the Industrial Workers of the World (IWW)," *Occasional Paper No. 24* (1977), American Institute for Marxist Studies, New York, 1977.

JOHNSTONE, JENNY ELIZABETH, *Women in Steel*, New York, 1957.

KELBER, HARRY, *Sexism in the Labor Movement*, New York, 1978.

LAWRENCE, KEN, "Mississippi's First Labor Union," mimeographed pamphlet, Tougaloo, Miss., Deep South People's History Project, n.d.

LAWSON, ELIZABETH, *The Jobless Negro*, New York, 1933.

LINDNER, WALTER, *The Great Flint Sit-Down Strike Against GM, 1936–1937: How Industrial Unionism Was Won*, Ann Arbor, Mich., 1970.

LONG, CLARENCE D., "The Labor Force in Wartime America," Occasional Paper 14, National Bureau of Economic Research, New York, March, 1944.

SEIU, *A Commitment to Women*, San Francisco, 1979.

Statement of Purpose, Structure and Guidelines Adopted by Coalition of Labor Union Women Founding Conference, March 23–24, Chicago, 1974.

Union WAGE: *Our Purposes and Goals*. Leaflet issued by Union Women's Alliance to Gain Equality, San Francisco, n.d.

United Electrical, Radio and Machine Workers of America. *UE Fights for Women Workers*, New York, 1952.

United Farm Workers Organizing Committee, "The Farm Workers' Struggle— The Delano Grape Strike," mimeographed sheet, n.p., n.d.

Women's Charter, What and Why, The, Washington, D.C., 1936.

Women's Work Project, *Separate and Unequal: Discrimination Against Women Workers in World War II: The UAW, 1944, 1947*, Silver Spring, Md., 1978.

Women Working: Meeting the "All-Craft Women," New York, 1978.

Films

Crystal Lee Jordan, produced by Joan Shigehawa for KERA–TV Dallas/Fort Worth in association with *Ms.* magazine. Written by Gloria Steinem.

Harlan County U.S.A. (The Brookside Miners' Strike). Produced and directed by Barbara Kopple.

I Am Somebody (The Charleston Strike of Hospital Workers). Produced by the National Union of Drug and Hospital Workers.

Like a Beautiful Child. Produced and directed by John Schultz (Moe Foner, executive producer), for the National Union of Drug and Hospital Workers.

Mother Is on Strike. Produced by the International Ladies' Garment Workers' Union.

Union Maids. Directed by James Klen, Miles Magulescu, and Julia Reichert.

With Babes and Banners (The Women's Emergency Brigade in the Sit-Down strike at General Motors, Flint, Mich.) Produced by L. Gray, L. Goldfarb, and A. Bohlen.

Articles

"Admission of Women to Union Membership," *Monthly Labor Review* 55 (November 1942): 100–106.

"Armstrong Association, The," *Opportunity*, August, 1923, pp. 28–30.

"Attack on Labor Laws Is Begun in Rush for Profits," *Advance*, Apr. 27, 1917, pp. 1–4.

BAER, BARBARA L., AND GLEN MATHEWS, "The Women of the Boycott," *Nation*, Feb. 23, 1974, pp. 233–34.

BAKER, ELLA, AND MARVEL COOKE, "The Bronx Slave Market," *Crisis* 42 (November 1935): 330–31, 340.

BAKER, RAY STANNARD, "Revolutionary Strike," *American Magazine* 74 (May, 1912): 30–35.

BAKER, ROB, "Women and Seniority," *People's World*, Nov. 22, 1975, p. 3.

BAKER, ROSS K., "Entry of Women into Federal Job World—at a Price," *Smithsonian* 8 (July, 1977): 83–85.

BARNES, MARY CLARK, "The Strike of the Shirtwaist Makers," *World-Today* 18 (March 1910): 260–70.

BASKIN, ALEX, "The Ford Hunger March—1932," *Labor History* 13 (Summer 1972): 331–60.

BAXANDALL, ROSALYN FRAAD, "Elizabeth Gurley Flynn: The Early Years," *Radical America* 8 (Jan.–Feb. 1975): 90–102.

BEDELL, BEN, "Clerical Workers on the Move," *Guardian*, Apr. 4, 1979, p. 5.

———, "CLUW: More of the Same," *Guardian*, Dec. 13, 1975, p. 5.

———, "Women Take Their Place in the Mines," *Guardian*, Nov. 29, 1978, p. 6.

BEECHER, JOHN, "The Sharecroppers' Union in Alabama," *Social Forces* 13 (October 1934): 124–32.

BLAAKAN, RENEE, "Labor Women Organizing," *Guardian*, Jan. 30, 1974, p. 6.

———, "Women Challenge Seniority," *Guardian*, Nov. 27, 1974, p. 4.

BLACKWELDER, JULIA KIRK, "Women in the Workforce, Atlanta, and San Antonio, Texas 1930 to 1940," *Journal of Urban History* 4 (May 1978): 331–58.

BLANK, ROSE, "Strike of the Furriers," *Life and Labor* 2 (December 1912): 360–61.

BLUMBERG, DOROTHY ROSE, "'Dear Mr. Engels': Unpublished Letters, 1884–1894, of Florence Kelley [Wischnewetsky] to Friedrich Engels," *Labor History* 5 (Spring 1964): 105–28.

BODE, KEN, "Unions Divided," *New Republic*, Oct. 15, 1977, p. 20.

BOLIN, WINIFRED D. WANDERSEE, "The Economics of Middle-Income Family Life: Working Women During the Great Depression," *Journal of American History* 65 (June 1978): 60–74.

CARROL, JANE LYNOTT, "Raising a Baby in Shifts," *Parents' Magazine*, 20 (October 1943): 77–79.

CHAMBERLAIN, MARY, "Women and War Work," *Survey* 38 (May 19, 1917): 153–54.

CHERNOW, RON, "All in a Day's Work," *Mother Jones* 6 (August 1976): 11–16.

CHEYNEY, ALICE S., "Negro Women in Industry," *Survey* 46 (Apr. 23, 1921): 119.

CHIVERS, WALTER R., "Effects of the Present War upon the Status of Negro Women," *Southern Frontier* 4 (December 1943): 1.

CLARK, SUE AINSLEY, AND EDITH WYATT, "The Shirtwaist Makers and Their Strike," *McClure's Magazine* 36 (November 1910): 70–86.

CLIVE, ALAN, "Women Workers in World War II: Michigan as a Test Case," *Labor History* 20 (Winter 1979): 44–72.

"Colored Women in Industry in Philadelphia," *Monthly Labor Review* 12 (May 1921): 1046–48.

COWLEY, MALCOLM, "King Mob and John Law," *New Republic*, Dec. 20, 1932, pp. 146–49.

CRATON, ANN WASHINGTON, "Working the Woman Worker," *Nation* 124 (Mar. 23, 1927): 311–13.

D'AGOSTINO, THERESA, "A Woman of Steel," *Daily World*, Mar. 8, 1975, p. 3.

DAHLBERG, EDWARD, "Hunger on the March," *Nation* 135 (Dec. 28, 1932): 542–44.

DAVIS, ALLEN F., "The Women's Trade Union League: Origins and Organization," *Labor History* 5 (Winter 1964): 3–17.

DAVIS, ANGELA, "Racism and Male Supremacy," *Political Affairs* 56 (March 1977): 2–8.

DAVIS, GEORGE, "A Healing Hand in Harlem," *New York Times Magazine*, Apr. 22, 1979, p. 58.

DAVIS, LEON J., AND MOE FONER, "Organization and Unionization of Health Workers in the United States: The Trade Union Perspective," *International Journal of Health Services* 5 (1975): 21–23.

DAVIS, PHILIP, "The Social Settlement and the Trade Union," *Charities and the Commons* 1 (April, 1904): 142–47.

DICKERSON, DENNIS CLARK, "Black Steelworkers in Western Pennsylvania, 1900–1950," *Pennsylvania Heritage* 4 (Dec. 1977): 52–58.

DONART, GRETCHEN, "Women Workers at J. P. Stevens," *Labor Unity*, March 1979, pp. 12–13.

DRATCH, HOWARD, "The Politics of Child Care in the 1940's," *Science & Society* 38 (Summer 1974): 167–204.

DREYFUS, CLAUDIA, "The Woman from 1199," *New York Daily News Magazine*, July 20, 1975, pp. 8–9.

DUBIN, MARSHALL, "Twenty Years in the Hospitals," *1199 Drug & Hospital News*, January, 1979, p. 15.

DYE, NANCY SCHROM, "Creating a Feminist Alliance: Sisterhood, Feminism or Unionism: The New York Women's Trade Union League and the Labor Movement," *Feminist Studies* 3 (Fall, 1975): 111–25.

EARL, DAVID, "Our Experience with the Employment of Women," *American Machinist* 68 (Feb. 7, 1918): 240–44.

ELIAS, ARTHUR, "The Charleston Strike," *New Politics* 7 (Summer 1968): 218–25.

ELLIS, EDWARD ROBB, "What the Depression Did to People," in Frazier, Thomas R., *The Private Side of American History: Readings in Everyday Life*, New York, 1975, 2: 205–33.

ELLIS, ELAINE, "Women of the Cotton Field," *Crisis* 45 (Oct. 1938): 333, 342.

"Female Labor Arouses Hostility and Apprehension in Union Ranks," *Current Opinion*, April, 1914, pp. 292–93.

FIELD, JANE, "The Coalition of Labor Union Women," *Political Affairs* 54 (March 1975): 7–11.

_____, "Women in the Trade Unions: Reality, Need, Potential," *Daily World*, Dec. 4, 1975, p. 3.

FILIPELLI, RONALD L., "UE: The Formative Years, 1933–1937," *Labor History* 17 (Summer 1976): 351–71.

FLYNN, ELIZABETH GURLEY, "A People's Health Center," *Sunday Worker Magazine*, Jan. 4, 1937, p. 10.

_____, "I.W.W. Call to Women," *Solidarity*, July 31, 1915.

_____, "The New Role of Women in Industry," *Communist* 22 (April 1943): 349–57.

_____, "Women and Socialism," *Solidarity*, May 27, 1915.

_____, "Women and Unionism," *Solidarity*, May 27, 1911.

_____, "Women in Industry Should Organize," *Industrial Worker*, June 1, 1911.

FONER, MOE, "'Like a Beautiful Child,': Film as an Organizing Tool," *Film Library Quarterly* 12 (1979): 64–65.

FOX, BONNIE R., "Unemployment Relief in Philadelphia, 1930–1932, A Study of the Depression's Impact on Voluntarism," *Pennsylvania Magazine of History and Biography* 84 (Jan. 1960): 102–24.

FRIEDAN, BETTY, "NOW–How It Began," *Women Speaking* (London), April, 1967, pp. 4–10.

FRIEDENBERG, EDGAR Z., "Another America," *New York Review of Books*, Mar. 3, 1966, p. 10.

GABIN, NANCY, "Women Workers and the UAW in the Post–World War II Period: 1945–1954," *Labor History* 21 (Winter 1979–80): 5–30.

GERBERT, BILL, "The Convention of 400,000," *Communist* 16 (October 1937): 891–905.

_____, "The St. Louis Strike and the Chicago Needle Strike," *Communist* 12 (August 1933): 800–809.

GILMAN, W. T., "Women and Heavy War Work," *Scribner's Monthly* 65 (1918): 113–16.

GINGER, RAY, "Labor in a Massachusetts Cotton Mill, 1853–1860," *Business History Review* 28 (March 1954): 67–91.

"Gloria Steinem Writes on Local 1199," *New York*, July 27, 1970, pp. 3–7.

GOMPERS, SAMUEL, "Don't Sacrifice Womanhood," *American Federationist* 24 (August 1917): 747–49.

_____, "Equal Rights Law Will Hurt Women," *Labor*, Jan. 21, 1922, p. 1.

_____, "Women Workers in War Time," *American Federationist* 24 (September 1917): 912–15.

GOODMARK, PAULINE, "The Facts of Women in War Industries," *New Republic*, Dec. 29, 1917, pp. 251–52 (letter to editor).

GORDON, MICHAEL A., "The Labor Boycott in New York City, 1880–1886," *Labor History Labor History* 16 (Spring 1975): 184–229.

GREENWALD, MAURINE WEINER, "Women Workers and World War I: The American Railroad Industry: A Case Study," *Journal of Social History* 9 (Winter 1975): 154–77.

HARMON, DUDLEY, "What Are These War Jobs for Women?" *Ladies' Home Journal* 34 (November 1917): 31, 91–92.

HAWES, ELIZABETH, "Do Women Workers Get an Even Break?" *New York Times Sunday Magazine*, Nov. 19, 1944.

HEATON, JAMES P., "The Legal Aftermath of the Lawrence Strike," *Survey* 28 (July 6, 1912): 509–10.

HEWES, AMY, "Women as Munition Makers," *Survey*, Jan. 6, 1917, pp. 381–85.

HOAG, M. E., "Phenomenal Increase in Production," *American Machinist* 68 (Jan. 10, 1918): 46–49.

HOBBY, DANIEL T., ed., "We Have Got Results : A Document on the Organization of Domestics in the Progressive Era," *Labor History* 17 (Winter 1976): 103–08.

HOLMES, LIZZIE SWANK, "Women Workers of Chicago," *American Federationist* 12 (August 1905): 508–09.

HOURWICH, ISAAC A., "The Garment Workers' Strike," *The New Review* 1 (March 15, 1913): 426–27.

HUNTER, J. V., "The Training of Women as Machine Operators," *American Machinist* 68 (Sept. 26, 1918): 565–70.

HUTCHINS, GRACE, "5,000,000 Women Workers Eligible for Trade Unions," *AFL Rank and File Federationist*, June 1934, p. 3.

HUTCHINSON, WOODS, "The Hygienic Aspects of the Shirtwaist Strike," *Survey* 23 (Jan. 22, 1910): 541–50.

JACKSON, AUGUST V., "A New Deal for Tobacco Workers," *Crisis* 4 (October 1938): 322–24, 330.

JOHNSON, OAKLEY C., "Helen Lynch, Organizer of the Unemployed," *World*, Mar. 19, 1974.

KANN, KENNETH, "The Knights of Labor and the Southern Black Worker," *Labor History* 18 (Winter 1977): 49–70.

KEERAN, ROGER R., "'Everything for Victory': Communist Influence in the Auto Industry During World War II," *Science & Society* 43 (Spring 1979): 6–23.

KELBER, MIM, "AFL–CIO for Men Only," *Nation* 229 (Nov. 17, 1979): 491–92.

KELLEY, FLORENCE, "The District Minimum Wage," *Survey* 45 (Feb. 12, 1921): 702.

———, "The War and Women Workers," *Survey* 39 (Mar. 9, 1918): 628–31.

KENNEALLY, JAMES, "Women and Trade Unions," *Labor History* 14 (Winter 1973): 42–55.

KESSLER-HARRIS, ALICE, "Organizing the Unorganizable: Three Jewish Women and Their Union," *Labor History* 17 (Winter 1976): 5–23.

_____, ed., "The Autobiography of Ann Washington Craton," *Signs* 3 (Summer 1976): 1021–24.

KLACZYNSKA, BARBARA, "Why Women Work: A Comparison of Various Groups—Philadelphia, 1910–1930," *Labor History* 17 (Winter 1976).

"Kopple Gets Things Done," *In These Times*, Feb. 2–8, 1977, p. 10.

LEAB, DANIEL J., "'United We Eat': The Creation and Organization of the Unemployed Councils in 1930," *Labor History* 8 (Fall 1976): 300–15.

LEIFERMANN, HENRY P., "The Unions Are Coming," *New York Times Sunday Magazine*, Aug. 5, 1973.

LESCAZE, L., "Bringing Culture to the Workplace," *Washington Post*, Apr. 23, 1979.

LEUPP, CONSTANCE D., "The Shirtwaist Strike," *Survey* 28 (Dec. 18, 1909): 383–86.

MACK, MARY, "The Emergency Brigade," *Sunday Worker*, May 14, 1937, p. 8.

McCONVILLE, ED, "The Southern Textile War," *Nation*, Oct. 2, 1976, pp. 292–96.

McDONALD, ALLAN, "Lowell: A Commercial Utopia," *New England Quarterly* 10 (March 1937): 37–62.

McDOWELL, MARY, "The Story of a Women's Labor Union," *Charities and the Commons* 7 (January 1903): 1–3.

McLAURIN, MILTON A., "The Racial Policies of the Knights of Labor and the Organization of Southern Workers," *Labor History* 17 (Fall 1976): 568–85.

McMICHAELS, LINDA, "Women Coal Miners Can Dig It Too," *Daily World*, June 14, 1979, p. 4.

MANN, ARTHUR, "British Social Thought and American Reformers," *Mississippi Valley Historical Review* 42 (March 1956): 682–92.

MARCY, LESLIE AND FREDERICK SUMNER BOYD, "One Big Union Wins," *International Socialist Review* 12 (April 1912): 625–29.

MAROT, HELEN, "A Moral in the Cloakmakers' Strike," New York *Call*, Aug. 7, 1910.

_____, "A Woman's Strike: An Appreciation of the Shirtwaist Makers of New York," *Proceedings of the Academy of Political Science in the City of New York* (1910): 122–28.

_____, "What Can a Union Do for Its Members?" New York *Call*, Jan. 27, 1913.

MILKMAN, RUTH, "Women's Work and Economic Crises: Some Lessons of the Great Depression," *Review of Radical Political Economy* 8 (Spring 1976): 75–97.

MONTGOMERY, DAVID, "Workers' Control of Machine Production in the Nineteenth Century," *Labor History* 17 (Fall 1976): 485–509.

NAISON, MARK D., "Black Agrarian Radicalism in the Great Depression: The Threads of a Lost Tradition," *Journal of Ethnic Studies* 1 (Fall 1973): 33–84.

PALMER, LEWIS E., "A Strike for Four Loaves of Bread," *Survey* 28 (Feb. 3, 1912): 1695–99.

PEARIMAN, LESTER M., "Ordinance Workers in 1918 and 1943," *Monthly Labor Review* 57 (December 1943): 1074–88.

PELLET, GAIL, "The Making of *Harlan County, U.S.A.*: An Interview with Barbara Kopple," *Radical America* 11 (March–April 1977): 32–37.

PERSONS, C. E., "Women's Wages in the United States," *Quarterly Journal of Economics* 29 (Feb. 1919): 201–34.

RAPHAEL, EDNA, E., "Working Women and Their Membership in Labor Unions," *Monthly Labor Review* 97 (May 1974): 27–39.

RASKIN, A. H., "A Union with Soul,'" *New York Times Sunday Magazine*, Mar. 22, 1970.

REVERBY, SUSAN, "Hospital Organizing in the 1950's: An Interview with Lillian Roberts," *Signs* 1 (Summer 1976): 1053–60.

RITTER, ELLEN M., "Elizabeth Morgan: Pioneer Female Labor Agitator," *Central States Speech Journal* 22 (Fall 1971): 228–49.

SCHAPPES, MORRIS U., "The Political Origins of the United Hebrew Trades of 1888," *Journal of Ethnic Studies* 5 (Spring 1977): 13–44.

SCHARNAU, RALPH, "Elizabeth Morgan, Crusader for Labor Reform," *Labor History* 14 (Summer 1973): 340–51.

SCHLOSS, CLARA F., AND ELLA JOAN POLINSKY, "Postwar Labor Turn-Over Among Women Factory Workers," *Monthly Labor Review* 6 (March 1947): 411–19.

SCHNEIDERMAN, ROSE, "A Cap-Maker's Story," *Independent* 58 (1905): 935–37.

———, "The White Goods Workers of New York: Their Struggle for Human Conditions," *Life and Labor* 3 (May 1913): 132–36.

SCOTT, EMMETT J., collector, "Letters from Negro Migrants, 1916–1918," *Journal of Negro History* 4 (July 1919): 296–319.

SCOTT, MIRIAM F., "The Spirit of the Girl Strikers," *Outlook* 94 (Feb. 19, 1910): 392–97.

———, "What the Women Strikers Won," *Outlook* 95 (July 12, 1910): 480–88.

SEXTON, PATRICIA CAYO, "Workers (Female) Arise! On Founding the Coalition of Labor Union Women," *Dissent* 21 (Summer 1974): 380–95.

SIMERAL, MARGARET, "Women and the Reserve Army of Labor," *Insurgent Sociologist* 8 (Fall 1978): 164–80.

SITKOFF, HARVARD, "The Detroit Race Riot of 1943," *Michigan History* 53 (Fall 1969): 187–204.

———, "Racial Militancy and Interracial Violence in the Second World War," *Journal of American History* 58 (December 1971): 661–81.

SQUIRES, BENJAMIN, "Women Street Railway Employees," *Monthly Labor Review* 6 (May 1918): 1049–56.

STEARNS, BERTHA, M., "Early Factory Magazines in New England," *Journal of Economic & Business History* 2 (August 1930): 685–705.

STRAUB, ELEANOR, "United States Government Policy Toward Civilian Women During World War II," *Prologue* 5 (Winter 1973): 246–70.

SUMNER, MARY BROWN, "The Spirit of the Strikers," *Survey* 23 (Jan. 22, 1910): 550–55.

TAYLOR, RONALD B., "Huelga! The Boycott That Worked," *Nation*, Sept. 17, 1970, pp. 167–70.

TEPPERMAN, JEAN, "Organizing Office Workers," *Radical America* 10 (Jan.–Feb. 1976): 3–6.

"There is No Shortage of Labor," *American Federationist* 24 (Oct. 1917): 22–25.

VORSE, MARY HEATON, "Elizabeth Gurley Flynn," *Nation* 102 (Feb. 17, 1916): 175–76.

_____, "Perkins This Way," *New Republic*, Feb. 1934, pp. 44–45.

WALKOWITZ, DANIEL J., "Working-Class Women in the Gilded Age: Factory, Community and Family Life Among Cohoes, New York Cotton Workers," *Journal of Social History* 5 (Summer 1972): 464–90.

WELTER, BARBARA, "The Cult of True Womanhood, 1820–1860," *American Quarterly* 18 (Summer 1966): 151–74.

WEST, REBECCA, "Mothering the Munitions Maker," *New Republic*, Oct. 6, 1917, pp. 266–69.

WHEELER, TIM, "Women in the Mines," *Daily World*, Dec. 29, 1977, p. 3.

"Where War Wages Do Not Reach," *Survey* 40 (June 22, 1918): 351–52.

"Why We Are Replacing Men with Women," *Factory Management* 18 (1917): 313–16.

"Wilmar 8: Equal Pay for Equal Work," *Wree-View*, May–June, 1978, p. 4.

WITHERN, ANN, "The Death of CLUW," *Radical America* 10 (March–April, 1976): 48–54.

WOLFE, ALLIS ROSENBERG, "Women, Consumerism, and the National Consumers League in the Progressive Era, 1900–1923," *Labor History* 16 (Summer, 1975): 378–92.

WOLFSON, THERESA, "Equal Right in the Union," *Survey* 57 (Feb. 15, 1927): 29–30.

_____, "Trade Union Activities of Women," *Annals of the American Academy of Political and Social Science*, May 1929, pp. 127–39.

"Working Conditions of Pecan Shellers in San Antonio," *Monthly Labor Review* 48 (March 1939): 549–51.

YOUNG, LOUISE, M., "Woman's Place in American Politics: The Historical Perspective," *Journal of Politics* 38 (Aug. 1976): 295–335.

Index

Ablowitz, Rebecca, 125
Abolitionists, 31–32, 46, 57–58
Abortion, 440
Abramowitz, Bessie, 159, 163
Abzug, Bella, 453, 457
Accidents, 43–44, 235
Adams, Graham, Jr., 157
Addams, Jane, 104–5, 112, 115
Address of the National Labor Congress to the Workingmen of the United States, 56
"Address to Working Girls and Women, An," 99
Adler, Felix, 105
Advocates for Women, 462
Affirmative Action, 33, 445, 448, 458, 459, 463
AFL–CIO News, 450
Agricultural workers: conditions of, 417; difficulties in organizing, 417–18; had no rights under the law, 417; importance of women in struggles of, 423–25; strikes and unions of, 417–28
Agricultural Workers Organizing Committee, 418–19
Albert, Marge, 480
Alinsky, Saul, 419
All-Craft Center, 461–64
All-Craft Foundation, 461–62
Allied Committees for National Defense, 346
Amalgamated Association of Iron, Steel & Tin Workers, 113, 329–30
Amalgamated Association of Street and Electric Railway Employees of America, 255–66, 363

Amalgamated Clothing Workers of America: factors leading to formation, 174–77; formation, 182–83; strikes, 185–88, 425–30
Amalgamated Clothing and Textile Workers of America, 425–30, 458
Amalgamated Meat Cutters and Butcher Workmen, 129, 246
American Association of University Women's Journal, 341
American Civil Liberties Union, 311, 313
American Communications Association, 369
American Equal Rights Association, 57
American Federationist, 131, 152, 248–49, 295, 374n.
American Federation of Labor (AFL): and black workers, 267; contradictory approach to organizing women during World War I, 247–48; craft unionism in discriminates against women workers, 99–100; decline during Great Depression, 315–16; discussions at conventions on exclusion of women, 277–78; does nothing to encourage organization of women, 396; early years, 98–102; favors equal pay for equal work, 99; growth in membership during World War I, 251; ignores needs of women workers, 124; ignores women in postwar report, 261; impossible to change, 184; indifferent to organizing office workers, 294; leaders believe women cannot be organized, 137–38; leaders refuse to adopt industrial unionism, 319–20; merges with CIO,

593

Condition of Women Workers Under the Present Industrial System, The, 107–8
Conductorettes, 255–66
Conference on Interracial Problems, 302
Congressional Union, 282
Congress of Industrial Organizations (CIO): Committee to Abolish Racial Discrimination, 365–66; criticized for not doing enough for women workers, 396; expels eleven progressive unions as "Communist dominated," 395; fights for equal pay for equal work, 376–79; merges with AFL, 396–97; no program for women workers after World War II, 392; and women workers, 362–73
Congress of Racial Equality, 412, 421
Congress of Women's Auxiliaries, 370–75
Consumers' League, 122, 140, 276, 282, 284, 288
Coolidge, Calvin, 290, 291
Cooperatives, 76–77
Council of Working Class Women, 307
Crisis, 366
Crowell, Benedict, 235
"Cult of True Womenhood," 2, 13–14
Curtis, Carl, 403
Curtis, Charles, 307–8
Curtis, Harriet F., 21

D'Agostino, Theresa, 464
Dagwell, May, 358
Daily Worker, 298–99, 362
Darin, Peg, 335–36
Darlin, Ellen, 46
Darrow, Clarence, 112, 163
Daughters of St. Crispin, 74
Daughters of the American Revolution, 269
Davis, Allen F., 126
Davis, Mrs. Hershell, 369
Davis, James, 290
Davis, Leon J., 403–4, 406, 411, 414, 416
Davis, Philip, 128–29
Day care centers, 351–55
Day, Clara, 411*n*., 442, 456*n*., 458
Day, Dorothy, 308
Delano strike: boycott in, 421–22; causes, 417–18; early history, 420–21; victory achieved, 422–23
Democratic Party, 60
Democratic-Republican Societies, 12–13
Denison House, 105, 123, 129, 131
Denton, David R., 402
Department of Women's Work (Knights of Labor), 83–92
Department Store Union, 457
Depression, after World War I, 296. *See also* Great Depression

Detroit Free Press, 310
Deverall, Richard, 381
Dewson, Mary, 287
Dias, Lily, 443
Dickason, Gladys, 369–70
Dickens, Charles, 21
Dielman, Henry B., 259
Disabled Miners and Widows of Southern West Virginia, 435
Displaced Homemakers Network, 497–500
Distributive, Processing and Office Workers of America, 399
District of Columbia, minimum-wage law in, 279, 286–89
District 31 Women's Caucus, USWA Bulletin, 465–66
District 1199: *see* Local 1199
District 65, 398–99, 480, 485
Division of Women in Industry, 360
Dix, Dorothy, 327
Dodge, Grace M., 103
Domestic Workers, 199–204, 229
Donahue, Bishop Hugh, 421
Donahue, Tom, 457
Donnelly, Michael, 129
"Don't Sacrifice Womanhood," 248
Dorr, Thomas, 24
Douglas, Stephen A., 49
Douglass, Frederick, 57
Draper, Ann, 421
Dreier, Mary E., 136, 140, 276, 293
Dress and Waistmakers' Union, Local 25, 181
Driver, Rev. Thomas, 46
Drug & Hospital News, 411
Dubois, Ellen Carol, 60, 61*n*.
Du Bois, W. E. B., 150
Du Chessi, William, 432
Dudley, Helena S., 128, 129
Duke Power Company, 435–38
Dunham, Dana, 442
Durham, Mary, 151
Dutcher, Elizabeth, 150
Dyche, John, 156–57, 164
Dye, Nancy Schrom, 170

Eastman, Mehitabel, 34, 35, 41–42
East St. Louis riot, 233
Effective Contract Language for Union Women, 459*n*.
Eight Hour Day, 103
Eight-hour day, 79, 274
Eight-hour laws, 118*n*.
Elastic Goring Weavers' Association, 278*n*.
El Diario, 407
Elliot, Emma, 270

Henning, Georgia, 443
Henrotin, Ellen M., 132
Henry Street Settlement, 105, 123, 125
Hernandez, Maria, 449
Hill, Joe, 187, 195, 199
Hillman, Sidney, 163, 340
Hillquit, Morris, 44–45, 146, 153
Hillstrom, Joseph: see Hill, Joe
Hinchley, Margaret, 291*n*.
Hobbes, Margaret A., 218
Hobby, Wilbur, 434
Hoboes, 302–3
Holland, James P., 269
Holmes, Oliver Wendell, 287
Holtzman, Elizabeth, 457
Homestead Strike, 113
Hoover, Herbert, 296
Hopedale, 32
Hopkins, Velma, 384–85
Horizon, 150
Hosiery Worker, 332
Hospital Employees Union, Local 151, 401
Hospitals: composition, 402; conditions in, 399–400
Hospital workers: conditions of, 399–401; excluded from protection, 402; wages, 403, 405, 409; first organized, 421–22; *see also* Local 1199
Hotel & Club Employees Union, 369
Hourwich, Isaac A., 177
Household Technicians of America, 486–87
Household workers, 486–87
Howe, Louise Kapp, 473–74, 478–79
Hoyt, Mary Frances, 74
Huelga, 418–37
Huerta, Dolores, 420, 422, 424, 428
Hugo, Victor, 82
Hull House, 104–5, 112, 115, 122, 123, 131, 158
Hunger Marches, 306–8
Hutchins, Grace, 297
Hutton, Barbara, 331

Iliong, Larry, 419
Illinois Factory and Workshop Inspection Act, 118
Illinois Manufacturers Association, 118
Illinois Supreme Court, 183
Illinois Women's Alliance, 102–3, 117
"Improvement Circles," 20
Industrial Commission, 124
Industrial Conference, 267–68
"Industrial Reform Lyceum," 30
Industrial Union Bulletin, 188, 199*n*.
Industrial unionism, as necessary to organize women workers, 319–20

Industrial Union of Marine Shipbuilding Workers, 392
Industrial Worker, 191, 193, 194
Industrial Workers of the World (IWW): advanced position on women workers, 204; analysis of prostitution by, 193; attacked by government in World War I, 203; attitude toward marriage, 194–95; attitude toward married women, 194–95; attitude toward women workers, 189; and black workers, 189; call to women, 204; and Chinese, 189; contradictions in approach to women workers, 190–98; criticizes AFL, 189–90; endorses birth control, 194; formation, 184–86; government campaign against, 200; ideology, 184–85; in several respects similar to AFL, 203–4; and Japanese, 189; and Lawrence strike, 205–18; male chauvinists in, 202–3; migratory workers in, 192–93; organizes domestic workers, 199–204; oversimplified view on woman suffrage, 197–98; position of toward women, 186–87; reasons for formation, 184–86; regards woman suffrage as irrelevant, 197; weakness, 218; Western locals and women workers, 199; Western members, 192–93; and women workers, 188–204
Injunctions, 158
International Assembly of North America, 54
International Association of Machinists, 387
International Brotherhood of Boilermakers and Iron Shipbuilders, 363, 364
International Brotherhood of Teamsters, 425
International Congress of Working Women, 275–76; *see also* International Federation of Working Women
International Federation of Trade Unions, 271
International Federation of Working Women, 275, 289–90
International Fur Workers of the United States and Canada, 174, 295
International Labor Conference, 275
International Labor Organization, 273
International Labor Solidarity, 428
International Labour Office, 361
International Ladies Garment Workers Union: absent at Industrial conference, 267; formation, 176–80; growth, 181–83; and role of women in leadership, 369–70; and education for women workers, 271–72, 295; and "un-

162, 164, 176, 179-80, 210-11, 214-17, 254, 305, 313, 330, 334
Political Equality League, 141
Powderly, Terence V., 71, 72, 73, 82, 86, 88, 89, 90, 91, 95, 96
Powell, Adam Clayton, 410
Pratt, Henry N., 406
"Prayer Pilgrimage," 413
Preferential Union shop, 157, 158
Premium System, 207
Prince, Laura, 259, 262, 263
Prostitution, 4, 193
Protective labor legislation: CLUW on, 442: dispute over, 282-94, 315; during World War II, 356-57; for women workers, 281-94
"Protocol of Peace," 158-59, 181
Provident Society, 8
Public Law, 414, 418
Puerala, Alice, 468
Puerto Rican workers, 40, 398-99, 407-10
Puett, Austin, 65
Putnam, Mary Kellogg, 61, 63

Quesada, Margaret, 427
Quill, Mike, 409

Race riots, 233, 350
Racism, 227-33, 365-66
Radical America, 454-55
Radical Republicans, 58
Radio Corporation of America, 334
Railroad Brotherhoods, 363-64
Railroads, 232-33, 241-43, 314
Rankin, Mildred, 252, 253, 294n., 346, 405, 412, 413, 450n.
Raskin, A. H., 407-8, 456
Rauh, Ida, 140
Rayburn, John, 143
"Rebel Girl, The," 187n.
Recession of 1974-75, effect on women workers, 445, 447-48
Reconstruction, 266
Reconstruction Conference, 266
Red Special, 171-72
Reece, Florence, 437, 438
R. E. Funsten Co., 310-14
Regan, Agnes, 286
Reichers, Charles F., 111
Republican Party, 58, 60
Retail, Wholesale, Department Store Workers, 398-99, 404
Reuther, Walter P., 393
Revolution, 58-59, 64, 68
Rickert, Thomas, 162, 176-77, 183
Rights of Labor, 117
R. J. Reynolds Tobacco Company, 383-85

Roanoke Rapids, 433-34
Robert F. Kennedy Farm Workers Medical Plan, 424
Robins, Margaret Dreier, 132, 149, 163, 164, 179, 252, 262, 273-74, 275-76, 366, 387
Robinson, Cleveland, 399
Robinson, Harriet F., 19-20, 32
Robinson, Mary, 343
Rockefeller, Nelson D., 413-15
Rodgers, Annie, 212
Rodgers, Elizabeth, 96
Rodgers, George, 83
Rodriguez, Dina, 449-50
Roosevelt, Eleanor, 245, 316, 367-68, 417
Roosevelt, Franklin D., 321
Roosevelt, Theodore, 180
Ruff, Jackie, 483
Risanowska, Margaret, 259
Russell Sage Foundation, 290
Rustin, Bayard, 405, 412
Ryan, William Fitts, 414

Sabadado, Marie, 424
Sadlowski, Ed, 465, 466
St. John, Vincent, 195
St. Louis, 310-14
St. Louis *Argus*, 313
St. Paul, 48
Samuel, Howard D., 492-93
Sanger, Margaret, 194
Sarnoff, David, 334
Sashon, Rose, 152
Saturday Evening Post, 339n.
Shackford, Reverend Charles C., 48
Schlesinger, Arthur M., Jr., 303
Schneiderman, Rose: activities during Great Depression, 315; at Paris Peace Conference, 272-73; cites gains of women garment workers, 182; contradictory stand on Socialist issue, 190; during World War II, 361n.; on difficulties in organizing women, 289-90; on Supreme Court decision, 288; president of WTUL, 281; relations with Eleanor Roosevelt, 316; role in Brookwood Labor College, 270n.; role in clockmakers' strike, 157; role in waistmakers' strike, 140, 150-51, 152; speech at Triangle fire memorial meeting, 169; supports ERA, 286; and women workers after World War I, 268
Schouler, William, 21, 24, 38-39
Schuble, Pam, 470-71
Scott, Melina, 152, 170, 272, 286, 291n.
Scott, Phebe, 7
Scott, Mrs. William, 346
Scudder, Yida, 128